The Collected Papers of James Meade

Volume III: International Economics

Also from Unwin Hyman

The Collected Papers of James Meade

Volume I: Employment and Inflation
edited by Susan Howson 0 04 331115 6

Volume II: Value, Distribution and Growth
edited by Susan Howson 0 04 445073 7

Volume IV: The Cabinet Office Diary of James Meade 1944–46
edited by Susan Howson and Donald Moggridge 0 04 445075 3

The Collected Papers of James Meade

Volume III: International Economics

Edited by

SUSAN HOWSON

University of Toronto

London
UNWIN HYMAN
Boston Sydney Wellington

330.1
M481
v.3

© James Meade, 1988
This book is copyright under the Berne Convention.
No reproduction without permission. All rights reserved.

Published by the Academic Division of
Unwin Hyman Ltd,
15/17 Broadwick Street, London W1V 1FP, UK

Unwin Hyman, Inc.,
8 Winchester Place, Winchester, Mass. 01890, USA

Allen & Unwin (Australia) Ltd,
8 Napier Street, North Sydney, NSW 2060, Australia

Allen & Unwin (New Zealand) Ltd
in association with the Port Nicholson Press Ltd,
60 Cambridge Terrace, Wellington, New Zealand

First published in 1988

British Library Cataloguing in Publication Data

Meade, J. E. (James Edward), *1907–*
The collected papers of James Meade.
1. Great Britain. Economic policies, 1929–1982
I. Title
330.941′082
ISBN 0–04–331119–9

Library of Congress Cataloging-in-Publication Data
(Revised for vol. 3)

Meade, J. E. (James Edward), 1907–
The collected papers of James Meade.
Vol. 3 has imprint: London; Boston: Unwin Hyman.
"Published writings of James Meade": v. 3, p.
Includes indexes.
Contents: v. 1. Employment and inflation –
v. 3. International economics.
1. Unemployment – Effect of inflation on.
2. Unemployment – Great Britain – Effect of inflation on.
3. Keynesian economics.
I. Howson, Susan, 1945–
II. Title.
HB33.M43 1988 330.1 87–15288
ISBN 0–04–331119–9 (v. 1: alk. paper)

Typeset in 10 on 11 Times by
Computape (Pickering) Ltd, North Yorkshire
and printed in England by
Biddles Ltd, Guildford and King's Lynn

19325

Contents

	Editorial Preface	*page* ix
1	International Economic Co-operation (1933)	1
2	The Exchange Policy of a Socialist Government (1934)	11
3	A Proposal for an International Commercial Union (1942)	27
4	The Post-War International Settlement and the United Kingdom Balance of Payments (1943)	36
5	Financial Policy and the Balance of Payments (1948)	67
6	Bretton Woods, Havana and the United Kingdom Balance of Payments (1948)	81
7	National Income, National Expenditure and the Balance of Payments (1948–49)	95
8	A Geometrical Representation of Balance-of-Payments Policy (1949)	133
9	Bretton Woods, GATT and the Balance of Payments: A Second Round? (1952)	148
10	The Case for Variable Exchange Rates (1955)	161
11	Benelux: The Formation of the Common Customs (1956)	177
12	The Price Mechanism and the Australian Balance of Payments (1956)	190
13	Wage-Rates, the Cost of Living, and the Balance of Payments (with E. A. Russell) (1957)	206
14	The Balance-of-Payments Problems of a European Free-Trade Area (1957)	212
15	The Future of International Trade and Payments (1961)	229
16	UK, Commonwealth and Common Market (1962)	244
17	The Common Market: Is There an Alternative? (1962)	274
18	International Commodity Agreements (1964)	285
19	Exchange-Rate Flexibility (1966)	297
20	A Strategy for Commodity Policy (1978)	313
21	Structural Changes in the Rate of Interest and the Rate of Foreign Exchange to Preserve Equilibrium in the Balance of Payments and the Budget Balance (1984)	324
22	A New Keynesian Bretton Woods (1984)	338
23	Monetary Policy and Fiscal Policy: Impact Effects with a New Keynesian 'Assignment' of Weapons to Targets (with David Vines) (1987)	354
	Published Writings of James Meade	388
	Index	406

UNIVERSITY LIBRARIES
CARNEGIE-MELLON UNIVERSITY
PITTSBURGH, PENNSYLVANIA 15213

Editorial Preface

This is the third volume of an edition of Professor Meade's papers. As with the first two volumes (*The Collected Papers of James Meade, Vol. I: Employment and Inflation*, *Vol. II: Value, Distribution and Growth*) it includes both previously published papers and hitherto unpublished memoranda written either for the Labour Party in the 1930s, while Meade was teaching in Oxford, or during his period of government service, 1940–7, in the Economic Section of the Cabinet Offices, of which he was Director 1946–7.

Over five decades Professor Meade has written and published on a wide range of topics in economic theory and policy: Keynesian unemployment theory, national income accounting, the control of inflation, exchange-rate theory, open economy macro-economics, international trade, price theory and welfare economics, growth theory, economic development, problems of income distribution, and some aspects of industrial organisation. The selection of his published and unpublished papers included in this edition has therefore been organised in five broad categories corresponding to the five parts of his *An Introduction to Economic Analysis and Policy* (Oxford: Clarendon Press, 1936; second edition, London: Oxford University Press, 1937). These he called Unemployment; Competition and Monopoly; The Distribution of Income; The Supply of the Primary Factors of Production; and International Problems. Volume I was devoted to the first of these categories, Volume II to the second, third and fourth groups. This volume comprises papers in international economics.

James Meade was awarded the Nobel Memorial Prize in Economics in 1977 (jointly with Bertil Ohlin) for his contributions in international economics. His major work in this field, *The Theory of International Economic Policy, Volume I: The Balance of Payments* and *Volume II: Trade and Welfare*, published with their *Mathematical Supplements* in 1951 and 1955 respectively (London: Oxford University Press for the Royal Institute of International Affairs), was written after he returned to academic life in 1947, as Professor of Commerce with special reference to International Trade at the London School of Economics. Several articles he produced while preparing these volumes are included in this edition (in this volume, Chapters 7 and 8, and in Vol. II, Chapters 6 and 7). Meade's related work on customs unions and free trade areas is also represented in this volume (Chapters 11, 14, 16, 17), though his seminal de Vries Lectures, delivered in Rotterdam in April 1955, on *The Theory of Customs Unions* (Amsterdam: North-Holland, 1955) have had to be omitted on account of their length. But Meade's interest in international economics goes back to the 1930s, as he has explained in his own account of his life (*Collected Papers*, Vol. I, Chapter 1), and has continued to this day. Both his earliest published papers and his unpublished papers for the Labour Party and the New Fabian Research Bureau before he went to Geneva to work for the League of Nations in 1937 were concerned with international economic policy. (Two of these are equally concerned with unemployment and appear in Volume I.) In the 1940s, in the Economic Section, he was heavily involved in the discussions and conferences on the post-war international economic order which led to the establishment of the International Monetary Fund, the International Bank for Reconstruction and Development and the General Agreement on Tariffs and Trade. Several papers in this volume reflect these activities; others indicate his views on the problems of the world economy as they evolved after 1947. The volume also contains Meade's most recent paper on open economy macro-economics, first presented in Cambridge in July 1987 to a conference which celebrated his 80th birthday.

The selection of published papers included in the three volumes of this edition has been based on two simple criteria: major articles in major academic journals on the one hand, and essays, lectures, and pamphlets that present Meade's policy proposals and his analyses of their effects, on the other. The unpublished papers have been selected mainly from the Meade Papers in the British Library of Political and Economic Science, which contain at least the first drafts of his Labour Party papers and copies of forty-five papers that he chose to take with him when he left government service in 1947, supplemented by research in the Public Record Office and Labour Party sources. The origins and reasons for inclusion of the individual documents are indicated in the introductory notes to the papers, which also provide the sources of the papers and of the information in the introductory notes themselves. Apart from the correction of minor inconsistencies of spelling and obvious typographical errors and the completion or correction of bibliographical references, the papers appear as they were originally typed or printed. This volume also includes a bibliography of Meade's published works, compiled with the enthusiastic assistance of Michael Gasiorek.

I am grateful to the Controller of Her Majesty's Stationery Office for permission to reproduce Crown Copyright Material in the Public Record Office, to the Fabian Society for permission to publish a paper written for the New Fabian Research Bureau, to the editors of *Economica*, *The Economic Journal*, *The Economic Record*, the *Journal of Agricultural Economics*, *Oxford Economic Papers*, the *Scandinavian Journal of Economics*, *Lloyds Bank Review*, and *The Three Banks Review* for permission to reprint articles from their journals, and to the Institute of Economic Affairs for permission to publish Meade's Hobart Paper on 'UK, Commonwealth & Common Market'. I also wish to thank Michael Gasiorek, Dr Angela Raspin of the British Library of Political and Economic Science, Dr Stephen Bird of the Labour Party, Professor Donald Moggridge of the University of Toronto, the Warden and

Fellows of Nuffield College, Oxford, and the Humanities and Social Sciences Committee of the Research Board of the University of Toronto, for their generous assistance of various kinds in connection with this edition. Most of all, I should like to thank Professor Meade for asking me to undertake the edition and for providing invaluable help and encouragement in its preparation.

Susan Howson
October 1987

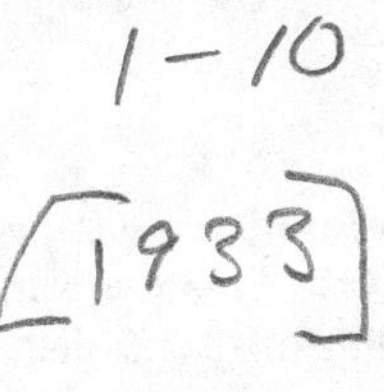

1

International Economic Co-operation

From the Journal of Proceedings of the Agricultural Economics Society, *vol. 2 (November 1933), pp. 275–82. Meade had presented the paper at the Society's conference held in London on 6–7 December 1932.*

My intention in writing this paper is to discuss what in my view are the broad principles upon which nations should co-operate in the economic sphere. I am not therefore going to discuss in any detail either the actual facts of the present economic situation in the world or the political difficulties, which are bound to arise as soon as any attempt at economic co-operation is made. Let us suppose that every politician, who may be responsible for any decision at the World Economic and Financial Conference [in London in June–July 1933], is a trained economist, animated by the highest motives for the general well-being of every country and able to act in the certainty that his decisions, whatever they may be, will be accepted by the country which he represents. What decisions should such persons make?

Now there is a very common view that the broad lines on which we should work for International Co-operation in the economic sphere, are simple and clear to anyone who looks upon the problem with an impartial mind. These principles are two in number: in the first place, we should co-operate to build up again an international monetary system, either by restoring the gold standard in its old shape or in some modified form, or else, perhaps even by devising a form of international currency; and in the second place, every effort should be made to free the trade of the world by co-operating to reduce tariffs and other forms of restriction on the movement of goods between nations, wherever such reductions are politically possible. The view that action in the monetary sphere and in the commercial sphere is necessary above all other forms of economic action, and that the principles of an international money standard, whether the standard be gold or not, and of free trade are clearly desirable, is a view held not only by a very large number of members of the public, which in any country takes an interest in international affairs, but also by many politicians, bankers, financiers and economists, who are more directly concerned with international affairs either from an administrative or technical point of view. In the Final Report of the Gold Delegation of the Financial Committee of the League of Nations, published in June 1932, those who signed the Report expressed the view that a return to a world gold standard was desirable, while even those who dissented from the majority view were all of the opinion that an international monetary standard of some kind was desirable if certain conditions were fulfilled. The League of Nations expert committees have, as far as I know, without exception expressed the view that free trade was preferable to the system of trade restrictions. This was certainly the opinion of the World Economic Conference in 1927. The Bank for International Settlements was set up largely to maintain and facilitate the operation of the Gold Standard; the central bankers who direct that institution are all advocates of such a standard. There can be no doubt that the members of the last Labour Cabinet [1929–31] desired to co-operate with other nations; clearly they were convinced that the maintenance of the Gold Standard and the freeing of international trade from restrictions of every kind were the fundamental principles of international co-operation in the economic sphere.

In this paper I wish to suggest some reasons why an international monetary standard and complete freedom of trade between nations may both be undesirable, and to suggest alternative principles, upon which nations can co-operate.

An international monetary standard means that the rate at which the currencies of any two countries exchange for one another is fixed at all events within very narrow limits. This is quite clear, if there is an actual international currency, so that the two countries use exactly the same currency, and in the case of the gold standard, if the two currencies are maintained both at a fixed gold value, the value of the one currency in terms of the other is also fixed. And this is all that an international monetary standard alone does involve. It does not necessarily mean that the general level of world prices will remain stable; prices may fluctuate violently up or down, as they have done in all the countries on a gold standard between 1929 and 1931. In order to maintain stability of prices, or to provide that prices shall not fall or rise undesirably quickly, some further control is necessary. The maintenance of an international monetary system is not enough to assure this.

Now, suppose that the rest of the world decides for some reason or another to lend less to a particular country, or suppose that the rest of the world decides to spend less on the exports of this particular country. This may happen either because of a change of taste on the part of the members of the country purchasing these goods; it may happen because other countries become more efficient in producing the goods which this particular country exports; or it may happen because the country in question becomes less efficient in producing the goods for export, if the demand for these goods is elastic, or because the country becomes more efficient in the production of goods for export, if the demand for its exports is inelastic. Or suppose that the members of this country decide, for some reason or another, to lend more abroad or to spend more on their imports from other countries.[1]

Any of these changes will lead to an exchange weakness and loss of gold on the part of this country. Even if the other countries aid the transition by allowing their prices and money incomes to rise, so that they tend to buy more from the particular country again and to export less to it, yet this particular country must itself do something to cut down its imports or to expand its exports to help to restore equilibrium. There are three things which it can do.

(*a*) It might let its exchange rate depreciate in terms of other currencies. This would naturally raise the price, in terms of its currency, of the goods which it imports, and would therefore cut down its expenditure on imports in terms of the currencies of other countries. The exchange depreciation would also make the price of the goods which it exports cheaper in the currencies of other countries, and would therefore increase the amount spent on its exports in terms of the currencies of other countries, so long as the elasticity of demand for its exports is greater than unity. Except in the rare case in which the elasticity of demand for its exports is so much less than 1, that as the exchange depreciates the decrease in the amount spent by other countries on its exports is greater than the decrease in the value of its imports in terms of other countries' currencies, exchange depreciation is of itself bound to help to restore the balance of payments. But this solution is incompatible with an international monetary standard.

(*b*) The country whose exchange weakened for any reason, and which began, therefore, to lose gold, could put the situation right by imposing a tariff or other form of restriction on its imports. By raising the price of its imports, it can cut down the volume of goods imported and thus cut down the amount it spends on imports. It can by this means restrict its expenditure on imports without letting its exchange depreciate. Since the exchange rate is in this case constant, the price of its exports in foreign markets will have remained unchanged and the amount spent by other countries on its exports will have remained constant. Now the same rise in price of imports will restrict imports by the same amount, whether the rise in price is due to exchange depreciation or to tariffs; on the condition that the demand of other countries for the exports of the country in question has an elasticity equal to unity, the same total amount will be spent on the exports in terms of the currency of other countries, whatever the price of these goods. In this case, therefore, both the tariff method and the exchange depreciation method of righting the trade balance will require the same rise in price of imports to correct a given primary excess of imports over exports. If, however, the elasticity of the demand for the country's exports is greater than 1, then as the exchange depreciates there will be some increase in the total value of the country's exports in

[1] The demand for a commodity is elastic or has an elasticity greater than 1, if a fall in the price of the commodity so increases the amount purchased that a greater total sum of money is spent on it than before. Conversely the demand for it is inelastic or has an elasticity less than 1, if a fall in its price leads to so small an increase in the amount purchased that the total amount of money spent on the commodity is less than before.

terms of other countries' currency. In this case, to right a given excess of imports over exports, the rise in the price of imports need be less with the method of exchange depreciation, since exchange depreciation will also increase the value of the country's exports, than with the method of tariff restriction. But conversely, if the demand of other countries for the exports of the particular country has an elasticity less than 1 – which may be the case in a country producing practically the whole supply of a commodity for which the demand is inelastic, and the export of which forms a large proportion of her total exports – the rise in price of imports necessary to obtain a given increase in the favourable balance of trade will be greater with the method of exchange depreciation, since this will lessen the value of the country's exports, than with the method of tariff restriction. In this case, tariffs are certainly preferable to exchange depreciation, and in the case in which the country, which has a certain unfavourable balance of payments to correct, owes to other countries interest on debt fixed in terms of other countries' currency, it may be absolutely necessary to use the method of tariff restriction, if at the same time the demand for her exports was very inelastic, and her demand for imports was very inelastic, so that exchange depreciation would only increase the excess of imports over exports. Moreover, if the country which has a certain excess of imports over exports to counter is at the same time indebted to other countries and the debt is payable in the currency of the other countries, the method of restricting imports by raising tariffs will not increase the fixed debt in terms of its own currency, but the method of exchange depreciation is in any case bound to increase the debt payments in terms of its own currency and will therefore cause it some budgetary difficulties. Further, the method of restricting imports by tariffs may be preferable because the exchange depreciation method will always turn the real terms of trade against the country, while the import restriction method will not do so. But if the world maintains a system of free trade, as well as an international monetary standard, this method must also be ruled out.

(*c*) A disequilibrium in the balance of payments between two countries can be corrected in a third manner, which is, in fact, the orthodox manner, and is the only method compatible with free trade and an international monetary standard. As the country whose exchanges are weak loses gold, her banking system should raise interest rates; this at first will attract more loans from abroad, which will ease the exchange position; but more important than this, the rise in interest rates will discourage producers at home from borrowing, will decrease their expenditure on commodities, and the employment of labour. This will lower prices and money incomes in the country, and will thus automatically tend to a decrease in imports and an increase in exports. The required increase in exports and decrease in imports will be obtained as soon as the increase in unemployment and the fall in profits have led to a sufficient fall in prices and in money incomes to reduce imports and encourage exports sufficiently; but full employment will not be obtained again until money costs and money wages have been reduced sufficiently. In the countries receiving gold the reverse movements take place. The banks lower interest rates. This encourages an increase in foreign lending, so relieving the exchange weakness of other countries. But secondly the lower interest rates encourage borrowing by producers for development of their production at home, and their increased expenditure raises first the price of commodities and later money wages and costs. This leads to an increased expenditure on imports and to a decreased exportation, and thus relieves the exchange position of other countries.

What conditions must be fulfilled for this orthodox method to operate smoothly?

(1) In the first place it is clear that money wages and costs must be easily reduced in the country which is in a weak exchange position. For otherwise the reduction in prices and incomes in that country will simply take the form of the disappearance of profits and an increase in unemployment. Such a general depression is necessary to right the trade balance, and can only be overcome by a ruthless and quick reduction in money costs including wage-rates. How much does this involve? Let us take the position of England in the years 1925–29, when her exchange position was weak, and the rest of the world was not depressed. Or consider the position of Australia in 1928 and 1929, when the slump in the price of wool and wheat, Australia's main exports, put her in a very weak exchange position. The trade unions' resistance to wage reductions must be overcome. Wage-rates fixed by Trade Boards or by awards of Industrial Conciliation Boards or Arbitration Courts must be revised. Probably also, if there is a moderately high rate of unemployment benefit, this too must be lowered, in order to force the unemployed by competing more strenuously in the labour market to lower the resistance of trade unions to wage reductions. In England in 1926 the clash of these opposing forces manifested itself in the General Strike. Australia more wisely allowed herself to be driven off the Gold Standard and let her exchange depreciate.

(2) In the second place the national banking systems must not attempt to stabilise general price levels or the general trade position in their single countries. If a country loses gold, its banking system must not offset this in any way, but must raise interest rates and intensify unemployment and depression in a vigorous and ruthless attempt to lower money costs, incomes and prices. If a country receives gold, its banking system must lower interest rates and encourage borrowing and raise prices and money incomes to aid the restoration of exchange equilibrium. It must do this, regardless of the fact that there may be an incipient or even developed boom in progress in its country. Compare the relative positions of England and America between 1925 and 1929, and more especially in the years 1928 and 1929. England was in a weak exchange position. Because her trade was already depressed and the structure of her money costs was rigid, the Bank of England attempted to offset in one way or another her exchange weakness without depressing trade still more. The Federal Reserve System in America was receiving gold throughout 1928 and 1929. But in that country a stock exchange boom was developing and there was a trade boom in progress, only concealed by the fact that prices

remained stable whilst costs fell quickly, because of increasing efficiency. The Federal Reserve System naturally attempted to offset the import of gold and to prevent it intensifying the rise in money incomes in America. But if both countries attempted thus to stabilise their internal position, international equilibrium would only have been maintained if the exchange value of the pound had depreciated, if England had raised a tariff or if America had lowered her tariff.

(3) The country which has a weak exchange to counter by lowering money prices, costs and incomes must not try to offset the necessary depression, which alone will bring about the required deflation of costs, by state action taking the form of borrowing for public works to employ the unemployed. This will only delay the readjustment and will probably intensify the subsequent exchange difficulties. Let me illustrate this point by the position of Germany between 1925 and 1929. The payment of reparations put a strain on Germany's exchange. Interest rates were very high in Germany, and this attracted a great deal of foreign lending to Germany, by means of which she was able to pay the indemnity. The high interest rates would in themselves have discouraged borrowing by German industrialists and would thus have led to a fall in German prices and incomes by causing a general depression. This, if carried far enough, would have led to a fall in Germany's money wages and costs, and thus to a fall in Germany's imports and a rise in her exports, which would have enabled her to pay the indemnity. But largely to prevent such unemployment and general business depression public authorities of every kind borrowed heavily in those years for expenditure, which maintained employment and so money incomes, prices and costs. At the same time their borrowing at high rates attracted foreign capital and so equilibrium was maintained. But all the time this was merely intensifying the difficulties of the necessary readjustment that would have to come some time in the future. As these loans were piling up, the interest payment which Germany had to meet to pay to other countries was increasing. When the lending of other countries ceased in 1929 Germany had to meet not only the reparations payments but the interest on these loans, and she had by deflating her prices and incomes to meet a much larger exchange weakness than she would have had to meet had she made the readjustment in 1925. It is an extremely shortsighted policy to encourage lending to debtor countries or countries with a weak exchange position simply in order to relieve their exchange position, since interest on these loans will grow and their position will only become weaker. Such a situation should only be met by a cancellation of debt, or else by the development of an export surplus on the part of the debtor, which can only come about by a deflation of costs and prices in the debtor and an inflation of costs and prices in the creditor countries, by a lowering of tariffs in the creditor and a raising of tariffs in the debtor countries, or by allowing the exchange rate of the debtor country to depreciate, thereby giving a stimulus to its exports and cutting off some of its imports. If a system of free trade and an international monetary standard are maintained, then the debtor country must deflate its prices, costs and incomes sufficiently.

(4) There are certain other ways in which prices and costs may be fixed and may make the process of reducing money incomes and costs a very difficult one. The more the state enters into the economic life of the community and plans and controls in this sphere, the more difficult readjustments of money costs and prices become. For all state economic action will be based on fixed costs. Thus salaries of civil servants, including the servants of local authorities, prices of commodities guaranteed or controlled by public authorities, such as electric power, railway rates, rates of unemployment benefit, health insurance contributions and payments, etc., would all need adjusting; the wider the economic activities of the state, the more important these prices become in the economic system, and at the same time the greater are the political difficulties of altering these prices. Moreover, frequent or violent alteration of these rates obviously makes the difficulties of state planning and control very great indeed. In this country, for instance, with a fixed internal charge for debt interest of some £300 million per annum – about one-twelfth of the national income – a fall in money prices and incomes greatly increases the budgeting difficulties of the state, and leads to higher rates of taxation or economies on social services. A stable and consistent budgetary policy is impossible in these circumstances. Where industries have financed their capital equipment largely by borrowing on fixed interest debentures instead of by the issue of ordinary shares, a fall of prices will lead to frequent bankruptcies, which are necessary to rid the firms of such fixed costs. For a deflation of prices, costs and incomes to be achieved with any degree of ease, few prices must be controlled by the state or other public authorities, the fixed debt of the state and public authorities must be small and private industry must not be financed to too large an extent by means of fixed interest debentures. Where these rigidities are great, a country will almost certainly be forced to face an exchange weakness not by deflating prices and costs but by letting its exchange rate depreciate.

I hope that I have been able to convince you that international economic co-operation based on an international monetary standard and free trade can only work smoothly if there is a very large degree of *laissez-faire* within every nation. Whether we deplore it or not, it is however a fact that there is already an almost complete lack of *laissez-faire* in certain countries which are Communist or Fascist, and a considerable degree of state or monopolistic control of prices, etc., in such countries as Germany, England and Australia. Even in France and the United States of America, the present strongholds of individualism, the tendency towards control is likely to develop; and already in the United States of America there are considerable attempts to control prices of particular commodities by trusts and combines, and by such bodies as the Federal Farm Board, while the Federal Reserve Board between 1924 and 1929 made a very successful attempt to stabilise the general level of prices irrespective of whether America was importing or losing gold. In my opinion there is not in fact a sufficient degree of *laissez-faire* to make me contemplate with any equanimity a return to an international gold standard and free trade.

But up to this point my paper has been almost entirely critical and destructive of certain important suggestions. If I am unwilling to advocate the principles of a return to an international monetary standard and the freeing of trade from restrictions of every kind, it is incumbent upon me to suggest alternative principles upon which the nations should co-operate in the economic sphere. I will attempt to do this very briefly. There are three spheres in which it is most important to obtain international co-operation, in monetary policy, in tariff policy, and in the policy of expenditure of money for capital developments on the part of states and public authorities.

Although I have suggested that in view of the present economic organisation of the different countries of the world there ought not to be an international monetary standard, yet international co-operation in monetary policy remains of supreme importance. At the beginning of or during a world depression it will be easier for the banking system of a single country by lowering interest rates and increasing the supply of money in that country to maintain prices and employment, if it can allow its exchange to depreciate. But it will still be extremely difficult for one country to act alone. If it lowers its interest rates, more will be lent abroad, and if it maintains its prices and incomes while prices and incomes fall in other countries, its exchange will for these two reasons depreciate very considerably. This may lead to considerable speculation in the exchanges, which is likely to be very important since there is, in the modern world, so large an amount of short-term money, which moves readily from one money market to another; this speculation might cause a lack of confidence, a flight from the country's currency, a tremendous and unjustified fall in its exchange rate and thus a very violent rise in the price of its imports. Such results could be avoided and the effective prevention of world depression by the lowering of interest rates and the increasing of the amount of money on the part of the banks greatly strengthened if the banking systems of different nations co-operated to stop a depression by acting together in this way, and to stop a world boom by raising interest rates and by decreasing the supply of money. In the case in which trade in one country is depressed and in another a boom is developing, the banks in the former can ease the situation and in the latter raise interest rates to prevent the boom; in this case the exchange rate would have to move against the former country, but the monetary authorities should co-operate in deciding how far the rate should move and in preventing and offsetting unjustified exchange speculation.

But once prices and profits have begun to fall, a lowering of interest rates and an easing of the monetary conditions may do little to stop the slump developing. Industrialists will not come forward to borrow to spend more on capital developments, just because money can be borrowed more cheaply, for the reason that they expect profits and prices to fall still further and do not know how far the movement of prices is going. They will sell stocks of commodities which are depreciating in value, and will prefer to hold money rather than securities, the prices of which are still falling. Such action will of course intensify the fall in prices. At this point if private producers will not come in and borrow, the state and the public authorities should borrow at the cheap rates offered in the market, and use these funds for capital developments of every kind, thereby increasing the expenditure on capital goods and the incomes of those thus employed, and so stopping the fall in prices. Conversely to stop a boom in prices and profits, public authorities should cut down their borrowing and expenditure to a minimum. Now if a single state carries out this policy, it will be liable to the same dangers as a single nation, which is attempting to prevent a world slump by adopting an easy money policy. The maintenance of prices and money incomes, while they fall in the rest of the world, will lead to exchange depreciation, which may be very great and lead to disastrous exchange speculation. This is probably the main reason why a policy of control and timing of public works expenditure has been tried so little in the past, although the principle is accepted by so many economists. No country dare attempt it alone. But if all countries, or at any rate the principal creditor countries, agreed together to co-operate in varying their expenditure on public works, speeding it up in bad times and cutting it down in good times, this could, I am sure, become a most important and effective instrument in the control of world booms and slumps.

All countries are not affected alike by a world depression. The debtor countries, as the value of their imports and exports falls, will be in a weak exchange position. Those countries which produce foodstuffs and raw materials as their chief export goods, since the supply of these commodities is less easily restricted, will find that the price of these commodities falls out of all relation to the price of the industrial products which they import. The value of their exports will fall much more heavily than the value of their imports, and they will be in a very weak exchange position. If they happen to be debtor countries as well, as many of them are, e.g. Australia, many of the eastern European states and some of the South American republics, their exchange position will be very dangerous. If they were borrowing heavily before the slump, as most of these states were, their difficulties will be still further intensified, since the difficulty which they will suddenly find in paying their existing debts will lead to a complete cessation of lending to them on the part of the creditors. It is essential that the creditor countries or the countries whose exchange position is strong for one reason or another should ease the situation by doing something to increase their imports from the debtor countries and to decrease their exports to them. If the creditor countries are themselves depressed, they can do this best by embarking upon an easy money policy together with a policy of public works expenditure, which will raise their prices and money incomes, allowing this increase in their prices and money incomes to lead to an increased importation from the debtor countries and a decrease in their exports to these countries. If the creditor countries wish to avoid an inflationary movement in their prices and incomes, because their trade is not depressed, they should allow the debtor countries to invade their markets by a depreciation of the debtor's rate of exchange and to raise tariffs against the goods, which they import from the creditor countries; and at the same time instead of retaliating by raising tariffs and putting on special 'exchange-dumping' duties on the commodities exported from the countries with depreciated exchanges, the creditor countries should aid by lowering their tariffs. This is perhaps the most important principle of all to be observed in international economic co-operation. The creditor countries must lead the way in a depression by an easy money policy, by a policy of public works and by lowering their tariffs in favour of the countries in a weak exchange position. Those countries in a strong exchange position must be willing to see an increase in their imports and a decrease in their exports in order to help the weaker countries. It is absurd to expect the debtor countries, which export commodities, whose price has slumped out of all proportion to other prices, and which are now unable to show any security for a loan although they were borrowing considerably before the slump, to start a world recovery by undertaking public works or by removing exchange restrictions and tariff barriers. The countries in strong exchange positions must take the first steps towards recovery and must agree to face an unfavourable balance of payments in order to relieve this situation. Until the financiers, industrialists and politicians in such countries realise that one country's favourable balance is another's unfavourable balance and that the weak countries have no security on which to borrow in order to finance an unfavourable balance of trade, it will be impossible for the nations to co-operate on sound lines to cure a world depression.

2

The Exchange Policy of a Socialist Government

While he was in Oxford (as a Fellow of Hertford College 1931–37) Meade was a member of the New Fabian Research Bureau, which was set up by G. D. H. Cole in 1931; he wrote the following paper for the NFRB's discussions in June 1934 (Meade Papers 2/7).

I. Internal Financial Policy

Before discussing the exchange policy of a Socialist Government it is essential to outline what we consider to be the necessary elements of the Government's internal financial policy. It is largely as a means of implementing this internal policy that we make our recommendations concerning the exchange policy of the Government. It is assumed throughout this memorandum that the Government is adopting an internal price policy designed to achieve and maintain a high level of employment.

If the Government comes into power during a period of slump and unemployment, or if a slump and general unemployment develop during its tenure of office, there are three important elements of financial policy appropriate to such a situation:

(a) The banks should lower interest rates and increase the amount of money. The Bank of England should lower the Bank Rate and should purchase securities in the open market. This will increase funds which are paid into the joint-stock banks and will thus increase their reserves held with the Bank of England. The joint-stock banks should then be in a position to lend more at lower rates to industry in the form of advances, or, if the demand for such loans is not forthcoming, will be in a position to purchase more securities in the open market. The result of this banking policy will be first to lower short-term interest rates directly; and secondly the purchase of long-term securities by the banks will tend to raise their price and so lower the long-term rate of interest and enable the Government, municipalities and industry to borrow on better terms for capital development. Such a fall in interest rates will probably not in itself cure the situation, but it is a necessary first condition.

(b) A National Investment Board should be set up to control and push forward expenditure by the Government, municipalities and industry on capital developments. In a period of unemployment it is the function of the Board not only to direct funds into the most desirable channels, but also to increase the total value of the funds borrowed for expenditure on development of the nation's capital equipment.

(c) The budgetary policy of the Government also has a large influence on the unemployment situation. The Budget should be divided into two accounts: an income account and a capital account. The income account, which should include all items of expenditure which do not add directly to the capital equipment of the country, e.g. social services, defence, interest on the national debt, should normally be financed from tax receipts or from the income of the Government derived from the public ownership of industrial undertakings. The capital account should include government expenditure on national capital development and on the redemption of the national debt (i.e. the sinking fund) and should be financed out of tax receipts, profits from Government industrial undertakings or from borrowing. In a period of unemployment the sinking fund should be reduced or abolished, expenditure on national capital development should be increased and a greater part of the income of the capital account of the Budget should come from borrowing and less from taxation.

There should be very close co-ordination between these three items of financial policy. The expansionist monetary policy of the banks will ensure that there are funds available to be borrowed for capital development, but this will not ensure that they are in fact borrowed; for during a slump most industries will be making losses or very small profits and in this case a reduction in the rate of interest will not give much encouragement to private enterprise to increase employment or expenditure on capital development. The actual borrowing by the Government for these purposes and the encouragement given by the Government through the National Investment Board to municipalities and private industries must ensure that these funds are spent on capital development and thereby increase employment in industries producing capital goods. This will lead to an increase in expenditure on consumption goods and employment in these industries. The reduction in taxation will also encourage expenditure on consumption goods and on capital developments.

If, when the Government is in office, there is no serious unemployment problem, and if at the same time a boom develops, so that prices are rising quickly, it is important to adopt a financial policy which will stop the boom. This is so for two reasons: first, there is reason to believe that a slump is likely to follow after the boom has broken, and, secondly, money wage-rates are likely to rise considerably less quickly than prices, thus giving the profit-maker an abnormally and unnecessarily high profit.

During a boom or as long as it is necessary to take steps to prevent such a boom in prices

(a) the banks should raise interest rates and restrict the amount of money by selling securities in the market
(b) the National Investment Board should allow no increase in, and if necessary decrease, the amount of funds spent on national capital development
(c) in the capital account of the Budget more funds should be raised by taxation and less by borrowing; at the same time less should be spent on capital development and more should be spent on the sinking fund to redeem the outstanding national debt.

Again very close co-ordination of these policies is necessary.

We shall also assume in what we have to say on the Government's exchange policy, that it has taken the steps necessary to obtain the controls essential for its internal policy. These are (i) control of banking policy, (ii) control of investment through a National Investment Board, and (iii) control of the Budget.

(i) What steps the Government would have to take to secure control of banking policy would depend on the attitude of the banks themselves. It is essential that the Government should formulate precisely and explain in clear terms to the banking authorities the objects and methods of its banking policy. If as a result of this explanation loyal co-operation could be secured, then no legislation with regard to the banks would be necessary, at least for this purpose.

It is possible, however, that co-operation could not be secured for one of two reasons. (a) The banking authorities might hold that they could not be responsible for a policy, however desirable in the national interest, on the grounds that they were obliged to put the interests of their shareholders or depositors before the national interest. This would be a perfectly legitimate objection from a narrow point of view and the one more likely to be raised. (b) The banks might refuse to co-operate on the ground that the policy outlined was not in the national interest.

If either of these objections were raised the Government would have to secure fresh banking legislation. In the former case it would be desirable to make a minimum change in the status of the banks required to ease the minds of those in charge. In the latter case more drastic measures of control would be desirable.

In either case it would be desirable to limit the control imposed to the minimum required to enforce a policy fully and clearly explained to the electorate. Otherwise the public would suspect that the powers asked for were designed to facilitate undefined and unspecified interference with individual banking accounts or some form of expropriation. This is a matter on which the individual citizen is naturally most prone to take alarm. Ignorant of the technical considerations involved, he is more likely to suspect arbitrary and discriminatory interference in this than in any sphere and to exaggerate the degree and scope of regimentation which 'monetary management' involves. Since the amount of control really required to carry out the proposals of this section is less than it would appear to be to the uninformed, it is both fair and expedient to reduce the apparent change to a minimum.

(ii) A National Investment Board should be set up to control the amount of money spent on long-term capital development. Once it was decided by the Government in its Budget how much was to be spent on national public works and on the development of industry which is directly or indirectly dependent on public authority, and how much of these funds were to be provided by borrowing, the National Investment Board should arrange for the borrowing on the best available terms of these funds. It should have the power of arranging for the flotation of loans in the market for private industry for approved purposes and also of vetoing the flotation of any private loan in the new issue market which did not pass the tests devised by the Board. It would not, however, normally give any Government guarantees on the loans floated by it on behalf of municipalities or private industry; it would merely examine their schemes of development, if they desired it, and by reporting favourably on them and aiding them in the new issue market with the close co-operation of the Bank of England would enable them to borrow on more favourable terms. If, however, the Government decided to guarantee the interest of loans floated by local authorities or by private enterprise for approved purposes, or to subsidise such loans, the National Investment Board would in these cases always act as the intermediary between these bodies and the new issue market.

The institution of the National Investment Board should present no difficulties. But it should be clearly realised that the mere institution of such a body will do very little good unless the Government has carefully planned beforehand schemes of expenditure on housing, slum clearance, roads etc. and on the capital development or reorganisation of controlled industries, and on the development of new industries in depressed areas. Again, it is not so much organisation in this body as the body's policy which is important.

(iii) The control of the Budget is already in Government hands.

It should be clear that a very close co-ordination of the three elements of financial policy – banking, investment and budgetary policies – is required, and that these policies in turn should be closely co-ordinated with the industrial policy of the Government. For this reason it is essential that a Supreme Economic Authority be set up, and that the authorities administering the national Budget, the National Investment Board and the Bank of England be subordinated to this authority and in very close contact with it.

The rest of our memorandum is written on the assumption that the above is in broad outline the internal financial policy of the Government. It is not here assumed that the Government's policy will be to stabilise the price level. This is a question of detail to be decided by another committee. It is simply assumed that the main purpose of its internal policy is to achieve and maintain a high level of employment on the lines suggested above. It is assumed moreover that whatever steps the Government may be adopting in the reorganisation and socialisation of particular industries, there is still a large amount of capital in private control and ownership.

II Undesirability of Fixed Exchange Rates

If the policy outlined above is adopted, it is essential that the exchange rates with other countries should not be rigidly fixed. Let us suppose that in other countries the price level is falling and that money incomes are being reduced by a fall in employment, wage-rates and profits. In these circumstances, if the English price level does not fall and English money incomes are maintained by the Government's internal financial policy, the consequence will be a fall in the volume as well as the value of English exports, since foreign incomes are smaller and foreign prices lower, and a rise in the volume of English imports, since foreign prices have fallen. To meet this situation it will be necessary for the Government either to abandon its internal policy of stabilisation and to reduce prices and incomes at home, or else to allow the pound to depreciate in the exchange market in order to lower the price of English goods to the foreigner and to raise the price of foreign goods again to the Englishman. Conversely, if foreign prices and incomes are rising, while English prices and incomes are maintained relatively stable, this will cause a large increase in English exports and a fall in English imports. In this case the Government again has the choice of abandoning its internal policy and letting English prices and incomes rise in line with the movement in the rest of the world, or else it must allow the pound to appreciate to offset the movement in foreign prices and incomes. It is thus clear that if the Government wishes to be free to prosecute its internal financial plans of controlling fluctuations, it must have the power of altering the exchange rates with other countries, if the other countries are not stabilising their economic position in the same way as the English Government.

Even if other important countries have determined to control fluctuations in prices and employment in the same manner as the Labour Government in England, the Government should be unwilling to fix its exchange rates even with these countries for more than a limited period at a time. There are many reasons why this is so, but two examples will show the kind of thing which will almost certainly, even in these circumstances, make fixed exchange rates undesirable.

(i) Let us suppose that both Great Britain and the USA have decided to stabilise their internal price levels, and that both countries are completely successful in this policy. There are still many things which may happen to make it undesirable to maintain fixed exchange rates between the two countries. If we suppose simply that the USA raise its tariff or impose new restrictions of another kind on our exports, Great Britain will then be selling less abroad, while she will have no immediate cause to buy less from the rest of the world. This situation can only be met (a) by Great Britain abandoning her policy of a stable price level, and so lowering her prices and money incomes that the USA will again buy more from her while Great Britain is restricting her imports, or (b) by Great Britain imposing tariffs or other import restrictions on a scale sufficient to offset the fall in her exports due to the rise in the American tariff, or (c) by Great Britain allowing the pound to depreciate so that American goods are automatically made more expensive in England and English goods cheaper in America. We regard the third of these policies as the right one.

Or we may assume that while the general price level both in America and in England remains stable, the prices of the principal US exports fall because of greatly increased efficiency in the production of these goods in the USA, this fall in price being offset by a corresponding rise in price of the goods, which the USA cannot export. If England competes with the USA in export markets or buys goods from the USA English exports may fall or her imports increase, because of the fall in price of American exports. Again England must do something to increase her exports and/or decrease her imports. If she is unwilling to abandon her internal policy of stable prices or to impose sufficient extra restrictions on imports, she must be in a position to allow her exchange rate to depreciate.

On the other hand we may suppose that there is a general increase in productivity in all industries in the USA – i.e. an increase in productivity which is not simply confined to the export markets. In this case if the price level is maintained stable in the USA there must be an increase in money wages and profits because of the increased productivity. Money incomes being greater and home and foreign prices being unchanged it is probable that Americans will spend some of the increase in their incomes on buying more imported goods. In this case English exports would rise without there being any immediate rise in her imports. England can therefore either abandon her policy of stabilisation this time by allowing her money prices and incomes to rise, or reduce her tariffs or import restrictions, so that her increased exports are for this reason counter-balanced by increased imports, or if she is unwilling to do either of these things she must raise the price of her exports to the American and lower the price to herself of American goods by allowing the pound to appreciate in the exchange market.

(ii) If we suppose that the internal financial policy of England and the USA is not to stabilise their respective internal price levels, but to maintain a high volume of employment at existing money wage-rates, the same type of argument against fixed exchange rates is valid, even if both countries are completely successful in their internal policies. Again if America were to increase its restrictions on imports, English exports would fall and England would have either to allow a fall in its own volume of employment or in money wage-rates or else to allow the pound to depreciate in the exchange market. Or if American industry generally became more productive, the American price level would fall, if the money wage-rate and employment in America were stabilised. This would cause England to buy more from America and would cause America to buy less from us; again England could only meet the fall in its exports and increase in its imports by either allowing employment to fall off or money wage-rates to be reduced or by allowing the pound to depreciate.

We have seen then that even if such economic co-operation is possible between the nations so that the financial policy in all the main countries is similar, it is still undesirable to have fixed exchange rates. *A fortiori* it is undesirable to maintain fixed rates of exchange, if this co-operation is not forthcoming.

III Alternatives to the Gold Standard

If the argument of the preceding paragraph is admitted, it follows that the Labour Government should refuse to operate a free gold standard. What are the possible alternative monetary standards?

(i) The first possibility is to have no standard at all other than the paper pound. In this case the Government is completely free to devise that internal financial and economic policy which it desires. It may then leave the exchange market relatively free so that the pound may find its own level; or it may interfere in the exchange market by use of an Exchange Equalisation Fund, buying and selling foreign currencies as it wishes to depreciate or appreciate the exchange value of the pound; or it may take more rigid controls over the exchange rate through the control of foreign trade and of foreign lending discussed in IV and V below. There are, however, certain disadvantages, particularly evident in any transitional period, in having no standard. (a) The absence of any standard is liable to increase the difficulties which may arise in controlling speculation in the exchanges. If there is no standard there will be a much greater fear and misunderstanding of the Government's financial policy, leading to a withdrawal of funds from England in the fear of exchange depreciation of the pound. Such speculative movements of funds would be diminished and their control simplified if some standard were adopted. (b) The existence of some standard would prevent violent fluctuations in the exchange rate, would diminish speculative buying and selling of pounds, would therefore simplify the problems of English importers and exporters, and would moreover provide a simpler mechanism than that of an Exchange Equalisation Fund to achieve these objects. (c) The existence of some standard would make it much easier to obtain economic and financial co-operation with other countries on desirable principles than if England refused to undertake any well-defined exchange policy in the prosecution of which other countries could co-operate.

(ii) The second possibility is a gold standard reformed in a very important way. It would be possible to allow the free import and export of gold, to fix the Bank of England's buying and selling prices of gold but to give the Bank of England the power of altering its buying and selling prices of gold in the same way that it can at present alter the Bank Rate. This would achieve the object of making short-period fluctuations in the exchange rate with gold standard countries smaller than under (i), and if and when sufficient co-operation could be obtained with other countries not on the gold standard to operate the same standard, it would open up great possibilities of stabilising for considerable periods the rates of exchange with these other countries, while giving each country the freedom to alter its exchange rate in accordance with the requirements of a fundamentally changed economic situation.

It should be one of the major objects of the Government to secure international monetary co-operation; and if this type of gold standard is accepted such co-operation might take the following form: each central bank should agree to keep funds with an International Bank – e.g. the BIS [Bank for International Settlements] – whose assets and liabilities would be reckoned in obligations fixed in gold units; the representatives of each central bank or government at the BIS should attempt to offset the movement of short-term funds from one centre to another, where this is desirable, by means of transferring funds with the BIS from one account to another, rather than by operating through national exchange equalisation funds. The central banks should in co-operation with one another, through the BIS, attempt to fix for certain periods of time their national buying and selling prices of gold. Debtor countries should be allowed a sufficiently high price for gold to generate a favourable balance of payments to meet their obligations; but it should be a clear principle in determining particular exchange rates that no country which wished to obtain a recovery in trade should do so by raising its price of gold in order to obtain a favourable balance of payments in excess of that required to meet its normal obligations. To achieve this recovery it should rely on its internal economic and financial expansion. On the other hand any country which is taking positive measures to raise its prices and money incomes to get out of a depression, while other countries are not doing so, or which is taking positive measures to maintain its prices and money incomes, while they are falling in other countries, should be allowed to raise its price of gold.

Such a standard would not of course eliminate exchange speculation, since people would speculate on a change in the Bank of England's price for gold. Thus, if people expected a rise in this price, they would buy gold or other currencies at the ruling price, in order to sell them again to the Bank at the higher price. Considerable difficulty may be avoided in this respect if there is a sufficient margin between the Bank's buying and selling prices of gold, so that after any raising of these prices the new buying price would still be below the old selling price, and alternatively after a lowering of these prices the new selling price would still be higher than the old buying price. If the Government monopolised dealings in foreign exchange, as suggested below in V, the problem of speculative movements of funds would solve itself.

(iii) The third possibility is that of fixing the value of the pound in terms of commodities; if the Bank of England were obliged to buy and sell at a fixed price in pounds a certain bundle of commodities (e.g. a given weight of gold plus a given amount of wheat plus . . . etc.). The Bank would be obliged to buy or sell a fixed bundle of these commodities at a given price in pounds, but it should be obliged only to deal in bundles and not in any individual commodities in the bundle. The suggestion that it should state its willingness to buy one of the commodities, e.g. so much iron for £1, if sufficient iron is presented to it to buy at current prices the 'bundle' of commodities whose value is fixed at £1, is open to the following serious objection: the Bank might find that its reserves were mainly in the form of iron, and then if the price of iron fell considerably, while the prices of other commodities in the bundle rose, this would cause the value of its assets to slump without causing any change in the value of its liabilities. The Bank should therefore deal always in the bundle of commodities alone. If this were done a group of merchants outside the Bank would soon be formed, or could easily be formed by the Government, to deal in these bundles between the Bank and the producers and the consumers of the individual commodities. We must discuss this suggestion first on the assumption that in the main the commodities are home-produced, and secondly on the assumption that they are foreign-produced.

(a) Where the commodities in the 'bundle' are home-produced, this standard would provide a very great aid to the Government in any attempt to prevent violent fluctuations in prices and money incomes. If prices are tending to fall people will sell commodities to the Bank at the fixed price; this will maintain their price and maintain the incomes of those producing them, thus keeping up the income which they have to spend on other commodities. It will also increase automatically the amount of money, provided that the persons selling the commodities to the Bank are paid with new money (i.e. notes or deposits) issued by the Bank against the Bank's purchases – i.e. provided that the Bank does not offset this transaction by selling some other asset. This money will be paid into the joint-stock banks, who will find that their reserves of cash are up by this amount and will attempt to lend nine times as much in order to preserve the ten per cent ratio between their cash and deposits. This will automatically lower interest rates considerably and make both Government and private capital development more profitable. The converse will hold true, if prices and money incomes are tending to rise. The Bank will therefore have to be ready to store the commodities until market prices tend to rise again and the commodities are bought from the Bank instead of in the market. It is necessary therefore to choose commodities which are standardised, durable and easily stored. It may be that in many cases the cost of storage would be excessive; but in other cases the Government should meet the necessary cost of storage out of the Budget. This would be a small cost to pay for so powerful a weapon of stabilisation. It should, however, be carefully noted that this automatic stabilisation of a certain price level should not take the place of other action mentioned in I above. If large sales or purchases of commodities are made to or from the Bank, this should act as a signal that the appropriate action of I is desired.

(b) If the commodities are mainly foreign-produced commodities, the effect of this policy will not be so directly to stabilise the internal position. It will directly mean that if the foreign price level of these goods falls, the pound will depreciate in terms of foreign commodities to sell at a profit to the Bank. This would provide an effective means of enabling the monetary authorities to adjust the exchange rate so as to stabilise the internal price level of our imports and so as to offset any change in the foreign demand for our exports due to a change in foreign prices and incomes.

In either case such a standard would provide a currency the commodity value of which was automatically kept stable, and if it were successfully operated by this country might lead to a similar change in monetary policy in other countries, which would provide at the same time stable exchange rates and which would do much to eliminate world booms and slumps.

This form of standard has so far been discussed in its most complete form. But it can be modified until it is reduced simply to an instance of symmetallism. If the bundle of commodities were simply a certain amount of gold plus a certain amount of silver, the standard would be simply a symmetallic standard. The greater the number of commodities and the more diverse are their uses and their conditions of production, the more effective this standard becomes. It is probably best for the Labour Government to adopt some standard, either that of (ii) or (iii) of this paragraph. If the cost of storage is not too great to obtain a really representative bundle of commodities the standard of (iii) is the best, though it might be necessary from time to time to change the buying and selling prices of the bundle of commodities and to alter its composition.

IV Foreign Trade

The object of foreign trade is to obtain imported goods in exchange for home-produced goods, whenever it is possible to obtain a greater amount of these goods by importing them than would have been obtained had the factors of production been withdrawn from the production of the exported goods and set to the production at home of the imported goods. This result is achieved if home-made goods are sold abroad whenever the price obtainable in the foreign market is, when converted into sterling at the ruling rate, not lower than the cost of production, and if all goods are allowed to flow in whenever the price at which they are offered by the foreigner, when converted into sterling at the ruling rate, is lower than the cost of producing the same goods at home. The exchange rate will be fixed at that level at which, when under the stimulus of the internal financial policy full employment is secured, the value of exports minus the value of imports is just equal to the amount which it is considered desirable to lend abroad. In this computation invisible items are included in exports and imports.

The same result could be obtained regardless of the exchange rate if the Government monopolised all external trade, assessed the cost of producing the imported goods at home and exported regardless of the exchange rate, whenever the amount of imports which, at the prices ruling in the rest of the world, it can get for a given amount of exported goods was greater than the amount of these imported goods that would be produced at home for the same cost as the exports. The first method is, however, preferable to the second because it is simpler to operate and gives to each individual industry an index of what its policy should be.

If the first method is adopted, the following further principles should be observed:

(a) A system of costing should be adopted in controlled industry, which will show as clearly as can be done the real marginal cost of labour, capital and land required in the production of each commodity. This cost must be expressed in money terms. Each controlled industry should sell in the export market as much as it can without loss at this cost and at the current rate of exchange. In this case each socialised industry can arrange through appropriate mechanism for its own marketing.

(b) There should be a progressive reduction of tariffs and elimination of import quotas and prohibitions.

V *Control of Capital Movements*

Lending abroad can be divided into two heads:

(1) Long-term loans, which take the form of the flotation in London of new issues by foreign governments, municipalities or companies, and the purchase by residents in this country of existing foreign securities. The incentive to lend abroad on long term will be greater the higher is the rate of return abroad and the higher it is expected to be compared with the return in home industry, the greater are the expectations of a boom in security prices abroad, and the greater are the expectations that the pound will depreciate in the exchange market.

(2) Short-term loans, which take the form of the purchase of foreign exchange for the purpose of holding deposits in foreign banks, foreign currency or short-term foreign bills. The incentive to make such short-term loans depends upon the relative rates of interest on such loans here and abroad, and also upon the expectation of a change in the exchange rate.

It is clear from this summary of the factors which determine how much people are willing to lend abroad that there may be very considerable and violent fluctuations in the amount which people decide to lend. Such changes may be due simply to the belief that it is more profitable to invest or speculate in a foreign country or at the other extreme may be due to a panic export of capital in the fear of confiscatory legislation at home. Even if such panics are completely avoided there would however remain many things – such as speculative movements on foreign stock exchanges, political changes in foreign centres or changes in the profitability of industry in foreign nations – which would cause considerable changes in the amount which people in this country would attempt to lend abroad.

If the Government is not in a position to control the volume of foreign lending, it will be forced either to abandon its internal policy of stabilisation or else to abandon the forms of temporary exchange stability which have been suggested in section III. For suppose that there is a considerable increase in the amount which people in this country desire to lend abroad. This will cause an increased demand for foreign currencies on the part of those who hold sterling. Such a movement of capital from this country can only be financed if our imports contract and/or our exports expand. This result can be obtained if English prices and money incomes are so deflated by means of an internal financial policy designed for the purpose that our imports are discouraged and our exports are encouraged sufficiently to finance the increased foreign lending. But this means that the internal policy of stabilisation must be abandoned, which is certainly too heavy a price to pay for the advantages of increased lending abroad.

But if the increased foreign lending is allowed and the internal policy of stabilisation maintained, the necessary increase in our exports and decrease in our imports can only be obtained by allowing the pound to depreciate so as to make our imports more expensive in England and our exports cheaper in the world markets. This might well mean abandoning the exchange policies suggested in section III.

Apart from this, however, there is a general argument of great importance against allowing unrestricted foreign lending. Increased lending abroad can only be financed by increased exports and decreased imports, and this result can only be achieved – whatever methods may be adopted – by lowering the price of our exports relatively to the price of our imports. In other words the greater the volume of foreign lending, the smaller the quantity of imports that we receive for a given amount of our exports; and this might prove an economic cost out of proportion to any advantage to be gained from increased investment in foreign countries.

It must be understood that the private investor is solely concerned with the prospective profit on his investment considered as a percentage of the capital sum. But if a considerable sum has to be financed (i.e. a considerable excess of exports over imports has to be generated) for the purpose of making this investment, this, like a reparations payment, may cause a considerable turn in the terms of trade against the country, and throw a corresponding burden on to the community as a whole, which is additional to the burden which the investor himself bears in providing funds for his investment. Whether in any particular case this secondary cost incurred through foreign investment is great depends on the elasticity of demand and supply at home and abroad for the goods which enter into our foreign trade. On this subject the Supreme Economic Authority should have collected data to enable it to judge.

The case for controlling the volume of foreign investment is strengthened by the possibility of sudden flights of capital owing to panic or unreasoning alarms and suspicions and by the large volume of floating balances which, under a system of free foreign exchanges, can be transferred abroad with ease. Big movements to and fro of such balances under the influence of casual rumours and suspicions are almost bound, if unchecked, to disrupt a system for maintaining internal stability combined with a reasonable steadiness in foreign exchange rates.

The only alternative is to take direct control over the volume of foreign lending, fluctuations in which are the primary cause of these problems. The Government or the Supreme Economic Authority of the Government must decide how much it is desirable shall be lent abroad each year. It is impossible to give any rule-of-thumb principles by which this decision should be governed; but the following are the main considerations which should be borne in mind:

(a) The extent to which a higher return can be earned on investment abroad rather than in England;
(b) The extent to which, if there is no alteration in the internal policy of stabilisation and in the existing rate of exchange with other countries, an excess of exports and other current receipts of foreign currrencies will automatically be generated. This will show the funds which *are* available for lending abroad, if there is no change in the existing financial policy;
(c) The extent to which it would be necessary, while maintaining the internal financial policy unchanged, to depreciate the pound to raise the price of imports and to lower the price of exports in foreign markets sufficiently to increase the funds available for foreign lending by a given amount. This will give some indication of the cost involved in any increase in foreign lending;
(d) The extent to which the borrowing country in each case is borrowing for a productive use. In this connection it must be clearly realised that, if the loan is a loan and not a gift, and if repayment of the loan and of interest on it is going to be demanded, the borrowing country must be using the loan in a productive manner which is likely to strengthen its position in the competitive markets of the world. If this is not the case, ultimate repayment is unlikely to materialise, and the attempt to repay by the borrowing country will cause very great economic difficulties and suffering in that country. In this connection it should always be remembered that where it is a question of maintaining a large volume of foreign lending with a low exchange rate, or a small volume of foreign lending with a high exchange rate, the low exchange rate will damage other countries' export trade by making our goods cheaper in foreign markets, while a high exchange will enable other countries to export more easily. If

this country wishes therefore to aid other countries in a time of depression, it can probably do more good by lending little to, but buying more from, foreign countries, rather than by lending more and allowing its exchange rate to depreciate, thereby competing more strongly with other countries in the export market and buying less from them;

(e) Any relevant political or other non-economic factors involved in lending abroad to particular countries or for particular purposes.

It appears then that there is a strong case for the complete control of foreign lending by the Economic Authority. But it may be that such control is only possible if the Government can through some appropriate organ (e.g. the Bank of England) monopolise the purchase and sale of foreign currency and of foreign securities. It is of course relatively easy to control new issues on the London capital market on the part of foreign borrowers, if the Government has set up a National Investment Board, whose sanction is necessary for any new issue. But this does not give the Government the requisite control over foreign lending. For it remains possible for individuals and institutions to buy foreign currency or deposits in foreign banks or existing foreign securities with English money without check. Such purchases can only be effectively controlled if the Government can control all purchases of foreign money, so that it is able to allow or disallow purchases according as they are made for approved purposes or not.

This involves further powers for the Government. In the first place the Government must have the power to see that persons who own foreign investments do not re-lend abroad the income derived from them without the approval of the Government, but surrender it in exchange for sterling. For in this country past foreign investments provide an important source of income, which can in present circumstances be lent abroad without the necessity of first buying foreign currencies. It is probable that the income-tax authorities have the requisite knowledge of the holding of foreign securities, but the Government must take the powers necessary to compel people to bring back to England the income from these securities.

In the second place the Government must have the power necessary to force English exporters to change into English money the foreign money which they receive in payment for their exports. For if these powers are not taken it is always possible for exporters to lend abroad the proceeds of their sale of exports in foreign markets without purchasing foreign currencies with sterling for this purpose. In this case the customs authorities would probably with comparative ease be able to obtain the necessary information relating to the receipts of foreign money by English exporters, but the Government must take the powers necessary to compel these exporters to repatriate their receipts.

Thirdly the Government must have similar powers by which it can ensure that those who have claims to foreign currencies arising otherwise than through the ownership of foreign investments or through the sale of exports, change these receipts into English money.

The Government should, then, aim at a complete monopoly in foreign exchange dealings. This can only be done by the following measures:

(a) Legislation which will make illegal the purchase or sale of foreign money through any organ other than the recognised Government institutions (e.g. the Bank of England) with heavy penalties for violations.
(b) Legislation which will require those receiving payments from abroad to sell the foreign currencies so obtained at the official price to the authorised institutions.

VI Summary

When this control has been obtained, we may summarise the suggested financial policy for the Government as follows:

(a) It should lay most stress on its internal financial policy directed to preventing unemployment (sec. I).
(b) It should then choose a fixed buying and selling price of gold (cf. sec. III, para. ii), or a fixed buying and selling price of some suitable composite commodity (cf. sec. III, para. iii), for the Bank of England on the principles discussed in section III. It must be borne in mind in choosing the suitable price of gold or of the composite commodity that it should be so chosen that in view of the fixed internal financial policy of this country and of the financial policy of other countries the English rate of exchange will be such as to provide just that volume of exports and of imports which is necessary to finance the volume of foreign lending which is held to be desirable in view of the considerations discussed in section V.

    The Bank's fixed buying and selling price of gold or the composite commodity should be revised from time to time in accordance with the principles of section III.
(c) If the arguments of V are regarded as cogent, further powers are required for the Government, in order to secure control over the volume of foreign lending. It cannot be predicted in advance whether the substantial policy outlined in (a) and (b) could be successfully operated without these further powers. It is possible that it could. In view of the opposite possibility, however, the Government should be forearmed with the following plan for securing control over foreign lending to be put into operation either at the outset or as soon as it became clear that speculative transfers of funds abroad were prejudicing the success of the internal policy.

    Having monopolised the purchase and sale of foreign currencies and having fixed the Bank of England's buying and selling price of gold or of the composite commodity, the Government should allow purchase and sale of foreign currency for the financing of imports and exports, and of invisible items on current account, though all such purchases and sales would be made through recognised institutions. Controlled industries should purchase abroad whenever that is cheaper at the official rate of foreign exchange and should sell abroad whenever it is profitable for them to do so at this rate. Further, the Government should by degrees remove all quotas and tariffs (cf. section IV).

(d) The Government must have power to ensure that exporters, whether these are private individuals or controlled industries, sell to the authorised institutions at the official rate all foreign currencies which they obtain in payment for exported goods; it must have similar powers to compel those earning income on foreign investments or from other foreign sources to sell the foreign money so obtained at the official rate for pounds (cf. section V).

(e) The funds which the Economic Authority or its representative organ (e.g. the Bank of England) should actually allow to be lent abroad must be simply the excess of the sales of foreign currency to it over the purchase of foreign money from it for the purposes already approved. This sum may be greater or less than the sum which the authority planned should be lent abroad in the first place. In this case the authority has the choice either of changing its exchange policy, so as to obtain a smaller or greater supply of foreign currency for foreign lending. Thus if it is lending abroad less than it wishes to lend it may now raise the official price of gold or of the composite commodity and so raise the appropriate official price for foreign currencies that the price of imports in this country rises and the price of English exports in foreign markets falls sufficiently to obtain the appropriate increase in the supply of funds for foreign lending.

Whether the authority operates by revising its plans about the sum to be lent abroad or by revising its exchange policy must depend in each case upon the consideration of the points discussed in section V. The important point, however, is that the authority should change either its policy of foreign lending or its exchange policy, and should not meet the situation by giving up its plans of internal stability. It is clear that the plans for foreign lending and for controlling exchange rates must come up for frequent revision if they are to be used in this way as a means of obtaining internal stability.

3

A Proposal for an International Commercial Union

Meade's proposal, first dated 25 July 1942, for a 'commercial union' to complement Keynes's plan for a 'clearing union' was adopted by the Board of Trade later the same year, and subsequently discussed with American officials in Washington by the Law Mission (of which Meade was a member) in September–October 1943. Further discussions in London and Washington beginning in December 1944 led to the 'Proposals for consideration by an International Conference on Trade and Employment' *published by the US and UK Governments in December 1945. Meade was then a British representative on the Preparatory Commission for the conference, which met in London in October 1946 and Geneva in April 1947 to produce a Draft Charter for an International Trade Organisation. Although the ITO Charter adopted at the UN Conference on Trade and Employment in Havana on 23 March 1948 was not ratified, many of its principles had been incorporated in the General Agreement on Tariffs and Trade negotiated in Geneva in 1947. (Public Record Office T230/14, 92, 125, 171, 172; Meade Papers 3/2 and Meade Diaries, 1943 and 1944–46; Richard N. Gardner,* Sterling–Dollar Diplomacy, *London: Oxford University Press, 1956, Chapters VI, VIII, XIV and XVII.)*

I Our Post-War Commercial Problem

1 The United Kingdom will be in a difficult commercial position after the war. As a community we depend upon imports of essential foodstuffs and raw materials, which we must purchase by the export of manufactured goods. Developments during the war, such as the loss of income from foreign investments, will have increased our need for an expanded export trade, while at the same time the industrialisation which has taken, or is likely to take, place in certain overseas territories may well have restricted some of our export opportunities. We import essentials; we export goods with which our customers can more easily dispense. If ever there was a community which had an interest in the general removal of restrictions to international commerce, it is the United Kingdom.

2 Our trade in the past has been very largely of a multilateral character. We have bought goods from the United States with income obtained from the sale of our produce in other less well developed territories. If many of our most readily available sources of supply of essential imports are not to be closed to us, it is important that the opportunities for beneficial multilateral trade should be preserved to their fullest extent.

3 Our export possibilities would thus be directly and indirectly greatly improved, if we could obtain the agreement, for example, of the United States to modify its pre-war excessive tariff barriers and of Germany to give up its pre-war policy of bilateralism and trade discrimination. These considerations suggest that we, above all other countries, stand to gain (i) from a policy of general world economic and financial expansion which will maintain a high level of buying power in export markets, (ii) from a general reduction of barriers and restrictions in international markets and (iii) from a removal of those discriminations and rigidly bilateral bargains which remove the opportunities for multilateral trading.

4 Multilateral trading the removal of trade restrictions do not, however, imply *laissez-faire*, and are in no way incompatible with a system of state trading. We shall wish to co-operate with the United States, on the basis of Article VII of the Mutual Aid Agreement of 23 February 1942, on 'action by the United States of America and the United Kingdom, open to participation by all other countries of like mind, directed to . . . the elimination of all forms of discriminatory treatment in international commerce, and to the reduction of tariffs and other trade barriers . . . ' At the same time we must aim at the formulation of such action by means, which do not automatically preclude countries such as the USSR which may be assumed to desire to continue a system of state trading nor prevent us, if we so desire, from continuing a system of state importation for certain products.

5 After the war we shall not be in a good position in which we can afford *unconditionally* to abandon all protective devices. We cannot readily indulge in a unilateral policy of removing our protective armour and shall thus desire to retain the right to restrict purchases from, and to discriminate against, those countries which themselves retain highly protective commercial policies or which discriminate against ours. We shall, moreover, need to retain the right to impose more general restrictions on purchases of inessential goods or on unnecessary payments abroad so long as we are faced with an acute problem of restoring equilibrium to our international balance of payments.

6 The essential features of our post-war commercial problem may, therefore, be summarised as follows:

(i) We shall need a large expansion of our export trade and shall stand to gain very greatly from a general world system in which there is a general expansion of world purchasing power and in which restrictions and discriminations on foreign trade are reduced or removed.

(ii) Apart from our interests we are committed under Article VII of the Mutual Aid Agreement to such a policy, and the future of our relations with the United States requires that we should implement this undertaking.

(iii) We need, however, to implement these undertakings in a way which leaves room for state trading and which does not preclude us (a) from imposing restrictions or discriminations against those countries which impose severe restrictions or discriminations against us or (b) from restricting our payments to other countries if and when balance-of-payments difficulties make such action inevitable.

II The Contribution of Other Proposed Institutions to the Solution of the Commercial Problem

7 The proposals which have already been made (RP(42)2 ['External and economic policy with special reference to the discussions with the US Administration, Note by the Treasury', 24 March 1942, PRO CAB87/2], paragraphs 51–3, 61–134) for the institution of an International Clearing Union, if they are adopted, should much simplify our tasks in formulating far-reaching and imaginative proposals for the reduction of restrictions to international commerce.

8 In the first place, these and similar proposals would greatly help – indeed this is the essence of the proposals – to adjust the balance of payments without undue strain on the debtor countries. Since a large number of protective devices are in origin essentially weapons of defence of countries which are faced with an undue pressure on their balances of international payments, an effective mechanism which makes the creditor nations responsible for a due part, if necessary, of adjustments of international payments should clear the way for attempts to mitigate protectionism.

9 But, in the second place, the machinery of the Clearing Union, through the debit and credit balances of its members, provides an effective and automatic measurement of existing maladjustments in balances of payments. A country which claims that it must be permitted to impose certain protective restrictions as a result of a serious maladjustment in its balance of payments can appeal to (or to be referred to) a reasonably unambiguous index – its debit balance with the Clearing Union. It should, for example, be possible for a country to commit itself in commercial agreements to remove various protective devices but, at the same time, to reserve the right to reimpose some of these devices when and for as long as its debit with the Clearing Union was in excess of a certain figure.

10 Thirdly, the Clearing Union may be expected to aid in promoting that general expansion of demand in world markets which, in Article VII of the Mutual Aid Agreement itself, comes before the removal of trade restrictions and discriminations as an objective of international co-operative action. Indeed, it is only in a general milieu of economic expansion that the pressure on the balances of payments of debtor countries is likely to be sufficiently relieved to make possible a really effective lowering of protective devices. There are other proposals under consideration which will help towards the same purpose of economic expansion. In particular, the proposals for the development of international investment (RP(42)2 paragraphs 36–50) and the proposals for a systematisation of buffer stock arrangements for primary products (USE (42)15 ['The International Regulation of Primary Products, Memorandum by the Treasury', 10 July 1942, PRO CAB87/60]) should provide effective support to an expansive international policy.

III Outline of a Possible Commercial Union

11 It is suggested, therefore, that the United Kingdom should propose the formulation of an International Commercial Union for the purpose of achieving a general reduction of restrictions on international commerce. The Commercial Union would be founded on the following principles:

(i) Membership of the Union would be open to all states which applied for membership and which were willing to carry out the obligations of membership. Membership of the Commercial Union would not be confined to members of the Clearing Union (just as membership of the Clearing Union would in no way be confined to members of the Commercial Union); but, as is indicated in (iv) below, members of the Commercial Union who were also members of the Clearing Union would obtain certain privileges in the Commercial Union.

(ii) Members of the Commercial Union would undertake not to grant preferences or other price advantages to any other member of the Union without extending it to all members, except that certain moderate and defined degrees of preference might be given as between members of a recognised political or geographical group of nations. A clause of this kind would permit discrimination of any degree desired against countries which were not members of the Commercial Union and which had not, therefore, pledged themselves in turn not to discriminate. It would also permit discrimination of a defined and moderate degree in favour of a recognised political or geographical grouping of states, and would thus permit the continuation of a moderate degree of Imperial Preference.

(iii) Members of the Commercial Union would undertake to remove altogether certain protective devices against the commerce of other members of the Union and to reduce to a defined maximum the degree of protection which they would afford to their own home producers against the produce of other members of the Union. A clause of this type would pledge members to eliminate or to limit their protective devices against other members of the Union who had undertaken a similar pledge, but would leave them free to introduce what protective measures they desired against non-members. Such an arrangement would be safeguarded by the right of any non-member state to join the Commercial Union.

(iv) Members of the Commercial Union, who were also members of the Clearing Union and whose accounts with the Clearing Union were in deficit by a certain defined amount, would be permitted to impose certain protective devices so long as their debt remained in excess of the prescribed amount.

(v) The Charter of the Commercial Union would expressly state that state trading by members of the Union was not precluded. An indication should be given of the way in which the provisions of the Charter of the Commercial Union should be applied both in the case of competitive trading and in the case of state trading.

(vi) The Charter of the Commercial Union would provide for the institution of an International Commerce Commission of a semi-arbitral semi-judicial nature. Members could refer complaints to this body in order to obtain an opinion on whether the Charter of the Union was being broken by any particular action of a particular member of the Union.

(vii) Membership of the Commercial Union would in no way preclude any member from concluding any type of commercial treaty or agreement with any other state – whether a member of the Union or not – provided only that the terms of the treaty or agreement were not incompatible with its obligations as a member of the Union.

12 If an attempt were made to draft a Charter for a Commercial Union of this type, one of the most important questions would be how precisely worded should be the definition of the discriminations and degrees of protection that would be disallowed to members of the Union and of the actions which would be permitted or disallowed to state trading organisations. It is in this connection that the major dilemma is to be faced. If an attempt is made to define very rigidly and precisely exactly what any member may or may not do in all possible circumstances, it is probable that as circumstances change and as states introduce new methods of trading organisation certain state measures may be precluded which it is not in the general intention of the Charter to disallow and certain other measures may be allowed which it is in the intention of the Charter to forbid. On the other hand, if the Charter is drawn up in much less precise terms and expresses only in the most general terms the types of protective device which it is intended to forbid and the general maximum degree of protection which it is intended to allow, then very great responsibility will rest upon the International Commerce Commission or similar body whose duty it was to interpret the Charter. The success of

the Union will depend upon the formulation of the Charter in terms which, on the one hand do not attempt to put international trade into an impossible straitjacket and, on the other hand, do not impose upon the International Commerce Commission such a burden of semi-legislative duties that it could not bear.

13 The following clauses are intended merely as an illustration of one possible set of conditions which might be included in that section of the Charter of the Commercial Union in which the limitations on members' discriminatory or protective policy are defined:

(i) Members would be forbidden to discriminate (whether by means of taxes, subsidies, preferential prices offered by state organisations, or other means) in the prices offered for the produce of other members of the Union.
(ii) Members would be bound to give other members of the Union as favourable prices for their produce as they gave for the similar produce from any non-member state.
(iii) As exceptions to clauses (i) and (ii) above members could give price preferences up to a maximum of, say, 10 per cent to the produce of another state with which it formed a special recognised geographical or political union.
(iv) Members would be forbidden to give a preference (whether by tax, subsidy, price offered by state trading body or other means) in price to their home producers which was more than, say, 25 per cent greater than the price offered for similar goods produced by other members of the Union.
(v) Members would be forbidden to impose quantitative restrictions or prohibitions, other than for reasons of public health or public safety, on the import of goods from other members of the Commercial Union.
(vi) Members would undertake not to impose restrictions on payments for current (as opposed to capital) transactions to other members of the Union, except that a country which was also a member of the Clearing Union and was a 'deficiency' country with the Clearing Union would be permitted to impose restrictions on current payments for as long as it remained a 'deficiency' country.
(vii) Members would undertake not to impose quantitative restrictions or prohibitions on exports except as part of a recognised international regulation scheme for primary products (as arranged for in the scheme outlined in USE (42)15).
(viii) Members would undertake not to impose open or hidden taxes or subsidies of more than, say, 10 per cent on exports to any country whether a member of the Commercial Union or not.

14 The purpose of these various provisions is clear. Clauses (i) to (iii) in the preceding paragraph would limit price discriminations for imports; clause (iv) would limit the degree of price protection which could be given to home production; clauses (v) and (vi) would prevent quantita-

tive or value restrictions on imports, except in the case of countries in a 'deficiency' position with the Clearing Union; and clauses (vii) and (viii) would cover export policy, preventing both undue restriction of export and export dumping, – the latter of which may be equally obnoxious whether it be to other member states or to non-member states.

IV The Problem of State Trading

15 The general principles of the application of these clauses to countries adopting a competitive trade organisation are clear, although there would, no doubt, be many difficult technical problems to be determined in border-line cases by the International Commerce Commission, as to what exactly did or did not constitute a price preference or a restriction on payments. The problem of applying these clauses to cases of state trading would probably in practice present more difficulties since it is as yet a less familiar problem; but in principle it should be no less capable of satisfactory solution.

16 It resolves itself into a two-fold problem:

(i) that of determining the degree of price preference or protection which is being offered by the state trading organisation and
(ii) that of deciding whether a quantitative restriction on imports (or on exports) is being imposed.

In the case of a state which, while its trading system is mainly competitive, monopolises for itself the trade of a limited number of commodities, the problem of judging the degree of price discrimination or of price preference given as between one source of supply and another or as between one market and another does not present any additional difficulties of principle. This problem may become somewhat more complicated in practice, but it still remains in essence the same, even in the case of a country which has socialised trade in all or the majority of products; such extreme cases are, however, in the post-war world likely to be relatively few in number; and they will be still less important from the point of view of their share in the total of international trade.

17 The regulation of price preferences is not, however, sufficient to prevent discrimination or protection. A state trading organisation might, for example, discriminate in favour of one source of supply as opposed to another by buying much in the first and little in the second, even though it paid a non-discriminatory price. It is necessary to determine what corresponds in the case of state trading to the obligations (suggested in clauses (v)–(vii) of paragraph 14 above) not to impose quantitative restrictions on imports or exports except in certain clearly defined cases. This limitation corresponds in the case of state trading to an obligation (i) to take from each foreign market as much imports as each such market would wish to supply at the price which the importing state organisation

is offering and (ii) to sell in all foreign markets as much foreign exports as each such market would wish to purchase at the price at which the goods are offered by the state exporting organisation.

18 These considerations suggest that the principles of membership of the Commercial Union should be applied in such a way as (i) to impose the same obligations both to competitive and to state trading in all matters of price discrimination and price preference, (ii) to forbid in the case of competitive trading quantitative restrictions on imports and exports and on current payments, and (iii) to impose in the case of state trading obligations to purchase from, or to sell to, each foreign market as much as that foreign market wishes to sell, or to purchase, at the prices offered by the state trading organisation. It would, however, be a matter for detailed consideration to determine the extent to which, and the conditions on which long forward contracts could be entered into by state trading organisations within the framework of these principles. Such contracts should not be excluded; but they should be undertaken in such a way as to maintain a reasonable approximation to the principles outlined above.

V The International Commerce Commission

19 The existence of some international body which had the competence to interpret the Charter of the Commercial Union, and to arbitrate or to give decisions in case of disputes among its members would be an essential part of the mechanism of such a Union. It would, however, be premature at this stage to make detailed suggestions about the constitution of such a body. Its members should, no doubt, be appointed by the governments of the states making up the Commercial Union. It should, no doubt, have the power of expressing an opinion upon any complaint brought to its notice by one member of the Union against another member, and of requiring members of the Union to provide it with the statistical and other information necessary to form a judgement in such cases. It might well be ruled that, in such cases, its findings – both its majority and minority findings – should be published. But it is a matter for further consideration how such findings should be binding on members of the Union. It might, for example, be provided, as a sanction against breaches of the Charter of the Union, that any member of the Union which refused to accept a majority finding of the Commission could be treated by other members as if it were no longer a member of the Union, in so far as the clauses prohibiting discriminatory practices were concerned. This, however, is a question which is probably best answered at a much later stage.

VI The Problem of the Transition

20 Membership of the Commercial Union (at any rate on anything like the terms suggested above for illustrative purposes) would require an

extensive readjustment of commercial policy in the case of a number of countries. If such major readjustments are desirable, there is much to be said for undertaking them after the cataclysm of a major war; for serious readjustments will be inevitable in such a period in any case, and it is surely better to readjust then to the conditions which are most desired than to rebuild to an ancient plan which it is intended in any case to reconstruct sooner or later. Nevertheless, it would be out of the question to suggest this or any other country should commit itself to an immediate acceptance of all the principles of the Commercial Union immediately after the war. What is required is some transitional arrangement whereby countries can become members of the Commercial Union during a period of, say, five years after the close of hostilities on condition:

(i) That they undertake to fulfil some of its obligations, such as the removal of quantitative import restrictions and prohibitions, within a short period of a year or two, and
(ii) That they undertake to fulfil the remaining obligations within a period of not less than, say, five years. Such an arrangement might serve to secure that certain protective devices were quickly eliminated, that a more gradual movement was initiated for the removal or reduction of others, and – most important of all – that each member could plan its economic development on the assumption that within a specified number of years other members would have contracted their protective and discriminatory devices within reasonably precise and clearly defined limits.

4

The Post-War International Settlement and the United Kingdom Balance of Payments

After the Law Mission to Washington in September–October 1943 (see above p. 27) further Anglo–American discussions on post-war economic policy were delayed until the end of 1944 by disputes within the British Government. The following paper, which Meade wrote in December 1943 during those disputes, is included here as an indication of Meade's views on the post-war international economic order at that time; for his views after the war see Chapters 6 and 10 below. (Meade Papers 3/2; Public Record Office T230/15 and CAB124/582; The Collected Writings of John Maynard Keynes, Vol. XXVI: Activities 1941–1946, Shaping the Post-war World: Bretton Woods and Reparations, *London: Macmillan, 1980, Chapter 2.)*

The joint official reports on the Washington discussions referred to in the paper are to be found on Public Record Office T230/92; records of the discussions on T230/172.

1 The purpose of this note is to show that the broad lines of the economic settlement discussed informally among United Kingdom and United States officials in Washington recently (September and October, 1943) make full allowance for the solution of the problem of the United Kingdom post-war balance of payments. Indeed, more than this will be claimed; for there is strong reason to believe that the proposed settlement provides a favourable set of conditions for the resolution of this difficult and esssential problem. The question may best be discussed in two separate parts: first as it will be affected by the proposed international economic arrangements in the long run after the immediate post-war dislocations have been surmounted, and secondly as it will present itself in the transitional period.

I The Long-Term Problem

(i) General Considerations

2 The United Kingdom exports manufactured goods which are less essential than the foodstuffs and raw materials which she imports. But

not only are her exports less essential in character than her imports; these manufactured exports are sold, to an increasing extent, in competition with the manufactures of the importing countries. For this reason also foreign customers can dispense more easily with United Kingdom exports than the United Kingdom can with her overseas supplies of essential primary products.

3 This essential factor must form the basis for any long-term policy for restoring equilibrium to the United Kingdom balance of payments. In short, since our exports are less indispensable to others than our imports are to ourselves, we must aim at a general settlement which lays at least as much, if not more, stress on preventing others from imposing unnecessary restrictions on their imports as it does on allowing us to take steps to restrict our imports.

4 This principle applies above all to the use of quantitative import restrictions. It is more important to ensure that other countries whose balances of payments are not unfavourable do not impose quantitative import restrictions (which inter-war experience proved to be the most serious obstacle to our export trade) than it is to preserve our right to impose quantitative import restrictions on our imports. It is, of course, true that there is an appreciable volume of manufactured imports with which we could dispense altogether or which at a price we could produce at home. The same is true, though to a more limited extent, of our imports of foodstuffs and raw materials, some of which could at a price be produced at home. But the simple fact is that the foreigner will be able to dispense still more easily with our exports. The ideal solution is one which permits the use of quantitative import restrictions to us if our balance of payments is unfavourable, but simultaneously prohibits the use of quantitative import restrictions by our customers if their balances of payments are not unfavourable.

5 A similar principle applies to adjustments of exchange rates. It is as important to ensure that foreign countries, whose balances of payments are not unfavourable, do not depreciate unnecessarily their exchange rates as it is to ensure that we are free to depreciate sterling if this is necessary for the adjustment of an adverse balance of payments. If we depreciate sterling, any consequent expansion of our exports may be nullified if our customers and our competitiors depreciate *pari passu* their own currencies, so that our exports obtain no advantage relative to the similar exports of our competitors or to the similar products of our customers. Here again the ideal solution is to permit a moderate degree of exchange depreciation to countries with an unfavourable balance of payments, but to deny it to countries whose balances are not adverse.

6 There has been some tendency recently to underestimate the important part which appropriate adjustments of exchange rates may play in restoring equilibrium to international balances of payments. Quantitative restriction of imports can do nothing to promote exports, which in

the case of a country like the United Kingdom are more flexible than imports. A depreciation of sterling, on the other hand, by reducing the price of our products in foreign markets will stimulate our exports, as well as operate on our imports by raising their sterling price. Quantitative import restrictions operate more promptly than a depreciation of sterling, since the desired restriction of imports can be brought about immediately. But a depreciation of sterling will have an extensive effect through its influence on the prices of all exports and of all imports. This effect will, however, work itself out fully only after a period of time in which foreign producers and purchasers, and home producers and purchasers, have become aware of the changed price relationships and have had time to adjust their behaviour accordingly.

7 The effectiveness of an exchange depreciation is, of course, dependent upon the circumstances in which it takes place. In so far as other countries, even though their balances of payments are favourable, impede our exports by high tariffs or by rigid quantitative import restrictions, a depreciation of sterling will not lead to an expansion of our overseas sales. In particular, in so far as these countries offset any advantage which we may obtain from a depreciation of sterling by raising their tariffs or imposing new import restrictions or by paying additional subsidies to their own competing exports, a depreciation of sterling will prove ineffective in expanding our external markets. Similarly, if countries with favourable balances of payments offset any depreciation of sterling by an unnecessary competitive depreciation of their own currencies, this method of adjustment will prove ineffective.

8 From the point of view of our standard of living it would, of course, always be preferable to expand our exports by improvements in our industrial efficiency, which would enable us to lower our costs of production and so to lower the prices at which our goods were offered in overseas markets. But from the point of view of the effect upon the value of our export trade it makes no difference whether the price reductions leading to an expansion of our exports are due to exchange depreciation or to increased efficiency. Both methods will prove equally ineffective in so far as they are offset by rigid quantitative restrictions on imports or by high or increased tariff barriers in other countries, by export subsidies paid by our competitiors, or by competitive exchange depreciation.

9 But in conditions in which strict limits are set upon the height of tariffs; in which quantitative import restrictions may be imposed by countries with unfavourable, but not by countries with favourable, balances of payments; in which export subsidies are outlawed; and in which depreciation of currencies is not permitted to a country whose balance of payments is already in equilibrium; – in these conditions a 10 per cent depreciation of sterling might after the necessary period of adjustment bring about a very substantial improvement in the United Kingdom balance of payments. The result depends upon the extent to which a 10 per cent reduction in the price of our exports in foreign

markets would expand our overseas sales, and the extent to which a 10 per cent rise in the price of foreign goods on our internal markets would restrict our imports.

10 Our exports are of such a character that (provided always that our customers and our competitors do not retaliate unnecessarily) a reduction in their price in foreign markets should, after a time, cause a large expansion in their volume. For, in the first place, the goods which we export are more easily dispensed with when their price is high, and are bought in considerably greater additional quantities when their price falls, than is the case with basic foodstuffs and other essentials. Secondly, we produce these goods in competition with many of our customers and with a number of other important competing exporters, so that when the price of our goods falls (without a corresponding fall in the price of the similar products of countries whose balances of payments are not unfavourable) there is a considerable shift of demand to our produce.

11 The sensitiveness of our imports to a rise in their price is not so great, since we import a considerable amount of essentials which we cannot readily produce at home. In so far as we cannot dispense with imports, the whole adjustment of our balance of payments *must* fall on our exports. In such a hypothetical case, there would be no case at all for quantitative import restrictions (since all imports are essential). But the real situation is not as rigid as this. Quantitative import restrictions can within limits help to adjust our balance of payments, since there is a range of imported manufactures and even of foodstuffs and raw materials which we can do without or, at a cost, produce at home for ourselves. For exactly the same reasons, a 10 per cent rise in the price of our imports will shift demand to home produce or will cause consumers to reduce somewhat their consumption of an appreciable range of our imports.

12 In the Annex [below pp. 63–6] a formula is given whereby the adjustment which a 10 per cent depreciation of sterling would bring about can be measured in relation to the sensitiveness of the foreign demand for our goods and services, and of our demand for foreign goods and services. It is certain that a rise in the price of our imports would cause some reduction in their volume. Let us assume that a 1 per cent overall rise in the price of our imports would cause a ½ per cent reduction in the overall volume of our imports. The foreigners' demand for our exports will be much more sensitive than this. Let us assume that a 1 per cent reduction in our prices in overseas markets leads eventually to a 2 per cent increase in the *volume* (or – what amounts to the same thing – a 1 per cent increase in the *foreign value*) of our overseas sales. In these circumstances if we started with £900 millions of visible and invisible exports and £1,000 millions of visible and invisible imports, a 10 per cent depreciation of sterling would change this adverse balance of payments of £100 millions into a favourable balance of £30 millions. If we made the very improbable assumption that, even after allowing full time for adjustments and even after banning all unnecessary retaliatory action, a

1 per cent reduction of the overseas prices of our exports would lead only to a 1 per cent increase in the volume of our exports (and thus to no increase in the foreign value of our exports), a 10 per cent depreciation of sterling would still improve our balance of payments by £40 millions.

13 There are other important desiderata to bear in mind in considering the sort of post-war world which will help to restore the United Kingdom balance of payments. A world of restriction schemes for primary products which rigidly limited the overseas supplies of our essential imports of raw materials and foodstuffs and which held up the price of these commodities against us would seriously intensify our difficulties. A world in which successful measures were taken to prevent catastrophic collapses of prices and purchasing power particularly in important industrialised countries such as the United States, and to maintain an even rate of expansion of world markets, would prevent sudden dislocations in international balances of payments such as those which occurred as a result of the Great Depression after 1929. A flow of international long-term lending from rich creditor countries with favourable balances of payments, such as the United States, for the development of more backward regions would ease the problem of international balances of payments. Such American lending would be of direct benefit to us, if any substantial part of the money lent were not tied to purchases of goods exclusively from the lender, but were available for expenditure by the borrowing countries upon United Kingdom produce. On the other hand, it is desirable that countries with an unfavourable balance of payments should be free to impose limitations on, or indeed to prohibit, the export of capital funds abroad. Finally, a satisfactory international economic settlement must provide for all countries a sufficient cushion of monetary reserves or of international credit to absorb temporary fluctuations in balances of payments or to give time to set more fundamental adjustments into motion when a more lasting change affects international economic relationships.

(ii) The Terms of the Proposed Settlement

14 If the argument of the preceding paragraphs is correct, the conditions most favourable for the solution of the United Kingdom balance-of-payments problem are as follows:

(a) The strict limitation of tariff barriers, of export subsidies and of quantitative import restrictions by any country (whether it be our customer or our competitor) whose balance of payments is not unfavourable.
(b) A system which permits an effective special use of import restriction to countries with an unfavourable balance of payments, but not to other countries.
(c) The strict prohibition of unnecessary exchange depreciation by countries which do not require to depreciate in order to restore equilibrium to their balances of international payments.

(d) A system which permits some degree of exchange depreciation to a country whose balance of payments is consistently unfavourable.
(e) A set of rules which prevents the unnecessary restriction of output or maintenance of prices of foodstuffs and raw materials.
(f) Agreement on the main principles of effective action to prevent world-wide depressions of prices and incomes.
(g) A flow of long-term loans, if possible untied to purchases in any particular market, from countries rich in capital and with favourable balances of payments to undeveloped countries.
(h) Freedom on the part of countries with an unfavourable balance of payments to control the export of capital funds.
(i) The provision of a sufficient stock of international monetary reserves to absorb temporary, and to give time to adjust more lasting, fluctuations in balance of payments.

15 Such are the desiderata. They were very largely met in the economic settlement which was the subject of informal discussion between British and American officials this autumn in Washington. It is true that in the conversations which have already taken place some of the desiderata have been more clearly achieved than others, and that in some cases more progress towards precision has been made than in others. But by and large the proposed settlement makes very adequate allowance for these points.

16 The joint report of the British and American officials on Commercial Policy proposes that (apart from a limited number of exceptional uses such as for the carrying out of approved international commodity agreements) the use of quantitative import restrictions should be prohibited to countries whose balances of payments are not unfavourable and should be permitted to countries whose balances of payments are substantially adverse or whose monetary reserves have fallen below a defined level of safety. In this connection, an interesting suggestion due to American Treasury officials is to be found in the joint report on the monetary discussions. It is proposed that when a country's balance of payments is so insistently favourable that its currency becomes scarce, then other countries should be permitted to impose discriminatory restrictions on imports from that country. This would mean that if the dollar became scarce all countries could impose discriminatory import restrictions against American goods. This would be an addition to the arrangement whereby a country with an unfavourable balance could impose non-discriminatory restrictions on its imports from all sources of supply. The joint report on Commercial Policy also proposes that the use of export subsidies (such as the pre-war German levy on industrial production for the subsidisation of her manufactured exports) should be prohibited. It is also made clear in the joint report that the United Kingdom officials do not consider that any far-reaching commercial policy agreement would be feasible unless it led to the radical reduction of high tariffs.

17 These commercial policy arrangements would be very favourable to us, if after the war we had to take measures to restore equilibrium in a world in which the United Kingdom balance of payments was unfavourable and the United States balance very favourable.

(i) We should be permitted to impose restrictions on our imports, while our competitors and our customers could not do so unless they had similar balance-of-payments difficulties.
(ii) Our competitors could not subsidise their exports against our products as Germany did before the war – greatly to our detriment – by means of an industrial levy for the subsidisation of her products.
(iii) High tariffs, such as the American tariff, would have been radically reduced, while our moderate tariff would have suffered merely a moderate adjustment.
(iv) We and all other countries would be in a position to impose special import restrictions on American goods so long as the American balance of payments remained excessively favourable.

18 Against these advantages, we should have to set a radical adjustment of Imperial Preferences; for it is clear that without such an adjustment, agreement on these commercial arrangements with the Americans would be out of the question. Such an adjustment would in itself probably tend to increase the strain on our balance of payments, since we should lose part at least of the preferences which we obtain for our exports in imperial markets. The closing of the preferences which we give to imports from other parts of the Commonwealth might to some extent offset this, since in part it might have to be done by raising the preferential rate towards the full rate of duty. In any case, when account is taken of the whole nexus of the proposed commercial arrangements – the radical lowering of high tariffs, the abolition of export subsidies, the right to put special restrictions on imports from a country whose currency is scarce, the right to impose restrictions on all imports if our own balance of payments is unfavourable, and – above all – the prohibition of quantitative restrictions on the imports of our goods into countries whose balance of payments is not unfavourable – there can be no doubt at all that the balance of advantage is immensely in our favour.

19 The joint report on Commercial Policy does not require that any quantitative import restrictions which we may impose on balance-of-payments grounds should be removed again, unless our balance has become favourable and our stock of monetary reserves has been fully restored. But it does require that after such restrictions have been in operation for a period of two or three years, discussions should take place 'in order to determine whether some other action (such as an adjustment of exchanges, alterations in the flow of international long-term capital or an expansion of money incomes in other countries) could not be appropriately taken'. It has already been argued at some length above (paras 6–12) that, in the conditions which would result from the

acceptance of the proposed commercial policy arrangements, an adjustment of exchange rates might prove an effective instrument for removing any long-term disequilibrium in our balance of payments. The proposed monetary arrangement leaves room for such an adjustment:

(i) A member country may adjust its exchange rate by 10 per cent without the permission of the proposed international monetary body; and the British officials at Washington maintained that a country should have the right to depreciate in this way by 10 per cent not merely once for all, but once in each successive ten-year period.

(ii) In the case of an application to the Fund for a further 10 per cent exchange depreciation, the proposed international monetary organisation must give its decision within two days of the application.

(iii) Countries can propose more extensive changes in the parity of their currencies. But they undertake not to do so, unless they consider it appropriate to the correction of a fundamental disequilibrium; on the other hand, the proposed international monetary authority is bound to approve a requested change if it is essential to the correction of a fundamental disequilibrium.

(iv) A country may withdraw from the proposed monetary organisation without previous notice and without penalty, so that it could always be free in the last resort to depreciate its exchange against the decision of the international body.

This set of rules is less precise than that proposed for the imposition of quantitative import restrictions on balance-of-payments grounds. It does not in all circumstances completely prevent unnecessary action by countries whose balance of payments is favourable, nor does it quite so precisely guarantee the right of a country with an unfavourable balance of payments to make the appropriate adjustment. Nevertheless it is calculated to make possible an exchange depreciation if that is essential for the restoration of equilibrium and – what is of equal importance from our point of view – in most cases to make difficult, if not impossible, unnecessary competitive exchange depreciation by our customers or our competitors.

20 The agreed proposals for an international monetary organisation make provision for a total international credit of some £3,000 millions, of which rather more than £300 millions would be at the disposal of the United Kingdom. About £80 millions of this could be used by the United Kingdom in any one year. These sums would not, of course, suffice in themselves to cover indefinitely any possible or probable maladjustment of balances of payments. They would, however, provide a most useful additional shock-absorber, while the necessary adjustments were being made.

21 The joint report of British and American officials on Commodity Policy suggests a set of rules to ensure that quantitative restriction of the

production or export of primary products would not be used unnecessarily to hold up the prices of such commodities at unnaturally high levels. This is particularly important for the balance of payments of a country like the United Kingdom, which relies upon the importation of essential foodstuffs and raw materials. Thus it is agreed:

(i) that the quantitative restriction of exports and/or production should be regarded as a transitory measure to facilitate orderly change during transitional periods;
(ii) that importing countries should have as large a voting power as exporting countries;
(iii) that the possibility of dealing with the root causes which have given rise to the proposal for a restriction scheme should be explored before any such scheme is approved;
(iv) that any restriction scheme should allow for a shift from the less economical to the more economical sources of supply of the product; and
(v) that no scheme should be approved for more than five years.

These principles if they can be effectively applied in international action should ensure that we are not held up to ransom by the organised monopolisation of our most essential imports.

22 Other matters which were discussed among British and American officials at Washington – though very much less exhaustively – were:

(i) the co-ordination of policies for the maintenance of employment; and
(ii) international cartels.

There was also one unofficial discussion on an American draft for an international institution to promote the flow of long-term capital. These subjects all have their relevance to the problem of the United Kingdom balance of payments. But the discussions in Washington on them were not carried to a point at which precise proposals emerged.

23 The importance of effective policies against unemployment cannot be overemphasised from the point of view of the maintenance of equilibrium in international balances of payments. Certain of the international policies discussed at Washington under other heads will make an important contribution to the maintenance of employment throughout the world. Thus the commercial policy proposals and the monetary proposals are such as to enable countries to go ahead with internal policies for the maintenance of employment with less concern for the immediate effect upon their international position; for these proposals enable a country to protect its balance of payments with quantitative import restrictions or, if necessary, by means of exchange depreciation and they provide a cushion of additional international credit. The proposals for buffer stock regulation of primary products introduce a

more direct means of injecting additional purchasing power into world markets when such markets slump, and of sucking back such purchasing power when markets boom. Schemes for international investment might be so planned and timed as to help to stabilise world expenditure upon capital developments at a high level.

24 These international arrangements may usefully help to preserve a high level of trade activity throughout world markets. But when all is said and done, it will be the internal policies in the major countries – and in particular in the United States and the United Kingdom – which will determine whether national incomes and world purchasing power are again to be allowed to slump disastrously as they did after 1929. The prevention of such catastrophic collapses in world purchasing power is one of the main ways of preventing a strain on national balances of payments. A serious American depression, with the collapse of external purchasing power which that would entail for us, would necessarily exercise a serious strain on our balance of payments whatever may be the form of the international economic settlement. It is, therefore, of the first importance for us and for other countries to promote an exchange of views with the Americans on the types of internal measure which may most appropriately be taken when a general depression once again threatens.

25 An American draft has been put before us on the subject of an international bank to promote long-term international investment. Our interest, from the point of view of the restoration of equilibrium to international balances of payments, is threefold:

(i) to encourage a flow of capital from countries rich in capital and with favourable balances of payments to the undeveloped countries;
(ii) to ensure as far as possible that capital development in undeveloped regions is planned and timed in such a way and on such a scale as to prevent general depressions of world trade activity; and
(iii) to ensure that such loans are tied as little as possible to expenditure in the markets of the lending countries.

The funds for international investment must at first be largely American; and it is appropriate that on this subject the Americans should have prepared a first draft. It remains for us to insist upon the development of those three essential ideas in any further discussions on the subject.

26 The Americans have also presented a case for the prohibition or rigid limitation of the restrictive practices of international cartels. The immediate effect of international cartellisation upon our balance of payments is uncertain. If the producers of the primary products which we import can be prevented from restricting their sales and at the same time the producers of the manufactured goods which we export are left free to restrict markets and to maintain prices, we might be able so to turn the

terms of trade in our favour as to reduce the strain upon our balance of payments. On the other hand it is questionable whether we can obtain whole-hearted American support for the principles (outlined in paragraph 21 above) limiting the restriction of primary products, unless we go some way to apply similar principles to manufactured exports. Moreover, after the war as a result of our losses of 'invisible exports' such as interest on foreign investments, we shall need to adopt an aggressive export policy; and it is doubtful whether the cartellisation of foreign markets, starting from the pre-war distribution of export markets, would leave us sufficient elbow room to restore equilibrium to our balance of payments. Clearly the probable effect of international cartels on our post-war balance of payments is one of the factors which must be carefully considered before any decision can be reached upon the answer to be given to the American initiative on this subject.

(iii) The Way the Proposed Settlement Might Work

27 In order to see how the proposed international economic settlement might work out concretely, it may be useful to inquire how it would have worked in face of a catastrophic decline in the American national income on a scale comparable to that experienced in the Great Depression after 1929. This is, of course, to take a most pessimistic view; for it assumes that the Americans will have learnt nothing from the inter-war experience and that all those parts of the proposed settlement which are aimed at preventing violent depressions in the general level of world activity will have proved completely ineffective. But if history were unfortunately to repeat itself, should we be so tied by the terms of the proposed economic settlement that we should have to abandon any internal attempts at stabilisation and to submit to being dragged down by the external collapse?

28 That an external collapse on the scale contemplated would severely affect us cannot be denied. The direct and indirect effects on our balance of payments of a collapse of American purchases and of a sudden cut in American money costs and prices would necessarily be very serious. But this would be inevitable whatever were the international economic arrangement. The only point at issue is whether the type of international economic settlement recently discussed among officials at Washington would give us the elbow room necessary to cope with the situation.

29 A collapse of external incomes and prices would reduce the demand for our exports and would tend to increase our imports by undercutting our own home production. Our balance of payments would become adverse; and the balance of payments of the United States and other countries would become favourable. This tendency would be intensified if (as we should) we courageously insisted on continuing to the best of our ability an internal policy designed to maintain and stabilise prices and purchasing power. But the proposed international economic settlement would, for the following reasons, help rather than hinder us in doing so:

(i) The proposed international monetary organisation would provide us with an additional reserve of credit which we would draw on up to about £80 million a year for some four years. This would not, of course, be sufficient to weather the storm, nor would it be appropriate to attempt to weather the storm merely by means of external credits of this kind. But it would provide a useful cushion to take the first shock while other measures were being put into operation.

(ii) There is nothing in the proposed settlement to prevent us from imposing the most rigid exchange controls against capital exports, so that a flight from the pound could be prevented.

(iii) As our balance of payments became markedly unfavourable we should be permitted to impose quantitative restrictions on our imports.

(iv) The Americans and others with favourable balances of payments would be precluded from imposing restrictions on imports or additional tariff barriers against our goods.

(v) If the American balance of payments became so favourable that the dollar became a scarce currency, we and all other countries could impose special discriminatory restrictions against purchases of American goods.

(vi) We could depreciate sterling by 10 per cent, could ask for a decision upon a further 10 per cent depreciation within two days, could ask for yet a further depreciation which the international monetary authority would be under an obligation to grant if it were necessary to restore equilibrium in the radically changed circumstances of relative prices and costs, and we could withdraw immediately from the international monetary organisation and so regain our freedom of action if such an application were refused.

(vii) Finally, the Americans would be largely bound not to depreciate the dollar.

30 Our experience in the 1930s might have been very different if we had had an additional cushion of international credit of £80 million a year, if we had immediately imposed restrictions on capital exports, if we had imposed restrictions on imports as well as adjusting the exchange rate, and if at the same time the Americans had been under an obligation not to increase their tariff or other trade barriers and not to depreciate the dollar. We should have retained all the freedom of internal action which we could desire for the prosecution of a vigorous employment policy; and the Americans would have been driven more promptly and inevitably towards the real solution of the problem – a restoration of their own purchasing power by similar policies of internal expansion.

(iv) The Alternative

31 The pound and the dollar have predominant influence as international currencies; and the Anglo–American countries (i.e. the British Commonwealth, the United States with the Philippines and Latin

America) accounted for 50 per cent of the pre-war world trade. Anglo–American agreement on international economic affairs is, therefore, essential if the chaos of the immediate pre-war years is to be dissipated. In the absence of such an economic agreement the prospects of a reasonable international political organisation may be endangered. For an atmosphere of economic friction and recrimination cannot lead to political harmony; and it is difficult to conceive that the United States could remain for long economically isolationist and politically co-operative.

32 If an extensive economic settlement is to be reached, acceptable to the Americans and, at the same time, compatible with our own interests, it must be on the lines of the settlement discussed at Washington. This settlement allows fully for our own long-term interests. It is, however, unthinkable (whatever may be the administration in power in the United States) that the Americans would adhere to any reasonable international settlement which was not based, at least to the extent of the proposed settlement, upon the principles of multilateralism and non-discrimination. If positive American co-operation in world economic affairs is desired, there is no alternative to this type of settlement.

33 The only other course is to rely upon a system of commercial and financial relationships which will allow us – and other countries – a much greater measure of freedom to control our external commerce. Such controls might in some cases take the form of increased customs duties. But the adherents of this alternative view would lay comparatively little stress on tariff protection. They would rather claim that the control of our imports which we could exercise by means of quantitative regulation and the stimulus which we could give to our export trade by means of payments agreements, clearing arrangements or similar methods of bilateral barter with our main suppliers, constitute the sole reliable weapon by means of which we (and other countries in similar balance-of-payments difficulties) can restore equilibrium to our balance of payments.

34 Such a system has a double aspect. It will allow for a greater measure of national 'protection' all round. It will also permit such 'discrimination' as is inevitable in any set of arrangements for the bilateral balancing of trade transactions between pairs of countries. There can be little doubt that a general all-round extension of national protectionism is against our interest. We export manufactured goods which are not indispensable and which the producers of primary products can produce for themselves if they have unlimited freedom to protect uneconomic industries; we rely upon essential imports of foodstuffs and raw materials, much of which we cannot readily produce at home. A general all-round protectionism will, therefore, hit our standard of life more severely than those of other countries; and it has also been argued (in paragraphs 2–4 above) that for similar reasons a general all-round reduction of protective barriers will be favourable also to our balance of payments.

35 The answer is, however, not so clear in the case of the retention by us and other countries of a power to 'discriminate', such as to enable us by quantitative import regulation, by payments or clearing agreements or by discriminatory state purchases to induce others to take our exports as a bilateral *quid pro quo* for our purchases from them. The United Kingdom has undoubtedly great bargaining strengh as the main importing country of many important commodities. In 1938 non-Continental Europe (i.e. the United Kingdom and Ireland) accounted for the following percentages of total world imports:–

Pork	81	Zinc	36
Beef and Mutton	80	Maize	33
Butter	78	Petrol	31
Tea	53	Wool	29
Wheat	40	Cotton	19
Citrus Fruit	36		

The conclusion of payments agreements or clearings with our principal suppliers of these and other products, many of whom do not spend on United Kingdom products anything like the amount which we spend on theirs, would compel these countries to take United Kingdom products; and this would greatly expand our exports and restore equilibrium to our balance of payments. The supplying countries could not readily submit to losing so important a market for their principal exports and would thus be obliged to fall in with such arrangements. Alternatively, in the absence of strict payments or clearing agreements they might be persuaded to purchase more of our goods in return for advantages for their exports in the United Kingdom market which we could guarantee by giving them favourable shares in a system of import quotas or by guaranteed purchases through a state trading organisation.

36 Such a system has, however, many disadvantages. In the first place, a generalisation of bilateral trading arrangements would sacrifice the very real advantages of triangular or multilateral trade, whereby A exports what B requires, B what C requires and C what A requires. In the 1920s some 25 per cent of total world trade was multilateral, in the sense that it represented payments for imports from one country to another which were not offset by reverse payments for 'visible' or 'invisible' exports between the same pair of countries. If bilateral arrangements became the rule, all such trade would have to disappear or be diverted into channels which were less economical. The real loss which this would entail should not be exaggerated, but it would nevertheless be substantial. The United Kingdom has a special interest in multilateral payments. Our receipt of dividends and interest, for example, from tropical countries has not been financed by an equivalent excess of imports from, over our exports to, such tropical countries. Indeed, in the 1920s in spite of drawing very considerable interest payments from these countries we had a surplus of commodity exports to them. This was financed by an excess of tropical exports to the United States, to

Continental Europe and to other countries from the tropical countries, and by our excess of imports from the United States, from Continental Europe and from other countries. A case in point is the way in which Malaya was able to make payments to us on United Kingdom investments in Malaya and for United Kingdom exports to Malaya through sales of tin and rubber in the United States, which in turn helped the United Kingdom to finance its excess of imports from the United States.

37 The system of bilateral bargaining in its fullest development is of German origin and it was grossly misused by the Germans before the war. This does not, of course, prove that it might not be better used in reasonable British hands. But we should not be misled by the partial success which the Germans undoubtedly achieved from this system in financing their heavy imports for war preparations, into thinking that we should necessarily be able to achieve a similar success in restoring equilibrium to our post-war balance of payments. Germany was able, by these means before this war, to obtain advantages for herself because, in the atmosphere of appeasement, many important countries did not seriously retaliate. But there will be no world movement to appease the British, if we start the same type of bilateral discriminatory commercial policy. We must, therefore, be prepared to adopt this policy in a world in which (i) all other countries, whether they be our customers or our competitors, are free to adopt – and assuredly will adopt – policies of high protectionism, autarky, and discriminatory bilateralism, and (ii) the Americans, with their exaggerated passion for the principle of non-discrimination, are angered by our action and prepared to take, in a spirit of spitefulness, whatever counter-measures they can readily adopt.

38 Any general increase in world protectionism will impose an additional strain on our balance of payments. Nor is this extra strain likely to be offset permanently by any freedom which we may retain for bilateral bargaining with our customers. For a time a country producing primary products which we threaten not to purchase, may be induced to take our goods in return for her surplus supplies. But this will last only so long as her exportable surplus lasts; and such a country is likely, sooner or later, to attempt to free herself from reliance on our market by industrialisation, encouraged by a policy of high protectionism and autarky. In this case, our supplies of essential imports will dry up, as our suppliers turn progressively to produce for themselves what we were previously exporting to them.

39 The United States would react most unfavourably if we were to develop a bilateral and discriminatory trading system. Quite apart from the fact that the Americans have an exaggerated and, in part, irrational distaste for such a system, it would be found sooner or later to lead to clashes with their exporters in particular markets. Any attempt to use our buying power to induce, for example, a South American country to discriminate against American and in favour of British manufactures would provoke violent resentments. American officials have warned us

that in such circumstances the United States would probably itself adopt bilateral forms of trading such as to impede our own trade; and we would certainly have to compete with similar action from our other main competitors, such as Germany. The Americans, in addition, would certainly use their influence as the richest source of foreign capital, to promote their own exports at our expense. There could certainly be no more certain way of encouraging the uneconomic industrialisation of our main suppliers of primary products than to attempt to tie them unduly to our own market for their purchases and to provoke the United States into offering them loans for unnecessary industrial developments.

40 If we do perpetuate a system of bilateral arrangements, we shall inevitably put a serious strain on imperial economic relations and on the coherence of the sterling area. In the first place, the position of Canada would be most invidious. Canada is not part of the sterling area, and her economy is very closely geared to that of the United States. The value of trade passing between her and the United States is the greatest that passes between any pair of countries in the world. If the United Kingdom is attempting to establish one type, and the United States another type, of commercial system, the strain placed on Canada will be obvious.

41 But the other Dominions and other countries of the sterling area will be subjected to a great strain, and might well break away economically from sterling. The United Kingdom would be in a very difficult position as the centre of the sterling area. We should ourselves be attempting to achieve a bilateral balance of our payments with other countries. We should in particular be subjecting to careful regulation our payments in dollars to the United States. To what extent could we provide dollars and other 'hard' currencies to the members of the sterling area which kept their monetary balances with us?

42 We could not undertake a limitless obligation to do so. We might attempt to persuade the other members of the sterling area to continue to control their dollar payments and to regulate their trade transactions with the United States so as to preserve a bilateral balance either for each member of the sterling area or for the sterling area as a whole *vis-à-vis* the United States. Such action may be possible within limits in the atmosphere of a common war effort. It is doubtful whether it could be long continued in times of peace – particularly in an atmosphere in which the United States was ill-disposed towards it and was willing to make commercial and other sacrifices to help it to break down.

43 We certainly could not limit the convertibility of normal sterling balances in this country into dollars. For in this case the sterling area would certainly break down, since no member would be willing to accumulate its monetary reserves in the form of a blocked balance. We might perhaps guarantee to convert the sterling balances of the sterling area into gold or dollars, holding a sufficient reserve expressly for this purpose, while we alone continued to regulate bilaterally the United

Kingdom trade with other countries (including the members of the sterling area). It would still be open to grave doubt how long the British Commonwealth could maintain its economic coherence. The United Kingdom could offer certain attractive advantages to some of the Dominions; for example, the purchase by us on long-term contracts at preferential prices of the wool, butter or similar products of some of the Dominions might induce them to give certain reciprocal advantages on a bilateral basis to our exports. But the United States by offering substantial tariff or other advantages to the Dominions on the condition that she received strict most-favoured-nation treatment at their hands might in many cases provide a very attractive counter-inducement, particularly if the Dominions realised that we could not in any case afford greatly to reduce our purchases of some of the goods in which they are interested as producers and imports of which are essential to our standard of living. As far as the Colonial Empire is concerned we should have committed ourselves to the development of a closed imperial economy, which – in contradistinction to the principle of the 'open door' – is most liable to produce the charge that we are exploiting the Colonies for our own purposes instead of holding them as trustees for the interests of the colonial peoples themselves and of the other countries which desire to trade with them.

44 A protectionist world of bilateral bargaining is one in which there are no rules of the economic game. We might ourselves act reasonably in such a world. But such a system could not work harmoniously for long. When every country is making bilateral arrangements with every other country (each bargain being at least potentially at the expense of other third countries), economic relationships will become a perpetual source of diplomatic friction. Only a bold lead from the United States and the United Kingdom on a commercial and financial system based upon reasonable 'rules of the game' and limiting the use of protective and discriminatory devices, can hope to lead the devastated countries of Europe away from the chaos which otherwise threatens, and to prevent the development of serious economic strain within the British Commonwealth itself. And the only type of imaginative settlement on which both we and the Americans can hope to agree is that which was the subject of the recent Washington discussions.

II The Transitional Period

(i) Transitional Arrangements under the Proposed Settlement

45 The recent Washington discussions were directed primarily to a long-term settlement; and little special attention was given to the peculiar problems of the immediate post-war transition. This does not mean that the attention paid to the long-term problems was premature. The transitional period is a period of transition from the war-time economy to something else; and unless one knows what that something is it will be difficult to order the transition properly.

46 Unless the countries commit themselves before, or as soon as possible after, the close of hostilities to the main structure of the long-term economic settlement, the psychological moment will pass at which a generous and imaginative solution is politically possible. Moreover, unless countries commit themselves in advance to the main principles of the long-term settlement, it will be impossible to guide national policies during the transition in such a way as to lead in the end to a reasonable world economic order. For example during the transitional period, special shortages and special problems of relief, rehabilitation, and foreign exchange will necessitate the use by some countries of rigid import restrictions; but unless there is in existence some future commitment to limit the use of such protective weapons the necessities of the transition are likely to lead to a proliferation of highly protective policies, carried out by a network of quantitative import restrictions and constituting a permanent obstacle to our own long-run commercial interests.

47 But while the main principles of the long-run settlement are for this reason of immediate urgency, it is equally important to make sure that there is broad agreement on the sort of measures which must be taken during the transitional period to reach these objectives, and indeed that it is possible to overcome the transitional difficulties in such a way as to make the long-run proposals ultimately attainable.

48 Although the economic settlement recently discussed at Washington refers primarily to the long-term situation, the various proposals recognise the fact that the transitional problems will require exceptional treatment and make some general references to the modifications of the long-term arrangements which will be necessary during the transitional period. Thus the joint report on Commercial Policy states:

> In the emergency period during and immediately following the war import prohibitions and quantitative limitations would be permitted when necessary to meet emergencies arising from (a) the necessity of rationing imports because of shortages of supplies, shipping or foreign exchange, and (b) a temporary surplus of stocks of the commodity to which the restriction applies. These temporary exceptions would be applicable for a specified limited period after the cessation of hostilities unless the period of their application were further extended by action of the proposed international commercial policy organisation.

A similar special exception during the transitional period is recognised for the suggested rules limiting the protective and discriminatory use of the instruments of state trading.

49 The principle is thus recognised that there must be an interim period of readjustment during which continuation of special restrictive controls over trade by some countries will be inevitable. There was, however, in discussion some difference of emphasis between the American and

British views on this subject. The Americans, who have not experienced the same difficulties of shortages of supplies, shipping and foreign exchange as the British and are further removed from the devastated economies of Europe, are apt to lay all their emphasis upon the desirability of limiting the exceptional transitional devices to a minimum in extent and in time. The British officials, on the other hand, laid great emphasis upon the problems of adjustment of the British and of the European economies as a result of shortages of raw materials, destruction of industrial equipment, transport difficulties, shortages of foreign exchange, need for special supplies for relief and rehabilitation, need for the restoration of export markets, etc.

50 The main point at issue is not likely to be the principle or the forms of special action permissible in the commercial policy field, but the time for which such special action should be permissible. The Americans started off by proposing the use of exceptional measures for a period of one year, extensions of which could be made by decision of the proposed international commercial policy organisation; the British proposed a transitional period of five years during the first two years of which countries would retain more or less complete freedom for import regulation and during the next two years of which they would have progressively to relax and finally to eliminate these special transitional restrictions. The gulf is not, however, so large as might at first sight appear. For it became apparent from discussions that the American year was to date from the end of all hostilities (i.e. after the close of the Japanese war) and that in any case the Americans expected that some extension would probably be necessary. Compromise might perhaps be made on, for example, a transitional period which ended either four years after the termination of hostilities in Europe or two years after the termination of hostilities in Asia, whichever was the later date, and which was capable of prolongation by international decision even beyond that date. In any case there was complete agreement among the American and British officials that, however the transitional period might be defined, an exceptional use of import restrictions on the grounds of balance-of-payments difficulties should form a permanent feature of commercial policy arrangements, so that import restrictions on this ground could in any case if necessary be continued beyond the transitional period.

51 The joint proposals for an international monetary organisation also recognise that controls over foreign payments cannot be immediately relaxed upon the termination of hostilities, but only as equilibrium is gradually restored to international balances of payments. It is accordingly proposed that member countries should be obliged:

> To abandon as soon as possible, when the member country decides that conditions permit, all restrictions on payments for current international transactions with other member countries (other than those involving capital transfers), and not to impose any additional restric-

> tions (except upon capital transfers, or in accordance with 10 above[1]) without the approval of the Fund. The Fund may make representations that conditions are favourable to the abandonment of restrictions.

Thus, while each country recognises an obligation to remove restrictions on current payments as soon as practicable, no exact time limit is laid down. The proposed international Fund may make representations, but the member country makes the final decision.

52 The monetary proposals suggest that in general the rules fixing exchange rates and regulating their subsequent variation should come into operation as soon as a country joins the Fund, – that is to say that the initial par value of each country's currency would have to be agreed with the Fund and subsequent changes in the parity would be subject to the limitations described in paragraph 19 above. It is, however, recognised that for a temporary period of three years during which exchange rates will have in many cases to be experimental in character, there must be special facility for exchange-rate adjustments:

> Because of the extreme uncertainties of the immediate post-war period and recognising that rates established during such period will of necessity be tentative in many instances, during the first three years the Fund shall recognise that there will be need for many changes and adjustments and shall resolve cases of reasonable doubt in favour of the country requesting changes in rates.

53 The proposed settlement thus makes special provision for the regulation of trade and of foreign payments and allows special temporary facilities for the adjustment of exchange rates during a post-war transitional period. Are these special arrangements flexible enough? For how long after the war should they continue? Are there any other special exceptions to the rules of the proposed settlement which should be added? Are there any other special positive measures for the treatment of the transitional problem, which are necessary conditions for the acceptance of a general settlement on the lines proposed?

(ii) The General Characteristics of the Transitional Period

54 The transition from war to peace will come in two stages, if the war with Germany is brought to an end before the war with Japan. The end of the war in Europe will release some resources from the war effort, since it will be impossible for us and for the Americans to bring the whole of our forces to bear on Japan alone. The period between the close of the European and of the Asiatic wars will thus present us with an opportunity of making at least a start in reorganising our internal economy towards

[1] i.e. for the apportionment of a scarce currency.

that appropriate to peace and, in particular, towards that appropriate to a great exporting country.

55 This first transitional stage will, however, put a very great strain on world resources for the relief and rehabilitation of Europe. Estimates of European requirements of the most essential foodstuffs and raw materials suggest that the supplies required and their finance and transport will for at least eighteen months or so impose a serious strain on the world economy.

56 The European balance of payments will not only be strained by the need for essential additional imports for relief purposes; European industrial production will be reduced to a low level in the occupied countries by shortages of skilled labour, materials and equipment as a result of German exactions and in Germany itself by aerial bombardment which may in the end have caused serious devastation. Germany is a part of Europe; and like other European countries she will not be able to support herself (much less to generate the substantial favourable balance necessary to make a net reparation to the rest of the world) until relief has been followed by some measure of rehabilitation. This imposes a double strain upon balances of payments, since additional imports of materials and equipment may be necessary for the purpose of rehabilitation and at the same time exports cannot be readily restored until productive capacity is rehabilitated.

57 Our own balance of payments will certainly remain a serious problem during this period. In the first place, we shall still be prosecuting the war against Japan with the utmost of our ability. The military considerations which this will involve combined with the continued joint planning of our exports on grounds of the most effective source of supply for different markets will severely restrain the redevelopment of our export trade – or at any rate of that part of our export trade for which we can expect to obtain immediate payment from our customers. It is by no means improbable that during this phase of the transition the Americans will be able to go further than us in the restoration of normal peace-time production and of export trade. Secondly, we shall ourselves be providing certain supplies for relief purposes. For some of these we shall receive payment. But many countries will be unable to pay. Recent negotiations of UNRRA [United Nations Relief and Rehabilitation Administration] suggest a reasonable limit to each country's commitment to make supplies for relief without payment, and only a small part of this sum is to be subscribed in free foreign exchange. The remainder is to represent merely the value of goods and services provided out of our own real resources for relief purposes. But, nevertheless, it will increase our difficulties in restoring our normal export markets. Thirdly, great shortages of every kind will continue in our own internal markets during the period; and it will require great determination not to allow internal pressure for the relaxation of existing restrictions on consumption from seriously impeding the development of our export trade. Fourthly,

pressure will be put on us by many of our best overseas customers to accept payment for our exports out of the sterling balances accumulated in London during the war, a process which would prevent our exports from making any immediate contribution towards the finance of our current imports.

58 These very real difficulties should not be exaggerated. First, recent calculations of the probable post-war internal income of this country suggest that within two or three years from the close of major hostilities we shall be able to produce in aggregate the required supplies to meet all the claims upon our national income including the restoration of export trade sufficient to put our balance of payments into equilibrium. Secondly, pent-up demand in overseas markets which have been starved of supplies during the war should enable us to find markets, at least at first, for whatever we can produce for normal export markets. This will at least provide us with an opportunity to restore our commercial connections in overseas markets. Thirdly, the cessation of hostilities in Europe will certainly release an appreciable part of our internal economic resources for production for export and will eliminate from our import programmes considerable supplies which will no longer be required for military purposes.

(iii) Policy during the Transitional Period

59 Some method must be devised for financing the unfavourable balances of payments of European countries and of the United Kingdom during the transitional period, until the necessary readjustments have been made. It is possible at the outset to dismiss one possible method of doing this. The resources of the proposed international stabilisation Fund should not be used on a large scale for these transitional purposes. The 'quotas' of additional international credit which the proposed Fund would provide for the member countries are to be regarded as cushions of credit which in more normal times could absorb shocks to a country's balance of payments. It would be most undesirable that these credits should be used up during the transitional period of exceptional strain to balances of payments. It may be satisfactory to require countries with considerable reserves of gold or foreign exchange to pay for their relief supplies, although even this is questionable if it goes beyond a certain point. But if the resources provided by the Fund are all used up for special transitional payments, the whole long-term object of the Fund will be nullified. Countries will embark on the more normal long-term period without that cushion of international credit which it is the purpose of the Fund to provide.

61 [sic] What then are the alternatives? In the first place there are a number of measures, for which the Washington discussions provide. Thus it will be essential during this period for countries with balance-of-payments difficulties to restrict and regulate their imports in order to ensure that scarce foreign currencies are spent only for the most

indispensable purposes; and express provision has been made for this in the joint report on Commercial Policy. It will be equally essential to ensure that control of the foreign exchanges is continued to prevent the export of capital or the transfer of funds abroad for other inessential purposes; and the monetary proposals resulting from the Washington discussions leave countries complete freedom for this purpose. In the case of this country it will be essential to block balances of sterling accumulated here during the war or to make special arrangements for their gradual release even for the purpose of purchasing United Kingdom goods. The American monetary proposals made express provisions for this purpose; and although the British officials prefer that we should be free to make special arrangements about such sterling balances with our creditors rather than organise a precise international scheme for the purpose, the principle that special measures will be necessary is firmly established and the Americans do not object to the procedure which we prefer.

62 The control of imports and the control of capital movements, including special arrangements for blocked balances, should greatly help. But neither in our case nor in that of the liberated European countries will these measures alone completely suffice. We shall need time to restore our exports sufficiently to pay for our essential imports, and in addition we shall be making some contributions to the relief of Europe. The countries of Europe, it is true, will for a time be getting their most essential supplies for relief and rehabilitation on terms which do not require payment where payment is impossible; but their productive resources and their whole economies will in some cases have been so badly disorganised that they will require very special treatment for recovery.

63 The simplest and most attractive method of meeting these difficulties would no doubt be to continue the principle of Mutual Aid during the transitional period, until the first essential stages in adjusting balances of payments had been completed. There will be at least a limited recognition of this principle in the provision of supplies for relief without payment to countries lacking the necessary resources of foreign exchange. But it would be unrealistic to hope that the system could be continued in a generalised form throughout the transitional period. The extent to which this may prove possible will depend upon the American attitude towards the continuation of Lend-Lease. It is most improbable that Lend-Lease supplies would be continued in any substance after the close of the Japanese war; and it is at least uncertain whether it would be continued in a generalised way even during the period between the ends of the wars in Europe and in Asia.

64 A second method of helping with the readjustment would be to reach agreement with the United States that the machinery of combined planning of exports should be so used during the transitional period as to help us and other countries to restore our balances of payments. If the

period between the close of the European and Asiatic wars is recognised as a period of partial demobilisation and partial reconstruction, it would be logical to maintain that the combined planning of exports should take into account not only the normal criteria of a war economy (which country can supply which essential exports at the least cost to the war economy as a whole) but also the main criterion of international reconstruction (which country needs the exports most to readjust international balances of payments). If it were possible during the transitional period to plan in this way in co-operation with the Americans the initial restoration of our export markets, we might thereby avoid a great deal of unnecessary friction and resentment.

65 Finally, it might be possible to arrange with the Americans for the flotation of special reconstruction loans for Europe, the proceeds of which, in conjunction with relief supplies, would give to those countries sufficient time and sufficient elbow room to restore their internal economies and so their export trade during a reasonably short transitional period. We ourselves might also be well advised to supplement our reserves of foreign exchange in a similar manner.

66 In fact, international policy for the transitional period may well have to take the form of a combination of these methods. Thus it might be advisable to ask the Americans to continue the principle of Lend-Lease for armaments and foodstuffs until the end of the Japanese war, and possibly for armaments alone somewhat beyond that date. It is probable that if we wish to be reasonably free to press the restoration of our export trade, we shall have to be prepared to see raw materials supplies excluded from Lend-Lease at an early date; otherwise the difficulties and resentments raised by the problems of not exporting goods containing Lend-Lease materials might well become intolerable. We might further hope to persuade the Americans to recognise to a greater or less extent that during this period the restoration of balances of payments should be at least one factor in determining the combined planning of civilian exports. We might hope to see these principles supplemented by some reconstruction loans. The length of the transitional period could be much shortened, and the prospect of coming through it in a way which would not prejudice the long-run success of the settlement discussed at Washington would be much improved, if policies of this kind could be adopted for the transitional period. We should emphasise the interconnection between policies for the transitional period and policies for the long run in our future discussions with the Americans.

67 On the assumption that a policy of this kind were adopted, we might contemplate a gradual return to more normal conditions during a few years of transition. As each particular commodity becomes less scarce it can be removed from the realm of combined planning and can cease to be allocated among different uses and different markets. As exports are restored and emergency imports for relief and rehabilitation fall off, each country can begin to relax its import restrictions. As its balance of

payments approaches nearer to equilibrium, each country need rely less and less upon relief supplies, Lend-Lease supplies, or foreign loans and can be asked progressively to substitute the principle of commercial payments for that of Mutual Aid. As the predetermined date for the close of the transitional period approaches, consideration can be given to the question whether there should be international agreement for its further extension; and if the transitional arrangements are not prolonged by international action, there will still remain the permanent arrangement whereby any particular country whose balance of payments is still seriously out of equilibrium can continue to regulate its import trade.

68 Provided that an appropriate period is allowed for the transitional period, it would appear that commercial policy proposals of the kind mentioned in paragraph 48 above would in no way stand in the way of a positive policy for the transitional period. It is also clear that the monetary proposals regulating the transitional use of exchange restrictions on current payments (cf. paragraph 51 above) present no obstacle to an adequate policy of transition.

69 It remains, however, to decide whether the other proposed arrangements of the international stabilisation Fund are appropriate for the transitional period. It has been argued above (paragraph 59) that the resources of the Fund should not be used extensively during the transitional period for the finance of special transitional maladjustments in balances of payments. If this is correct, there is much to be said for a formal recognition of this principle. Thus it might be well to place special limitations on the use of the resources of the Fund during the transitional period. For example, it is proposed as a permanent rule of the Fund to limit the drawing by any particular country of the Fund in any one year to 25 per cent of its total 'quota'. It might be ruled that during the transitional period no country should draw upon more than 5 per cent of its 'quota' in any one year. This would permit the Fund to be set up and the proposed subscriptions to be paid into the Fund at the outset, thereby removing the danger that, if the Fund is not instituted immediately, the psychological moment for its institution will have been lost. But it would mean that the Fund would not actually operate as an important source of international credit until the close of the transitional period.

70 It is also necessary to decide whether the proposed international monetary arrangements allow sufficient flexibility of exchange rates in the transitional period. There will be great difficulty in determining during that period what is the appropriate rate at which European and other currencies should be fixed. There will be great uncertainties about the movements which have actually taken place in some of these countries in prices and costs, and still more uncertainty about the level at which they will ultimately settle in relation to price and cost levels in other countries; the war will have induced considerable changes in the structure of world production and trade, the ultimate effect of which upon the relative demand for different national currencies will be

uncertain; and the gradual application of more liberal types of commercial policy will bring about further changes in the relative demand for different currencies. The right to adjust a currency by 10 per cent will not necessarily prove sufficient in the transitional period; and although the proposed international monetary arrangements suggest that during this period the Fund should give specially favourable consideration to an application for an exchange adjustment, it may be wiser to consider an even more flexible arrangement for the transitional period.

71 In the first place, if – as is suggested above – it is wise during this period to limit severely the use which may be made of the resources of the proposed Fund, it would be difficult to ask countries during this period very seriously to limit their freedom in fixing exchange rates. Secondly, from our own point of view it is important to avoid the development of a state of affairs in which the currencies of our European customers and competitors are seriously undervalued in relation to sterling; for this might seriously impede our efforts to restore a long-term equilibrium to our balance of payments. It may be easier to induce European countries not to fix too low a value for their currencies if they know that for a period they will be free to adjust downwards if this proves necessary; if subsequent downward adjustments of currencies are possible, the Americans may be less anxious to fix them on the low side in order to be generous in giving the European countries elbow-room for their reconstruction. Finally it may be safer for us not to be fully committed to any particular value for sterling until it becomes clearer how far European currencies are likely to be under- or over-valued.

72 If these arguments are correct, the best procedure might be to arrange that the Fund should be set up and the subscriptions paid in as early as possible; that during a predetermined transitional period there should be a severe limitation on the extent to which countries could draw on the Fund; that during this same period member countries should be under an obligation merely to consult with the Fund before fixing or altering the value of their currencies, and that at the end of this period countries would have to agree the exchange value of their currencies with the Fund, before they were permitted to have the full use of the resources of the Fund. Since all countries during the transitional period would have in view this final stage requiring full agreement with the Fund on the value of their currencies, the consultations with the Fund during the transitional period would probably be taken seriously.

(iv) Conclusions

73 If the analysis of the preceding paragraphs is correct, a policy for the transitional period which would meet the requirements of that period without sacrificing the ultimate application of the principles of the final settlement discussed recently at Washington might be devised on the following lines:

(a) There would be an agreed date for the termination of the transitional period. Such a date might be four years after the end of European hostilities or two years after the end of Asiatic hostilities, whichever was the later. This period would be capable of extension by international agreement, if this was thought desirable when the time came.

(b) General agreement should be sought for the continuation of the principle of Mutual Aid at least for certain supplies at least during the first part of the transitional period.

(c) General agreement should be sought for the recognition of the need to restore balances of international payments as one principle to be taken into account in the combined planning of exports during the transitional period.

(d) Consideration should be given to the possibility of help through special international loans for reconstruction.

(e) The international monetary Fund should be set up, but no substantial use of its resources should be made for financing supplies during the transitional period.

(f) During the transitional period there would be exceptional permission for the use of quantitative import restrictions and similar measures of trade control, and for restrictions on current payments overseas. The proposed international commercial policy organisation would be set up during this period to supervise those parts of the proposed multilateral commercial convention which were not affected by these special exceptional measures, and to provide a mechanism for consultation and conciliation on the national use of these exceptional and temporary powers.

(g) At the end of the transitional period the full obligations to remove restrictions on imports would come into force. But there would, of course, continue to be recourse to the permanent exception in favour of the use of quantitative import restrictions by countries whose balances of payments were seriously out of equilibrium.

(h) Controls on the export of capital would be continued, and special measures for dealing with sterling balances should be devised, during the transitional period.

(i) During the transitional period, while the use of the resources of the proposed international monetary Fund was severely limited, as proposed in (e) above, countries should be free to vary their exchange rates merely after consultation with the Fund. At the end of the transitional period they would be required to agree an exchange rate with the Fund before they could make full use of the resources of the Fund.

(j) The proposed international commodity organisation should be set up during the transitional period. It could help to determine the principles which should apply temporarily to any commodity requiring special treatment during this period, and would be prepared to introduce the principle of buffer stock regulation for the purchase of commodities as scarcities gave way to incipient surpluses.

(k) During the transitional period the opportunity should be taken to set up institutions to deal with international investment and with co-ordinated policies for the maintenance of employment. These institutions would be in a position, after the period of general scarcities, to prevent the recurrence of world-wide depressions, by initiating schemes for the capital development of undeveloped regions and for the stabilisation of incomes and prices. It may well be necessary to be ready with schemes of this kind for the stimulation of general economic activity at an earlier date than is commonly expected.

Annex

Effect of a Change in the Foreign Exchange Rate on the Balance of Current Payments

1. If $E =$ the value of United Kingdom exports (visible and invisible);
$I =$ the value of United Kingdom imports (visible and invisible);
$-e =$ the elasticity of the foreign demand for United Kingdom goods and services;
$-i =$ the elasticity of home demand for foreign goods and services; and
$r =$ the rate of exchange (i.e. the amount of sterling paid for a unit of foreign money);

it may be shown that

$$\mathrm{d}(E - I) = \frac{\mathrm{d}r}{r}\left[E - e + I(i - 1)\right].$$

2 The above equation is a mere truism. It remains to evaluate the various quantities in order to judge the probable effect of a change in the exchange rate upon the balance of payments. Let us suppose that after the war the value of exports (E) is £900 millions and the value of imports (I) is £1,000 millions, so that the balance of payments ($E - I$) is negative or adverse to the extent of £100 millions. We wish to examine the effect upon this adverse balance of a depreciation of sterling by, say 10 per cent (i.e. $\mathrm{d}r/r = 10\%$). The result depends entirely upon (i) 'the elasticity of the foreign demand for United Kingdom goods and services' – i.e. the extent to which a reduction in the price of United Kingdom goods and services on foreign markets would lead to an increase in the purchase of United Kingdom goods – and (ii) 'the elasticity of home demand for foreign goods and services' – i.e. the extent to which a rise in the sterling price of imported goods and services would reduce our demand for such goods and services.

3 Reason has been given in the main text (paragraphs 6–12) for believing that, in view of the character of the goods and services which the United Kingdom exports, a reduction in the price in foreign markets of such goods and services (after the lapse of the necessary period of time for adjustment) is likely to be very great, provided (i) that the expansion

of our exports is not impeded by prohibitive tariffs or quantitative restrictions on imports in foreign markets and (ii) that the expansion of our exports cannot be offset by competitive exchange depreciation or by increased tariffs and newly imposed restrictions on imports or by the subsidisation of exports by countries which do not need to improve their balances of payments. It is also argued that, while the response of our demand for imported goods and services to a change in their price is likely to be less marked, it will nevertheless be appreciable in so far as there is any possibility of dispensing with inessential imports or of producing essentials at home instead of importing them.

4 Let us assume, by way of illustration, that a 1 per cent fall in the price of our goods and services in foreign markets would lead to a 2 per cent increase[2] in the volume of their sales and that a 1 per cent rise in the price of foreign goods and services in our home market would lead to $\frac{1}{2}$ per cent reduction in our imports of such goods. In this case if we start with exports of £900 millions and imports of £1,000 millions, a 10 per cent depreciation of sterling would change this *adverse* balance of £100 millions into a *favourable* balance of £30 millions. Even if we were to make the very improbable assumption that, after allowing time for all adjustments, a 1 per cent fall in the price of our goods and services abroad would cause the volume of our exports to increase only by 1 per cent, it would still be true that a 10 per cent depreciation of sterling would reduce the adverse balance of payments from £100 millions to £60 millions.

5 The above paragraphs are written on the tacit assumptions that the expansion of our export industry can be brought about without any significant increase in the sterling price offered for our export goods, and that a contraction of our demand for imports does not cause any decline in terms of foreign currency of the prices at which our imports are offered to us. In other words, it has been assumed that the elasticities of our supply of goods for export and of the foreign supply of our imports to us are infinite.

6 In fact this may not be the case. Our exports are of a type which we probably could supply, at least after a period of readjustment, in greater amount without any very large rise in costs per unit, since they are largely manufactured goods capable of large-scale production. Our imports, on the other hand, are of such a character that a contraction of demand in such an important market as the United Kingdom might cause an appreciable reduction in the foreign price, since primary production is of a less elastic character than manufacture.

7 In so far as there was any tendency for our supply price of exports to rise as the volume of our exports was expanded, this would probably be unfavourable to our balance of payments; for, since the foreigners'

[2] This is an extremely moderate figure to choose. On the basis of the assumptions made in the preceding paragraph, the elasticity of demand for our exports should be considerably higher than this, if sufficient time is allowed for the necessary adjustments to be made.

demand for our exports is likely to be elastic, anything which tends to keep up the price at which we are prepared to supply exports will tend to reduce our total receipts from exports. On the other hand, in so far as the foreign supply price of our imports tended to fall as the volume of our imports declined, this would probably be favourable to our balance of payments; for, since our demand for imports is likely to be inelastic, anything which tends to keep down the price of our imports will tend to keep down our total expenditure on imports.

8. If $-e_d$ = the elasticity of the foreign demand for our goods and services;
e_s = the elasticity of our supply of goods and services for export;
$-i_d$ = the elasticity of our demand for foreign goods and services; and
i_s = the elasticity of the foreign supply of our imports of goods and services,

the formula given in paragraph 1 above takes the following form:–

$$d(E-I)=\frac{dr}{r}\left[E\frac{e_d(1+e_s)}{e_d+e_s}-I\frac{i_s(1-i_d)}{i_d+i_s}\right].$$

9 If, by way of illustration, we assume as before that

E = £900 millions
I = £1,000 millions
$e_d = 2$
and $i_d = \frac{1}{2}$

and now also assume that (instead of $e_s = i_s =$ infinity)

$e_s = 10$
$i_s = 1$,

then a 10 per cent depreciation of sterling would turn the unfavourable balance of payments of £100 millions into a favourable balance of £31$\frac{2}{3}$ millions instead of into a favourable balance of £30 millions. In other words, what is lost by assuming a less elastic supply of exports is in this case more or less exactly offset by assuming a less elastic supply of imports.

10 In these calculations our exports must include our invisible as well as our visible exports. The elasticity of the foreign demand for some of our invisibles, such as shipping services, is probably great, since a reduction in our shipping costs is of great importance in enabling us to compete with foreign shippers. But there is one special form of invisible export, namely our receipt of income from foreign investments, which requires some special consideration. In so far as we receive income fixed in terms of foreign currency, a 10 per cent depreciation of sterling would cause no

change in the foreign currency paid to us on our investments; and in this case the elasticity of the foreign demand for our service must be regarded as equal to unity. In so far as we receive income payable in sterling, a 10 per cent depreciation will be accompanied by a 10 per cent reduction in the amount of foreign money paid in interest on our overseas investments; and in this case the foreigners' elasticity of demand for our 'invisible exports' must be regarded as zero.

11 If out of £900 millions of 'invisible' and 'visible' exports £100 millions represented income from overseas investments, of which half was payable in sterling and half in foreign currencies, then the elasticity of demand for our exports of other goods and services would have to be $2\frac{3}{16}$ in order to make the elasticity of demand for all our goods and services 2. If the whole of the £100 millions of income from overseas investments were payable in foreign currencies, then the elasticity of foreign demand for our other goods and services would have to be $2\frac{1}{4}$ in order to make the elasticity of demand for all our visible and invisible exports together equal to 2.

12 A depreciation of sterling, while in appropriate conditions it will help greatly to rectify a disequilibrium in our balance of payments, is likely to cause some change in the terms of international trade against us; for it is likely to lead to a decline in the price of our exports in foreign currencies relative to the price in foreign currencies at which we can acquire our imports. It remains, therefore, to determine how great this adverse movement is likely to be. The proportionate change in the ratio of export prices to import prices consequent upon a depreciation of sterling is given by the following formula:–

$$\frac{\mathrm{d}r}{r}\left(\frac{e_{\mathrm{d}}}{e_{\mathrm{d}}+e_{\mathrm{s}}}-\frac{i_{\mathrm{s}}}{i_{\mathrm{d}}+i_{\mathrm{s}}}\right).$$

From this it follows that a 10 per cent depreciation of sterling, which on the assumption made in paragraph 9 above would improve the balance of payments by £$131\frac{2}{3}$ millions, would on the same assumptions be accompanied by a 5 per cent change in the terms of trade against this country. Since foreign transactions affect only a limited part of the total national income, the reduction in real income associated with this would be much smaller – probably only of the order of 1 per cent. Moreover, in fact the elasticity of demand for our exports would probably prove to be considerably more than 2 in the conditions foreshadowed by the settlement recently discussed at Washington. If this elasticity were 3 instead of 2, then the 10 per cent depreciation of sterling discussed in paragraph 9 would have improved our balance of payments by some £195 millions (instead of only £$131\frac{2}{3}$ millions) at the cost of a movement in the terms of trade against us of only about $4\frac{1}{3}$ per cent (instead of 5 per cent).

5

Financial Policy and the Balance of Payments

Meade's inaugural lecture as Professor of Commerce with special reference to International Trade at the London School of Economics on 16 February 1948 was published in Economica*, vol. 15 (May 1948), pp. 101–15. Meade pointed out that it was his 'intention to treat the subject of this lecture, and in particular the relationship between internal policy and the balance of payments, rather more fully' in his book* Planning and the Price Mechanism *(London: Allen & Unwin, 1948). A revised version of the lecture was published in the book (as Chapter V), as was the article on 'Bretton Woods, Havana and the United Kingdom Balance of Payments' (as an appendix), which is reproduced as Chapter 6.*

I deliver this Inaugural Lecture with a great sense of the honour conferred upon me by my appointment to this Chair and with a profound realisation of my inadequacies for this position. I cannot vie with my predecessor, Professor Benham, in his great and robust gifts as a teacher and in his extensive knowledge of trading conditions throughout the world. These qualities of his are well known here in the London School of Economics where he both learned and taught his subject for so many years.

I have come to this great School as an outsider and with interests which differ somewhat from those of some of my predecessors. My main concern in economics has always been, not with descriptive or institutional studies, but with theoretical analysis and, in particular, with the contribution which economic analysis has to make to the solution of problems of practical economic policy. Accordingly I have selected as subject matter for this lecture an outstanding, perhaps *the* outstanding, problem of practical economic policy in the field of international trade – namely the present balance-of-payments disequilibrium of the United Kingdom. And it is my intention to discuss it this evening from the point of view of economic analysis.

Throughout the many economic problems which confront us one common question arises: should we rely upon direct quantitative controls to achieve our ends or upon using the money and price mechanism so as to induce persons to do what is socially desirable? Should we, for example, direct workers from inessential to essential uses or should we attract them by higher wage-rates in the latter and lower wage-rates in the former? Should we achieve an equitable distribution of wealth by the direct guarantee of a fair share of each essential commodity to each citizen or by measures which ensure a tolerably equitable distribution of general monetary purchasing power exercised in a relatively free market? Should we restrain the inflationary pressure of the too much money chasing the too few goods by a system of direct licensing and rationing of each commodity or by general measures which reduce money purchasing power to the desired degree? The same question arises in the case of our balance of payments. Should we exercise a system of direct quantitative controls over the import of each commodity and the exports of each of our industries, or should we so rig the market that our producers have such incentives to sell abroad and our purchasers such disincentives from buying from abroad that we restore the balance that way?

I cannot now argue the general issue. The case against direct controls is that they are costly in administrative manpower; that they are often clumsy and uneconomic in their effects; that they may threaten personal freedom; that they encourage spivery and corruption; and that they are often destructive of economic incentives. I would not be misunderstood. Of course I am not advocating instantaneous decontrol. No one but a lunatic would say that tomorrow we should remove all import restrictions and exchange controls. Nor am I suggesting that the state should not try to foresee future developments and plan ahead to meet them. Of course, in present conditions it is sensible to plan export and import programmes ahead in the sense of having a target date for the closing of our balance-of-payments gap and an idea how much we shall have to close by import restriction and how much we shall be able to meet by export expansion. But I do maintain that we should consider carefully how at every stage we can supplement, and in appropriate cases replace, direct quantitative controls with a planned use of the monetary and pricing mechanisms which will induce private citizens to do what it is in the social interest that they should do.

Accordingly, I address myself this evening to this specific problem: What answer has economic analysis to give to the question whether the monetary and pricing mechanisms can be used to help us to close our balance-of-payments gap?

First and foremost there is the problem of making the goods and services available to the foreigner. This in my opinion is above all a question of an internal disinflationary financial policy.

I am not now referring to direct controls limiting wage-rates, profit margins and prices. It is, of course, of importance to ensure that the cost of the goods which we do make available for export enables them to be sold abroad in competition with foreign products; and I shall revert to this question later. But measures which reduce money prices as quickly as they reduce spendable incomes do nothing to reduce the real purchasing power of domestic consumers or the amount of our produce which they will demand for their own consumption.

In order to reduce the pull of internal demand and to make more goods available for export, measures are required which directly reduce the domestic demand for goods and services or which indirectly do so by reducing spendable incomes more than money prices or by raising prices to domestic consumers without raising their spendable incomes. Such measures include economies in public expenditure on goods and services; discouragement of expenditures on capital developments of all kinds; increases in direct taxation which reduce spendable incomes; and increases in indirect taxation or reductions in subsidies which raise the price of goods and services to domestic consumers without raising their spendable incomes.

Measures of this kind, by restricting the demand for goods and services, would incidentally put the most effective brake on the upward spiral of money prices and costs; but they could also be used to limit internal demand to the extent necessary to prevent supplies required for export from being pulled on to the domestic market. They would powerfully reinforce and might well eventually replace attempts to force exports by clumsy direct controls which require each industry to export an arbitrarily determined proportion of its output.

There is a second task which seems to me to be equally clearly a matter for financial policy – in this case for external financial policy. Having made certain that the goods will not be bought on the internal market, one must next ensure that they are not bought by overseas purchasers except for money which will enable us in turn to purhase the imports which we require. It is frequently argued that we require some system of direct control over our exports for the purpose of directing them away from 'soft' currency markets where their sale will not earn us currencies which we can readily use for purchasing essential supplies.

But such a system of direct export controls would be superfluous if we insisted that overseas purchasers of our goods should pay for them in gold, convertible currencies, or sterling acquired currently by them through the sale of useful goods to us. This result would be achieved if the large balances of liquid sterling funds accumulated by overseas countries as a result of war-time finance were blocked or otherwise effectively prevented from being run down, and if no export of capital were allowed from this country to any overseas territory. In such conditions foreigners could obtain sterling for the purchase of our goods only through the sale to us either of their goods or of other currencies which were useful to us for the purchase by us of imports from other sources. Exporters would automatically find that only those overseas markets were profitable which gave us the power to import needed supplies.

I do not intend to maintain that there should be literally no movement of capital abroad. Even in our present critical position we may be under some moral obligation to make a token payment on account of the indebtedness which we incurred during the war. We must sometimes be prepared to run up our holdings of a foreign currency or to allow the foreign holdings of our currency to decline moderately and temporarily in a clearing or payments account. It may occasionally be economical for us on a moderate scale to allow a country to purchase our exports on some form of credit if thereby we obtain an export trade which is likely soon to become repaying and which we might lose permanently if we did not enter it promptly. We may be wise occasionally to invest abroad on a moderate scale in economic schemes for the development of new sources of cheap supply of essential imports, provided that we can get no other country or international institution to advance the necessary funds. But on these and similar grounds we can consciously decide how much credit should be granted, or how much debt should be repaid, to each overseas country and can make our financial arrangements accordingly. That done, there is no need for any further control to guide exports to repaying markets.

Our exports tend at present to go to non-dollar markets and we draw a large surplus of imports from dollar markets. Indeed, the Chancellor of the Exchequer stated recently that for 1948 we hoped to attain substantially an overall balance in our balance of current payments; but he added that there would still be 'within this total balance a deficit with the Western Hemisphere of nearly £300 million sterling which, of course, cannot be set off against our surplus from the other areas. That could only be tackled by cutting off imports from or extending exports to the Western Hemisphere.' In other words, the prospect was that we should export £300 millions more to non-dollar markets than our imports from those markets. How might our excess exports to the non-dollar markets be financed?

First, these excess exports might be sold in the non-dollar markets in return for gold or dollars which the non-dollar countries would have to have earned by their excess exports to dollar countries or by untied loans or other untied aid from dollar countries. But in this case we would be able to set off our surplus with the non-dollar world against our deficit with the Western Hemisphere. We should have nothing to worry about: our overall balance of payments would balance and we should face no loss of gold or dollar reserves – unless, of course, we were prepared to allow other countries to obtain funds from us on capital account for conversion into gold and dollars to finance their excess imports from dollar markets.

Secondly, however, we might ourselves provide to the non-dollar countries by some form of capital export the funds necessary to purchase our excess exports. But it would be surprising if, in the present parlous plight of our balance of payments, we were to contemplate an export of capital of no less than £300 millions in one year.

The figures for 1947 show that in that year our net loss of gold and other monetary reserves was £972 millions while our adverse balance of payments on current account was £675 millions. The difference of about £300 millions must have represented a movement of capital funds directly or indirectly lent or repaid by us to overseas countries to enable them to purchase goods from us without immediate repayment or to enable them to obtain from us gold and dollars to finance their excess imports from other countries. About one half of this export of capital represented a repayment of sterling balances. These are huge figures. A capital export of £300 millions in a year would have been very large in the best days of our balance of payments; it represents between one-quarter and one-third of the whole United States Loan [the Anglo–American Financial Agreement of December 1945]; it is perhaps as much as the total aid we can hope to get from the Marshall plan; it is three-fifths of the reserves of gold and dollars which remained to us at the end of 1947; and it may be compared with the £43¾ millions which in the United States Loan Agreement was laid down as the annual rate at which after 1951 we might repay the accumulated sterling balances without losing the benefit of the waiver of interest on the United States Loan.

We come now to the third main question concerning the use of financial policy as a means of adjusting our balance of payments. Suppose that we have restricted internal monetary demand and have set close limitations on the purchase of our exports by overseas buyers out of funds acquired on capital account. The goods will then be available for export and for export only to repaying markets. If there is no special difficulty in selling our goods in those markets, well and good. The job is done. Two heroic measures of financial policy, one domestic and one external, have done the trick and our balance of payments is balanced.

But suppose that we have taken these steps and that we then find that we cannot sell the goods in the repaying markets? What then? Are there further adjustments of financial policy available to solve this problem? Or must we rely on trade controls?

Let us first consider the nature of the trade controls which would be appropriate. We might restrict imports to the extent necessary to bring them into balance with the limited amount of exports which we find that we *can* sell in repaying overseas markets. What does this imply?

When imports are restricted quantitatively below the level which would otherwise be brought into the country, the price which consumers would be willing to offer for the goods will be in excess, and often greatly in excess, of the price which the foreign suppliers would be willing to take for the goods. Who gets the benefit of this potentially substantial rake-off?

First, it may accrue to the final consumers of the imports. This is the more likely if there is an effective domestic price control. But price control is a difficult matter, and there are many goods where it may prove not to be practicable. When it is practicable it means either a consumers' scramble for the limited supplies with the resulting shop shortages, queues, etc., or a scheme of rationing or licensing to ensure an equitable distribution of the short supplies. This method is not compatible with the reinstatement of the pricing system domestically.

Secondly, the rake-off may accrue to those lucky middlemen to whom the controllers hand out the valuable pieces of paper called import licences which give permission to the privileged few to purchase in the cheap foreign market for resale at scarcity prices at home.

Thirdly, the price charged by the foreign suppliers may be raised to correspond with the higher price at home. This has often happened in the past and is a constant danger; and in so far as it does happen the saving in foreign exchange which is the object of the restriction of imports is frustrated by the rise in the price paid to the foreign suppliers. Indeed, if the domestic demand for the imports is sufficiently irresponsive to price changes, the reduction in supplies will so raise the price of the imported goods that the foreigner will obtain a larger sum of money for a smaller volume of goods. The import restriction in that case will actually increase the bill which we must pay for our imports. A cure which may simultaneously reduce our supplies of essential imports and make our balance of payments worse cannot perhaps be considered in every respect ideal.

The rake-off is the more likely to accrue to foreign governments, foreign producers or foreign middlemen, the more easily the foreign suppliers can form a monopoly and, by restricting or threatening to restrict their sales, can obtain a price corresponding to the scarcity price in the country of import. Foreign suppliers may, of course, in any case attempt to indulge in such monopolistic exploitation of the importing market; it does not require import restriction by the importing country to make successful export restriction profitable. But import restriction often makes export restriction by the foreign suppliers much easier to organise. This is particularly the case if the import restriction is administered by the allocation of a fixed quota to each supplying country. For in that case, the exporters in one exporting country cannot be undercut by competition from another exporting country, since the latter will be restrained by its own fixed quota. All that each exporting country need do in order to exploit the scarcity in the importing country is to organise a separate national export monopoly. No comprehensive international restriction scheme is necessary, as would be the case in the absence of import quotas in the importing country.

But import licensing is not inevitably prone to the dangers indicated above. They would be completely removed by quite a moderate change in the method of applying import restrictions. I refer, of course, to the possibility that import licences should be sold to the highest bidder. This would ensure that the rake-off between the scarcity selling price and the foreign purchase price of the imported supplies accrued, as it should, to the community in the form of an increased public revenue, part of which could of course be used, if it were so desired, to supplement the incomes of the poorer consumers so as to offset the rise in the price charged for the imported goods. It would enable a system of strict quantitative control of imports to be integrated into a domestic price mechanism. It would not involve the selection of a privileged few importing middlemen, since all firms, old and new, domestic and foreign, could take part in the auction. The licence to import need not tie the importer to a single source of supply, and this would fully maintain the incentive and the power of the importers to keep down the price offered by them to the foreign suppliers.

Any experiments in auctioning import licences could be initiated on a limited scale. One or two commodities for which the conditions were considered most suitable could be chosen in order to see how such a system might work. But the really interesting possibilities would arise when the system became more general. This is so not merely because a large amount of imports would then be covered by all the individual schemes, but because there would be great possibilities of extending the range of goods covered by each individual scheme. One of the great difficulties involved in drawing up any quantitative import programme is to decide how much of each particular commodity should be imported. How much wheat and how much maize should be imported? There is nothing to prevent the organisation of a single auction for the right to import such and such a total value of cereals. Indeed, the principle could go much further than this. There is nothing to prevent the organisation in the end, by the successive merging of small groups, of a single auction for the right to import such and such a total value of all imports. To the extent that it was desired to use the pricing system as a means of following consumers' choice in the home market, the same principle could be applied in the selection of imports even though the total value of imports were rigidly controlled.

There remains, however, a much more serious criticism of the use of import restrictions – namely, that it does nothing to expand our exports. It means that we balance our international accounts at an uneconomically low level both of imports and of exports. This is very serious for a country which like us relies upon the import of essential foodstuffs and raw materials which we cannot produce at home. Quantitative restriction of imports is clearly a second best arrangement for us and one which we should accept only if we cannot arrange to sell our exports of manufactured goods in repaying markets on a scale sufficient to finance all the imports we need of the goods which can be produced relatively more cheaply abroad.

Import restrictions should not be dismissed on these grounds until they have been examined in the form which is least open to this sort of objection. In conditions in which there are a number of separate countries suffering from an adverse strain on their balances of payments, import restrictions, if they are to be used to correct the balance of payments with the least restrictive effect on world trade, should be used discriminatorily. For suppose that France and the United Kingdom are both suffering from serious balance-of-payments deficits, while the United States has a large balance-of-payments surplus. If both France and the United Kingdom restrict their imports on a non-discriminatory basis, then France must restrict her purchases of British as well as of American goods and the United Kingdom must restrict her purchases of French as well as of American goods. If, however, France discriminates in her import restrictions in favour of the United Kingdom and the United Kingdom in favour of France, the division of labour between France and the United Kingdom can have full scope. Because we purchase more from France, France will be able to pay for more of our exports and we shall have a larger volume of remunerative export sales.

But while this mitigates the evil restrictive effect of import controls, it by no means removes it completely. Balance between Western Europe and North America would still be reached by a restriction of imports of North American goods into Western Europe rather than by an expansion of Western European exports into North America. Nor is this the end of the problem. It is easy to say that a new balance should be reached by means of trade discriminations against the exports of a country with a persistent balance-of-payments surplus. But what form should this discrimination take? Should each member of a group of deficit countries which are making, as it were, a common dollar pool discriminate against dollar purchases only in so far as necessary to ensure that each particular member does not take more dollars out of the pool than it puts in, or should each of the members discriminate equally against dollar purchases, regardless of its own particular contribution to the pool? As Mr G. D. A. MacDougall has recently pointed out,[1] these are very different propositions. Discrimination against dollar purchases may be a polite periphrasis for going without the most essential imports; and the members of the dollar pool which contribute most dollars to it will want a quite different principle of discrimination from that desired by the members of the pool who contribute few dollars to it.

And the above is only one simple example of a clash of interests which might arise even if there were only three countries – one surplus and two deficit. But there are in fact some fifty countries, and at least a dozen countries of commercial importance, with a highly complex pattern of trading relationships between them. Suppose there are a number of deficit and a number of surplus countries. Against which surplus country shall which deficit country discriminate to what degree? I fear that if I carried this analysis very far it would become too complicated to be readily intelligible. Professor Ragnar Frisch has recently pointed out[2] that by the application of the mathematical method of matrices one might determine even in the most complicated trading patterns that system of discriminatory import restrictions which would restore equilibrium to every balance of payments with the minimum reduction in the total of world trade. But even this will not, I fear, get one so very far. This might mean that one country must restrict imports only from country X and not at all from its other suppliers Y and Z. But if it bought all its essential foodstuffs from X and its luxuries from Y and Z, it might not console its own inhabitants to know that they were starving in order that statistically the volume of world trade might suffer a somewhat small diminution.

In fact, discriminatory import restrictions are likely to descend into a welter of bilateral trade bargains with a more or less exact balancing of trade between each pair of countries. However enlightened and able the officials of the future International Trade Organisation may be, they will not be able to prevent such a system from deteriorating into a chaotic game of international barter causing real hardships to many unfortunate countries and imagined grievance to many more. We in this country, who stand so much to gain by the international division of labour, whose trade has hitherto run so much in multilateral channels, and who have learned from our inter-war experience that the import restrictions of other countries constitute the most inexorable barrier which our exports can confront, may indeed shrink from the prospect of a world in which many

[1] 'Notes on Non-Discrimination', *Bulletin of the Oxford University Institute of Statistics*, vol. 9 (November 1947), pp. 375–394.

[2] 'On the Need for Forecasting a Multilateral Balance of Payments', *American Economic Review*, vol. 37 (September 1947), pp. 535–551.

bilateral deals will be taking place which result in the restriction of, and discrimination against, our exports.

It is time to return to financial policy and to ask whether there is not a financial means by which the problem might be tackled. There is, of course, such a means in the adjustment of exchange rates. Let me make one thing clear at the outset. I am not advocating that here and now the pound sterling should be depreciated. Far from it. My argument up to this point has been that we should first restrain our own internal demand to match the supply of goods and services which would still be available to us if our exports were so increased or our imports so decreased that our balance of payments balanced, and that we should make sure that we sold our exports only in return for gold, convertible currency, or sterling newly acquired from the sale of useful goods to us. Such action might, I have said, cure our problem. It is only if we are then unable to find sufficient remunerative overseas markets for our exports that we should have to choose between import restrictions and exchange depreciation. And this choice may well never arise. An upward movement of money wage-rates is proceeding and may well continue in the United States. On the other hand, the effective application in this country of those measures for reducing excess demand which are in any case necessary to release our products for export would greatly restrain the upward tendency of our money prices and costs. If, in addition, we can start to close the existing gap between the technical efficiency of American and British industry, we may well find that we can undercut United States products to a sufficient degree without any exchange depreciation. Loose talk about an exchange depreciation which may never prove necessary is to be deprecated in view of the foreigners' hesitation to purchase our goods or to hold our money which would result from any expectation that our goods and our money were just about to be cheapened in terms of foreign currency by a depreciation of the pound. Nevertheless it is important to consider whether, in the hypothetical case of a country being unable to find sufficient remunerative markets to sell all the exports necessary to finance unrestricted imports, it would be wise to choose import restrictions or exchange depreciation.

Now, appropriate exchange-rate adjustments give just the correct degree of discrimination against the 'hard currency' sources of supply. Let us revert to the example of France and the United Kingdom, both of which we assume to be countries which have brought their internal inflations under control, have stopped the export of capital, but still have adverse balances of payments; and let us consider their commercial relations with the United States, which we assume to have a surplus on its balance of payments. If the franc and the pound sterling were both depreciated by 20 per cent, this would make American goods 20 per cent more expensive in both France and the United Kingdom without making French goods more expensive or more difficult to purchase in the United Kingdom or British goods more expensive or more difficult to purchase in France. In this way if each country with a deficit on its balance of payments were to depreciate, and each country with a surplus on its balance of payments to appreciate, to the extent necessary to achieve a balance in its own balance of payments, there would be just that degree of 'discrimination' in the sources of imports which is required to correct the balance. And this would be done without any loss of multilateral trade or any of the complexities and arbitrary clashes of interest of bilateral barter arrangements.

In this respect the method of exchange-rate adjustment is to be greatly preferred to that of direct trade controls. But there remain two further essential differences between import restriction and exchange depreciation which require some examination.

In the first place, discriminatory import restriction provides the state with an opportunity for exercising a monopolistic bargaining power which is not the case with exchange depreciation. Exchange depreciation discourages all imports from all sources equally. With discriminatory import restriction the state can attempt to obtain its imports on favourable terms by playing one supplier off against another. We can refuse to take these particular goods from this particular country unless the country in question will sell very cheaply or will take our exports in return at a good price. By exercising pressure on those countries which could least readily sell their produce elsewhere or turn to the production of other commodities, we could undoubtedly obtain an advantage, provided of course that no one tried the same trick on us.

But there is the rub. A country like ours which imports essentials which it cannot produce for itself and exports inessentials which others can fairly readily produce is not in the long run likely to come off well in a generalised system of monopolistic barter between sovereign states, even though it may be able in the short run to pick up one or two good bargains from countries which in the more liberal days of the past had been organised to serve this market and had not yet had time to extricate themselves from such a bad bargaining position. In the longer run if we wish to survive we must achieve a general set of rules, such as those adumbrated in the present Draft Charter for an International Trade Organisation, which ensures a general all round renunciation of discriminatory bargaining through import controls, although in the absence of such a set of rules we shall no doubt go bravely under stoutly asserting to ourselves as well as to others that our extensive market for essential raw materials and foodstuffs, though they are at present in short supply, though they come largely from underdeveloped countries determined in any case to switch from their production to that of industrial products, and though without them we must close down our industries and cease to eat, puts us in a peculiarly strong bargaining position.

In the second place, a depreciation of the exchange rate will make our exports cheaper in terms of foreign currency as well as making our imports more expensive in terms of sterling, whereas import restrictions will do nothing to cheapen our exports in foreign markets. Does this difference tell in favour of import restrictions or of exchange-rate adjustment?

It is not possible to give an absolutely unequivocal answer to this question. If the foreign demand for our exports were very irresponsive to price changes, a reduction in their price might so little stimulate the total amount which we sold that we should receive actually less foreign currency than before. Even though the elasticity of the foreign demand for our exports is likely to be sufficiently great to ensure that this does not happen, we should almost certainly suffer some movement in the real terms of trade against us, in the sense that an exchange depreciation would cause a greater reduction in the price of our exports than in the price of our imports in foreign currencies so that the country could obtain less real imports per unit of the commodities which it exported.

But against this must be set the fact that there would be an increase in our total exports; and if the increased volume of our exports were large in relation to the fall in the price which we could get for them in foreign currencies, we should stand to gain more from the increased volume of trade than we should lose from the smaller gain per unit of trade.

The question then comes down to this. Would a relatively small reduction in the price of our exports in foreign markets cause a relatively large increase in the volume of goods which we could sell? If so, the case for exchange-rate adjustment is conclusive.

Now, a reduction in the price of our exports should normally lead to a very considerable increase in the demand for them. For we produce manufactured goods in competition with the similar products of many other countries. A reduction in the price at which we can offer our goods can be expected, therefore, sooner or later, to lead to a considerable shift of demand in foreign markets in favour of our products.

This conclusion would, of course, be modified if many other countries depreciated their currencies and cheapened their exports simultaneously with us. For we obtain competitive advantage only over the products of those countries which do not depreciate; and for this reason it is of great importance to obtain international agreement to outlaw exchange depreciation by countries whose balances of payments are not in deficit.

But at present a number of other countries are in deficit simultaneously with ourselves, so that some simultaneous depreciation of their currencies would be legitimate. What the world suffers from is primarily a dollar shortage. If we and all the other non-dollar countries of the world could expand our exports to dollar markets and restrict our purchases from dollar markets, the remaining problems of adjustment between the members of the non-dollar area would be relatively easy to solve. What we have, therefore, to examine is the effect on the balance of payments between the non-dollar countries and the dollar countries as a whole of a simultaneous depreciation of, say, 20 per cent of all the currencies of the non-dollar group of deficit countries. Or in other words, would an appreciation of the dollar by, say, 20 per cent, remove the favourable balance of payments of the United States?

There is, in my opinion, no reason for believing that simultaneous depreciation by a large group of deficit countries will be less effective in restoring equilibrium than depreciation by a single small deficit country. Depreciation by the large group is likely to operate mainly on the imports of that group whereas depreciation by the small single country is likely to operate mainly on that country's exports. A small single country normally produces goods for export which compete with the exports and the home production of many other countries. A relatively small reduction in the price at which it offers its goods for export may enable it to undercut a large volume of foreign production.

The exports of a large group of countries will make up a much larger proportion of the total production of the rest of the world. The large group cannot, therefore, expect to obtain any given proportionate increase in its exports without a much greater danger of spoiling the foreign market for its goods. But on the other hand a large group of countries is likely to include countries which produce many diverse commodities including agricultural and industrial products. For this reason their imports from the rest of the world will be much more sensitive to price changes than in the case of a small single country which is likely to be much less self-sufficient. For example, suppose that we and a large group of deficit countries, including both agricultural and manufacturing countries, depreciated simultaneously. The rise in the price of dollar foodstuffs to us would enable us, without deliberate discrimination against United States produce, to switch our imports of foodstuffs to non-dollar sources of supply. The rise in the price of dollar manufactures in the agricultural members of the depreciating group would enable them, without deliberate discrimination, to switch to the purchase of our manufactured goods instead of United States products. The group's imports from the United States would as a whole be responsive to price changes, though its total exports to the United States would be less responsive than would the exports of a single country to the whole of the rest of the world.

It will be observed that I am assuming that both we and the agricultural members of the deficit group have adopted disinflationary domestic policies on a scale sufficient to release our products for sale to each other. In these conditions there is no reason to believe that a simultaneous depreciation by a large group of countries will be any the less effective in putting the group into equilibrium than a depreciation by a single country in putting that country into equilibrium, though it is probably true that the large group of countries will have a greater incentive to choose the method of import restriction. For it has less chance of expanding the total volume of its export trade by exchange depreciation; and it will probably lose less real welfare by a large restriction of imports, since its imports are less likely to be irreplaceable by home production.

But it must never be forgotten that the very possibility that deficit countries may improve their balances of payments or terms of trade by means of import restrictions rests upon the assumption that the surplus countries will not retaliate by themselves restricting imports. If the surplus countries refuse to buy the deficit countries' goods as quickly as the deficit countries refuse to take the surplus countries' goods, the deficit countries will not, of course, succeed in improving their own position. Their export markets will be spoiled by the surplus countries' restrictions just as badly as they spoil the surplus countries' export markets by their own restrictions. Such retaliation by the surplus countries is ruled out in the present Draft Charter for an International Trade Organisation; and that is a main reason why it should be one of our chief objectives to seek general acceptance for that Charter. But it is a hard doctrine for the surplus countries to accept. And while we can legitimately ask the surplus countries to agree that something effective must be done by both deficit and surplus countries to remove disequilibria in international balances of payments we cannot expect the surplus countries long to accept a solution which is unnecessarily destructive to world trade and particularly opposed to their own interests.

Indeed, what answer could we give to the following offer by the surplus countries if it were ever made to us? 'You are imposing discriminatory restrictions against our exports. We wish rather to get rid of the disequilibrium by appreciating our currency. This will enable you to continue to purchase each others' goods rather than ours because it will make our goods more expensive to you, but we shall get the benefit of the higher price charged for our goods. Moreover, the appreciation of our currency will reduce the price of your goods to us and we shall then spend more on them. This will enable you to afford to purchase more of our exports. If you will not agree to this very reasonable solution, we shall not be able to continue our one-sided restraint from the use of import restrictions.'

The challenge would be difficult to meet since, from the international point of view, there is always a net advantage in replacing import restrictions by an exchange-rate adjustment; for what one country loses by any adverse movement of its terms of trade must be gained by the favourable movement in the terms of trade of other countries, whereas the increased volume of remunerative international trade brings a net advantage to every country. In any case, it would be better for the deficit countries to accept reasonable arrangements for the restoration of balance through exchange-rate adjustments rather than to risk a decline into a world in which all countries, surplus as well as deficit, were making an uncontrolled use of discriminatory import restrictions. In such a world this country above all would find it difficult to survive.

If the preceding analysis is correct, appropriate exchange-rate adjustment should in any normal case go a long way towards the effective restoration of equilibrium, provided that it is not accompanied by unnecessary competitive exchange depreciation by the surplus countries, that the new channels of trade made profitable by the resulting price adjustments are not clogged up with trade barriers of all kinds and that the invasion by the deficit countries of the markets of the surplus countries is not accompanied by a general depression and collapse of internal demand in the surplus countries.

Indeed, these are the vital conditions. The possibility of using the price mechanism effectively to correct disordered balances of world payments depends upon the general rules of the game accepted not only by us but by other countries for the conduct of international commercial and financial transactions. If we can obtain agreement to a set of rules which recognises the principle that deficit countries should prevent all forms of capital export; which allows deficit countries to depreciate their exchange rates but does not allow surplus countries to do so; which ensures that surplus countries reduce their trade barriers to imports and do not raise them to keep out new imports as the deficit countries restore their position; and which ensures that the surplus countries maintain a high and stable level of internal demand; then we shall have achieved a situation in which the price mechanism can properly perform its international task. But these are precisely the conditions which the Articles of Agreement of the International Monetary Fund and the Draft Charter for an International Trade Organisation are aimed at ensuring and, for this reason, if for no other, these international instruments are of vital importance to us and should command our wholehearted support.[3]

[3] I have discussed the relevance of these international instruments for the restoration of equilibrium to our balance of payments in more detail in an article entitled 'Bretton Woods, Havana and the United Kingdom Balance of Payments' in *Lloyds Bank Review* for January 1948 [Chapter 6 below]. There is one point, not mentioned in that article, which needs to be carefully watched. It is possible to interpret the present draft of the Charter for an International Trade Organisation as ruling out the right to administer import licensing through the method advocated above of auctioning such licences to the highest bidder. This would be a serious blemish; but it is difficult to believe that the auctioning of licences is really out of line with the spirit of an International Trade Charter which does after all attempt to restore in some measure the international working of the price mechanism.

81-94
[1948]

6

Bretton Woods, Havana and the United Kingdom Balance of Payments

U.K.
4220
4313

From Lloyds Bank Review, *no. 7 (January 1948), pp. 1–18. With respect to the 1947 draft Wheat Agreement mentioned in footnote 3 below, Meade had been involved in interdepartmental discussions in Whitehall surrounding the conference. He was also consulted, even though he had left government service, by the UK delegation when negotiations on an International Wheat Agreement resumed in Washington in January 1948. (His suggested amendments to the draft Agreement were adopted by the UK delegation but not accepted by the other participants.) (Public Record Office MAF83/1665 and MAF84/817 and 818; Meade Papers 3/2, 3/6 and 3/13.) For his continuing interest in commodity schemes see Chapters 18 and 20 below.*

I Introductory

Since the end of the war one of the main issues in international policy has been that of the basic system of international commercial and financial relationships which this country should adopt. Should we attempt to rebuild our external position on the basis of a set of internationally recognised 'rules of the game' designed to reduce commercial and financial obstacles to international commerce and to promote multilateral trading to the maximum possible extent? Or should we preserve our freedom from any such set of international rules in order to build up a system of bilateral deals with other countries as a means of restoring our balance of payments by forcing others to buy from us as much as we buy from them and of insulating ourselves, to some extent at least, from the external instabilities which may arise in the future if there is another world slump spreading, for example, from a major depression in the United States?

The first alternative is associated with three great international projects – the International Monetary Fund, the International Bank for Reconstruction and Development and the International Trade Organisation, of which the first two, on which Lord Keynes so unreservedly expended his energies, are already born and the last is confidently expected by all concerned shortly to be the subject of an interesting event at Havana. In spite of much controversy on the subject the Government have consistently adopted this first alternative. The two Bretton Woods financial institutions were accepted at the end of 1945 at the time of the acceptance of the Loan Agreement [the Anglo-American Financial Agreement of December 1945]. At the same time Trade Proposals, drafted by the United States authorities after the closest consultation with United Kingdom officials, were published and the Government expressed their agreement with the main principles of these Proposals. At two successive sessions of the United Nations Commission which has been preparing for the World Conference on Trade and Employment (now meeting in Havana) there has been elaborated a Draft Charter for an International Trade Organisation, clearly based in large measure on these trade proposals.

Was the decision to support these institutions the right decision? The issue is of supreme importance to the United Kingdom. The prosperity and greatness of this country depend so essentially upon overseas supplies of essential foodstuffs and raw materials that the restoration of our balance of international payments must be our main pre-occupation; and clearly these new international economic and financial instruments will profoundly affect the solution of this problem. My own personal opinion is that the acceptance of these instruments is unquestionably in the interest of our balance of payments. There are those who see in these instruments inflexible rules for the restoration of Free Trade and the Gold Standard imposed upon us by a United States which is ignorant of the economic realities of a world of disordered balances of payments and which is prepared to make unscrupulous use of its present powerful position to force its doctrinaire ideas down our and other throats. There are those who see in these instruments ideas which are desirable as a long-term Utopian goal and which may possibly prove practicable at some fairly distant (but, they hope, not utterly remote) future date. Let these people study the actual texts. They will find there practical international provisions which may be initiated here and now and which ensure international rules for economic and financial conduct expressly constructed according to the designs of the most streamlined modern economic thought, to facilitate the restoration of equilibrium to disordered balances of international payments. The purpose of this paper is to produce some evidence in support of this claim.

II The Limitation of General Protectionism

The Articles of Agreement of the International Monetary Fund and the Draft Trade Charter (particularly in Chapter IV) set limits to the use of protective devices, whether the character of these be monetary (such as exchange controls limiting the purchase of foreign goods and services) or commercial (such as tariffs, quantitative import restrictions, subsidisation, or the undue restriction of imports by a state trading monopoly). These international instruments do not prohibit the use of any of these devices.[1] They attempt to set limitations to their use, limitations which vary in severity and in method according to the protective device in question. In particular, there are special provisions included in the rules governing the use of these protective devices, which are specifically designed to enable countries to use exchange and trade controls for balance-of-payments reasons.

It would be out of place here to discuss at length whether each of the various rules for the limitation of each protective device has been wisely conceived or is technically capable of more or less precise application. But one general point does require consideration. Is an all-round limitation of protection helpful or harmful to the United Kingdom's balance of payments?

If we wish to restore our balance of payments without either closing down our industries or starving, there can, I think, be no ground for doubting the interest of this country in a general limitation on protectionism. We import essential raw materials, which we cannot to any great extent replace with home production but without which we could not maintain our industrial production and employment. We import foodstuffs, which we should find it most difficult to replace with home production, but without which we should starve. We export manufactured goods, many of which are not essential to the importing countries, being of a luxury or semi-luxury character and many of which can, without too much difficulty or economic loss, be produced in other countries. In fact, we maintain a large population at a high standard of living in this country by relying on the international division of labour. Can there be any sane inhabitant of these islands who does not at least start with a strong prejudice in favour of the existing set of international institutions designed primarily to set reasonable limits to protectionism? Our balance of payments will, of course, be restored, as soon as we have either increased our exports or, having failed to do so, have cut down our imports because we have used up our reserves and can persuade no one else to lend or to give us any more. The only question at issue is whether the balance will be one which gives us sufficient imports of foodstuffs and raw materials to avoid malnutrition and serious industrial unemployment.

Anyone familiar with the present compelling desires of under-developed primary producing countries to industrialise and to turn to the domestic production of manufactures will realise the special dangers which now confront the balance of payments of a country in our position. I do not wish to deny the advantages which will accrue to the world as a whole from a sensible policy of industrial development of under-developed countries, or to argue that there is no justification for any temporary special protection for this purpose. There is, no doubt, in many countries at present a real 'infant industry' argument in favour of state aid for the first stages of industrialisation. Nor do I wish to assert

[1] Nor, of course, do they prohibit state trading as opposed to private trading. The Trade Charter merely attempts to ensure that state trading shall not be used to give greater protection or more discrimination than is permitted to private trading through tariffs, import restrictions, subsidies, etc.

that such industrialisation is all loss to the older industrialised countries like the United Kingdom. The increased real income of those countries which, by sensible and economic industrialisation schemes, have really raised their incomes (and have not, in fact, merely lowered their standards by uneconomic obstacles to the international division of labour) will, to some extent – and possibly wholly – replace their previous demand for the simpler types of manufactured imports with a new demand for higher quality manufactured imports which they could not previously afford. But in underdeveloped countries there is a fashionable enthusiasm for industrial development schemes which in some cases perhaps somewhat impedes the nicely reasoned calculations of economy; and in other cases it is doubtful whether the pressure behind the drive for industrialisation is purely economic.[2]

In all this there is room for a sensible bargain between the developed and underdeveloped countries. The developed countries can provide 'know-how' and, in some cases, capital. The underdeveloped countries, moreover, can, for the purpose of promoting industrial development, be given limited exemptions from certain of the rules and procedures limiting protectionism. In return they can agree to co-operate with developed countries in the consideration and determination of what are really sensible and economic development projects. This is the basis of Chapter III of the Draft Trade Charter.

III International Commodity Agreements

We export manufactured goods and we import primary products consisting of essential supplies of raw materials and foodstuffs. It is as important for our balance of payments that our foreign suppliers should not put up the prices of our supplies to us unduly as it is that we should have unimpeded access to the foreign purchasers of our products. But if we were to insist upon unfettered freedom to make our own trading arrangements, our suppliers would of course insist on freedom to make such arrangements as they pleased. One of the most dangerous forms which such arrangements might easily take is the institution by producing countries of international commodity agreements which, in effect, restrict the production or the export of foodstuffs and raw materials and thereby raise their prices to the consuming countries.

Our vital interests are not hurt by the institution of 'buffer stock' types of commodity control which stabilise prices to primary producers by holding supplies off the market and maintaining prices when prices would otherwise slump, and putting extra supplies on to the market and restraining prices at times of excess demand. Although the maintenance

[2] In the case of many underdeveloped countries it is, in fact, an improvement in agricultural techniques and equipment which is the first essential from their own point of view, food still being their greatest need and agriculture being in a backward state capable of great technical improvement and expansion as a result of capital development. Any such agricultural development which increases supplies and reduces costs of the primary products which we import would, of course, be also to our interest.

of world prices might come at a peculiarly inconvenient time from the narrow point of view of our balance of payments (for example, during a world slump when a reduction in our exports has imposed a strain which might be relieved by a fall in the price of our imports), the increased price which we should have to pay for our imports at one time would be offset by a lower price at other times. And we should gain indirectly by the stabilisation of buying power in the primary producing countries.[3]

But it is quite another matter if commodity agreements take a form which restricts quantitatively the amounts which suppliers may produce or export or which disposes of surplus supplies by sales in certain favoured markets at a lower price than the price charged to us. Such arrangements mean that the price which we pay for our imports is higher than it would otherwise be; and a 10 per cent rise in the price of our imports would, of course, raise the notorious 70 per cent increase needed on our pre-war exports by another 17 points.

It is an essential interest for our balance of payments to avoid such undesirable forms of commodity agreement. Chapter VI of the Draft Trade Charter lays down principles for the institution and operation of commodity agreements which will enable us to protect our vital and legitimate interests in this respect. Countries which are members of the Trade Organisation will not be able to institute restrictive commodity agreements except through an internationally recognised procedure which gives the consumers as much influence as the producers.

IV The Best of Both Worlds on Import Restrictions and Exchange Controls

Among the most important provisions from the point of view of our balance of payments are those which relate to the use of commercial restrictions on imports and financial restrictions on payments for current transactions. During the inter-war period there was no obstacle so harmful to our exports as the restrictions which other countries placed either upon the quantities of manufactured goods which could be imported into their markets or upon the value of the manufactured goods for which their importers might make payment. To get rid of these obstacles to our exports is perhaps an even more important interest in the present post-war period. We have now to undertake an aggressive export policy to obtain a vast increase in our exports which we shall only be able to obtain if we achieve a larger share in world exports of manufactures; for, however much total world trade in manufactures may rise, and however much we may benefit from reduced German and Japanese competition, we cannot hope to achieve a 70 per cent increase in our

[3] Similar considerations apply to international commodity schemes which consist of 'internationalised long-term contracts', i.e. of arrangements which, without restricting the total quantities which may be supplied, guarantee to exporters a certain demand at minimum prices in times of slump and to importers a certain supply at maximum prices in times of boom. The draft Wheat Agreement produced by the London Wheat Conference in the spring of 1947 was of this nature.

exports without an aggressive export policy. Quantitative restrictions on imports, particularly if they take the form of quotas of trade based upon performance in some earlier (probably pre-war) representative period, are the most rigid and inexorable barrier which our exports could encounter. No matter how much we improve the efficiency and lower the costs of our export industries or depreciate the value of our currency there can be no increase in exports over barriers which fix predetermined volumes or values for our trade.[4]

On the other hand, it is important that we should retain the right to control our imports so long as our acute balance-of-payments problem continues. The Draft Trade Charter and the Articles of Agreement of the International Monetary Fund are nicely calculated to give us the best of both worlds in a situation of this kind. The Draft Trade Charter lays it down that as a general rule there should be no quantitative import restrictions; but it immediately excepts the use of trade controls which are necessary to protect a country's monetary reserves. It lays down a procedure whereby the Trade Organisation in consultation with the Monetary Fund can on complaint judge whether such import controls are necessary for this purpose or not; and it can impose sanctions against a country which fails to accept its judgement. Thus we preserve our right to control imports so long as our position makes this necessary; but we acquire a powerful instrument for challenging the unnecessary use of such controls against our exports.

In the Articles of Agreement of the International Monetary Fund it is laid down that for a transitional period of some years countries can use exchange controls on current payments as long as these are necessary for its balance-of-payments problems. The Fund can, however, put increasing pressure upon countries to make their currencies convertible for current payments as their balance-of-payments position makes this possible; and as soon as a country has accepted the Fund obligation of making its currency convertible for current purposes, it can re-introduce such restrictions only with the permission of the Fund. It is of the greatest importance to us that the pressure to make currencies convertible for current transactions should, in fact, be exercised on those countries which are important export markets for our goods, as soon as they are in any position to start paying us gold, dollars or other convertible currencies for our goods. One of our most difficult problems at present is that our exports tend naturally to go to countries whose currencies are inconvertible and our imports tend to come from 'hard' currency sources.

There is much misunderstanding on this point. There is nothing in the Trade Charter or the Monetary Fund[5] at any time to force this country to make any funds convertible on capital account or to prevent the stoppage of any form of capital export. It is permissible to block all accumulated balances of sterling and to prevent all capital exports to any part of the

[4] This point should also be borne in mind in considering Chapter V of the Draft Trade Charter which deals with the problem of 'international cartels'. Some private business arrangements (e.g. the division of export markets on the basis of past performance) are probably inimical to a country which has got to invade its competitors' markets.

[5] Or, for that matter, in the United States Loan Agreement.

world. The only obligation which convertibility of sterling for current payments would impose upon us is not to try to force countries to receive additional balances of inconvertible sterling in payment for their sales to us – a thing which we might in any case find it difficult to do in the present seller's market for the things we want. And the Trade Charter and the Fund[6] do not in present circumstances even impose this obligation on us, but merely give the Fund some power of putting pressure on us and other countries to accept this obligation as our conditions improve.

Broadly speaking then, the Trade Charter and the Articles of Agreement of the Fund permit countries in balance-of-payments difficulties to restrict imports by trade or financial controls while they considerably limit the freedom of action in these respects of those countries which enjoy a favourable balance of payments. We stand, therefore, to gain much from the general acceptance of these instruments, since freedom for us to restrict imports will not comfort us much, unless those countries with favourable balances are prevented from similar restrictions on our sales to them.

V *The Problem of Non-Discrimination*

If trade or exchange controls are being used for the purpose of adjusting the balance of payments, circumstances may arise when their application on a non-discriminatory basis would unnecessarily damage world trade and limit the international division of labour. If a group of deficit countries confronts a group of surplus countries or a single large surplus country, the imposition of import restrictions by the deficit countries on a strictly non-discriminatory basis would mean that they would have to restrict their imports from each other (which would do nothing to restore equilibrium) as well as their imports from the surplus countries (which would help to restore a balance).

Both the Fund and the Trade Charter recognise this important problem. In the well-known 'Scarce Currency Clause' (Article VII of the Fund) it is laid down that if the Fund runs out of the currency of a particular country (a fate which should sooner or later overtake any country which continues to sell abroad without purchasing or lending abroad), the other countries can restrict imports from the country whose currency is scarce without restricting imports from each other. The principle is thus fully recognised; but the technical details of its application in the Fund are defective.

In the first place, a currency can only become scarce in the Fund when other countries exercise their drawing rights under the Fund and use their 'quotas' to purchase the currency in question from the Fund in exchange for their own currencies. But there are strict limitations on the extent to which, and the speed with which, other countries may exercise these rights, with the result that any currency of which there is at the start

[6] But the United States Loan Agreement does, of course, do so.

a large amount in the Fund can only become technically scarce after the lapse of a period of time. This has the result that even in present conditions the United States dollar cannot become technically scarce for many months and perhaps some years. Secondly, countries using the resources of the Fund must pay increasingly high rates of interest as they use their drawing rights, so that it may become very expensive for the deficit countries to maintain the technical scarcity of a currency in the Fund, even in conditions in which it is unquestionably extremely scarce in reality. Thirdly, the technical scarcity of the currency could be removed by the Fund borrowing more of that currency; and if that were done at a time when a number of the deficit countries had exhausted their powers of drawing from the Fund, the currency in question might continue to be in good supply in the Fund though it was still basically scarce in reality.[7]

The need for discrimination in such circumstances is, however, also recognised in the latest draft of the Trade Charter, and in a way that is not open to similar technical defects. It is there laid down that import restrictions should in general be on a non-discriminatory basis. But it is recognised that when there is a basic disequilibrium in international payments deficit countries, if they discriminate in favour of each other, may be able to obtain additional imports from each other, without thereby being able to afford less imports from the surplus countries. Safeguarding principles and procedures are, however, laid down to ensure that such discriminatory trade arrangements are not used to promote the protection of highly uneconomic lines of production by barter deals at prices widely divergent from world prices or to canalise trade in such a way as substantially to divert the exports of the deficit countries away from the markets of the 'hard' currency surplus countries, thereby restricting total trade with such countries.

Here again these safeguards are as important to us as the right to discriminate. We might well otherwise ourselves be the victims of unjustifiable discriminations in the purchasing policies of other countries which would harm our export trade. The system of financial and commercial relationships contemplated by the Fund and the Charter is not one of pure non-discrimination; it is one whereby international rules are enunciated for the legitimate uses of discriminatory devices,[8] and which presents an international forum for the continuing discussion and development of rules of international good conduct on this subject. Such a settlement is undoubtedly in the interests of the United Kingdom balance of payments.

7 All these are deficiencies which the Executive Directors of the Fund could avoid in any particular instance if they so decided. They may relax the limitations on drawings by deficit countries, may reduce interest charges, and may refuse to borrow fresh supplies of a scarce currency.

8 Space prevents me from discussing the other uses which are permitted, such as discriminations in favour of each other between territories (e.g. the United Kingdom and the Colonies) having a common quota with the International Monetary Fund or temporary discriminations in favour of economies which have been shattered by the war.

VI The Best of Both Worlds on Exchange-Rate Adjustments

Perhaps the greatest unresolved issue in international economics is the extent to which reliance should be placed on trade controls or on exchange-rate adjustments as a means of restoring equilibrium to balances of payments. This question is not resolved in the Articles of Agreement of the Fund and the Trade Charter. The Fund lays it down that, beyond a small movement, a country cannot adjust its exchange rate without the permission of the Fund, but that the Fund, regardless of that country's domestic policies, must give its consent if the country in question is in a 'fundamental disequilibrium'. The Trade Charter, as we have seen, allows a country to use trade controls for this purpose. It also provides a procedure for organised international consultation between the Trade Organisation, the Fund and the countries concerned about the use of these and other alternative devices for restoring equilibrium to balances of payments.

I will not hide my own opinion that, where exchange depreciation would enable a deficit country to find markets for considerably more exports than it could otherwise discover, this method is greatly preferable to that of trade controls. For, in the first place, unlike trade controls, it does not reduce the real income of the world by obstructing international trade and the international division of labour; and, secondly (though this is not a purely economic consideration), it is less liable to lead to friction between countries and to international administrative difficulties. Since the Monetary Fund and the Trade Organisation leave this issue quite unresolved, this is not an appropriate occasion to produce arguments in support of these assertions. There are, however, two basic points which must be made in the present context.

First, the general limitations on protectionism and, in particular, the prohibition on the use by surplus countries of inflexible protective devices such as quantitative import restrictions should greatly increase the effectiveness of exchange-rate adjustment as a method of restoring equilibrium. An exchange depreciation is useful in so far as the consequent change in price relationships expands the country's exports and contracts its imports; and its exports will expand much more if, in the surplus countries in whose markets they will be cheapened, there are no rigid obstacles to prevent a competitive invasion of those markets and no possibility of raising new protective barriers to keep out the increased imports. Exchange depreciation should, therefore, be a much more effective weapon with the Trade Organisation in existence than it would be without it.

But, secondly, an exchange depreciation can only begin to be effective if it is not offset by a competitive exchange depreciation by other countries; and this is exactly what the Fund achieves. Countries with very unfavourable balances of payments are permitted to depreciate, and countries with favourable balances of payments will not be permitted to offset this by an unnecessary competitive exchange depreciation. Have we forgotten so easily the history of the 1930s when our depreciation (entirely necessary for our balance of payments) was followed by as great an exchange depreciation of the United States dollar (entirely unnecessary from the point of view of their balance of payments)? What should we then have thought of an internationally agreed set of rules which would have allowed us to depreciate and to restrict imports and would have permitted them neither to depreciate, nor to restrict imports, nor substantially to raise their tariff? And all this without any loss of our rights to control the flight of capital. Should we then have considered this a loss of our financial and commercial freedom?

VII International Capital Movements

It has already been observed that neither the Fund nor the Trade Charter limits our rights to prevent an export of capital. On the other hand, the Fund does, of course, give us the right to draw some £80 millions a year for four years in defence of our balance of payments, and gives other countries in similar difficulties a corresponding supplement to their monetary reserves. And the Bank is an institution for the promotion of long-term lending, mainly by the United States, for the reconstruction and development of countries which are in need of capital. The Bank is clearly not in a position alone to provide finance on a scale adequate to meet the present need for dollars. It does, however, make a definite, if limited, contribution; and it introduces for the first time into the rules of international good behaviour a principle of considerable importance to us, namely, that of the untied loan. None of the loans which the Bank supports can be tied, in the sense that their proceeds must be spent on purchases in any particular country.

If the United States undertakes an adequate programme of lending, it is of the first importance to us that this principle should be observed. We sell capital equipment to countries at present short of dollars. If they can borrow dollars and, where we are truly competitive suppliers, can use these dollars to purchase our goods, we shall get that indirect benefit from United States lending which is our proper due in a multilateral world. It is, accordingly, wise for us to see that as much emphasis as possible is placed upon the principles upon which the Bank was instituted in any future international arrangements for capital finance.

VIII The Maintenance of Full Employment

There are provisions in the Draft Trade Charter to bind a country to take appropriate measures to stimulate its domestic demand for goods and services if a deficiency in its internal purchasing power is causing a deficiency in its buying from other countries and is thus imposing a strain on other countries' balances of payments. Chapter II of the Draft Trade Charter lays it down that a country 'shall take action designed to achieve and maintain full and productive employment and large and steadily growing demand' domestically; that if a country is nevertheless exercising a deflationary pressure on the balances of payments of other countries it 'shall make its full contribution . . . towards correcting the situation,' or, in other words, shall do something (e.g. reduce tariffs or other barriers to imports, appreciate its exchange rate, lend more abroad, etc.) so as to make a greater use of its external purchasing power; that countries shall participate in arrangements for exchange of information and for consultation on policies for the maintenance of demand; and that the Trade Organisation in exercising its functions under the other provisions of the Trade Charter 'shall have regard . . . to the need of Members to take action . . . to safeguard their economies against deflationary pressure in the event of a serious or abrupt decline in the effective demand of other countries.'

All this might in the not far distant future be very relevant to our balance of payments. A major internal depression in the United States would, as in the 1930s, reduce United States buying power in many markets and thus seriously intensify the problem of a world shortage of dollars. It would, of course, give some compensating relief to us, since the reduced demand for foodstuffs and raw materials would substantially reduce their price, while the price of our manufactured exports would probably not decline so rapidly. But if a United States depression were at all severe or prolonged it is virtually certain that any such counterbalancing advantages would fail to offset the difficulties caused by the decline in United States purchases from the rest of the world. It would in any case cause localised unemployment in our export industries; its effect on the external buying power of other countries would be very severe and would promote protectionism and import restrictions, to the further detriment of our exports; and the primary producing countries would have a strong incentive to organise restriction schemes to maintain the prices of their exports of foodstuffs and raw materials. Whatever protectionism against our exports and price maintenance of the primary products supplied to us was permitted within the framework of the Trade Charter would certainly be used, and the pressure might become so great that the defences which the Charter provides for us might themselves be destroyed.

The Draft Trade Charter, by creating an international obligation to maintain external purchasing power in such circumstances and by outlining an international organisation for the promotion of action for this purpose, is a big step in advance. How helpful it might have been to the balance of payments of this and other countries in the depression of the early 1930s if the responsibility of countries which exerted a deflationary influence and a balance-of-payments pressure on other countries through an uncontrolled domestic depression had been clearly recognised in a freely negotiated international instrument, if a permanent international organisation had existed for the discussion of the implications of this responsibility, and if the organisation had had both the power and the obligation to release those countries which were the victims of such deflationary pressure from the obligations which would otherwise have prevented them from taking the necessary defensive measures without permitting the countries with favourable balances of payments to retaliate.

IX Conclusions

Any international agreement is bound to be a compromise. Apart from a number of technical blemishes in these international instruments which one would like to see removed, there are points of substance on which concessions have had to be made to obtain the many solid advantages enumerated above. In particular, in obtaining the tariff reductions granted by the United States and other countries in the General Agreement on Tariffs and Trade negotiated last summer in Geneva and closely connected with the Draft Trade Charter, we and the Dominions have had to make concessions not only on tariffs but also on Imperial Preference, that bugbear of the United States administration. We shall thereby lose some preferential protection for some of our manufactures in some Commonwealth markets, and this taken alone would, no doubt, increase our balance-of-payments difficulties. But preferences have been bargained against tariffs on the basis that the preference–tariff adjustment must itself constitute a mutually advantageous arrangement. Those who are aware of the staunch loyalty and hard-headed ability of our negotiators will be aware what this implies.

But it must be remembered that, into the bargain, so long as our balance-of-payments difficulties persist, we can replace tariffs with import restrictions (which the United States cannot do). And so long as the general world disequilibrium of payments remains, 'deficit' Commonwealth countries can, regardless of concessions on tariff–preferences, arrange to discriminate in favour of each other through their import controls so far as this is necessary to enable them to obtain 'additional imports' on the conditions discussed in Section V above. What the United States have gained – and from their point of view it is, of course, an important achievement – is that particular Imperial Preferences should be effectively reduced or eliminated in so far as and as soon as discriminatory trade arrangements are no longer justifiable on balance-of-payments grounds.

Nor, of course, do these international instruments provide a panacea for all our ills or a magic formula for removing our balance-of-payments difficulties. That herculean task cannot in any case be achieved without many unpleasant domestic measures necessary to make available the supply of more goods for export and to reduce the consumption of imports. On the nature of some of these internal measures there is now widespread agreement. We must, in particular, by heavy taxation, by reduced public expenditure and by strict economy in projects for capital development, reduce and hold in check the ever-threatening excess of domestic purchasing power which, quite apart from any other disadvantages which it may bring, pulls goods into domestic consumption and so diminishes the supplies available for export.[9] A few days ago at

[9] In present conditions a reduction in internal purchasing power would probably not greatly reduce imports. That is already done by our import controls. But one must not overlook the fact that many forms of internal consumption use imported raw materials, and once the raw materials are imported it is not possible to prevent all seepages into less essential domestic consumption. The elimination of such domestic demands would

my bank I was standing beside a man who was paying a series of cheques into his account. The clerk asked him how his business flourished and whether he had many export sales. He replied that business was fine, that he could obtain any amount of export orders but that he was too busy to undertake that sort of thing. We must reduce the internal pressure of demand, not, of course, to such an extent as to cause serious unemployment, but sufficiently to make it profitable for many more businesses to go all out for the alternative export orders which they could in fact fairly readily obtain.

There is nothing, of course, in the Trade Charter or elsewhere to prevent us from adopting the necessary internal measures. But, on the other hand, there is nothing which puts pressure on us to do so. It is arguable that this is a defect in the existing provisions of the Draft Trade Charter. During the 1930s it was to the disadvantage of the United States' own internal prosperity that they failed to take measures to increase and maintain their internal purchasing power; such a failure was a main cause of the then disequilibrium in international balances of payments; and it exerted a deflationary pressure on other countries which were already suffering from heavy unemployment as a result of a deficiency of monetary demand for the goods and services which they could produce. But the wheel has now turned full circle. Countries with unfavourable balances of payments which are not sufficiently restraining a domestic excess of monetary purchasing power are inflicting on themselves the wastes of an uncontrolled inflationary pressure; their failure to restrict excess domestic demand is a major contributory factor to present disequilibria in balances of payments; and they are exerting an inflationary pressure on other countries which are already suffering from the evils of inflation. Chapter II of the Draft Trade Charter severely discourages the former type of criminal folly: but it does nothing about the latter.[10]

In this paper I have confined myself to adducing evidence to support the claim that these international instruments provide a reasonable international background against which we can work out our own measures for the salvation of our own balance of payments. I have made no attempt to discuss the question whether we should have a still better chance of restoring our balance of payments in the free-for-all (and the absence of special dollar assistance) which would result from a refusal to accept any of the commitments of the Fund or the Trade Charter. It is my opinion (for reasons which have been ably stated by Mr G. D. A. MacDougall in two recent articles in the *Economic Journal* ['Britain's Bargaining Power', vol. 56 (March 1946), pp. 27–37, and 'Britain's Foreign Trade Problem', vol. 57 (March 1947), pp. 69–113]) that our

release raw materials for the manufacture of exports or reduce the need for their importation.

10 Criticism of the Draft Charter on similar lines was made by Mr Gunnar Myrdal when he was socialist Minister of Commerce in Sweden. (See Supplement B to Svenska Handelsbanken's *Index*, December 1946 ['The Reconstruction of World Trade and Swedish Trade Policy', a paper read before the Swedish Economics Society in December 1946].)

bargaining power in such circumstances would not suffice to enable us to restore our balance of payments at a tolerable standard of living.

Any such alternative would, of course, make economic co-operation with the United States impossible. I do not wish to discuss the political implications of this incontrovertible fact. The Fund, the Bank and the Trade Organisation constitute, broadly speaking, the only set of international economic and financial principles on which there is any hope of achieving agreement between Western Europe, the British Commonwealth and the United States, a group which accounted for rather more than two-thirds of pre-war world trade. Serious economic friction between these countries would entail serious diplomatic and political friction. It might split the Commonwealth. How, for example, could Canada choose between the Mother Country and her great American neighbour? And the United Kingdom would indeed develop a split personality. For how should we choose between Europe, the Commonwealth and that other great English-speaking entity?

Finally, it must never be forgotten that international instruments, such as those which have been discussed above, can only operate if there is sufficient will on the part of a sufficient number of countries of sufficient importance to co-operate in a spirit of constructive compromise so as to make the agreed arrangements work practically in a reasonably just and efficient manner. However well the agreements may be drafted and however suitable their provisions may be for a world of countries which desire the ends which the agreements are designed to serve, they are bound to break down, to be evaded and to cause friction and frustration if they are not operated with a will to make them succeed. The claim which is made in this article is that the ends which these instruments are designed to serve are so much to our interest that we should apply ourselves to see that, so far at any rate as the issue depends upon us, their provisions are observed not only in the letter but in the spirit.

95 - 132
[1948]

7

National Income, National Expenditure and the Balance of Payments

U.K.
~~3212~~
4312
4110
0230

This article, which was published in two parts in The Economic Journal, *vol. 58 (December 1948), pp. 483–505, and vol. 59 (March 1949), pp. 17–39, was written, according to Meade, 'largely as a by-product of work . . . under the auspices of the Royal Institute of International Affairs in preparing a volume on "International Economic Policy"'* (The Theory of International Economic Policy, Volume I: The Balance of Payments, *London: Oxford University Press, 1951).*

I The Limitations of 'Multiplier' Technique

This article has a very limited purpose. It seeks to elucidate certain relationships between the national income, the national expenditure and the balance of payments on the assumption that all domestic and foreign money prices and all rates of foreign exchange remain constant. That is to say, it deals with the effects which a change in the balance of payments may have on the national income and expenditure, and with the effects which a change in the national income and expenditure may have on the balance of payments, if we abstract from the substitution effects of changes in the relative prices of various goods and services. This article, in other words, assumes away all equilibrating mechanisms due to changes in the international flow of capital resulting from variations in relative rates of interest, or changes in the flow of international trade resulting from variations in exchange rates or in domestic wage-rates and prices. It assumes that if the national income is changed as a result of a change in the domestic or foreign demand for a country's produce, then output and employment are changed *pro rata* and all money prices remain unchanged. It investigates the effects only of changes of this type.

'Multiplier' analysis of this type is, of course, very strictly limited. It should never be used alone as a basis for prescription of policy in the real world. Nevertheless it has some use. Provided that its limitations are carefully remembered, it is a useful preliminary analytical device, in that it can isolate for explanation certain of the basic forces which are at work and which must be understood before the working of the whole system can be comprehended. 'Models' of the balance of payments can be later developed which, while they make room also for the effects of changes in relative prices, still contain the basic 'multiplier' relationships which it is the purpose of this article to investigate.

II Three Basic Forms of Disturbance

In what follows we shall confine our attention to the balance of payments between one country (which we shall call country A) and the rest of the world (which we shall call country B). We start in a position of rest. Some 'primary' or 'spontaneous' disturbance occurs; and we then ask what is the final effect on the balance of payments between country A and country B and on the national incomes of countries A and B when this 'primary' or 'spontaneous' disturbance has worked out all its secondary 'multiplier' effects upon both countries' income, expenditure, imports and exports.

We shall, in fact, attempt to find the answers (always on the basis of our simplifying 'multiplier' assumptions) to many questions concerning many kinds of international disequilibrium; but these questions can all be resolved into questions about three basic types of 'primary' or 'spontaneous' disturbing forces, though these may take different particular forms and may be combined in different ways.

(i) The first basic type of 'primary' disturbance is some internal change in the level of a country's effective demand for goods and services which is associated with the given level of national income in that country. (ii) The second basic type of 'primary' disturbance is a shift, within the given level of effective demand, from the goods and services produced by one of the two countries to the goods and services produced by the other – a shift which may occur in either or both of the two countries concerned. (iii) The third basic type of 'primary' disturbance is some change in the amount of money transferred from one country to another not in payment for an increased demand for goods and services, e.g. an increased lending or an increased reparations payment by one country to another. Let us consider each of these types of 'primary' disturbance in turn.

(i) The general level of a country's demand for goods and services which is associated with a given level of national income in that country may change for a number of reasons. People may decide to save less and spend more of their incomes on goods and services for personal consumption; the state may reduce taxation (without reducing its public expenditure) so as to leave persons with a larger tax-free income to spend on goods and services for personal consumption; the state may, without raising taxation or reducing the spendable incomes of others, itself spend more on goods and services for current state purposes or in prosecution of a larger public investment programme; or private investment, i.e. expenditure on goods and services by private enterprise for purposes of capital development, may increase because of some favourable change in the capital market (e.g. an expansionist banking policy leading to lower rates of interest) or because of an improved expectation of the yield to be reaped on capital development. For any of these reasons the demand for goods and services for domestic purposes (i.e. for personal consumption, for public consumption, for private or public investment) may show a 'spontaneous' primary change. In what follows we shall call the domestic demand for goods and services used for current consumption by persons or by public authorities or for domestic capital construction by private or public concerns 'domestic expenditure'; and we shall talk of a 'spontaneous change in domestic expenditure' when some such change as those enumerated above occurs so as to raise or lower the level of domestic expenditure which is associated with any given national income.

(ii) Now it is to be observed that 'domestic expenditure' is *not* expenditure on domestically produced goods and services. It is expenditure on goods and services, whether produced at home or abroad, for the satisfaction of domestic consumption or domestic investment whether private or public. Having decided how much to spend for such purposes out of any given national income, the next decision is how much of this 'domestic expenditure' should be spent on home-produced goods and services and how much on imports. We shall speak of a given 'propensity to import' as relating the total of imports to any given total of domestic expenditure. There is a 'spontaneous change in imports' when this propensity alters and when there is a change in the level of imports associated with any given level of total domestic expenditure. Such a 'spontaneous change in imports' in either country is the second basic type of disturbance.

(iii) There remains the third basic type of primary disturbance. Country A lends more to country B or has to pay increased reparations to country B. This will have no direct effect upon the balance of trade[1] of country A (though it will, of course, have a direct effect upon country A's total balance of payments including the loan or other financial transfer) unless it directly or indirectly causes a change in the demand for country A's or for country B's goods. In the 'pure' case of this type of 'spontaneous' disturbance there is no 'spontaneous' change either in domestic expenditure or in imports in either country. All we have to deal with as the 'primary' or 'spontaneous' cause of trouble is an increased transfer from country A to country B, causing a corresponding loss of monetary reserves from country A to country B.

But many disturbing occurrences which we shall wish to examine can be handled only as instances of combinations of these three 'pure' types. A few examples may serve to illustrate the many possibilities.

In the first place, country A may impose an import duty which both reduces its demand for imports and also raises an increased revenue for its state budget. If this increased revenue were added to the budget surplus it would cause a reduced demand for goods and services at factor cost out of any given national income. Such an occurrence would be a combination of disturbing forces Nos. (i) and (ii) above. It would

[1] In what follows by the balance of trade we shall mean the balance of all current payments (i.e. for visible and invisible trade).

represent a 'spontaneous' reduction in imports and a simultaneous 'spontaneous' reduction in total domestic expenditure at factor cost.

A second example would be afforded by an improvement in the investment prospects in country B which not only caused a 'spontaneous' increase in the domestic demand of country B for the goods and services needed to carry out a larger investment programme but also attracted a larger flow of lending from country A to country B to take advantage of the increased opportunities of profit in country B. Such an occurrence would represent a combination of primary disturbances (i) and (iii).

A third example would be afforded by the payment of reparations from country A to country B. There would be a 'spontaneous' increase in this form of financial transfer to be made from A to B. But the raising of tax revenue in A to acquire the funds to pay to B, and the tax remissions which might occur in B as the reparations were received into B's budget, would cause a simultaneous increase in A's, and decrease in B's, domestic expenditure by the taxpayers. There would thus be 'spontaneous' changes in both countries' domestic expenditures concurrently with the 'spontaneous' change in financial transfer between them.

III Three Basic Forms of Domestic Economy

We have defined what we mean by the 'primary' or 'spontaneous' changes in a country's domestic expenditure, imports or lending (or similar financial transfers) which will form the starting-points of the developments which we wish to examine. These 'primary' changes will be followed by certain 'secondary' changes in domestic expenditure, imports or lending in the two countries.

We must now examine these secondary changes. They fall into two classes which we shall call, respectively, 'induced' changes and 'policy' changes in domestic expenditure, imports and lending. The 'induced' changes do not at this stage require much explanation. The general repercussions following any given 'spontaneous' change may cause a country's national income to rise or to fall. But a change in the national income is likely itself to 'induce' a change in domestic expenditure and thereby to 'induce' a change in imports. For example, when income rises persons and institutions are likely to increase their demand for goods and services and, among such goods, for imported goods and services. Such increases (or decreases) in domestic expenditure and in imports as occur simply because the national income has risen (or fallen) we will call 'induced' increases (or decreases) in domestic expenditure and imports.

There may similarly be induced changes in foreign lending. An increase in country A's income will mean an increase in her savings. There may be some increased lending abroad by A simply because A has a larger volume of savings from which to lend at home or abroad. On the other hand, the increase in country A's national income may increase the prospect of profit in A's industries and so reduce the incentive for savers in A to lend to B and increase the incentive for savers in B to lend to A. The net change in A's lending abroad which was due to the sum of these two influences (and which might, therefore, be positive or negative) would represent country A's net 'induced' foreign lending.

But there is another class of secondary changes in domestic expenditure, imports or lending. We shall not assume throughout our analysis that the government or the monetary authorities of each country adopt a purely passive rôle when a 'spontaneous' change occurs. The authorities may themselves cause changes (which we will call 'policy' changes) in domestic expenditure or imports, in order to offset certain of the effects of the 'spontaneous' changes. There are three main types of 'policy' reaction to such 'spontaneous' changes.

First, the authorities in the affected country may take no conscious measures to adapt the level of its own domestic expenditure or imports to the changed conditions. On our strict assumptions that all prices and wage-rates are constant, a 'spontaneous' decline in its own domestic demand for its own products or in the external demand for its exports would cause a decline in its production and employment and a decline in the value of its national product (i.e. in its national income). This would then have 'multiplier' effects leading to further decline in national income and employment. Similarly, a 'spontaneous' increase in the internal or external demand for its products would lead to increases in its employment, national production and national income. A 'spontaneous' decline in the demand for its products would thus lead to increased unemployment in the country in question; and a 'spontaneous' rise in the demand for its products would lead to reduced unemployment in the affected country.[2] We call such an economy a Neutral Economy.

Secondly, the authorities in the affected country may take domestic measures so to control its total domestic expenditure or, within that total, its demand for imports that the total demand for its own produce is kept in a nice balance with its total potential production. In this case, if there is a 'spontaneous' decline in the internal or external demand for its products, the authorities in the affected country will take measures (e.g. by an intensified public works programme or by a reduction in taxation which stimulates personal demand for consumption or by a restriction of imports which diverts demand on to home-produced goods) to bring about such a 'policy' increase in the demand for its products that there is no net decline in the total demand for its products. It has a conscious 'Full Employment' policy aimed at stabilising the total demand for its production and so the total value of its national income. We will call it an Internally Balanced Economy.

Thirdly, the authorities in the affected country may take measures so to control its total domestic demand for goods and services or, within that total, its demand for foreign goods that the excess of its imports over its exports is kept equal to the net lending or similar financial transfers of the

[2] In order that the expansionist effects of a 'spontaneous' increase in the demand for its products may have their full 'multiplier' effects in increasing the national income and expenditure without leading to any rise in prices (i.e. consistently with our underlying assumption of constant prices) we must assume that the economy starts off with a sufficient volume of unemployment to meet the full effects of any 'spontaneous' increase in the demand for its products.

rest of the world to it. In this case if there is a decline in the external demand for its exports or an increased net lending to foreign countries, the authorities in the affected country will take measures (e.g. by a reduced expenditure on public works or by a rise in taxation which reduces the personal demand for consumption goods or by a restriction on imports) to bring about a 'policy' reduction in its imports as great as the fall in its exports or the increased net lending abroad. Such a country maintains a constant equilibrium in its balance of payments regardless of the consequential changes in the level of its own national income. We will call it an Externally Balanced Economy.

In the case of Neutral Economies and Internally Balanced Economies a primary disturbance may well leave the country with a balance-of-payments disequilibrium. For example, a primary increase in domestic expenditure in country A may so stimulate its demand for imports that it has an excess of imports which cannot be financed by any increase in the normal lending to it by country B. The disturbance will have led to a net unfavourable movement in country A's balance of payments with country B, counting in that balance both its net excess of exports to B and its net excess of normal borrowing (or other transfer receipts) from B. The change in a country's balance of payments in this sense is one of the things which we desire to examine. Such a balance can be financed in either of two ways: by the use of monetary reserves or other special funds by the monetary authorities, or else by means of exchange controls over capital movements which prevent the outflow of 'normal' capital funds from being as large as they otherwise would. The size of the increase in a country's total adverse balance of payments will thus measure the extent to which that country must rely either on the use of monetary reserves or on the control of capital movements to finance its payments with the rest of the world.

IV The Purpose of the Succeeding Analysis

We have now the following four forms of 'spontaneous' change, which may occur alone or in various combinations:–

(i) a 'spontaneous' change in A's domestic expenditure;
(ii) a 'spontaneous' change in B's domestic expenditure;
(iii) a 'spontaneous' shift of demand in either or both countries from A's goods to B's goods and vice versa; and
(iv) a 'spontaneous' change in the net amount of normal lending or other transfers from A to B.

We wish to examine the ultimate effect of these changes on the following eight variables:–

(i) A's national income;
(ii) B's national income;
(iii) the 'policy' changes which A must initiate in her domestic expenditure or

(iv) in her imports to maintain Internal or External Balance;
(v) the 'policy' changes which B must initiate in her domestic expenditure or
(vi) in her imports to maintain her economy in Internal or External Balance;
(vii) the balance of trade between A and B; and
(viii) the balance of payments (i.e. balance of trade less net lending or other similar transfers) between A and B.

This analysis we must carry out on the following nine 'policy' assumptions:–

(i) both A and B may have Neutral Economies;
(ii) A may have a Neutural and B an Internally Balanced Economy;
(iii) A may have a Neutral and B an Externally Balanced Economy;
(iv) A may have an Internally Balanced and B a Neutral Economy;
(v) both A and B may have Internally Balanced Economies;
(vi) A may have an Internally Balanced and B an Externally Balanced Economy;
(vii) A may have an Externally Balanced and B a Neutral Economy;
(viii) A may have an Externally Balanced and B an Internally Balanced Economy; and
(ix) both A and B may have Externally Balanced Economies.

V *The Underlying Equations*

The following set of equations represents the fundamental relationships for our two countries A and B:–

$$Y_a = D_a + T \quad (1a)$$
$$Y_b = D_b - T \quad (1b)$$
$$D_a = D_{as} + D_{ap} + D_{ai} \quad (2a)$$
$$D_b = D_{bs} + D_{bp} + D_{bi} \quad (2b)$$
$$T = -I_a + I_b \quad (3)$$
$$I_a = I_{as} + I_{ap} + I_{ai} \quad (4a)$$
$$I_b = I_{bs} + I_{bp} + I_{bi} \quad (4b)$$
$$L = L_s + L_{ai} - L_{bi} \quad (5)$$
$$P = T - L \quad (6)$$
$$D_{ai} = (1 - \lambda_a) Y_a \quad (7a)$$
$$D_{bi} = (1 - \lambda_b) Y_b \quad (7b)$$
$$I_{ai} = \pi_a(1 - \lambda_a) Y_a \quad (8a)$$
$$I_{bi} = \pi_b(1 - \lambda_b) Y_b \quad (8b)$$
$$L_{ai} = \gamma_a Y_a \quad (9a)$$
$$L_{bi} = \gamma_b Y_b \quad (9b)$$
$$\pi_{as} = \frac{I_{as}}{D_{as}} \quad (10a)$$
$$\pi_{bs} = \frac{I_{bs}}{D_{bs}} \quad (10b)$$
$$\pi_{ap} = \frac{I_{ap}}{D_{ap}} \quad (11a)$$
$$\pi_{bp} = \frac{I_{bp}}{D_{bp}} \quad (11b)$$

In these equations the subscript *a* refers the quantity concerned to country A and the subscript *b* to country B. The subscripts *s*, *p* and *i* respectively refer to a 'spontaneous', 'policy' or 'induced' change in the quantity. Each of the quantities Y, D, I, L, T and P refers to a small increment in a basic quantity, thus Y denotes a small increment in national income, D a small increment in domestic expenditure, I a small increase in imports, L a small increase in lending by A to B, T a small increment in the balance of trade and P a small increment in the total balance of payments of country A with country B. Thus D_{as} denotes a 'spontaneous' increase in country A's domestic expenditure.

Equations (1*a*) and (1*b*) express the basic relationship between the national income and national expenditure of any country. An increase in country A's national income (Y_a) can be generated only by an increase in the demand for its products. This increase in the demand for its products is analysed in the two terms D_a and T. D_a represents the total ('spontaneous', 'policy' and 'induced') increase in country A's domestic expenditure (i.e. in the country's demand for goods and services, whether home-produced or imported, which are needed for personal and public consumption and for private and public investment). From this we must deduct imports, since the increment of domestic expenditure (D_a) includes the increased demand for imports which does not generate increased income at home. To it we must add the value of exports, since the foreign demand for the country's goods and services helps to generate its national income, and this foreign demand has not been included in the increment of domestic expenditure (D_a). But T is the total increment in the country's balance of trade, i.e. the increment in its visible and invisible exports minus the increment in its invisible and invisible imports. It follows that $D_a + T$ represents the total increment in the demand for the country's produce, and thus is equal to Y_a, the increment in its national income.[3]

Similarly, $Y_b = D_b - T$, since T, which represents the increment of country A's exports minus the increment of country A's imports, equals the increment of country B's imports minus the increment of country B's exports.

Equations (2*a*) and (2*b*) merely express the fact that the total increment of domestic expenditure in each country (e.g. D_a in country A) is equal to the sum of the 'spontaneous' (D_{as}), the 'policy' (D_{ap}) and the 'induced' (D_{ai}) increment of domestic expenditure.

Equation (3) expresses the fact that the increment of country A's

[3] A simplification has been made to the relationship $Y = D + T$ through the elimination of a term for indirect taxes and subsidies. Y is the national income at factor cost, since in what follows this is the term which is assumed to be stabilised in order to provide full employment. Any net indirect taxes less subsidies must, therefore, have been deducted from the right-hand side of the equation. In so far as indirect taxes are levied on (or subsidies paid in respect of) goods and services, whether home-produced or imported, which are included in domestic expenditure (D), there is no difficulty. Domestic expenditure is reckoned at factor cost (i.e. after the deduction of indirect taxes and addition of subsidies) and is so treated in what follows. But in so far as indirect taxes or subsidies relate to exports there is a difficulty. In order that T should measure the balance of current payments, exports must be reckoned at market prices, i.e. at what the foreigner pays for our goods. This, however, differs from the contribution of exports to the generation of the national income (Y) by the indirect taxes or subsidies which relate to exports. For the present purpose we merely assume no indirect taxes or subsidies on exports.

balance of the visible and invisible trade (T) is equal to the increase in country A's exports (i.e. I_b, the increase in country B's imports) less the increase in country A's imports (I_a).

Equations (4*a*) and (4*b*) show that each country's increment of imports (i.e. I_a in the case of country A) is made up of the sum of the 'spontaneous' (I_{as}), the 'policy' (I_{ap}) and the 'induced' (I_{ai}) increases of imports.

Equation (5) shows that the total increase in the normal lending or other financial transfers from A to B is made up of the net 'spontaneous' increase in financial transfers from A to B (L_s), plus any net increase in 'induced' transfers from A to B (L_{ai}) induced by a rise in A's national income, minus any net increase in 'induced' 'transfers' from B to A (L_{bi}), induced by a rise in B's national income.

Equation (6) shows that the net favourable movement in country A's overall balance of payments (P) is the improvement in her balance of trade (T) less any net increase in her 'normal' lending or other financial transfers to B (L).

Equations (7), (8) and (9) express certain structural relationships and we must spend rather more time over them.

Equations (7*a*) and (7*b*) express the 'induced' increase in a country's domestic expenditure (e.g. D_{ai}) as dependent upon the increment in that country's national income (Y_a) and the propensity (λ_a) of that increment of income to leak away and not to cause any increment of domestic expenditure. A rise in the national income (Y_a) will itself induce some increase in domestic expenditure (D_{ai}), but not, probably, an exactly equivalent increase. Some part (λ_a) of the increased national income will leak away in the form of tax payments, increased savings and the like and only the remainder ($1 - \lambda_a$) will cause an increase in the demand for goods and services.

The increased demand for goods and services $(1 - \lambda_a) Y_a$ may take any of three forms: an increase in the demand for goods and services for personal consumption due to the fact that consumers have larger incomes to spend; an increased demand for goods and services by the public authorities, caused by the improved budgetary position which the increase in the national income will bring with it; and finally, an increase in the demand for capital goods for purposes of home investment due to the fact that the expectation of profit on home production has been improved by that increased demand for home-produced goods and services which itself generated the increase in the national income. Let us write

$$1 - \lambda = c_1 + c_2 + c_3$$

where c_1 = the proportion of any increase in the national income which causes an increase in the demand for goods and services for personal consumption, c_2 = the ratio which any increase in state expenditure on goods and services bears to the increase in the national income which has induced that increase, and c_3 = the ratio which any increase in expenditure on capital development that may be induced by a given increase in the national income bears to that increase in the national income.

As far as c_1 is concerned, an increase in the national income causes some increase in the demand for goods and services for personal consumption, but probably not an equal increase (i.e. $0<c_1<1$) for the following reasons:–

(i) Some part of the increased income associated with greater employment will merely replace the unemployment benefit of previously unemployed labour, and this will not lead to any increased incomes at the disposal of consumers. Public expenditure out of the Unemployment Insurance Fund will be reduced by this amount, and the surplus or saving of the Fund will be correspondingly increased.

(ii) A part of the net increase in income may be taken by the government in increased direct taxes and added to a budget surplus, and this again does not lead to any increase in the tax-free incomes at the disposal of consumers.

(iii) Some part of the increased income remaining after direct taxes are paid may be saved, either in the form of being added to reserves of undistributed profits by companies which are earning a larger income or in the form of savings of one kind or another by private individuals.

(iv) Of the remainder which is spent on goods and services some part may represent indirect taxes levied on those goods and services, and this increased revenue of the government may also be added to a budget surplus. On the other hand, if any part of personal consumption is subsidised, the demand for goods and services at factor cost will go up by more than the increased expenditure out of the incomes of the private consumers, and allowance must be made for this in calculating the final effect upon the demand at factor cost for additional goods and services for personal consumption.

For these reasons, the consumption element c_1 in the expression given for $1-\lambda$ above may be written as

$$(1-u)(1-d)(1-s)(1-i)$$

where $u=$ the proportion of any increase in income which merely replaces unemployment benefit, $d=$ the proportion of any net increase in income which is paid in direct taxes, $s=$ the proportion of any increase in income after payments of direct taxes which is saved, and $i=$ the proportion of any increased expenditure on personal consumption which is taken in net indirect taxes, i.e. in indirect taxes less subsidies.

As far as c_2, the state expenditure element in $1-\lambda$, is concerned, the improvement in the state budget as a result of the increased revenue from direct and net indirect taxes and of the reduced expenditure on unemployment benefit which follows a unit increase in the national income is

$$u + (1-u)(d + [1-d][1-s]i)$$

and we may then write

$$c_2 = e\{u + (1-u)(d - [1-d][1-s]i)\}$$

where e represents the proportion of any increase in its budget surplus which the state uses to increase its expenditure on goods and services.

The new investment element c_3 in $1-\lambda$ presents certain difficulties. The extent to which home investment will be stimulated depends upon internal monetary policy. If, for example, the policy of the monetary authority is to keep the rate of interest constant (the only policy which is strictly compatible with our rigid 'multiplier' assumption that all prices remain unchanged) the increase in domestic investment will be greater than if the amount of money is kept constant and the rate of interest allowed to rise as the internal demand for money to finance the increased business turnover itself increases. Moreover, the extent to which home investment is stimulated will also depend upon the period which we are considering. The increased domestic activity may require some period during which new capital is installed to meet some of the increased demand; but when this period is over, home investment will fall back again. These factors must be borne in mind in considering c_3.

In what follows we shall assume that $0<1-\lambda<1$. The sum of $c_1 + c_2$ is almost certainly <1 and $1-\lambda$ is, therefore, likely to be <1 unless c_3 is appreciable. If, however, $1-\lambda$ were >1, then the equilibrium of a closed economy would be unstable since, for example, any chance primary increase in domestic expenditure in A would set up so large a series of repercussions on its national income and so again on its domestic expenditure as to cause the national income to rise indefinitely. In an open economy $1-\lambda_a$ might be somewhat greater than 1 without causing instability in A because at each round of expansion part of the increased domestic expenditure in A would represent an increased demand for B's products, not all of which would come back onto A's goods unless B adopted a policy of External Balance. We shall disregard the possibility of instability in what follows.

Equations (8*a*) and (8*b*) show how each country's 'induced' imports are determined. We assume that there is a given 'marginal propensity to import' in each country (π_a and π_b) which expresses what fraction of any induced increase in domestic expenditure (i.e. $[1-\lambda_a]Y_a$ and $[1-\lambda_b]Y_b$) will be spent on the purchase of imported as opposed to home-produced supplies.[4]

[4] The normal import content of the various elements making up the total 'induced' increase in domestic expenditure may differ considerably. For example, the normal import content of an induced increase in personal consumption might be markedly greater (or less) than the normal import content of an induced increase in public or private investment. We can write π_a and π_b in terms of weighted averages of the normal import

Equations (9*a*) and (9*b*) show how each country's induced net foreign lending is determined. If there is a rise in income in any country (e.g. Y_a) this may have a twofold effect upon that country's net foreign lending. On the one hand, it may increase it because when the national income rises people will save more, and when they save more they may naturally lend some part of their increased savings abroad. On the other hand, the increase in the national income must be caused by an increased demand (whether internal or external) for that country's products and that must mean that the country's production has become more profitable. For this reason those with funds to invest may decide to lend a larger amount than they would otherwise have done to this country instead of to other countries. If the first influence outweighs the second, γ_a and γ_b will be positive, but will probably be less than unity; if the second outweighs the first, they will be negative. If the two factors cancel each other out, they will be zero.

Equations (10*a*), (10*b*), (11*a*) and (11*b*) merely define terms (π_{as}, π_{ap}, π_{bs} and π_{bp}) which may on occasion prove useful for expressing the ratio between a 'spontaneous' (or 'policy') increase of imports and the 'spontaneous' (or 'policy') increase of domestic expenditure with which it is associated. In some cases these π's may truly express the normal 'marginal propensity to import' which is associated with a given 'spontaneous' or 'policy' increment of domestic expenditure. Consider π_{ap}, for example. There is a 'policy' increment of domestic expenditure D_{ap}, undertaken to preserve the Internal or External Balance of the economy of country A; if there is no attempt to control imports or to select for the 'policy' increase an element of domestic expenditure which has a peculiarly high or low import content, then there will be directly associated with this increment of domestic expenditure (D_{ap}) an increment of imports (I_{ap}) which bears a normal relationship to it. In other words, in this case π_{ap} will equal π_a.[5] But the 'policy' decision may not be of this character. There might, for example, be a decision to increase domestic expenditure, but in a peculiarly 'protective' manner which meant that the increment of domestic expenditure was directed solely on to home-produced goods. In this case $\pi_{ap} = 0$. Or the policy decision might be simply to allow more imports into the country (e.g. by relaxing an import restriction) without doing anything to increase domestic expenditure as a whole. In this case $1/\pi_{ap} = 0$. And similarly with a 'spontaneous' change in domestic expenditure on imports. The change

contents of the three elements (c_1, c_2 and c_3) which we have already distinguished in the proportion $(1 - \lambda)$ of any increment in the national income which represents an induced increase in domestic expenditure. Let π_1, π_2 and π_3 represent the normal import contents of an increment of personal consumption, government consumption and public or private investment respectively. Then

$$\pi = \frac{c_1\pi_1 + c_2\pi_2 + c_3\pi_3}{c_1 + c_2 + c_3}.$$

[5] Or, more accurately, will equal that element in the weighted average comprising π_a which corresponds most nearly to the type of 'policy' increase in domestic expenditure with which we are concerned. (See footnote 4.)

may be solely in domestic expenditure with a normal import content, in which case $\pi_{as} = \pi_a$. Or there may be a simple shift from home-produced to imported goods within a given level of domestic expenditure, in which case $1/\pi_{as} = 0$. And so on. There are an infinite variety of 'spontaneous' disturbances or of 'policy' decisions which may lead to changes in imports and in domestic expenditure in many varied combinations. In some cases π_{as}, π_{bs}, π_{ap} and π_{bp} will represent the normal propensities to consume associated with D_{as}, D_{bs}, D_{ap}, and D_{bp}. In other cases they will merely express the particular relationship between increments of imports and increments of domestic expenditure which rules in a more complicated situation. The context of each problem as it arises must determine their nature.

In discussing equations (8), (10) and (11) we have considered the factors determining a country's demand for imports as if all imports were for domestic consumption. But this is not the case. Imports may be needed not only to consume directly at home or to work up into products for such domestic consumption, but also for the purpose of making goods to be sold for export. For this reason the gross demand for imports must be related not only to the total of domestic expenditure but also to the export element in the country's balance of current payments.

It is very simple to make allowance for this fact in the preceding equations. The balance of current payments is itself a net figure and represents only the net excess of exports over imports, in the sense that it includes on the export side all the direct or indirect re-exports of the imports enumerated on the import side so that only the imports less these re-exports count as a net subtraction to the favourable balance of current payments. Any increment of imports (whether 'spontaneous', 'policy' or 'induced') must be treated in the same net way. If, for example, the domestic expenditure of country A shifts from home-produced to imported goods, then this represents a net shift of demand to country B's goods only in so far as the additional goods which country A imports from country B do not contain raw materials which country B must import from country A.[6] In so far as they do contain such raw materials the shift of country A's demand does not represent a shift away from her own home-produced products.

Let p_a = the proportion of country A's exports which represents a raw material or other content purchased from country B, and p_b = the proportion of country B's exports which represents a raw material or other content purchased from country A. Then if there is a gross increment of imports by A equal to $\bar{I}_a$ only $(1-p_b)\bar{I}_a$ represents a net increment in the demand for country B's goods, while $p_b\bar{I}_a$ represents an

[6] The raw material content of exports is not the only possible example of this factor. Another case would be where one country (e.g. the United Kingdom) imported for her own use additional quantities of some product (e.g. rubber) in the production of which she had significant overseas investments so that part of the increased expenditure on the rubber came back to her as an invisible export in the form of increased profits on overseas investments. An increased interest on its overseas investments due to the increased purchase by country A of imports of some product is the same, for our purposes, as the export by country A of a material for inclusion in a finished product which is to be exported by country B to country A.

increment in the demand for A's goods. In the equations on page 101 above the terms for imports must all be interpreted in this 'net' sense. In other words, $I_{as}=(1-p_b)\bar{I}_{as}$, $I_{ap}=(1-p_b)\bar{I}_{ap}$ and $I_{ai}=(1-p_b)\bar{I}_{ai}$, where $\bar{I}_{as}$, $\bar{I}_{ap}$, and $\bar{I}_{ai}$ represent gross increments of imports of a 'spontaneous', 'policy' or 'induced' character. And similarly, $I_{bs}=(1-p_a)\bar{I}_{bs}$, $I_{bp}=(1-p_a)\bar{I}_{bp}$ and $I_{bi}=(1-p_a)\bar{I}_{bi}$.

The π's in the equations on page 101 must be similarly interpreted in a net manner. If $\bar{\pi}_a=$ the gross propensity to import associated with any given 'induced' increment of domestic expenditure, then π_a as used in those equations $=(1-p_b)\bar{\pi}_a$. Similarly, $\pi_{as}=(1-p_b)\bar{\pi}_{as}=(1-p_b)\bar{I}_{ab}/D_{as}$, and so on. All the π's used in this article are in this sense 'net'.

In what follows we shall assume that π_a and π_b[7] are positive fractions lying between 0 and 1. This is undoubtedly the normal case. It is, however, conceivable that if a country imported 'superior goods' it might, when its real domestic expenditure went up, spend on imports more than the whole of the increment of its domestic expenditure as it shifted away from the 'inferior goods' which it produced at home. In this case π would be >1. Alternatively, if a country imported 'inferior goods' it might actually import less when its total domestic expenditure increased; and in this case π would be <0. The reader is left to apply for himself, if he so wishes, these abnormal conditions to the conclusions of this article, which will be based on the normal assumption that $0<\pi<1$.

Equations (1) to (9) can be reduced to the following four equations:

$$\lambda_a Y_a \qquad - D_{ap} \qquad - T = D_{as} \tag{12}$$

$$\lambda_b Y_b \qquad - D_{bp} \qquad + T = D_{bs} \tag{13}$$

$$\pi_a(1-\lambda_a)Y_a - \pi_b(1-\lambda_b)Y_b \qquad + I_{ap} \qquad - I_{bp} + T = -I_{as} + I_{bs} \tag{14}$$

$$-\gamma_a Y_a \quad + \gamma_b Y_b \qquad + T - P = L_s \tag{15}$$

Of the nineteen terms in these four equations, eleven are always known; namely, the five 'spontaneous' disturbances (D_{as}, D_{bs}, I_{as}, I_{bs}, L_s) and the six structural parameters (π_a, π_b, λ_a, λ_b, γ_a and γ_b). This leaves eight unknowns to be determined in terms of our known quantities; namely, the two increments of national income (Y_a and Y_b), the four 'policy' changes which must be made to offset the spontaneous disturbance (D_{ap}, D_{bp}, I_{ap}, I_{bp}) and two terms showing the final effect on the balance of payments (T and P). We have so far four equations and eight unknowns.

The missing four relationships are given by the various possible policy assumptions, as indicated in the table on the opposite page.

It may be useful very briefly to go through the various policy choices shown in the above table for a country (e.g. country A). If it has a Neutral Economy it will take no positive steps to offset any initial disturbance either by inflating or deflating domestic expenditure or by restricting or encouraging imports. D_{ap} and I_{ap} will all be zero.

[7] And for that matter also the elements (π_1, π_2 and π_3) from which the weighted averages π_a and π_b are obtained. (See footnote 4.)

New Relationships Introduced by Various Policy Assumptions

Policy Assumed	*Country*	
	A	*B*
Neutral	$D_{ap}=0$ $I_{ap}=0$	$D_{bp}=0$ $I_{bp}=0$
Internal Balance	$Y_a=0$ $I_{ap}=\pi_{ap}D_{ap}$	$Y_b=0$ $I_{bp}=\pi_{bp}D_{bp}$
External Balance	$P=0$ $I_{ap}=\pi_{ap}D_{ap}$	$P=0$ $I_{bp}=\pi_{bp}D_{bp}$

If A has an Internally Balanced Economy it will take steps to ensure that its national income is unchanged and Y_a will be zero. There would still remain the choice whether the authorities should attempt to preserve a constant demand for the country's produce mainly by an internal inflation or deflation of domestic expenditure or mainly by taking measures to shift demand to (or from) home-produced goods away from (or on to) imports. In other words, we need to know one more thing: the relationship between D_{ap} and I_{ap}. This relationship is obtained by assuming as known π_{ap} ($=I_{ap}/D_{ap}$), the ratio of the 'policy' change in imports to the 'policy' change in domestic expenditure. If the authorities act solely by way of the internal deflation or inflation of domestic expenditure which contains a normal import content, then π_{ap} is this given normal import content. If the authorities do not act at all on domestic expenditure but solely on a shift of demand between home-produced and foreign goods, then $1/\pi_{ap}=0$. And so on with more complicated forms of policy. In any case there are two additional relationships ($Y_a=0$ and $I_{ap}=\pi_{ap}D_{ap}$) due to the policy assumption.

If country A has an Externally Balanced Economy, then it will take care to ensure that its total balance of payments is not disturbed, so that $P=0$. To do this it may operate by an internal inflation or deflation of its domestic demand (in which case $I_{ap}/D_{ap}=\pi_{ap}$ measures the given normal propensity to import), or solely by a shift of demand between home-produced and foreign goods (in which case $1/\pi_{ap}=0$), or by more complicated combinations of I_{ap} and D_{ap} (which will be represented by other values of π_{ap}). In any case there are once more two additional relationships introduced by the policy assumptions regarding country A.

The same is also true of country B. Each policy assumption which is made about country B also introduces two additional relationships. The two policy relationships introduced for country A with the two introduced for country B thus provide the four additional relationships to determine the system.

There is, however, one exception to this conclusion. Each of the three policy assumptions for country A can be combined with each of the three policy assumptions for country B. Thus A and B can both have Neutral Economies; or A Neutral and B Internally Balanced; or A Neutral and B

Table I *The General Equations*

Policy Combination 1

Neutral Economy in A $(D_{ap}=0,\ I_{ap}=0)$
Neutral Economy in B $(D_{bp}=0,\ I_{bp}=0)$

$$Y_a = \frac{1}{\lambda_a}\cdot\frac{(1+\mu_b)D_{as}+\mu_b D_{bs}+T_s}{1+\mu_a+\mu_b}$$

$$Y_b = \frac{1}{\lambda_b}\cdot\frac{\mu_a D_{as}+(1+\mu_a)D_{bs}-T_s}{1+\mu_a+\mu_b}$$

$$T = \frac{-\mu_a D_{as}+\mu_b D_{bs}+T_s}{1+\mu_a+\mu_b}$$

$$P = \frac{-\left(\left[1-\frac{\gamma_b}{\lambda_b}\right]\mu_a+\frac{\gamma_a}{\lambda_a}[1+\mu_b]\right)D_{as} + \left(\left[1-\frac{\gamma_a}{\lambda_a}\right]\mu_b+\frac{\gamma_b}{\lambda_b}[1+\mu_a]\right)D_{bs}+\left(1-\frac{\gamma_a}{\lambda_a}-\frac{\gamma_b}{\lambda_b}\right)T_s}{1+\mu_a+\mu_b} - L_s$$

Policy Combination 2

Neutral Economy in A $(D_{ap}=0,\ I_{ap}=0)$
Internally Balanced Economy in B $(Y_b=0,\ I_{bp}=\pi_{bp}D_{bp})$

$$Y_a = \frac{1}{\lambda_a}\cdot\frac{(1+\pi_{bp})D_{as}-\pi_{bp}D_{bs}+T_s}{1+\mu_a-\pi_{bs}}$$

$$T = \frac{-\mu_a D_{as}-\pi_{bp}D_{bs}+T_s}{1+\mu_a-\pi_{bp}}$$

$$P = \frac{-\left((\mu_a+\frac{\gamma_a}{\lambda_a}[1-\pi_{bp}]\right)D_{as}+\left(1-\frac{\gamma_a}{\lambda_a}\right)(-\pi_{bp}D_{bs}+T_s)}{1+\mu_a-\pi_{bp}} - L_s$$

Policy Combination 3

Neutral Economy in A $(D_{ap}=0,\ I_{ap}=0)$
Externally Balanced Economy in B $(P=0,\ I_{bp}=\pi_{bp}D_{bp})$

$$Y_a = \frac{1}{\lambda_a}\cdot\frac{\left(\mu_b+\pi_{bp}+\frac{\gamma_b}{\lambda_b}[1-\pi_{bp}]\right)D_{as}+\frac{\gamma_b}{\lambda_b}(-\pi_{bp}D_{bs}+T_s)+(\mu_b+\pi_{bp})L_s}{\left(1-\frac{\gamma_a}{\lambda_a}\right)(\mu_b+\pi_{bp})+\frac{\gamma_b}{\lambda_b}(1+\mu_a-\pi_{bp})}$$

$$Y_b = \frac{1}{\lambda_b}\cdot\frac{\left(\mu_a+\frac{\gamma_a}{\lambda_a}[1-\pi_{bp}]\right)D_{as}-\left(1-\frac{\gamma_a}{\lambda_a}\right)(-\pi_{bp}D_{bs}+T_s)+(1+\mu_a-\pi_{bp})L_s}{\left(1-\frac{\gamma_a}{\lambda_a}\right)(\mu_b+\pi_{bp})+\frac{\gamma_b}{\lambda_b}(1+\mu_a-\pi_{bp})}$$

Table I (*continued*)

$$T=\frac{\left(\frac{\gamma_a}{\lambda_a}[\mu_b+\pi_{bp}]-\frac{\gamma_b}{\lambda_b}\mu_a\right)D_{as}+\frac{\gamma_b}{\lambda_b}(-\pi_{bp}D_{bs}+T_s)+(\mu_b+\pi_{bp})L_s}{\left(1-\frac{\gamma_a}{\lambda_a}\right)(\mu_b+\pi_{bp})+\frac{\gamma_b}{\lambda_b}(1+\mu_a-\pi_{bp})}$$

Policy Combination 4

Internally Balanced Economy in A $(Y_a=0, I_{ap}=\pi_{ap}D_{ap})$
Internally Balanced Economy in B $(Y_b=0, I_{bp}=\pi_{bp}D_{bp})$

$$T=\frac{\pi_{ap}D_{as}-\pi_{bp}D_{bs}+T_s}{1-\pi_{ap}-\pi_{bp}}$$

$$P=\frac{\pi_{ap}D_{as}-\pi_{bp}D_{bs}+T_s}{1-\pi_{ap}-\pi_{bp}}-L_s$$

Policy Combination 5

Internally Balanced Economy in A $(Y_a=0, I_{ap}=\pi_{ap}D_{ap})$
Externally Balanced Economy in B $(P=0, I_{bp}=\pi_{bp}D_{bp})$

$$Y_b=\frac{1}{\lambda_b}\cdot\frac{-\pi_{ap}D_{as}+\pi_{bp}D_{bs}-T_s+(1-\pi_{ap}-\pi_{bp})L_s}{\mu_b+\pi_{bp}+\frac{\gamma_b}{\lambda_b}(1-\pi_{ap}-\pi_{bp})}$$

$$T=\frac{\frac{\gamma_b}{\lambda_b}(\pi_{ap}D_{as}-\pi_{bp}D_{bs}+T_s)+(\mu_b+\pi_{bp})L_s}{\mu_b+\pi_{bp}+\frac{\gamma_b}{\lambda_b}(1-\pi_{ap}-\pi_{bp})}$$

Policy Combination 6

Externally Balanced Economy in A $(I_{ap}=\pi_{ap}D_{ap})$
Externally Balanced Economy in B $(I_{bp}=\pi_{bp}D_{bp})$ $\Big\}$ $(P=0,\ Y_b=-mY_a)$

$$Y_a=\frac{\pi_{ap}D_{as}-\pi_{bp}D_{bs}+T_s-(1-\pi_{ap}-\pi_{bp})L_s}{\lambda_a(\mu_a+\pi_{ap})+m\lambda_b(\mu_b+\pi_{bp})+(\gamma_a+m\gamma_b)(1-\pi_{ap}-\pi_{bp})}$$

$$T=\frac{(\gamma_a+m\gamma_b)(\pi_{ap}D_{as}-\pi_{bp}D_{bs}+T)+(\lambda_a[\mu_a+\pi_{ap}]+m\lambda_b[\mu_b+\pi_{bp}])L_s}{\lambda_a(\mu_a+\pi_{ap)+m\lambda_b}(\mu_b+\pi_{bp})+(\gamma_s+m\gamma_b)(1-\pi_{ap}-\pi_{bp})}$$

Externally Balanced; and so on. Each of the possible nine policy combinations provides the four additional relationships which we require, with the exception of the policy combination, External Balance in A with External Balance in B. In this case, as can be seen from the table on page 109, only three additional relationships ($P=0, I_{ap}=\pi_{ap}P_{ap}$ and $I_{bp}=\pi_{bp}D_{bp}$) are introduced, because $P=0$ is in this case common to both A's and B's policy assumptions.

The economic meaning of this is clear. Suppose some primary disturbance (e.g. a shift of demand away from A's goods on to B's goods) takes place which causes A to have an adverse balance of payments. Both A and B have Externally Balanced Economies. A therefore deflates and/or restricts imports. B inflates and/or removes obstacles to imports. But how much of the adjustment must fall on A and how much on B? If A deflates or restricts imports a lot, B will have to inflate or expand imports only a little; and vice versa. Clearly some additional information is required to know how much of the adjustment must fall on each country.

In what follows we shall introduce this additional piece of information by assuming as given m ($= - Y_b/Y_a$) which measures the ratio between the inflation (or deflation) of national income in B and the deflation (or inflation) of national income in A. Those who like to do so can think of this in terms of an old-fashioned gold standard. There is a primary improvement in country B's balance of payments and gold flows from A to B. In B gold has an income velocity of circulation of V_b and in A it has an income velocity of circulation of V_a. When an amount of gold, G, has flowed from A to B, $Y_b = V_b G$ and $Y_a = - V_a G$ so that $m = - Y_b/Y_a = V_b/V_a$.

VI The General Solution

The equations in Table I give the values, derived from equations (12), (13), (14) and (15), for the changes in national incomes of countries A and B (Y_a and Y_b) and for the changes in the balance of trade and the balance of payments between them (T and P), in terms of simultaneous spontaneous changes in domestic expenditure (D_{as} and D_{bs}) and imports (I_{as} and I_{bs}) in each country and in the net foreign lending between them (L_s). The value of the policy changes in domestic expenditure (D_{ap} and D_{bp}) which are required in each country on the various policy assumptions made can be obtained from these by writing $D_{ap} = \lambda_a Y_a - D_{as} - T$ and $D_{bp} = \lambda_b Y_b - D_{bs} + T$. From this I_{ap} and I_{bp} can be derived by writing $I_{ap} = \pi_{ap} D_{ap}$ and $I_{bp} = \pi_{bp} D_{bp}$.

In these equations T_s is written for $-I_{as} + I_{bs}$ since these two terms always appear together in that combination. T_s represents the net 'spontaneous' improvement in A's balance of trade, i.e. it measures the net 'spontaneous' shift in demand from B's on to A's goods. For deriving multipliers for special cases T_s may be broken down in the following formulæ into its two components $-I_{as} + I_{bs}$.

Moreover, for purposes of simplification, in the equations in Table I μ_a is written for $\pi_a(1 - \lambda_a)/\lambda_a$ and μ_b for $\pi_b(1 - \lambda_b)/\lambda_b$.

In Table I six of the possible nine policy combinations are examined. We have omitted to give the general solutions in the remaining three cases because these can readily be derived from the six cases which have been given. Thus we give the solutions for the case in which country A has a Neutral Economy and Country B an Internally Balanced Economy, but we do not give the solution for the case where it is A which has the Internally Balanced Economy and B the Neutral Economy. The latter can be derived from the former by writing throughout each equation the subscript a for the subscript b and vice versa and changing the signs of T_s, T, P and L_s.

What do these equations for the general solution show us? We must assume that there is some primary disturbance affecting simultaneously the imports and the domestic expenditure of both countries and the net amount of financial transfers (e.g. for foreign lending) between them. In other words, I_{as}, I_{bs}, D_{as}, D_{bs} and L_s are all given.[8] The equations then show the effect of the complex primary disturbance on the national incomes of the two countries and on their balance of trade and their overall balance of payments on the various policy assumptions.

The equations in Table I are in too general a form for it to be at all easy to use them to point out the main results of this multiplier analysis. It has, however, been thought best to give these general formulæ because some readers may be interested to use these equations for the solution of their own pet problems on their own pet simplifying assumptions.

For this purpose the following points may be useful:–

(i) A great deal of the complication of the multipliers in Table I is due to the complexity of the type of primary disturbance there assumed. We shall in the next section examine the effects of much simpler types of primary change.

(ii) Much of the complication of many of the multipliers given in Table I is removed if it is assumed that $\gamma_a = \gamma_b = 0$, i.e. that changes in the national income in countries A and B do not induce any significant changes in net foreign lending.

(iii) Much complication can be removed from many of the formulæ by assuming that $\pi_{as} = \pi_{ap} = \pi_a$ and $\pi_{bs} = \pi_{bp} = \pi_b$, or, in other words, that the proportion of any 'spontaneous' or 'policy' increment of domestic expenditure has the same import content as an 'induced' increment of domestic expenditure. For some purposes it is, of course, of the nature of the problem to assume that this is not the case. π_{as}, π_{ap}, π_{bs} and π_{bp} may range from 0 (when there is no import content in the 'spontaneous' or 'policy' change of increment of domestic expenditure) to ∞ (when there is merely a 'spontaneous' or 'policy' shift of demand from home-produced to imported goods without any 'spontaneous' or 'policy' increment of domestic expenditure). But where the nature of the problem allows it to be reasonably assumed that the π's for any one country are all equal, great simplification is often possible.[9]

[8] For example, suppose that there were an increase in investment opportunities in country A leading to a spontaneous increase in its domestic expenditure for home investment (D_{as}). With this is associated a certain increased demand for imports (I_{as}). But the increased investment opportunities encourage people to lend more to A rather than B so that there is a fall in net foreign lending from A to B (L_s). People in B save somewhat more to make the best of this new opportunity for investment and there is a fall in B's domestic expenditure (D_{bs}) with which is associated some fall in B's imports (I_{bs}). Suppose that a proportion π of D_{as} is spent on imports; that a proportion l of D_{as} is financed by a net increase in B's lending to A; that a proportion s of this increased net lending to A comes from reduced domestic expenditure in B; and that a proportion π_{bs} of this reduced domestic expenditure in B represents a reduced demand for imports. Then $I_{as} = \pi_{as} D_{as}$; $L_s = -lD_{as}$; $D_{bs} = -slD_{as}$; and $I_{bs} = -\pi_{bs} slD_{as}$. By substituting these values for I_{as}, I_{bs}, D_{bs} and L_s in the equations of Table I the effect of the primary change D_{as} on the various unknowns could be obtained.

[9] In this connection it should be observed that since $\mu_a = \pi_a[(1-\lambda_a)/\lambda_a]$, $\mu_a + \pi_a$ (which frequently occurs in the formulæ) $= \pi_a/\lambda_a$. And similarly with $\mu_b + \pi_b$. Also, for example, since $T_s = -I_{as} + I_{bs}$, $T_s + \pi_{ap} D_{as} - \pi_{bp} D_{bs} = 0$, if $\pi_{ap} = \pi_{as}$ and $\pi_{bp} = \pi_{bs}$. (Cf. equations in Table I Policy Combinations 5 and 6.)

In the following section of this article these general formulæ will be applied with appropriate simplifying assumptions to give the answers to certain specific 'multiplier' problems.

VII The Analysis Applied to Certain Illustrative Problems

We are now in a position to apply the general analysis of the preceding sections to certain specific and simplified 'multiplier' problems. We will consider four examples: (i) a 'pure' disturbance due solely to a 'spontaneous' change in domestic expenditure in one of the two countries (e.g. country A); (ii) a 'pure' disturbance due solely to a 'spontaneous' shift in either country, within any given level of domestic expenditure, from B's goods on to A's goods; (iii) a 'pure' disturbance due solely to a 'spontaneous' change in net foreign lending from A to B; and (iv) a 'combined' disturbance due to the payment of reparations from A to B which represents a 'spontaneous' increase in net foreign transfers (cf. case (iii) above) and simultaneously causes 'spontaneous' changes in the level of domestic expenditure in both countries (cf. case (i) above).

In the tables which illustrate these four cases we shall give values only for Y_a, Y_b and P. That is to say, we shall confine ourselves to the effects of the change on the three basic quantities: the national incomes in the two countries and the total balance of payments between them. It is from the behaviour of these quantities that we can answer the two basic questions: will the change affect the level of employment and economic activity in the two countries, and will the change cause a balance-of-payments problem between them? The tables will omit giving the values of D_{ap}, D_{bp}, I_{ap} and I_{bp}. In other words, we shall not give the values of the 'policy' changes which will be required in either of the countries to preserve Internal or External Balance, although these can, of course, readily be derived from the equations in Table I. These quantities are, however, not so fundamental. We can regard them as being reached by a process of trial and error: some internal or external change in demand takes place in country A which requires some 'policy' inflation or deflation of domestic expenditure in order to maintain Internal or External Balance; and the authorities accordingly inflate or deflate domestic expenditure by a process of trial and error to the extent necessary to preserve whichever balance they intend to achieve.[10]

Case (i): a 'spontaneous' change in country A's domestic expenditure. There is some 'spontaneous' increase or decrease in domestic expenditure in country A. This might be due to a boom or slump in private

[10] Throughout what follows a main theme will be the dilemma of choice between the action which is aimed at achieving Internal, and that which is aimed at achieving External Balance. When, for example, the foreign demand for A's goods falls, should the authorities in A inflate their domestic expenditure in order to preserve A's national income and employment or should they deflate in order to preserve A's balance of international payments? The sharpness of this dilemma is, of course, due to the rigid multiplier assumptions which we are making. If relative prices can be changed, either by changes in exchange rates or by internal inflations and deflations of cost and price levels, the dilemma in large measure disappears.

investment or to some governmental measure of reflation or disinflation through a change in public expenditure or a change in the amount of taxes levied. We wish to examine the effect of the 'spontaneous' change in country A's domestic expenditure (D_{as}) on her national income (Y_a), on country B's national income (Y_b), and on the total balance of payments between the two countries (P) on the various policy assumptions which we are making.

In this case it is possible to derive from the equations given in Table I the values given in Table II for Y_a, Y_b and P, all of which are there expressed in the form of the 'multipliers' which must be applied to the 'spontaneous' change in country A's domestic expenditure (D_{as}). Let us first confine ourselves to the case of a Neutral Economy in country A (i.e. rows (1), (2) and (3) of the Table) and consider each of the multipliers in turn.

In a closed economy the 'multiplier' Y_a/D_{as} would have the value $1/\lambda_a$. If country B is an Externally Balanced Economy and if changes in country A's and country B's national income do not induce any changes in foreign lending, this for country A is tantamount to being a closed economy. For no part of any increase in country A's expenditure on imports 'leaks' permanently abroad, since country B takes deliberate steps to ensure that its own expenditure on country A's exports expands just to the extent necessary to keep her in balance-of-payments equilibrium. And since there is assumed to be no induced change in foreign lending, country B will keep her balance of payments in equilibrium only by expanding her demand for A's goods to exactly the same extent as A's imports from her have increased. We find, therefore, that when country B has an Externally Balanced Economy and $\gamma_a = \gamma_b = 0$, the multiplier Y_a/D_{as} has the closed-economy value of $1/\lambda_a$ (see row (3) of Table II).

But this closed-economy multiplier is modified by the factor $(1 - \pi_{as} + \mu_b)/(1 + \mu_a + \mu_b)$ if there is a Neutral Economy in the rest of the world and by the factor $(1 - \pi_{as} + \pi_{bp})/(1 + \mu_a - \pi_{bp})$ if there is an Internally Balanced Economy in the rest of the world. (See rows (1) and (2) of Table II.) As the general case, let us suppose that the import content of the 'spontaneous' and 'policy' increases in domestic expenditure are of the 'normal' size in both countries (i.e. $\pi_{as} = \pi_a$, $\pi_{bp} = \pi_b$). Suppose, for the sake of numerical illustration, that $\lambda_a = \lambda_b = 0.5$, $\pi_{as} = \pi_a = 0.25$ and $\pi_{bp} = \pi_b = 0.1$. Then the closed-economy multiplier $= 2$, and this is the same as the multiplier with an Externally Balanced economy in the rest of the world, if $\gamma_a = \gamma_b = 0$. The modifying factor with a Neutral Economy in the rest of the world is 0.63 and with an Internally Balanced Economy in the rest of the world is 0.57, so that in the former case the multiplier $Y_a/D_{as} = 2 \times 0.63 = 1.26$ and in the latter case $= 2 \times 0.57 = 1.14$.

This shows how in the two latter cases the 'closed-economy' multiplier $1/\lambda_a$ is damped down by the foreign leakage through the increased imports which the growth of domestic expenditure in country A involves. Not all of the increased demand in country A is an increased demand for home-produced goods; and this import 'leakage' reduces the extent to which an increase in domestic expenditure stimulates national income and domestic expenditure still further. But with a Neutral Economy in

Table II *A 'Spontaneous' Change in Domestic Expenditure in Country A*

(D_{as} given. $I_{as} = \pi_{as} D_{as}$. $I_{bs} = D_{bs} = L_s = 0$)

Policy assumed in A	B		$\frac{Y_a}{D_{as}}$	$\frac{Y_b}{D_{as}}$	$\frac{P}{D_{as}}$
N	N	(1)	$\frac{1}{\lambda_a} \cdot \frac{1-\pi_{as}+\mu_b}{1+\mu_a+\mu_b}$	$\frac{1}{\lambda_b} \cdot \frac{\mu_a+\pi_{as}}{1+\mu_a+\mu_b}$	$-\frac{\left(1-\frac{\gamma_b}{\lambda_b}\right)(\mu_a+\pi_{as})+\frac{\gamma_a}{\lambda_a}(1-\pi_{as}+\mu_b)}{1+\mu_a+\mu_b}$
N	IB	(2)	$\frac{1}{\lambda_a} \cdot \frac{1-\pi_{as}-\pi_{bp}}{1+\mu_a-\pi_{bp}}$	$\boxed{0}$	$-\frac{\mu_a+\pi_{as}+\frac{\gamma_a}{\lambda_a}(1-\pi_{as}-\pi_{bp})}{1+\mu_a-\pi_{bp}}$
N	EB	(3)	$\frac{1}{\lambda_a} \cdot \frac{\mu_b+\pi_{bp}+\frac{\gamma_b}{\lambda_b}(1-\pi_{as}-\pi_{bp})}{\left(1-\frac{\gamma_a}{\lambda_a}\right)(\mu_b+\pi_{bp})+\frac{\gamma_b}{\lambda_b}(1+\mu_a-\pi_{bp})}$	$\frac{1}{\lambda_b} \cdot \frac{\mu_a+\pi_{as}+\frac{\gamma_a}{\lambda_a}(1-\pi_{as}-\pi_{bp})}{\left(1-\frac{\gamma_a}{\lambda_a}\right)(\mu_b+\pi_{bp})+\frac{\gamma_b}{\lambda_b}(1+\mu_a-\pi_{bp})}$	$\boxed{0}$
IB	IB	(4)	$\boxed{0}$	$\boxed{0}$	$\frac{\pi_{ap}-\pi_{as}}{1-\pi_{ap}-\pi_{as}}$
IB	EB	(5)	$\boxed{0}$	$\frac{1}{\lambda_b} \cdot \frac{\pi_{as}-\pi_{ap}}{\mu_b+\pi_{bp}+\frac{\gamma_b}{\lambda_b}(1-\pi_{ap}-\pi_{bp})}$	$\boxed{0}$
EB	EB	(6)	$\frac{\pi_{ap}-\pi_{bp}}{\lambda_a(\mu_a+\pi_{ap})+m\lambda_b(\mu_b+\pi_{bp})+(\gamma_a+m\gamma_b)(1-\pi_{ap}-\pi_{bp})}$	$-m\frac{Y_a}{D_{as}}$	$\boxed{0}$

Notes. (i) N, IB and EB signify Neutral, Internally Balanced and Externally Balanced Economies respectively.
(ii) The values given in a square □ merely state the policy assumed.

the rest of the world this damping-down factor in country A will itself be reduced. The increased demand in country A for the products of country B will stimulate the national income of country B which will stimulate country B's demand for goods and services which will stimulate country B's demand for imports from country A. Part of the foreign leakage of demand in country A will come back indirectly as a demand for country A's exports.

But this will not occur if there is an Internally Balanced Economy in country B. Indeed, the reverse will happen. When country A spends more on country B's goods as a result of the inflation of country A's domestic expenditure, country B, having a conscious policy of maintaining a stable national income, offsets the increased foreign demand for her goods by a policy of deflating her domestic expenditure. If the domestic expenditure which she deflates contains some imported goods ($\pi_{bp}>0$), then her deflation of domestic expenditure will cause a *reduction* in her imports from country A. The foreign leakage for country A, far from being itself diminished, will be intensified by the repercussions in country B. It is for this reason that the multiplier Y_a/D_{as} in row (2) of Table II is smaller than the corresponding multiplier in row (1).

Indeed, it can be seen from Table II that if there is an Internally Balanced Economy in country B and if $\pi_{as} + \pi_{bp} = 1$ the multiplier Y_a/D_{as} will be zero. There is a primary increase of domestic demand in country A equal to D_{as}. Of this $\pi_{as} D_{as}$ causes a rise in demand for imports from country B. Country B experiences an increase in the foreign demand for her goods equal to $\pi_{as} D_{as}$ and she reduces her domestic expenditure by an amount D_{bp} sufficient to cause just that decrease in her own demand for her own goods ($[1 - \pi_{bp}] D_{bp}$) to offset the increased foreign demand for her own goods, $\pi_{as} D_{as}$, so that $(1 - \pi_{bp})\ D_{bp} = \pi_{as} D_{as}$ or $D_{bp} = \pi_{as} D_{as}/(1 - \pi_{bp})$. But the reduced domestic expenditure in country B (D_{bp}) causes a reduction in the demand in country B for country A's goods equal to $\pi_{bp} D_{bp}$ or $\pi_{bp} \pi_{as} D_{as}/(1 - \pi_{bp})$. If $\pi_{as} + \pi_{bp} = 1$, $\pi_{bp} \pi_{as} D_{as}/(1 - \pi_{bp}) = (1 - \pi_{as}) D_{as}$, which is exactly equal to the primary increase in the demand for country A's goods caused by the primary increase in country A's domestic expenditure (D_{as}) which started the whole set of repercussions. In other words, the increased demand for country A's own goods caused by country A's 'spontaneous' inflation of her domestic expenditure is exactly offset by the reduction in country B's demand for country A's goods which is caused by country B's policy of deflating her domestic expenditure to the extent required to offset the increased demand for her goods by country A. There is no net change in the demand for country A's products and thus no net change in country A's national income.

Let us turn now to the multiplier P/D_{as}. If country B has an Externally Balanced Economy this will, of course, be zero, as is shown in row (3) of Table II. In the two other cases it will be seen that the inflation of demand in country A due to the 'spontaneous' increase in her domestic expenditure will directly (and indirectly through the induced effects upon domestic expenditure in country A) raise her demand for imports. The balance of payments will move against her, both because the balance of trade will thus move against her, and also (if $\gamma_a>0$) because with a larger income she may lend more abroad. This last effect will be partly or wholly offset (if $\gamma_b > 0$) in the case in which country B has a Neutral Economy, because country B will lend abroad more as her income rises. But with an Internally Balanced Economy in B, since B's income will not rise there will be no offset of this kind.

If we assume $\gamma_a = \gamma_b = 0$, we have $P/D_{as} = -(\mu_a + \pi_{as})/(1 + \mu_a + \mu_b)$ and $-(\mu_a + \pi_{as})/(1 + \mu_a - \pi_{bp})$ in the cases of a Neutral and Internally Balanced Economy in B respectively.[11] (See rows (1) and (2) of Table II.) These expressions make it clear that, so far as the trade elements in the balance of payments are concerned, with a Neutral Economy in country B the unfavourable movement will be less than with an Internally Balanced Economy in country B, since in the former case, as has already been argued, there will be some inflation of domestic expenditure and increased demand for country A's exports in country B, while in the latter there will be a reduced domestic expenditure and a reduced demand for country A's exports in country B. To continue the previous numerical example with $\lambda_a = \lambda_b = 0.5$, $\pi_{as} = \pi_a = 0.25$, $\pi_{bp} = \pi_b = 0.1$ and $\gamma_a = \gamma_b = 0$, Table II shows that with a Neutral Economy in country B the unfavourable movement in country A's balance of payments will be 0.37 times the primary increase in her domestic expenditure and with an Internally Balanced Economy in country B will be 0.43 times this primary increase in her domestic expenditure.

So far we have only considered the effect of a primary increase in domestic expenditure in country A which itself has the 'normal' import content ($\pi_{as} = \pi_a$). Let us now consider the effects on country A's balance of current payments and national income of a public works policy which is consciously devised so that the primary increase in domestic expenditure (D_{as}) which it represents is spent solely on goods and services produced in country A. In this case $\pi_{as} = 0$. The multipliers Y_a/D_{as} and P/D_{as} given in Table II show that in this case the adverse effect of a reflationary policy in country A on its balance of current payments is by so much reduced, and the favourable effect upon its national income is by so much increased, by ensuring that the whole of the primary increase in domestic expenditure is spent on home-produced goods. With our numerical illustration with $\lambda_a = \lambda_b = 0.5$, $\pi_a = 0.25$, $\pi_{bp} = \pi_b = 0.1$ and $\gamma_a = \gamma_b = 0$, the values of the multipliers showing the effect of a primary change in domestic expenditure upon the balance of payments and the national income, (*a*) with $\pi_{as} = \pi_a$ and (*b*) with $\pi_{as} = 0$, may be shown as follows:

	With $\pi_{as} = \pi_a$	With $\pi_{as} = 0$
Neutral Economy in country B:		
Y_a/D_{as}	1.26	1.63
P/D_{as}	−0.37	−0.19
Internally Balanced Economy in country B:		
Y_a/D_{as}	1.14	1.57
P/D_{as}	−0.43	−0.22

[11] These expressions measure the change in the balance of trade even if γ_a and γ_b are $\neq 0$. This can readily be seen when it is remembered that $P = T - \gamma_a Y_a + \gamma_b Y_b - L_s$ (see equation (15)). Indeed, by means of this equation the multiplier for T can easily be obtained from the multipliers for Y_a, Y_b and P in any of the Tables II to V.

Let us next consider the internal effects upon country B of the primary inflation or deflation in the domestic expenditure of country A, as measured by the multiplier Y_b/D_{as}.

With a Neutral Economy in country B, D_{bp} as well as D_{bs} will be zero. In this case the national income in country B will rise by an amount obtained by applying the closed-economy multiplier of country B $(1/\lambda_b)$ to the improvement in country B's balance of trade. We have already seen that a primary inflation of country A's domestic expenditure will cause an unfavourable movement in country A's balance of trade equal to $(\mu_a + \pi_{as})/(1 + \mu_a + \mu_b)$ times the primary increase in A's domestic expenditure; and this will measure the favourable movement in country B's balance of trade to which the multiplier $1/\lambda_b$ must be applied to obtain the consequential inflation of country B's national income.

With an Internally Balanced Economy in country B, Y_b/D_{as} will, of course, be zero.

With an Externally Balanced Economy in B there will be no change in the balance of trade except in so far as is required to offset induced changes in foreign lending. Let us assume no induced foreign lending (i.e. $\gamma_a = \gamma_b = 0$). In this case, it will be seen from row (3) of Table II that $Y_b/D_{as} = 1/\lambda_b \cdot (\mu_a + \pi_{as})/(\mu_b + \pi_{bp})$. To prevent any change in the balance of payments, B will in this case need to prevent any change in the balance of trade; and for this purpose country B must engineer such a primary increase in her own domestic expenditure as to cause an increase in country B's demand for country A's goods equal to the increase in country A's demand for country B's goods which has resulted from the primary inflation in country A. The 'policy' inflation required in country B's domestic expenditure is $(\mu_a + \pi_{as})/(\mu_b + \pi_{bp})$ times the 'spontaneous' increase in country A's expenditure,[12] and the increase in country B's national income is obtained by applying the closed-economy multiplier $1/\lambda_b$ to this quantity. It is interesting to observe that if the marginal propensity to import in each country which is associated with 'spontaneous' or 'policy' increases in domestic expenditure is equal to the marginal propensity to import in each country which is associated with the 'induced' increases in domestic expenditure (i.e. if $\pi_{as} = \pi_a$ and $\pi_{bp} = \pi_b$) a further simplification is possible. In this case, $Y_b/D_{as} = \pi_a/\pi_b \cdot 1/\lambda_a$.

So far we have only considered the cases in which there is a Neutral Economy in country A (rows (1), (2) and (3) of Table II). It can be seen from the rest of Table II[13] that if country A has an Internally Balanced or

[12] This can be seen clearly in the following way. $\pi_{as} D_{as}$ is the increase in country A's imports due to the primary increase in its domestic expenditure. $(1/\lambda_a) D_{as}$ is the increase in country A's income, $[(1 - \lambda_a)/\lambda_a] D_{as}$ the 'induced' increase in its domestic expenditure, and $[\pi_a(1 - \lambda_a)]/\lambda_a$ or $\mu_a D_{as}$ the 'induced' increase in its imports, so that $(\mu_a + \pi_{as}) D_{as}$ is the total increase in country A's imports. Similarly $(\mu_b + \pi_{bp}) D_{bp}$ is the total increase in country B's imports; and since D_{bp} is such as to make $T = 0$ these two quantities are equal.

[13] This table does not show the values for Y_a/D_{as}, Y_b/D_{as} and P/D_{as} for those cases in which there is a Neutral Economy in B and an Internally or an Externally Balanced Economy in A, or an Internally Balanced Economy in B and an Externally Balanced Economy in A. These results could be obtained from the values of Y_b/D_{bs}, Y_a/D_{bs} and P/D_{bs} obtained from Table I for policy combinations 2, 3 and 5 respectively, and then writing throughout subscript *a* for subscript *b* and altering the sign of *P*. But the general argument in the text would remain unchanged.

an Externally Balanced Economy a 'spontaneous' increase in domestic expenditure in country A will have no effect at all on either country's national income or balance of payments, if the import content of the 'spontaneous' increase in domestic expenditure is the same as the import content of the 'policy' decrease in domestic expenditure which is undertaken to offset it (i.e. if $\pi_{as} = \pi_{ap}$). The reason should be clear. If there is a 'policy' decrease in domestic expenditure equal in magnitude to the 'spontaneous' increase in domestic expenditure and if each has the same import content, then the 'policy' change will exactly offset the effects of the 'spontaneous' change on income and imports. Nothing will change. It is only in so far as the import contents differ that there will be further repercussions of any kind.

Case (ii): a 'spontaneous' shift of demand in either country from country B's goods on to country A's goods. We can now turn to the second type of primary disturbance. Either in country A or in country B – it makes no difference – there is a shift of demand, within the ruling level of domestic expenditure, from country B's goods on to country A's goods. This is defined as a 'spontaneous' increase in country A's balance of trade (T_s) equal in size to the primary increase in expenditure on country A's goods and decrease in expenditure on country B's goods. What is the final effect on the national incomes of both countries and on the balance of current payments between them?

Let us first compare the position of a Neutral Economy in both countries (row (1) of Table III) with that of an Internally Balanced Economy in both countries (row (4) of Table III); and let us first consider the final effect of the 'spontaneous' shift in the balance of trade (T_s) upon the balance of payments between the two countries. Let us once more simplify by assuming no 'induced' foreign lending (i.e. $\gamma_a = \gamma_b = 0$), so that in both cases the change in the balance of trade is equal to the change in the total balance of payments, expressed by $1/(1 + \mu_a + \mu_b)$ in the case of the Neutral Economies and by $1/(1 - \pi_{ap} - \pi_{bp})$ in the case of the Internally Balanced Economies.[14]

It has already been pointed out by a number of authors[15] that, in the world of Neutral Economies, any primary improvement in a country's balance of payments will be 'damped down' before a new equilibrium is reached. Consider the relationship of country A with the rest of the world (country B). Assume that there is a change of taste which causes purchasers to shift their demand away from the goods of country B to the goods of country A. There is an increase in country A's exports and in country B's imports. The balance of current payments of country A becomes more favourable and that of country B less favourable. But the increased demand for country A's exports increases the incomes of those employed in country A in producing exports; they spend some part of

14 Applying equation (15) to rows (1) and (2) of Table III it is clear that these are the expressions for the change in the balance of trade even if γ_a and $\gamma_b \neq 0$.

15 See, for example, A. J. Brown, 'Trade Balances and Exchange Stability', *Oxford Economic Papers*, vol. 6 (April 1942) pp. 57–75, and Joan Robinson, 'The Foreign Exchanges' in *Essays in the Theory of Employment*. (London: Macmillan, 1937), pp. 183–209.

Table III *A 'Spontaneous' Shift of Demand from B's Goods to A's Goods*

(T_s ($= -I_{as} + I_{bs}$) is given. $D_{as} = D_{bs} = L_s = 0$)

Policy assumed in A	B		$\frac{Y_a}{T_s}$	$\frac{Y_b}{T_s}$	$\frac{P}{T_s}$
N	N	(1)	$-\frac{1}{\lambda_a}\cdot\frac{1}{1+\mu_a+\mu_b}$	$-\frac{1}{\lambda_b}\cdot\frac{1}{1+\mu_a+\mu_b}$	$\frac{1-\frac{\gamma_a}{\lambda_a}-\frac{\gamma_b}{\lambda_b}}{1+\mu_a+\mu_b}$
N	IB	(2)	$\frac{1}{\lambda_a}\cdot\frac{1}{1+\mu_a-\pi_{bp}}$	$\boxed{0}$	$\frac{1-\frac{\gamma_a}{\lambda_a}}{1+\mu_a-\pi_{bp}}$
N	EB	(3)	$\frac{1}{\lambda_a}\cdot\frac{\frac{\gamma_b}{\lambda_b}}{\left(1-\frac{\gamma_a}{\lambda_a}\right)(\mu_b+\pi_{bp})+\frac{\gamma_b}{\lambda_b}(1+\mu_a+\pi_{bp})}$	$-\frac{1}{\lambda_b}\cdot\frac{1-\frac{\gamma_a}{\lambda_a}}{\left(1-\frac{\gamma_a}{\lambda_a}\right)(\mu_b+\pi_{bp})+\frac{\gamma_b}{\lambda_b}(1+\mu_a+\pi_{bp})}$	$\boxed{0}$
IB	IB	(4)	$\boxed{0}$	$\boxed{0}$	$\frac{1}{1-\pi_{ap}-\pi_{bp}}$
IB	EB	(5)	$\boxed{0}$	$-\frac{1}{\lambda_b}\cdot\frac{1}{\mu_b+\pi_{bp}+\frac{\gamma_b}{\lambda_b}(1-\pi_{ap}-\pi_{bp})}$	$\boxed{0}$
EB	EB	(6)	$\frac{1}{\lambda_a(\mu_a+\pi_{ap})+m\lambda_b(\mu_b+\pi_{bp}+(\gamma_a+m\gamma_b)(1-\pi_{ap}-\pi_{bp})}$	$-m\frac{Y_a}{T_{as}}$	$\boxed{0}$

Notes.—See bottom of Table II, p. 116.

their increased incomes on purchases of more goods and services; some of this increased expenditure is on imported goods and services, some on home-produced goods and services; this causes another round of increased purchases both of imports and of home-produced goods; and so on. In the end home incomes and imports will have risen. Conversely, in country B the increased imports will have attracted purchasing power away from expenditure on home-produced goods; the incomes of those producers whose products are replaced by the imports will fall; there will result a decline in incomes in country B, and the imports of country B will decline again by an amount determined by country B's propensity to import. Thus the primary improvement in country A's balance of current payments will be dampened down by this secondary increase in country A's imports, and secondary decline in country B's imports, due to the repercussions on incomes and expenditures in the two countries.[16]

This is shown by the multiplier P/T_s in row (1) of Table III, which with our illustrative numerical values of $\lambda_a = \lambda_b = 0.5$, $\pi_a = 0.25$, $\pi_b = 0.1$ and $\gamma_a = \gamma_b = 0$, has the value of 0.74. In other words, as a result of the secondary increase in imports in country A and decrease in imports in country B only about three-quarters of any primary improvement in country A's balance of payments will result in a lasting improvement in that balance.

But the position is completely changed if countries A and B both have Internally Balanced Economies. Assume again a primary change of taste within any given level of domestic expenditure in the two countries which increases country A's exports and/or decreases her imports. This will mean that there is an increased demand for country A's products and a decreased demand for country B's products. Country A, in order to avoid an inflationary pressure of demand, must take domestic measures to reduce the internal demand for goods and services. Thus it may raise interest rates or take other measures to reduce domestic expenditure on new capital development; or it may reduce government expenditure without reducing taxation; or it may reduce spendable incomes by raising rates of taxation, or take other measures to reduce private expenditure on goods and services for personal consumption. Whichever method it adopts, there will result a reduction in demand not only for home-produced goods and services but also for imported goods and services. At the same time country B must be adopting the opposite policy of stimulating its domestic expenditure on goods and services in order to offset the primary reduction in demand for its products. But this 'reflation' of domestic expenditure in country B will increase country B's demand for imported goods and services as well as her demand for her own home-produced goods and services. Thus the primary increase in country A's balance of current payments, far from being 'damped down', will be 'magnified up' in these conditions by the restriction of domestic

[16] If we allowed for 'induced' foreign lending and assumed γ_a and $\gamma_b > 0$, there would be a further factor 'damping down' the improvement in A's total balance of payments, since the increase in A's income would induce her to lend more abroad and the decline in B's income would induce her to lend less abroad. The influence of this factor can be seen in the expression for the multiplier P/T_s in row (1) of Table III.

demand in country A which will lead to some further reduction in her demand for imports and by the reflation of domestic demand in country B which will lead to some further increase in her demand for imports.[17] Moreover, in this case since the national incomes of both countries are constant there can be no damping effect on the improvement in A's total balance of payments from an increased net lending from A to B, however great γ_a and γ_b may be.

This result is illustrated by the multiplier P/T_s in row (4) of Table III which with $\pi_{ap} = 0.25$ and $\pi_{bp} = 0.1$ would equal 1.54.[18] In other words, the final improvement in country A's favourable balance of trade would, as a result of the repercussions of the increased domestic expenditure required in country B to keep country B's national income stable and of the reduced domestic expenditure required in country A to keep country

[17] It is an interesting conclusion from this that in a world of Internally Balanced Economies various measures will be made more effective in restoring equilibrium to disordered balances of payments than they would be in a world of Neutral Economies. Thus, suppose country A's balance of current payments to need to be increased. Assume some change (e.g. a depreciation of country A's currency, a reduction in country B's tariff, etc.) which increases country A's balance in the first place by 100. In a world of Neutral Economies the secondary inflation of domestic expenditure in country A and deflation in country B will damp this down to, say, 75. In a world of Internally Balanced Economies the secondary deflation of domestic expenditure in A and inflation in B will magnify this up to, say, 150.

[18] This multiplier becomes very large as $\pi_{ap} + \pi_{bp}$ approaches unity, becomes infinite if $\pi_{ap} + \pi_{bp} = 1$ and becomes negative if $\pi_{ap} + \pi_{bp} > 1$. This last condition is improbable but not impossible. It would occur, for example, if both countries spent on imports more than 50 per cent of any marginal changes in their total domestic demands. This would mean that if there were a primary increase in the balance of trade of country A, country A should 'plan' its domestic expenditure on the assumption that there was, in fact, going to be ultimately a net *decrease* in its balance of trade and should accordingly *inflate* its domestic expenditure; and country B, enjoying a primary *decrease* in its balance of trade, should adopt the apparently perverse policy of *deflating* its domestic expenditure. The inflation in country A will very little increase the demand for country A's goods but will very greatly increase demand for country B's goods; similarly, the deflation in country B will very little decrease the demand for country B's goods but will very much increase the demand for country A's goods. These readjustments of domestic expenditure will, therefore, cause a net *decrease* in the demand for country A's goods and a net *increase* in the demand for country B's goods, which will work in the opposite direction to the primary increase in country A's balance of trade. The ultimate position will be one in which there is a net *decrease* in country A's balance of trade; her domestic expenditure will have risen to counterbalance this; and the effect of the rise in her domestic expenditure on imports will have been so great as to remove the whole of the primary increase in her balance of trade and to have turned it into a net decrease equal to the increase in her domestic expenditure. This may be regarded as a 'perverse' case. The 'normal' case is where $0 < \pi_{ap} + \pi_{bp} < 1$. The ingenious reader may be amused to ring the changes on the combinations of 'perverse' and 'normal' effects of the values for $\pi_{ap} + \pi_{bp}$ with the 'perverse' and 'normal' effects of an exchange depreciation on a country's balance of current payments. Suppose price elasticities of demand for imports in both countries to be so small that a depreciation of country A's currency has the perverse effect of causing a *reduction* in her favourable balance of trade. If both countries had Internally Balanced Economies and $\pi_{ap} + \pi_{bp} > 1$, then none the less the final effect would be to improve country A's balance of trade. A normal exchange-rate effect (*i.e.* depreciation causing a primary improvement in the balance of trade) plus a normal $\pi_{ap} + \pi_{bp}$ effect, or a perverse exchange-rate effect plus a perverse $\pi_{ap} + \pi_{bp}$ effect will enable exchange depreciation to improve the balance of trade. But if one effect is normal and the other perverse, exchange depreciation with Internally Balanced Economies will worsen the balance of trade.

A's national income stable, be about 50 per cent greater than the primary shift of demand from country B's goods to country A goods.

The illustration that has been given assumes that the 'policy' changes in domestic expenditures in countries A and B which are undertaken expressly to offset changes in the foreign demand for each country's products, themselves contain the 'normal' net import content (i.e. $\pi_{ap} = \pi_a$ and $\pi_{bp} = \pi_b$). But this might not be the case. Suppose that each country selected policies for stabilising demand which affected only the demand for their own home-produced products so that $\pi_{ap} = \pi_{bp} = 0$. This might be the case, for example, if when there was a primary improvement in country A's balance of current payments of, say, 100, then country A decreased a public investment programme which had no import content by 100 and country B increased a public investment programme which had no import content by 100. The increased public investment demand in country B for country B's goods of 100 would exactly offset the primary reduction of 100 in the net demand for country B's exports (or in her own net shift of demand from home-produced to imported goods). And similarly in country A. There would be no 'magnifying up' of the primary involvement of the balance of current payments of 100, and P/T_s would equal 1. But if country A chose to deflate in a way which meant that it had to reduce domestic expenditure by 133⅓ in order to reduce its own demand for its own products by 100, the remaining 33⅓ would represent a reduction in imports and so a further improvement in its balance of current payments.

The effects of these changes in the balance of trade on the levels of national income in the two countries are readily explained. In the case of Neutral Economies in both countries (row (1) of Table III), the final improvement in country A's balance of trade is $1/(1 + \mu_a + \mu_b)$ times T_s; and there is an inflation of the national income in country A equal to $1/\lambda_a$ times, and a deflation of the national income in country B equal to $1/\lambda_b$ times, this sum. With Internally Balanced Economies (row 4) there is, of course, no change in either national income.

Row (2) of Table III shows a final effect upon the balance of payments (P/T_s) intermediate between those of rows (1) and (4). In country A there is a Neutral Economy; the 'spontaneous' improvement in her balance of trade leads to a rise in her national income; this leads both to some increase in her imports and also, if γ_a is >1, to some increase in her foreign lending; and these are factors damping down the primary improvement in her balance of payments and are shown in the term $+ \mu_a$ in the denominator, and in the term $- (\gamma_a/\lambda_a)$ in the numerator, of the multiplier P/T_s. On the other hand, in country B there is an Internally Balanced Economy; the primary worsening of her balance of trade causes her to engineer an offsetting primary increase in her domestic expenditure; this leads to some further increase in her imports; and this is a factor 'magnifying up' the primary worsening of her balance of trade, which is shown in the term $- \pi_{bp}$ in the denominator of the multiplier P/T_s. Whether there is a net 'damping' or 'magnifying' effect depends upon whether $\mu_a + \gamma_a/\lambda_a >$ or $<\pi_{bp}$. The final internal changes are easily seen. In country A the national income rises by an amount, shown by applying the multiplier $1/\lambda_a$ to $1/(1 + \mu_a - \pi_{bp})$, which is the final improvement in her balance of trade; and in country B there is no change in the national income.

We may next consider rows (3) and (5), which, it will be seen, lead to the same final outcome if $\gamma_b = 0$. For in these conditions $Y_a/T_s = 0$ and $Y_b/T_s = -1/\lambda_b \cdot 1/(\mu_b + \pi_{bp})$ in both cases. In both cases country B so deflates her domestic expenditure, and thereby her national income, as to cause a reduction in her demand for imports sufficient to offset the primary worsening in her balance of payments and to ensure that there is in the end no net change in that balance. Now if $\gamma_b = 0$, B will not need to offset any change in foreign lending induced by her own adjustments of her national income. She will only have to adjust her national income so as to induce a change in her imports sufficient to offset the 'spontaneous' change in the balance of trade and any changes in the balance of trade or foreign lending induced by a change in country A's national income. But there will in fact be no such 'induced' changes of A's imports or foreign lending, because in the case of row (5) country A adopts a conscious policy which prevents any such changes, while in the case of row (3) if country B just offsets the 'primary' shift in demand to A's goods by a 'policy' deflation of her own demand for A's goods of exactly the same magnitude there will in fact be no net increase in the demand for A's goods. So far as A is concerned nothing will have happened and her national income will not rise. But if $\gamma_b > 0$, then, whereas in the case of row (5) it will still be A's policy to keep her national income constant, in the case of row (3) there will now be some rise in her national income. For as B deflates her national income in order to reduce her imports so as to offset the effect on the balance of payments of the primary shift of demand away from her goods, there will be an 'induced' decline in her lending to A. The reduction in her demand for imports need not, therefore, go quite so far as the primary shift of demand from her goods, since part of her balance-of-payments gap will now be filled by her reduced lending to A. A, therefore, will experience some net increase in the demand for her goods, and with a Neutral Economy will, therefore, experience some net rise in her national income.

There remains row (6) of Table III. In view of the primary shift of demand from B's to A's goods, A adopts a policy of inflating her domestic expenditure and so her national income to restore equilibrium to the balance of payments, and B deflates for the same purpose. B's deflation is m times as large as A's inflation. As a special case it may be interesting to see what happens as A takes less and less of the responsibility for restoring equilibrium by inflating and leaves more and more of the responsibility to B to restore equilibrium by deflating. At the limit when A will do nothing and $1/m = 0$, then, it can be seen from Table III, the multipliers in row (6) become exactly the same as those in row (5). A in fact keeps her national income constant and B has to make the whole change in her own.

Table IV *A 'Spontaneous' Change in Net Foreign Lending*

(L_s is given. $T_s = D_{as} = D_{bs} = 0$)

Policy assumed in *A*	*B*		$\frac{Y_a}{L_s}$	$\frac{Y_b}{L_s}$	$\frac{P}{L_s}$
N	N	(1)	0	0	-1
N	IB	(2)	0	$\boxed{0}$	-1
N	EB	(3)	$\frac{1}{\lambda_a} \cdot \frac{\mu_b + \pi_{bp}}{\left(1 - \frac{\gamma_a}{\lambda_a}\right)(\mu_b + \pi_{bp}) + \frac{\gamma_b}{\lambda_b}(1 + \mu_a + \pi_{bp})}$	$\frac{1}{\lambda_b} \cdot \frac{1 + \mu_a - \pi_{bp}}{\left(1 - \frac{\gamma_a}{\lambda_a}\right)(\mu_b + \pi_{bp}) + \frac{\gamma_b}{\lambda_b}(1 + \mu_a - \pi_{bp})}$	$\boxed{0}$
IB	IB	(4)	$\boxed{0}$	$\boxed{0}$	-1
IB	EB	(5)	$\boxed{0}$	$\frac{1}{\lambda_b} \cdot \frac{1 - \pi_{ap} - \pi_{bp}}{\mu_b + \pi_{bp} + \frac{\gamma_b}{\lambda_b}(1 - \pi_{ap} - \pi_{bp})}$	$\boxed{0}$
EB	EB	(6)	$-\frac{1 - \pi_{ap} - \pi_{bp}}{\lambda_a(\mu_a + \pi_{ap}) + m\lambda_b(\mu_b + \pi_{bp}) + (\gamma_a + m\gamma_b)(1 - \pi_{ap} - \pi_{bp})}$	$-m\frac{Y_a}{L_s}$	$\boxed{0}$

Notes.—See bottom of Table II, p. 116.

As another special case, let us assume that $\pi_{ap} = \pi_a$ and $\pi_{bp} = \pi_b$ (i.e. that the 'policy' changes in domestic expenditure have the normal import content). If in addition $\gamma_a = \gamma_b = 0$, the multipliers for the two national incomes reduce to the following simple formulæ which give the 'weights' to be attached to the inflation in A and the deflation in B:

$$\frac{Y_a}{T_s} = \frac{1}{\pi_a + m\pi_b} \quad \text{and} \quad \frac{Y_b}{T_s} = -\frac{1}{\frac{\pi_a}{m} + \pi_b}.$$

Case (iii): a 'spontaneous' change in foreign lending or some similar financial transfer from A to B. The multiplier effects of a 'pure' case of primary disturbance due to a change in net foreign lending can be fairly quickly discussed. By a 'pure' case of this type we mean one in which there is not associated with the increased lending from A to B any 'spontaneous' change in the demand for domestic or foreign goods either in A or B. People purchase securities in B's capital market instead of in A's capital market, and that is all there is to it.

Table IV shows the multipliers which result from the application of these strict assumptions to the equations of Table I. In those cases in which neither country is adopting an Externally Balanced Economy (see rows (1), (2) and (4) of Table IV) there will be a change in the final balance of payments exactly equal to the primary change in net foreign lending and nothing else will alter at all. The reason for this is clear. The primary change in foreign lending does not itself directly cause any change in the demand for the goods of either country. There will be no forces causing any change unless the disequilibrium in the total balance of payments which results from the foreign lending causes some country to adopt a 'policy' change in its domestic expenditure or imports in order to restore an External Balance.

In the case in which country B inflates its domestic expenditure and national income to bring about an increase of imports to preserve an External Balance, country A will also experience some rise in its national income as a result of the increased demand for its exports, if it has a Neutral Economy. (See row (3) of Table IV.) If country A has an Internally Balanced Economy, then country B, in order to preserve an External Balance, need carry its inflation less far, since A will deflate its domestic demand in order to prevent B's increased demand for its exports from inflating its national income and this will reduce A's demand for B's goods and thus help to restore equilibrium to the balance of payments. Moreover, in this case since there will be no rise in A's income there will be no 'induced' increase in A's lending abroad, even if $\gamma_a > 0$. Indeed, if $\pi_{ap} + \pi_{bp} = 1$, B will not in fact experience any net inflation of her national income. The inflation which she will carry out in her domestic expenditure to preserve an external balance will be followed by a deflation in A to prevent B's increased demand from affecting A's income. But this reduced demand in A will just offset the increased demand in B as far as B's income is concerned, if $\pi_{ap} + \pi_{bp} = 1$. (See row (5) of Table IV.) If both A and B have Externally Balanced Economies, there will be a deflation of domestic expenditure in A and an

Table V *A Reparations Transfer from A to B*

(Reparations Transfer $= L_s. - D_{as} = D_{bs} = L_s.\ I_{as} = \pi_{as} D_{as}.\ I_{bs} = \pi_{bs} D_{bs}$)

Policy assumed in A	B		$\frac{Y_a}{L_s}$	$\frac{Y_b}{L_s}$	$\frac{P}{L_s}$
N	N	(1)	$-\frac{1}{\lambda_a} \cdot \frac{1 - \pi_{as} - \pi_{bs}}{1 + \mu_a + \mu_b}$	$\frac{1}{\lambda_b} \cdot \frac{1 - \pi_{as} - \pi_{bs}}{1 + \mu_a + \mu_b}$	$-\frac{\left(1 - \frac{\gamma_a}{\lambda_a} - \frac{\gamma_b}{\lambda_b}\right)(1 - \pi_{as} - \pi_{bs})}{1 + \mu_a + \mu_b}$
N	IB	(2)	$-\frac{1}{\lambda_a} \cdot \frac{1 - \pi_{as} - \pi_{bs}}{1 + \mu_a - \pi_{bp}}$	$\boxed{0}$	$-\frac{\left(1 - \frac{\gamma_a}{\lambda_a}\right)(1 - \pi_{as} - \pi_{bs})}{1 + \mu_a - \pi_{bp}}$
N	EB	(3)	$-\frac{1}{\lambda_a} \cdot \frac{\frac{\gamma_b}{\lambda_b}(1 - \pi_{as} - \pi_{bs})}{\left(1 - \frac{\gamma_a}{\lambda_a}\right)(\mu_b + \pi_{bp}) + \frac{\gamma_b}{\lambda_b}(1 + \mu_a - \pi_{bp})}$	$\frac{1}{\lambda_b} \cdot \frac{\left(1 - \frac{\gamma_a}{\lambda_a}\right)(1 - \pi_{as} - \pi_{bs})}{\left(1 - \frac{\gamma_a}{\lambda_a}\right)(\mu_b + \pi_{bp}) + \frac{\gamma_b}{\lambda_b}(1 + \mu_a - \pi_{bp})}$	$\boxed{0}$
IB	IB	(4)	$\boxed{0}$	$\boxed{0}$	$-\frac{1 - \pi_{as} - \pi_{bs}}{1 - \pi_{ap} - \pi_{bp}}$
IB	EB	(5)	$\boxed{0}$	$\frac{1}{\lambda_b} \cdot \frac{1 - \pi_{as} - \pi_{bs}}{\mu_b + \pi_{bp} + \frac{\gamma_b}{\lambda_b}(1 - \pi_{ap} - \pi_{bp})}$	$\boxed{0}$
EB	EB	(6)	$-\frac{1 - \pi_{as} - \pi_{bs}}{\lambda_a(\mu_a + \pi_{ap}) + m\lambda_b(\mu_b + \pi_{bp}) + (\gamma_a + m\gamma_b)(1 - \pi_{ap} - \pi_{bp})}$	$-m\frac{Y_a}{L_s}$	$\boxed{0}$

Notes.—See bottom of Table II, p. 116.

inflation in B. This will cause a deflation of A's income and an inflation of B's income, as shown in row (6) of Table IV, unless once more $\pi_{ap} + \pi_{bp} = 1$, in which case the deflation of domestic demand in A and the inflation of domestic demand in B will just cancel out so far as the national incomes of both A and B are concerned.

Case (iv): a reparations payment is made from A to B, which represents a 'spontaneous' financial transfer from A to B; but the raising of the revenue in A and its disposal in B causes a simultaneous 'spontaneous' decrease of domestic expenditure in A and increase of domestic expenditure in B. This is another case of combined primary disturbance, an event which simultaneously causes an increased financial transfer from A to B and a decrease of domestic expenditure in A and an increase in B. Now it is probable that in fact the 'spontaneous' decrease in domestic expenditure in A would be rather less than the reparations payment even if there were an increased tax revenue equal to the whole of the reparations to be paid, since some part of the revenue raised to make the payment to B would probably come out of savings rather than expenditure in A. Similarly, the 'spontaneous' increase in domestic expenditure in B might well be rather less than the total reparations received from A. But for the purposes of simplification we shall assume that there is a reparations payment to be transferred equal to L_s, and that there is a 'spontaneous' decline in A's domestic expenditure equal to the whole of this $(-D_{as} = L_s)$ and a 'spontaneous' increase in B's domestic expenditure of the same size $(D_{bs} = L_s)$. On these assumptions the multipliers given in Table V can be derived from the equations given in Table I.[19]

Table V has one quite outstanding feature, and we will confine our comments to remarking upon it. In every case[20] (except where A has an Internally Balanced Economy) the payment of reparations by A will mean a deflation of A's national income if $\pi_{as} + \pi_{bs} < 1$, no change if $\pi_{as} + \pi_{bs} = 1$ and actually an inflation if $\pi_{as} + \pi_{bs} > 1$. In every case (except where B has an Internally Balanced Economy) the receipt of reparations by B will mean an inflation of B's income if $\pi_{as} + \pi_{bs} < 1$, no change if $\pi_{as} + \pi_{bs} = 1$ and actually a deflation if $\pi_{as} + \pi_{bs} > 1$. In every case[21] (except where one or both countries have an Externally Balanced Economy) the transfer will cause an unfavourable movement in A's balance of payments if $\pi_{as} + \pi_{bs} < 1$, no movement if $\pi_{as} + \pi_{bs} = 1$ and actually a favourable movement if $\pi_{as} + \pi_{bs} > 1$. Clearly the size of $\pi_{as} + \pi_{bs}$ is of crucial importance.

A little reflection will show the reasonableness of the above-mentioned conclusions. We are assuming that the transfer L_s causes a primary decrease in domestic expenditure in country A of L_s and a primary increase in domestic expenditure of country B also of L_s. $(1 - \pi_{as}) L_s$ therefore represents the direct reduction in country A's

19 The reader can work out for himself from the equations given in Table I what the multipliers would be if it were assumed that only a proportion, k_a, of the reparations caused a 'spontaneous' decline in A's domestic expenditure $(-D_{as} = k_a L_s)$ and that only a proportion, k_b, of the reparations caused a 'spontaneous' increase in B's domestic expenditure $(D_{bs} = k_b L_s)$.

20 Assuming in the special case of row (3) of Table VI that $\gamma_b > 0$.

21 Assuming in the case of row (4) of Table VI that $\pi_{bp} < 1$.

demand for country A's goods and $\pi_{bs} L_s$ the direct increase in country B's demand for country A's goods, i.e. a total direct reduction in demand for country A's goods of $(1 - \pi_{as} - \pi_{bs}) L_s$. Similarly, there will be a total direct increase in the demand for country B's goods of $(1 - \pi_{as} - \pi_{bs}) L_s$. And there will be a direct decrease in country A's imports of $\pi_{as} L_s$ and increase in country B's imports of $\pi_{bs} L_s$, i.e. a direct improvement in country A's balance of trade of $(\pi_{as} + \pi_{bs})$. L_s If, therefore, $\pi_{as} + \pi_{bs} = 1$, there will be an immediate change in the balance of trade equal to L_s and no net primary change in the total demand for country A's goods or for country B's goods; and there will thus be no further repercussions on national income. And if $\pi_{as} + \pi_{bs}$ were actually >1, there would be direct improvement in the balance of payments of A greater than L_s and there would actually be a direct net increase in the total demand for country A's goods and a decrease in the total demand for country B's goods, so that there would be a resulting inflation in country A's income and deflation in country B's income. And vice versa in the more normal case in which $\pi_{as} + \pi_{bs} < 1$.

VII *Conclusion. Comparison with Professor Machlup's* International Trade and the National Income Multiplier

I have to confess that I had worked out my formulæ before I read Professor Machlup's admirable study on this same subject [Philadelphia: The Blakiston Company, 1943]; and in many respects I find that I have merely repeated his earlier work. I have nevertheless considered it worth while publishing my results for a number of reasons.

First, Professor Machlup does not make room for state revenue and expenditure in his analysis, and he assumes away all secondary effects of changes in national income upon investment. I do not make such severely simplifying assumptions. But this difference is purely formal. If Professor Machlup's factor s is defined in the same way as my factor λ, this difference disappears.

But, secondly, there is a more important difference between his marginal propensity to import (m) and my marginal propensity to import (π). He relates the marginal propensity to import to the national income, whereas I relate it to what I have called domestic expenditure. He says that of any unit increase in the national income a proportion, s, will be saved, a proportion, c, will be spent on home-produced goods and services and a proportion, m, will be spent on imported goods, where $s + c + m = 1$. I say that a unit increase in the national income will, as to a proportion λ, not lead to any increase in domestic expenditure whether for public or private consumption or investment, and that of the increased expenditure $(1 - \lambda)$ a proportion $(1 - \pi)$ will be spent on home-produced goods and the remainder π on imports. Thus, subject to the difference between s and λ to which reference has been made in the preceding paragraph, Professor Machlup's $s = \lambda$, $c = (1 - \lambda)(1 - \pi)$ and $m = (1 - \lambda)\pi$.

I claim an advantage for my notation. Professor Machlup's notation suggests that a person who has more income decides whether to spend it on savings, home products or imports, much as he might decide whether to spend it on apples, oranges or nuts. I divide the decision, I believe more realistically, into two parts. There is first the set of factors which determines whether an increase in the national income shall lead to an increased expenditure on goods and services or not. This decision depends upon matters such as the rate of direct and indirect taxes, state policy as regards the budget surplus or deficit, rates of unemployment benefit and the sensitiveness of the demand for capital goods to an increased demand for final products, as well as upon those factors such as the rate of interest and the distribution of income which determine private savings. But when this decision has been made there is a second question whether the extra goods which are purchased for public or private consumption or investment should be purchased abroad or at home; and here a quite different set of factors is at work, namely, whether home goods or foreign goods are 'inferior' or 'superior', whether they are complements or substitutes, whether the price relationship is favourable to imports or not, and what commercial policy is adopted. To relate imports to the total domestic expenditure and total domestic expenditure to the national income brings out this distinction.

A third difference is to be found in the fact that I have tried to discuss the 'multiplier' problems of the total balance of payments and not only of the balance of trade. By allowing for 'induced' foreign lending (in my terminology) as well as for 'induced' imports, I have tried to give a more extensive scope to the 'multiplier' formulæ. I have allowed everywhere as much for the effects of income changes on foreign lending as for their effects on trade. And this, as will be seen from the relevant equations, makes a substantial difference to the results. For whereas a unit of 'induced' foreign lending has the same immediate effect upon the balance of payments as a unit of 'induced' imports, the ultimate effect is quite different because they have quite different 'multiplier' effects within the country receiving payment and lead, therefore, to quite different foreign repercussions so far as the paying country is concerned.

There remains the fourth and most substantial difference between Professor Machlup's treatment and my treatment of these problems, namely, that Professor Machlup, like other authors on this subject, deals only with what I have called Neutral Economies. I have dealt also, wherever relevant, with the difference made to the formulæ by assuming Internally or Externally Balanced Economies in either or both of the countries concerned. Indeed, the main point of the particular examples examined in Section VII is to undermine the importance of these alternatives. The detailed application is bound to appear somewhat involved; but the guiding principle is clear. Something happens in A (a depression or a shift of demand) to cause a reduction in the demand for B's products. How will B react? Will she let her national income decline until a new equilibrium is reached with a lower level of employment but a somewhat reduced adverse balance of payments? Or will she reflate her national income, thereby exercising an inflationary pressure on A and exacerbating the balance-of-payments difficulty? Or will she take positive measures to carry her internal deflation to the point of removing entirely the strain on her balance of payments, thereby exercising a deflationary pressure on A? The multiplier technique is applicable in all three cases, though the results are very different. For each practical problem we must be careful to select the most appropriate assumption.

8

A Geometrical Representation of Balance-of-Payments Policy

From Economica, *vol. 16 (November 1949), pp. 305–320. The model and the diagrams (pp. 142–7 below) in this article were also used in Chapter VIII of the* Mathematical Supplement *to* The Theory of International Economic Policy Volume I: The Balance of Payments *(London: Oxford University Press, 1951).*

In my paper on 'National Income, National Expenditure and the Balance of Payments' in *The Economic Journal* for December 1948 and March 1949 [Chapter 7 above] I attempted to show algebraically certain 'multiplier' relationships between income, expenditure, imports and exports on the assumption that all prices were constant. In this paper I intend to use the geometric technique to introduce certain changes in price relationships into the general structure used in my *Economic Journal* paper. But this technique will be used in this paper for the sole and limited purpose of comparing exchange-rate variation and commercial policy (e.g., import restrictions or export subsidies) as a means of removing an existing balance-of-payments disequilibrium between two countries both of which, in the terminology of my *Economic Journal* paper, are adopting policies for Internal Balance.

We assume (i) that there are only two countries A and B, of which one may, of course, represent the rest of the world; (ii) that A produces only one product which we will call Wheat, and B only one product which we will call Machinery or, more realistically, that the prices of A's various products do not vary in relation to each other so that we can think unambiguously of a representative A product, and similarly with B; (iii) that both A and B adopt domestic fiscal or monetary policies for the maintenance of what I have called Internal Balance or, in other words, that the authorities in each country take steps to cause such an inflation or deflation of its domestic expenditure (i.e. of its total money expenditure on goods and services for final use at home, whether these be home-produced or imported products) as to maintain constant the total demand for its own product and so for its own labour; (iv) that the money wage-rate and so (with constant employment and output) the money price of the product of each country in terms of the currency of that country is constant; and (v) that imports of Wheat from A into B and of Machinery from B into A are the only elements in the balance of payments except where the contrary is expressly stated.

We have left room in the above assumptions for two important types of price change. First, we do not assume a constant rate of exchange between A's money which we will call dollars and B's money which we will call pounds. The pound price of B's Machinery and the dollar price of A's Wheat are fixed (see assumption iv); but as the pound may depreciate in terms of dollars, so a unit of B's Machinery may exchange for a smaller amount of A's Wheat than before. Secondly, we do not assume free trade or an unchanged commercial policy. The price of A's Wheat may rise in pounds and so in terms of B's Machinery in B's market without rising in A's market, because B imposes an import duty on Wheat.

Let us start off then with free trade but a rate of exchange between the pound and the dollar which leaves B with a deficit on her balance of trade. This position is depicted in Figure I. Let BO measure the amount of Machinery produced by country B, and since the pound price of Machinery is given it can also measure the value in B's currency of B's national income. But B's domestic expenditure (i.e., the amount of purchasing power which she has available to spend at home for domestic purposes on goods and services of all kinds whether home-produced or imported) is equal to her national income + her imports − her exports. So if B has a deficit of OR in her balance of trade, her total domestic expenditure will be equal to BR. Let the slope of the line α represent the £–$ rate of exchange (or the real terms of trade between Machinery and Wheat). Country B has her national income (BO) plus her 'Marshall Aid' (OR) to spend on home-produced or imported goods and services at a market price corresponding to the slope of α. She moves from R up this price line to the point Q_{ma} where this price line is a tangent to her highest indifference curve (I_b). At this point B is in equilibrium. She consumes BC of her own Machinery and uses CR of her domestic expenditure to purchase CQ_{ma} of A's Wheat.

Similarly, country A has a dollar national income (or Wheat national product) equal to AO. But of this OR' is used to finance a balance-of-trade surplus ('Marshall Aid') so that her own domestic expenditure is AR'. On the price line α she uses $R'G$ of her domestic expenditure to consume GQ_{ma} imported Machinery, because Q_{ma} is also the point at which the price line α is a tangent to A's highest indifference curve (I_a). Q_{ma} is our initial point of balance-of-payments disequilibrium, which becomes a position of equilibrium through the payment of 'Marshall Aid' on a scale exactly equal to B's balance-of-payments deficit at the given rate of exchange.

Let us now suppose that the balance-of-trade deficit is removed. Country B's domestic expenditure in terms of her own money or products must now be confined to her national income BO. The foreign exchange value of the pound is altered (in Figure I we have shown it as depreciated) to the slope of the price line β. From O country B moves up this price line until it is a tangent to her highest indifference curve I_b' at

Q_{ed}, where she uses DO of her domestic expenditure to spend on DQ_{ed} of imported Wheat and consumes the remainder (BD) in terms of her own product. Similarly, country A now starts with a domestic expenditure of AO; she moves from O up the price line β to the point of tangency with her highest indifference curve I'_a at the same point Q_{ed}, where she uses OF of her domestic expenditure in consuming FQ_{ed} imported Machinery and consumes the remainder (FA) in the form of her own product Wheat. Q_{ed} is the point of equilibrium obtained by exchange depreciation. It is to be observed that both Q_{ma} and Q_{ed} lie on the contract curve KK which is the locus of the points at which an A indifference curve is tangential to a B indifference curve.

The movement from Q_{ma} to Q_{ed} may be regarded as taking place in two parts. Since B is going to lose an excess of imports over exports of OR, she must take steps to deflate her domestic expenditure by this amount in order to keep her demand for goods and services in line with the reduced supplies which will be available when she has sufficiently increased her exports and reduced her imports. Conversely, A must inflate her domestic expenditure by OR' to take up the excess supply of goods on her domestic market which will be available when she is no longer exporting more than she is importing. But this deflation of domestic expenditure in B and inflation in A will certainly decrease B's demand for imports and increase A's demand for imports, if the marginal propensity to import in both countries is greater than zero. Why should any depreciation of B's currency be necessary?[1] Why should not these expenditure effects alone be sufficient to restore equilibrium? If they are sufficient, then the point Q_{ed} in Figure I will coincide with the point H at which the price line α' (which is parallel to the price line α but passes through O instead of R and R') cuts the contract curve KK. It is clear from Figure I that an exchange depreciation will be required as well as the expenditure effect only if as we move North-West up the contract curve the slopes of the successive points of tangency between A and B indifference curves do not remain constant but become steeper and steeper. If the slope of the tangent to the A and B indifference curves at H were equal to the slope of the tangent at Q_{ma} (i.e., to the price line α) then the price line α' would at H describe the new position of equilibrium since it has the same slope as α. Only if the price line α' is less steeply sloped than the tangent to the indifference curves at H must we move up towards the price line β at the point Q_{ed} in order to reach equilibrium.

[1] We are carrying out the whole analysis of this paper in terms of a system of variable exchange rates. We could do it just as well in terms of variable wage-rates (i.e., the Gold Standard). In this latter case a deflation of B's and inflation of A's domestic expenditure would take place because without Marshall Aid B would lose gold to A. This deflation in B and inflation in A would cause B to purchase less of A's goods and less of B's goods and A to purchase more of A's goods and more of B's goods. Why should not these income effects just cancel each other out? Why should there be a *net* decline in the demand for B's goods and increase in the demand for A's? Only in this latter case will it be necessary for there to be a fall in prices and money wage-rates in B and rise in money prices and wage-rates in A (and so a movement of the real terms of trade against B) in order fully to remove the deficit on B's balance of trade.

What does this mean? In the terminology of my *Economic Journal* paper it means that the sum of A's and B's marginal propensities to import must be less than unity. This is shown in Figure II. Country B's domestic expenditure goes down by an amount equal to OR or MQ_{ma}. Let us suppose that with prices unchanged (i.e. α' parallel to α) B's marginal propensity to import is equal to ML/MQ_{ma}, so that of the decrease in her domestic expenditure LQ_{ma} represents a decrease in her demand for her own Machinery and NL (with a Machine value of ML) a decrease in her demand for imported Wheat. This means that one of B's indifference curves must be tangential to the price line α' at the point N. Now MQ_{ma} also measures, in terms of B's currency, the increase in A's domestic expenditure. If the sum of A's and B's marginal propensities to import is less than unity, then, at unchanged prices, A must spend on imports a proportion of her increase in domestic expenditure which is less than LQ_{ma}/MQ_{ma}. Suppose that A's marginal propensity to import is only JQ_{ma}/MQ_{ma} (i.e., $ML/MQ_{ma} + JQ_{ma}/MQ_{ma} < 1$), so that she spends only JQ_{ma} more on Machinery and PJ (with a Machine value of MJ) more on her own Wheat. Then there must be an A indifference curve tangential to α' at P. It is clear from the shape of the indifference curves at P and N (i) that there must be a point H on the price line α' between P and N at which an A indifference curve is tangential to a B indifference curve, and (ii) that the slope of the tangent to the two indifference curves at this point H must be steeper than the slope of α', i.e., than the slope of α which is equal to the slope of the tangent to the A and B indifference curves at Q_{ma}. If we start from the point Q_{ma}, by taking successively larger changes in the domestic expenditure of each country we can trace out the loci of the points N and P which we will call respectively B's expenditure curve (E_b) and A's expenditure curve (E_a). It is clear from Figure II that as we move North-West from Q_{ma} along the contract curve KK, E_b will lie to the East of us and E_a to the West. This is the fundamental proposition which arises from the assumption that the sum of the two marginal propensities to import is less than unity.

There is a second fundamental geometric proposition which we must establish before we proceed. This arises from the familiar assumption that the sum of A's and B's price elasticities of demand for imports is greater than unity. It is illustrated in Figure III. Let us start from the point Q_{ed} where the balance of trade between A and B has been brought into equilibrium by means of exchange depreciation to a price line β. Suppose now that the exchange rate were appreciated again to α'. How much of each commodity would each country purchase, *assuming that each country's domestic expenditure were kept equal to its national income* (i.e., BO for B and AO for A)? This is, of course, shown by each country's familiar offer curve. When the price of imports falls for B from β to α' we assume that B purchases some more of A's products (i.e. her elasticity of demand is greater than zero and her consumption combination on the line α' would lie North-East of N'.) If her elasticity of demand for A's products were greater than unity she would not only consume more of A's products but would also give up a larger amount of her own in return, so that her new consumption combination would lie on

α' at some point North-East of P'. In other words, B's offer curve (O_b) will run from Q_{ed} to cut α' at a point N somewhere North-East of N' and at this point a B indifference curve will be tangential to α'. Similarly, A's offer curve will run from Q_{ed} to cut α' at a point P somewhere South-West of P', and at this point an A indifference curve will be tangential to α'.

It is a familiar proposition, which we shall not prove here, that if the sum of A's and B's elasticities of demand for imports is greater than unity, then N will lie to the North-East of P, and a fall in the price of A's product from the equilibrium point Q_{ed} will generate an excess demand for A's product or money (DN demanded by B and PC by A) and a deficient demand for B's (BD demanded by B and CA by A). In Figure III both A's and B's demands have been depicted as having an elasticity less than unity; but their sum is greater than unity and N lies to the North-East of P. Now it can be seen from the shape of the indifference curves at P and N that there will be a point H on α' in between P and N at which an A indifference curve will be tangential to a B indifference curve. In other words, the contract curve KK will run from Q_{ed} Southwards with O_a to the West and O_b to the East of it.

In Figures IV (*a*) and (*b*) the two expenditure curves (E_a and E_b) and the two offer curves (O_a and O_b) have been drawn on a single diagram, the only material difference between these two figures being that in IV(*a*) the elasticity of demand for imports for each country is greater than, and in IV(*b*) is less than, unity. It should be observed that each country's expenditure curve will cut the price line α' at the same point as its own offer curve. This is so because both the expenditure curve and the offer curve must cut the price line α' at the points at which the price line α' is a tangent to one of that country's indifference curves, as can be seen from Figures II to III. Take, for example, the point Q_{isa} where B's offer curve and expenditure curve cut the price line α'. Starting from Q_{ma} and moving up B's expenditure curve (E_b) as B's domestic expenditure declines from BR to BO, we move to the consumption point Q_{isa} at which α' is a tangent to the highest possible B indifference curve. Or starting from Q_{ed} on the price line β and allowing the price of B's imports to fall towards α' with a constant domestic expenditure in B of BO, we move along B's offer curve O_b; and the point Q_{isa} on this offer curve also describes the point at which the new price line α' is tangential to the highest possible B indifference curve.

We are now in a position to consider commercial policy as a means of restoring equilibrium to the balance of trade between A and B. We start from the Marshall Aid point Q_{ma}, the point of intersection of the two expenditure curves (E_a and E_b). We have shown that Q_{ed}, the point of intersection of the two offer curves, will describe the equilibrium as obtained by exchange depreciation. We now propose to show that Q_{itb}, the point of intersection of A's offer curve and her expenditure curve, describes the equilibrium obtained by an import tax in the deficit country B; that Q_{isa}, the point of intersection of B's offer and expenditure curves, describes the new equilibrium obtained by an import subsidy in the surplus country A; that the point of intersection (if any) of B's expenditure curves and A's offer curve (Q_{esb} in Figure IV(*a*) and Q_{etb} in Figure IV(*b*)) will describe the equilibrium (if any) brought about by an export subsidy (Q_{esb}) or tax (Q_{etb}) imposed by B; and that the point of intersection (if any) of A's expenditure curve and B's offer curve (Q_{eta} in Figure IV(*a*) and Q_{esa} in Figure IV(*b*)) will describe the equilibrium (if any) brought about by A's taxing (Q_{eta}) or subsidising (Q_{esa}) her exports.

Let us consider first the point Q_{itb} which describes how country B can get rid of the deficit on her balance of trade without depreciating her currency but by imposing a tax on imports. This is shown in more detail in Figure V. After the balance-of-trade disequilibrium has been removed A's domestic expenditure will rise from AR' to AO. But since B's prices are unchanged and the rate of exchange is unaltered A will now move up the price line α' from O until she reaches the point Q_{itb} at which one of her indifference curves is tangent to α', which point is, of course, where both her expenditure curve and her offer curve cut the line α'. This then determines the amount of Machinery which A will import from B and the amount of Wheat which she will offer in return. But how is B to be induced to demand just this amount of Wheat? Through the point Q_{itb} there is a B indifference curve, the slope of which is steeper than the slope of the A indifference curve and so of the price line α', because Q_{itb} lies to the West of KK. Draw the price line γ through Q_{itb} tangential to the B indifference curve at Q_{itb} and let it cut B's Machinery axis at S. Then OS will represent in terms of machinery or pounds the amount of revenue raised in B on imports of Wheat into B, and γ will be the price line which represents the price of Wheat in B cum import duty while α' represents its price ex import duty.

B now has a total domestic expenditure at factor cost of BO but a total domestic expenditure at market price of BS. In other words, she has available to spend on goods and services at their market price (including duty) not only her national income at factor cost (BO) but also the total revenue from the import duties (OS). Let us suppose that the government which receives this revenue distributes it out as a *pro rata* subsidy to everyone's income in B.[2] Then consumers in B have BS to spend on home-produced goods or on imports at a market price corresponding to γ. They move up the price line γ from S till they reach their highest indifference curve at Q_{itb}. Thus they consume BC of their own Machinery and CQ_{itb} of imported Wheat. For this Wheat they pay CO to obtain the necessary dollars to give to suppliers in A and OS in import duty, which is then paid back by their government to them to subsidise their incomes.

If the point Q_{itb} is compared with the point Q_{ed}, it can be seen that for

[2] This method of dealing with the import duty revenue is quite realistic. A government which was already raising revenue (e.g. by proportionate income tax) to cover its governmental expenditure could use the revenue which accrued from an import duty whose primary purpose was to remove a deficit on the balance of trade merely to replace other revenue (e.g., for the reduction of its proportionate income tax). But this means we can allow B's indifference map itself to determine how much of the revenue from the import tax is spent on B's Machinery and how much on A's Wheat. A. P. Lerner in his article on 'The Symmetry between Import and Export Taxes', *Economica*, vol. 3 (1936), pp. 306–313, has shown the crucial importance of determining this point.

A exchange depreciation will always be better than import restriction by B, since Q_{ed} and Q_{itb} both lie on A's offer curve and β is a better price than α' for A. The point Q_{itb} may be better for B than the point Q_{ed}. This is bound to be so if A's demand for imports has an elasticity less than unity; for in this case Q_{itb} will lie both South and East of Q_{ed}, so that B will get more Machinery and more Wheat than at Q_{ed}. But if A's elasticity of demand for imports is greater than unity Q_{itb} will lie South and West of Q_{ed}. B will have more Machinery but less Wheat than at Q_{ed}. In Figure V B's indifference curve which passes through Q_{ed} is shown as I_b. It cuts the price line α' at D. If A's demand is so elastic that Q_{itb} lies to the West of D then B as well as A would be better off at Q_{ed} than at Q_{itb}.[3]

Figure VI shows how an import subsidy in the surplus country A would close the balance-of-trade gap. Country B now has a domestic expenditure just equal to its national income, BO; for it has now no 'Marshall Aid' (i.e. no excess of imports) nor any revenue from imports to supplement its national income. Since A's prices and the rate of exchange are unchanged, B moves up the price line α' from O until it reaches Q_{isa} which is the point on its expenditure and offer curves. But through Q_{isa} there is an A indifference curve which, since Q_{isa} lies East of KK, has a steeper slope than α'. Draw the price line γ through Q_{isa} tangential to A's indifference curve at that point. Then A has a national income at factor cost of AO from which must be deducted the proportionate income tax OT which she levies to pay the subsidy on her imports of Machinery. Her consumers have then the limited purchasing power AT to spend, but enjoy the very favourable subsidised price for imports corresponding to the line γ. They move up this line γ from T till they also reach the point Q_{isa} at which the line γ is tangential to the highest possible A indifference curve. For the imports of Machinery CQ_{isa}, consumers in A pay TC in the subsidised price and the government of A pays OT in subsidy on its imports, so that the suppliers in B get OC.

Now if one compares Q_{isa} with Q_{ed} it is clear that B is better off at Q_{isa} since both points are on her offer curve (O_b) but Q_{isa} is at the more favourable price. A is, however, invariably worse off at Q_{isa} than at Q_{ed}, since Q_{ed} which lies on β must be to the South-East of A's indifference curve I_a which passes through Q_{ed} and is a tangent to β; and α' is always South-East of β.

Let us turn now to the possibility that country B should remove the deficit on her balance of trade by subsidising or taxing her exports. It is clear that if A's demand for imports is sufficiently elastic an export subsidy by B without any change in the rate of exchange should remove B's deficit because the consequential reduction in the price of B's products in A's market will increase the value of A's expenditure on B's products. Simultaneously, the raising of the tax revenue in B to finance the subsidy will cause consumers in B to cut down their purchases of imports (as well as of home-produced products) and this will also help to close the gap in the balance of trade.

[3] Q_{itb}, like all the 'commercial policy' points but unlike Q_{ma} and Q_{ed}, both of which are on the contract curve, is in any case an 'inefficient' solution in the sense that another solution

This outcome is illustrated in Figure VII. The new position of equilibrium will be at Q_{esb} where A's offer curve cuts B's expenditure curve. The proof of this is as follows. Through Q_{esb} draw the price line α' which is tangential to the B indifference curve passing through Q_{esb} and let this line cut BO at U. Now BO is B's national income; and OU represents the amount of this income which is raised by the government of B in a proportionate income tax to finance the export subsidy. Consumers in B have BU to spend and they can buy imports at the old rate of exchange (slope of α' = slope of α because both Q_{ma} and Q_{esb} lie on E_b). They proceed from U up the price line α' to their highest indifference curve at Q_{esb}. Now through Q_{esb} there passes also an A indifference curve the tangent to which (the line γ) passes through the origin O because Q_{esb} lies on A's offer curve (O_a). The price line γ represents the amount of B's Machinery which A can obtain per unit of her own Wheat after allowing for the subsidy by B to the price of Machinery. In exchange for CQ_{esb} of her Wheat A obtains CU of B's Machinery at the unsubsidised price of Machinery but CO at the subsidised price. And at the price of Machinery of CQ_{esb}/CO (i.e. the slope of γ) A is also in equilibrium at Q_{esb}.

If we compare Q_{ed} with Q_{esb} A is certainly better off at Q_{esb} because both points lie on A's offer curve (O_a) but Q_{esb} is at the more favourable price (γ as compared with β). B is certainly worse off at Q_{esb} because the B indifference curve (I_b) which passes through Q_{ed} lies to the South-East of the line β whereas Q_{esb} being on γ lies to the North-West of β.

If A's demand for imports is inelastic, then an export subsidy in B cannot remove B's deficit, because the value of B's exports will fall instead of rising as their price in A's market declines. If, however, A's demand were sufficiently inelastic then an export duty in B might put B's balance of trade right, because at the higher price of imports A would spend a greater total amount on them.[4] The inelasticity of A's demand must, however, be sufficient to offset the fact that as B obtains a revenue from the export tax her consumers will be able to spend not only B's national income but also the proceeds of the export duty, so that B's demand for A's goods at the unchanged exchange rate will rise somewhat.

This possibility is illustrated in Figure VIII where O_a cuts E_b below Q_{ma} at Q_{etb}. The proof is similar to that given in the immediately preceding case and will not be repeated here. It must serve merely to indicate what the various points signify. BO is again B's national income; but consumers in B have available to spend not only BO but also OV, the proceeds of the export duty. This they spend at the unchanged rate of exchange (α' parallel to α) on the price line α', settling at the point at which α' cuts E_b. Consumers in A have only their national income OA to

(e.g., a combination of 'Marshall Aid' and exchange depreciation) could be found at a point on the contract curve at which both A and B were better off than at Q_{itb}.

4 It is quite possible that no solution to the balance-of-trade problem is possible by means of any subsidy or tax on B's exports. An inspection of Figures IV(a) and (b) will show that if A's elasticity of demand for imports is about unity, O_a may never cut E_b. This is particularly likely if, as it is often drawn, O_a curves back towards O below Q_{itb} and towards the axis BO above Q_{ed}.

spend; but they must buy imports at the taxed price corresponding to the price line γ. They purchase CQ_{etb} of B's Machinery and pay for it CV' to meet the untaxed price of this amount of B's products and OV' (the Wheat value of OV) to pay the export tax in B.

Q_{etb} is clearly better than Q_{ed} for B but worse for A, since it lies both to the South and the East of Q_{ed}.

An export duty in A would remove the surplus on A's balance of trade if B's demand for A imports were sufficiently elastic (Figure IX); and an export subsidy in A would remove the surplus on A's balance of trade if B's demand for imports were sufficiently inelastic (Figure X). But it is clear from an inspection of Figures IV(a) and IV(b) that, if B's demand for imports is sufficiently close to unity, O_b and E_a may never meet and no tax or subsidy on A's exports might be effective in closing the balance-of-trade gap.

The explanation of Figures IX and X runs on lines similar to those of Figures VII and VIII. Here a very brief description must suffice.

In Figure IX country A has her national income (AO) plus the proceeds of her export tax (OW) to spend on her own goods or on imports at the same rate of exchange (α' parallel to α). She moves from W up the price line α' to Q_{eta} which is on E_a and where she, therefore, reaches her highest indifference curve. B has simply her national income BO to spend at a price of imports which, including the export duty in A, corresponds to γ. For the amount of Wheat CQ_{eta}, B pays an untaxed price of CW' plus a tax of $W'O$. For B Q_{eta} is worse than Q_{ed}, because both points lie on B's offer curve with Q_{eta} at the less favourable price. In Figure IX Q_{eta} is better than Q_{ed} for A because it lies on a higher A indifference curve. But this outcome is not absolutely necessary. Inspection of Figure IV(a) suggests that if B's elasticity of demand for imports became sufficiently large as B's imports diminished (i.e. O_b moved sufficiently rapidly Southwards as one moved from Q_{ed} Westwards along O_b) and if A's marginal propensity to import were sufficiently small (i.e. E_a rose sufficiently slowly Northwards as one moved Westwards along E_a from Q_{ma}) the point Q_{eta} might lie on a lower A indifference curve than the point Q_{ed}.

In Figure X country A pays an export subsidy. Her consumers have, therefore, only her national income less the revenue which has to be raised to finance the export subsidy (i.e. AO minus $OX' = X'A$) to spend on her own or imported products. She starts from X' and moves along the price line α' to the point (Q_{esa}) where α' cuts E_a, since the price ratio for her has not changed (i.e., α' parallel to α). B has neither more nor less than her national income BO to spend, and she can dispose of it along the price line γ which corresponds to the subsidised price of A's exports. She moves along γ until this line cuts her offer curve at Q_{esa}. She purchases CQ_{esa} of A's exports and pays for them a net price of CO, made up of an unsubsidised price of CX less the subsidy of OX in terms of her own currency (OX' in terms of A's currency). The point Q_{esa} must be South and East of Q_{ed} because, since B's demand must be inelastic, O_b slopes South East from Q_{ed}. Q_{esa} must, therefore, be better than Q_{ed} for B and worse than Q_{ed} for A.

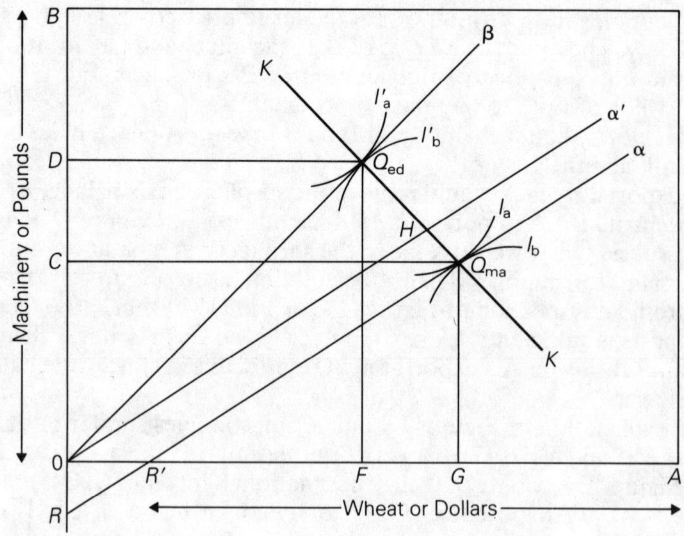
B
β
K
I'_a
I'_b
α'
D
Q_{ed}
α
Machinery or Pounds
H
I_a
C
I_b
Q_{ma}
K
0
R'
F
G
A
R
Wheat or Dollars

Fig. I

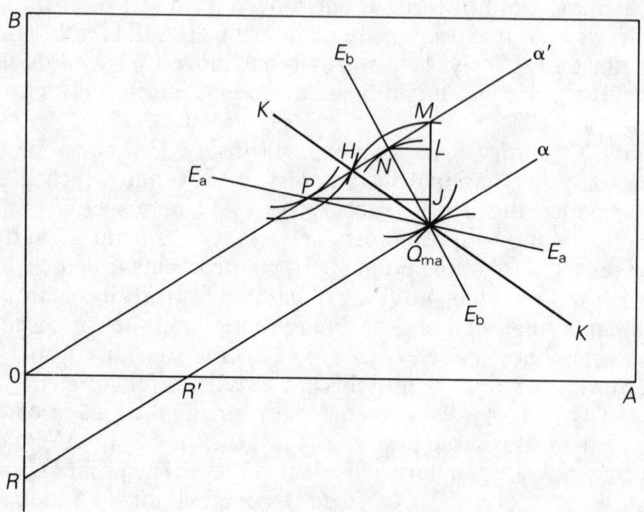
B
E_b
α'
K
M
H
L
N
α
E_a
P
J
Q_{ma}
E_a
E_b
K
0
R'
A
R

Fig. II

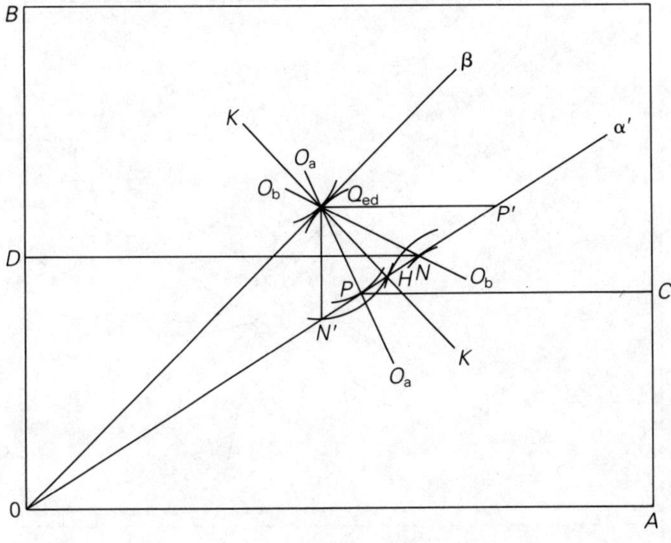

Fig. III

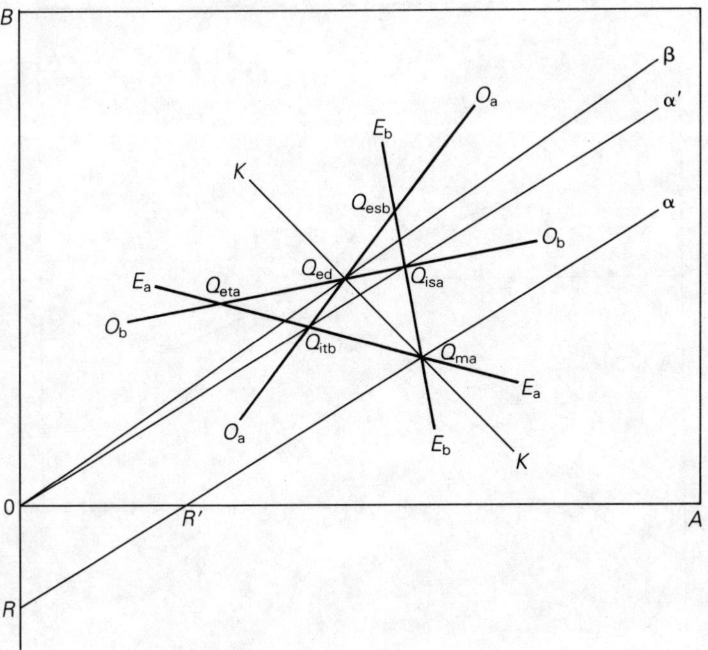

Fig. IV (*a*)

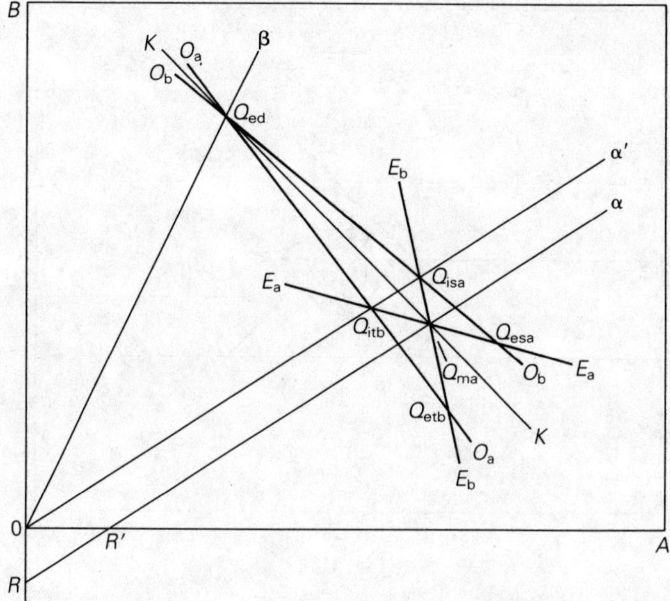

Fig. IV (*b*)

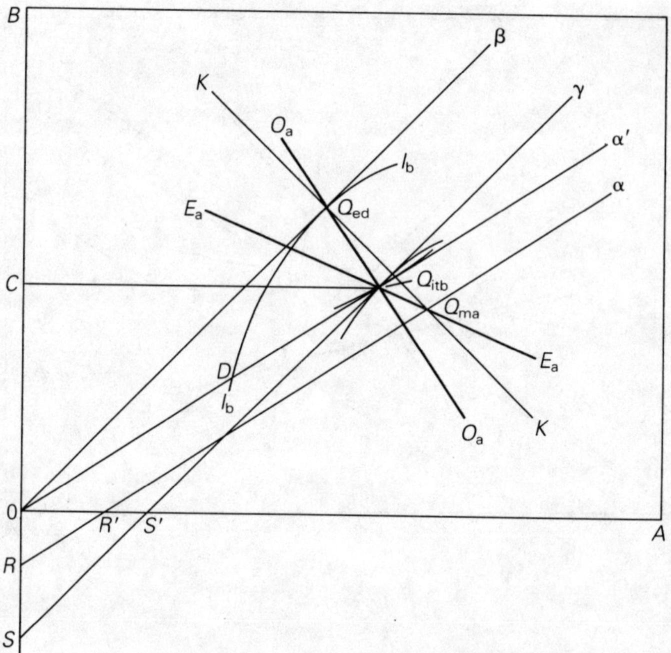

Fig. V Import Tax in B

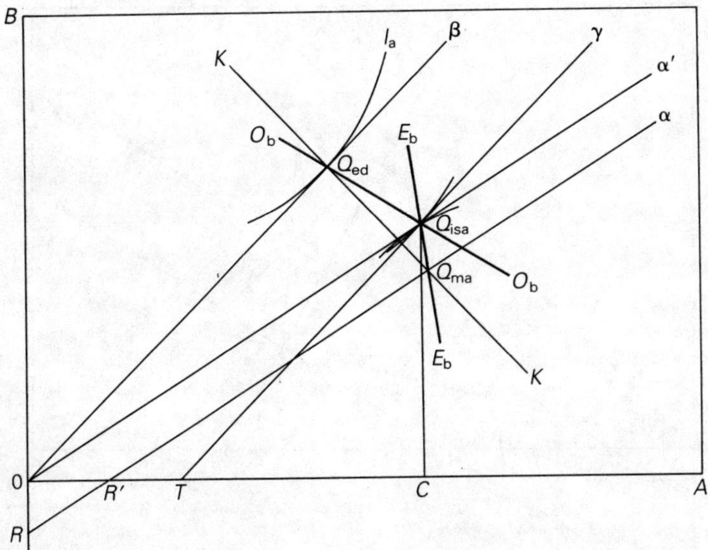

Fig. VI Import Subsidy in A

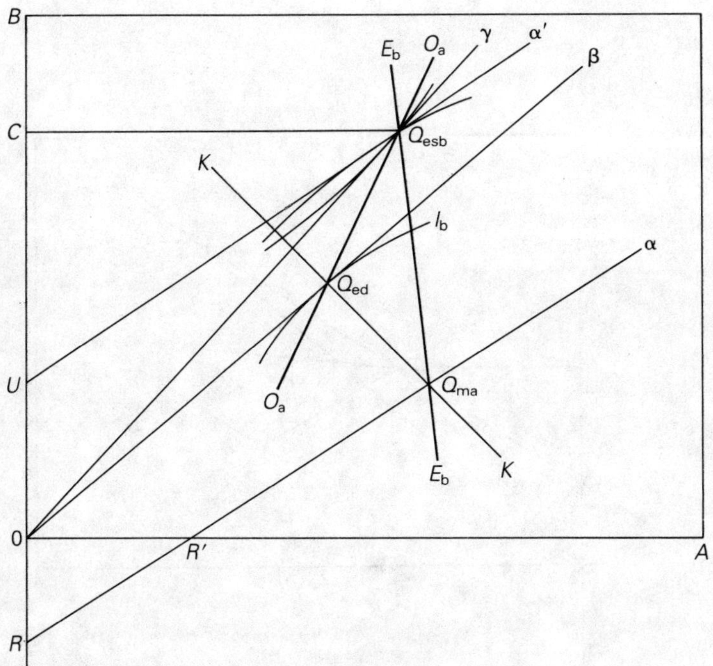

Fig. VII Export Subsidy in B

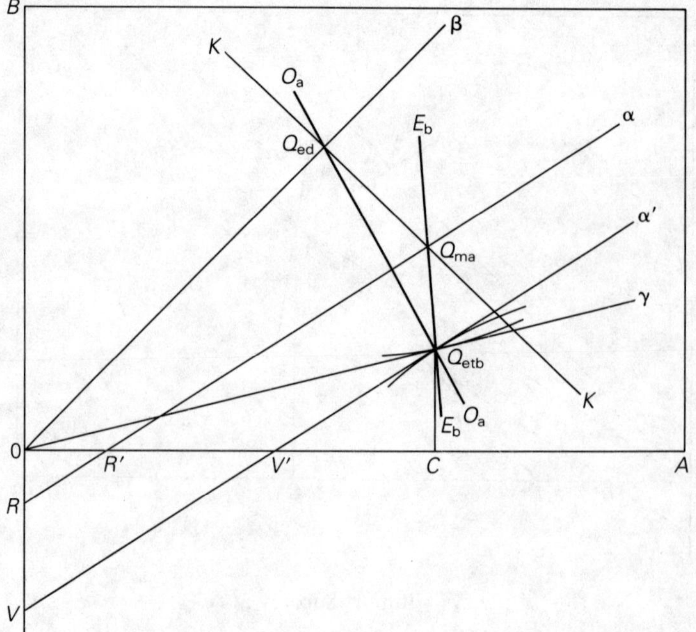

Fig. VIII Export Tax in B

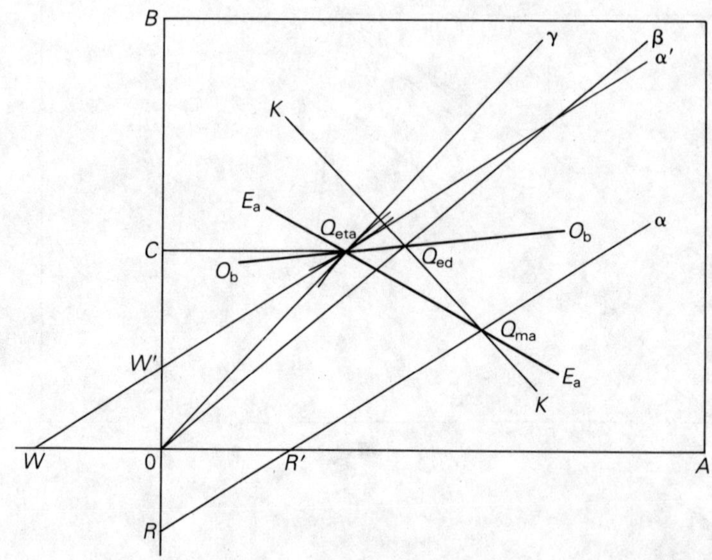

Fig. IX Export Tax in A

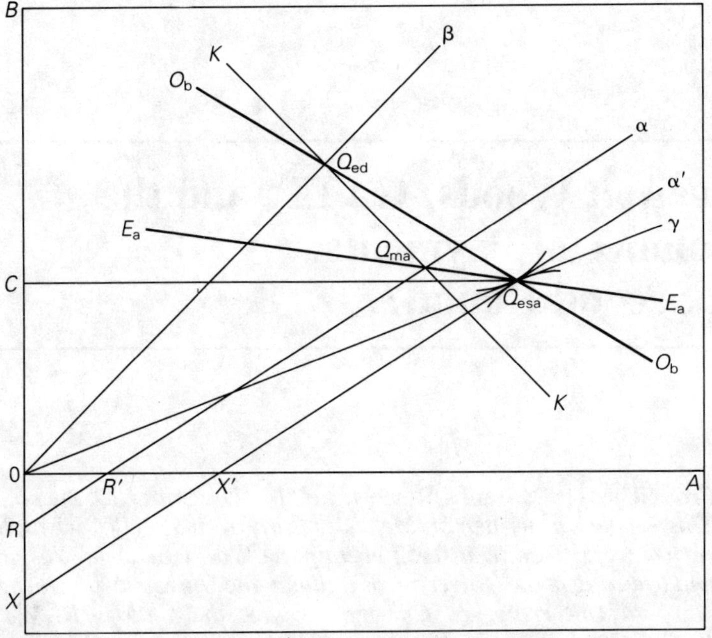

Fig. X Export Subsidy in A

148-60

[1952]

9

Bretton Woods, GATT, and the Balance of Payments: A Second Round?

U.K.
4220
A313

From The Three Banks Review, *no. 16 (December 1952), pp. 3–22. This article was written on Meade's return from the USA where he had spent several months in 1952 visiting the World Bank in Washington, and lecturing at the University of Indiana, the University of Chicago and Harvard University. At Chicago he gave the Charles R. Walgreen Foundation lectures on* Problems of Economic Union *(Chicago: University of Chicago Press; London: Allen & Unwin, 1953).*

1 *Reasons for a Second Round*

After the Second World War an attempt was made to devise a general set of principles to govern international trade and payments in such a way as to maintain equilibrium in the balance of payments in domestic conditions of full employment and in an international atmosphere of relatively free trade. This attempted settlement was particularly associated with the International Monetary Fund, the International Bank for Reconstruction and Development, the Anglo-American Loan Agreement, and the General Agreement on Tariffs and Trade. There are a number of reasons why the next year or two may present an opportune time for an attempt to reconsider and renegotiate some of the general principles involved.

First, the United Kingdom has got into the habit of having a balance-of-payments crisis every odd year – the convertibility crisis in 1947, the devaluation crisis in 1949, and the crisis of 1951. The idea that there would be a transitional post-war period of strain followed by a reasonable equilibrium has worn pretty thin. There is considerable disappointment and disillusionment both in London and in Washington over these recurrent crises. The atmosphere on both sides of the Atlantic is thus suitable for a reconsideration of the whole sterling–dollar problem.

Second, there is the change in the United States administration. It is much too early to say how far the internationalist outlook of Mr Eisenhower will prevail over the isolationist elements in the Republican

Party. We can only wait and see. But we can be sure that the new administration will want to do something different from the old and this *may* present a new opportunity. In any case, the United States Trade Agreements Act under which all the commercial policy concessions given by the United States under the General Agreement on Tariffs and Trade have been negotiated comes up for renewal by Congress in 1953. To this extent the new administration must formulate its ideas on commercial policy in the near future.

Third, natural disappointment with the recurrent balance-of-payments crises tends, on both sides of the Atlantic, to obscure the fact that the United Kingdom is now in a much stronger basic economic position than it was at the time of the Round 1 economic settlement (1944–46). The balance-of-payments crisis of 1951 appeared as serious as those of 1947 and 1949. But it should be remembered that we were struggling to achieve a balance which included the use of the Anglo-American Loan in 1947 and of Marshall Aid in 1949. But in 1951 there was no loan or Marshall Aid; we were really concerned with standing on our own feet. The following figures suffice to show the underlying change:

	Pre-War	*1946*	*1951*
UK Industrial Production	100 (1935)	102	145
UK Volume of Exports	100 (1938)	99	182

An important part of our necessary structural adjustment has already been achieved. We ought now to be able to talk more sensibly about a 'normal' system.

Fourth, there are now two new problems of first-rate importance which ought to be brought into any general international settlement and which were not on the agenda in Round 1. I refer to the problems of the joint defence effort under NATO and the problems of the finance of the economic development of underdeveloped territories, which are discussed below.

Some arguments for caution in the approach to a new settlement will be considered at the end of this article. Meanwhile, the following paragraphs present a list of the main principles which, in my opinion, should be observed if an attempt is made in the near future to negotiate a basically new settlement.

2 *Domestic Economic Policies and the Balance of Payments*

Experience between 1945 and 1952 should have taught us all that it is quite impossible to divorce domestic monetary and fiscal problems from the balance of payments. But the Articles of Agreement of the International Monetary Fund and the Articles of the General Agreement on Tariffs and Trade are both at pains to emphasise the independence of national governments in their choice of domestic financial and economic policies. I do not for one minute wish to suggest that a country with a deficit on its balance of payments should be obliged to undertake an absolute deflation domestically, nor a country in surplus to undertake an absolute inflation domestically. But there ought to be a quite clear international obligation on the part of deficit countries to prevent a general domestic inflation (which will keep goods off the export markets and swell the demand for imports without being necessary for the maintenance of employment at home) and on the part of surplus countries to prevent a general domestic deflation (which will contract the international markets of the deficit countries without being necessary for the avoidance of the domestic evils of domestic inflation).

It is a matter for negotiation how far each national Government should be free to decide for itself whether it is fulfilling this obligation, or how far some international body should be empowered to pass judgement and even to sanction the obligation. Personally, being an unrepentant internationalist, I should like to see the international supervision of this obligation go a considerable way – provided that the other principles mentioned in this article are also accepted.

It can, of course, be persuasively argued that the avoidance of domestic booms and slumps is not an appropriate subject for international obligations. Lord Keynes once put it this way. 'You can legislate against sin but not against stupidity. Do you really believe that the Americans want to indulge in a depression?' But in fact an organised international forum in which the financial policies of the deficit countries could be legitimately criticised on the grounds that they are inflationary and those of the surplus countries on the grounds that they are deflationary could be very useful. In Round 1 the United Kingdom, backed by many other countries and in particular by Australia, pressed one side of this case, namely, the duty of the surplus country (i.e. the United States) to prevent deflation and to maintain full employment. The Americans made the wrong reply. They half admitted the obligation, but tried to whittle it all away. They ought to have replied: 'What a good idea. Certainly we accept an obligation on the part of surplus countries to avoid depression and unemployment. Naturally in return deficit countries must undertake an obligation to avoid inflation. In our Employment Act of 1946 we have legislated on our side of such an obligation. What equally convincing evidence can you give us that you will really strive to prevent inflationary pressures so long as you have a deficit?' This might have ended in a really desirable mutual obligation of the kind suggested above.

Since 1945 the problem of maintaining full employment has been the subject of much thought – some of which, in the deficit countries at least, would have been better spent on the problem of preventing inflation from perpetuating the deficit in the balance of payments. The emphasis is beginning to change both in domestic policies and in international discussion. Anti-inflationary policies are increasingly the subject of official thought and discussion. Let us hope that the atmosphere of discussion is not changing too much and too late. There are now in this and many other countries perhaps the first signs since 1945 of some real relaxation of inflationary pressures. The spectacle of the new United

States administration during the first months of the Second Great Depression of 1955–60 boasting of its successful anti-inflationary policy would be even more distressing than that of a Government on this side of the Atlantic boasting of its successful policies for full employment during the Great Inflation of 1945–50. How much more flexible and well-timed our stabilisation policies might be if there were a clearly formulated reciprocal international obligation for the avoidance of domestic inflations by deficit countries and of domestic deflations by surplus countries.

3 Import Restrictions and Variable Exchange Rates

The second fundamental intellectual muddle in the Round-1 settlement was the failure to realise that in the modern world it is impossible to restore free convertibility of currencies except in a system of variable foreign exchange rates. There are, after all, only four possible systems for looking after the balance of payments:

(i) The first set of principles is that of the *Gold Standard*, namely, that a deficit country should deflate so long as it is in deficit and that a surplus country should inflate so long as it is in surplus. None of us now works on this principle. The Americans do not say: 'We are in surplus on our balance of payments, therefore we must engineer a domestic inflation.' They say: 'We are threatened by a domestic inflation. How shall we prevent it?' Nor do we in the United Kingdom say: 'We have a deficit, therefore we must go on deflating till the deficit is removed even if that implies a 10 per cent level of unemployment.' It is one thing to say, as is argued above, that the surplus country should avoid a domestic deflation and the deficit country a domestic inflation. It is quite another thing to say that, if this is not sufficient to restore external balance, the surplus country should proceed to engineer an absolute domestic inflation and the deficit country an absolute domestic deflation. This latter set of principles is happily dead and buried and will not be resurrected.

(ii) The second possibility is to accept a continuing disequilibrium and for the surplus countries perpetually to provide the *Accommodating Finance* necessary to cover the deficits of the deficit countries. I personally would strongly support the continuing payment of sums into a common defence pool on the principle of a fair sharing of a common burden and the payment of continuing grants-in-aid by rich developed countries for the economic development of poor undeveloped areas. But it is quite another matter for a country because it has a surplus on its balance of payments to make a grant to cover the deficits of the countries which happen to be importing more than they are exporting. The deficit country is not necessarily poor, underdeveloped, or bearing an undue share of some joint international burden. It may simply suffer from inappropriate fiscal, exchange-rate, and commercial policies at home and abroad. The principle of perpetual hand-outs from surplus to deficit countries, as such, will never be accepted and I, for one, do not regret it.

(iii) A third possibility is for the deficit countries by *Quantitative Import Licensing and Exchange Controls* to restrict their payments to match their receipts of foreign currencies. This is the present procedure which the world has inadvertently adopted as its normal and orthodox balancing mechanism. Moreover, it is gradually being realised that if quantitative restrictions on trade and payments are going to be used as the main instrument for equilibration of international payments they must be discriminatory. The deficit countries must restrict imports from the surplus countries and not merely hand their deficits on to each other by economising foreign exchange at each other's expense. These restrictions and discriminations have the grave disadvantage of interfering with that freedom of commerce which will enable each country to concentrate on the production of the things which it is comparatively best fitted to produce. This I recognise to be a shamefully old-fashioned sentiment. But that is not a conclusive proof that it is untrue. In the long run a wide adoption of the free-trade principle is of essential importance for the United Kingdom whose whole economic life rests upon exporting manufactures in order to earn the means of paying for essential imports of foodstuffs and raw materials. We should, accordingly, attempt to find a solution which is compatible with the removal of import restrictions and with the convertibility of currencies on current account. The removal of controls over capital movements is another matter; and it is not the purpose of this article to suggest that it should be an objective of the next Round of discussions.

(iv) There remains only the method of *Variations in Exchange Rates*, whereby the currencies of the deficit countries would be depreciated in terms of the currencies of the surplus countries, thus enabling the deficit countries to undercut the products of the surplus countries. Such a system could take either of two forms: the fixing of parities between the various currencies as at present under the rules of the International Monetary Fund with the recognition, however, that frequent and substantial alterations of these parities was a normal part of the mechanism of international balance; or the complete freeing of exchange rates in a free exchange market combined, probably, with some steadying of the market through official stabilisation funds. The choice between these two methods raises some most important questions. But I do not intend to discuss them in this article, which is concerned only with the more basic choice between exchange-rate variations and import restrictions.

If the above argument is correct it is impossible to get rid of import restrictions or to make sterling convertible in any real sense except in conditions in which variations in exchange rates have become a principal instrument of equilibration.

But it by no means follows that the adoption of a system of variable exchange rates will alone suffice to justify convertibility. The purpose of a depreciation of the exchange rate of a deficit country is so to expand its exports (by lowering their price in foreign currencies) and to decrease its imports (by raising their price in its own currency), as to improve its balance of trade. But there are at least two reasons why this may not happen.

In the first place, if there is an uncontrolled inflationary situation in the deficit country and the depreciation of its currency is regarded as an alternative to domestic measures for the control of inflation, then money prices, costs and incomes may continue so to rise in the deficit country that its exports are not in fact cheapened in terms of foreign currencies and its demand for imports is not in fact restrained by the higher price of imports. There is even a danger that the rise in the price of imports might set off a domestic round of inflation of money wages, which would necessitate a further depreciation, which would stimulate a further dose of inflation, and so on until the domestic currency had lost all value. Corresponding dangers exist in the surplus country, where the deflationary effects of the appreciation of its currency might be allowed to intensify a domestic recession which would cause a reduction in its demand for imports and would cheapen its own exports. A system of variable exchange rates can work only if it is combined with effective domestic measures for the avoidance of inflations in deficit countries and of deflations in surplus countries.

But, secondly, even if all national economies were stabilised domestically, the exchange-rate depreciation of a deficit country would make its deficit worse, and not better, if the price changes caused by the exchange-rate variation led to only a small expansion of its exports and reduction of its imports. If a reduction in the foreign-currency price of British exports leads to only a small increase in the amount sold abroad, we should collect less foreign currency than before; and if at the same time a rise in the sterling price of our imports leads to only a small fall in the amount imported, the loss of foreign currency on our exports might outweigh the saving of foreign currency on our imports. Only if flows of trade can be made reasonably sensitive to changes in prices, could we abandon import-restriction-plus-fixed-exchange-rates for convertibility-plus-variable-exchange-rates, although if the change could be successfully made the greater freedom of trade all round the world would be greatly to our long-run interest.

A high sensitivity of trade flows to price changes depends upon three conditions, and it is the establishment of these three conditions which we in the United Kingdom should make a major objective in any Round-2 discussions.

(i) The first condition is that the price and cost changes due to exchange-rate variations should be given time to work out their effects. If sterling is depreciated and this enables British motor-cycles to undercut American motor-cycles, the immediate increase in sales of British motor-cycles may not be enormous. But when the British manufacturers have been given time to build up their selling organisations and the American firms have been given time to contract, a much larger expansion of the market will follow.

(ii) The second condition is that commercial policies should be such as to enable the changes in prices due to exchange-rate variations to have their full effect. Imports of British motor-cycles into the United States must be allowed eventually to replace the home-produced American product in the American market, if the underlying comparative costs make that appropriate.

(iii) The third condition is that all major international monetary transfers should be untied so that, for example, dollars paid out by the United States for economic development in Brazil can be used for the purchase of British hydro-electric plant, if the sterling–dollar exchange rate makes the British product the cheaper.

In the following four sections something will be said about the items which should be put upon the agenda of the Round-2 talks in order to establish these three conditions.

4 International Liquidity

Since an exchange depreciation might not immediately lead to a sufficiently large shift in the channels of trade and might develop its beneficial effects upon the balance of trade only over a considerable period of time, deficit countries could make the leap in the dark from import restrictions to exchange-rate variations only if they were assured of sufficient foreign-exchange reserves to tide over any intermediate periods of continuing excess of imports over exports. This is the basic reason for the need for greater international monetary reserves if a new start is to be made. But there are two other reasons for holding the view that the present reserves of the Sterling Area are not anything like sufficient for the adoption of the principles proposed in this article.

First, the experience of 1949 shows how large an effect even a moderate recession in the United States may have in reducing the supply of dollars to other countries. If the policy of freedom from exchange controls on current transactions and from import restrictions is to be maintained during periods in which the United States administration is coping with the problem of preventing a domestic recession from developing into a slump, a large buffer of foreign-exchange reserves will be required by the outside world. It is, of course, a matter for negotiation whether this need should be met by an increase in general reserves or by the provision of special finance in the event of a recession in a surplus country.

Second, any final settlement must take account of the problem of the sterling balances (see pages 158–9). Any settlement which involved the removal of exchange controls and import restrictions by the other countries of the Sterling Area would mean that the United Kingdom's final reserves of gold and dollars would have to be greatly enlarged.

To wait until the United Kingdom by direct controls, austerity at home and so on, has so improved its external position as not merely to have balanced its external accounts but to have accumulated a sufficient increase in its external reserves to justify the changes proposed in this article, would be to put the new settlement off to the Greek Kalends.

One part of the new settlement would have to be a very substantial increase in international liquidity.

Many possible methods suggest themselves: a stabilisation grant or loan by the United States; the use of much enlarged quotas under a revised and revivified International Monetary Fund; an all-round rise in the price of gold; the formation of some instrument in the United States, such as a United States exchange equalisation fund, whereby in co-operation with the British and other exchange equalisation funds desirable temporary support can be given to currencies which are under exceptionally heavy temporary pressure.

5 Commercial Policy

A second way in which variations in the channels of trade can be made responsive to variations in relative prices and costs is by the removal of trade barriers particularly in the surplus countries. The United States tariff is now perhaps as low as ever in its history. Due credit is not always given to the United States administration for the extent to which the average rate of duty levied on dutiable imports has fallen, as a result of its Trade Agreements programme and of the general rise in prices which has greatly reduced the *ad valorem* incidence of the specific element in many duties. Nevertheless, much remains to be done.

(i) The United States administration should obtain powers to go as far as the elimination of those duties (e.g. on British woollens) which really do still greatly impede trade. Some part of the statistical reduction in the United States tariff has undoubtedly been due to cutting out the unimportant, because unnecessary, parts of the tariff system.

(ii) Perhaps more important is the elimination from the General Agreement on Tariffs and Trade of the escape clause which enables a government to remove a concession if as a result of it imports come in in such amounts as seriously to injure the domestic industry. If the industry is in fact uneconomic, it ought to be injured and even eliminated by imports. It is a serious deterrent to potential exporters of the United States to know that the United States administration, however enlightened in its approach may be, is actually required by Congressional legislation to remove a concession if by their selling efforts the foreign exporters do really effectively cut into an American market.

(iii) The simplification of the United States customs procedure is another way in which an important contribution might be made to the elasticity of the United States demand for imports. Legislation on this matter has been bogged down in Congress.

(iv) The removal of subsidies on United States shipping and shipbuilding and of regulations which require that parts of United States trade should be carried in United States ships would free to price-and-cost competition another important market in which the

United States would often find itself at a serious comparative disadvantage.

Such are the main demands which we should make in commercial policy. But there is one case in which the United States has itself made demands, the granting of which would, in fact, be to our own long-term advantage. I refer to action to prevent international cartels from dividing up international markets, fixing prices and so on. Such cartels rigidify international trade and make elasticities of demand smaller, because they prevent a change in relative prices from leading to an easy change in the direction of trade. I will not discuss whether it is wise in negotiations with the United States to scream with pain as they extract our false teeth, as Lord Keynes once put it. But however much we may scream over this one, it remains a false tooth.

6 The Finance of NATO Rearmament

One of the most important new developments that has occurred since the immediate post-war attempt at building an international economic system is the idea that the free countries of the world should work out a common policy for defence and a common programme for its finance and execution. The economic principles of this joint effort need to be integrated into the general economic settlement. There are two ways in which they might make a most important contribution to the solution of the problem of international economic equilibrium.

First, one of the main reasons often given, and sometimes a valid reason, for national protection is the defence argument. The protection of United States shipping and shipbuilding is a good instance. No one who lived in the United Kingdom between 1939 and 1945 will belittle the military importance of a large Atlantic shipping fleet. But if NATO could develop an effective system whereby it was really guaranteed that in case of war all NATO shipping – Norwegian, Greek, French, British and American – would be operated jointly in a common pool, there would be no defence argument for the protection of United States shipping, though some argument might still remain for the protection of United States shipbuilding. NATO should be developed in such a way as to remove every avoidable reason for national protection on defence grounds and to ensure that the grounds which it could not remove were not misused for purely protective purposes.

Second, an efficient and equitable system of defence requires that the rich pay taxes which are used to purchase weapons in the cheapest market to be used by troops in the most threatened positions. In 1940 the citizens of London were taxed to purchase weapons made in Birmingham for Scottish troops to use in the defence of Kent. If this principle could be truly applied in our joint defence arrangements, a great new flexibility would be introduced into the balance of payments. If a depreciation of the pound made British uniforms or guns cheaper than similar American products and if this in due course could lead to a shift of purchases of such articles for the American, French and British armies away from American on to British products, the efficacy of exchange-rate adjustments would be greatly enhanced. The development of NATO so that certainly all foreign military aid and, one would hope, a large part of the national funds used to equip national armies were – with due regard to the security aspects of the location of the industries concerned – spent in the cheapest market would add to the efficiency of the defence arrangements. It would purchase more defence per dollar. But it would also help greatly to make adjustments of balances of payments more responsive to price changes. In other words, money payments into, and drawings from the joint defence budget – what we now call Military Aid – should not be calculated directly with reference to gaps in balances of payments. They should be determined on the principle of a fair sharing between rich and poor countries of the common defence burden. The balance-of-payments problem should be met by allowing variations in exchange rates to determine, among other flows of trade, the markets in which it was cheapest to purchase the physical military supplies out of the given national financial contributions.

7 *The Finance of Economic Development*

Another set of ideas which might play a much more important role in Round 2 than they did in Round 1 is the organised economic development of underdeveloped countries by joint plans in which both the developed and underdeveloped countries participate. There is probably no other field of international economic policy in which more could be done by bold constructive action both to increase economic welfare (by the relief of stark poverty) and to consolidate the free way of life (by demonstrating that the free world can effectively cope with such problems). If it is tackled in this spirit, this joint endeavour, after preliminary stages of blueprinting and training, would eventually involve the transfer of very large sums by way of grant, loan or direct investment from the developed to the underdeveloped countries.

Arranged in one way this might merely put yet one more strain on the balances of payments of deficit countries. Arranged in another way – and a way which would also enable more economic welfare to be purchased by each dollar spent on economic development – it might in two respects considerably alleviate the balance-of-payments problems of countries like the United Kingdom.

First, just as in the case of a joint defence programme, the principle of not tying the finance to the products of any particular country would be of great assistance. Thus if the United States is the country rich in capital, if Britain – at equilibrium rates of exchange – has the comparative advantage in producing steam locomotives, and if Ruritania is the country which most needs such railway equipment, the most economic arrangement is for capital from the United States to be spent on British locomotives for use by the Ruritanian railways. You get more economic development per dollar that way. And this principle of untied finance will, of course, enable deficit countries by exchange depreciation to compete for the orders for the capital equipment regardless of the source of the finance or of the country in which the goods are to be used.

Second, it is important to ensure that the funds are spent on the most economic lines of development. More welfare per dollar spent on development is, of course, achieved that way. But this will also help to ease balance-of-payments adjustments. If, for example, a depreciation of the United Kingdom's exchange rate should lower the price of United Kingdom manufactured exports relatively to the price of United Kingdom imports of primary products, this would make it relatively more profitable in other parts of the world to develop the production of raw materials and foodstuffs rather than of manufactured goods. In development programmes, in the process of the continuous review which will in any case be necessary, due attention should be paid to the relative emphasis on industrial and on agricultural development, as shifts in the terms of trade make the one or the other the more profitable line.

8 Regional Arrangements

Such are the principles which might be adopted to put new life into the building of a more or less universal system for international economic relations in the free world. The formation of purely regional arrangements is always a second best, particularly for the United Kingdom which for the reasons given above has a special long-run interest in the widest system of free multilateral trade. But this is not to say that regional arrangements – such as the partial liberalisation of intra-European trade from import restrictions under the Organisation for European Economic Co-operation, the freeing of the Continental European market for coal and steel through the Schuman Plan, the multilateral clearing of European and Sterling Area payments through the European Payments Union, and the maintenance of freedom of payments from exchange control within the Sterling Area – may not be better than nothing. This note simply does not deal with them. It is an attempt to consider the main items which would be on the agenda for any second attempt to establish a more universal system. But even so one negative point can be made. These regional arrangements need not be scrapped simply because a more universal attempt is made. They will, however, become less important if the universal solution succeeds. Thus if all trade were freed from import restrictions on balance-of-payments grounds the liberalisation programme of the Organisation for European Economic Co-operation would automatically lose its point.

A new settlement on these lines would, of course, raise fundamental questions for the future of the Sterling Area, of which the following would perhaps be the two most important. First, should there be some attempt to make the leap in the dark more possible for the United Kingdom by an agreed restriction of the rate at which the holders of existing sterling balances would make use of them, or should an attempt be made so to increase the general scale of the United Kingdom's reserves as to enable the existing sterling balances to be freely floated off? Second, should the principle of variable exchange rates be applied within the Sterling Area, for example, as between the Australian pound and the pound sterling, as a main means of maintaining equilibrium in the balances of payments of the individual members of the Sterling Area, or should we rely for the solution of balance-of-payments problems within the Sterling Area upon the principles of Accommodating Finance (variations in the size of the sterling balances) or of the Gold Standard (relative domestic inflation or deflation in the different parts of the Area)? These questions are too extensive to be discussed here. I can only indicate my own personal preference for a sufficient increase in general international liquidity to float off the existing balances and for the application of the principle of exchange-rate variations within the Sterling Area itself. All that can be asserted with assurance is that these two questions would be central items on the new agenda.

9 Conclusion

To summarise: any new attempt to build a more or less universal system for a freer international economy for the free world must be based on the following principles.

First, an obligation on the part of deficit countries to avoid inflationary pressures and on the part of surplus countries to avoid deflationary pressures at home.

Second, a serious shift of emphasis away from the use of import restrictions and exchange controls on to variations in exchange rates as the basic means of preserving equilibrium in balances of payments.

Third, the provision of a much larger fund of international liquidity to cushion temporary deficits in balances of payments while a depreciated exchange rate is allowed to have its effect in changing the channels of trade, or while a surplus country is coping with a domestic recession.

Fourth, a further reduction of import barriers, simplification of customs procedures, removal of commercial policy escape clauses, and removal of national quantitative regulations over shipping and other services, by all countries but more particularly by the surplus countries in return for the shift from import restrictions by the deficit countries.

Fifth, a development of NATO in such a way as to remove the need for, and to control the use of, protective devices on security grounds.

Sixth, a development of the principles of the joint responsibility for the military defence of the free world in such a way that, with due regard to military security, all supplies for the armed forces are purchased in the cheapest market.

Seventh, the application of the same principle to funds provided by developed countries for the economic development of underdeveloped countries, namely, that such funds should be untied and free to be spent on the purchase of the appropriate capital and other goods in the cheapest market.

Eighth, recognition of the principle that funds supplied for the economic development of undeveloped countries should be used for economic forms of development, that is to say for the development of sources of primary products when the terms of trade between primary products and manufactured products are such as to make this economic.

In my view, such is the long-run interest of the United Kingdom in the development of a free international market for goods and services that the type of world economic system outlined in this article should certainly constitute our ultimate objective. It is another question whether we should attempt to achieve it through an immediate brave new settlement or whether we would all be wise to hurry more slowly to our final goal through a series of more tentative and particular adjustments. A new settlement which promptly broke down would leave us further away than ever from our objective. And this might happen if the settlement were quickly followed by a serious American recession; or if trade flows were not made sufficiently responsive to price changes, so that any new fund of international reserves disappeared like the post-war Anglo-American loan; or if for similar reasons the dismantling of our import controls were allowed to cause such a sharp deterioration in our terms of trade as seriously to threaten domestic standards of living or the stability of money wages and prices. It cannot be too strongly emphasised that the various items in the proposals made in this article are not alternatives to each other.

This fact makes the present timing of negotiations a matter of vital importance. The Commonwealth economic conference (of November–December 1952) will have taken place by the time this article is published. It must not lead to a wholesale one-sided dismantling of our protective controls, though it is greatly to be desired that it will have resulted in proposals to start dismantling our controls as part of a bargain with the United States for further appropriate action by that great surplus country. The whole programme stands or falls together.

10

The Case for Variable Exchange Rates

From The Three Banks Review, *no. 27 (September 1955), pp. 3–27.*

I still hold the old-fashioned view that the freeing of world trade is in the interests of this country. We import essential raw materials and food-stuffs, which we cannot make for ourselves; and in return we export manufactured goods which other countries can more and more readily make for themselves. This is not to say that there are no valid exceptions to the free-trade rule. In the first place, there is some force in the 'infant-industry' argument; the underdeveloped countries have a good case for giving some special state help to the introduction of some new lines of activity into their economies. Secondly, while greater freedom of trade all round is undoubtedly to our interest, unilateral freedom of trade is not necessarily good for us; we might turn the terms of trade against us if we greatly increased our demand for the products of other countries without their liberating simultaneously their own demand for our goods. The moral of all this is simply that we should take our place once more as the leading country which is working for a negotiated all-round reduction of barriers to world trade and payments.

But how are we to make this compatible with the maintenance of full employment inside this country and of equilibrium in our balance of payments with other countries? It was on this rock that the ship of British free trade finally foundered in the early 1930s. We had returned to the gold standard and a fixed rate of exchange with other countries in 1925. When, with the Wall Street crash of 1929, a great deflation of incomes, prices, and costs started in the outside world, there were only two ways in which we could defend the fixed rate of exchange without a loss of all our reserves: the first was to deflate our own money expenditures and so prices, profits, and employment until our money demand for imports had fallen *pari passu* with the outside demand for our products, and the second was to restrict our demand for outside products by imposing tariffs or other direct barriers on our imports from outside. The old-fashioned liberals took the first line, implying that a temporary rise of unemployment figures well above the then ruling 10 per cent was worth the preservation of free trade, and the Keynesians argued for the abandonment of free trade as means to give us elbow room to fight the depression at home. With a few notable exceptions like Mr Hawtrey, no one made the point that the only way to combine a fight against depression at home with continued freedom of trade was to let the exchange rate go. And when in the autumn of 1931 we were finally driven off the gold standard, the free-trade policy was, alas, already dead.

The extreme depression of the 1930s is most unlikely to recur. There can be no reasonable doubt that all important countries, and not least the United States of America, would react with effective domestic measures of reflation against any heavy fall of demand and rise in unemployment domestically. We can count upon not being faced with so sharp, so great, and so prolonged a fall in the external demand for our products. But this does not mean that there is no longer any conflict between free trade and full employment. On the contrary. The reason why we can be sure that we shall not again have to face so great an external depression is simply that other countries in the future are going to use their domestic monetary and budgetary policies not exclusively, indeed not mainly, in order to maintain equilibrium in their external balances of payments, but in order to prevent internal inflations and deflations which are undesired on domestic grounds.

This will be true in particular of the United States. Her reserves are so great and the value of her external trade is so small relatively to her total domestic income and expenditure that she can, if she wants, largely ignore her balance of payments in deciding upon her domestic financial policy. And this in fact is what she is doing. The authorities in the United States do not argue (as they should in a free-trade fixed-exchange-rate world): 'We have a surplus on our balance of payments, therefore we must have cheap money, budget deficits, and inflation in order to increase our demand for imports.' In fact they argue: 'There is a threat of inflation in the domestic economy, therefore we must have dear money and budget surpluses', or 'There is a recession in our business activity, therefore we must reflate through cheap money and budget deficits'.

Let us greatly rejoice that this is so. Big fluctuations in activity in the United States would be the worst possible economic background for the progress and stability of the free world. But we must be clear about its implications for us and for other countries. If we were to choose a free-trade fixed-exchange-rate system, we should become the economic satellites of the United States in so far as our own domestic financial policies were concerned. Personally I think this would be an unfortunate development. But I need not argue that case now. The simple point is that it is not going to happen. For, consider what it means. Suppose that money incomes do not rise much in the United States but that productivity increases so that prices fall somewhat; suppose that we are going through a period of rather aggressive wage-raising activity on the part of the trade unions; and suppose at the same time that for technological reasons world demand is shifting a bit away from the sort of things which we are producing. Then to maintain fixed exchange rates and free trade our authorities would have to disinflate to an extent that might cause the level of unemployment in this country to rise from its 1 per cent to 2, 3, 4,

5 per cent. World developments which would require this degree of domestic disinflation are not at all unthinkable; and yet it is quite unthinkable that any government would disregard such a rise of unemployment. The policy of domestic disinflation would be abandoned, and either the exchange rate would be allowed to fluctuate or direct controls over imports or payments would be reimposed. Free trade and fixed exchange rates are incompatible in the modern world; and all modern free traders should be in favour of variable exchange rates.

The story would be somewhat different if we had a world government, a supranational authority, or even a strong international organisation whose purpose it was to conduct a monetary and budgetary policy for the free world as a whole. In such circumstances we might perhaps feel sufficient confidence that world demand was going to be maintained at a level which paid adequate regard to our own problems, so that we could abandon any national effort to control our own domestic level of money expenditure. Personally I think that, even if this were a real possibility, it might be found less advantageous than a system under which each national government fashions its own monetary and budgetary policy to fit its own plans for domestic stability, international trade and payments being then conducted in relatively free markets at uncontrolled prices for the various national currencies. It is really a very sensible division of economic functions, which devolves upon the local national governments freedom to pick and choose and to experiment in policies for domestic stabilisation. It is certainly, in my view, far and away the best solution in the actual situation in which to make financial policy for economic stability a function of some world authority is a mere pipe dream.

Now it is well known that no system of variable exchange rates will work efficiently as a long-term method of adjustment unless the channels of international trade are sufficiently sensitive to price changes. A depreciation of a country's currency will raise the price of imported goods in terms of the depreciated currency; the country in question will then presumably buy a smaller quantity of imports, and this will presumably save foreign exchange; but it will not save much foreign exchange if the demand for imports falls off very little when the price of imports rises in terms of the depreciated currency. The depreciation of the currency will also tend to lower the price of the depreciating country's exports in terms of foreign currencies; the foreigners will then presumably purchase a larger amount of the country's exports; but if they purchase only a little more in volume when the price falls a lot, they may spend less foreign money on the depreciating country's exports. If the depreciating country buys only a little less imports and sells only a little more exports, when the currency is greatly depreciated, then it may lose more foreign exchange on its exports than it saves on its imports; and its balance of trade will actually be worsened. But if there is any appreciable sensitivity of imports and exports to price changes, the depreciation will improve the balance of payments because considerably less foreign exchange will be spent on imports and considerably more will be earned from exports.

It should be realised that if conditions are such that the depreciation of a country's exchange rate would then have this perverse effect upon its balance of payments, then, the use of the 'gold-standard' mechanism of fixed exchange rates without exchange controls and import restrictions would be ruled out just as effectively as the use of the mechanism of variable exchange rates. Thus suppose that a country keeps its exchange rate fixed but deflates its domestic level of money prices, incomes, and costs. It will then presumably purchase less imports (which are now relatively high in price) and foreigners will presumably purchase more of its exports (which are now relatively low in price). But if the reactions to price are very small, it will save very little foreign exchange on its imports but will lose considerable foreign-exchange earnings on its exports, since it will be selling only a very little more at a substantially lower price. Thus if price elasticities of demand for imports are low, we shall have to rely on exchange controls, import restrictions and the like in order to preserve equilibrium in balances of payments. The conditions would be fatal both to exchange-rate variations and to internal inflations and deflations as methods of adjustment.

But personally I have no doubt that sensitivities to price adjustments are likely to be amply large enough to make the price mechanism workable in international trade if certain simple conditions are fulfilled. Since a large amount of products which are exported from any one country compete with similar goods produced in other parts of the world, the sensitivity to price changes of the world demand for a country's exports is likely to be potentially very great. And similarly, though perhaps to a somewhat lesser degree, since a large amount of products which are imported into any one country normally compete with similar goods produced in that country, the sensitivity to price changes of the local demand for imports is also likely to be potentially very great.

But for these potentially large changes in trade flows to be realised, two conditions must be fulfilled. First, they must not be obstructed by a lot of rigid barriers to trade flows. If there is a host of quantitative restrictions in world markets over the amounts of particular products which are permitted to be imported into particular countries, then, of course, price changes cannot be expected to do their work of adjustment of balances of trade and payments. There is thus a double relationship between the freeing of trade and the use of variable exchange rates as the major mechanism for maintaining equilibrium in balances of payments. I argued at the outset that the United Kingdom had a major real interest in seeing that world trade was as free as possible from artificial barriers, and that the use of exchange-rate fluctuations as the means of balance-of-payments adjustment was the only way in which one could hope to make free trade a workable system. I am now arguing that the greater is the freedom of trade from rigid barriers, the more workable the system of variable exchange rates becomes. The United Kingdom should for this reason lead a double crusade in international economic relations: for freely fluctuating exchanges and for the removal of rigid trade barriers. The two will together form a workable system, advantageous to this country.

But there is a second condition which is necessary in order to enable the potential adjustments of trade flows to exchange-rate variations to be realised – namely, adequate time for adjustment. If a country's exports become cheaper in world markets because of a depreciation of that country's currency, we cannot hope for an immediate realisation of the full increase in the amount which it will thereby be able ultimately to sell. Time must be allowed for the foreign consumers to realise the full implications of the price change and to make their own domestic adjustments to it. In particular producers of the commodity or of closely competing commodities in the importing country will find their markets less profitable; they will gradually shift their resources into other lines of production; but for familiar reasons such shifts of productive resources take time; and the full increase of the foreign market for the exporting country's products will be realised only when these shifts of productive resources have taken place in the importing countries.

Now with a system of fixed exchange rates without exchange controls or other direct restrictions on imports or payments it is the domestic deflation in the deficit countries relative to the surplus countries that brings about the basic structural changes in relative prices and so in the long run in trade flows and the balance of payments. In the short run it may not cure the problem; the fall in the money price of the deficit country's exports may not at first cause any large increase in its earnings of foreign exchange and the relative rise in the price of its imports may not cause any large saving in its expenditure on imports. With such a system the short-term gap which may thus persist in the balance of payments may in part be filled by a movement of short-term capital funds to the deficit country. But in the last resort any remaining gap can in the short run always be financed by the movement of gold or of other reserves of foreign money from the deficit to the surplus countries.

Is there anything to play this essential role in a system of variable exchange rates? In order to answer this question we must consider the different forms which a system of variable exchange rates may take and the effect of these different forms upon the movements of speculative funds between the currencies concerned.

There are, broadly speaking, two extreme types of system which may be adopted for a system of variable exchange rates. The first may be called the system of the adjustable peg. Under this system each country fixes its rate of exchange in terms of some common standard of value such as gold; and thus rates of exchange between national currencies are also fixed. But the countries do not then undertake so to order their internal financial policies as to maintain this exchange rate unchanged. On the contrary, they are free to undertake domestic financial policies which aim at the prevention of domestic inflations and deflations or at the prevention of the growth of unemployment at home. When as a result of this, they find – as they certainly will from time to time – that their external balances of payments are in serious or fundamental disequilibrium, they can make the necessary adjustments by a substantial shift of the peg between their national currency and the common standard of value, gold, and thus indirectly by altering the rate of exchange between their national money and the currencies of other countries. This is, broadly speaking, the system which was formally put into writing in the Articles of Agreement of the International Monetary Fund, and which the most important countries in the free world with the exception of Canada have been operating in the last few years.

The alternative system is not to peg exchange rates at all, but to allow the values of one national currency in terms of another to vary from day to day, indeed from hour to hour, according to the forces of supply and demand for each currency in a free market. This is a system which, so far as I am aware, has never yet been tried for any major currency as the normal method of adjustment.

These two methods are only the extreme forms of a whole range of possible systems of variable exchange rates. Suppose that a country has instituted a national Exchange Equalisation Account. The monetary authorities then have a fund consisting partly of the home currency and partly of foreign currencies. If the authorities never intervene in the foreign exchange market, then we have the extreme form of a completely free foreign exchange rate. But the authorities may support the home currency by selling foreign currencies for the home currency when the home currency seems to be temporarily unnaturally low in value, and they may sell the home currency for foreign currencies if the home currency seems to be abnormally high in value. In doing so, they may or may not fix precise upper and lower limits at which for the time being they will sell and buy the home currency; and such limits may be fixed far apart or close together, may be publicly stated or remain undisclosed, and may be frequently or infrequently revised. If the authorities fix only a narrow margin between these limits, announce them publicly, and revise them infrequently, we are right back at the other extreme, namely, the adjustable peg.

We will, however, start by discussing the relative merits of the two extreme forms: the freely fluctuating exchange rate without any official intervention in the foreign exchange market, and the system of the adjustable peg. This comparison should help us to decide what ingredients, if any, from each system we would like to have for any mixture which we may finally choose.

In regard to the long-run effects upon the structure of the national economies and the flows of international trade, there is little or nothing to choose between the two systems. The exchange rate can under either system be altered in response to basic changes in the balance-of-payments position of the various countries; and the price adjustments under each system will presumably have similar long-run effects upon trade patterns. It is in their short-run effects, that is to say, in their contribution to the transition from one basic pattern of trade and payments to another, that they differ fundamentally from each other. And in this respect, if I may somewhat oversimplify my position, I find virtue in the freely fluctuating exchange rate and vice in the adjustable peg.

The adjustable peg cannot be operated without exchange controls, import restrictions, and the rest of the paraphernalia of direct controls, unless the countries concerned have exceptionally large reserves of gold or foreign currencies. For, in the first place, under this system any adverse movement in a balance of payments will have to be met by a loss of reserves during an initial period while the exchange rate remains pegged at the old value and domestic financial policies continue to be conducted with an eye mainly to domestic stability. During this period the authorities concerned will be making up their minds whether the adverse movement is a permanent one which requires one of those infrequent earthquakes of a change in the par rate of exchange. Secondly, the underlying adverse factors in the balance of payments will continue to exert their influence for some time after the exchange rate has been changed, until the changed price relationships have worked out their long-run effects upon the flows of international trade.

But, thirdly, very large reserves will be required because of the pernicious effect which this system is likely to have on the speculative movements of capital. A country runs into balance-of-payments difficulties; it looks as if these are likely to be lasting; it becomes clear that the currency may be depreciated – perhaps by 20, 30, or even 40 per cent at one fell swoop; it is quite certain that it will not be appreciated; speculators have every incentive to move out of this currency into others; if the depreciation does take place they will make a very large profit overnight; if it does not take place, they will not lose. Meanwhile, the authorities of the country in question will have to finance this speculative outflow of funds by a loss of reserves additional to that which is necessary to finance the current deficit which is the basic cause of the whole problem. If the depreciation takes place and the speculators bring back their funds, the monetary authorities buy them back at a much higher price. No useful purpose has been served by the movement, which has merely enriched the private speculator at the expense of the monetary authority.

Nor is it at all sensible to suggest that this problem can be met by the imposition of exchange controls over short-term capital movements without any serious interference with current payments. In the case of a currency like sterling which is so widely used in so many and varied transactions the difficulties would be especially great. But in any case any exchange control must give importers some latitude in deciding exactly when they will buy the foreign exchange for their permitted imports, and must give the exporters some latitude in deciding exactly when they will bring back the foreign exchange proceeds of their exports. When a substantial depreciation is expected, importers will buy foreign currencies at the earliest possible date and exporters will surrender the foreign currencies which they have earned at the latest possible dates; and these leads and lags in the United Kingdom may alone account for a speculative capital export of as much as £300 to £400 million.

With freely floating rates of exchange the position of the speculator is very different. When something happens to put a strain on a country's balance of payments, the excess of supply over demand for that currency in the foreign exchange market will cause an immediate depreciation in its value. At first this depreciation will go further than is necessary to achieve a long-run equilibrium in the country's balance of payments; and thereafter the currency will appreciate again as the price adjustments due to the depreciation work out their favourable effects upon the balance of payments. Speculators will, therefore, have an immediate incentive to purchase the currency with their holdings of foreign currencies; and this will represent an inflow of short-term capital which, like movements of official reserves under the gold standard, helps to fill the gap in the balance of payments while the longer-run price effects are working themselves out.

Now if one is trying to run a system of convertible currencies on very small gold reserves, it is essential to have a system in which private speculators may – as in the case just quoted – themselves play at least some of the useful role which must be played under other systems by official monetary reserves. This consideration cannot be ignored in the case of a country like the United Kingdom whose reserves before the Second World War were considered by many to be rather inadequate, when they were equal to about 100 per cent of the then short-term sterling liabilities and to about 75 per cent of a year's imports into the United Kingdom, and whose reserves now cover less than 25 per cent of the short-term sterling liabilities and some 25 to 33⅓ per cent of a year's imports into the United Kingdom.

Of course, speculation may not always have this sort of useful effect. In order that it should do so, it must be both competitive and well-informed. That is to say, it must not be possible for the majority of all the potential speculators to get together and to exert a monopolist's influence over the rate fixed for any particular currency. This, however, is a danger which we can presumably ignore. In a really free market there would presumably be a sufficient number of independent sharp-witted persons in London, New York, Zürich and elsewhere for there always to be a pretty competitive market for sterling in terms of other currencies. But speculation of this kind will be useful only in so far as it is well-informed. It is only in so far as the speculation comes in to support a currency when it is in fact undervalued relatively to its real future prospects that the movements of funds will be on the right scale and in the right direction. This is, of course, a crucial – perhaps the crucial – question: will private speculators be less well-informed and more excitable and hysterical about the probable future movements underlying a country's balance of payments than the operators of an official equalisation fund? I shall return to this in due course.

So far I have tried to put what I consider to be the basic case in favour of a system of freely fluctuating exchange rates. I now intend to consider briefly the main criticism which can, I think, be made of the use of this system.

A serious argument against a system of fluctuating exchange rates is that it adds to the risk and uncertainties of foreign trade. The exporter's costs are incurred in pounds sterling; he contracts for a selling price in, say, dollars; but he does not know what will be the dollar price of sterling when he brings home the foreign exchange proceeds of his exports. If, to avoid this risk, he insists on fixing his selling price in sterling, then the risk is, of course, merely shifted on to the shoulders of the foreign importer.

But this argument, while it is true as far as it goes, completely ignores the risks to trade which are removed by the adoption of a system of fluctuating exchange rates. If my basic argument is right, we must regard fluctuating exchange rates as an alternative to policies of exchange control and import restriction. For example, in 1951, when the United Kingdom had a balance-of-payments problem, continental producers of many products for our markets suddenly found themselves debarred from sales to us, because we were restricting imports on balance-of-payments grounds. The sterling–franc exchange rate was stable enough, but ask the French exporters of tinned peas whether there were any risks involved in the export trade which they had rather laboriously built up with this country. Or, to take another example, in 1952 when Australia was faced with a serious balance-of-payments problem, she suddenly made great cuts in the quantities of our manufactured goods which were to be admitted into Australia. The rate of exchange between the Australian pound and the pound sterling was stable enough; but ask our exporters of motor-cars whether there were any risks involved in their export trade with Australia.

In this evil world risks in foreign trade cannot be eliminated. Their burden can, however, be diminished. The use of a system of freely fluctuating exchange rates spreads the necessary adjustments all round at the margin of all exports and all imports with all countries, whereas the use of large and sudden variations in the quotas for particular products from particular countries concentrates the whole adjustment on one set of people – the choice of victims being, however, unsettled until the bureaucrats make their final decisions.

Moreover, specialised institutions can bear those risks which cannot be eliminated. A market in forward exchanges enables the United Kingdom exporter to the United States, for example, to get rid of his exchange risk by selling forward the dollars which he expects to get from his exports. The risk is then borne directly or indirectly by some professional foreign-exchange dealer. Now it may well be true that, under the present foreign-exchange regulations, forward markets of this kind do not at present exist of a kind and on a scale which will fully enable traders to cover their exchange-rate risks, though the specialised institutions already provide the necessary technical facilities. Any existing deficiencies are mainly due to the fact that we have not used the system of freely fluctuating rates as the normal equilibrating mechanism. I peer into my crystal and see a world of freely fluctuating exchange rates in which the sharp-witted people in London, New York, Zürich, and elsewhere are busy devising all sorts of useful ways in which they can make a profit on their hunches as to what will happen to future exchange rates, and some of these will be ways of relieving other people from this concern. My crystal becomes a little clouded and dimmed; I cannot see whether they are getting the fullest possible encouragement in these activities from the authorities concerned; I very much hope that they are.

Fluctuating exchange rates are similarly criticised on the grounds that they will greatly impede foreign lending. The lender will not know what he is going to receive in his own currency if the debt is fixed in terms of the borrower's currency; and the borrower will not know what he will have to pay in his currency if the debt is fixed in terms of the lender's currency.

This again is a perfectly true argument so far as it goes. But once again it ignores the fact that fluctuating exchange rates are the alternative to direct controls over trade and payments. It is not clear that risks and uncertainties are increased when the possibilities of exchange-rate fluctuations are greater but those of exchange controls over transfers of interest and sinking funds are less. And once again it ought not to be impossible to develop special arrangements for sharing out the risks involved. Foreign investment can take the form of equities or of fixed debts, which can be expressed in the lender's money, the borrower's money, in gold, or in the currency of a third country; and it might be possible for some foreign investment to take place through specialised institutions which could bear a part or a whole of the risk of exchange-rate variations.

Another argument against a system of freely fluctuating exchange rates is that it will increase the probability of domestic inflations. A country's balance of payments is in difficulties; the exchange rate depreciates; this raises the price of imports and so the cost of living; money wage-rates rise in consequence; the maintenance of full employment then involves a domestic financial policy which allows the general level of money incomes and prices to rise *pari passu* with the wage-rate; this puts a further strain on the balance of payments, which necessitates a further depreciation; and this in turn starts another round of the same process. I think that this is a very serious consideration. Certainly in this respect our own domestic situation is very far from perfect; and my own view is that one of the most fundamental problems which we have still to solve is the marriage between trade unions, full employment, and the prevention of inflation in a free society.

Now it may well be that a change from a system of fixed to a system of fluctuating exchange rates would increase the danger of domestic inflation. But it is by no means certain that it would do so. At present one has to preach wage restraint and disinflation in order to stop a threat to the gold reserves. Under the new system one would have to preach wage restraint and disinflation in order to stop a depreciation of sterling and a continued rise in the cost of living. It is not impossible that the second argument would in fact prove more telling than the first. In any case, I am sure that in the end we must fight this battle on the straightforward ground that a perpetual inflation of money prices is bad for the distribution of incomes and for economic incentives in our own domestic economy.

The system of fluctuating exchange rates will operate with fully smooth effectiveness only if it is built on the fairly solid foundation of reasonable domestic stability in the main countries. Professional speculators will probably be able to judge as well as anyone what are likely to be the future changes in the real factors like industrial productivity and commercial opportunity which affect a country's balance of payments and so the value of its currency; it is indeed their specialised job to make such assessments; and they may be able to do it even as well as officials of Ministries of Finance and Central Banks. In so far as they are speculating about the future course of such real underlying technological and commercial factors their speculation will often be of that well-informed character which, as I explained earlier, will help to reduce the short-run difficulties of long-term adjustments.

But if they cannot rely upon reasonable stability in the general level of domestic prices and costs, then they will have to speculate not only on the future of the underlying real factors, but also upon the future of domestic financial policies. They may decide to sell rather than to buy a currency which, at current prices and costs, is already more than sufficiently depreciated to put a balance of payments back into equilibrium, for the very good reason that they fear a further inflation of prices and costs in that country. If they prove wrong in their fears, then their speculation will merely have caused a further unnecessary downward fluctuation in the currency with all the attendant drawbacks and none of the attendant advantages of such a fluctuation.

But the danger is much worse than that. It is possible that this speculation against the currency may itself give rise to the very evils whose expectation has motivated the speculation in the first place. Consider the following possible case. There is some basic adverse movement against a country's external position; its currency depreciates to a point which is already more than sufficient, in the absence of domestic inflation, to restore it in the long run to external balance; this depreciation is not itself sufficient in fact to touch off any serious spiral of domestic inflation; but speculators fear some substantial domestic inflation, and therefore continue to sell rather than to buy the currency; and this further depreciation is sufficient to start off a serious round of domestic inflation, so that the speculators' fears are after all justified.

The danger of speculative developments of this kind is an important reason for a careful choice of the time for initiating a system of variable exchange rates. If the system were started during a period of excessive inflationary pressure domestically combined with a weakness in the external balance of payments, speculators would be sure that when the rate was freed it would depreciate and not appreciate and they might well fear that this would merely intensify the domestic inflation. This would mean that the first, and perhaps decisive, impressions which speculators would form of the new system would be one in which there were real dangers of a vicious spiral of depreciation. It is very important to initiate the system only when inflationary domestic pressures have been brought well under control.

But while first impressions are important, the recurrence of a real danger of cumulative inflation and depreciation cannot be avoided merely by a good timing for the start of the new system. Underlying real conditions may be such that from time to time there will be dangerous speculation against the currency because of fears of a cumulative domestic inflation. It is against speculation of this kind that official counter-speculation through some form of exchange equalisation account may have to be organised. In my view private competitive speculation will probably do the job of adjusting exchange rates to long-run changes in the underlying real conditions of production and exchange at least as well as an official speculative fund of foreign currencies. But if a speculative movement against a currency might itself cause a domestic inflation which in turn would justify the speculation, there is a strong argument for an official fund to offset the movement of funds and to stop the spiral of deterioration at the outset.

One particular way of dealing with this problem is to allow complete freedom of exchange rates between a fixed upper and lower limit, the margin between the limits being wide and the rates at the limits being held fixed by the operations of an Exchange Equalisation Fund. If the rates at these limits are confidently expected to be immutably fixed, then this compromise might be a useful one. The margin between the limits might give room for much of the benefits of a variable exchange rate, and the existence of the limits might give speculators a firm assurance that there would be no cumulative spiral of inflation against which they should speculate.

But if the limiting rates are not expected to be maintained, this compromise might well give the worst of both worlds. The limits would no longer give any firm assurance against the possibility of a cumulative inflationary process. But as soon as they were reached, they would stop the adjusting mechanism of exchange-rate variations so long as they were held. Moreover, since speculators would now expect the limiting rates themselves to be changed, many of the speculative disadvantages of the adjustable peg mechanism would come into operation once more.

Operations by an exchange equalisation account of one kind or another may well be necessary for the prevention of cumulative inflationary processes. But it is very much to be hoped that sufficient confidence in a basic domestic stability can be built up to make the use of official equalisation funds unnecessary.

The reasons for this view are simple. If a number of independent national authorities are intervening in foreign exchange markets in this way, their operations may be conflicting and inconsistent; and they may also be – or, what is perhaps as important, they may be thought to be – aimed at obtaining some national advantage for the country in question at the expense of other countries. We can perhaps usefully illustrate this general principle by referring to two particular cases.

One is given to understand in press reports of the recent discussions about the future of the European Payments Union that many representatives of continental countries objected to a system under which the exchange value of the pound sterling was allowed to fluctuate. One reason for this objection was that the British monetary authorities could then arbitrarily manipulate the value of the pound sterling, which was a matter of considerable direct interest to the continental countries. The best answer to this fear would be to say that the British authorities were not going to manipulate the value of the pound sterling at all, but that that was going to be left to the forces of supply and demand as between private operators in a free market. The answer which runs in terms of setting certain pre-determined limits to the extent of future variations in the value of sterling may, for the reasons which have just been given, be regarded as a bad second-best.

The other illustration of the disadvantages of the intervention of Exchange Equalisation Funds which I shall mention is the dread of competitive exchange depreciations which arose from the experience of the 1930s and which must bear so great a part of the responsibility for the incorporation at Bretton Woods of the fundamentally ill-judged system of the adjustable peg into the International Monetary Fund. At certain periods during the late 1930s important countries, including the United Kingdom, were rightly or wrongly thought to have operated in the following manner. They set up important Exchange Equalisation Funds richly endowed with their own national currencies; these funds were used on a massive scale to buy foreign currencies; this kept the national currency at an unduly depreciated rate; this cheapened the exports of the country in question and enabled it to undercut its competitors to an extent which was not required to keep its balance of payments in order; and this enabled it to increase its own level of employment and economic activity, but only at the expense of other competing countries.

Now there are two ways of meeting this danger. One is to say that there must be international agreement about the rates at which the national exchange equalisation accounts will buy and sell national currencies, and that these rates must only be altered occasionally and by some mechanism of international agreement. This is the bad method of the adjustable peg. The other method is to say that the national exchange equalisation accounts will not intervene at all in the foreign exchange markets except occasionally and then in accordance with some process of international agreement. If my argument is correct, this is the more hopeful principle which we should now try.

But in any case the dangers of competitive exchange depreciation are now much smaller than they were in the 1930s. Those were days of deflation and unemployment; nations sought to extend their export markets and to contract their imports as much as possible in order to give employment to domestic resources; as far as exchange-rate manipulation was concerned, this required a copious supply of the domestic currency (which could always be made available) for sale through an exchange equalisation fund against foreign currencies, so as to keep the national currency undervalued. Today we live in a world of inflation; nations seek to provide their home markets as liberally as possible with home-produced and imported goods in order to mop up inflationary pressures at home; the sort of exchange-rate manipulation that this requires is to sell foreign currencies against home currency through an exchange equalisation fund so as to keep the home currency overvalued and to finance an excess of imports over exports; but this sort of manipulation is strictly limited, since supplies of foreign currencies unlike supplies of national currencies cannot be made available *ad lib* to national exchange equalisation accounts.

Finally, there is one special problem which we must consider in the application of the principle of fluctuating exchange rates to sterling. Sterling is an important international currency. Not only do balances of sterling provide the actual central monetary reserves of the sterling area countries. Sterling is also widely held and used by individuals and by monetary authorities in other countries. How would the use of sterling as an international currency be affected if the major countries of the world went over to a system of fluctuating exchange rates?

The answer to this question would very largely depend upon whether or not the other members of the sterling area themselves fully adopted the system of fluctuating exchange rates and allowed their local currencies to vary in value in terms of sterling according to the play of the forces of supply and demand. Personally, I believe that on balance it would be to their interest to adopt the system fully themselves. For example, if the Australian pound were allowed to appreciate when there was a heavy world demand for Australian export products like wheat and wool, Australia would both isolate herself from the inflationary forces coming from the outside world and would tend to keep a closer balance in her balance of payments; and conversely, the Australian pound should be allowed to depreciate if the world price of her staple exports fell.

It would, of course, be for the sterling area countries themselves to choose whether they would adopt such a system or not. But clearly the greater the number of sterling area countries which do choose to operate the new system, the more serious would be the consequent threat to the use of sterling as an international currency. I shall, therefore, discuss this issue on the assumption that all important sterling area countries do join in the new system.

In these circumstances there would be bound, I think, to be some reduction in the demand for sterling by overseas monetary authorities to hold as an international currency, and this would be bound to exercise for a period some pressure on the foreign-exchange value of sterling as these sums were being worked off through some additional surplus on the balance of payments of the United Kingdom. This, I think, is in the end an inevitable price which we should have to pay for the inauguration of the new system which, once it had been inaugurated, would in my opinion be much more to our advantage than the existing system. Personally I think the ultimate gain would be well worth the price.

But we must not exaggerate the price that would have to be paid. If my basic argument is correct, a system of fluctuating national currencies would reduce the need for official monetary reserves. Since sterling is widely used as a monetary reserve, this would *pro tanto* reduce the demand for sterling and for other major currencies by overseas monetary authorities. But against this must be set three considerations which would at least partially offset this reduction in the official demand for sterling.

In the first place, there would be some counter-balancing reduction in our own need to hold reserves of other currencies. Fluctuations in the gold and dollar reserves in London have in large measure been due to deficits and surpluses in dollar balances of payments of the sterling area countries. If the adoption of a variable-exchange-rate system by Australia meant that there were less violent fluctuations in the Australian balance of payments, they might need to hold less sterling, but we also would need to hold less gold and dollars.

Second, while the system of variable exchange rates might well reduce the overseas demand for official reserves and so for sterling, an essential feature of the new system would be the growth of organised private speculation in the major currencies. The increased demands for working balances of sterling and of other major currencies by private professional speculators would at least in part offset the decline in the official demand.

Thirdly, whether or not monetary authorities in overseas countries would on balance hold a larger or smaller proportion of their remaining reserves in sterling cannot be answered *a priori*. It would depend very closely upon the answer which must be given to the basic question: can we successfully maintain a reasonable degree of domestic stability of money prices and costs? If so, then there will in fact be no reason why the pound should not be as likely to appreciate as to depreciate in terms of dollars or of other important currencies. Overseas monetary authorities would probably wish to spread their risks and to keep some of their reserves in sterling and some in dollars. Initially this would reduce the demand for sterling by countries which at present keep their reserves principally in the form of sterling balances; but on the other hand, it might somewhat increase the demand for sterling by countries which at present keep their reserves principally in the form of gold or dollars.

Subsequently the overseas monetary authorities might shift parts of their reserves from the one currency to the other if they thought that the one or the other was appreciably overvalued or undervalued. But in so far as this movement was well-informed, it would play exactly the same useful role as the similar movements of private speculators which we have already discussed. The bigger the corpus of funds ready to move in a well-informed way from one currency to another in order to anticipate future adjustments in exchange rates, the better the system will work.

But the use of sterling as an international currency is not merely a question of the amount of sterling held by overseas monetary authorities or professional dealers in foreign exchange. It is also a question of the amount of current international business which overseas traders, shippers, bankers, insurers, borrowers and lenders elect to carry out in terms of sterling rather than in terms of other currencies. On this score we can, I think, be more optimistic about the future of sterling under a general system of fluctuating exchange rates. For, as I have argued at an early stage of my analysis, a general system of fluctuating exchange rates should lead to all sorts of developments in which transactions between countries whose currencies are expected to be peculiarly liable to fluctuation will be expressed in terms of the currencies of third countries. The City of London with its traditions and its continuing strengths in this sort of business might well provide some of the most important services of this kind to traders and others in the rest of the world – provided, once more, that the sterling price level in the United Kingdom itself is not expected to be subject to rapid inflations or deflations.

This problem of domestic stabilisation is indeed our basic problem.

The more nearly we can solve it, the more unreservedly we should take the lead in building a new world system of freer trade, domestic financial policies for domestic stability, and freely fluctuating foreign exchanges in markets which are not manipulated by national monetary authorities.

11

Benelux: The Formation of the Common Customs

From Economica, *vol. 23 (August 1956), pp. 201–213. Meade's study of the formation of the customs union between Belgium, Luxembourg and the Netherlands, referred to in footnote 1 below, was published as 'The Building of Benelux, 1943–1960' in J. E. Meade, H. H. Liesner and S. J. Wells,* Case Studies in European Economic Union: The Mechanics of Integration *(London: Oxford University Press, 1962), pp. 59–193. Meade also published* The Belgium–Luxembourg Economic Union 1921–1939: Lessons from an Early Experiment, *Princeton Essays in International Finance no. 25, March 1956, which was reprinted in that volume, and* Negotiations for Benelux: An Annotated Chronicle, *Princeton Studies in International Finance no. 6, 1957, as well as his famous Professor Dr F. de Vries Lectures of April 1955 on* The Theory of Customs Unions *(Amsterdam: North-Holland, 1955) and his earlier lectures at the University of Chicago on* Problems of Economic Union *(London: Allen & Unwin, 1953).*

A first and basic step in the formation of an economic union is the formation of a customs union in the sense of the imposition of a single uniform tariff of duties on imports into the partner countries from third countries and the removal of such duties on the flow of trade between the partner countries. It is the purpose of this article to give an account of some of the problems which arose when the Benelux countries, on 1 January 1948, took this first step towards the formation of their economic union.[1]

This first step has proved to be the easiest task in the building of the full Benelux economic union. But even so some important problems arose. There were technical difficulties due to the fact that in a number of points

[1] This article has been written in the course of the preparation for the Royal Institute of International Affairs, with the help of the Economic Research Division of the London School of Economics, of a study on the formation of the Benelux economic union. Much of the material has been taken from two admirable books on the subject: Max Weisglas, *Benelux: Van Nabuurstaten tot Uniepartners* (Amsterdam: Elsevier, 1949); and Institut National de la Statistique et des Etudes Economiques, *Le Bénélux* (Paris, 1953). I would also like to thank the many Belgian, Dutch and Luxembourg officials who have helped me both in providing documents and also in conversation on the subject.

the pre-existing Dutch and Belgium–Luxembourg tariff systems differed greatly from each other.

In the first place, the classification of commodities for customs purposes was quite different in the pre-Benelux Dutch and Belgium–Luxembourg tariffs. The Dutch had a short list of products under 160 headings with 850 sub-headings, the order of the products on the list being simply alphabetical and without reference to the nature of the goods themselves. On the other hand, the Belgium–Luxembourg tariff was a much more elaborate and scientific structure starting off with 21 main divisions by type of product, sub-divided into 1,200 main headings and then into 3,600 sub-headings according to the nature of the products within the main divisions. Indeed, this systematic classification, which had been introduced by a Belgian law of 8 May 1924, had, together with the French tariff, served as a model on which the systematic League of Nations Draft Customs Nomenclature of 1937 had been based. The Benelux negotiators adopted in this respect the Belgian principle; and the common Benelux tariff was based, with minor modifications, upon the League of Nations classification.

Secondly, only the relatively few products named on the Dutch list were subject to import duty. Everything which did not appear on the list was free of duty. The Belgium–Luxembourg list on the other hand attempted to classify all products whether they were dutiable or not. Any product which was found not to appear on the list was to be treated for import duty purposes in the same way as the named product to which it was most similar. This latter principle was adopted for the Benelux tariff. Any product not included on the list was to be assimilated for tax treatment to the most similar product already on the list; and, in addition, in case of doubt it was to be assimilated to the product which paid the highest rate of duty.

A third problem was presented by the fact that the Dutch tariff was mainly on an *ad valorem* basis, while the Belgium–Luxembourg tariff was in the main specific. Thus of the 850 dutiable items in the Dutch tariff some 700 were taxable on an *ad valorem* basis, some 100 on a specific basis, and the remainder on a combined specific and *ad valorem* basis. But in the Belgium–Luxembourg tariff of more than 3,000 dutiable items only 400 were taxable on an *ad valorem* basis. The solution adopted for this problem was to impose most of the Benelux duties upon an *ad valorem* basis; indeed, in the final Benelux tariff specific duties were even rarer than in the old Dutch tariff.

The choice of an *ad valorem* basis for the new tariff was, no doubt, greatly influenced by the desirability of such a system in order to maintain the protective effect of a given tariff, and to preserve the real value of the customs revenue, in a period of rapidly moving commodity prices. Indeed, the Belgians and Luxembourgers with the inflation of commodity prices between 1939 and 1945 had already had a sharp experience of the way in which a substantial rise in commodity prices can lower the protective effect of, and the real value of the revenue from, a system of specific duties.

But there was another reason why the choice of the *ad valorem* principle for the Benelux tariff turned out to be a most fortunate one. In September 1949, less than two years after the imposition of the common Benelux tariff, the guilder was devalued in terms of the franc. At this time sterling was devalued in terms of the dollar; and the Dutch (who were experiencing a heavy deficit on their balance of payments) devalued with the United Kingdom, while the Belgians (whose balance of payments was more or less in equilibrium) followed sterling only part of the way in its devaluation. This adjustment of the rate of exchange between the two Benelux currencies involved an adjustment of all the specific items in the common tariff; either the duty expressed in guilders had to be raised or the duty expressed in francs had to be lowered, in order to keep the duty at the same level in the two re-aligned national currencies. Fortunately most of the duties were on an *ad valorem* basis and needed no such adjustment. But the few existing specific duties had to be adjusted; in some cases the duties were raised in terms of guilders, in some the duties were lowered in terms of francs, and for others the guilder duty was partially raised and the franc duty partially lowered. There can be no doubt that, if variations in exchange rates are ever likely to be used as a weapon of equilibration in balances of payments, it is important that the common tariff for the partners in any economic union should be fixed on an *ad valorem* basis.

A fourth, but minor, technical difference between the Dutch and the Belgium–Luxembourg tariffs was that in the Dutch system excise duties were collected separately, the customs duty representing only the additional protective element in the tax on the product concerned, whereas in the Belgium–Luxembourg system the rate of customs duty itself included both any relevant domestic excise duty and any additional protective element in the import duty. Since the Benelux excise duties were not unified at the same time as the imposition of the common Benelux customs duties in 1948, it was inevitable that the Dutch system should be applied to the Benelux tariff. That is to say, the Benelux customs duties expressed only the additional protective element in import duties; and additional excise duties on the relevant imports were to be collected by each partner in accordance with the scale of excise duties levied domestically on its own produce.

The full application of this principle involved one particular adjustment in the taxation of Luxembourg products in the Belgian and Dutch markets. Under the treaty of economic union of 1921 between Belgium and Luxembourg, Belgium undertook to exempt Luxembourg wines from excise duty in the Belgium–Luxembourg market. Belgium herself was not a wine producer and did not, therefore, produce wines to be subject to her own excise duty. The result was frankly to protect Luxembourg wines in the Belgium–Luxembourg market against imports of wines from outside countries which would be subject to the excise duty. But by the general obligations of the General Agreement on Tariffs and Trade signed in Geneva in 1947 Belgium become bound not to levy excise duties on foreign products within the Belgium–Luxembourg Economic Union at a higher rate than those levied on Belgian and Luxembourg products themselves. In order to avoid this difficulty it was necessary that the Belgium–Luxembourg excise duties on wines should be included in the customs duties payable on imports of wines from third countries. Apart from the fact that this change would make these duties, like all other customs duties, subject to GATT tariff negotiations, this would have been a purely formal alteration if it had not been for the entry of the Netherlands into the Benelux customs union. French wines, for example, on import into the Belgium–Luxembourg Economic Union would have paid as a customs duty what previously they paid as an excise duty, but in both cases Luxembourg wines would have been exempt. But it was now necessary to incorporate this new customs duty into the Benelux tariff; and this was done by a protocol between the three partner countries of 22 December 1947, whereby they all agreed to raise the customs duty on wines in the proposed Benelux tariff so as to incorporate in it the previous Belgium–Luxembourg excise duty. This, of course, had the effect of giving Luxembourg wines this degree of tariff protection against French and other wines in the Dutch as well as in the Belgian market.

A fifth problem arose from the fact that with a common tariff of *ad valorem* duties it is desirable to have a common principle for the valuation for tax purposes at the point of import of the dutiable products. In the pre-Benelux Belgian system the rule had been to value imports at the highest of three possible figures: the normal wholesale price abroad, the normal wholesale price in Belgium, or the price actually paid by the importer. Under the pre-Benelux Dutch system the importer had a free choice of declaring *either* the current price (i.e. a price corresponding to the normal wholesale price abroad of the Belgian system) *or*, even though it was lower, the actual price paid provided that it was fixed under normal conditions. In both the Belgian and the Dutch systems the time and place relevant for the valuation was the same, namely, the time and place of the passage of the goods through the customs, the only difference in this respect being that the Belgian system did and the Dutch system did not include in the value of the goods any *inland* cost of transport of the goods to the point of passage through the customs. For the Benelux tariffs the principle was adopted of valuing imports at the price which the exporter would normally obtain for them on delivery at the place of passage through the customs; and it was agreed that, save for exceptional cases, this value could be considered as equivalent to the actual price paid for the goods with the addition of all charges (e.g. for transport, insurance, etc.) incurred in addition to the purchase price up to the passage through the customs.

Another secondary technical problem was raised by the fact that the pre-Benelux Belgian tariff was a double-column structure with two rates of duty – a lower and a higher – applicable to each dutiable product. The lower rate of duty was to be regarded as the normal rate of duty; and the higher rate was to be applied only in exceptional cases against the products of particular countries who discriminated against Belgium. In fact since 1935 the column of higher rates had not been applied. The Dutch tariff, on the other hand, had only one column of duties, although existing legislation gave the power (which had in fact never been used) to apply specially heavy rates on products coming from some countries. The Benelux tariff has a double column of maximum and minimum rates, the minimum rate being the normal rate and the maximum rate (equal to double the minimum rate with a lower limit of 10 per cent) being applicable only in exceptional cases against the products of countries which discriminate against Benelux products.

The actual administration of the customs has not been unified; the customs administration of the Netherlands or of the Belgium–Luxembourg Economic Union imposes the duty according to the point of entry of the goods into the Benelux area. Nor have the general legislative provisions governing customs and excise been unified throughout the Benelux countries. For example, in Belgium appeal can be made to the ordinary courts against decisions of the customs authorities, whereas in the Netherlands appeal must be made to a special Tariff Commission. But the intention of the Benelux countries is ultimately to unify their customs legislation; and a Draft General Law on Customs and Excise has been prepared to act as a statement of principles in these matters for the three partner countries. There have in fact been some measures of close co-operative action between the two customs authorities. Thus, while it is necessary to maintain a customs control at the common Belgium–Luxembourg frontier so long as domestic excise and turnover taxes have not been unified and there are agricultural or other exceptions to the principle of free trade within the Benelux area, at a number of points on the common frontier these customs inspections are carried out at the same place as a single joint operation by both authorities. Moreover, in September 1952, a Benelux Convention was signed making provision for joint administrative action to simplify customs and excise procedures, to prevent and punish fraud, and to collect the relevant taxes.

So much for the technical problems of forming a single customs system out of two separate and in many respects divergent national systems. The formation of a common customs also raised some problems of rather more basic economic importance. Three such problems should be noted in the case of the Benelux duties: first, the determination of the general level of the duties to be imposed on imports from the outside world; second, the preferential arrangements to be made in regard to imports into the Benelux area of products from the overseas territories of Belgium and the Netherlands; and third, the arrangements to be made for the division between the governments concerned of the revenue raised by means of the common customs duties.

As far as the height of the Benelux import duties was concerned, the main principle adopted was to take the Dutch and the Belgium–Luxembourg duties as they existed in 1939, converting specific duties in force at that date into *ad valorem* equivalents at the prices of the products ruling in 1939, and to take an average of these two national rates of duty to determine the *ad valorem* rate of duty for the product concerned in the joint Benelux tariff. Two subsidiary principles were also generally to be observed: first, that in no case should the final Benelux duty be higher than the higher of the pre-existing Belgian and Dutch duties; and, second, that where there had previously been free entry into one of the partners free entry should be maintained in the final Benelux tariff. None of these principles was to be applied automatically in every case and without any exceptions; they were regarded rather in the light of guiding principles; and in the fixing of a number of rates account was taken of special circumstances of the special industries or occupations concerned.

In normal conditions the choice of a single rate of import duty might in many cases have been expected to give rise to serious conflicts between the national interests involved. But in the case of the Benelux tariff the necessary process of reaching agreement between the governments and of obtaining the consent of the parliaments concerned was made much easier by the special post-war conditions ruling at the time at which these negotiations took place. In these immediate post-war years rates of import duty had temporarily at least lost much of their importance. It was scarcity of overseas supplies and scarcities of overseas currencies for the purchase of supplies which caused imports to be limited in amounts. In the conditions of extreme scarcity of supplies then ruling the countries concerned would gladly have welcomed greater imports rather than have desired to protect domestic producers by means of import duties. Indeed, since the liberation no import duties had been levied in the Netherlands; and in Belgium hardly any import duties had in fact been imposed. The operations of the two tariffs were largely suspended in order to avoid rises in prices of imports (particularly of necessities and of goods required for reconstruction) which would have made more difficult the existing attempts to control upward movements of prices and wages. Indeed, when the new Benelux tariff was itself put into force on 1 January 1948, the application of many of the duties in this tariff was, for these reasons, also postponed for a further period.

Even so, cases of serious conflict of interest were not lacking. The most marked example of this occurred in the fixing of the Benelux import duty on tobacco. The previous Belgium–Luxembourg import duty was a heavy one, namely 500 francs per 100 kg. of unstripped and 900 francs per 100 kg. of stripped tobacco. On the other hand, the Dutch duty was a light one, namely Fl. 1.40 (the equivalent of only 23 francs) per 100 kg. of leaf tobacco. This great difference reflected a real and marked divergence of interest. The high Belgian duty protected a substantial high-cost domestic production of tobacco which accounted for about one-third of domestic consumption in a normal year. On the other hand, the Dutch had no domestic production to protect but provided an important international market for dealings in tobacco. For the purpose of facilitating transit traffic, dealings in samples, and the storage of tobacco a low rate of import duty on raw tobacco was desirable; and the problem of raising revenue was met by the Dutch through the excise on finished tobacco products – cigarettes, cigars, pipe tobacco. This conflict of interest led to serious difficulties. Finally in the Benelux tariff a compromise was reached with duties of 413 francs per 100 kg. of unstripped leaf and 578 francs per 100 kg. of stripped leaf. Since the average value of raw tobacco had risen some four times since the pre-war years, the mere maintenance of the old pre-war duties would have represented a very big cut in the protective incidence of the duty to

Belgian domestic growers. The new duties thus marked a considerable reduction in Belgian protection; nevertheless they meant for the Dutch a very substantial change from their previous policy of almost free import.

The fixation of a common Benelux rate of duty for each imported product threatened at first to raise another considerable difficulty. Both the Netherlands and Belgium had a number of important commercial treaties with other countries. These treaties contained, among other things, two important undertakings in so far as rates of duty on imports into the Netherlands or the Belgium–Luxembourg Economic Union were concerned: first, the most-favoured-nation undertaking to give treatment to imports from the country concerned at least as favourable as that given to imports from any other country; and second, undertakings not to levy import duties above a certain level on certain specified imports from the country concerned in return for undertakings by that other country not to raise above a stated level its duties on certain imports from the Netherlands or from the Belgium–Luxembourg Economic Union. Both these undertakings were capable of raising serious difficulties in the Benelux proposal to remove their customs duties on each other's products and to strike an average between the Dutch and the Belgian rates of duty for the formation of a joint tariff for imports from outside countries.

It is, of course, the most-favoured-nation obligations which raise the most familiar and obvious obstacle to such a proposal. If, for example, Belgium totally removes her import duties on imports from the Netherlands but has a commercial treaty with the United Kingdom in which she has undertaken to give United Kingdom products as favourable treatment as any other foreign products on the Belgian market, must Belgium also totally remove her import duties on imports from the United Kingdom? If this were so, then the Netherlands and Belgium could form a customs union only if they adopted a completely free-trade policy as regards imports from all countries with which either of them had a commercial treaty containing a most-favoured-nation clause. It was on this rock that the proposal for mutual tariff reductions between the Netherlands and the Belgium–Luxembourg Economic Union contained in the Ouchy Convention of 1931 had foundered. But while this is the basic theoretical difficulty, it was not expected in the Benelux case to prove a formidable obstacle in fact. There was a general expectation and understanding that the main commercial powers regarded the formation of the Benelux Economic Union with a sufficiently favourable eye not to insist in this way on any theoretical most-favoured-nation rights of this kind which they might possess.

A much more real problem was presented by the fact that the Netherlands and Belgium had undertaken not to raise their duties on imports of particular products from particular countries with which they had commercial agreements. For example, for motor vehicles Belgian import duties had an incidence of roughly 35 per cent. But the Dutch duties were bound in an agreement with the United States at 15 per cent. If an average had been struck between the Belgian rate of 35 per cent and the Dutch rate of 15 per cent, the Benelux import duty would have been

25 per cent. But this would have meant the raising by the Dutch of their duty on American cars to 25 per cent, though they were bound by their existing agreement not to raise it above 15 per cent. In other words, in so far as the existing duties on imports into the Belgium–Luxembourg Economic Union or into the Netherlands were bound under existing commercial agreements, the Benelux tariff would have had to incorporate in each case not an average between the two duties but the lower of the two duties, unless one of the partner countries was to disregard its obligation.

A further difficulty of exactly the same kind threatened to arise in the application of the Benelux tariff formula from the fact that the Belgian duties were largely specific and commodity prices had risen greatly since 1939. For the majority of products the *ad valorem* incidence of the Dutch duties in 1939 was appreciably lower than that of the Belgian duties. The averaging principle thus meant that in most cases there would be some reduction in the protective incidence of the Belgian duties below its 1939 level. But most of the Belgian duties were specific in nature and the mere rise of commodity prices between 1939 and the years immediately after the Second World War had very greatly reduced the *ad valorem* value and so the protective incidence of the Belgian duties. Indeed, the averaging formula in very many cases meant that, while there would be an appreciable reduction in the protective incidence of the Belgian tariff as compared with 1939, there would be an actual rise in the import duties levied in terms of Belgian francs on any particular product. But in those cases in which Belgium had a commercial treaty with some third country which bound a Belgian specific duty against increase, the application of the Benelux tariff formula would again be incompatible with an existing commercial obligation.

These serious difficulties were overcome by the good fortune that in 1947 the main commercial countries met together in Geneva at the meeting of the Preparatory Commission for the International Conference on Trade and Employment to draft the Charter for a proposed International Trade Organisation. In the course of this conference the countries concerned negotiated reductions and bindings of duties on the trade between them in a series of bilateral tariff agreements based on the most-favoured-nation principle and supported by a multilateral trade agreement known as the General Agreement on Tariffs and Trade. This gave the Benelux countries the opportunity not only to ensure that there would in fact be a let-out from any most-favoured-nation obligations for a customs union such as the Benelux Economic Union, but also to re-negotiate their tariff agreements with all the other members of the General Agreement on Tariffs and Trade on the basis of a new and joint Benelux tariff of import duties. 1 January 1948, the date on which the joint Benelux tariff came into effect, was also the precise date on which the General Agreement on Tariffs and Trade came into force.[2] It cannot

[2] The problem remained unsolved in so far as the Netherlands and Belgium were bound by commercial treaties with countries not represented at the Geneva negotiations. The Benelux countries in fact applied the joint Benelux tariff to all third countries, whether or not they were members of the General Agreement on Tariffs and Trade, at the same time

be expected that countries which are forming a customs union will always be presented with such a golden opportunity for making the necessary revisions in their commercial agreements with third countries.

The institution of the joint Benelux tariff also raised a problem of preferential rates of duty. The Benelux Economic Union is intended to be an economic union between three partner countries in respect of their metropolitan European territories; it is not intended to include the overseas dependent territories of the three partners. The ultimate aim is to ensure complete freedom of movement for goods, men, and capital within the European area comprising Belgium, the Netherlands, and Luxembourg without implying complete freedom of movement between this area and the overseas dependent territories of Belgium and the Netherlands. Nevertheless, the fact that each partner country may have special economic or financial relationships with its own overseas territories may raise complicating issues when the partners form a complete economic union between themselves.

One such issue was raised for the joint Benelux tariff by the question of preferential import duties. Broadly speaking, before the formation of Benelux the Dutch treated their imports from Dutch overseas territories on the same terms as they treated similar imports from third countries; there were no preferential rates of import duty. Similarly, the Dutch overseas territories treated their imports from the Netherlands on the same terms as imports from third countries. The Belgian arrangements were different. Products from the Belgian Congo were admitted into Belgium duty-free, even if similar products from third countries would have been dutiable. On the other hand, Belgian products sent to the Belgian Congo were subject to the same treatment as goods sent from third countries, since the 'open-door' principle of equal treatment for the trade of all countries in the Congo basin was guaranteed under the General Act of Berlin of 1885. Thus the existing position was that the Dutch treated imports from the Dutch overseas territories and from the Belgian Congo on the same terms as imports from any other third country; but the Belgians admitted goods from the Belgian Congo duty-free, while they treated goods from the Dutch overseas territories on the same terms as goods from any other third country.

For the common Benelux tariff it was, of course, necessary either that preferential treatment on the Belgian market of the products of the Belgian Congo should be abolished or else that both the Netherlands and Belgium should give the same preferential treatment to the products of both the Dutch and the Belgian overseas territories. The difficulty of the problem was much mitigated by the fact that the type of products (raw materials and foodstuffs) imported from the overseas territories were in any case likely to enjoy free entry or very low duties in the Benelux tariff, whatever their origin might be. The final solution reached was that goods from the overseas territories of both countries on import into any part of

declaring themselves ready to negotiate on the basis of the joint Benelux tariff with any country which considered itself hurt by this action. Only Switzerland asked for such negotiations, which resulted at the end of 1948 in the conclusion of a new treaty of commerce between Switzerland and the Benelux countries.

the Benelux area could obtain whole or partial exemption from the relevant duties of the common Benelux tariff, such exemptions to be given to the extent determined by the relevant Ministers on the advice of the Benelux Official Council for Customs Regulations.[3] Thus automatic free entry of the products of the Belgian Congo onto the Belgian market has disappeared and has given place to a system of limited and partial preferences for certain products coming from the Dutch as well as the Belgian overseas territories into the Netherlands as well as into Belgium or Luxembourg.

In the arrangements for the institution of the joint Benelux tariff no special provisions were made for the distribution between the three participating Governments of the revenue raised by import duties. Each Government retained for its own Budget the revenue from the duties levied on imports entering the Benelux area through its own customs houses. This is at first sight surprising. In previous customs unions there has normally been some pooling of the customs revenue and its distribution between the participating governments on some more logical principle than the mere geographical position of the port or railway station by which the products happen to have entered the common market. For example, in the Belgium–Luxembourg Economic Union since 1921 revenues from the common customs duties and from the unified excise duties have – with certain exceptions – been pooled and distributed between the Governments of the two participating states in proportion to the size of the populations of those states.

The principle that the revenue from the customs should accrue to the government of the country through which the dutiable products first enter the common market has little basic logic and may lead to considerable unfairness, since products might naturally enter one partner country for transport to, and consumption in, another partner country. There is one circumstance which at first sight might seem to make this principle particularly dangerous in its application to Benelux. There is a very great commercial competition between the Belgian port of Antwerp and the Dutch port of Rotterdam; this acute competition has made the settlement of conditions (port dues, wage-rates for dock labour, the construction of harbour facilities and, in particular, of waterways feeding the two harbours) a matter of great concern to, and of considerable dispute between, the Governments concerned. Under the existing Benelux system (or lack of system) for the distribution of the revenue from the joint customs the Governments might be expected to add a direct budgetary interest to the other commercial considerations which have from time to time heated the controversy between them about the conditions in which the two great ports compete. For it is now true that if products are imported from, say, the United States for consumption in, say, Belgium, the revenue from the relevant Benelux import duty will accrue to the Belgian Government if the ship docks in Antwerp but to the Netherlands Government if the ship docks in Rotterdam.

[3] This Council is the permanent committee of senior officials from the three countries which has been set up to supervise, and advise upon, the working of the common customs arrangements.

Nevertheless, the existing system seems to have worked well enough in practice and there is certainly no evidence that it has in fact exacerbated the problem of competition between the Belgian and Dutch ports. The reason for this is that the geographical situation and the transport conditions are such that, broadly speaking, goods for consumption in Belgium are in any case likely to enter through a Belgian port and goods for consumption in the Netherlands through a Dutch port. The acute competition between Belgian and Dutch ports is over transit traffic rather than over imports for consumption in the Benelux countries themselves.

The position is different as regards the revenue from excise duties. It is very probable that in conditions of complete free trade within the Benelux area a dutiable product will be made by one partner country for export to, and consumption in, another partner country. If the rates of excise duty for the product concerned are the same in all the partner countries, there is no need to control the trade in the product at the common frontier in order to see that the rates of tax are adjusted to the rates ruling in the imported partner country. But if the excise duty is levied in the first instance on the production of the product the revenue will all accrue to the Government of the country in which the commodity is produced; none of it will go to the Government of the country where it is consumed. If it is desired to distribute the revenue on any basis other than that of the location of the production of the product within the economic union, it will be necessary in some way to pool the revenue from these unified excise taxes in order to distribute it on some other principle.

In Benelux there has not as yet been great success in the final unification of excise duties. In many cases, therefore, a control has had to be maintained at the common frontier between the Netherlands and Belgium. When a product which is subject to excise duty is exported from the Netherlands to Belgium it is exempt from Dutch excise duty on export from the Netherlands but is subject to Belgian excise duty on import into Belgium. But certain excise duties have been unified – in particular, a Protocol of December 1947 unified the duties on sparkling fermented drinks, and in this case no tax control is exercised on the common frontier. Nevertheless, the control at the common frontier must even in this case still be maintained for statistical purposes. For by a Convention of February 1950 it is agreed that the revenue from unified excise duties should be distributed between the Governments concerned according to the location of the consumption, and not of the production, of the product. Thus for every product passing from Belgium to the Netherlands on which the excise is unified an account must be kept, so that the Belgian Government, which will have received the excise revenue from the production of the product, may be made accountable for this sum to the Dutch Government, in whose territory the product is consumed.

Thus the principle of distributing the revenue according to the amount consumed is already in application for the few excise duties which have already been formally unified; and it was certainly the intention of the

Governments of the three Benelux countries in the final Benelux Economic Union when all important excise duties, as well as the customs duties, have been unified, to pool the revenue from both sources and to distribute it between the Governments of the three countries on some agreed basis.

Quite apart from the system or lack of system on which the revenue is divided between the partner countries, the mere fact that uniform rates of duty are imposed by the partner countries raises an important budgetary problem. A substantial part of the budgetary revenue for each national Government is then determined not by the decisions of the particular Minister of Finance and Government of each country, but by a common agreement which implies, first, that changes in tax rates can only be made occasionally and with considerable delay since each partner must agree to the change and, second, that if one Government is to increase its revenue by raising the relevant rates of tax the revenue of the other partner Governments must be increased simultaneously and in the same manner.

This problem which is already an appreciable one in Benelux with the unification of customs duties would become a very serious one if all customs, excise, and turnover taxes were unified. In that case some 50 per cent of tax revenue (rather more for Belgium and rather less for the Netherlands) would no longer be under the direct control of the Minister of Finance of the country concerned. Suppose there were, for example, a general intensification of world inflationary pressures or a general recession in world economic activity; and suppose further that the Belgian and Dutch Governments wished to react in rather different ways to these situations. For example, the Dutch authorities in a time of recession might wish to stimulate demand by the use of a rapid fiscal instrument, such as a reduction in the rate of turnover tax. But if the Belgian authorities wished to rely on monetary rather than on budgetary policies to maintain equilibrium, the Dutch would be unable to act in this way. In the modern world, the unification of the rates of all the main indirect taxes for the 'commercial' purpose of promoting free trade between the partners intensifies, through its effects upon budgetary revenues, the case for an extension of co-operative action into 'financial' spheres concerned with the control of inflation, the maintenance of full employment, and the preservation of equilibrium in the balance of payments.

Finally, it may be of interest to point out two administrative implications of the formation of the common Benelux tariff.

In the first place, at the Geneva tariff negotiations in 1947 it was necessary for the three Benelux countries to have a single joint delegation which negotiated the new joint Benelux tariff with the large number of other countries concerned. Separate national delegations were sent to Geneva for the purpose of the rest of the commercial negotiations, that is to say for the negotiation of the general articles concerning quantitative restrictions, subsidies, state trading, and the rest, for inclusion in the Charter of the proposed General Agreement on Tariffs and Trade. But as the Benelux tariff was a completely joint and unified structure, it could be negotiated with other countries only by a single mixed delegation which received a single set of instructions on the basis of agreements reached between the Dutch and the Belgian Governments in the Hague and Brussels.

In the second place, in order to make it possible to negotiate changes in the joint Benelux tariff in commercial agreements with other countries without intolerable delays and uncertainties a special parliamentary procedure was devised for each partner country. In the legislation enacted by each of the three parliaments concerned for the ratification of the customs union each Government was empowered by its legislature to agree upon, and to put into force, changes in the joint Benelux tariff, only with the obligation to obtain subsequent parliamentary approval of the changes. The duties would be restored to their previous level if the parliament of one of the countries failed to approve the change. It was also thought that some such procedure for facilitating changes in the joint tariff was especially necessary in view of the rapidity with which the final Benelux tariff had to be drawn up and in view of the necessarily experimental nature of so novel a tariff structure.

12

The Price Mechanism and the Australian Balance of Payments[1]

In 1956 Meade spent six months at the Australian National University in Canberra; during his stay he wrote this article, from the Economic Record*, vol. 32 (November 1956), pp. 239–256, and, jointly with Eric Russell of the University of Adelaide, the following one.*

In recent years Australia has been experiencing simultaneously a domestic inflation and a deficit on her balance of payments. There can be no doubt what is the correct policy to adopt in a situation of this kind. Total domestic monetary expenditure should be deflated by means of monetary and/or budgetary policy. In so far as the reduction in expenditure causes a fall in the demand for home-produced products it relieves the domestic inflationary pressure or releases for export goods which were being consumed at home; and in so far as it causes a fall in the demand for imports it directly relieves the balance-of-payments position.

Professor Downing in his article 'The Australian Economy, March, 1956', in the *Economic Record* for May 1956, [vol. 32, pp. 1–27] analysed the then existing position in Australia; and this position is still substantially unchanged. In the course of the last twelve months disinflationary monetary and budgetary policies have been adopted in Australia which have caused a very considerable improvement in the domestic situation. The acute strain in the labour market has eased; but there has been less success in restraining the upward movement of money prices and wage-rates.

There is, however, some room for doubt whether the disinflationary process has yet been carried quite far enough. There are a number of reasons for holding this view.

In the first place, there is still probably some element of overfull employment in the Australian economy which may seriously impede the structural changes of Australian industry which, as we shall argue later, are necessary to put the balance of payments into equilibrium. The number of unemployed in Australia is still only a fraction of 1 per cent of

[1] The ideas contained in this article owe their origin to many conversations with many economists in Australia. I would in particular like to thank Professor Swan and Professor Arndt for helpful suggestions.

the labour force. Putting the balance of payments right involves, as we shall see, the adoption of an economic policy which will make production for export or to replace imports more profitable relatively to the production of non-tradeable products for the home market, in order to induce labour and other factors of production to move from the latter to the former groups of industries and occupations. Now this movement will not take place unless there is some moderate push out of the contracting industries as well as a strong pull into the expanding industries. And if labour is to move from one occupation to another, there is bound to be a certain number in the process of movement at any one moment of time. The authorities concerned should take all measures possible to ease the process of movement with generous unemployment benefits, with help in finding suitable new posts, with facilities for retraining, and with aid in geographical movement; and financial policy should never be so disinflationary as to cause any massive volume of unemployment. But it would not appear to be unreasonable to disinflate so as to give greater flexibility to the economy, even if this involved temporary unemployment of up to 2 per cent of the total number of workers.

There is a second consideration which strongly reinforces this conclusion. For reasons which are obvious enough, but which we shall discuss in detail later on, it is much more difficult to deal with a balance-of-payments deficit if there is a continual inflation of money wage-rates and costs in process than if there is reasonable stability of wage costs. Whatever may be the process of wage-fixing, money wage-rates are likely to rise more quickly the greater is the excess of demand for labour over the supply of labour. A disinflation of total domestic expenditure could be an important factor in moderating the rate of rise in money wage-rates as well as in commodity prices.

There is a third reason why some intensification of the present disinflationary policies would be wise. The deficit on the balance of payments is held in check now only by the imposition of fairly severe restrictions on imports. As long as a deficit on the balance of payments still exists, in the sense that a loss of overseas funds can be avoided only by means of strict import licensing, there is a strong argument for weighting the scales rather more heavily in favour of disinflation than would otherwise be the case. It is difficult to say whether the current rate of import is already sufficiently restricted to avoid any further loss of overseas reserves. This depends upon other unknowns such as the future price of wool and the amount of capital which will in fact flow into Australia from abroad. But, in any case, the existing restrictions on imports have not yet had their full effect in reducing the volume of imports; and the volume of imports is, therefore, likely to be further reduced in the course of the next year. This in itself will restrict the total supplies of goods available for purchase and, unless something else happens to restrict the amount of domestic expenditure or to increase the domestic supply of goods and services, this will lead to an increase in inflationary pressure and so to the need for some further disinflationary measures.

Of course, in the coming months things other than a further shortage of imported supplies will occur to affect the general balance between money expenditure and available supplies. The price of wool, the rate at which merchants and business men will desire to build up their stocks, the actual rate of immigration, and – closely connected with that – the future rate of expenditure on house-building or other forms of investment, the amounts which people will wish to save out of their incomes, changes in output due to changes in the productivity of labour – all these are unknown factors which may operate to increase inflationary pressures or to mitigate them.

But these things are too uncertain for it to be possible to predict with any confidence how on balance they will affect the inflationary situation. It is necessary at the time of the annual Budget to make the best possible guess in order to set rates of taxation which are most likely to be suitable for conditions over the coming year. But it is most undesirable to adhere rigidly to any policy which is so set. Certainly there should be complete readiness to change monetary policies from month to month in order to impose a stricter policy if in the event inflationary forces should gather force or to relax credit conditions if any serious unemployment should begin to appear. Personally I am driven more and more to the less orthodox conclusion that it would be most desirable if some form of tax could be found (say a sales tax or a pay-roll or an income tax) which was technically capable of frequent variation and if some political and administrative arrangements could be found whereby this tax could be promptly raised or lowered at any time of the year (and not merely at Budget-time) as a means of controlling the total level of domestic expenditure. However that may be, it is essential by monetary and/or fiscal means to be able and ready to make prompt and frequent effective adjustments of financial policy. This would strengthen the case for adopting a rather more disinflationary policy now; for it could then be promptly reversed if it should prove too severe.

So much for the case for some intensification of present disinflationary financial policies. In present Australian conditions the problem of the balance-of-payments deficit seems to be more acute than the remaining domestic problem of overfull employment; and it would almost certainly prove necessary to put a stop to the process of disinflation in order to prevent the growth of serious unemployment before the point was reached at which the balance-of-payments problem was fully solved, that is to say, before the point was reached at which import licensing could be virtually abolished without danger to Australia's overseas funds. This I will call the residual balance-of-payments problem. The question to which I must now turn is how to deal with this residual deficit. What should one do when, in the interests of preventing excessive unemployment, exclusive reliance can no longer be placed upon further use of the weapon of general disinflation of demand at home?

There are four possible answers to this question:

The first line of action is to let the deficit continue and to find some way of financing it.

The second possibility is to suppress the deficit through the maintenance of direct controls over foreign transactions and, in particular, through quantitative restrictions of imports.

Third, it is possible to cheapen home production, and thus to encourage exports and to discourage imports, by a reduction of money wage costs combined with a further disinflation of domestic money expenditure so as to bring prices down in line with reduced costs.

Fourth, the exchange rate may be depreciated so that imports are discouraged and exports encouraged as a result of the rise in the prices of these products in terms of Australian pounds.

Let me say something about the possibilities and relative merits of the application of each of these methods in the present conditions of the Australian economy.

It is clearly impracticable for Australia to finance any substantial deficit on her balance of payments out of her remaining London funds or her drawing rights on the International Monetary Fund or other similar sources of special 'accommodating' finance. But it is very reasonable to reduce the residual balance-of-payments problem through the inflow of other capital into Australia. It is very proper and natural that a relatively new and sparsely populated continent which is being rapidly developed and is experiencing a rapid growth of population by natural increase and by immigration should finance part of its development by an inflow of capital funds, as Australia has in fact been doing in recent years. There are those who are now arguing that Australia should relieve her inflationary pressure and her balance-of-payments problem by reducing the rate of immigration. If I were an Australian, for non-economic reasons I should not want to see the pace of immigration reduced. I would much prefer to see the pace of capital inflow speeded up, if that were possible and were the alternative to a slackened rate of immigration. The easy profits associated with inflation may be attractive to the investment of foreign equity capital in Australia; but the transfer of the high profits made in such conditions by the concerns which are technically successful may place a severe burden on the future Australian balance of payments. Borrowing of foreign capital at fixed interest is less open to this objection; and it is possible that some intensification of disinflationary policies domestically would help to raise the flow of such capital into Australia. In the first place, if the disinflationary policy takes the form of a stricter monetary policy it will lead to a scarcity of monetary funds on Australian capital markets and to some rise in rates of yield on such capital funds; and this might help to attract funds to Australia. Secondly, the more effective the fight against domestic inflation in Australia, the less the prospect that the Australian pound will ultimately be depreciated or the smaller the depreciation that will be expected; and this may keep some capital funds in Australia which might otherwise be removed. But it is not probable that any substantial new source of foreign capital can be found in the near future and even if some contribution to the problem were made from an increased flow of capital into Australia, it seems most improbable that that could, in the near future at any rate, cover the whole of the residual balance-of-payments deficit. We must examine the other remaining measures.

Professor Lundberg and Mr Hill in their article entitled 'Australia's Long-Term Balance of Payments Problem' in the *Economic Record* for May 1956, [vol. 32, pp. 28–49] have enumerated some of the economic inefficiencies which a permanent system of quantitative import licensing may entail: the bottleneck situations which may develop, the encouragement which may be given to monopolistic situations, the rise in the costs of export production which may result, and the protection which may be given to really inefficient lines of production. These criticisms were directed specifically against the use of quantitative import licensing. But I would like to add two more general considerations which would tell against the discouragement of imports by a general duty or other levy on all imports as well as against the selective control of imports by quantitative import quotas.

First, a reduction in Australian costs relatively to overseas costs (whether it was brought about by a fall in Australian wage costs, a rise in foreign wage-costs, or a depreciation of the foreign exchange value of the Australian pound) would do something to encourage Australian exports as well as to discourage imports. Moreover, it would also do something to affect invisible as well as visible trade. To give one example of this last point, a reduction in Australian costs relatively to United Kingdom costs would reduce freight rates on coastal shipping from Sydney to Fremantle relatively to sterling freight rates from London to Fremantle and would thus help to divert Western Australian demand onto the manufactured products of the Eastern States shipped in Australian ships. As one who believes that there are still important economies to be obtained from concentrating output where comparative costs are lowest and who thinks that the price mechanism in the market is still the most efficient and rapid calculating machine yet devised for the solution of the rather complicated economic riddles involved, I start favourably disposed to general price changes which adjust conditions in all markets rather than to import restrictions or duties which concentrate their effects on one group of products or prices.

Second, we should look for a system of balance-of-payments adjustment which, if generalised for all countries, would work smoothly and effectively. For reasons which I cannot now develop I believe that, if Australia uses the general price mechanism rather than concentrating on the limitation of imports to solve her balance-of-payments problems, it will be easier for the United Kingdom and other countries to adjust their foreign trade to the corrective adjustments taken by Australia, just as it will be easier for Australia to solve her balance-of-payments problems if the United Kingdom and other countries use the general price mechanism rather than the limitation of imports to deal with their difficulties. In other words, I think a generalised system of exchange-rate variation or wage-rate adjustment is better than a generalised system of import restriction.

Accordingly I propose to turn now to a consideration of the two basic 'price-mechanism' methods of dealing with a residual balance-of-payments problem, namely (1) wage policy, which will adjust Australian wage costs to foreign costs, and (2) exchange-rate policy, in order to consider whether either or both of them can be expected to work satisfactorily in the Australian case. If our answer is No, then we shall be driven back on to import restrictions as the only remaining effective method. I shall start by considering a basic question which is common to both types of price-mechanism policy; namely, is the structure of the Australian economy such that a general price adjustment, however brought about, can be effective in removing a residual balance-of-payments deficit?

Now a depreciation of the exchange rate and a cut in wage-rates are best regarded as alternative means of raising the price of imports and exports relatively to the price of other products in the Australian economy.

The way in which a depreciation of the rate of exchange brings about this change in relative prices is clear. An increase in the number of Australian pounds payable or receivable for a given amount of sterling or dollars will tend to raise the price of imports and exports in Australia, since nothing will have happened directly to change the price of these products in overseas markets in terms of overseas currencies; but the depreciation will not itself have done anything to raise the price of other goods and services produced in Australia. (It must be remembered that we are assuming a sufficiently disinflationary financial policy in Australia to prevent the price of such products from being driven up by an excess of money demand over and above their costs of production.)

A similar change in relative prices could have been brought about by a general reduction of money wage-rates in Australia. Such a reduction would reduce the costs of goods produced in Australia and, on the assumption of a sufficiently disinflationary financial policy to adjust demand to what is sufficient to cover costs, the prices of such goods when consumed in Australia would be reduced. On the other hand, the prices of imports and exports would tend to be kept up to the level at which these products were being traded in overseas markets. Once again the prices of imports and exports would tend to be raised relatively to those of other products in Australia.

This change in relative prices might help in various ways to increase the volume of goods made available for export or to reduce the volume of imported goods which people wished to purchase.

First, the rise in the profitability of producing exportable products relatively to other products might increase the volume of exports. Wool and other rural products account for the greater part of Australia's exports; but the production of these rural products uses such different resources from the production of non-rural output that there is not likely to be any appreciable quick increase in output of rural products consequent upon a rise in the price of rural relatively to non-rural products. Of course, if the price of one rural product (say, wheat) rises relatively to that of another rural product (say, wool), then at the margin there may be some significant shift of land and other resources from the latter to the former line of production. But the problem we are now considering is where the price of all rural exportable products together rises relatively to that of non-rural products; and this will not lead to any great immediate expansion of total rural output. On the other hand, it may well be that there is a significant range of manufactured goods which Australia might well begin to produce for export to some of the neighbouring countries as they develop their economies, if Australian costs were brought more in line with costs in other manufacturing countries; the expansion of these industries would use resources of labour and capital which might well be attracted from other lines of domestic production.

Second, the rise in the price of Australian exports will raise their cost to the Australian consumer, who may thus be induced to shift his own purchases on to cheaper alternative products and thus to release more exportable goods for actual export. In the case of Australia's great export product, wool, this cannot be of any great importance. Australia already exports over 90 per cent of her output of wool, so that, even if a rise in the price of raw wool did cause Australians to consume appreciably less of it at home (which is not very probable), it could not release much more for export. But Australia herself consumes some two-thirds of her production of butter, half of her cheese, a third to a quarter of her canned fruit, two-thirds of her eggs, three-quarters of her meat, and over a third of her wheat. If a relative rise in the price of these exportables did cause any significant shift of demand on to alternative home-produced products (and why should not a rise in the price of butter, for example, be allowed to cause a shift of demand on to margarine?), the effect in increasing supplies available for export might be considerable. There may also be some real significance in the shift of Australian demand away from manufactured goods which she exports or might export on to other home products which could not be exported.

On the import side the picture is more encouraging. A rise in the price of imports relatively to other goods can be expected to have a very considerable effect upon the volume of goods which Australians will wish to import. Direct import replacements in many cases in Australia do not require very specialised factors for their production; and many imports compete in consumers' purchases fairly directly with many other home-produced products. A rise in the price of imports relatively to other products is, therefore, likely to cause a considerable reduction in the demand for imports both because the demand for these types of product will fall and because the output of them in Australia itself will rise. Less will be wanted; more will be produced at home, and for both reasons the demand for imports will be reduced.

The scope for a further reduction of actual Australian imports in present conditions must not be exaggerated. Import licensing has already caused Australian imports to be confined more and more to imports of raw materials and producers' equipment which cannot be produced at home. But we are, of course, considering the use of the price mechanism as an alternative to import licensing; and a rise in the price of imports relatively to other products would, for the reasons which we have just discussed, reduce the demand for those replaceable imports which are at present excluded by administrative licensing. In so far as the future Australian balance-of-payments problem should turn out to be so serious as to require still further limitation, the price-mechanism method will have the advantage of raising the price of all imports equally and thus will induce throughout the community an economy of the direct or indirect use of imported supplies of all kinds, the further savings of imports being thus automatically concentrated on those lines of production where the import content of home output is greatest and where, therefore, a further saving of imports causes least damage. Such a result could, of course, be obtained by substituting a general *ad valorem* charge or duty on all imports for the present system of selective import licensing. But if Australia's situation is such that she is likely to have real difficulty in financing the import of adequate supplies of indispensable materials and producers' equipment, then her future must lie in expanding her exports (including exports of manufactured goods) in order to finance a more adequate volume of imported materials and equipment; and this requires a general price adjustment which will stimulate exports as well as restrict imports.

Of course, all the various shifts of output and of demand which we have discussed above will take time to develop. We cannot expect any substantial shift of resources into the production of exportable and of import-replacing products to take place immediately upon a change in relative prices and profitabilities. Some small changes requiring only a movement of unskilled labour from one firm to another in the same district may take place practically immediately; but substantial shifts which require the retraining of labour, the movement of labour from one district to another, or the installation of new equipment will take time. Shifts of demand between final products are less liable to delay for technical reasons, but patterns of consumers' expenditure will be modified only gradually in response to price changes. We can expect a general price adjustment in Australia to exert its full effect on the volume of goods offered for export and the volume of goods desired by importers only after the lapse of some considerable time. I shall return later to the problem of filling the gap during the process of change.

So far we have argued as if the price of Australian exports and imports on world markets would remain unaffected by the steps which were being taken to put her balance of payments right. Would this necessarily be so? A reduction in Australia's purchase of imports would probably not cause any very appreciable fall in the price at which she could obtain these goods in foreign markets; for in general Australia makes up only a small part of the total world market for them. This is no longer universally true of Australia's imports; she provides, for example, a very substantial market for United Kingdom motor-cars; and a sharp reduction in Australian purchases may significantly keep down the price of such cars. We may conclude that a considerable reduction of imports by Australia might cause a moderate, but only a moderate, fall in their price. On the other hand, Australia does produce a relatively large part of the world supply of some export products like wool and an appreciable increase in the amount which she put on the world market might cause an appreciable fall in the world price. But wool is becoming increasingly subject to the competition of synthetic fibres and the overseas demand is probably for this reason already considerably more responsive to changes in price than used to be the case. In the case of some of Australia's exports, like wheat, imports into the buying countries are seriously impeded by quotas and other rigid import barriers. In such cases any attempt on Australia's part to increase the volume of her sales would inevitably lead to a substantial fall in the price of the product with only a small increase in the amount sold. But in the case of these staple export products we have seen that Australia is not in fact likely to put much more on the world market as the result of a general price adjustment. Exports of manufactured products by Australia have to compete with similar exports from other countries, and an increase in the amount exported is not likely to cause a substantial change in their price. So Australia's terms of trade are not likely to be seriously affected by a general price adjustment. The price in foreign exchange of her imports is not likely to change much because of the high elasticity of supply of these products to her. The price of her exports in foreign exchange is not likely to be affected very significantly because the elasticity of her supply of exports to the outside world is likely to be rather low in the case of those products for which the overseas elasticity of demand is low.

The Australian economy is such that a general adjustment of Australian prices and costs relatively to world prices and costs would effectively improve Australia's balance of trade. It would considerably decrease her demand for imports and somewhat increase her supply of exports at not very different terms of trade between imports and exports.

But in Australian conditions the choice between import restrictions and the price mechanism will have a considerable effect on the internal distribution of income. An exchange depreciation or a reduction of the general level of money wage costs in Australia will, as we have seen, raise the price of imports and of *exportable* products relatively to other products; import restrictions or a rise of import duties will raise the price of import products relatively to that of all other products, including *exportable* products, and will then have its effect by reducing the demand for and encouraging the output of imports and import-competing products. The price mechanism will, therefore, result in a higher price for exportables than will the method of import restriction. Because many exportables (like wool and wheat) depend so largely for their production on a factor of production (land) which is little needed for the production of other products, the use of the price mechanism will cause a distribution of income more favourable to landowners than will the use of import restrictions.

This problem is not, of course, unique to Australia. A policy of import restriction in any country will normally increase the demand for home products which can replace imports at the expense of the demand for products which might otherwise be exported, and will thus improve the position of the producers of the former relatively to the position of the producers of the latter. But the problem is specially severe in Australia for two reasons: in the first place, there is so sharp a difference between the factors used in producing primary products for export and those used in producing goods to replace imports that it is specially difficult to move from the one to the other line of production; and, secondly, wool growing contains what is already by far the richest and most prosperous class of citizens.

A further redistribution of income in favour of the producers of primary products for export may well be regarded as an undesirable feature of the use of the price mechanism. If so, the rational and logical step would be to combine with the use of the price mechanism some fiscal arrangements to offset this undesired redistribution of income. For example, the institution of some special scheme for the stabilisation of wool prices, or the removal of special leniencies in the way in which pastoral incomes are taxed, or a general recasting of the tax system whereby richer persons pay a rather larger and poorer persons a rather smaller proportion of their incomes in tax. If the avoidance of quantitative restrictions would in fact in itself help to raise total real incomes (on the old-fashioned free-trade grounds that it would enable Australia to concentrate more on the production of things in which she is most efficient), it is likely that some other more direct and effective method of redistribution could be found to prevent the excessive enrichment of landowners.

There is one other, closely related, reason why the method of import restriction may be more easy to apply in Australia than the general price-mechanism method. As we have seen, the latter method consists in getting Australian costs and, in particular, wage costs lower than before in relation to costs in other countries. This can be brought about by a reduction in Australian wage costs in terms of Australian pounds with a corresponding fall in the price of the general range of Australian products but without a corresponding fall in the price of importable products (i.e. of imports and of import-competing products) and of exportable products. Or else it can be brought about by a depreciation of the rate of exchange which leaves wage costs and the price of a wide range of domestic products unchanged but raises the price of importables and exportables in terms of Australian pounds. In both cases the real wage-rate tends to fall in so far as the prices of importables and exportables enter into the wage-earners' cost of living. I shall have more to say later about the question whether it is easier to achieve this restraint on real wage-rates by the one or the other method of applying the price mechanism. At the moment I want to address myself to the question whether the use of import restrictions enables one to avoid this problem completely.

There is in fact a similar problem with import restrictions. These by making imported products scarcer on the home market will tend to raise their price and so the cost of living. If wage-rates were raised as a result of this rise in the cost of living, domestic costs and prices would be raised and a vicious spiral of inflation might ensue. The dangers of a system of variable exchange rates in such conditions of a cumulative domestic inflation are well known; it would lead to a perpetual cumulative tendency for the Australian pound to lose its value in terms of other currencies. But strangely enough the equally bad – and possibly worse – effects of import restrictions in similar circumstances are often overlooked. If there is a continuing domestic inflation of costs relatively to foreign costs at a fixed rate of exchange, exports will continually decline. Import restrictions will, therefore, have to be made more and more severe, and there is no logical end to this process until imports and exports are both reduced to zero. A system which tends to reduce trade to nothing must be compared with one which tends to reduce the foreign-exchange value of the currency to zero; and this is an awkward choice which is best avoided. It can be avoided only by the avoidance of a cumulative domestic inflation. Import restriction is preferable to exchange depreciation on these grounds if, but only if, import restriction will make it possible to avoid a domestic wage inflation which cannot be avoided with exchange depreciation.

There are some grounds for believing that in the Australian economy the wage problem may be somewhat more tractable with import restrictions than with the use of the price mechanism.

First, there is the implication of the point which we have already made about the effects of import restrictions upon the distribution of income. Import restrictions will raise the price offered for importable products but not for exportable products, whereas the use of the price mechanism will raise the price offered for exportable as well as for importable products. This latter will, therefore, raise the real incomes of the owners of land relatively to the real incomes of wage-earners. The real wage-rate (before payment of tax) in Australia can be maintained more easily with import restrictions, even though – if a suitable fiscal method of distribution could be found which kept the real incomes of the owners of land constant – the real incomes of wage-earners (after payment of tax) could probably be maintained at a higher level with the use of the price mechanism.

Second, it is sometimes argued that quantitative import licensing can be used to reduce imports, without raising their prices to consumers to the same extent as would occur if the same limitation of imports was achieved by other methods. Now import restrictions will make goods scarcer relatively to demand than they were before and, therefore, in the absence of price controls and rationing (which are difficult on constitutional grounds in Australia) either the price will go up or there will be scarcities and shop shortages. In the first case the consumer loses because the cost of living is higher, and in the second case he loses because the goods he wants are just not available at the prices quoted in the market. It would seem improbable that scarcities and shop shortages could last for any very considerable time without leading to rises in price; but as long as they did last, and to the extent that the wage-earner demands a higher money income to compensate him for a rise in the cost of living but not to compensate him for the inability to buy certain goods, the wage problem may be more tractable with import restrictions than with the use of the price mechanism.

Third, import restrictions can be applied selectively to those products which enter least into the cost of living; and this provides an opportunity of avoiding part of the wage trouble. But theoretically the trouble could, of course, be as well or better avoided by the use of the price mechanism combined with a system of indirect taxes and subsidies which kept up the prices of goods which did not enter into the cost of living and kept down the price of those which did.

If it is decided to use the price mechanism rather than the quantitative control of imports as the means of adjustment for the residual balance-of-payments deficit, we have to ask whether the necessary adjustment of real wage-rates would be more easily achieved in Australian conditions with a fixed exchange rate combined with a direct attempt to adjust money wage-rates or with more or less stable money wage-rates combined with an appropriate adjustment of the rate of exchange. There are three reasons why the latter method is often considered likely to be the easier.

The first reason we may call the 'summer-time illusion'. When to save daylight we want to get everyone to do everything an hour earlier, we put the clock on one hour; we do not attempt to persuade first family A, then factory B, then shop C, then office D, and then farmer E to start and to stop all operations one hour sooner by the clock. So when we need to get all real costs down by 10 per cent, it may be easier to alter the exchange rate than to reduce each money cost in turn. This argument probably has more force in a country like the United Kingdom where the wage-rate is fixed independently for each trade and occupation by separate processes of collective bargaining than in Australia which until recently has been used to the concept of a single basic wage applicable directly or indirectly to practically all workers and capable of adjustment up or down by a single decision of an arbitration court.

Second, there is what may be called 'the money-wage illusion'. In so far as wage-earners and other recipients of income think of their incomes primarily in terms of money – so many pounds and shillings per week – they will feel more concerned about a reduction in a money wage-rate than about an equivalent rise in the cost of living. This would make an adjustment of real wage-costs easier by an exchange-rate variation than by an adjustment of money wage-rates. Once again this consideration is likely to have more force in the United Kingdom where the formal tying of wage-rates to the cost of living is exceptional than in Australia where until very recently both in Commonwealth and State awards wage-rates have been subject to automatic quarterly adjustment to changes in a cost-of-living index, so that the wage-earner has become much less subject to any money illusion.

Third, there is what we may call 'the money-tax illusion'. In Australia income taxes have a high degree of progression in their incidence. The higher is a citizen's *money* income, the higher is the proportion of his income which he must pay in tax. Now a general price adjustment which operates by a depreciation of the exchange rate, a rise of the prices of importable and exportable products, and no fall in money wage-rates will result in a higher level of *money* incomes than one which operates by a fall in money wage-rates and in the price of the general run of domestic products without any fall in the price of importable and exportable products. Since progressive scales of tax are fixed in terms of *money* incomes, the former method will automatically result in a higher average rate of tax than the latter. Since, as we have seen, the success of a general price adjustment in removing a residual balance-of-payments deficit depends upon its being accompanied by some intensification of domestic disinflationary pressure, this is a strong point in favour of the use of an exchange-rate adjustment.

Against these considerations and in favour of the method of the direct adjustment of money wage-rates with a fixed rate of exchange must be set what may be called 'the financial-stringency illusion'. So long as the exchange rate is fixed there will be certain interests in the community, namely the producers of exportables and of import-competing products, who will have a direct interest in keeping down domestic money costs, because they have to compete at a fixed exchange rate with similar products produced in other countries. Moreover, it is clear and obvious that, with a fixed exchange rate, to remove a balance-of-payments deficit without using import restrictions requires a disinflation both of money costs and of money demand and prices. For reasons which have already been given above, it is in fact also true that a depreciation of the exchange rate requires a disinflationary domestic financial policy if it is to succeed in removing a balance-of-trade deficit; for it is necessary to restrict domestic demand when domestic supplies become scarcer as exports expand and imports contract. But this may be less obvious to the man in the street, who may be subject to the illusion that domestic financial restraint is unnecessary if the effects of higher prices and costs can always readily be offset by a further depreciation of the exchange rate. If this is so, final success may be more probable if some attempt is made to adjust money wages directly at a fixed rate of exchange.

This method is, however, bound to be slow and uncertain. The present need in Australia is to bring about an appreciable reduction in Australian money wage costs relatively to foreign money wage costs, if import restrictions are to be removed. It is quite uncertain what will happen to foreign wage costs; they will rise in so far as foreign money wage-rates go up and they will fall in so far as foreign currencies may be depreciated or the productivity of foreign labour rises. All these developments are uncertain and beyond Australia's control. She can only hope that foreign wage costs will rise so that her adjustment can be made with smaller pressure on Australian wage-rates. The best that can probably be expected from Australian wage policy is that for some time money wage-rates should not actually rise. It would seem to be fanciful to expect that an appreciable reduction in actual money wage-rates could be achieved in the modern full-employment Australian economy.

If this is so, the adjustment of the Australian balance of payments by this method is at best likely to be a relatively slow affair. First, the fall in Australian wage costs relatively to foreign wage costs is likely to be slow; and, second, as was pointed out above, the necessary adjustments of the flows of imports and exports to this change in relative costs and prices is itself likely to take considerable time. During this prolonged process import licensing will have to be maintained and can only be tailed off as and when imports are in fact restrained and exports promoted by the price adjustment. An exchange-rate adjustment, *provided always that it can be combined with a sufficiently disinflationary financial policy and with a restraint of money wage-rates*, would adjust relative prices and costs very quickly – indeed, more or less instantaneously – and the process of removal of import restrictions could start that much the quicker.

It is arguable that a slow and gradual adjustment is in any case preferable to the more rapid adjustment which an alteration in the exchange rate might make possible. The argument runs as follows: it is impossible to predict with certainty the future course of any balance of payments, and particularly of the Australian balance of payments with its great reliance on the price of wool which is subject to wide fluctuations. If something sometime goes wrong with the Australian balance of payments, it is impossible to say with certainty whether the change is permanent (and requires, therefore, a vast structural change) or mainly temporary (and requires, therefore, only a small structural change but presents a serious problem of filling a short-run gap). If the problem is in fact of the latter type, one does not want to make a vast price change through a large depreciation of the exchange rate, with all its difficult and disturbing reactions on the cost of living, merely in order to have to reverse it next year or the year after. But since one never in fact knows whether a given change will lead to long-lasting trouble or not, the best policy is to see that the price adjustment is always being made at a moderate pace in the direction which the present situation demands. Meanwhile, the short-run gap must be controlled by import restrictions.

But against this it may be argued that a sharp deterioration in the balance-of-payments situation may turn out to be permanent and to require an appreciable structural change in the economy. If in these circumstances the price adjustment starts off only at a snail's pace in the correct direction, import restrictions will become almost a permanent feature of the economic system. In my opinion, the argument from uncertainty presents a strong case against the use of the instrument of the variable exchange rate in the form of alterations from time to time in the rate at which the Australian pound is pegged to other currencies. For in that case the authorities will naturally and properly avoid making a once-for-all (or perhaps one should say, a once-for-some-considerable-time) change in the exchange rate until it is unequivocally clear that an appreciable change is required; and even then a guess will have to be made at what is the correct level for the new peg; and the chances are very high that this guess will turn out to be wrong. In the end the exchange rate might be subject to spasmodic and substantial alterations, each change taking place only when an alteration was clearly overdue. This would constitute a speculator's paradise. At each of these critical points it would become clear that a big profit might be made by selling the currency (if a depreciation were overdue) or by buying the currency (if an appreciation were overdue). In neither case would any good social purpose be served by the speculation.

The position would be different with a freely fluctuating exchange rate. In this case if something went wrong with the balance of payments, the rate of exchange of the Australian pound would immediately fall. As it fell, more and more people with their varying assessment about the underlying real factors, such as the long-run outlook for Australian produce in world markets, would pass from the category of those who thought that the Australian pound was overvalued to those who thought that the current value of the Australian pound was so low that, when the new price relationships had had time to work out their full favourable effects upon Australian imports and exports, the value of the Australian pound would rise again. In other words, as the value of the Australian pound fell, more and more speculators would stop selling and would start buying Australian pounds, until a point was reached at which a temporary deficit on the balance of payments was being financed by an inflow of speculative funds. Thereafter, the rate of exchange would rise or fall from month to month as events helped to show the true seriousness of the initial disturbance or as new disturbances, favourable and unfavourable, occurred and demanded new estimates of Australia's long-run prospects.

In order that such a system should have a real chance of working effectively two conditions need to be fulfilled.

First, there must be a number of clever and rich men or institutions who are able to make well-informed and intelligent judgements about future commercial prospects and are prepared to back their judgement in the foreign exchange market. On this score I would be optimistic. Funds have in the past moved into or out of the Australian pound on a considerable scale in expectation of an alteration in the exchange rate, as witness the considerable inflow of capital into Australia in 1949/50 and 1950/51 when an appreciation of the Australian pound was expected. There are many clever men of the right kind in London, and probably also in New York, Zürich, Amsterdam and Paris, to say nothing of Sydney and Melbourne who might perform this useful speculative function.

But in order that they should do so one further condition must be satisfied. It must be confidently expected that there is not going to be a domestic inflation of money incomes, prices, and costs in Australia. Our clever men must be asked to speculate on such commercial matters as the long-run prospects of the world demand for wool and not on such political–financial matters as whether there is going to be a runaway domestic inflation in Australia. For in the latter case, when something went wrong with the balance of payments and the Australian pound started to fall in value, our clever men might sell Australian pounds simply because they expected the trouble to lead to an inflation inside Australia which would make further depreciation of the exchange rate necessary; and the speculators' flight from the Australian pound might itself cause an unnecessary depreciation of the exchange rate and a consequent rise of the Australian cost of living of such a magnitude that it in fact caused the domestic inflation which itself in turn justified the speculators' pessimism.

So whatever way one looks at the problem, one comes back to the same basic conclusion. In order to achieve a satisfactory solution of her balance-of-payments problems it is essential that Australia should operate from a firm domestic financial base. This involves three elements. First, there must be a monetary and budgetary disinflationary policy, quickly and promptly adjustable to changing circumstances, such as to avoid too great a tension in the domestic markets for commodities and for labour but without causing any substantial unemployment. Second, there must be some machinery for the settlement of wage problems which is capable of keeping increases of Australian wage-rates at least down to the rates at which the productivity of Australian labour is rising, without any tie to the cost of living. Thirdly, there must be some fiscal arrangements for obtaining desired effects upon the distribution of income without having to rely on import restrictions as the only practicable method of affecting the incomes of rich landowners.

This is perhaps enough to be getting on with! When these conditions have been achieved, experience will show whether it is possible to bring about necessary alterations in Australian prices and costs relative to foreign prices and costs at a reasonable speed by means of the direct control of wage-rates at a constant rate of exchange. My own guess would be that, if and when the conditions for a firm domestic financial base have been achieved, the situation will be such that the sharper instrument of a freely fluctuating exchange will also be found to have lost its dangers. But these are issues for solution in the future.

206-11
[1957]

13

Wage-Rates, the Cost of Living, and the Balance of Payments

Australia
4312

By J. E. Meade and E. A. Russell, from the Economic Record, *vol. 33 (April 1957), pp. 23–28.*

Australia is a country in which the following three conditions are all fulfilled: (1) her main exports (wool, wheat, meat, etc.) are the products of land rather than of labour; (2) these same products enter into the worker's cost of living; and (3) the money wage-rate is likely to vary upwards and downwards with the cost of living. In such circumstances an improvement in the overseas demand for Australia's products will have rather complicated effects upon the distribution of incomes in Australia and upon the Australian balance of payments. The impact effect of the increase in overseas demand for Australian products will, of course, be (i) to shift the distribution of income in favour of the owners of the land used for the production of Australian exports and (ii) to improve the Australian balance of payments. But it will also lead to a rise in the price of these export products and so in the cost of living. This will lead to a rise in wage-rates which will (i) redistribute income once more rather more favourably to wage-earners and (ii) will raise costs in the industries producing goods in competition with imports. As a result of this imports from abroad will be able to compete more easily with Australian products. There will be a rise in the value of imports; and, as is argued in the following paragraphs, it is by no means impossible that this increase in imports will be greater than the initial increase in exports. In such a case a permanent increase in the demand for Australia's exports could lead to a long-term strain on the Australian balance of payments.

Consider a country A which has only two factors, land and labour, and produces only two products, food and clothing. It exports food and imports clothing, food being very land-intensive and clothing very labour-intensive.

Suppose that the money price of food and of clothing are determined abroad in B (the rest of the world) in terms of the foreign currency of B. Suppose that B is so large relatively to A that A must take the prices ruling in B as given. Suppose that the rate of exchange between the currency of A and the currency of B is fixed at par and that there is a given 10 per cent *ad valorem* duty on imports of clothing into A. Then the price of food in A equals the price of food in B and the price of clothing in A is 10 per cent above the price of clothing in B.

Suppose that at these prices money wage-rates and money rents in A find levels which give full employment of land and labour in A and a balanced balance of payments between A and B.

Suppose now that the price of food rises in B by, say, 20 per cent because of an increased demand for food there, the price of clothing in B remaining unchanged. The demand for A's exports rises, and the terms of trade move permanently in A's favour by 20 per cent. We want to know what effect this has on the balance of trade, the prices of food and of clothing in A, the outputs of food and of clothing in A, the volume of employment in A, and the level of money and of real wage-rates and rents in A.

Consider first what will happen if money wage-rates in A are permitted to find their new equilibrium market level, i.e. without any tie to the cost-of-living index. The price of food will go up by 20 per cent in A and the price of clothing will remain constant in A. Food production will become profitable relatively to the production of clothing and factors of production will be attracted from clothing production to food production. But increased food production requires much land and little labour, while reduced clothing product releases little land and much labour. There will be a shortage of land and a plenty of labour. The rate of rent will rise relatively to the rate of wages. A higher proportion of labour to land will be used in both industries, since producers will try to economise the use of the expensive factor land and to use instead the cheap factor labour. Since the ratio of labour to land will have increased in both industries, the marginal production of labour and so the real wage-rate will have fallen in terms of both food and clothing. An improvement of A's international terms of trade will have made A's workers worse off, and A's landowners will have gained the whole and more than the whole of the increase in A's real income. In so far as A's producers of food exchange their exports of food on better terms with B's producers of clothing, A's producers of food enjoy the whole of the increase in A's real income due to the improvement in A's international terms of trade; and in so far as A's producers of food exchange another part of their output of food on better terms with A's own home producers of clothing, there is a further rise in the real incomes of A's producers of food at the expense of an absolute fall in the real income of A's producers of clothing.

In the conditions now under examination in A, the rise in the price offered for A's food in B will lead not only to a fall in the real wage-rate in A but also to a fall in the money wage-rate in A. The money price of clothing will be unchanged in A, because its money price in B is unchanged and the 10 per cent *ad valorem* rate of duty on its import into B is unchanged. In order that clothing should be produced in B, the money cost of clothing in B must be unchanged.[1] Since land and labour

[1] This is on the assumption that the rise in the price offered for food in B is not so great as to cause A to specialise totally on the production of food.

are the only two factors of production and since the rent of land has gone up relatively to the rate of wages, a constant cost of production of clothing in B involves an absolute rise in the money rate of rent and an absolute fall in the money rate of wages.

It might be considered more realistic to build a model for Australia in which no shift of factors were possible from the clothing to the food industry. This is easily done, and does not alter our basic conclusion that a rise in the price offered for food in B will cause a reduction in the real wage-rate in A, though it will no longer involve a fall in the money wage-rate in A. Suppose that land can be used for the production of food but for no other purpose, and suppose that labour can be used for the production of clothing but for no other purpose, this being merely the limiting case of extreme differences in factor proportions in the two industries. Then the amount of land in A being fixed, the output of food in A is fixed; and, similarly, the amount of labour being fixed, the output of clothing is fixed.

If now the price of food goes up by 20 per cent in B and in consequence rises by 20 per cent in A as well, the money rate of rent will also go up by 20 per cent. With the price of clothing in B and the rate of import duty into A constant, the price of clothing in A will be unchanged and in consequence the money wage in A will be unchanged. The real wage-rate measured in terms of clothing will in this case be unchanged, the money wage-rate and the money price of clothing both being unchanged. But the price of food has risen; and in so far as the workers who produce clothing in A purchase food from the landowners in A, the real wage-rate will have fallen in A and the real incomes of the landowners will have gone up by more than the total increase in A's income due to the improvement in A's international terms of trade.

Let us start once more from the initial equilibrium before the rise in the price offered for food in B. But let us now suppose that the money wage-rate in A is tied to a cost-of-living index which includes the price of clothing and of food with the result that the real wage-rate is kept constant in terms of some composite bundle of these two commodities. Suppose then that as before there is a 20 per cent rise in the price offered for food in B. What will now happen?

In A once more the money price of food will rise by 20 per cent and the money price of clothing will remain unchanged, since these prices are determined by the new market conditions in B. The rate of rent of land in A will rise because the increased world demand for food will represent indirectly an increased demand for land which is the factor most needed to produce food. But now the money wage-rate of labour will also be forced up because the rise in the price of food has raised the cost of living and the wage-rate is tied to the cost of living. But since the money rate of rent and the money rate of wages have both been forced up, the cost of production of clothing will have been raised. On the other hand, the price of clothing imported from B has not risen. A's domestic clothing industry will be priced out of the market by a flood of cheaper imports. Indeed, in our simple model there will be no end to this process until A's clothing industry has been eliminated, and A is importing all her clothing. A deficit will thus appear on A's balance of trade and unemployment will grow in A's clothing industry.

But A's government, we may suppose, has a domestic monetary and budgetary policy aimed at preventing the growth of unemployment. Total domestic expenditure is stimulated in order to maintain employment; but this only increases the demand for imports and worsens the balance-of-payments deficit. The only remaining cure is to restrict imports either by raising the existing 10 per cent import duty on clothing or else by adding to this duty a supplementary structure of import restrictions. When the tariff has been sufficiently raised or imports have been sufficiently restricted to raise the price of clothing in A to a level which makes A's clothing industry once more profitable, employment and the balance-of-payments equilibrium can be once more restored. We reach, therefore, the rather paradoxical conclusion that an increase in the overseas demand for A's exports of food which will permanently improve A's terms of trade and which will have the impact effect of improving A's balance-of-payments position will, after all its repercussions upon domestic prices and wage-rates have worked themselves out, lead to a permanent balance-of-payments problem which can be solved only by permanent import restrictions or a permanently higher tariff.

What will have happened to real incomes in A as a result of these changes? The first point to realise is that if the initial change is a 20 per cent increase in the price offered in B for A's exports of food, then final equilibrium of employment and the balance of payments will be restored only if the pre-existing import duty is increased sufficiently to raise the price of clothing in A by 20 per cent,[2] or if import restrictions of equivalent severity are imposed. In this case the money price of clothing as well as of food would be 20 per cent higher in A than before the change. The cost of living will be 20 per cent higher and because of its tie to the cost of living the rate of money wages will also be 20 per cent higher. Equilibrium in the market now demands that the money rate of rent should also be 20 per cent higher. In this case in A's domestic productive system nothing will have changed in real terms. Outputs will be unchanged; the ratios in which the factors are employed in each of the two industries will be unchanged; and the real marginal product of each factor in terms of each of the products will be unchanged. But the money price of every factor and every product will be inflated by 20 per cent. The community as a whole will, of course, be better off because of the improvement in A's real terms of trade. Each unit of A's food exports will purchase 20 per cent more in volume of imported clothing. This gain will, however, accrue directly neither to the landowner nor to the worker whose real rewards will be unchanged in terms of both products. It will accrue to the government of A in terms of the increased revenue derived from the additional import duty – unless, of course, a system of import licensing is employed, in which case it will accrue to those lucky citizens who have received the valuable limited rights to import. The distribution of the ultimate gain thus depends upon what the government does with

2 This involves a rise in the existing import duty from 10 per cent to 32 per cent *ad valorem*, so that prices in A rise by 20 per cent from 110 to 132.

the margin between the unchanged price in B and the higher price in A of the clothing imported into A from B.

There are two alternative mechanisms which with our model would have exactly the same real effects as the system which we have just examined, though the monetary effects would be different.

Suppose first that when the price of A's food in B rises by 20 per cent the foreign-exchange value of A's currency is appreciated by 20 per cent so as to keep the price of food constant in A. Then the price of clothing in A will fall by 20 per cent because the price is the same in B but 20 per cent more of B's currency is exchanged for a unit of A's currency. As a result the cost of living, and in consequence, the money wage-rate will be reduced in A by a fraction of 20 per cent, this fraction depending upon the weight of clothing in the cost-of-living index. But while the price obtainable for clothing has fallen by 20 per cent, the wage cost will have fallen by less than 20 per cent. Imported clothing will undercut home-produced clothing; a deficit will develop on the balance of payments; and unemployment will threaten in the clothing industry. If an expansionary financial policy is adopted to maintain full employment, this will only make the balance-of-payments deficit worse. The only cure is a higher tariff or import restrictions which will restore the domestic price of clothing to what it was. The cost of living and the wage-rate will then also be restored to their previous level. Everything will be exactly as it was at home – prices of food and clothing, the wage-rate, the rate of rent, and output and employment in both industries. The one real difference will be the increased revenue accruing to the government (or to the lucky recipients of import licences) from the margin between the lower prices (in A's currency) paid to the foreign producers of clothing and the unchanged prices inside A. The real result will be exactly the same as that which was achieved when the exchange rate was fixed; the only difference is that in the present case there is no rise in the general level of money prices and costs in A.

There is a second alternative mechanism which in our model will achieve exactly the same real result without any rise in the general levels of money prices and costs in A, even though the rate of exchange between A's and B's currencies remains unchanged. Suppose that an export levy or a stabilisation scheme were instituted for A's food exports, such that A's food producers received an unchanged price in terms of A's currency for their exports of food when the price in B rose by 20 per cent, the 20 per cent levy on food exports accruing in revenue to A's government. Then there would be no change in the wage-rate or the rate of rent in A either in money terms or in real terms; and the prices of food and of clothing would remain unchanged in A. The community would gain through the increased revenue to the government accruing from the higher price received for A's food in B.

In the preceding paragraphs we have been concerned with the effects upon the distribution of income and the balance of payments of a wage policy which maintains a given real wage-rate by tying the money wage-rate to the cost of living. It should be noted that our argument would apply without any modification if a wage policy were adopted (as is more nearly the case in New Zealand) to maintain the worker's share of the national income relatively to the farmer's share. Indeed, in this case our argument would have rather more general validity, since our conclusions would follow even if the price of A's exports did not enter into the cost of living of A's workers. Thus a rise in the price of A's food exports will increase the incomes of A's landowners. From this point onwards in our analysis it makes no difference whether the money wage-rate in A is raised to offset an adverse effect of the rise in the price of food on the cost of living in A or to ensure to the wage-earners in A a rise in money incomes proportionately as great as that enjoyed by the landowners.

Finally, we wish to stress the great oversimplifications which we have made in our model. In the real world it may not be true that a change in the volume of Australian export and import trade will not affect the prices of her exports or imports in B's markets; it may not be true that Australian import-competing products are perfect substitutes for Australian imports; Australia exports some products which are much less land-intensive than her main primary exports; there are the factors 'capital' and 'enterprise' to be considered as well as 'land' and 'labour'; there are groups of Australian industries producing 'non-tradeable' products (e.g. houses) which are neither import-competing nor exportable; and perfect competition is not the rule in all Australian markets. For this and for other reasons we have not tried to draw any conclusions about the desirability of different forms of policy in Australia. We have tried only to show that, because of certain features in the Australian economy, the good fortune of an improvement in the Australian real terms of international trade may tend to cause a fall in the absolute level of real wages, the prevention of which by a rise in money wage-rates may give rise to balance-of-payments problems and so to increased restrictions on Australia's foreign trade. It is no part of our purpose in this note to attempt to answer the question whether there are alternative and preferable methods of influencing the distribution of income. The answer to this question would involve assessments of the economic, administrative, and political advantages and disadvantages of many different measures in the particular circumstances of the actual Australian economy.

14

The Balance-of-Payments Problems of a European Free-Trade Area

Meade's Presidential Address to Section F of the British Association for the Advancement of Science, delivered in Dublin on 5 September 1957; from The Economic Journal, *vol. 67 (September 1957), pp. 379–396.*

I do not propose in this lecture to inquire into the effect of the institution of a free-trade area in Western Europe upon productivity, standards of living and so on. I propose only to raise some of the financial issues which are involved. Is it possible in Western Europe to combine free trade with full employment and balance-of-payments equilibrium?

Balance-of-payments problems as between the members of a European free-trade area can be avoided if each member takes steps to keep its own overall balance of payments in equilibrium. It will not matter if France, for example, is in deficit with the rest of the free-trade area provided she is in overall balance, i.e. in equal surplus with outside countries. She can then use the outside currencies which she earns to pay her debts within the free-trade area. And these outside currencies will be needed by the other members of the free-trade area; for if France is in deficit inside the free-trade area, some other member or members (say, Germany) must be in equal surplus within the free-trade area. But if Germany is also in overall balance, then the German surplus in the free-trade area must be matched by an equal German deficit with outside countries. If France has no overall deficit on her balance of payments, she can pay Germany with her earnings of outside currencies; and if Germany has no overall surplus on her balance of payments, she will need these outside currencies to pay her debts to the outside world.

This multilateral principle is well illustrated by the history of Benelux. Within Benelux the natural structure of trade and other transactions is such that the Netherlands is practically always in bilateral deficit with the Belgium–Luxembourg Economic Union. In the early post-war years the Dutch balance of payments was in overall deficit; and in these conditions the finance of her bilateral deficit with Belgium gave rise to problems which could be solved only by restricting Dutch imports from her partner. But from 1951 onwards the Dutch international payments regained an overall balance; and the Dutch were earning a surplus with outside countries which matched their deficit with the Belgium–Luxembourg Economic Union. The Dutch could pay the Belgians with the currencies of third countries.

Consideration of the payments problems of Benelux suggests that the maintenance of overall equilibrium in the balance of payments of each partner country is not merely a possible, but also the only acceptable, method of dealing with payments between the partners. Consider the alternative principle that each partner should keep its payments with the other members of the union (rather than with all the other countries of the world) in balance. This result could be achieved in Benelux without restrictions on intra-Benelux trade if there were a very great rise in Belgian prices and costs (brought about by inflation in Belgium or by an appreciation of the Belgian franc) so as to cause an increase in Belgian purchases from, and a decrease in Belgian sales to, the Dutch on a sufficient scale to bring the bilateral Belgian–Dutch balance of payments into equilibrium. But this would have threatened to put the Belgian overall balance of payments into serious deficit, since the rise in Belgian prices and costs would have increased Belgian imports from, and would have decreased her exports to, the rest of the world as well. Belgium would have had to impose strict controls over payments to other countries. Or if the Dutch–Belgian balance of payments were put into bilateral balance by such a deflation in the Netherlands as to reduce Dutch purchases from, and to increase Dutch sales to, Belgium to the required extent, then this would have caused a great decrease in Dutch imports from, and an increase in Dutch exports to, the outside world as well. The Dutch would have to deal with a large undesired surplus in their overall balance of payments.[1] In conditions in which the structure of trade and payments is such that some members of a free-trade area naturally have deficits with their partners matched by surpluses with outside countries, while other members are in the opposite situation, the principle that each member should be primarily concerned with its overall balance of payments is the only acceptable one.

Our first and basic principle is, therefore, that each member of the free-trade area should maintain equilibrium in its overall balance of payments. But before proceeding further I would like to make two comments on this general principle.

First, the maintenance of overall equilibrium in a country's balance of payments is nothing like so precise a criterion as might at first sight appear. Obviously, since some countries will naturally and properly be lending abroad or borrowing from abroad for ordinary commercial and

[1] Suppose that the Netherlands were in overall surplus (its deficit with Belgium being less than its surplus with the outside world), while Belgium were in overall deficit (her surplus with the Netherlands being less than her deficit with the outside world). Suppose then that the Dutch inflate and the Belgians deflate. The Dutch will get rid of their overall surplus by decreasing their surplus with the outside world but *increasing their deficit with Belgium*, while the Belgians will get rid of their overall deficit by decreasing their deficit with the outside world and *increasing their surplus with the Netherlands*. The solution of a balance-of-payments problem of a free-trade area may thus well involve the increase of the deficits and surpluses within the area itself.

developmental purposes, by equilibrium in the balance of payments we do not mean an equality between current payments and current receipts. We are concerned with the balance of all normal current and capital payments and receipts. Even so, we cannot make an exact equality between payments and receipts our criterion. A country which has very inadequate reserves of gold and dollars may properly aim at some surplus of normal receipts over payments which will enable it to bring its reserves to a reasonable level. We can only lay down a general principle that it is the duty of each member of the free-trade area to avoid a continuing deficit or surplus on its overall balance of payments which threatens to result in the unreasonable accumulation or loss of its reserves.

Second, we must allow for the fact that not all outside currencies are convertible into each other. To return to my Benelux example, suppose that the Netherlands and Belgium are both in overall equilibrium, but that the Belgians have a deficit with the outside world and a surplus with the Netherlands, while the Dutch have a deficit with Belgium but a surplus with the outside world. If the outside currency which the Dutch are earning is a 'hard' currency which is convertible into the outside currency which the Belgians are spending, all is well. The Dutch can pay the Belgians with this currency, and the Belgians can use it to finance their outside debts.

But trouble might arise if Benelux as a whole, while it is in overall balance, has an outside surplus of 'soft' currencies and an outside deficit of 'hard' currencies. The Netherlands might be earning a surplus of outside 'soft' currencies which were not convertible into the 'hard' currencies needed by Belgium for the finance of her outside deficit.

There are in fact two very different types of case in which a European free-trade area as a whole might be earning a surplus of 'soft' currencies.

In the first case the surplus earnings of the free-trade area may be in terms of a currency which is not freely convertible into other outside currencies but is more or less freely convertible into the currency of one of the members of the free-trade area. The outstanding example of this is, of course, the overseas members of the sterling area. Suppose that in the European free-trade area the Germans have a dollar deficit and that the French are in debt to the Germans but are earning a surplus in Australian pounds, which are freely convertible into United Kingdom pounds, the United Kingdom being a member and Australia not a member of the free-trade area. If sterling is not freely convertible into dollars, the French cannot pay the Germans in an outside currency which the Germans need. The basic cure in this type of case is, of course, that the sterling area as a whole, rather than just the United Kingdom, should be in overall balance. If the free-trade area (excluding the United Kingdom) has a surplus with the sterling area, then the sterling area (including the United Kingdom) will be in overall balance only if it has a surplus with some country outside the free-trade area and the sterling area, e.g. with the dollar world. Once again the circle is closed. France can pay Germany with her sterling earnings and, since the sterling area has a dollar surplus, Germany can convert this sterling into dollars for the finance of her dollar deficit without putting a strain on the sterling area's dollar reserves.

The basic balance-of-payments rule for the free-trade area must thus be modified to the effect that each national government undertakes to maintain overall equilibrium in the balance of payments of the monetary area of which it is the centre rather than merely overall equilibrium in its own national balance of payments. This puts the United Kingdom in a special position which has become a familiar problem in the European Payments Union and the Organisation for European Economic Co-operation. The United Kingdom, as banker for the sterling area, has cleared all sterling-area payments through EPU, but in the adjustment of the OEEC trade liberalisation programme to maintain balance-of-payments equilibrium she has been able to enter into commercial policy commitments only for the United Kingdom and not for the other members of the sterling area such as Australia.

A different type of problem might arise if the outside deficits of the free-trade area were in dollars and the outside surpluses were in some currency like the Brazilian cruzeiro, which is convertible neither into other outside currencies (such as the dollar) nor into the currency of a member country (such as sterling). But the countries of Western Europe are now in a sufficiently strong position to deal with this type of problem in a simple but decisive manner. If the monetary authority of each European country does not undertake to exchange into its own European currency any Brazilian cruzeiros which its exporters may earn, then in self-defence the individual European exporters to Brazil will demand from the Brazilian importers to be paid in their own European currencies or in other acceptable convertible currencies. This means that the Brazilian authorities have to take steps to see that their importers do not purchase more from Western Europe as a whole than Brazil can finance out of the proceeds of her exports or other earnings. Immediately after the war each country of Europe dealt with this problem by a separate bilateral payments arrangement with Brazil or with similar 'soft' currency countries. This is now unnecessary; and, through the so-called Hague Club, arrangements are now being made whereby the Brazilians can transfer any earnings which they may obtain in one European currency into another European currency for the purchase of goods from that second European country. In these conditions while one European country alone may have an excess of exports to Brazil and another an excess of imports from Brazil, there can be no problem of an excess of earnings of the 'soft' Brazilian currency by the free-trade area as a whole.

But let me return to my main problem. By what means can each member of the free-trade area keep its overall balance of payments in equilibrium? There are at least five possible lines of approach to this problem which I shall call the liquidity approach, the gold-standard approach, the integration approach, the direct-control approach and the exchange-rate approach.

By the *liquidity approach* I mean that steps might be taken to increase the availability of liquid reserves to the European countries which are in overall deficit so that they can thereby tide over temporary balance-of-payments difficulties. This cannot, of course, provide a full cure for lasting and permanent balance-of-payments deficits. But it can deal with temporary balance-of-payments problems and, above all, it can provide a buffer which will enable other measures for dealing with permanent difficulties to have time to work out their effects. Reserves of some European countries and particularly of the United Kingdom are still lamentably low. An increase in liquidity is an essential ingredient in a satisfactory solution of our problem.

How can this best be achieved? One's thoughts naturally turn to the European Payments Union, which provides a mechanism whereby, according to the credit element in the monthly settlements, European countries with a surplus in their payments to other European countries automatically provide credit, and so liquidity, to those European countries which have a deficit in their payments with other European countries. Could the European liquidity problem be solved by a development of this European instrument whereby European surplus countries provide credits to European deficit countries?

There are two serious objections to reliance upon an EPU type of mechanism.

In the first place there may well be times when the European free-trade area as a whole is in deficit with the outside world. This means that the overall deficits of the European deficit countries are greater than the overall surpluses of the European surplus countries. In such circumstances, it is impossible to cover the deficits of the deficit members by the surpluses of the surplus members. For this reason it would be much more satisfactory to proceed by means of a more 'universal' approach (such as an extension of drawing rights with the International Monetary Fund) which would give each European country, regardless of the position of its European partners, greater international liquidity to deal with its own overall balance-of-payments problems.

If, however, this more 'universal' approach is for any reason ruled out, it is possible to do something by methods whereby European surplus countries lend temporarily to European deficit countries. But there is now a second objection to an EPU type of mechanism. My basic theme has been that if each member is in overall balance-of-payments equilibrium, then the settlement of payments within the free-trade area should be possible. Suppose that the Netherlands has a dollar surplus matched by a deficit with Belgium, while Belgium has a dollar deficit matched by its surplus with the Netherlands; it should be possible for the Dutch to pay the Belgians with dollars. But with the EPU arrangements the Netherlands will continuously pile up reserves of gold and dollars, since their surplus is earned wholly in that form, while their deficit is payable through the EPU partly in book credit. But Belgium will run out of gold and dollar reserves, since her dollar deficit must be financed wholly in that form while her surplus is with EPU and will be financed partly by a book credit with EPU. This difficulty is avoided if settlements through EPU are 100 per cent in gold; but in this case EPU does not fulfil the function of providing additional credit by overall surplus to overall deficit members.

It is, of course, possible to devise methods for European surplus countries to lend to European deficit countries, which are not open to this objection. This might be done merely by arrangements between the exchange equalisation accounts or similar authorities of the members to the effect that the authorities of an overall surplus member would hold more of the currencies of an overall deficit member. Or it might be rather more institutionalised in the form of a European Monetary Fund into which all members paid certain amounts of their own currencies, and possibly also of their reserves of gold and dollars, and from which members with overall deficits were able to make temporary drawings. Or it might take the extreme form of the payment of all the gold and dollars of all the members into a common single pool, payments between members being financed by the transfer of claims on this pool, and payments to the outside world by drawings from the pool. This last system would, of course, have special implications for the United Kingdom, since it would mean pooling with the Europeans the reserves held against the claims of the whole sterling area; and although there is nothing inherently illogical (indeed there is much positively desirable) in extending the payments mechanism to cover a wider region than the commercial free-trade area, the political difficulties involved are obviously very great.

In any case an increase in international liquidity for European countries is not a complete cure for our problem. What methods could be used to deal with persistent balance-of-payments problems in the European free-trade area? Let us consider first what I have called the *gold-standard approach*.

By this I mean the application of the principles of the old gold standard as they are expounded in the textbooks. Any member of the free-trade area which is in overall deficit will lose reserves of foreign exchange; it should allow this to lead to a restriction of the domestic supply of its money until its domestic money incomes, prices and costs are so deflated that it has put its overall balance of payments into equilibrium by buying less imports and supplying more and cheaper products for export. Simultaneously any surplus member of the free-trade area should allow its receipt of foreign-exchange reserves to cause a monetary inflation domestically, which should lead to an increase in its imports and a decrease in its exports. This solution is dangerous. It requires that each European national government should devise its domestic monetary and budgetary policies essentially with regard to its balance-of-payments situation and with little or no thought for its domestic situation. Financial policies to prevent domestic inflations or to preserve full employment must be more or less abandoned.

This would mean that Germany, so long as she has an overall balance-of-payments surplus, must inflate her domestic money incomes, prices and costs. But Germany, with her memories of past hyperinflation, is very unwilling to do this. And, as recent events show, a surplus country like Germany is always able to restrain an inflation; she can, through restrictive domestic monetary and budgetary policies, offset the domestic inflationary effects of a balance-of-payments surplus and continue to pile up balances of gold and foreign currencies. But this means that a potentially deficit member of the free-trade area such as France might have to make an undue share of the adjustment by a domestic deflation of its money incomes, prices and costs; for it cannot indefinitely postpone the adjustment, since its stock of gold and foreign currencies is limited and exhaustible. It might have to abandon a domestic financial policy of expansion for full employment just at the time that the structural adjustment of its industries due to the removal of trade barriers within the free-trade area may be causing some redundancy of labour in its less efficient industries, so that it was especially desirable to have a domestic background of financial expansion to ease the development of its more efficient industries. Governments are nowadays so wedded (and, in my opinion, rightly so wedded) to the idea that it is one of their duties to preserve full employment that the probable outcome of this solution would in fact be the breakdown of the free-trade-area arrangements.

Many who accept these criticisms of the gold-standard approach may ask whether we could not get rid of payments difficulties, at least within the free-trade area, by combining with the building of a free-trade area in Western Europe the integration of European financial arrangements so as to make it as easy for a Frenchman to pay a German within Europe as it is for a Welshman to pay an Englishman within the United Kingdom.

The logic of this *integration approach* is unassailable. But it is not, I think, always realised how far-reaching this proposal is. This we can best see by asking why it is that the adjustment of payments between England and Wales is so much easier than that between Germany and France. There are at least five elements to the answer.

In the first place, the fact that goods, labour and capital can move freely between England and Wales makes adjustments easier. Suppose Wales is in economic difficulty. A deflation of prices and incomes in Wales relatively to prices and incomes in England will have more effect in inducing consumers to buy Welsh rather than English products and in inducing workers to work in England rather than Wales, because there are no restrictions on the movement of goods or workers from Wales to England. Moreover, any rise in interest rates in Wales caused by a scarcity of money capital due to the deflation of money supplies in Wales would have more effect in attracting new capital funds from England because there are no barriers to the movement of capital within the United Kingdom. Indeed, the Welsh and the English share in common the London capital market. A complete common market for goods, labour and capital throughout Western Europe would similarly make the mechanism of adjustment of payments easier. There is some truth in the contention that the gold-standard approach is less dangerous when it is applied to the payments between the members of an economic union than when it is applied to payments between national states which maintain impediments to the movement of goods and services between them.

But this is not the whole of the story. A second reason why the adjustment of payments between England and Wales is much easier than between Germany and France is because the United Kingdom has, while

Western Europe has not, got a single common currency and banking system. If the Welsh balance of payments with England is £1 million in deficit, then this means that £1 million of currency or bank deposits passes from the ownership of Welshmen to that of Englishmen. This deflation of £1 million in Wales and inflation of £1 million in England is the end of the direct monetary adjustment. But if the French balance of payments with Germany is 1 million francs in deficit, then the French central bank loses 1 million francs of foreign-exchange reserves and the German central bank gains an equivalent amount of reserves. There are many reasons why a change of 1 million in a country's foreign-exchange reserves may cause a change of many millions in its total domestic supply of money. In particular, if France has only a small proportion of her total domestic supply of money covered by foreign-exchange reserves, she may have to deflate her domestic supply of money by many times any loss of her reserves, in order to prevent a dangerous fall in her foreign-exchange reserve ratio. In other words, the absence of a single money means that the abruptness and speed of adjustment in France and Germany may have to be much greater than in Wales and England. Much of this problem would, of course, be solved by sufficiently far-reaching arrangements for increasing international liquidity between the members of the European free-trade area. In the example just given, if France had foreign-exchange reserves equal to 100 per cent of her domestic money supply, then any given loss of reserves would no longer make it necessary for her to deflate her domestic money supply by many times that loss of reserves.

Thirdly, England and Wales have a single national government which by the adoption of a stricter or easier central-banking monetary policy or by running a budget surplus or deficit can pump monetary purchasing power out of or into the system as a whole. This means that there can be an effective anti-inflation or anti-deflation financial policy for the United Kingdom as a whole which can take into account the interest both of Wales and of England. Trouble with the Welsh balance of payments need not be intensified by a failure of monetary demand in England to expand sufficiently. This is a most far-reaching difference between interregional and international payments. In Europe at present it is the function of each national government by control of its central bank's monetary policy and through its own budgetary policy to prevent undesirable domestic inflations and deflations. Free trade combined with fixed exchange rates (the gold-standard approach) would prevent European governments from devising their domestic financial policy for the purpose of preserving domestic stability. But the prevention of widespread booms and slumps is an essential feature of modern government. To entrust this task to a supranational European authority would require a very far-reaching surrender of powers by the national governments to ensure a single central-bank policy and a single budgetary policy for Western Europe as a whole.

Fourthly, suppose that the balance-of-payments deficit of Wales is greater than the balance-of-payments surplus of England, so that the United Kingdom as a whole has a deficit with the outside world. There exist central authorities for the United Kingdom which will then do something to correct the United Kingdom balance of payments. Restrictions on imports into the United Kingdom as a whole would cause consumers in the surplus area, England, to purchase from the deficit area, Wales, goods which could no longer be procured from abroad. Similarly, a depreciation of the pound would cause outside goods to rise in price relatively to goods inside the United Kingdom, and England would buy more from Wales and less from outside countries and would sell more to outside countries and less to Wales. This also is a very far-reaching point. A European supranational authority with extensive governmental powers would be needed to devise and administer a single programme of control over imports into the free-trade area from outside (we shall return to this problem at a later stage) and to decide upon any changes in the exchange rate between all European currencies, on the one hand, and all outside currencies, on the other.

Fifthly, if in the United Kingdom (in spite of the factors which we have just mentioned) some economic adjustment does bring concentrated depression in a single region (like South Wales in the 1930s), then the Central Government in London exists to take special measures to bring new investment and enterprise to South Wales and to help to move labour out of South Wales. No such supranational authority exists to take such 'special-area' action on the part of Western Europe as a whole for the promotion of economic development in, say, a particular region of Europe, like Southern Italy.

The integration approach thus involves – in addition to the formation of a common market for goods and for factors of production and the provision of much greater international liquidity for European monetary authorities – a very extensive range of powers for what would amount to a single European Government. Such a Government would have to be able to control central bank monetary policy and governmental budgetary policy throughout Europe, to determine a single European commercial and exchange-rate policy *vis-à-vis* third countries, and to carry out an effective special-area policy for depressed regions in Europe.

This is in my opinion ultimately desirable; let us hope that it will prove ultimately practicable; but it is not a starter at the moment, and it would be a great shame to sacrifice the present real political possibilities of building a commercial free-trade area to this ideal of simultaneous monetary and budgetary integration.

Let us consider next the possibility of dealing with a deficit in a country's balance of payments by imposing restrictions on imports from abroad or on payments to other countries. This *direct-control approach* is more desirable than sole reliance on the gold-standard approach, with its potential threat to full employment; and it is more practicable than the integration approach with its very far-reaching political implications. But in so far as it involves a deficit member of the European free-trade area restricting imports from another member of that area, it cuts deeply into the idea of a true free-trade area. Its interference with the free-trade principle is not to be measured merely by the amount of restriction of imports which actually exists at any one moment of time. The mere knowledge that trade may be restricted in this way in the future will discourage the large-scale investments that may be necessary to build up localised specialised mass production for the whole European market. The mass production of motor cars in Detroit in the United States involves the investment of huge sums of capital in plant and equipment in Detroit, which is undertaken because the producer knows for certain that the whole United States market will always be freely open to him.

If restrictions on trade between the members of a European free-trade area are to be avoided, it must, of course, be possible for traders to make payments for such purposes. This does not in itself imply the absence of all exchange controls over the currencies of the countries concerned. Thus any one member country, say France, could maintain strict exchange controls; every Frenchman who wanted a foreign currency, say, German marks, to purchase goods from Germany, might be required to obtain the currency from a central French exchange-control authority or its agent; and every Frenchman who acquired any foreign currency, say, German marks from the sale of French products to Germany, might be required to surrender the currency to the central French exchange-control authority or its agent in exchange for francs. All that is necessary to ensure the free entry of German products into France is that the French exchange-control authority should in fact always grant a Frenchman's request for foreign currency if he can show that it is required to finance the import of German products into France.

But the problem is very different if it is intended that there should be freedom of capital movements between the member countries. Full freedom of movement of capital funds from France to Germany, for example, means that the Frenchman must be free to buy German marks for all purposes, capital as well as current. But suppose that the German exchange control differs from the French, the French forbidding and the German allowing the movement of capital funds into dollars. If the Frenchman is free to lend to the German, and the German is then free to lend to the American, it does not require great ingenuity on the part of financiers (who are not conspicuously lacking in that quality) to devise means whereby in effect the Frenchman is lending his money to the American by way of a German intermediary. The control of the movement of capital from France to the United States will become much less effective if there is freedom of movement of capital funds from France to Germany and the German mark is fully convertible. To make one member's control over exports of capital to countries outside the free-trade area effective, the exchange-control regulations of all the members must be harmonised, if freedom of capital movement within the free-trade area is to be maintained. This is a very difficult operation. If it should prove too difficult, then freedom of movement of capital funds cannot be allowed in Europe so long as some members are in heavy deficit and need to control the outflow of capital at least to the outside world, while others are in strong surplus and wish to make their currencies convertible into outside currencies.

But let us return to the problem of trade controls. Is it possible for a member of the European free-trade area to deal with a deficit in its overall balance of payments by restricting imports from outside countries without restricting imports from the other members of the free-trade area?[2]

The use by the members of the European free-trade area on balance-of-payments grounds of restrictions on imports from third countries can be organised in either of two ways which I will call the *national* and the *supranational* methods respectively. By the national method I mean simply that each individual member of the free-trade area might restrict imports from outside countries into its own national market as an aid to the preservation of equilibrium in its own overall balance of payments. By the supranational method I mean that the members of the free-trade area should set up some joint authority which would determine the total amount of outside goods which could be imported into the free-trade area as a whole, using this instrument to preserve equilibrium in the balance of payments of the area as a whole with the outside world.

There can, I think, be little doubt that in the circumstances of the European free-trade area it is the national method which must be employed, at least until there is some further movement towards extensive European integration. There is great difficulty in the supranational method. Suppose that Germany is in overall surplus and France in overall deficit, but that France's deficit is greater than Germany's surplus and the area as a whole is in deficit. To get a single joint programme of control of imports into the area from outside agreement has got to be reached on at least three basic points. First, how severe should the total restrictions be? Germany may want the problem solved mainly by deflation or depreciation by France with little common import restriction, and France may want it solved mainly by inflation or appreciation by Germany with much import restriction. With the supranational method this choice would have to be made by common agreement. Second, given the degree of total restriction, which particular imports should be restricted? France may want severe restrictions on the import of wheat which she produces, but not on chemicals which she does not produce; and Germany may want the opposite type of import programme. Thirdly, given the degree of restriction of each particular import, how many of the import licences should be given to German and how many to French importers? If we may draw any conclusions from the history of the Benelux economic union, we can safely conclude that the formation of a common programme of restriction of imports from third countries is one of the most difficult things to achieve even when there are only two trading partners to be considered.

Let us then consider the case of a member of the European free-trade area which is in an overall balance-of-payments deficit and which is trying to deal with this by restricting imports from outside countries without restricting imports from the other members of the free-trade area. In these conditions too much reliance cannot be placed upon the weapon of

[2] I do not propose to consider on this occasion which, if any, of the systems of import control discussed below would require a special waiver under the General Agreement on Tariffs and Trade.

import control. In any free-trade area comprising the main countries of Western Europe each individual member would in fact purchase a large proportion of its total imports from other members of the area. In 1955 the United Kingdom purchased 28 per cent, Western Germany 51 per cent, France 33 per cent, Italy 46 per cent, the Belgium–Luxembourg Economic Union 59 per cent and the Netherlands 59 per cent of its imports from other countries of Western Europe. Import restrictions which were confined to imports from other sources would thus be limited in their scope.

Moreover, the limitation of this weapon is rather greater than these crude figures suggest. For the imports of the typical Western European country from outside Europe consist very largely of raw materials and foodstuffs which are less easily dispensable than many manufactured goods which it imports from its Western European partners.

There is a further reason why restrictions on imports from outside countries imposed on what I have called the national as opposed to the supranational principle may in certain circumstances prove a rather weak weapon of control. Suppose that France restricts imports of United States products because she is in deficit, but that Germany does not do so because she is in surplus. Then if United States products can move freely from Germany to France, the French restrictions become very ineffective. Indeed, for the system to have any sense at all it must be open to France to restrict the import of United States produce whether it comes into France directly or *via* Germany. But even if this is done, French restrictions on some United States products (say, motor-cars) may mean that more such cars are imported into Germany, thereby releasing for export to France some German cars which would have been wanted in the German market if Germany had also been restricting the import of United States cars. The national method will, because of such substitutabilities, be somewhat less effective a device for causing a net reduction in total imports than the supranational method. France will have to rely rather more on disinflation or depreciation than would otherwise be the case, when France is in deficit and Germany in surplus.

But when all the members of the free-trade area are simultaneously in overall deficit, when – that is to say – the free-trade area is in deficit because the outside world is in surplus with all the individual members, then the national method will work very effectively. If Germany is restricting the import of United States cars because she (Germany) is in overall deficit, then the restrictions which France is putting on the import of United States cars will not be offset by the increased import of German cars which are being replaced by United States cars in the German market. If and when developments in the outside world (and, of course, in particular in the United States) impose an almost universal strain on European balances of payments, then the national method will automatically regain its full effectiveness. I personally regard the fact that it will be rather an ineffective tool, except in circumstances such as these, as a strong recommendation of it.

Because of the difficulties involved in operating the supranational method, even the six countries forming the full European customs union would probably have to operate their restrictions on imports from outside countries by the national method. They would then have to maintain a customs control at their common frontiers to prevent the products of outside countries from entering a member country with severe import restrictions indirectly *via* a member country with lax restrictions on the products of outside countries. But the experience of Benelux suggests that, unless they are successful not only in imposing a single tariff of duties on imports from outside countries, but also in unifying all domestic excise duties and turnover taxes and in removing all their domestic agricultural support policies, they will in any case have to maintain customs controls at their common frontier.

But whatever the members of the full customs union may do, the United Kingdom must employ the national method for her restrictions on imports from outside countries. She will wish as far as possible to avoid discriminating against the products of Commonwealth countries, particularly if they are members of the sterling area; but if she joined in any common European supranational import-control plan, she might be forced to restrict imports from sterling-area Commonwealth countries, even though she had to admit similar European products without restriction.

Incidentally, because of the special relationship both to Europe and to the sterling-area countries the United Kingdom will find restrictions on imports from outside countries a particularly weak weapon. In 1955 the United Kingdom purchased 28 per cent of her imports from Western Europe and 38 per cent from the sterling area, leaving only 34 per cent from other sources for restriction; and much of this 34 per cent consists of basic materials and foodstuffs which it would be undesirable to restrict.

There remains the *exchange-rate approach* to the problem. A simple process of elimination leads inevitably to the conclusion that if the European national governments are going to use monetary and budgetary policies for purposes of domestic stabilisation – if, for example, in their present situation of balance-of-payments surplus the German authorities are nevertheless going to use their monetary policy to prevent a domestic inflation – and if it is desired to avoid the use of quantitative import restrictions on trade within the free-trade area, a greater use of the weapon of exchange-rate variation will have to be made. Some realignment of exchange rates may be particularly necessary during the initial stages of building the free-trade area. The removal of trade barriers of varying degrees of severity and the consequential development of import and export trades of varying degrees of expansibility may leave some members in deficit and others in surplus. The correction of this initial structural disturbance may require some exchange-rate adjustments quite apart from any need for exchange-rate variations to maintain equilibrium when once it has been achieved. Members of the free-trade area with a persistent surplus in their overall balance of payments will have to be ready to appreciate, and those with a persistent deficit will have to be ready to depreciate, the foreign-exchange values of their currencies.

This question is a difficult and controversial one, and it is not possible to discuss it at length in this lecture.[3] There are, of course, serious disadvantages in variations of exchange rates. There is the possibility that anti-social speculative movements of funds will be generated by the expectation of depreciations. There is the danger that a depreciation by raising the price of imports and so the cost of living will itself cause a rise of wage-rates which, by making exports more costly, will give rise to yet a further depreciation.

These dangers will be much less if the European governments adopt effective domestic measures to prevent domestic inflations as well as to prevent domestic deflations. Speculation against a currency is most serious and dangerous when speculators think that a depreciation may set in motion the vicious inflationary spiral of higher import prices, higher wage-rates, higher money costs, more depreciation and so on without end. Exchange-rate variations are certainly not a substitute for sensible and effective domestic policies to prevent inflation; on the contrary, they can be expected to work only if they are accompanied by such domestic policies.

The governments of all the countries of Western Europe are nowadays technically and politically in a position to control the total money demand within their countries by means of suitable budgetary and banking policies. What is much less certain is their ability to cope with inflation arising on the side of costs. If the institutions for the fixing of wage-rates are such that, so long as there is reasonably full employment, money wage-rates are pushed up more quickly than output per head, the European governments will be faced by an unhappy dilemma: through their control over banking and budgetary policies either they must allow an increase in the total money demand for goods and services which will provide employment for all workers at the higher money wage-rates (in which case prices will rise as rapidly as costs) or else they must restrict monetary demand so as to prevent domestic purchasers from offering higher prices for the country's output (in which case higher money costs are likely to lead to unemployment). Only if suitable wage-fixing arrangements can be devised will the European governments be able to use their control over banking and budgetary policies in such a way as to combine full employment with sufficient stability of prices to reassure their own citizens and foreign holders of their money that it is not necessary perpetually to speculate against a further loss of value and depreciation of the national currency concerned.

This problem of control of inflation from the cost side as well as the demand side is perhaps the most important economic issue which now faces the governments of Europe. In present circumstances it can be tackled only on a national basis, since trade unions are national organisations and wage-fixing methods and habits vary widely from country to country. There are sure to be some divergences in its treatment; and differences in the annual percentage rate of change of prices and costs in different European countries, though very moderate in amount, could give rise to serious balance-of-payments problems as they accumulate at

[3] For my own views on the subject, see J. E. Meade,'The Case for Variable Exchange Rates', *The Three Banks Review*, no. 27 (September 1955), pp. 3–27 [Chapter 10 above].

compound interest over a period of years. For this reason, if for no other, rates of exchange between the European currencies must be variable, if it is desired to avoid more or less permanent restrictions on imports from being used as the way of meeting a growing divergence in levels of prices and costs.

But while exchange-rate variations are a necessary weapon in the armoury, it is of the utmost importance that they should not be regarded merely as another name for exchange-rate depreciations. Strong currencies should be expected to go up as much as weak currencies to go down. In order to establish this principle, it is especially important to initiate the use of this weapon in Europe with the appreciation of a strong currency rather than with the depreciation of a weak currency. There should probably be some depreciation of the French franc; but first and foremost at this moment there should be a substantial appreciation of the German mark.

I think that my attitude to exchange-rate variations is very much like Sir Winston Churchill's attitude to democracy, which he once described as the worst of all possible forms of government except the others. And I am reminded, too, that Mr E. M. Forster once wrote a book entitled *Two Cheers for Democracy*, so I ask you to join with me in giving one cheer for a depreciation of the French franc and two cheers for an appreciation of the German mark.

I will conclude by outlining my own tentative conclusions on this difficult problem.

Full employment is more important than free trade for Europe; and financial policies to prevent booms and slumps must for some time remain primarily the function of the European national governments. In order to ensure that they could not be forced to abandon their full-employment policies on balance-of-payments grounds they should for the time being be able to restrict imports even from their partners in the free-trade area, until experience has shown that alternative balance-of-payments arrangements can be made to work. But such restrictions are a serious derogation of the principle of European free trade; they should be used only as a very last resort; and their imposition and use should be subject to the close supervision of an appropriate European authority.

A workable positive arrangement which would enable full employment to be maintained without restrictions on intra-European trade could meanwhile be worked out on the basis of three main principles. First, the European national governments must carry out effective domestic stabilisation policies, the surplus countries putting the emphasis on the avoidance of deflation, and the deficit countries on the avoidance of inflation. Second, the foreign-exchange values of the currencies of countries in a persistent balance-of-payments surplus must be appreciated and of those in a persistent balance-of-payments deficit must be depreciated. Thirdly, greater foreign-exchange reserves must be extended to the deficit countries to tide over the process of readjustment.

There are many ways of implementing these three general principles; but by way of illustration I will tentatively recommend one particular method.

As I have said, domestic monetary stabilisation would remain essentially the concern of the national governments; but something can be done to encourage suitable national action by international discussion and co-operation. Each member of the free-trade area should formally recognise that its partners had a legitimate interest in the successful stabilisation of its own domestic incomes, prices and costs, and, in particular, in the avoidance of deflations by surplus members and of inflations by deficit members. There should be some European institution like the Organisation for European Economic Co-operation at which the national governments would regularly consult each other about their domestic financial policies.

Against a background of domestic stability the exchange rates of the national currencies of the members of the free-trade area should be allowed to float in a more or less free foreign-exchange market. This suggestion is liable to raise up a picture of wildly fluctuating European currencies, many of them losing their value completely. If reasonable domestic policies for domestic stabilisation are applied, nothing could be more absurd; and unless such policies can be applied, no sensible balance-of-payments policies for a true free-trade area can be devised. If reasonable domestic policies for domestic stabilisation are applied, there will still be some moderate external disturbances or some moderate divergences in price and cost levels requiring adjustment. To meet these, exchange rates will float moderately upwards or downwards; and every encouragement should be given for the development of a free market in forward exchange, so that the moderate inconveniences and uncertainties for traders resulting from these moderate fluctuations in exchange rates may be minimised.

In such circumstances there should be no essential difficulty for the countries of continental Europe in allowing their exchange rates to float. There would be more difficulty in the case of sterling, which is a currency used extensively by traders in other countries, held in large amounts by residents in other countries, and backed by inadequate reserves. There are, therefore, much greater possibilities of speculation by non-resident holders against sterling than against other currencies. But this is a difference of degree rather than of kind. It means that it is more important for the United Kingdom to obtain greater reserves or a greater degree of international liquidity by one means or another; and it means that it is especially important for the United Kingdom to devise an effective domestic policy for the avoidance of inflation from the cost as well as from the demand sides. In such conditions the pound could be confidently expected to float up as often as to float down; and there is no reason why in such circumstances a floating pound should not continue to be used as an international currency.

But what would be the use of a country's international reserves of gold and foreign exchange in such a system, in which its currency was allowed freely to find its own level in the foreign-exchange markets? The foreign-exchange markets, though in general free, might be subject to the intervention of the exchange equalisation account or similar authority of each member country, the authority selling some of its reserves of foreign exchange for its own domestic currency to mitigate what it considered an unreasonable speculation against its currency, or *vice versa*. Cushioned in this way by the use of a country's reserves, the necessary fluctuations in a country's exchange rate could be taken at a very moderate speed.

Such a system is, of course, open to misuse if the authority in one country attempts to manipulate the exchange rate between its currency and the currencies of its partners to obtain some commercial or other advantage which its balance-of-payments position does not really need. Partly to avoid this danger and partly to provide greater liquidity for European countries there might be instituted a European Monetary Fund into which each member would pay an amount of its own national currency. This fund would be under some form of independent 'supranational' management of a technical banking character; and its management would be empowered on its own initiative to buy and sell the currencies in the fund to ease the balance-of-payments adjustments of the members. This fund would also provide a forum at which the policies of the fund itself and of the national exchange equalisation funds could be continuously discussed and integrated. To avoid speculation such integration would, of course, have to take the form of secret discussions between the central monetary authorities of the member countries. Such a system would be capable of almost indefinite development. As an integrated Europe became more and more of a reality, so the member states could pay greater and greater sums of their own currencies into the European fund and could start also to pay into it part of their reserves of gold and dollars as well, until finally the supranational fund had superseded the national exchange equalisation funds. And as their domestic financial policies became more and more harmonised and integrated, so smaller and smaller fluctuations in exchange rates need be permitted, until finally the conditions for what I have called the integration approach to the balance-of-payments problems have been fully met and exchange-rate variations can be abandoned.

The proposals which I have just made are, of course, riddled with difficulties and imperfections. I put them forward only as a challenge to others to produce something which is simpler, but equally effective, for dealing with European balances of payments without preventing European free trade or destroying European full employment.

15

The Future of International Trade and Payments

From The Three Banks Review, *no. 50 (June 1961), pp. 3–26. The paper, with some revisions, was included in US Congress, Joint Economic Committee,* Factors Affecting the United States Balance of Payments *(Washington, DC: Government Printing Office, 1962), pp. 241–252.*

Present conditions call for a reconsideration by the highly developed, industrialised, wealthy countries of the Western world[1] of the future of their arrangements for the conduct of their international trade and payments. There are many reasons why such a review is now needed. The dollar has ceased to be a universally scarce currency and seems liable now, like other currencies, to recurrent periods of weakness; the new administration in the United States is in any case engaged in a review of the principles of United States economic policies at home and abroad; in Europe a solution is sought for the problem of reconciling the European Economic Community (the Six) with the European Free-Trade Area (the Seven); and throughout the Western countries there is a growing realisation of the need both to stimulate economic growth at home and to aid the economic development of the underdeveloped countries of Asia, Africa and South America. Perhaps as important as any of these factors is the possibility of a far-reaching disarmament agreement between the Communist and the Western countries; if this greatly desired event were to be realised, there would be many inevitable disturbances and strains in international trade and payments as resources were, by one means or another, transferred from military to peaceful uses. It is of the first importance that there should be a system of international trade and payments which could cope in a flexible manner with the very extensive readjustments that such a large disturbance would involve.

The basic problem is no doubt the machinery for international payments, and the real purpose of this article is to suggest some

[1] The countries which I have in mind are basically the countries of Western Europe and North America, though for some purposes we should add to the list some other countries like Australia and New Zealand – and possibly also Japan. Purely for the purposes of simple exposition I will call these 'the Western countries'.

improvements in the machinery for international payments between the main national currencies of Western countries. But a financial system is only a means to an end; and in order to decide what principles one wants to adopt for a payments system one must first know what are the basic objectives which one wishes to achieve by means of it. Now in my view the basic objectives of a reformed system of payments between the Western countries fall into three main groups: Freer Trade; more liberal Foreign Aid; and a higher rate of domestic Economic Expansion.

In commercial policy the Western countries should now negotiate among themselves a substantial further reduction of all the obstacles which they place on imports from each other, and they should extend these reductions of barriers to imports on a most-favoured-nation basis to their purchases from the underdeveloped countries of Asia, Africa and South America without demanding any very substantial *quid pro quo* in the form of much freer access to the markets of these underdeveloped countries. It is not, of course, practical politics to expect an immediate jump to the ultimate free-trade ideal; but it might well be practical politics for the Western countries to use the newly instituted Organisation for Economic Co-operation and Development and the General Agreement on Tariffs and Trade for a substantial organised move in this direction.

There are many arguments in favour of such a policy. As between the Western countries themselves there are the straightforward, old-fashioned free-trade arguments. There is no doubt real economic gain to be achieved if each country specialises further on the production of the goods which it is best fitted to produce. In addition to this, the vast market which free trade between the Western countries would provide would enable producers to reap the maximum benefits from economies of large-scale production. Moreover, the fact that the individual producers were subject to free competition from their rivals in other countries would make it more difficult to maintain monopolistic and restrictive arrangements within any one national market. This increased threat of competition might stimulate enterprise and efficiency. In brief, the Western countries might reap together on a much larger scale the advantages which the Six hope to gain from the European Economic Community and the Seven from the European Free-Trade Area.

The greater freedom of entry into the markets of the Western countries should be extended to the products of the underdeveloped countries of Asia, Africa and South America without any comparable commercial *quid pro quo*. In this case a vast market would exist in the Western countries for the cheap labour-intensive manufactures which it was relatively simple for many densely populated underdeveloped countries to learn to produce. In return the Western countries could concentrate on the production and export of the more complicated capital goods and consumption goods and, in the case of countries like the United States, Canada, Australia and New Zealand, on the export of those foodstuffs which need much land and capital for their production.

There are some good reasons why the underdeveloped countries should be freer than the developed countries to restrain their imports by one means or another. They may need to protect an infant industrial system until it has achieved a scale and a maturity which will justify its establishment. Moreover, in many of the densely populated, underdeveloped countries the employment in industry of a large unemployed or underemployed labour supply may require special encouragement and protection of labour-intensive manufactures. Finally, in so far as the restriction of imports can in some cases turn the real terms of trade in favour of the restricting country, there is some weight in the argument that the poor countries should be freer than the rich countries to impose controls over their imports.

All this does not imply that the underdeveloped countries have no reciprocal obligations to the developed countries. On the contrary, if the developed countries provide a free market for the products of the underdeveloped countries and if, as will be argued later, they provide substantial financial aid to the underdeveloped countries, it is reasonable that the underdeveloped countries should also undertake commitments towards the developed countries. But these should be concerned with certain features of their development plans (for example, the adequate development of the exports of the raw materials and other primary products needed by the developed countries) rather than take the form of a simple free-trade obligation.

A concerted movement towards freer trade on the part of the Western countries would incidentally be the best way of reconciling the commercial systems of the Six and the Seven in Europe. There are in my view real difficulties in the way of the United Kingdom simply joining the Six. One of the most important of these difficulties concerns the position of the underdeveloped countries in the British Commonwealth. At present there is free entry into the United Kingdom market for the products of such countries. At a time like the present, when there is increasing hope that the British Commonwealth can become more and more a real club of developed and underdeveloped countries from all parts of the world, it would be particularly unfortunate if the United Kingdom instead of letting in Indian manufactures free and taxing German manufactures had to let in German manufactures free and to impose the common European tariff on Indian manufactures. The best way of avoiding conflicts between the commercial systems of the Six and the Seven is a general movement towards freer imports from all sources, as well as from each other, into all the developed countries of the West.

There is a need also for a substantially increased programme of financial aid from the developed countries of the West to the underdeveloped countries of Asia, Africa and South America. These countries are more and more determined to start a process of economic growth through industrialisation and heavy investment in capital development. A large-scale flow of financial aid from the rich countries to these poorer and underdeveloped countries is the only way in which this process can be initiated without the rigid controls over private consumption and the grinding poverty which the finance of their own capital development solely out of their own domestic resources would involve. Moreover, there are now some very important underdeveloped countries, of which India and Brazil may be quoted as examples, who are sufficiently advanced in their development plans and are endowed with a sufficiently efficient administrative machine to be able to absorb very large amounts of capital to good effect.

It is important that such aid should be given in an untied form – the rich countries should provide financial aid to the poor countries, and the poor countries should be free to spend the aid on procuring the sort of capital equipment which they most need from whatever is the cheapest source. The country which should provide the aid because it is rich is not necessarily the country which can produce most cheaply the particular goods most needed by the country which receives the aid. Moreover, a system of tied aid may well cause the developing country to employ most wasteful forms of technique in its economic development. Machinery made in the United States, for example, is probably specially designed to save labour (which is scarce in the United States) even at the expense of employing much capital (which is relatively plentiful in the United States). Machinery to be used in India, for example, should be specially designed to save capital (which is scarce in India) even at the expense of requiring much labour for its operation (since labour is plentiful in India). Dollar aid which is tied to dollar machines may, therefore, be an inappropriate way to encourage capital development in India. It might, for example, be much better that a dollar loan to India should be spent on Japanese machinery, or should be used to finance the wages of Indian workers employed to produce by very labour-intensive methods a dam for irrigation purposes in India. In this latter case the dollar proceeds of the loan to India would be available to finance a general excess of India's imports over her exports during the process of capital development. Such Indian imports might well include some of the foodstuffs which the workers employed on constructing the dam would purchase with their wages.

There is one more basic requirement for a reformed system of international payments. In present-day conditions it is necessary that the national governments of the Western countries should feel free to use their domestic financial policies for the promotion of full employment, price stability and economic growth in their economies without having to pay too much regard to their balances of international payments. The simultaneous achievement of the three domestic goals of full employment, price stability and economic growth is difficult enough. The principles which must govern such action are now fairly well known. To maintain full employment the total level of money demand must be raised (by a cheap money policy, lower taxation and higher government expenditure) so long as there is not sufficient demand to absorb the whole of the economy's potential output and must be lowered (by the opposite financial measures) if there tends to be too high a level of money expenditure relatively to the available output of goods and services; to prevent a high level of demand from leading to a perpetual inflation of money prices and costs steps must be taken (perhaps the most difficult task of all) to prevent money wage-rates rising more quickly than the general productivity of labour; and to set the financial background for economic growth monetary and fiscal measures must be taken to stimulate expenditure upon new capital development and to restrain expenditure upon goods and services for current consumption.

In all conscience this task is sufficiently difficult. It becomes impossible if the national governments have, in addition, to make it a primary objective of their banking and budgetary policies to maintain an equilibrium in their international balances of payments. According to the rules of the old-fashioned gold-standard game, a country with a surplus on its international balance of payments should inflate its domestic money incomes, prices and costs until its demand for imports had so grown and the availability of its exports so declined that its balance of payments was in equilibrium once more; and, conversely, a deficit country should deflate its domestic incomes, prices and costs. But in fact this no longer happens. As the histories of the United States in the first ten years after the war and of Germany in the last five years show, a country which has a surplus on its balance of payments does not inflate domestically in order to get rid of this surplus; on the contrary, it uses its monetary and budgetary policies so as to achieve as far as possible domestic full employment, price stability and economic growth. Germany, for example, in recent years has been very successful in achieving this combination of domestic objectives, and she has shown no signs of willingness to abandon these domestic objectives for a domestic inflation which would remove the surplus on her balance of payments. Deficit countries which are losing their reserves of gold and foreign exchange have not, of course, found it so easy merely to disregard their balance-of-payments situation. But they have in recent years been extremely unwilling to give up their domestic monetary and budgetary policies for full employment and economic growth. They have tried often to avoid the need for deflation by imposing restrictions on their imports, cutting down their obligations of foreign aid, tying the aid which they give to expenditure on their own products, borrowing from abroad themselves, and so on.

In my opinion it is right that the national governments of the Western countries should use their domestic monetary and budgetary policies primarily to achieve their domestic aims of full employment, price stability and economic growth. These are outstandingly important objectives and their attainment requires the well-planned use of effective weapons. In the modern world these functions are the functions of *national* governments; there are no *supranational* governments or agencies designed for this purpose; even in the European Economic Community the objectives of full employment, price stability and economic growth will remain primarily the responsibility of the national governments of the constitutent countries; and until we have some form of supranational government for these countries with its own single currency, its own central bank, and its own system of taxes and public expenditure, these functions must remain primarily the responsibility of national authorities.

What is needed for the Western countries is a system of international payments that will allow the deficit as well as the surplus countries to devote their domestic monetary and budgetary policies primarily to the maintenance of domestic full employment, price stability and economic growth. Moreover, the system must be such as to enable them to press ahead with the removal of tariffs and other obstacles to imports; they must not, that is to say, be driven to restrict imports simply in order to restore equilibrium to their balance of international payments. Finally, the system must be such as to enable them to develop an enlarged programme of untied financial aid to the underdeveloped countries; they must not be under any compulsion to cut down their foreign aid, or to tie their foreign aid to their own national exports, as a means of putting their balance of payments into equilibrium and stopping a drain on their monetary reserves of gold and foreign currencies.

How far-reaching these requirements are can perhaps best be seen from the experience of the United States over the last year or so. The United States balance of payments has been in deficit. She has not yet actually increased her tariffs or intensified her restrictions on imports to put a stop to her loss of gold reserves; and she is much to be commended for not having done so. The underdeveloped countries may legitimately control their imports from developed countries; but we must not return to the undiluted principle that deficit countries can restrict imports from surplus countries. This might well mean that the USA being in deficit could restrict imports from the underdeveloped countries. The United States has refrained from actually restricting her imports on balance-of-payments grounds; but it would have been an admirable development if she had been able to go further and if at the meeting of the contracting parties to the General Agreement on Tariffs and Trade, now in session, she had been in a position to give a strong lead to the other Western countries to join together in reducing their barriers to imports. No doubt the new administration would in any case need more time to prepare such an initiative, which, to be really effective, would require new Congressional legislation on the vexed question of the United States tariff. But is there any hope that the United States could take such an initiative in reducing the barriers to her imports while she is engaged in putting right a serious deficit on her balance of payments?

Recently the United States has tended to tie the aid which she has given to underdeveloped countries more and more to United States products, as a method of reducing the strain on her balance of payments; and attempts have been made to persuade the Germans and other European countries with surpluses on their balances of payments that they should take over an increased share of the burden of the finance of aid to underdeveloped countries. No doubt a strong case can be made out for the view that the Germans and others should contribute more to the finance of foreign aid; but this case should rest on the fact that the Germans are rich and have a high standard of living and not on the fact that they have a surplus on their balance of payments. The principle that the countries with surpluses on their balances of payments should aid the countries with deficits on their balances of payments can lead to the ridiculous result that a poor territory (like Ghana) should aid a rich territory (like the United Kingdom) if the former happens to have a surplus on its balance of payments (due to a high world demand for cocoa) while the latter has a deficit (because the money cost of its manufactured exports is unduly inflated). Untied aid should be planned on an enlarged scale from the rich to the poor countries, and balances of payments should somehow be made to conform to these requirements. But can the United States with the present strain on its balance of payments be expected to take the lead in initiating such a reform, unless some alternative system for adjusting international payments can be found?

Finally, it is of the utmost importance that the United States Government should take early and effective monetary and budgetary measures to reflate demand inside the United States, to stimulate capital investment and economic growth, and generally to expand the domestic economy to absorb the quite appreciable amount of unemployed labour that has appeared in the recent economic recession. Such action is of central importance not only for the citizens of the United States themselves but also for the rest of the Western countries and of the underdeveloped countries. The maintenance and expansion of demand in the United States can greatly affect the exports of those other countries. In my view there is no doubt that the United States Government can organise a domestic economic expansion by means of its monetary and fiscal controls over the general level of demand, and there is little doubt that the new administration will in fact do so. But may not the domestic expansion in the United States by expanding the United States demand for imports put a further strain on her balance of payments? Will the United States be in a position at the same time to give the necessary lead to the other Western countries in reducing their barriers to imports and in enlarging a programme of untied aid to the underdeveloped countries?

The answer to this set of problems must, I think, be that the Western countries should make a freer use of alterations in the rates of exchange between their national currencies in order to preserve equilibrium in their balances of payments. Extreme advocates of this remedy would argue that if the rates of exchange between the main Western currencies – the dollar, the pound, the mark, the franc and so on – were allowed to fluctuate completely freely in uncontrolled foreign exchange markets, the problem would be easily solved. I shall proceed in this article: first, by stating as convincingly as I can the case for holding this extreme view; second, by examining certain criticisms which have been made of this view; and, thirdly, by proposing an actual scheme for international payments which attempts to take account of the many points made on both sides of this argument.

First, then, the case for freely fluctuating exchange rates. The statesmen of the Western countries, so it is argued, should concentrate their attention upon commercial negotiations for a general removal of their trade barriers against imports, upon a concerted programme of untied foreign aid, and upon domestic financial policies to promote full employment, price stability and economic growth. Let them forget their balance-of-payments problems. Of course, from time to time some of them will be in deficit and some in surplus on their balances of international payments. But in this case the currencies of the countries with strong balances of payments will appreciate in terms of the currencies of the countries with weak balances of payments. These alterations in exchange rates will look after the balance-of-payments problem by a double mechanism.

(1) The appreciation of the strong currency and the depreciation of the weak currency will make the products of the former country relatively more expensive and the products of the latter country relatively cheaper to all purchasers. The products of the former will tend to give way to the products of the latter in all consuming markets, that is to say, in the domestic markets of the two countries concerned and also in the markets of the other countries to which these two countries are exporting. In the end the consequential expansion of the exports of the country with the balance-of-payments deficit relatively to the exports of the country with the balance-of-payments surplus will corrrect the disequilibrium in international payments.

(2) But this adjustment will not, of course, be immediate. It will take time for the exports of the country whose exchange rate has depreciated to expand at the expense of the products of the country whose currency has appreciated. Meanwhile the excess demand for the currency of the surplus country and the excess supply of the currency of the deficit country will cause the former currency to appreciate very markedly and the latter currency to depreciate very markedly in the foreign exchange markets. But this will induce the private speculator to move funds from the former into the latter currency. The excessive appreciation of the former currency in terms of the latter will be known to be only temporary; for, as soon as it begins to have its basic effect in stimulating the exports of the deficit country relatively to the exports of the surplus country, the change in the exchange rates will be in large measure reversed. The speculator, so the argument runs, in search of private profit will thus move funds out of the surplus (and excessively appreciated) currency into the deficit (and excessively depreciated) currency. This movement of private funds will serve to finance the temporary deficit on the balance of payments of the deficit country until the exchange-rate variations have had time to carry out their basic role of adjusting the underlying elements in the balance of payments.

In fact any effective mechanism for adjustment of the balance of payments must perform a double function. The first function, which we may call the function of Liquidity, is to provide a temporary support for the currencies of the deficit countries to meet short-run fluctuations in balances of payments or to finance temporarily a more fundamental disequilibrium in balances of payments, while a more permanent adjustment is being carried out. Freely fluctuating exchange rates provide such liquidity through the mechanism of private speculation, as funds are moved out of currencies which have appreciated unduly as the result of the immediate impact of a change and into currencies which for similar reasons have depreciated unduly. The second function, which we may call that of Adjustment, is to bring about long-run basic changes in imports, exports and other items in balances of international payments; and this is done by the effect upon imports and exports of permanent moderate alterations in rates of exchange.

Are there any snags in this argument? The weaknesses of the system can be examined under four heads.

(1) The system will work only if the products of the countries concerned are competitive with each other. An appreciation of the German mark will reduce the surplus on the German balance of payments only if the resulting higher price of German products relatively to British, American, French and other products causes purchasers to buy considerably less German products and considerably more of the products of other countries. If this were not so, the change might do more harm than good; the higher prices of German products might cause the Germans to earn more, not less, foreign exchange for their exports; and if the Germans did not increase their imports of foreign products very appreciably, the result might be an increase rather than a decrease in the surplus on the German balance of payments. But the main industrialised countries of the West are in fact rather highly competitive in their manufactured exports; and if time is given for the adjustments to be made by the producers, traders and consumers concerned in all the countries of the world, there is, I think, little doubt that exchange-rate variations could cope with the long-run problem of adjustment between the Western countries. This would be even more certain if, as I have suggested, there were also freer trade between these countries and if the foreign aid which they gave were in an untied form. For both these reforms would make it easier for buyers of the products of these countries to shift their purchases from the more expensive to the cheaper suppliers; and this is what is needed in order to make a system of variable exchange rates work effectively.

(2) An essential part of the mechanism is the movement of short-term speculative funds from a currency which has temporarily appreciated excessively into a currency which has temporarily depreciated excessively. Such speculation would, of course, turn out to be profitable to the speculator. But whether or not it actually occurs will depend upon the speculators having a good understanding of what is going to happen, that is to say, upon their being able to decide when a currency is 'temporarily excessively' appreciated or depreciated and when it is not. In the absence of such well-informed speculation the system might be very unstable. Consider the following example. Suppose that there is a deficit on the United States balance of payments; the dollar depreciates; since it takes time for dollar exports to drive sterling and mark exports out of world markets, the dollar depreciates at first excessively; this gives an enormous price advantage to dollar products; producers, traders and consumers after a time-lag shift their demands very substantially away from sterling and mark products on to dollar products; this shift is so great as not merely to remove the deficit on the United States balance of payments but to cause a surplus; the dollar now appreciates excessively; this causes sterling and mark products to have an enormous price

advantage over dollar products; after a time, therefore, there is a swing back in the opposite direction. The system might proceed by a series of ever-increasing excessive swings now in one direction and now in the other. The trouble could, of course, be prevented if there were a sufficient volume of well-informed speculative funds, which would mitigate the excessive swings in the exchange rates which lie at the root of the trouble.

(3) The position might, however, be even worse if speculators not merely refrained from operating at the right time in the right direction, but actually operated in the wrong direction. Suppose once more that there is a deficit on the United States balance of payments and that the dollar depreciates in consequence. If speculators judge that simply because it has already depreciated a lot, it is likely to depreciate still further, they may themselves sell dollars and buy other currencies long after the dollar has depreciated sufficiently to put the United States balance of payments into equilibrium in the long run. They may, if they operate on a sufficiently great scale, make the position even more unstable than it would have been in the absence of all speculation. If speculators act in this way, they are liable in the end to make very considerable financial losses, because they will be left in the end in the position of holding no dollars but only marks and pounds when at last the excessive depreciation of the dollar comes to an end so that it regains value in terms of other currencies. But not all speculators will necessarily lose – only those who are in the end left carrying the baby. Some persons may speculate against the dollar when they know it is already depreciated below its true long-term value, simply because they think that others are going to continue to speculate against the dollar and that they themselves will be able to get out of dollars before the downward movement comes to an end.

(4) But there is one further danger which may intensify the instability of uncontrolled fluctuating exchange rates. Suppose that the United Kingdom has a deficit on its balance of payments, so that sterling depreciates in terms of other currencies. Suppose that the depreciation is at first rather excessive. The depreciation of the pound will cause the price of imports to go up in terms of pounds; this will cause the cost of living to go up; and this may in turn cause the money wage-rate to go up. If all this happens sufficiently quickly and on a sufficiently large scale, the result may be to cause a rise in money costs of production in the United Kingdom which largely or wholly offsets the competitive advantage gained by the depreciation of the pound itself. In this case the strain on the United Kingdom balance of payments would cause a further round of currency depreciation, followed by a further round of internal cost inflation, and so on. And in this case the speculators who speculated against the pound, while they would intensify the trouble, would not lose money, because their own speculation would help to cause the internal cost inflation and thus to justify the speculation itself. This danger can, I believe, very easily be exaggerated; for even in the United Kingdom the price of imports accounts for only a small part of the cost of living, and the effects of the rise in the price of imports upon the cost

of living and of the cost of living upon the wage-rate are both likely to be delayed.

However great or small these dangers may in fact be, they are real possibilities. For this reason the authorities of the Western countries are extremely unlikely to adopt an uncontrolled system of freely fluctuating exchange rates. It may be, as I personally greatly hope, that exchange-rate variations will be used more readily and frequently than in the past as a means of maintaining equilibrium in balances of payments; but if so, these variations will certainly be controlled to a greater or lesser degree by the authorities. The normal instrument for such control is the national exchange equalisation account; the national monetary authority holds a fund made up partly of its own national currency and partly of a reserve of gold and of other foreign currencies; if it wishes to prevent an appreciation in the value of its own currency it buys gold or foreign currencies in order to sell its own currency, and *vice versa*.

In the bad old days of mass unemployment in the 1930s, before the governments of the Western countries had learnt by Keynesian financial policies to maintain their internal domestic demands at adequate levels, this system led to complaints of competitive exchange depreciation. The authorities in one country would purchase gold and foreign currencies with their national currencies simply in order to make their national currencies depreciate (even though there was no deficit on their balance of payments), in order to cheapen their exports in foreign markets, in order to undercut the products of their competitors, in order to give employment to their own workers at the expense of foreign workers.

This danger is now little more than a bogy. National governments now know how to control total demand and there are so many useful things that each can do with unemployed resources that they are exceedingly unlikely to try to depreciate their currencies competitively against each other simply to find employment for their workers in export markets. But it was largely to fight against this danger that the rules of the International Monetary Fund were devised, whereby national governments undertook to peg their currencies in terms of gold and only to alter the peg from time to time in order to remove a fundamental disequilibrium in their balance of payments. This system is, in my opinion, a bad one. It means that if, for example, a deficit appears on the United Kingdom's balance of payments, the British authorities are under an obligation to maintain the value of the pound (by selling gold and dollars and buying pounds in the exchange equalisation account) until some once-for-all cataclysmic depreciation of the pound by 20, 30 or 40 per cent takes place to remove a fundamental disequilibrium. This provides a golden opportunity for useless anti-social speculation. During this period of support of the pound all speculators can see that the pound will certainly not be appreciated and may be very substantially depreciated. They sell pounds and buy dollars, knowing that at the worst they will not lose and at the best may make a quick profit of 20, 30 or 40 per cent. And such speculation serves no useful purpose; on the contrary, it merely piles an extra unnecessary strain on the pound.

This sort of danger is particularly great in the case of currencies like sterling and dollars which are held as international reserve currencies by other countries. The amount of sterling balances held as liquid reserves by foreigners is, as is well known, greatly in excess of the total gold and dollar reserves held by the United Kingdom authorities. If overseas holders of sterling lose confidence in the pound and try to move their funds out of sterling into gold and dollars, this can put a quite intolerable strain on sterling. The dollar is more and more reaching a similar position. In recent years international liquidity has been increased largely by other countries holding more and more of their reserves not in gold, but in dollars. The consequence is that against the gold reserves of the United States there is now a large liquid debt of dollar balances held by other countries. Lack of confidence in the dollar which caused these foreign holders to shift from dollars into gold or sterling can now put a very great strain on the United States gold reserves.

In my opinion, then, the Western countries need a reformed system for international payments in which (1) much greater use is made of variations in exchange rates than has been the case in recent years, (2) exchange-rate variations are, however, subject to some public control to avoid the dangers of misguided speculation, and (3) the special problem of potential instability of the great international currencies like the pound and the dollar are met. I will close this article by making some proposals which would meet these points. I shall put my proposals forward in the form of a precise 'ideal' scheme in order to be able to explain the principles briefly and clearly. In the real world it would, of course, be capable of many modifications.

I suggest, then, the following scheme.

(1) All the national monetary authorities of the Western countries would agree to pay all their monetary reserves (gold, dollars, sterling etc.) into a reformed International Monetary Fund. They would receive in exchange Gold Certificates at the current gold value of their reserves which they had paid into the IMF. They would agree in the future to hold only Gold Certificates as their reserves, and all newly mined gold which was not taken up by the private market (for industrial purposes or for private hoarding) would be paid into the IMF.

(2) The national monetary authorities would then let the value of their national currencies fluctuate in value in terms of Gold Certificates according to changes in supply and demand in the foreign exchange markets. Each national monetary authority would now possess a national exchange equalisation account made up partly by a holding of its own currency and partly by a holding of the Gold Certificates which it had acquired from the IMF in exchange for its foreign exchange reserves. It could, therefore, if it so decided, moderate the fluctuations in the value of its national currency in terms of Gold Certificates by buying or selling its own currency for Gold Certificates in its exchange equalisation account. But it would no longer be in a position to shift its foreign-exchange reserves from one form of foreign exchange to another (e.g. to sell pounds in order to buy dollars or to reduce its dollar balances in order to hold gold).

(3) The IMF would now hold an enormous additional fund of gold and national currencies (in particular pounds and dollars) which were paid into it from the reserves of the national monetary authorities. These would be in addition to its present holding of the gold and national currencies which were paid into it on its inception. It could now act as a most important supranational exchange equalisation account. If in its opinion, for example, the pound was temporarily unduly depreciated in terms of dollars, the IMF could sell dollars and purchase pounds out of its holdings of these currencies.

(4) Moreover, the IMF could now purchase (or sell) national currencies (such as pounds, dollars, marks, francs, etc.) for Gold Certificates. Gold Certificates would be held by the national monetary authorities as their sole form of monetary reserve and private operators might also hold Gold Certificates as a convenient form of reserve of external currency. The IMF by issuing new Gold Certificates to purchase national currencies (or by buying up existing Gold Certificates with some of the national currencies which it held) could thus control the total issue of Gold Certificates. By doing so it could ensure that the total amount of international liquid reserves was kept in line with the needs of international trade and payments.

How might such a system work in practice? Let me give a short account of how I personally would hope that it might be made to work. The national governments of the Western countries would concentrate on national policies for the maintenance of full employment, price stability and economic growth and on reaching international arrangements for agreed reductions in their trade barriers and for agreed programmes of untied aid to the underdeveloped countries. They would not concern themselves too much with the consequences upon their balances of international payments, but would rely upon variations in the rates of exchange between their national currencies (under the control and guidance of a reformed International Monetary Fund) to bring about the necessary adjustments.

The reformed IMF would in this case become a real supranational exchange equalisation fund. It could use its large fund of various national currencies to give temporary support to one currency in terms of another if such temporary support was desirable. It would itself have to judge, no doubt in close consultation with the national monetary authorities, whether private speculation should be supplemented or offset in order to prevent an excessive temporary depreciation or appreciation of particular currencies.

These operations of the reformed IMF could always be supplemented by the operations of the national exchange equalisation accounts which could buy (or sell) Gold Certificates with their own national currencies in their own national exchange equalisation accounts, if they wished to prevent an excessive temporary appreciation (or depreciation) of their national currency. But it would be greatly to be hoped that national exchange equalisation accounts would be used less and less frequently. In modern conditions it would be a most appropriate division of functions between national governments and a supranational monetary authority, if the former concentrated on policies for economic expansion, foreign aid and the removal of trade barriers while the latter concerned itself with the control of foreign exchange rates. Such a system could be made to work efficiently and would remove any possibility that the national governments might use their national exchange equalisation accounts for purposes of competitive exchange depreciation in order to obtain national advantages for their trade.

In addition to its functions of offsetting temporary excessive fluctuations in exchange rates by buying one national currency and selling another, the reformed IMF would also be able by buying (or selling) national currencies for Gold Certificates to increase (or to decrease) the total amount of liquid international funds available in the form of Gold Certificates. The IMF could buy and sell national currencies for Gold Certificates with the aim of keeping the value of Gold Certificates constant, not in terms of any single national currency (for the national currencies would be varying in terms of each other), but in terms of national currencies in general. Such stability of the value of Gold Certificates in terms of a composite index of national currencies would make it an admirable form of international liquid asset. In so far as national monetary authorities operated their national exchange equalisation accounts Gold Certificates, having a more or less constant value in terms of national currencies in general, would be an admirable form for holding their reserves of foreign exchange.

Even if, as is to be hoped, the operations of the national exchange equalisation accounts withered away as the system developed, the controlled provision by the IMF of international liquid reserves in the form of Gold Certificates would still remain of major importance. For Gold Certificates could be held by commercial banks and by other private institutions and individuals who, because their business involved them in international transactions, needed to hold their own reserves of foreign exchange.[2] Indeed, there would be no reason why those who wished to do so should not express their business contracts in terms, not of any single national currency, but of Gold Certificates. In particular, this possibility might greatly ease the flow of international loan capital in a regime of fluctuating rates of exchange between national currencies.

There is nothing absurd in modern conditions in having an international currency of this kind, controlled by a truly supranational authority, and at the same time having a number of national currencies whose values may fluctuate in terms of each other and in terms of the international currency. As long as we entrust to the national governments the main functions of public finance and of policies concerned with the maintenance of full employment, the control of inflation, and the stimulation of

[2] National monetary authorities would have undertaken to hold only Gold Certificates and no gold, but private individuals and institutions would be free to demand from the IMF the redemption of Gold Certificates with actual gold. But against this liability the IMF would now hold the whole of the present gold reserves of the monetary authorities of the Western countries. In the unlikely event that such reserves proved insufficient for this purpose the IMF would have to restrict the supply of Gold Certificates and to allow the price of Gold Certificates and of gold to rise in terms of national currencies in general.

economic growth, we cannot preserve *both* a liberal co-operative system of international trade and of foreign aid *and also* fixed exchange rates between national currencies. But this does not mean that there is no proper function for a really powerful supranational monetary authority. Those who, like myself, wish to move in the direction of effective world government will welcome this fact. All federal or confederal arrangements rest upon a sensible division of functions between the 'central' and the 'local' governments, suitable to the practical problems of the real situation. I suggest that for the Western countries the division of functions in monetary matters should be of the kind which I have outlined in this article.

Such proposals raise, of course, the most far-reaching questions of the proper nature for the management and governing body of an IMF that was transformed into so powerful a supranational instrument. It would be inevitable that it should be operated, in its day-to-day decisions about the purchase and sale of national currencies, by a small body of expert international servants, recruited no doubt largely from the treasuries and central banks of the constituent countries; but at the same time the principles of its operations should be supervised by a governing body of ministers or high officials from the governments of the member countries. But these matters cannot be discussed in this article.

244-73
[1962]

16

UK, Commonwealth and Common Market[1]

U.K.;
E.C.
4210
4233

Meade's Hobart Paper *(No. 17, London: Institute of Economic Affairs, April 1962) went into three editions. The first edition is reprinted here followed by Meade's* The Common Market: Is there an Alternative? *which appeared as the prologue to the second and third editions* (UK, Commonwealth & Common Market: A Reappraisal, *London: Institute of Economic Affairs, November 1962 and December 1970) and as a separate pamphlet in December 1962.*

I European Unity

Should the United Kingdom join the Common Market? As soon as one thinks of this issue one is confronted with a mixture of political and economic considerations that are difficult, if not impossible, to unscramble. In my view the political issues are ultimately more important than the economic. But the European Economic Community (EEC) is after all an *economic* institution; it has implications which are of importance from the purely economic point of view; and its political implications can be understood only in terms of its economic effects. I shall start by stating my attitude to the political issue but shall then concentrate on the economic problems, pointing out in the course of the analysis the political relevance of some of the economic choices.

The fundamental objective of the architects of the EEC is quite frankly the political unification of Western Europe into a federation or confederation of states. Many Europeans remember that a short while ago Europe, with its common cultural heritage, was the centre of world influence. They realise how much Europe has fallen in power and stature, as a result partly of a series of hideous civil wars between the European states and partly of the natural growth of influential civilisations in other parts of the world – in North America, in Russia, and now in Asia and Africa. They realise already that by coming together the European states have considerably restored their stature in a world in

[1] I should like to thank the Editor of the *European-Atlantic Review* for permission to reproduce several paragraphs from an article by the author in the March–April 1961 number ['Solution cannot be found by Britain and Europe alone', vol. 11, no. 1, pp. 24–26, 30].

which no one of them alone can have much influence. The resurgence of continental Europe through its reunion is already a substantial reality.

But such a European union could develop in either of two directions. It might strive to become a closely knit, inward-looking, compact Great Power. It could, on the other hand, become a liberal, outward-looking, confederation of like-minded communities, which exercised influence in building a bridge between East and West, between developed and underdeveloped countries, between socialism and free enterprise, and thus make a major contribution towards the building of the One World which, in my view, with present technological changes must necessarily be our main political objective.

Now we in the United Kingdom have also fallen from the status of a Great Power in comparison with the present giants, the USA and the USSR. We have a common heritage with the continental European countries. We also must forget our romantic dreams of grandeur. Moreover, we must fight against our tiresome fault of self-satisfied priggishness; for there are many very liberal men and women actively engaged in the construction of the new European institutions on the continent of Europe and many illiberal and narrow-minded persons exercising influence in the UK. Nevertheless, there are two facts in UK political life which could enable us to make a significant contribution to the political structure of Europe.

First, while we are bad at many things, we are good at Habeas Corpus, parliamentary democracy, one-man-one-vote, and freedom of speech. This set of Gladstonian virtues may be old-fashioned; but the recent history of Europe makes one realise how foolish it would be to belittle them. Moreover, the Scandinavians and the Swiss – our present partners in the European Free-Trade Association (EFTA) – are also good at these same things. If our entry into the EEC brought them in as members or as associates, these liberal forces in Europe would be further strengthened.

Second, both the development of the British Empire into a loose Commonwealth covering all races, all continents, all creeds, all stages of economic development, and most types of economic system and also the use of sterling as a world currency mean that we in the UK have necessarily a habit of looking outward over the world which is less ingrained in most of the continental Europeans.

In view of all this I would strongly favour our joining in Europe if there is at least a fair prospect that it will move in the liberal outward-looking direction I have described; and if we joined Europe we could hope to exercise a very considerable influence in steering developments in this direction. The main fear in this connection is not so much that we should not succeed, as that we might give up trying. If, therefore, there were little or no prospect of the European Community developing in this way, if it appeared that it was unalterably designed as yet one more monolithic, inward-looking Great Power, then we should stay outside. It would, of course, be ridiculous to demand, as a condition for our entry, cast-iron guarantees about the future development of the European Community. We must in the end reach our decision on the basis of probabilities, not of certainties.

But the economic conditions on which the UK can gain admission to the EEC will themselves be important pointers about the direction in which the EEC is more likely to develop. In this broad political context, what strictly economic, commercial, and financial issues would arise from a possible UK membership of the EEC?

II Economic Gains

First, it is widely held that, whatever the political arguments may be, the UK for her own economic salvation must join Europe. The argument is that the EEC provides a large and rapidly expanding economic system with a rate of growth considerably faster than that of the UK and that we cannot afford to be excluded from this market. The formation of the EEC will, for example, mean that German manufacturers will be able to sell freely all over the larger part of Western Europe, whereas UK producers will have to face appreciable import duties when they try to compete against such sales of German products. The rate of economic growth in our traditional export markets of the Commonwealth is much lower than in Europe; we need free entry to Europe as a basis of the much needed expansion of our export trade. Moreover, so it is argued, our export costs are high; our industries are riddled with restrictive practices; our rate of technical progress is low because of our happy-go-lucky attitude to work and business; and producers make no serious effort to resist the inflation of money costs caused by the trade unions' incessant demands for increased money wages. The draught of open competition with the vigorous continental producers would give just that shock which our Government, our producers, and our trade unions need to make British industry competitive.

There is, no doubt, some truth in all this; but there is less force in it than is believed by some of the less restrained enthusiasts for UK membership of the EEC. Let us try to unravel the various strands.

There is no evidence that the rate of economic growth in the six countries of the existing EEC is itself due to the formation of the Community. The rate of growth in these countries was exceptionally high long before the Community was even conceived; and there has recently been a noticeable decline in their rate of economic growth. The fact that their economies were active and expanding made it easier for the Six to face the adjustments in their economic structures which the removal of trade barriers made necessary. The high rate of economic growth may have led to the Community rather than the Community to the high rate of growth.

Special reasons (such as delayed economic recovery from the ravages of the Second World War) may explain much of the exceptionally high rate of growth in the EEC countries over the last decade; and it would be very rash to assert that in future years the rate of growth of demand in the EEC countries (to which the UK sells only about 15 per cent of her exports) will continue to be markedly higher than the rate of growth of demand in, say, the countries of the Commonwealth (to which the UK sells almost 50 per cent of her exports). Association with the EEC instead of the Commonwealth means *perhaps* association with a more rapidly growing market; it means *certainly* association with what is at present a much smaller market.

What then are the positive advantages which might be gained for UK industry by joining the EEC? There would, of course, be increased possibilities of trade with Europe; and this might be of advantage to us in three ways. First, it might enable us to concentrate on making those things in the production of which we have a comparative advantage and to exchange them for things in the production of which we had a comparative disadvantage. Second, by expanding the size of the total free-trade market for our manufactures, it might be possible to reap economies of large-scale production by specialising on the production of certain lines of output. Third, the close competition which our producers would face at home and in continental Europe would make it exceptionally difficult for them to maintain restrictive practices and would give them both an exceptional motive and an exceptional opportunity to reduce costs of production; and this might lead to changes in the attitudes of UK producers which would indirectly stimulate our rate of growth.

The first of these advantages is the straightforward classical argument for free trade. It is real enough. But in its present application it is not perhaps of much quantitative importance. One can look at it this way. Suppose that our terms of trade, the prices at which foreigners offer us their exports and the prices we charge for our exports, remain unchanged. We can then measure the increase in our welfare on an additional £100 of trade by the rate of duty on our imports. We export something which costs us £100; with it we purchase something for which we pay £100 to the foreigner; but the UK consumer will pay, say, £120 for the product because there is an import duty of 20 per cent which has made it that much scarcer or more costly in our own market. An export of what costs us £100 gains for us something which the consumer values at £120. As we reduce our duties from 20 per cent to zero, trade expands. The increase in our welfare is equal to something between 20 per cent and zero per cent (say, 10 per cent on the average) on this additional import trade. If the additional trade with Europe due to our adherence to the EEC were 25 per cent of our national income (a truly gigantic figure) the increase in our welfare would be equal only to 10 per cent of 25 per cent or 2½ per cent of our national income – the gain which we achieve from one year's economic growth at our present rather limited rate of growth. Such a figure does not mean the difference between national prosperity and economic calamity.

But in freeing trade on a regional as contrasted with a world-wide basis, the advantages of freer trade within the economic union may be offset, partially or wholly, by diversions of trade away from outside countries.

Thus, if the UK joined the EEC, some of the increased imports into the UK from Europe would be due to a diversion of trade from other sources. When we admit German products free we may purchase imports from Germany instead of imports from Canada, Sweden, or the United

States. There would be no loss in welfare to us from any reduction in imports from countries whose products we already admitted freely – such as many Canadian products which enjoy free entry under our Commonwealth arrangements or such as products from Sweden if we already admitted them freely under EFTA arrangements. For from every £100 of exports which we sold for the purchase of such imports from Canada or Sweden we should already be receiving goods which consumers in the UK valued at only £100. But if we diverted our import demand from, say, the USA on whose products we levied an import duty of, say, 30 per cent, we would be giving up imports which were worth to consumers 30 per cent more than their cost to us. We would thus have to set against the calculation of the gain from our trade with Europe a loss of a whole 30 per cent on the value of the trade diverted from the USA.

Moreover – and this is of the first importance – joining the EEC would oblige us to raise duties or levies on imports from the Commonwealth which at present enjoy free entry to the United Kingdom market. In so far as this caused us to purchase less from these markets, there would be, on the basis of our present calculations, a loss of economic welfare equal to about one half of the increased rate of duty or levy reckoned on the whole of the Commonwealth trade which was cut off by this rise of duty.

It has so far been assumed that the UK terms of trade would remain unaffected by our joining the EEC; but this may not be so. There would be many influences pulling both directions. That we would no longer enjoy a preference over German products in an EFTA country like Sweden would tend to reduce the demand for our exports and to turn the terms of trade against us; but this would presumably be at least matched by the fact that the German exporters would no longer enjoy a preference over British exporters in France, which would tend to raise the demand for our exports and to improve our terms of trade. But it is possible that all the members of the enlarged EEC would improve their terms of trade with outside countries – the USA, Japan, South America and so on – through the preferences which they would be giving to each other's products. On the other hand, a special factor which might tend to worsen the UK's terms of trade is the loss (for reasons I discuss later) of the preferences given to UK exports in the other Commonwealth countries. In so far as Australian demand was, for example, thereby diverted from UK to German cars, the UK's terms of trade would tend to worsen. But taking it all in all I can see no reason to believe there would be a very substantial movement one way or the other in the prices offered for UK exports.

The standard classical free-trade gain which we might expect from joining the EEC is for these reasons difficult to assess accurately. But it would appear that it cannot be a decisive argument for joining the Community. The economic argument for joining the Community must be based on the two other considerations, the possibility that it would give scope for economies of scale in production and that it would give a competitive jolt to our stagnant economy, thus stimulating the rate of growth in the UK economy.

These two arguments must be taken together. The economies-of-large-scale argument cannot be dismissed by asserting that the UK's present markets already provide sales for the output of at least *one* plant of a size sufficient to enjoy all important economies of scale. To have a truly dynamic, competitive economy one needs a market sufficiently large to contain a *large number* of competing plants each of a size sufficient to enjoy all important economies of scale. It may well be that the whole of Europe is a better sized basic home market than the UK alone if one applies this criterion. This argument (namely that a larger market is needed to provide a truly competitive stimulus for many firms each operating on a sufficiently large scale) may be important. We may have something substantial to gain here. But I would not like to guess how large it is or how far the competitive stimulus would in fact raise our rate of economic growth. I would merely at this point make two comments.

First, these gains can be appreciable only if the stimulus of the wider market can be combined with financial conditions which do not require the UK authorities to restrict investment and demand in general to prevent a balance-of-payments crisis. It is a wide market without stagnation that we need. The gain is subject to a satisfactory set of financial and balance-of-payments arrangements in the EEC, a matter considered in VI below.

Secondly, competition with manufacturers in other countries may be needed to promote the competitiveness of UK industry; but joining the EEC is not the only way of reducing duties on the import of manufactured goods into the UK. We have had many opportunities since the end of the Second World War to bargain reductions in our duties through the GATT against reductions in other countries' duties. We have in fact just completed one such tariff-reduction bargain through the GATT. If President Kennedy's attempt to gain substantially increased powers from Congress to bargain reductions in the US tariff is successful, we shall have even better opportunities in the future. It is no doubt true that at this moment joining the EEC presents us with the best opportunity of getting substantial reductions of other countries' obstacles against our exports in return for a reduction of our own barriers to imports into the UK. But if we take a slightly longer view this is by no means the only possible way of bargaining for substantial reductions in trade barriers. It is suggested in V below that we should in any case treat our negotiations for adherence to the EEC as part of a much wider exercise for the reduction of trade barriers. If the negotiations for entry into the EEC do not succeed, we shall have to rely on the other methods.

III Effects on EFTA Countries

Let us turn to the economic and financial problems with which the UK would be confronted by becoming a member of the EEC. These problems are those of:

(1) The other members of the European Free-Trade Association (EFTA);

(2) UK agricultural protection;
(3) Commonwealth trade;
(4) Sterling and the balance of payments;
(5) Labour migration.

In order to understand the present EFTA problem it is necessary to make a brief reference to its origin. When the Six were working out the Treaty provisions for the EEC, the UK proposed the association of the UK and of other countries of Europe with the EEC by means of a free-trade area. The UK proposals would have left agricultural products outside the terms of any agreement; there would have been free trade throughout the free-trade area in the manufactured products of the member countries; but each member country could have determined its import duties and general commercial policy arrangements *vis-à-vis* outside countries. These proposals were designed to enable the UK to be closely associated with Europe without breaking the UK links with the Commonwealth, as will be explained later.

As a result of the breakdown of these free-trade area proposals seven countries of Europe, of which the UK was by far the largest in scale of international trade, formed a European Free Trade Association built on the basis of the UK free-trade area proposals. Some of these countries, in particular the Swiss, the Austrians, and the Swedes, felt unable to join the EEC because to do so might compromise their position of neutrality in international politics. The EEC has many supranational overtones. In particular, the EEC is a customs union which means that there is a common tariff of duties on imports from outside countries. Full membership of the EEC means that a member country's import duties and quotas on trade with third countries are no longer decided as an act of sovereignty by the national government of the country concerned but become a matter to be decided supranationally by some single European governmental authority.

The UK clearly cannot now use the EFTA simply as a bargaining weapon to get terms from the EEC convenient to herself. She is under a clear moral obligation not to break the EFTA up and join the EEC unless the other members of the EFTA can also come to satisfactory arrangements with the EEC. I shall say little on this subject, not because I think the principle unimportant but because I doubt whether there would be very serious difficulty in reaching satisfactory terms. Some of the EFTA countries (in particular Norway and Denmark) are likely to want to become full members of the EEC if the UK does so; and there is no reason to believe that their membership would be refused. Others, as we have seen (in particular Sweden, Switzerland, and Austria) because of their neutrality in international politics may feel unable to become full members of the EEC. But their major economic requirements could be met by a form of association with the EEC which gave them free entry to the EEC market and which gave the EEC countries free entry to their markets. Provided these neutral countries kept their tariffs with third countries not too far out of line with those of the EEC countries, little harm could be done to the EEC structure. If the major problems of UK membership of the EEC can be overcome, the countries of the EEC will presumably not be so doctrinaire as to cause the breakdown of the whole structure by refusing to contemplate special arrangements with the neutral countries of Western Europe.

IV Problem of UK Farmers

The problem of UK agricultural protection itself raises three questions:

(1) Would there be a marked change in the degree of protection given to UK farmers?
(2) What would be the effect within the UK of any change in the methods of protection afforded to the farmers?
(3) What would be the effect of the change in the degree and methods of protection upon the Commonwealth suppliers of agricultural produce to the UK?

The third of these questions is a central part of the problem of Commonwealth trade, and will be discussed in V.

The protection at present given to UK farmers now costs almost £350 million a year in subsidies. Economically it could be thought a desirable development from the community's point of view if joining the EEC moderated this protection. But the domestic political problem in the UK is, of course, the farmers' vote; and it depends upon the level of agricultural protection.

At present there are wide differences in the degree of protection given to farmers in the various countries of the EEC. In particular, for many products the price paid to the German farmer is considerably higher than that paid to the French farmer. The general shape, though not the details, of future EEC agricultural policy has now been determined. After a period of transitional adjustments:

(1) there will be complete freedom of movement of agricultural produce within the EEC;

(2) for some products prices for EEC farmers will be maintained above world prices by ordinary fixed import duties;

(3) for a number of basic agricultural products stable target prices for EEC farmers will be set by a supranational agricultural authority and import levies charged on them will be varied from time to time to maintain the stable target domestic prices within the EEC in spite of fluctuations in world prices; and

(4) the proceeds of the import levies will eventually be paid into a common EEC agricultural pool and will be available for such purposes as the finance of investment in new equipment and methods in the backward agricultural regions of the EEC and for the payment of export subsidies to make possible the sale of surplus agricultural output at the lower world price in markets outside the EEC.

Suppose we were to join in this system. How would it affect the UK farmer? We should, of course, have to give up the process of our annual review of agricultural support prices and the fixing of prices which took into account the costs of production solely of the UK farmer. But for fixing the EEC target prices there would have presumably to be something like a periodic European price review. And there is no reason to believe that the prices likely to come out of that review would be very unfavourable for our farmers. At present the average price received by EEC farmers is above the UK support price for some products, notably cereals; but it is lower for other products, such as eggs and milk. But would the EEC price be likely to be set above or below the present EEC average? That is the great unknown. At first sight it would appear much easier politically to set the EEC price nearer the high German level which will enable the inefficient German peasant to continue to scrape a living than near the lower French level which would be adequate for efficient French farmers. But many of the influential leaders in the EEC have a much less protectionist bias than this; and in any case there will be some products, such as fruit and vegetables, the free entry of which from the continent of Europe would certainly hit the UK producers very seriously. The transitional period would have to be used in this country to find something else for many of our horticulturalists to do and to shift the emphasis on various products within our farming. But in my view it would be very wrong to refuse to join the EEC because of the uncertainties caused thereby to our farmers.

There would, however, be an important change in the methods of protection whereby any given level of support prices was made effective to our farmers; and while the method, as opposed to the degree of protection, would not affect the prosperity of our farmers it would have other effects in our economic system.

At present in the UK the main agricultural products are admitted freely at the relatively low world price at least from the large Commonwealth producers and support is given to the UK farmer by a direct subsidy from the Budget to the extent necessary to close the gap between the world price and the guaranteed support price. In consequence the price of food to the consumer is low, but general tax rates are high enough to raise the funds necessary to pay the subsidies to the farmers. If the EEC system were substituted for the UK system, the cost of living to the consumer would be raised because import levies would be imposed to raise the price to the home consumer as well as to the home farmer.

On the other hand, since it would no longer be necessary to subsidise the farmer directly from the Budget, there would be an opportunity for a cut in taxes or an increase in other forms of expenditure (e.g. old age pensions) which could in part offset the burden to the consumer of a rise in the cost of foodstuffs. But it would be only a very partial offset. The rise in the cost of living would be due to the rise in the price of imported as well as of home-produced supplies; the rise in the price to the consumer of home-produced supplies would result in an equivalent saving of agricultural subsidies and improvement in the UK budgetary situation; the rise in the price of imports, however, would result in a rise in revenue from import levies on agricultural produce; if, as is at present proposed in the EEC, these levies were paid into a common pool to be used to subsidise the export surpluses of other members of the EEC or to invest in agricultural improvements in other parts of the EEC the revenue would not be available to the UK Budget and there could be no easy offset to the burden of increased food prices to the consumer.

The first disadvantage of the EEC proposals to the UK is obvious. The UK is by far the largest importer of foodstuffs. The EEC import levies would be taxes, charged mainly on the UK consumer of foodstuffs and spent mainly on the subsidisation either of inefficient continental peasant production or of exports to third countries of agricultural surpluses from continental Europe. This would impose a heavy burden on the UK, which would show itself in a strain on the UK's balance of payments equal to the rise in the market price of all her food imports (whether from the EEC or from third countries) less whatever subsidies UK agriculture itself might receive out of the levies.

Second, a change of protective system from the UK production subsidies to the continental import levies would in one sense be a retrogressive step for the achievement of the basic objective of agricultural protection. Presumably, the object of agricultural protection is to encourage the domestic production of agricultural produce but not to discourage the domestic consumption of foodstuffs. There would, therefore, be a real economic inefficiency involved in using a method (e.g. that of import levies) that discouraged the domestic consumption of foodstuffs relatively to that of other products and encouraged the domestic production of agricultural products relatively to other products. Direct subsidies on production would have the desired effect on production without the undesired effect on consumption.

Third, a rise in the price of foodstuffs might fall very much on the poorer consumers, so that there would be real danger that the change would have an undesirable effect upon the distribution of income within the UK.

Fourth, if a rise in the cost of living led to increased demands for increased money wage-rates, it would have undesirable effects upon the level of money costs of production in the UK and thus upon the UK balance of payments.

These would be real difficulties; but if they were properly handled, they should not in my opinion present an insuperable obstacle to the UK joining the EEC.

In the first place, it is perfectly reasonable for the UK to ask that the EEC system of agricultural protection should be a compromise between production subsidies and import levies. The degree of agricultural protection depends upon the divergence between the lower world import price and the higher price assured for the domestic farmer; with the UK system the price to the consumer is at the low world import price and the gap is filled by subsidies to the domestic producer; with the continental system the price to the consumer is at the high domestic cost price and the gap is filled by the import levies. There is no reason why the price to the consumer should not be intermediate between the low world price and the high domestic cost price. A self-financing scheme of this kind could be devised if the revenue from moderate import levies was paid into a common EEC agricultural pool which used the proceeds to pay deficiency payments to the agricultural producers. Part of the gap between low world prices and high domestic farm prices would be filled by the import levies which would raise the price to the consumers above the world price and part would be filled by the deficiency payments which would raise the price received by the farmer above that paid by the consumer. It is not reasonable that the levies on the large UK imports of overseas foodstuffs should be used primarily, if not exclusively, to support continental agricultural production and export. The UK farmers should enjoy subsidies at least as large as those paid to continental producers. Of course, since the ratio of imports to home production is so much higher in the UK, the compromise proposal to tax imports in order to subsidise production would leave the UK as the main contributor and the other EEC countries as the main beneficiaries. Though it is better than the present EEC proposals, it is still a very generous arrangement from their point of view.

Any remaining adverse effect which the partial shift from production subsidies to import levies on foodstuffs might have on the distribution of income in the UK would have to be consciously planned by adjustments in tax burdens and social security benefits in the UK Budget. The whole of the budgetary saving on the present UK agricultural deficiency payments would be available for this purpose; and any remaining budgetary problems should not be unmanageable.

The effect of the change of system of agricultural protection on the cost of living and so on money wage-rates and money costs should not therefore present an insuperable problem. Its quantitative importance is limited. Even if the complete change were made from UK production subsidies to continental import levies, the cost of living would in the end be only some 2½ to 3 per cent higher than it would otherwise have been. If the transition to the new arrangements were spread over five or six years, the UK cost and price structure would have to absorb an additional rise of ½ per cent per annum. This is by no means a negligible problem; but it would be reduced if a compromise on the lines already discussed between the UK and the continental systems of agricultural protection were reached. But even with such a compromise, there would remain some rise in the cost of the UK's food imports with a strain on the balance of payments.

V Effects on Commonwealth Trade

One of the two really major problems is the difficulties connected with Commonwealth trade. The fact that these difficulties have on occasion been used as an excuse by those citizens of the UK who, on quite other grounds, want to stay out of Europe, does not mean that they are unreal. They are, in fact, very substantial.

The problem of UK trading relations with the rest of the Commonwealth concerns the treatment of UK products in the other parts of the Commonwealth and the treatment in the UK of the products of other parts of the Commonwealth.

The preferential treatment which UK products receive in the rest of the Commonwealth are of some importance to UK exporters. But their importance has much diminished since the 1930s. Their existence should not be allowed to present an insurmountable obstacle to the UK becoming a full member of the EEC. There is force in the argument that the UK would be trying to have it both ways if by joining the EEC she obtained one-hundred-per-cent preference in German, French, Italian, Dutch, Belgian and Luxembourg markets over US products, and at the same time sought to maintain her partial preferences in Commonwealth markets over European and US products. The preferences which the UK enjoys in Commonwealth markets are one of the things which the UK should be prepared to give up if an otherwise satisfactory solution of the problem of the Commonwealth can be found. Moreover, the surrender of these preferences by the UK is a necessary part of any attempt on the part of the Commonwealth countries to obtain commercial advantages to offset the losses which (as we shall see) they will sustain in the UK market. Australia, for example, may hope to obtain somewhat easier entry for her products to the EEC market and to the USA if in return she offers to cease to give UK manufactures preference over American, German, French, etc., manufactures in the Australian market.

It is the treatment which Commonwealth products receive in the UK which presents the really difficult problem. It is true in this case also that the preferences which Commonwealth countries enjoy in the UK are less important than they were in the 1930s; and if it were simply a matter of ending these preferences, it would be relatively innocuous for the UK to become a member of the EEC. But UK membership of the EEC would mean much more than this. It would involve not only removing the preferences given to Commonwealth products over continental European products but also in addition instituting a set of preferences for continental European products over Commonwealth products. At present the UK admits New Zealand butter on better terms than Dutch butter; in future she would have to admit Dutch butter free but keep out New Zealand butter to the extent necessary to maintain the agreed EEC price of butter within the EEC. At present the UK admits Indian textiles free of duty and taxes the import of German and Italian textiles; in future she would have to admit German and Italian textiles free and would have both to tax Indian textiles at the rate of EEC customs duty on textiles, and also to submit the import of Indian textiles to any quota restrictions laid down as part of the EEC's common commercial policy. The problem is not simply one of facing the abolition of Imperial Preferences as it is so often falsely presented; it is one of facing not only the abolition of Imperial Preferences but also the institution of an important system of discriminations against Commonwealth products.

In a number of Commonwealth products this problem would not arise. Many raw materials admitted free into the UK would also be admitted free into the EEC. Australian wool, for example, would enjoy free entry into the enlarged EEC.

There are, however, some raw materials which in their processed forms (aluminium, leather, newsprint, for example) are admitted freely into the UK but would be taxed under the present EEC tariff on import into the EEC. If these arrangements were continued, the UK would have to import aluminium from France free of duty while Canadian aluminium would be taxed. Such duties are proposed in order to protect the relevant processing industries in the EEC countries. It is reasonable for the UK to ask as a condition of her joining the EEC that they should be removed.

The products of tropical agriculture present a rather different set of problems. They are not produced in the EEC countries nor in the UK; but there is real danger that the EEC arrangements would be such as to use the EEC market including the very important UK market as a means of protecting the French ex-colonies against other, including Commonwealth, producers of similar products. This danger stems from the fact that certain French overseas African territories are associated with the EEC in such a way that they enjoy free entry into all the EEC markets. Unless, therefore, the Commonwealth producers of these products were similarly associated, the EEC market (including the UK market) would be used to protect French overseas territories against competing Commonwealth producers.

Temperate zone foodstuffs – cereals, meat, dairy produce, certain fruits and vegetables – present a very different and much more intractable problem since they are produced in the EEC countries themselves and in the Commonwealth countries like Australia, New Zealand, and Canada on a very large scale. The EEC agricultural proposals I have outlined could very seriously hit these Commonwealth producers. The EEC agricultural proposals imply that any change in the balance between supply and demand for such foodstuffs within the enlarged EEC will be met by an offsetting change in the amount imported from outside countries. There are two ways in which the EEC agricultural arrangements might affect the balance of supply and demand adversely from the outside countries' point of view.

First, the change in the methods of agricultural protection in the UK would, as explained, raise the price of foodstuffs in the UK. In so far as this caused a reduction in the amount of foodstuffs that would otherwise have been consumed the whole difference would be met by an exclusion (through raised import levies) of imports from outside countries including the Commonwealth suppliers, unless it were accompanied by a reduction in the amount produced by EEC farmers brought about by an appropriate reduction in the support price.

Second, political agreement on a common agricultural policy may be more easily reached in Europe if the common agricultural support prices are set at higher rather than lower levels so that all types of farmer have a chance of survival. But this may involve guaranteed stable prices at a high enough level to enable really efficient farmers throughout the EEC (including many efficient UK farmers) very substantially to expand their output. Such an expansion might exceed the expansion of demand within the EEC and the whole of the balance would have to be met by an equivalent exclusion of supplies from third countries. With butter, for example, a very large proportion of the outside supplies to the EEC market (including the UK) comes from New Zealand; and the New

Zealand economy is very largely dependent upon the production for overseas sale of dairy produce. New Zealand would face the risk of economic catastrophe if the forces in the European market went against her; for the adverse effect of all the marginal changes in supply and demand would be concentrated on her in order to preserve stability at a highly remunerative price for UK and other EEC farmers.

It is important in this connection to realise how fundamental from the point of view of the present EEC countries is the adherence of the UK to the common agricultural policy of the EEC. Both in absolute quantities and also as a percentage of total domestic consumption the UK is a larger importer of foodstuffs than any EEC country. Indeed, in some foodstuffs the EEC excluding the UK is supplying more or less enough for its domestic consumption and, if it produced much more, would have a surplus for export. This fact would put a serious restraint on the degree of protection which the EEC agricultural authorities might plan for EEC agriculture. The disposal of surpluses above the level of domestic requirements would have to be at the low world price level; this would raise awkward questions of export subsidies in their commercial relations with other countries, and would involve a budgetary problem since the difference between the lower world price and the higher price paid to the domestic producer would have to be met from general taxation. But the addition to the EEC system of a large net importer of foodstuffs like the UK would make it possible to dispose of the export surpluses of continental Europe at a high guaranteed price in the UK market at the expense of New Zealand and other outside producers who were formerly supplying the big import demands of the UK. And if this were not sufficient, the present proposals for the pooling of the EEC import levies would enable the revenue from the taxes on imports of Australian wheat and New Zealand butter into the UK to be used to subsidise surplus exports of French wheat and Dutch butter to undercut Australia and New Zealand in outside markets. It is not, of course, certain that EEC agricultural policies would develop in this illiberal manner. But it is not unreasonable for the Commonwealth suppliers to seek some assurance about the degree of agricultural protection in the enlarged EEC market.

In manufactures also there are dangers for Commonwealth producers, particularly for present and potential exporters of cheap labour-intensive manufactures from the overpopulated and underdeveloped parts of the Commonwealth. The UK grants free entry to cheap labour-intensive manufactures from Hong Kong and India. This principle is often challenged by competing producers in the UK, and it has sometimes been partially compromised by *ad hoc* unofficial private trading arrangements limiting the quantities of such goods which are exported to the UK. For example, there are arrangements between the UK textile industry and the exporters of textiles from Hong Kong and India limiting the export of textiles from these two sources to the UK market. But the principle of freedom from government restrictions on these imports stands; and all those who are liberally minded and wish to promote the welfare of the underdeveloped countries should do all they can to defend the principle and ensure its full application. The underdeveloped, overpopulated countries of Asia should be able, as Japan has been, to produce and to sell abroad the cheap labour-intensive manufactures which will enable them to buy capital equipment, foodstuffs, and raw materials from the developed countries of Europe, North America, and Australasia. I would oppose a change that meant giving up free entry for Indian manufactures in order to allow continental European manufactures freely into the UK with the obligation to impose the common European tariff on Indian manufactures, unless it were combined with other arrangements that offset the restrictive effect upon the market for Indian manufactures.

The future wealth of the poorest countries is at stake. The heavily populated underdeveloped countries can in many cases achieve reasonable progress only if they can find rapidly expanding markets. To restrict them now is not merely to inflict some immediate damage on Commonwealth countries that have gone some way with this sort of development. It is, above all, to damage the future prospects of countries that will need to develop in this way in the future. The sensible development of trade patterns is that the highly developed, industrialised countries of Western Europe should produce and export more of the capital goods and consumption goods that require much technical know-how, skill, and specialised equipment and should import more of the easily made manufactured consumption goods from the industrialising overseas countries. It would be a bad beginning for the UK to give up the principle of free entry for such products from the industrialising parts of the Commonwealth in order to protect the manufacture of such products in Germany, Italy, France, and the UK itself.

There are, of course, some exports from Commonwealth countries (and in particular from Canada) of the more elaborate, expensive manufactures. The UK would be obliged, if she joined the EEC, to import German chemicals free of duty but to tax the import of Canadian chemicals. This is in principle the same problem as that of New Zealand butter and of Hong Kong textiles, except that it is less extensive and less vital to the exporting countries. The contraction of the UK market for dairy produce and for cheap textiles could be an economic catastrophe for New Zealand and Hong Kong. The contraction of the UK market for its manufactures would be a setback but could not be a catastrophe for Canada.

How then might we deal with these problems of Commonwealth exports if the UK joined the EEC? The free-trade area proposals which the UK put forward in 1957 were designed to meet the problem. By excluding agriculture from their scope the problems of tropical and temperate zone foodstuffs would not have arisen. The UK would have been under an obligation to give free entry to European manufactures. But she would have remained free to give free entry also to Commonwealth manufactures. This would have meant the end of Imperial Preference on such goods. It would no longer have been possible to protect Indian and Hong Kong textiles in the UK by excluding German, French, and Italian textiles. But there would have been no obligation to have instituted a system of discrimination against Commonwealth products – to admit Italian textiles free but to tax Indian textiles at the EEC rate of import duty.

But these free-trade area proposals have been ruled out. Are there any alternatives?

Under the Rome Treaty creating the EEC, means have been devised for meeting the rather similar problems involved in the treatment of the overseas territories of the existing member countries and, in particular, of the French African territories. Forms of association have been worked out whereby:

(1) the products of these French African territories will enjoy free entry into the domestic markets of the six existing EEC countries;

(2) in order to protect their infant industries these territories will, however, be allowed to maintain duties on their imports of the products of the six existing EEC countries; but

(3) these territories will cease to give preferential treatment in their import duties to one EEC member over another.

In other words, a French associated territory will be able to export freely to France, Germany, Italy, and the Benelux countries; it will be able to impose import duties on French, German, Italian, and Benelux products; but it will have to charge on its imports of French products a duty as high as that which it charges on the import of German, Italian, and Benelux products. What is sauce for the goose is sauce for the gander. Cannot the problem of the British overseas Commonwealth territories be solved in the same way?

It is clear on consideration that no general solution can be found on these lines. If this principle were applied to all the overseas members of the Commonwealth, it would involve Germany and France and the other members of the Six giving free entry to New Zealand butter, Australian wheat, and similar temperate-zone agricultural products from the Commonwealth and free entry to the cheap textiles and other manufactures of Hong Kong and India. The Six would not for one moment consider such a powerful competitive blast on their protected agriculture and industry. In fact there is in this respect no analogy at all between the French Union and the British Commonwealth. Free entry into continental Europe from the French Union involves moderate supplies mainly of tropical or semi-tropical products which do not significantly compete with the produce of the European countries themselves. Free entry of Commonwealth products into the Common Market would involve potentially very large supplies of cheap manufactures from many Asian countries, very large supplies of temperate-zone agricultural products from Australasia, Africa and Canada, and quite appreciable supplies of more expensive highly manufactured goods from Canada and elsewhere.

But even if the Six would face extending to the British Commonwealth the arrangements which they offer to the French Union, the USA would do everything in their power to prevent it. Not only would this very extensive discrimination of Europeans in favour of Commonwealth products against closely competing US products cause a real blow to US exports (and that at a time when the US was facing a deficit on its balance of payments) but, being a form of discrimination involving the

British, it would arouse the quite irrational degree of distrust and hatred which the US feels towards the partial British Imperial Preferences, instead of arousing the favourable emotions which the hundred per cent preferences of a European Continental Customs Union stir up in the United States of the North American Continental Customs Union. Anything which had this effect would destroy all prospects of a liberal US commercial policy which – as I argue later – is so much to be desired.

A more promising suggestion is that a certain limited number of Commonwealth countries should be associated with the EEC in the same way as the French associated territories of Africa. In particular it may be hoped to solve the problem of tropical foodstuffs in this way. If the French African territories have free entry into the whole EEC market for their products (which are mainly tropical foodstuffs such as cocoa, coffee, bananas, etc.), the similar members of the Commonwealth (e.g. the African territories and the West Indies) must be offered similar treatment.

But in fact this partial solution would inevitably give rise to serious problems of discrimination between different Commonwealth countries. If bananas can be freely imported into the EEC territories from the African associated territories, both British and French, then the West Indies must be also given the status of associated territories in order to allow West Indian bananas as easy entry into Europe as African bananas. But the association of the West Indies would mean that the cheap labour-intensive manufactures of the West Indies which, we must hope, will grow in importance would also enjoy free entry into Europe. But then in order to avoid giving Jamaican manufactures preference over Hong Kong or Indian manufactures, Hong Kong and India would have to be given free entry to Europe. It is impossible to draw an arbitrary line between which territories and which products should and which should not enjoy free entry into Europe without introducing a serious element of discrimination between Commonwealth countries. The UK market (as well as the markets of the existing six EEC countries) will be being used to help some Commonwealth producers against other Commonwealth producers.

Indeed in my view the very idea of a solution through associated overseas territories is out of joint. Although the Americans are often very emotional and irrational about the evils of Imperial Preference, there is real substance in their present objections. For example, if the enlarged EEC admitted all coffee from all their overseas territories free and imposed serious restrictions on imports of coffee from other sources this would amount to something rather like the simple exclusion of Brazilian coffee from Europe. I share many of the objections to this discriminatory method of aid to developing countries. Moreover, the whole idea is already distasteful to many ex-colonial countries and will become increasingly so. Newly independent countries of Africa certainly want ready markets in developed countries for their produce, but they dislike, for obvious reasons, the political implications of obtaining them by being associated with one particular group of ex-colonial powers. Better than instituting any special association between the EEC and

British Commonwealth countries would be to put an end to the special association of the French overseas territories with the EEC and to search for a more general solution. I will return to this topic in due course.

One solution to the problem of the temperate-zone foodstuffs which has been proposed is that the Commonwealth countries should be granted some quotas of such foodstuffs which they could send into the EEC market free of the EEC import levies and could thus sell at the higher internal EEC price. It has been proposed that the size of such quotas should be fixed at a certain proportion of the existing sales of these suppliers in the EEC market; and some have proposed that the levy-free quotas should be gradually tapered off over a transitional period, at the end of which these Commonwealth producers would be in the same position as all other outside suppliers.

If these quotas were only temporary and were gradually tapered off we should in fact be saying to the New Zealand farmers: 'You have been loyal members of the Commonwealth and on the best free-trade principles of comparative cost you have organised your productive system to produce the goods we need. We are about to take measures which may result in a large shift in our custom to your continental high-cost competitors. This may hit you very hard. But we will pay you, at a diminishing rate, some unemployment benefit to tide you over the period while you look for something else to do.' I do not find this proposal attractive.

If the levy-free quotas are made permanent and not temporary, they would be in one sense too generous and in another sense too restrictive towards the Commonwealth suppliers. On these quotas the Commonwealth suppliers would now get an over-generous price, namely, a price as high as the domestic EEC price which would presumably be considerably above the lower world price at which under present arrangements the supplies are provided to the UK. The UK consumers would in fact be being 'taxed' on these supplies by an amount equal to the difference between the world price (at which the Commonwealth producers would be selling all their output over and above the levy-free quotas) and the domestic EEC price; and the revenue from this 'tax' would be being handed over to the lucky Commonwealth farmers who were selling the quota supplies.

But as far as quantities are concerned the Commonwealth suppliers would have no guaranteed share in the growth of consumption in the enlarged EEC market. In the longer run this element of participation in the growth of demand in the UK and the rest of Europe is of the utmost importance to the Commonwealth producers.

A possible quota arrangement which would meet both these objections is that the special quotas offered to the Commonwealth suppliers should be calculated not as a fixed amount but as a fixed proportion of the total consumption of these products in the enlarged EEC market. The quotas would rise as European consumption rose. But these quota supplies could be admitted into the EEC not entirely free of tax but at a fixed moderate import duty. They would thus be exempt from all the variable import levies designed to keep out overseas supplies; but they would be subject to some moderate rate of fixed duty which would mean that not the whole of the gap between the internal EEC price and the lower world price accrued to the Commonwealth producers. A scheme of this kind would be a real recognition of the Commonwealth problem. It would, of course, imply a limit to the degree of agricultural protectionism in Europe. It would no longer be possible to maintain prices for domestic farmers which so stimulated domestic output as not to leave room for the quota supplies from the Commonwealth producers.

Apart from these *ad hoc* solutions of particular Commonwealth problems, we need a solution which is more general in its scope and more permanent in its application. In my view there is only one such possibility. It is necessary that at the same time as the UK joins the EEC all the highly developed, industrialised countries of the North Atlantic should together reduce their restrictions on imports from each other and from the rest of the world.

If the UK joins the EEC the other Commonwealth countries will suffer because the UK will not only cease to discriminate in their favour against the continental Europeans, but will start to discriminate in favour of the Europeans against them. The only satisfactory way of dealing with this is to make arrangements whereby the Commonwealth countries gain by easier access to other markets what they lose by harder access to the UK market. One possibility is a general reduction of the common customs duties and other protective arrangements of the enlarged EEC. The Commonwealth countries could then sell somewhat more easily in the markets of continental Europe so that they would make up for their loss of markets in the UK.

But, for reasons we have already discussed, this reduction of EEC protective measures should be on a non-discriminatory basis. If this were so, then the reduction in EEC protection against outsiders would have to be very drastic indeed – so drastic that it might well be unacceptable. For example, India would have to be compensated by easier entry into continental Europe for the loss of free entry for her labour-intensive manufactures into the UK. But if the EEC had to reduce its import restrictions on a non-discriminatory basis, it might have to let in a flood of similar manufactures from Japan side by side with the increased imports from India. The 'price' paid by Europe to Japan and India would be much higher than the 'compensation' received by India alone.

This difficulty would be immensely reduced if all the highly developed, industrialised countries and not only the enlarged EEC took part in the operation – in particular, of course, if the USA joined in the exercise. This operation would consist of a general agreement on tariffs and other trade barriers between the enlarged EEC and the USA, whereby both parties reduce their barriers to imports from each other but on a most-favoured-nation basis so that the concessions which they gave to each other were extended automatically to imports from all other outside sources. Other highly developed or industrialised countries (Canada, Australia, New Zealand, Japan for example) might well take part in the agreement; but in general the highly developed industrialised countries would not ask for much in the way of commercial concessions from the underdeveloped countries. The exercise would in fact be to a large extent an exercise in aid through trade given on general non-discriminatory principles by the developed to the underdeveloped countries. It might be planned in the new Organisation for Economic Co-operation and Development (OECD) and negotiated finally through GATT.

I would, therefore, propose that the UK should make the ultimate acceptance of the results of its current negotiations with the EEC dependent upon the success of some such general re-shaping of commercial policy. It should become a member of the EEC if as a result of such a general settlement the Commonwealth countries agree that they stand to gain as much by this easier access to the whole North Atlantic areas as they lose in the UK market. Otherwise the UK should postpone its application for membership of the exclusive European club.

One card which the UK can play in this game is, of course, the preferences given by the overseas Commonwealth countries to UK manufactures. Part of the inducement to the Germans and Americans to reduce their protective measures against Indian and Australian produce would be that the Indians and Australians would cease to give preferences in their domestic markets to UK over German and American products. If in 1947 we had been prepared to sell Imperial Preferences for what they would fetch, what an immense clearance of the barriers of trade we might then have achieved. There was at that time a quite passionate desire by the Americans to get rid of these preferences. Now apparently the UK Government is prepared not only to abolish all Imperial Preferences but also to institute a severe system of anti-Imperial Preferences for no return at all from the United States, but simply to ensure that the Germans, French, Italians, and Beneluxers will not institute a new system of discrimination against us. The value of Imperial Preferences as a bargaining counter is certainly lower now than it was in 1947; but has it really fallen to zero?

This solution might until recently have been considered so utopian as not to merit serious consideration. But President Kennedy's recent proposals on commercial policy could transform the outlook. It is not merely that we should do everything we can to make President Kennedy's political task in the United States easier – for example, by emphasising that the acceptance of his proposals makes possible the total abolition of the abhorred Imperial Preferences. There are, it would seem, two sets of ideas behind the proposals themselves, and we should do everything we can to see that they develop in the way which helps the solution of the Commonwealth problem.

There is in some American quarters a desire that the USA itself should, as it were, join the Common Market or rather that it should not be too badly excluded from the Common Market. This stream of thought is symbolised by the President's proposal that the US administration should be empowered to bargain the complete elimination of tariffs on products for which the USA and the enlarged EEC are together the principal suppliers and account for 80 per cent or more of world trade in the products concerned. Motor-cars are a good example. There would result a complete free-trade area in the North Atlantic region for motor-cars. There is no proposal that these tariff reductions by the US should be on a discriminatory basis. Not only German and British, but also Hong Kong motor-cars would be admitted freely into the United States. But by limiting this extreme concession to the products which are not made in large amount outside the North Atlantic area, this part of the proposals cannot give much help to the overseas Commonwealth countries.

The rest of the President's proposals could be of much greater help in solving the Commonwealth problem. He is asking Congress for power to bargain for the total elimination of US duties on imports of tropical products which do not compete with US products. Free entry for tropical foodstuffs (such as coffee, cocoa, tea, bananas) from all sources into the whole of the enlarged EEC and the North American continent would without doubt provide the best solution for this part of the problem; and it must now be regarded as a political possibility. The President is also proposing to Congress that on the rest of the US import trade the administration should be empowered to make cuts of up to 50 per cent in all tariffs on a non-discriminatory basis. This proposal is of real importance from the Commonwealth point of view. If the USA reached a bargain with the enlarged EEC for a large cut in duties on these products, the automatic extension of this cut to the products of the rest of the world could be of the utmost significance to outside countries. But for two reasons such measures would in themselves not be sufficient.

In the first place, in labour-intensive textiles and some similar products, the developed countries restrict imports by quota restrictions rather than by tariffs. Any general tariff reductions would have to be accompanied by agreement between the developed countries to enlarge these quotas.

Secondly, in temperate-zone agricultural products the real damage to the interest of Commonwealth producers is done not so much by tariffs as by other forms of protection – by special variable import levies, by special quota restrictions on imports, by special subsidies and deficiency payments, and so on. The USA has as big a programme of this kind for the protection of her temperate-zone agricultural output as the EEC or the UK. It is only if the enlarged EEC and the USA are prepared to negotiate some effective limit to the total apparatus of their agricultural protection (for example, if they will set upper limits to their domestic support prices for the major agricultural products) that the problem can be solved in this manner.

To the extent that this is impossible we should have to rely for the solution of the problem of temperate-zone agricultural products on the special quotas in the EEC for such Commonwealth produce, which have already been discussed. This quota method would set an effective limit to the degree of agricultural protection in Europe, but would involve some discrimination by European importers in favour of Commonwealth against other (including US) suppliers. Much better would be a general limitation of agricultural protectionism in which the US also played its part.

The UK should make it clear that it is joint action by the EEC, the

USA, and the UK on these general liberal lines which will make possible not only the end of Imperial Preference and the entry of the UK into the EEC, but also a great reform in the commercial relationships between the developed and the underdeveloped countries of the world.

VI Sterling and the UK Balance of Payments

The commercial policy problem of Commonwealth trade which we have just examined is the fundamental problem on which precise decisions have to be taken immediately. There remains the equally important financial policy problem of the UK balance of payments and of the position of sterling; on this set of problems the commitments which we should in fact incur by joining the EEC are much less detailed, but the general issues are of no less importance.

As shown in Section IV, the proposed agricultural arrangements of the EEC would certainly put a heavy extra charge on our food imports. Another danger is that the removal of barriers to trade in manufactures would increase our purchases from Europe much more than our sales to Europe of such products. It is difficult to forecast whether this will in fact happen or not. There is considerable dispute whether UK money prices and costs at current rates of exchange are at the moment too high relatively to continental prices and costs. It is clear that at the moment the UK has the competitive edge in some products and the continentals have the competitive edge in others. In the former products we shall enjoy an increase in exports and in the latter an increase in imports. It is impossible to predict with certainty what would be the result on our balance of payments even if all barriers were going to be removed tomorrow.

But in addition there is much uncertainty about what changes in money prices and costs will take place in the UK and in the present EEC countries over the next months before the process of removal of trade barriers will even be started, much less completed. The position could improve in our favour. Already in the EEC countries and, in particular, in Germany money wage-rates have started to rise more quickly, and productivity less quickly, than in recent years; money costs are rising. In the UK itself we have the experiment of the Chancellor of the Exchequer with money wage-rates. Whatever views one may hold about the wisdom of this incursion by the Government into the processes of collective bargaining about wages, things will never be quite the same again. Whether the end result will be a delayed explosion of wage-rates or the introduction of some agreed form of wage restraint is difficult to foretell. But if it is the latter, then our competitive position *vis-à-vis* the continent could be radically improved.

But the basic financial danger which I wish to discuss does not depend upon the conclusion that joining the EEC *will* in fact put a serious strain on the UK balance of payments, but merely on the conclusion (which is quite unavoidable) that it *may* do so. Indeed, the basic danger would still be there even if it could be demonstrated with certainty that at the moment when the trade barriers fell our prices and costs would not be out of line with continental prices and costs. For the EEC obligations are designed to last forever, and he would be a bold prophet who was willing to assert that the UK will never again experience a serious balance-of-payments problem. In brief, we should not join the EEC unless we think that its provisions allow for an effective and acceptable mechanism for the adjustment of the balance of payments.

The balance-of-payments provisions of the EEC can be summarised under four heads:

(1) There will after the transitional period be a general obligation not only to remove restrictions on imports from EEC partners and on payments for current purposes to EEC partners, but also to allow free movement of capital between EEC countries. The weapons of import restrictions and of exchange controls over capital movements will in general be ruled out, at least for European transactions, as methods of maintaining equilibrium in the UK balance of payments. There is a provision for their use in severe balance-of-payments crises; but a member country can be required by a majority vote of a supranational EEC authority to desist from the use of these weapons. We would be free to use these weapons only if our partners thought we were making reasonable use of alternative weapons; and there is a clear implication in the provisions of the Treaty that they should not be used so long as the other members of the EEC are willing to provide temporary financial assistance to tide over the balance-of-payments difficulties of the deficit member.

(2) It is not clear that we would incur any such precise obligations to prevent us from imposing restrictions on imports from, and on payments to, countries outside the EEC in order to cope with a UK balance-of-payments deficit. But whatever our EEC obligations, there would be strong reasons why we should not rely much on this method.If we are not restricting imports from EEC countries, we should be discriminating against Commonwealth countries if we restricted our imports from them on balance-of-payments grounds. But imports from Western Europe and the Commonwealth together account for two-thirds of our total imports. If this two-thirds is free of restriction, the weapon of import restriction is clearly a very blunt one; and to be at all effective it would have to be extremely discriminatory against the few remaining sources of supply.

This point is even more important for exchange controls. The sterling area arrangements and the use of sterling as the reserve currency of many overseas countries is based on the freedom of payments within the sterling area. In the past when we have tried to protect our reserves by means of exchange control we have allowed payments to sterling area countries free but have restricted payments to other, including continental European, countries. If we now protected our balance of payments by allowing payments to Europe free and restricting payments to sterling area countries, there would be two serious consequences. First, we would be investing capital in the rich developed countries of Europe instead of in the comparatively poor and underdeveloped countries of the sterling area. Second, we might well break up the sterling area.

Sterling would no longer be anything like such an attractive currency for the sterling area countries to hold; they would shift progressively into gold or dollars. Since the short-term sterling liabilities of the UK are well in excess of her readily available assets of gold and dollars, this would not be a very effective way of avoiding balance-of-payments problems for the UK. Moreover, it would lead to a position of illiquidity in world payments on an enormous scale. I have argued elsewhere that the sterling area arrangements be merged into a reformed system of world payments.[2] But simply to destroy the sterling area is not the way to proceed.

(3) The Treaty sets up an EEC Monetary Commission; and there is a clear obligation on member countries to use it to consult one another on co-ordinating national monetary and financial policies so as to avoid balance-of-payments problems. There is no binding obligation here to commit any national government to any particular policy. But the overtones of this part of the Treaty and one's knowledge of the background of financial ideas make it clear that the purpose is to ensure as far as possible that deficit countries do not indulge too much in expansionary financial policies and, one hopes, that surplus countries do not indulge too much in deflationary financial policies.

(4) There is in the Treaty no rigid obligation about the maintenance of fixed exchange rates between the national currencies. There is merely an obligation 'to treat its policy with regard to exchange rates as a matter of common interest' with the additional provision that if one member does in fact alter its exchange rate unilaterally so as to distort the conditions of competition, the other members of the EEC may be permitted to take special counter-measures (presumably of import restriction or of export subsidisation) for a strictly limited period. Moreover, the EEC in its short history has hardly proved to be an institution of rigidly fixed exchange rates. It was founded on a large depreciation of the French franc to make it possible for the French to take part in free competition with their EEC partners; and it has witnessed the subsequent moderate appreciation of the German mark and of the Dutch guilder, changes which the Germans and Dutch did not, so we are told, even discuss in advance with their EEC partners. Neither the rules nor the history of the EEC militate very strongly against exchange-rate adjustments.

One can fairly summarise these provisions as:

(1) making it very difficult to use direct controls over trade and payments for the preservation of balance-of-payments equilibrium;

(2) leaving broadly open the choice between financial deflation in deficit countries, financial inflation in surplus countries, and variations in exchange rates as balance-of-payments weapons; and

(3) committing the partner countries to close consultation on this choice of methods.

I personally have no quarrel at all with this set of rules.

The danger lies in the philosophy that may lie behind the written rules. Those who have built the EEC have a definite prejudice in favour

[2] J. E. Meade, 'The Future of International Trade and Payments', *The Three Banks Review*, no. 50 (June 1961), pp. 3–26 [Chapter 15 above].

of fixed rates of exchange partly on orthodox financial grounds and partly on the grounds that this is a necessary first step towards a single European currency – which perhaps more than anything else would be the symbol of real European Union. The immediate danger to the UK is that by the time the barriers to intra-European trade are removed our prices and costs will be almost but not quite in line with continental European prices and costs; that we shall consider that we can deal with the problem by a continuation of monetary and fiscal restraints in the UK in order to keep down incomes and demand; that, to allay the anxieties of our future continental competitors, we shall consent to a special *ad hoc* undertaking not to depreciate sterling; and that, in consequence, this situation will drag on year after year, not quite bad enough to make inevitable the depreciation which we had said we would avoid, but bad enough to damp down seriously the expansion of domestic demand necessary to ensure a high rate of growth and a high level of employment in the UK economy. It could be rather like the economic consequences of returning to the gold standard in 1925.

On this there is one simple, clear comment to make. We should on these matters refuse to incur, as a condition of our entry into the EEC, any undertaking in addition to those written into the Rome Treaty itself.

How should we try to see the very broad financial rules of the EEC applied in practice? We have to cope with a situation in which direct controls over trade and payments are not going to be a major instrument of balance-of-payments policy. At the same time the national governments will be left (as they certainly are in the EEC) with the prime responsibility for devising basically independent national financial and economic policies for the control of inflation and deflation, for the preservation of full employment, and for the promotion of economic growth. There must in such a situation be some weapon other than direct controls over international trade and payments and other than domestic financial policies for the maintenance of balance-of-payments equilibrium. This means that there must be a more frequent resort to variations in the exchange rates between national currencies. We must enter the EEC in this frame of mind.

But this does not mean that in exchange-rate policy we should behave as small-minded defenders of national independence and sovereignty. On the contrary this is certainly one of the fields in which a large measure of supranationalism is most desirable. In my view the supranationalist is wrong in believing that the next step that should be taken is the rigid fixing of exchange rates between national currencies. But national governments should certainly not be left free to buy and sell their currencies for foreign currencies at whatever exchange rate they consider convenient from time to time. Public intervention in the foreign exchange markets for national currencies is a power which it is most desirable to submit to supranational control so that the general interest of all countries concerned can be considered. We should tell our European partners that, while we are not prepared to accept rigidly fixed exchange rates, we are prepared to co-operate with them in the most intimate manner on the joint use of European monetary reserves and of

European exchange equalisation accounts. We would reach joint decisions whether or not to intervene in the market for each others' currencies – that is to say to support the currency of a member who is temporarily abnormally weak and to prevent the appreciation of a currency that is temporarily abnormally strong.

But we should have to add to any such proposition that intimate co-operation on exchange equalisation could not and should not be considered solely from the point of view of the interests of the partners in the EEC. Because sterling is held as their monetary reserves by many countries outside Europe it is impossible to consider the desirable policy for the sterling exchange rate exclusively from the point of view of the members of an enlarged EEC. The interests of New Zealand, Australia, India, Ceylon, Pakistan, Malaya and the new African states are vitally affected. It is not possible to put the control of sterling into commission among all the many members of the sterling area. But if the guilder, the mark, the franc, the lira, and sterling are all to be managed by a close European co-ordination of exchange equalisation, then those concerned must consider the problems of the sterling area with as much care as the UK authorities have done in the past.

I have explained how the Treaty of Rome leaves open the choice between exchange-rate variations on the one hand, and domestic financial inflation or deflation on the other hand, as methods for adjusting the balance of payments. As explained my view is that as long as general domestic financial policies remain the concern of the independent national governments, there must be the possibility of resort to exchange-rate variations. But the two methods are not exclusive alternatives. It should be perfectly possible at the same time to move in the direction of a single European currency system provided that we all recognise the far-reaching implications of the ultimate goal. These implications can be examined under three heads.[3]

In the first place, an increasing measure of intervention in each others' domestic monetary and budgetary policies is a necessary condition for making the system of fixed exchange rates work. Suppose that in the EEC one member (the UK, for example) were in deficit and others (including, for example, Germany) were in surplus. If direct controls of trade and payments are ruled out and if exchange rates are fixed, then Germany can if she wishes just do nothing. The only result for her will be an accumulation of perhaps unwanted foreign exchange reserves. But if Germany does nothing, the UK must severely deflate her internal monetary demand for goods and services (by a dear money policy and by higher rates of taxation); for the UK cannot sit back and watch all her limited reserves of gold and dollars disappear. The system can work only if the surplus members inflate at least as much as the deficit countries deflate. We can rely less and less on exchange-rate variations if, but only if, we move to a situation of such close and effective co-ordination of domestic monetary and budgetary policies that the surplus members

[3] The basic issues are analysed more fully in J. E. Meade, 'The Balance-of-Payments Problems of a European Free-Trade Area', *Economic Journal*, vol. 67 (September 1957), pp. 379–96 [Chapter 14 above].

inflate more than they would want to do on the grounds of their domestic requirements alone.

The second implication of moving in the direction of a European currency concerns the formation of a single European financial policy *vis-à-vis* the outside world. So far in this part of the analysis I have assumed tacitly that a UK deficit was offset by an equal surplus on the overall balance of payments of the rest of the EEC, so that the EEC as a whole was in balance-of-payments equilibrium with the rest of the world. But suppose that while the UK had an overall deficit on her balance of payments, each of the other EEC countries was in equilibrium. The EEC as a whole would be in deficit with the rest of the world. Suppose that the rest of the world (e.g. the USA) will not help to put the balance right by indulging in a domestic inflation specially engineered for this purpose. What now should the EEC countries do if they want to preserve the exchange rates between their currencies?

We suppose that the UK will not undertake a sufficient domestic deflation to remove her overall deficit. If the other EEC countries will not help solve the UK problem by some domestic inflation, then sterling will be depreciated and the movement towards a common EEC currency will be halted. If the idea of a common European currency is to succeed, the other EEC countries should in such circumstances inflate so that the need for deflation in the UK would be mitigated by an inflation of money incomes and prices in the rest of the EEC. But in these circumstances the EEC deficit with the outside world would remain unchanged. It would, however, now be shared among all the EEC countries instead of being concentrated on the UK alone.

The EEC countries must now take some joint supranational decision how to get rid of the EEC deficit. Broadly speaking they have a choice of two methods. Either they could impose a joint programme of controls on imports from, and on payments to, outside countries or they could decide, while maintaining fixed exchange rates between the European currencies, to depreciate all these currencies simultaneously in terms of dollars and other outside currencies.

The choice between these two measures is a very difficult supranational task since the one method may suit one member and the other method another member. But at least three special difficulties would arise from the choice of a joint programme of import restrictions.

(1) It will be difficult to decide which imports should be restricted. One partner country may wish to keep out one product (which competes with its own manufactures), while another partner country relies heavily on imports of this same product.

(2) Having decided on a common programme of import restriction, difficulty would arise in deciding upon an equitable distribution of the import licences among the potential importers in the different partner countries – unless the import licences were auctioned throughout the EEC.

(3) The UK could not consent to take part in a supranational scheme of this kind unless the members of the sterling area were treated as being inside and not outside the EEC for these balance-of-payments controls.

Otherwise we should have to apply balance-of-payments restrictions on imports of Indian textiles and New Zealand butter without applying them to Italian textiles or Dutch butter. We should also have to apply exchange control on balance-of-payments grounds which would restrict the flow of UK capital to the underdeveloped parts of the Commonwealth without restricting its movement for investment in continental Europe.

For all these reasons any effective movement towards a European currency would mean that the EEC as a whole would have to keep the balance of payments of the EEC (including the sterling area) in equilibrium with the outside world in large measure by means of alterations in the rate of exchange between the European currency or group of currencies on the one hand and the currencies of outside countries on the other.

Finally, any move towards a European currency would be much helped by a pooling of all the gold and dollar reserves of the EEC countries. If some EEC countries then find themselves in balance-of-payments deficit and others in balance-of-payments surplus, the surplus members will be automatically lending funds to the deficit members, and this will help to tide over the time required for the other measures (of domestic inflation in the surplus countries and of domestic deflation in the deficit countries) to put the balances of payments back into equilibrium. Thus if Germany and the UK have paid all their gold and dollars into a single European pool and if Germany has a surplus and the UK a deficit on the balance of payments, Germany will be paying gold and dollars into the pool and the United Kingdom will be drawing gold and dollars out of the pool; at the same time Germany will be running up her credit, and the UK will be running down her credit or even running into a debit, with the pool. Such a system will, of course, do no more than provide a breathing space for the other adjustments which we have discussed to become effective; and it will not, of course, help to deal with a simultaneous deficit of all EEC countries with the outside world.

There remains one special problem for a European pool of monetary reserves, arising from the difference between sterling and the continental European currencies. In March 1961 the existing EEC countries possessed $16,000 million worth of monetary reserves of gold and dollars against which they had short-term liabilities of $2,000 million, a 'net' reserve of $14,000 million. The UK, on the other hand, held gold and dollar reserves of only $3,000 million, against which she had short-term liabilities (the 'sterling balances' which include the liquid monetary reserves of the sterling area) of no less than $10,900 million – a net reserve of *minus* $7,900 million! Even if one allows for any unused UK drawing rights with the IMF and any similar additional resources, it is abundantly clear that, if a common European currency pool were formed, the continentals would contribute the larger part of the assets.

There is nothing for the citizen of the UK to be ashamed of in this. Indeed, it should be a source of pride for him. The UK is one of the two great bankers of the world. In any national economy the great banks have large outstanding deposit liabilities, payable on sight, against which they hold small liquid cash reserves. It is those whose credit as bankers is not so universally trusted who have small liquid liabilities and must conduct their business on a substantial holding of ready cash.

This is not, of course, to deny that the UK reserves are undoubtedly too low relatively to her liabilities for the UK to have the ease of manoeuvre in her balance-of-payments policies which would be desirable from her point of view. It would, of course, be an immense advantage to the UK if the other EEC members were prepared to form a European pool of gold and dollar reserves. The UK would then have its sterling liabilities covered indirectly by the combined reserves of the European pool. But the arrangement would be compatible with the UK obligations to overseas sterling area countries only if it were recognised that the Indians, the Australians, the New Zealanders, the new African states, and the rest of the overseas members of the sterling area could freely convert their sterling balances into gold and dollars and that this use of the European pool of reserves was as proper as its use to finance the balance-of-payments deficits of Germany, France, or the UK itself.

VII Labour Migration

The EEC treaty requires the member countries eventually to allow the free movement of persons within the EEC. But it does not lay down a precise requirement that the EEC countries should institute a common system of control over the immigration of labour from outside. This means that the UK would be obliged to allow free migration from any EEC region, such as South Italy, even if there were a rapid rate of population growth there. She would also be permitted, but not obliged, to admit freely labour from similar Commonwealth regions, such as the West Indies.

As a result, there might develop a conflict between the interests of European and of Commonwealth immigrants into the UK. If the UK decided that she could not absorb unlimited immigration from both sources, it would be the Commonwealth and not the European immigrants whom she would have to restrict. There would then be a discrimination against the Commonwealth and in favour of Europe in migration as well as in trade.

But the difficulty would not be wholly on the side of the UK. West Indians who have settled in the UK are full British citizens and UK residents. The principle of the free movement of persons within the EEC would thus presumably involve freedom for West Indians after settlement in the UK to move to jobs throughout the EEC countries.

It would, therefore, seem inevitable that there should be a special arrangement by which the UK should be able to impose at least as severe controls over immigration from Europe as over immigration from Commonwealth countries. And in this case, of course, the other EEC countries would have to be allowed to control immigration into their countries from the UK.[4]

[4] Ultimately, in my view, this difficult problem can be solved satisfactorily only by the extension of effective family planning into both European and Commonwealth regions of uncontrolled population growth.

VIII Conclusions

The general moral is clear. The UK could and should join the EEC if it has real promise of becoming a liberal, outward-looking institution. But she should not join if it is designed as a tight, parochial European bloc. For the UK the treatment of the Commonwealth and of the sterling area must be the test.

In labour migration this condition presents an issue for which it is difficult to see any solution other than some exception to the principle of the free movement of labour within the EEC.

In commercial matters the UK would be obliged to discriminate against Commonwealth products; and she should be prepared to do so if, but only if, by some moderation of the general level of EEC protection and by agreement on a liberal commercial policy with the USA, compensation is found for Commonwealth exporters in other markets for what they would stand to lose in the UK market. President Kennedy's proposals on trade policy may present a unique opportunity here; indeed they could lead to a transformation of trading conditions so that not only Commonwealth countries but also many other developing countries in Latin America and elsewhere obtained on balance larger markets for their products. But success would depend upon the EEC countries, including the UK itself, being willing to moderate the degree of their existing protective systems in agriculture as well as in industry.

In financial matters there are no specific obligations in the EEC rules as they stand that would require the UK to discriminate against sterling area countries. But in this field the rules remain in large measure to be made. Important conflict could develop in the future between financial arrangements for payments and capital movements within the EEC and within the sterling area. But such conflict is avoidable; and these are problems for which it should still be possible for the UK to insist upon a satisfactory solution after she has entered the EEC.

Failure in the negotiations between the UK and the EEC may make it more difficult for President Kennedy to obtain the agreement of the US Congress to his new trade proposals. This is an important reason for the UK and for the continental Europeans to work for a successful outcome to the present negotiations with the EEC. Nevertheless, if it is impossible for the UK to achieve an agreement with the EEC on the liberal lines discussed in this paper, the UK should be prepared for the time being at least to remain outside the Community. She should then work, perhaps in less dramatic manner and at a somewhat slower pace, for the reduction of trade barriers, on a non-discriminatory basis, by general agreement between the developed countries of the North Atlantic.

17

The Common Market: Is There an Alternative?

Since the first edition of this *Hobart Paper* was published in April of this year (1962), three important developments have occurred. First, there has been a round of negotiations between the United Kingdom and the Six about the terms on which the UK might enter the European Economic Community (EEC). Second, a conference of Commonwealth Prime Ministers has been held in London to discuss the issue. Thirdly, the trade legislation proposed by President Kennedy has been finally passed by the United States Congress.

The Objectives of Commercial Policy

It is not my intention at this stage to comment in detail on the terms so far provisionally agreed with the Six for the UK's entry to the EEC. The negotiations are still in progress and the complete set of final terms is not yet known. But while some concessions of importance have been made to ease the position of the Commonwealth countries, it looks as if the final terms may well fall far short of what the analysis in this paper (Chapter 16 above) suggests as desirable.

It is, therefore, important to consider whether there is really any alternative course now open to the UK other than to join the EEC on the best terms available. The main text of this *Paper* has been left unchanged as presenting still an accurate picture of the basic Commonwealth issues which are involved in the UK's application for membership of the EEC. This Prologue is devoted to a consideration of the underlying question whether, if the final terms are bad, there is any alternative policy open to the UK.

It is frequently asserted that there is no alternative means by which we can achieve our major economic objectives. Is this true? To answer this question we must know what our major objectives in international commercial policy are. I venture to assert what these objectives should be, namely the formation of a huge free-trade community by the highly developed, industrialised countries of the free enterprise world. Basically this would imply that the North Atlantic countries of North America and of Western Europe (including, of course, the UK) would progressively remove their restrictions on imports of products from each other *and from other outside sources* until they had all adopted a policy of virtually free importation from all sources.

Such an outcome would achieve two results of great importance. First, the North Atlantic developed countries would achieve a vast free-trade area in which to sell their manufactures to each other, gaining thereby on a truly gigantic scale all the advantages of large-scale production and marketing, of specialisation, and of the competitive spur to efficiency which the protagonists of the Common Market have made familiar to us. But, secondly – what is in my view still more important – the outside underdeveloped countries would thereby gain unrestricted entry to the huge market of the rich developed countries without themselves having to give up the protection of their own infant industries. The greatest economic problem which now confronts the world is this task of pulling the economies of the underdeveloped countries up towards those of the developed countries; and this joint free-trade policy by the developed countries would make an immense contribution towards its solution.

No doubt we cannot expect to move at once tomorrow to the final achievement of this great goal. But its ultimate attainment is not, one feels, any longer a mere pipe dream. The successful passage through the US Congress of the trade legislation proposed by President Kennedy is a pointer in this direction and is by far the most important and exciting development in international commercial policy since the end of the Second World War. The right attitude towards the immediate choice with which we are now confronted – whether or not to join the EEC – is to search for that course of action which is most likely to lead towards the ultimate objective. There are three possible paths which we could choose to take towards this final goal: the first leads through the Common Market; the second is by means of unilateral action by the UK; and the third is through multilateral negotiations.[1] Which should we take?

1 Through the Common Market

Let us consider first the case for choosing the path through the EEC. By this means we should immediately create a very large free-trade market for industrial and agricultural products within a greatly enlarged Western European customs union. We should achieve the free-trade advantages of specialisation, large-scale markets, and a competitive spur to efficiency on a very substantial scale. If one considers narrowly the selfish economic interests of the UK, it is the possible economic effects of the jolt to our arrangements caused by free competition with the Six which provides the one strong argument that entry to the Six may be to our own immediate economic interests. The purely 'static' calculus of commercial gain and loss is probably very evenly balanced when one sets against the advantages to our exports of free entry to the Six the disadvantages to our exports of the loss of preferences in Commonwealth and EFTA markets

[1] Yet another possible course is to do nothing, but to continue as we are at present. I shall not discuss this possibility myself as I am an inveterate explorer of improvements in economic arrangements. But it is not a ridiculous alternative, even though those who tell us that we have never had it so good suggest that continuing as we are are spells disaster.

and the disadvantages to our imports of paying more to Europe than we do to the Commonwealth for our foodstuffs. But the much less easily measured 'dynamic' effects of confronting our industries with unhampered competition from efficient, growing industries in Germany, France, Italy, and Benelux could be of great importance.

Furthermore, by joining the EEC we would show that we had no insular prejudices against this kind of joint endeavour. And, since nothing succeeds like success, we might through the example of a successful enlarged EEC greatly encourage the US to join in the building of a North Atlantic free-trade community, the first steps towards which could be taken through the powers which the President has recently acquired by the new trade legislation.

But there is one feature of the path through the EEC which is most undesirable. The UK's present trading arrangements involve the granting of relatively easy access to the UK market for a vast range of manufactures, raw materials, and foodstuffs from the Commonwealth countries and eventual free entry for all manufactures from the EFTA countries (Norway, Sweden, Denmark, Switzerland, Austria, and Portugal). Our entry into the EEC would mean that while we would admit the products of Germany, France, Italy, and Benelux freely into the UK we would have to raise barriers (to the level of the common EEC commercial policy) on goods which we now admit freely from the Commonwealth and EFTA countries, except in so far as special arrangements were made with the Commonwealth countries or the EFTA countries were themselves admitted into the free-trade arrangements of the EEC. The final conditions on these matters which will result from our present negotiations with the Six are still unknown. Some important concessions have been agreed to meet the interests of Commonwealth producers; but nevertheless it remains tolerably certain that our entry into the EEC would involve the imposition of many substantial discriminatory barriers against the import of Commonwealth products which would have the effect of protecting EEC producers against Commonwealth producers in the UK market.

This is in principle bad. The move towards the North Atlantic free-trade community should be one in which these countries reduce existing import barriers without imposing new ones. We should not wish to replace one set of import restrictions with another. And in this case the actual exchange of barriers has certain specially unfortunate features. In the first place many of the Commonwealth countries are poor and underdeveloped relatively to many of the EEC countries; and it is not attractive that we should keep out the produce of the poor in order to protect the rich. In the second place, the Commonwealth countries have in the past been our closest friends and allies. One feature of the EEC which is especially attractive is that it is the beginning of a true and complete integration of countries which in the past have engaged in murderous wars, in which – after all – we have ourselves been involved. Our adherence to a European community which will make such conflicts impossible is itself most desirable; and on this basis I am an ardent supporter of it. But while we should do all we can to forget the past with our past enemies, I for one am not prepared to forget the past with our present friends. In 1940 the Commonwealth countries alone were fighting with us against fascism, while other countries were otherwise active – or inactive. I strongly support any move which means that German and Italian agricultural and manufactured products should be freely admitted into the UK to compete with our own and with Commonwealth products here. But I feel the greatest distaste in keeping Australasian foodstuffs and Indian textiles out of the UK market in order to protect high-cost European producers.

We have ourselves largely to blame for this dilemma. For at least ten years after the end of the war we could have achieved an integration of Western Europe on lines which would not have involved us in giving preferences to European countries against the Commonwealth countries. Our free-trade area proposals of 1956 were on these lines, but alas! they came too late; and on the insistence of the French, backed by the Americans, they were rejected by the Six. They were, however, adopted by seven European countries; and the European Free-Trade Association came into being. This might appear to put us under an obligation not to join the Six on terms which involve us in giving preferences to the manufactures of the Six against the manufactures of the Seven.

If then we are finally presented with the choice either of staying out of the Common Market or of going in on terms which may oblige us to impose serious discriminatory restrictions on the imports of products from some Commonwealth and some EFTA countries in order to protect the producers in the EEC, what should we do? In spite of what has been said above, a very strong case can still be made out for the view that we should nevertheless join the Common Market.

In the first place, the new trade legislation which President Kennedy has obtained from the US Congress could, if used, make a great step forward towards a North Atlantic free-trade community. But these powers can be fully used by the President only if the UK joins the Common Market. The legislation gives the President powers to negotiate with other countries:

(i) for the total elimination of import duties on tropical products which do not compete with US domestic production;
(ii) for the total elimination of import duties on manufactures of which the USA and the EEC countries account for 80 per cent or more of the world's trade; and
(iii) for the halving of duties on other products.

These tariff reductions would all be on the basis that the countries which agreed to reduce or eliminate their duties on each others' products would extend the benefit of these tariff reductions to other outside countries as well; and they could, therefore, result in a great increase in export markets for outside underdeveloped countries. If the UK joined the EEC, many goods would move from category (iii) above, on which the President has power only to halve import duties, into category (ii), on which the President has power completely to eliminate import duties. I for one regret this particular American pressure on us to join the EEC; but we must face the facts of life and this is now one of them.[2]

In the second place, if the UK joins the Common Market, she will be able to exercise a direct influence on the commercial policy of the enlarged EEC. This influence would probably be very substantial. One would hope (but can one be sure?) that it would be exercised in the direction of a liberalisation of the commercial policies of the Common Market *vis-à-vis* outside countries. There are many liberal forces of this kind in Europe for whom support for such policies might be enlisted. It can be argued with great force that, provided we throw our weight on the side of liberal commercial policies within the EEC, in the end the Commonwealth countries are likely to gain more from the liberalisation of US and European commercial policies which would result from our joining the Common Market than they would lose from the increased restrictions on their imports which the UK would herself be forced to impose.

But these developments are problematical and it is important, therefore, to ask whether there are any other paths towards a North Atlantic free-trade community which do not involve us in the initial step of erecting substantial new barriers against outside products, a step which entry to the Common Market now seems likely to involve.

2 *Through Unilateral Free Trade*

An alternative which we ought to consider very seriously is the unilateral reversal of our policy of protection. The National Government made a great mistake in the abandonment of our traditional free-trade policy in 1930. It is worth recalling this history because it has many lessons for our present choice. At that time the Great Depression was starting in the US; the consequent fall in our export markets all over the world had the two-fold effect of putting a strain on our balance of payments and of reducing the already low level of economic activity and employment in the UK itself. We were then faced with the choice between three lines of policy:

(i) of maintaining freedom of import of foreign products and the fixed rate of exchange between sterling and gold and other currencies, in which case we should have had to let the domestic slump develop unchecked until there was sufficient unemploy-

[2] Its importance must not, however, be exaggerated. For there are influential persons in the United States who, in the event of our not joining the EEC, wish to amend the trade legislation so that the category of goods on which the President could bargain for the elimination of all duties applied to manufactures of which the USA, the EEC, and the EFTA account for 80 per cent or more of the world's trade. An amendment of this kind had already been inserted into the Act by the Senate, but it was dropped during the final joint House–Senate conference on the Act; but the chairman of the House Ways and Means Committee explained that the legislation could be amended later if the UK did not join the Common Market. If such an amendment could be relied on, a decision not to join the EEC would not eventually in any way diminish the President's powers to reduce the US tariff.

ment and poverty at home to reduce our demand for imports to our reduced level of exports;

(ii) of stimulating the expansion of demand and so of employment at home by monetary and fiscal measures and of maintaining the fixed rate of exchange between sterling and other currencies, in which case we had to abandon our policy of free imports in order to keep our imports in balance with our exports; or

(iii) of stimulating the expansion of demand at home and of maintaining our policy of freedom of import, in which case we should have had to let the rate of exchange between sterling and other currencies depreciate as the means of dealing with the balance-of-payments problem.

I have no doubt whatsoever that policy (iii) would have been the right policy both from our own point of view and also from the point of view of the rest of the world. This policy would have given us the freedom to plan for economic expansion at home without abandoning the outward-looking, internationalist, radical attitude of the free trader. Unfortunately we went in for the abandonment of free trade (policy (ii)) in what proved to be a vain attempt to avoid the necessary adjustment of the exchange rate (policy (iii)). When in the autumn of 1931 the policy of the fixed gold value of sterling had to be abandoned and the basic *raison d'être* for protection was removed, it was alas! too late to put the protective apparatus into reverse.

We have now no serious threat of anything like the Great Depression, though there may be some moderate recessions ahead in economic activity in the USA and elsewhere. But we certainly could not contemplate the combination of a domestic policy for economic expansion and growth with an external policy for the unilateral removal of our protective restrictions on imports without being prepared to allow adjustments in the rate of exchange to deal with any strain which high domestic demand combined with free imports might impose on our balance of payments.

Provided that we were prepared to make such adjustments, I have no doubt that this policy would have very great advantages. We could gain thereby the free-trade advantages of specialisation, of larger markets, and of the competitive jolt to efficiency; a European customs union is not essential for this purpose. Moreover (apart from direct aid and capital loans), the two policies by developed countries which are of basic importance for the trade of the underdeveloped countries are that the developed countries should maintain a high and steadily expanding demand for goods and services in general (and so for the goods and services of the underdeveloped countries) and that the developed countries should not impose commercial policy barriers against imports (and so against the exports of the underdeveloped countries.) By combining a domestic policy for economic growth with an external free-trade policy we should be making our maximum contribution to a viable world trading system.

There are, of course, disadvantages to this unilateral free-trade policy.

As has already been argued, it would be quite likely to impose some immediate strain on our balance of payments which would have to be offset by some depreciation of sterling. This in itself presents serious problems. Even if these were overcome, there might be some more or less permanent movement in the terms of trade against us. The increased demand on our part for imports, caused by the removal of our barriers to imports, might well mean that we should have to pay the outside suppliers rather higher prices for their products relatively to the prices received from the sale of our exports. A given volume of exports might purchase rather less imports than before. In my view these disadvantages would be likely to be much more than offset by the free-trade advantages of greater efficiency and of specialisation on what we were best fitted to produce; but it would, of course, be nice to avoid them if it were possible.

They would be in large measure avoided if the other developed countries of the North Atlantic reduced their barriers on imports as quickly as we reduced ours. The demand for our exports in their markets would be rising as they reduced their barriers to imports simultaneously with the increase in our own demand for imports. No substantial strain on our balance of payments or terms of trade need then occur. Now it is possible that a unilateral move by us towards free imports would at this juncture of world affairs be a most effective stimulant for the liberalisation of the commercial policies of the other countries of the North Atlantic. If we really set this example, the present mood in the US which is typified by their recent trade legislation might be very greatly encouraged. On the other hand, we should have abandoned without immediate return all our commercial bargaining power. The fact that European and American producers could in any case obtain free access to our markets might make the EEC and the US administration less anxious to bargain away their import duties as a means of obtaining easier access to the UK market. Whether the setting of a unilateral and successful example or hard bargaining is the more likely to deliver the goods is a question to which I do not profess to know the answer.

3 Through Multilateral Commercial Bargaining

But it is at least useful to examine the method of hard multilateral commercial bargaining, which is the third possible path to the North Atlantic free-trade community. In this case the UK should consult with the Commonwealth and EFTA countries (possibly by the convening of a joint Commonwealth–EFTA conference) to take the lead in proposing trade negotiations with other countries and, in particular, with the USA and the EEC. The object of these negotiations, which would presumably be organised under the General Agreement on Tariffs and Trade (GATT), would be to make the most of President Kennedy's new trade powers to get a general reduction of trade barriers by all the developed countries of the world on a basis which would make it easier for all underdeveloped countries to find expanded markets in the developed countries.

These Commonwealth–EFTA consultations should *not* be designed to agree on any increases in Imperial Preferences or other discriminatory trade arrangements which are disallowed under the present rules of the GATT, however ridiculous those rules may be in blessing the 100 per cent discriminations involved in a customs union but cursing the lesser discriminations of a partial preferential system. The purpose of the consultations would be to use the existing mechanisms (the present GATT, the existing EEC, and the new US trade legislation) to achieve a large further reduction of trade barriers on a non-discriminatory basis by the developed countries.

This should not, however, debar the Commonwealth–EFTA countries from considering ways in which, consistently with the rules of the GATT, they can jointly counter the adverse effects upon themselves of any illiberal acts by other trading groups. For example, if the EEC adopts a policy of highly protected domestic prices for European agriculture, European agricultural output might be so expanded as to cause large agricultural surpluses which they might be driven to dump on the outside world at prices below the European domestic prices. It would be in complete conformity with the existing GATT rules that the EFTA–Commonwealth countries, provided that they themselves avoided such practices, should impose anti-dumping duties on such supplies.

Domestic Policy in the UK

If by any of these paths the UK is to make an effective contribution to the formation of the North Atlantic free-trade community, there are certain aspects of her own domestic economic arrangements which need attention.

In the first place, the policy of free importation will hit some groups of people unless special measures are taken to promote alternative uses for the workers and the businesses previously engaged in the protected occupations. It is important that the move towards freer trade should be combined with a policy of general economic expansion and growth at home; for it is very much easier for structural changes to take place in industry when there is rapid general expansion. Relative contraction can then take place simply by not growing as rapidly as other industries; and if absolute contraction must occur, there will be plenty of alternative expanding demands for labour, equipment, and enterprise. But general economic expansion is not enough. Unless alternatives are planned in advance, particular sections of the community may be hit by the move to free imports; and it is not just – or politically expedient – that particular persons should be hit by a general reversal of commercial policy.[3] The

[3] If, as is greatly to be hoped, the UK should set an example by expanding her markets especially for the products of the underdeveloped countries, particular groups of producers in the UK would be directly affected. Indian textiles might compete even more severely with Lancashire; Pakistan jute manufactures with Dundee; and West Indian and Mauritian cane sugar with East Anglian sugar beet. It would be wrong that these particular persons should bear the brunt of these structural changes; but it is equally wrong to put off these structural changes as the means of preserving the interests of these particular producers. Free trade must be combined with a planned shift of domestic resources which is organised and financed by society (see below).

relaxation of import restrictions should be gradual; and it should be combined with newly designed measures to finance redundancy and retraining schemes and to bring new appropriate industries to the affected areas. Properly planned there need be no individual hardship. Indeed, if new industries are introduced before the old are allowed to shrink, the total demand for labour and other resources can actually be increased in the affected areas.

Up to this point I have said nothing about UK agriculture. At present, broadly speaking, we have the free importation of agricultural products combined with the protection of our domestic producers by a system of direct subsidies, the so-called 'deficiency payments'. It is desirable that our policy of free import should be continued. Its abandonment is one of the disadvantages to us of joining the EEC. I am not suggesting that our system of support to domestic farmers by deficiency payments should be abandoned (though it is, of course, a protective system); but I do suggest that some reasonable upper limit must be set to the amount which we pay in subsidies to our farmers for cereals, meat, dairy produce, and other temperate-zone agricultural products. With increases in agricultural efficiency given level of support prices tend to produce surpluses of agricultural output. This is already happening in some lines of production in the UK. It may be tempting to meet this situation by imposing obstacles against the import into the UK of overseas supplies from Commonwealth and other sources; but this temptation must be resisted; it is indeed a main purpose of any search for an alternative to the Common Market to avoid such import restrictions. On the contrary it is essential that some moderate upper limit be set to the total amount paid in subsidies to UK farmers without the abandonment of the policy of free imports from outside sources, even if this involves the reduction of the level of support prices for some agricultural products. Any individual hardship which might otherwise be caused thereby must be met by special schemes for redundancy, retraining, and the introduction of alternative activities into the communities concerned.

As has already been emphasised, it is of the greatest importance that a policy of freeing imports should be combined with a domestic policy for economic growth and expansion. Experience has shown that necessary structural changes in our economy can be made quite easily in an atmosphere of general economic expansion, though they are acutely difficult in periods of general economic stagnation. Moreover, economic expansion in the UK and in other developed countries is a major instrument for the maintenance of export markets for the under-developed countries and so for the promotion of their development.

This is not the occasion to discuss in detail the monetary, fiscal, and other measures necessary to achieve economic expansion and growth. But one implication for our commercial policy must be discussed. What of our balance of payments? Can economic expansion at home be combined with freedom of import without the risk of balance-of-payments crises? It is a fact of life – whether it be a fortunate or an unfortunate one – that the UK's national currency, sterling, is used as the international monetary reserves of many other countries. This makes any run on sterling which may be encouraged by a balance-of-payments deficit particularly dangerous. Is it possible by any means to combine a steady policy of domestic economic expansion (no more 'Stop–Go–Stop' at home) and freedom of imports from restrictions (a sure export market for the underdeveloped countries) with the avoidance of balance-of-payments crises and periodic runs on sterling?

There is only one answer and that is a really effective policy of restraint for money wage-rates. If money costs are to be kept uninflated, money wage-rates in general must not rise more rapidly than the productivity of labour in general, in spite of the maintenance of a high and expanding demand for labour. If this restraint could be achieved, then sterling would become the safest and most desired currency in the world. If not, then the whole policy of combining free imports with planned economic expansion must collapse.

An effective policy of real wage restraint is absolutely essential. But it will be neither politically acceptable nor morally justifiable in the absence of an effective policy to deal with other forms of personal income. I do not believe that it is administratively possible or economically desirable to deal with this part of the problem by a system of direct controls over selling prices and profit margins. The proper approach is through a reform of the general system of direct taxation and of social benefits to deal with the distribution of incomes and – a most strangely neglected problem – with the distribution of property. Wage restraint should be combined with drastic changes in these other fiscal arrangements.

But wage restraint, although it is the essential key to the balance-of-payments problem, does not remove the need for greater flexibility in the rate of exchange between sterling and other national currencies. Variable exchange rates must be regarded *not* as an alternative to, but as a complement of, effective wage restraint; and the UK should set the example of looking after the balance of international payments by the combined use of these two instruments. There will certainly be disequilibria from time to time in international payments. It may well be – indeed if we succeed in achieving stable money costs and prices, it certainly will be – that disequilibrium on the UK balance of payments would show itself at least as often in a surplus as in a deficit. If we have a surplus, in order to avoid our imposing an excessive drain on the monetary reserves of other countries we should let sterling appreciate – just as we urged Germany to appreciate the mark in recent years when she had an undue surplus on her balance of payments and was draining gold reserves away from us. From time to time there may be pressures on sterling which should be allowed to lead to some depreciation of the exchange rate rather than to the abandonment either of domestic policies for steady economic expansion or of external policies of free imports from the ouside world.

There is indeed much to be done: a progressive freeing of imports from all sources and especially from the underdeveloped countries; a modernisation of our subsidisation of agriculture; planned schemes to deal with redundancies and to promote new enterprise where structural change is necessary; domestic fiscal and financial policies for economic expansion; effective wage restraint; fiscal and similar measures to ensure a more equal distribution of income and of property; and a system of greater flexibility in foreign exchange rates. We are no longer a great world power in any military or power-political sense. But we have a great tradition of innovation and experiment in social, political, and economic institutions; and history has given us many contacts with many different countries. If only we could throw off our present self-satisfied sloth, we might still be able to play an important role in combining progressive economic and social policies at home with the building of a great liberal North Atlantic free-trade community. This is the fundamental objective. To join or not to join the EEC is a question of the means to this end.

18

International Commodity Agreements

Meade's paper was submitted and circulated to the members of the first United Nations Conference on Trade and Development (UNCTAD) held in Geneva 23 March–15 June 1964, and was subsequently published in Lloyds Bank Review, *no. 73 (July 1964), pp. 28–42, as well as in the* Proceedings of the Conference (Volume III: Commodity Trade, *New York: United Nations, 1964, pp. 451–7) and (in its first version) in* World Agriculture, *vol. 13 (April 1964), pp. 20–26.*

I The Need for Action

The prices of primary products, when they are traded freely on uncontrolled world markets, are subject to violent fluctuations. Both the amounts produced and the amounts consumed of such products are typically rather insensitive to price changes, so that quite moderate shifts of world supply or demand may cause very great price changes before supply and demand are brought back into balance. Well-informed professional speculation, by carrying supplies from periods of low to periods of high price, can partially, but only very partially, offset these fluctuations. Ill-informed and perverse speculation may accentuate the fluctuations in price.

Moreover, there have in the past been periods of years during which the prices of primary products have shown a persistent trend (downwards or upwards) relatively to the prices of manufactured products, these price trends being determined by the balance of many structural changes in demand and supply conditions, both in primary production and in manufacture. Such price trends can be of the utmost importance to the countries producing primary products. A downward trend in the price of a particular primary product relatively to the prices of manufactures may well deprive a particular developing country of purchasing power over manufactured imports which is considerably greater than the total financial aid which it has been receiving for its economic development; and in recent years such downward price trends have been much in evidence, though the movement has now been reversed, at least for the time being.

The damage which may be done by a price fall to a country which is producing a primary product can take three distinct, though closely related, forms.

First, a fall in a primary-product price can put a very severe strain on the balance of payments of a country whose exports consist very largely of that product.

Secondly, the financial problem of the balance of payments can (though often only with great difficulty) be overcome (*a*) by a drastic monetary deflation which discourages investment in new machinery and makes the citizens unable to afford the purchase of imported consumption goods or (*b*) by a governmental restriction of imports which directly deprives the country either of consumption goods or of capital goods needed for economic development or (*c*) by so great a depreciation of the country's currency in terms of other countries' currencies that the citizens can no longer afford the excessively high prices for imports of manufactured consumption goods or of capital goods for economic development. But in all these cases there would, of course, be a great reduction in the standard of living in the country or in its programme of capital development. Its real income will have been greatly reduced. In the extreme case of Mauritius a single product (sugar) accounts for virtually the whole of Mauritian exports and these exports account for virtually one half of the Mauritian national income. A 50 per cent fall in the price of sugar would case a 25 per cent fall in the real income available in Mauritius for consumption or capital development.

Finally, apart from the general impact on the producing country's balance of payments and real income, there may well be a very serious problem for the particular section of the community which produces the primary product. Even if sugar exports were a relatively small proportion of a country's total exports and total national product, a fall in the price of sugar might inflict great damage on a concentrated and isolated group of producers who were unable to move readily to alternative occupations. This may cause concentrated distress which requires some relief. Fluctuations and uncertainty in selling prices may also discourage efficient planned production in the industry concerned.

These three forms of damage which primary-producing countries may suffer from falls in the prices of primary products have, of course, their obverses in the three forms of damage which the importing countries may suffer from rises in such prices.

A rise in the price of a primary product will increase the cost of its imports and so the strain on its balance of payments of an importing country if it cannot readily produce the supplies for itself or turn to the use of a substitute product. Even, however, if it is successful in meeting the balance-of-payments strain, the rise in the cost of its imported supplies of the product will reduce its real income; while those of its citizens who rely to an exceptional degree on the use of this product may be exceptionally hard hit.

But there are two reasons for believing that the damage done to the importing countries by a given rise in price is much more tolerable than the damage done to the exporting countries by an equal fall in price.

First, in a number of cases the real income per head is higher in the importing countries (which are often the highly developed industrialised countries) than in the exporting countries (which are often the underdeveloped unindustrialised countries). In these cases, a dollar's loss to the former countries with a high standard of living can properly be counted as of less importance than a dollar's gain to the latter countries with a low standard of living.

But this argument must be applied with great care. There is a very serious risk that it may be tragically misapplied in the coming years. For a very large and important group of primary products (namely, the temperate-zone foodstuffs such as wheat and similar cereals, meat, and dairy produce) the net exporters are those wealthy developed countries which are rich both in capital and land (for example, Canada, the United States, Australia, New Zealand). Many less developed countries with lower standards of living are net importers. Moreover, with the present population explosion and pressure on natural resources in many of these latter countries, it is greatly to be hoped that the wealthier temperate-zone countries will open their markets more and more widely to the simpler labour-intensive manufactures of the less developed countries and will provide aid to these countries. This will enable the latter to purchase not only the more elaborate manufactured capital goods but also some of their needed supplies of foodstuffs in increasing quantities from the wealthy temperate-zone granaries of the world. It would be a tragic mistake to regard the maintenance of the prices of temperate-zone foodstuffs as a way of helping the poor at the expense of the rich; the position is already the reverse and in a sane commercial world will become increasingly so.

Moreover, within a primary-producing underdeveloped economy there are quite likely to be much greater disparities in the distribution of income and wealth than in the industrialised developed economies. In some sugar-producing territories a rise in the price of sugar will raise the real incomes of the extremely poor cane-cutter and the extremely rich owner of the land and processing equipment on the sugar estate in a sugar-producing community; in the industrialised importing countries it will lower the real incomes of many working and middle-class families who are nothing like as poor as the cane-cutters nor as rich as the estate owners in the sugar-producing community. A rise in the price of sugar probably transfers income from the moderately well-off to the very poor and the very rich.

There is, however, a second and much more generally valid reason why the damage caused to consumers of primary products by a rise in the price of the product is more tolerable than the damage done to the producers by an equal fall in price. The former is much less concentrated than the latter. This is outstandingly true of individuals. The producer, whether he be the poor cane-cutter or the rich estate owner, may rely almost 100 per cent on the price of sugar for his income; there is no family in the importing countries which spends the whole of its income on sugar. A fall in the price of sugar will ruin a limited number of persons. A rise in the price of sugar will slightly raise the cost of living to a very large number of persons. This difference in the degree of concentration is true also of whole economies. Practically 100 per cent of Mauritian export earnings are sales of sugar and 50 per cent of Mauritian income is derived from sugar production; in an importing country like the United Kingdom, imports of sugar account for only small fractions of total imports and of total national expenditure. A fall in the price of sugar would play havoc with the Mauritian balance of payments and national income, while it would have a very limited effect upon the overall balance of payments and national income of each importing country.

II Buffer Stocks and Restriction Schemes

It is for these reasons most desirable that, as part of any new arrangements for world commerce, steps should be taken to offset the damaging effects of sharp fluctuations in the price of primary products and to mitigate the effects of any persistent downward trends in such prices. What measures could be taken for this purpose? International commodity arrangements in the past have been in the main based upon either or both of two principles.

First, a buffer stock arrangement can be used to mitigate fluctuations in the price of a particular primary product. The management of the stock is endowed in the first place with certain financial resources which can be used to buy up the commodity for storage when its price is abnormally low and for resale later when its price is abnormally high. Such action can undoubtedly be of great use in suitable cases. It is to be hoped that the use of this weapon will be extended in the future. But this weapon has its limitations.

The success of such schemes rests upon the wisdom (and resistance to pressure from interested parties) of the management or the designers of the rules for the operation of the scheme. It can succeed only if there is sufficient foresight and independence of action to ensure that purchases are made only when present prices are low relatively to future prices, and sales are made only when present prices are in fact high relatively to future prices. Such foresight is by no means easy. A buffer stock scheme, moreover, can operate only in the case of commodities for which the cost of storage is not excessive. There is always some cost involved in the interest on the capital invested in the stock; but in the cases in which warehousing space, refrigeration, protection against vermin, and other similar costs are concerned, the scheme may well become excessively costly. Buffer stock schemes should in any case be operated only so as to mitigate fluctuations in price. They cannot be properly used to mitigate or offset the damaging effects of a persistent trend in price. Thus if there is a persistent downward trend in the price of a product, purchases by a buffer stock could reduce the rate at which the price is allowed to fall, but would lead only to an accumulation of stock which must be sold at a still lower price in the future.

The second type of arrangement is the agreed restriction of the quantity produced or exported by the primary-producing countries. When a world surplus supply of a product occurs or threatens to occur, the governments of the countries which produce the product can get together and agree that each will intervene in its own national market in such a way as to restrict the amount produced or the amount exported to some agreed quota. By thus restricting the supplies coming forward for sale the price of the product can be maintained at a higher level; and if, as is usually the case at least in the short run, the demand for the product is inelastic, the exporting countries receive a larger total value for a smaller volume of exports and the producers a larger total income for a smaller volume of output.

If no alternative action is available, such an arrangement may often be better than doing nothing, particularly in an emergency situation in which the price of a product on which many economies largely depend would otherwise totally collapse. In this sense such schemes may often deserve every support. But it will be argued later (in the next section) that the alternative arrangements there described provide a good basis for dealing with situations of this kind, that they may make it unnecessary to resort to restriction schemes, and that they are at the least a most helpful supplement to any restriction schemes.

Restriction schemes are in any case subject to important difficulties. Such schemes are in fact extremely difficult to maintain. Past experience suggests this and the reason is easy to understand. If all producers are withholding supplies and thus maintaining a profitable price, it becomes exceedingly attractive to any individual producing country to refuse to join the scheme and to enjoy the high price on an unlimited output and export volume. A restriction scheme may start with all the producers in it except for one or two small producers; but this may give an opportunity for these outside producers greatly to expand their output and export. The quotas of the producers in the agreement will have to be reduced to maintain the prices as the sales of the outsiders expand. It becomes more and more attractive to the individual insider to join the outsiders. Attempts may be made to prevent this by means of an agreement which includes the main importing countries which, in return for the opportunity thus gained in controlling the degree of restriction exercised by the producers, agree to police the scheme by undertaking to purchase only from the inside producers. The outside producers will then be selling at lower prices than the inside producers and there will be a great incentive on individual importing countries to stay out of the agreement in order to purchase these cheaper supplies. This product may well be a raw material which enables an industrialised country that obtains cheaper supplies to undercut on the export market for manufactures those rivals purchasing their raw material supplies at the higher price; and in such a case there will be a great incentive for the importer countries to withdraw from their obligations to police the scheme. A pure restriction scheme is thus unlikely to be able to maintain for any very long period of time a price substantially above the price which would otherwise clear the world market.

There is a second reason why a restriction scheme, though it may be feasible and necessary as an emergency rescue operation, may be unsuitable for permanent operation. The elasticity of demand for most primary products is certainly small in the short run; but in the long run the response of purchasers to the price may be much greater. A rise in the price of natural rubber in the short run is unlikely to affect very appreciably the amount of natural rubber which is purchased for use in the motor-car and other industries. But if the higher price persists and is expected to persist it may make profitable a substantial expansion in the manufacturing capacity for synthetic rubber. It is an outstanding feature of modern technological advance to devise alternative ways of producing a needed material or to devise ways in which a need can be satisfied by the use of an alternative material.

Finally, restriction schemes, if they are maintained for long, make it very difficult to prevent serious inefficiencies in the production of the primary product concerned. Production or export quotas are likely to be fixed on the basis of past performance. Each producing country has a limited quota and it is thus impossible for the producing countries in which costs of production are reduced to expand at the expense of those in which costs of production rise, or fall less rapidly. Moreover, this phenomenon is likely to appear within each producing country. If the government of a country undertakes that its private-enterprise producers will not in total produce or export more than a given national quota, it must introduce some licensing or similar scheme to restrict the output or exports of each individual producer. The allocation of these sub-quotas within the country if, as is likely, it is arranged on the basis of past performance, will make it difficult for the progressive producer to expand at the cost of the stagnant.[1] Attempts can be made from time to time to revise the distribution of international quotas between the producing countries and of national quotas between the individual producers with the purpose of allowing low-cost producers to expand at the expense of their high-cost rivals. But attempts to do this by governmental agreement and administrative action are much less likely to be effective than the spur of competition in a world market.

III Price Compensation Agreements

The price mechanism always plays a dual rôle. A rise in a price affects the distribution of income, benefiting producers at the expense of consumers. It also affects the efficiency of the economic system, encouraging the more effective production and the more economical use of what is especially scarce. In no set of markets is this distinction more noticeable than in the world markets for primary products. Because of the concentration of production and the short-run inflexibilities of outputs and of demands, the 'distributional' effects of price changes may play havoc with the balance of payments and the real income of whole communities, and may thus greatly impede the programmes for economic development of such countries. But, at the same time, to prevent the longer-run trends of supply and demand from determining the prices of the products in world markets may not only be a difficult task but, if successful, may introduce serious 'inefficiencies' into the world economy. In any case there is no reason whatever for believing that the prices which are desirable on 'distributional' grounds are the same as those which are desirable on 'efficiency' grounds.

[1] This difficulty could be surmounted by the auctioning of licences to produce to the individual producers. The more efficient would outbid the less efficient. But this method of allocation of quotas is not a popular one and it would, of course, mean that the actual producers of the product did not get the advantage of the higher price of the product. Their competition for licences could ruin them just as effectively as their competition for markets.

It is the purpose of this paper to suggest an extremely simple method of divorcing these two aspects of price variation. Consider a case in which one country (Urbania) imports a primary product (that – following Lord Keynes – may be called Commod [as in 'The International Regulation of Primary Products' (1942), reprinted in *The Collected Writings of John Maynard Keynes*, vol. 27 (London: Macmillan, 1980), pp. 135–166]) which another country (Ruritania) exports. Their two governments agree upon a sliding scale whereby as the world price of Commod falls further and further below a certain figure the Government of Urbania will pay an increasing sum of money to the Government of Ruritania, and as the world price of Commod rises further and further above a certain figure the Government of Ruritania will pay an increasing sum of money to the Government of Urbania. One possible sliding scale – but by no means the only possible one – could be devised on the following lines. The two governments would agree on what was a 'normal volume' of exports of Commod from Ruritania to Urbania; and they would then devise a sliding scale so that the Government of Urbania was paying to the Government of Ruritania each month an amount of money which was equal to the shortfall below the 'standard price' of the world price of Commod on the 'normal volume' of trade in Commod between the two countries. Conversely, the Government of Ruritania would pay to the Government of Urbania an amount equal to any excess of the world price over the 'standard price' as reckoned on the 'normal volume' of trade between them.

The scheme has been illustrated in the above example in a form which gives complete compensation. But this is, of course, not necessary. The two governments might agree on a sliding scale whereby, say, only one half of the variation in the price of the 'normal volume' of trade between them was compensated by inter-governmental transfers.

Arrangements of this kind would directly divorce the 'distributional' from the 'efficiency' effects of changes in the world price of Commod. The two governments could allow their citizens to buy and sell Commod freely in world markets at the ruling world price. But as far as the balances of payments and national incomes of Urbania and Ruritania were concerned, the effect of a change in the world price of Commod would be entirely or partially offset, in so far as the normal volume of trade between Urbania and Ruritania was concerned. For example, if the world price of Commod fell below the agreed standard, Urbanian citizens would obtain cheaper supplies of Commod, but the Government of Urbania would have to raise additional revenue from them to pay over to the Government of Ruritania. At the same time the Ruritanian producers of Commod would be receiving smaller earnings from their sales of Commod, but the Ruritanian Government would be receiving an income from Urbania. The two governments would be entirely free to raise, and to dispose of, the funds transferred between them in any manner they choose. The Urbanian Government could, if it is so desired, raise the additional revenue by a levy on its citizens' consumption of Commod, in which case the consumers who would have gained from the fall in price will to this extent no longer do so. The Ruritanian Government could, if it is so desired, use its receipt of revenue from Urbania to supplement the incomes of its producers of Commod; but, if it so desired, it could use the revenue so received to finance other forms of economic development; or it could use the revenue partly for the one and partly for the other purpose.

The scheme thus copes with the distributional aspects of price changes; but it begs no questions about the efficiency aspects of price changes. What is done in that respect depends upon the action of the national governments concerned. They can offset the price changes to the particular consumers and producers concerned or they can allow world price changes to have their full effect in their own national markets for Commod.

The scheme has been expounded above in the simplest form of a bilateral agreement between one importing and one exporting country. It is a great virtue of the scheme that it could take this limited form without in any way discriminating in world trade in Commod, even if there were many other importers and exporters of Commod. In this case it would simply be an arrangement whereby these two countries agreed to offset the 'distributional' impact between them of a change in the price of Commod. But on the other hand there is, of course, nothing to prevent a fully multilateral international agreement on these lines. The governments of all the exporting and all the importing countries of Commod could jointly agree on a standard price and, for each participating country, on a normal quantity of import or of export of Commod for that country (the total of normal imports being equal to the total of normal exports). They could agree on a sliding scale according to which, when the world price of Commod was low, the governments of the importing countries paid contributions into a fund from which the governments of the exporting countries drew out an equal total sum; and conversely, if the price of Commod was high.

Many intermediate groupings are possible, covering more than two countries but less than all the countries concerned. Thus a Commonwealth Sugar Agreement could be arranged in which all Commonwealth imports and exports of sugar take place on the world market at the world price, but in which the governments of the importing members made transfer payments to the governments of the exporting members (and *vice versa*), according to the world price of sugar at which the trade was actually conducted. An outstanding advantage of the proposed scheme is that a bilateral or limited multilateral arrangement can be maintained without breakdown and can be arranged in such a way that it does no damage to outsiders and in no way discriminates in the flows of world trade.

A further advantage of compensation schemes of this straightforward direct type is that they are no way incompatible with other schemes. Thus if the world price of Commod is being partially stabilised by a buffer stock scheme or if it is being maintained by a restriction scheme, this in no way prevents the operation of direct compensation schemes, though, of course, the actual payments of compensation may be smaller because of the effect of the buffer stock or of the production or export quotas on the world price. It is, however, to be hoped that the successful initiation of a compensation scheme might often avoid the necessity for a restriction scheme, thus allowing the 'efficiency' effects of price movements to have their full play.

It is not, of course, claimed that compensation schemes will automatically make restriction schemes pointless. Thus a fully multilateral compensation scheme for wheat might set as the standard price what was expected to be the price which would equate supply to demand for wheat over the average of, say, the next five years. Its effect would then be to offset the repercussions on balances of payments and national incomes of day-to-day divergencies of the world price from the standard price. But this would not, of course, prevent unforeseen adverse changes in the underlying conditions of world supply and demand from causing a persistently low world wheat price. If, at the end of the five-year period, when the compensation scheme came up for renewal, the 'standard price' were not reduced, then the compensation scheme would become one under which the importing countries persistently subsidised the exporting countries. If the 'standard price' were reduced to correspond with the now lower expected world price, then a persistently lower value of exports and of national income would be experienced by the producing countries, unless this was offset by a restriction scheme.

There would then be three possibilities: to accept the long-run reduction in the export receipts and incomes of wheat producers; or to maintain these by a compensation scheme which set a 'standard price' on the average persistently above the world price ruling over an average of years; or to agree to a restriction scheme. But there is no reason to believe that the importing countries would lose more by accepting a 'standard price' rather unduly favourable to the producers (the second alternative) than by accepting the raising of prices against them by the restriction of production or export (the third alternative.).

Thus in its treatment of a persistent trend in the price of a primary product a compensation scheme can be very flexible. For example, the 'standard price' could be set at what was initially a generously high level (in order to provide funds to the governments of the exporting countries to maintain the incomes of their producers), but at the same time it could be agreed that this standard price should be gradually lowered from year to year so that this persistent subsidy to the producers by the consuming countries was gradually tapered off. In any case, even if a restriction scheme were operated, it would be possible and perhaps desirable to operate simultaneously a compensation scheme to offset the effects of fluctuations in the world price around the higher average level maintained by the restriction.

There is one other way in which a compensation scheme could show great flexibility. At the one extreme, it might constitute a purely stabilising device for offsetting the effects of a fluctuation in price on the balances of payments and national incomes of a group of importing and exporting countries. At the other extreme, it could be turned into a device for the grant of financial aid from a group of industrialised importing countries to a group of unindustrialised exporting countries, the amount of the aid varying, however, according to the balance of payments and national income needs of the latter countries.

To take a possible example of the former type of agreement: wheat is a commodity which is produced largely by one group of rich highly developed countries and consumed largely by another group of rich highly developed countries. A compensation agreement for wheat might, therefore, be expected to be based on a sliding scale which, on the average, caused the transfers from exporters to importers (in times of high prices) to be equal to the transfers from importers to exporters (in times of low prices).

But there may be a primary product (let us call it Commod) which is produced by relatively poor underdeveloped countries and consumed by relatively rich developed countries; and it may be the desire of the latter to grant financial aid to the former. Nevertheless, it may be very desirable that more aid should be given if the price of Commod is low and less aid if the price of Commod is high, since the needs of the exporting countries and the ability to pay of the importing countries will both be lower when the price of Commod is high. This result can, of course, be brought about by an appropriate choice of sliding scale under a compensation agreement.

The basic idea of compensation agreements is not, of course, new. This was the principle which lay behind the first Wheat Agreements after the Second World War. Trade in wheat could be conducted at world prices; but when the world price fell below a certain level the governments of the importing countries were obliged to pay a higher price for a certain quota of their imports and exporting countries had the right to sell corresponding quotas of their exports at a similar higher price; and conversely when the world price of wheat rose above a certain predetermined level. In essence, this was compensation by the governments of importing countries to the governments of exporting countries when the price of wheat was low; and *vice versa* when the price of wheat was high. But the arrangement was unnecessarily complicated by making the government-to-government compensation operate through obligations by exporting governments to provide some relatively cheap wheat when the world price was high and by importing governments to accept some relatively expensive wheat when the world price was low. These provisions constituted a set of quite unnecessary obligations for governmental interventions in the wheat markets. Much simpler is direct financial compensation, leaving it open to national governments to intervene or not to intervene in their national markets as they think fit.

IV Compensatory Finance

More recently, important proposals for more general schemes of compensatory financing have been made by two groups of experts.[2] Under such arrangements countries whose export earnings fluctuated widely as a result of fluctuations in their trade in primary products would receive special financial support in times of low export earnings, all or part of

[2] United Nations, *International Compensation for Fluctuations in Commodity Trade* (Report by a Committee of Experts, New York, 1961); Organization of American States, *Final Report of the Group of Experts on the Stabilization of Export Receipts* (Washington, DC, 1962).

which they would repay in times of high export earnings. Partly in response to these suggestions, the International Monetary Fund has made special arrangements to enable countries whose export earnings decline as a result of fluctuations in the trade in primary products to borrow for short periods more readily from the Fund.[3] These comprehensive and general financial arrangements have one great advantage over the price compensation agreements proposed in the previous section of this paper. They take account of fluctuations in the volume, as well as in the price, of exports of a primary-producing country.

What one wants to offset are fluctuations and declines in the total value of a country's export earnings. The commodity compensation agreements proposed above offset only fluctuations in the price of exports. Whether or not this is satisfactory will depend upon the conditions which have caused the change in export prices. Changes in the world price of a commodity must arise either from changes in conditions of demand or from changes in conditions of supply for that commodity. In so far as price changes are due to changes in demand in the importing countries, price compensation agreements are bound to be helpful. If the demand for a primary product falls, exporting countries may suffer both from a fall in price and from a fall in the quantity sold. An agreement which compensated for the fall in the price but not for the fall in the volume would at least work in the right direction. Moreover, if the elasticity of supply is small, the price will fall much more than the volume; and a price compensation scheme would, therefore, make a correction in the right direction and for the greater part of the change.

But in so far as a change in the world price of a commodity is due to a change in conditions of supply, a price compensation scheme might conceivably work in a perverse manner. For example, suppose that there were exceptionally good harvests of wheat throughout the world; world supplies of wheat are increased and the price of wheat falls. If, however, the elasticity of demand for wheat were high – as is almost certainly not the case – the price might fall only a little, so that the increased volume of exports of wheat more than offset the fall in the price of wheat, with a rise in the export earnings of the wheat-producing countries. To compensate for the price fall would add still further funds to their already inflated export earnings. If, however, as is more probable, the price elasticity of demand for wheat is low, the increased volume of exports will lead to a heavy fall in price and total export earnings will fall. Price compensation would supplement the fallen export earnings; but in this case, if price compensation were complete, export earnings would, of course, be over-compensated, since exporting countries would be getting the equivalent of the previous price on the larger volume of exports. A sliding scale which gave only partial price compensation would be needed to stabilise export earnings.

3 International Monetary Fund, *Compensatory Financing of Export Fluctuations* (Washington, DC, 1963). The United Kingdom Government has put forward proposals to the United Nations Conference on Trade and Development whereby such short-term finance might be supplemented by longer-term finance in those cases in which the export earnings of an underdeveloped country suffered a protracted decline which threatened to impede its programme for economic development.

While the elasticity of demand for the world's exports of a primary product is likely to be low, this may well not be true for the exports of a single country. Suppose that as a result of local cyclones Mauritian exports of sugar are halved. This may have only a moderate effect in reducing world supplies and so only a moderate effect in raising the world price of sugar. The value of Mauritian exports would be disastrously reduced, in spite of a small rise in the world price. It would be perverse in the extreme if, because of the rise in the world price of sugar, the Mauritian Government had to pay compensation to the United Kingdom Government at a time when the value of her exports had slumped.

General schemes for compensatory finance would not be subject to these dangers. They would compensate for a worsening or an improvement in the total *value* of a country's exports and not merely in the *price* of its exports. On the other hand, one of the main attractions of price compensation agreements is their simplicity and ease of administration. Intergovernmental transfers of funds according to changes in a world price index are easy to administer and it would not normally be possible for an individual country to affect the world price in a way which would enable it to gain improperly from the arrangement. This, unfortunately, would no longer be true if the arrangement were based on the value of a country's exports. A country might well be more ready to adopt policies which would in fact result in a decline in the value of its exports if it knew that such a decline would automatically be compensated by an intergovernmental transfer of funds to it.

We may conclude (i) that a price compensation agreement is wholly appropriate for a commodity primarily subject to fluctuations on the demand side; (ii) that, provided that the elasticity of demand for the world supply is low, a price compensation agreement can be devised to maintain and stabilise total world export earnings in the face of changes in world supply conditions; but (iii) that price compensation agreements cannot cope with (and indeed may even somewhat intensify) the problems which arise from local fluctuations in the supply conditions in individual producing countries. Problems of this kind must be covered by other measures. Price compensation agreements have the great advantage of extreme simplicity and flexibility. Above all, they could be started on a very restricted scale but be gradually expanded into a world-wide network covering many products and many countries. The ideal system would no doubt be to combine such a network of particular agreements with a general scheme for compensatory finance. There is no incompatibility between price compensation agreements and a general scheme of compensatory finance. The two measures complement each other; the existence of a network of price compensation agreements would greatly reduce the financial calls on any fund set up to provide general compensation against fluctuations in total export earnings. The fund would thus be able to use its limited resources in a more effective manner to deal with those cases which the network of price compensation agreements did not, and perhaps could not, cover.

19

Exchange-Rate Flexibility

From The Three Banks Review, *no. 70 (June 1966), pp. 3–27. This paper is a slightly revised version of one Meade presented to a symposium on international payments problems organised by the American Enterprise Institute in Washington in September 1965 (*International Payments Problems, *Washington DC: American Enterprise Institute for Public Policy Research, 1966, pp. 67–82).*

Introduction

Exchange-rate flexibility covers a multitude of sins and of virtues. My main purpose in this paper is to catalogue the various forms of sin and virtue and to comment as objectively as is possible upon the merits and demerits of each form. But I will not disguise the fact that I am one of those who favour a much greater measure of exchange-rate flexibility than is practised by the countries of the free world today. Accordingly I shall arrange my paper in the following three parts. First, I will outline the reasons why in my view we need to consider very seriously the adoption of a greater measure of exchange-rate flexibility. Second, I will catalogue the various forms which exchange-rate flexibility can take and will note the arguments for and against each form. Finally, I will describe the form of exchange-rate flexibility which I would personally advocate in present circumstances and will try to put it into the framework of the present discussions on the possible reform of the International Monetary Fund.

The Case for Greater Flexibility

The basic case for variations in exchange rates is fairly familiar and I have myself on other occasions argued it at some length. I shall, therefore, on this occasion state the case very briefly.

When a country has a surplus in its overall balance of international payments, it can go on accumulating foreign-exchange reserves indefinitely. If it is in deficit, it can go on as it is so long as its foreign-exchange reserves last or so long as it can beg, borrow, or steal additional reserves from some external source. But there are very good reasons for rejecting such do-nothing solutions. Overall surpluses or deficits in international *payments* are, broadly speaking, indications of maladjustments in the general structure of relative *money* prices, incomes and costs in the various countries; and there is no reason to believe that a desirable use of the world's *real* resources is obtained if the countries which happen at any one time to have international surpluses of *money* receipts automatically continue indefinitely to finance those countries which happen to have international *money* deficits. It is, for example, very possible for wealthy countries which are rich in capital to find themselves in deficit, while poor countries are in surplus, on their balance-of-payments current account. A continuation of such a situation could mean a continuous flow of real resources from the poor and underdeveloped to the rich and developed countries.

One can tackle the problem of adjustment of balances of payments through direct interventions or controls of a more or less drastic kind on international trade, capital movements and foreign aid. The authorities in deficit countries can restrict imports from lower-cost sources by import quotas or import surcharges; they can subsidise their own exports against the better-quality or lower-cost goods of their competitors; they can restrict or tax the flow of capital funds from their own country where capital is plentiful and the rate of return on it is low to countries where capital is scarcer and rates of return higher; they can cut down on their foreign aid; they can insist that the aid which they give must be spent on their own products even though some other country's products might be even more suitable for the recipient's needs. But to those of us who, like myself, sincerely wish to see the principles of the market mechanism and of the competitive price system appropriately extended not only within the countries of the free world, but in the economic relations between those countries as well, these methods of balance-of-payments adjustment should be anathema. Particular goods should be imported or exported according to their relative costs and qualities, not in order to adjust an overall balance of payments. Countries should give or receive foreign aid according to their real wealth and real needs, not according to the state of their overall balance of payments. Capital should move to the place of highest economic return, not necessarily to the country with the largest overall balance-of-payments deficit. Funds received in aid or by loan should be spent on the goods which are most efficient for the recipient's purposes, not necessarily on the goods of the country which happens to have a deficit.[1] And so on and so on.

Balances of international money payments should be corrected by adjustments in the general levels and structures of money prices, incomes and costs in the countries of the free world. Such general adjustments can be effected either by a general upward movement in surplus countries of their domestic prices, incomes and costs in terms of their domestic currencies combined with a general downward movement (or at least a slower upward movement) in the deficit countries' prices, incomes and

[1] An Indian friend who is in a position of great responsibility in these matters told me that in his judgement, if all the aid which India received were completely untied in its use, this would make up for a cut of one-third in the total amount of aid to India.

costs or else by an adjustment in the rate of exchange between the domestic currencies of the surplus and the deficit countries. Let us briefly consider these two methods.

The truly orthodox type of solution is that the authorities in the deficit countries should by restrictive monetary and budgetary policies reduce money expenditures on goods and services within their countries, while the opposite expansionary policies are adopted in the surplus countries. If all domestic prices and costs, and in particular money wage-rates, were readily and quickly adjustable, this orthodox solution might well be the most desirable one. The deflation of demand in the deficit country leads to a reduced demand for labour; there is some increase in unemployment and underemployment of both men and machines. But if a short period of very moderate slack is all that is required to obtain a considerable weakening of all money prices and costs, and if correspondingly in the surplus countries a short period of very moderate excess demand suffices to obtain a large rise in the basic structure of money prices and costs, an international system could well be built on this foundation.

But the facts of life are otherwise. You may well have a situation in the modern world in which there is considerable slack in the domestic economy of a particular country, but the whole structure of domestic money prices and costs does not as a result decline. If at the same time this country is internationally in deficit, there is a tragic dilemma. It will be desired to expand demand for domestic reasons to encourage growth and full employment; but it would be necessary to restrict demand and to increase unemployment still further in order to put sufficient downward pressure on money wage-rates and other prices. May this not have been the position of the United States in some recent years?

Such is the simple, straightforward, and in my view decisive argument against the orthodox solution. There is possibly a secondary argument against it which is worth mentioning in passing. Suppose that a relative downward pressure on money prices, incomes and costs is needed in one country on balance-of-payments grounds. Suppose that the authorities in that country do adopt the severe deflationary policy necessary for this purpose, but that money wage-costs do not respond very rapidly. During this process the profitability of industry will be greatly reduced since each producer's selling market is restricted but cost per unit is not immediately reduced. This profit squeeze may induce owners of capital to invest in other countries where no such profit squeeze is in process, with the result that during the perhaps prolonged process of adjustment the outflow of capital makes the balance of payments worse. Of course, when the process of downward adjustment of wage and other costs has been successfully concluded and the deflationary policies are ended, the country's balance of payments will be in better shape. Its price–income–cost structure will have been adjusted and the profit squeeze will have ceased. But during the process of adjustment the strain of the capital items on the balance of payments may be very great. May it not be that there has been an element of all this in the United States' experience in some recent years?

Many persons who recognise the force of these arguments would nevertheless still hope to be able to use successfully the method of adjustment of domestic price–income–cost structures to remedy balance-of-payments problems. They hope that we can learn to make the necessary adjustments of money prices – and in particular of money wage-rates – by means other than prolonged deflations of demand. This is called nowadays the use of an 'incomes policy'. I am afraid that I am very sceptical about the efficacy of such an approach to the problem. Consider once more the problem of a country which already has considerable unemployment and at the same time is in deficit. One needs expansionary fiscal and monetary policies to promote growth and full employment. Could one really hope to combine with that an incomes policy which will cause this *greater* level of employment and output to take place at a *lower* level of money wage-costs and prices? If it were seriously proposed to exercise a strict governmental control over a myriad of wage-rates of different types of labour in different occupations and over a myriad of prices of products of various kinds and qualities, I would reject the policy on other grounds. It may be possible to achieve something by moral suasion and by much less severe measures of governmental interest in wage-bargaining and price-fixing, but surely one cannot hope to achieve the main instrument for balance-of-payments control by such innocent means.

If this assessment is correct, we are left with the possibility of adjusting relative price–income–cost structures by adjustment of the rates of exchange between the various national currencies. The basic principles of this method are simple. The authorities in each country should use their monetary and budgetary policies and whatever influence they can exert over the fixing of money wage-rates and prices to attain the best combination within their powers of the domestic goals of full employment, economic growth and price stability. Long-run adjustments in the balance of payments can then be facilitated by variations in the rates of exchange between their own national currency and those of other countries. This does not, of course, mean that there is no connection between domestic financial policies and the balance of payments. On the contrary, there is a very close connection.

Consider a country which domestically is in equilibrium but suffers from a balance-of-payments deficit. A depreciation of its currency by making its exports cheaper in foreign currencies and its imports more expensive in terms of its own currency may successfully increase the value of its exports relatively to its imports. But if foreigners now spend more on its export products and if its own citizens now spend less on imports and more on home products, there will have developed an excess demand for its own products. To prevent domestic inflation some degree of restriction in domestic financial policies is now necessary. In this way to reduce a balance-of-payments deficit without leading to domestic inflation requires a combination of exchange-rate depreciation with deflationary domestic financial policies.

Or consider a country which has an unemployment problem domestically but is in balance-of-payments equilibrium. It needs to adopt expansionary domestic financial policies to engender the necessary degree of economic expansion domestically. But this expansion will cause its balance of trade to deteriorate as the demand for imported goods rises and as goods which would otherwise have been exported are sucked into the expanded home market. The rise in domestic incomes may also mean that its citizens have more savings available for investment abroad; but on the other hand, as we have already observed, the greater measure of profitability of industry at home may attract for domestic investment some funds which would otherwise have been invested abroad. Thus the net effect of the domestic expansion on the balance of payments may be unfavourable or favourable. If, as is most probable, it is unfavourable, then the domestic expansion must be accompanied by some depreciation of the currency; if favourable, then by some appreciation.

It is not possible to trace all the possible permutations and combinations of appropriate policies. But the general principles of such a system are clear. There are three targets: full employment, price stability and balance-of-payments equilibrium. The authorities have three weapons: domestic budgetary-cum-monetary policies; incomes policies; and the rate of exchange. Three stones can be used to kill three birds. (1) More or less inflationary domestic policies as the level of employment threatens to fall or rise; (2) more or less restraint in incomes policy as the general level of money prices threatens to rise or to fall; and (3) an upward or downward movement of the exchange rate as serious long-run surpluses or deficits appear on the balance of payments – such a threefold prescription will make possible a serious attempt (not merely a pious hope) to attain all three targets simultaneously.

The Various Forms of Exchange-rate Flexibility

So far I have noted the merits of exchange-rate variations and the demerits of other instruments for balance-of-payments adjustment. This is, of course, not playing fair. Life in this wicked world is a choice of evils and it may be that the evils of exchange-rate variation, when one comes to look at them, are worse than those of some of the other methods. I do not myself believe this to be the case, but it is only fair to have a good look at the difficulties. Accordingly in this section of my paper, I will consider in turn each of the six main forms which, in my view, a system of exchange-rate flexibility might take and shall search for the snags in each case.

(1) The first is what has come to be known as the *Adjustable Peg* system, and is the system under which we are supposed to be living at the present time according to the rules of the International Monetary Fund. Each country fixes the value of its national currency (within very narrow upper and lower limits) in terms of some common unit (such as an ounce of gold) and undertakes to maintain the value of its national currency at this level by buying it (with gold or other foreign currencies) if it tends to fall below its par value and by selling it (for gold or other foreign currencies) if it tends to rise above its par value. But if a country's balance of payments falls into fundamental disequilibrium, then it can

make a suitable adjustment in the rate at which it pegs its currency to gold – raising the price of gold in terms of its own currency if it is in deficit, and *vice versa* if it is in surplus.

As this system has in fact developed the stress has come to be put upon the fixity of the peg rather than upon its periodic adjustment. Certainly exchange rates have been very much less variable than many persons hoped at the initiation of the Fund. One reason for this is probably the very grave disadvantages of this method of exchange-rate adjustment. Its use builds a paradise for anti-social speculation. A country is in balance-of-payments deficit: if it is widely known that such countries are very liable to raise the pegged price of gold (and so of other currencies) in terms of their own currency, speculators have every reason to sell the currency of the deficit country and hold other currencies; the currency concerned may be depreciated, it is certain that it will not be appreciated; if the peg is changed, they gain a quick and large profit; if the peg is not changed, they lose at the very most a small margin on their money.

As the present rules of the IMF are drafted, countries must in general obtain the permission of the Fund before adjusting their pegs. If such a Fund decision were to be based upon a profound international inquiry into the alleged 'fundamental disequilibrium' of the country wishing to adjust its peg, the system would become wholly unworkable. The idea of a really meaningful inquiry and discussion in an international organisation of the pros and cons of altering, for example, by a large percentage the value of the dollar or sterling while all holders of dollars or sterling proceeded to take their one-way speculative option is so ridiculous as not to be capable of being taken seriously. Permission of the Fund must mean little more than overnight snap agreement with a decision which a handful of the responsible men have brooded over in extreme secrecy in the inner councils of the country concerned.

Such adjustments will tend to be rare events. In order to discourage speculation against its currency, the improbability of change will be stressed and change will appear improbable if it is in fact infrequent. If, however, as a last desperate resort a change is made, it is likely to be very large for two reasons: first, because a great deal of disequilibrium must be built up before the fatal step is admitted to be inevitable; and, second, because a new fixed peg must be chosen and – hung for a lamb, hung for a sheep – if a depreciation is undertaken it will be considered wise to err on the safe side and to choose a rate which really will insure a surplus for the depreciating country – and, therefore, incidentally a deficit for someone else.

It was not perhaps inevitable that the IMF system should have developed in this way. With a looser and in my view more useful interpretation of the phrase 'fundamental disequilibrium' one can imagine a state of affairs in which a regular use was made of exchange-rate variation as an instrument of balance-of-payments control in the form of frequent small movements in the pegs – a currency being put up or down by, say, 2 per cent without any implication that it might not next month or next quarter be moved by another 2 per cent in the same direction if a greater movement seemed necessary or back to its original position if developments suggested that the former move had been unnecessary. Such a system would to some extent keep the speculators guessing; there need never build up those positions in which a huge potential one-way option is presented to operators in the foreign exchange markets; only small movements would be expected and they might quite well be reversed. Nevertheless, even in this form the system would be subject to grave disadvantages. It would still present speculators with substantial opportunities, since it would still be clear from time to time that a currency's peg might be moved in one direction but not in the other. And the system would need very close, continuous and intimate co-operation between the representatives of the main national monetary authorities to reach agreement upon the frequent small adjustments.

(2) The present IMF system is thus one of pretty rigidly fixed rates subject from time to time to substantial and disturbing adjustment. Let us next consider a system at the other extreme, namely one of *Freely Floating Exchange Rates* in which the prices of the various currencies are determined from day to day by the free play of competition between private buyers and sellers of currencies in foreign exchange markets which are subject to no controlling intervention either by national monetary authorities or by any international institution. With such a system the national authorities would devise and use their monetary, fiscal and wage-determining institutions in whatever way they considered to be most appropriate to achieve full employment and economic growth and to avoid instabilities and fluctuations in money incomes and prices. The would let the balance of payments look after itself.

Now the advocates of this system argue that the balance of payments would satisfactorily look after itself. Consider, for example, a country – such as the United States or the United Kingdom in recent years – which developed a deficit on its balance of payments. There will be an excess of domestic purchasers of foreign currencies to make payments abroad over the foreign purchasers of the domestic currency to make payments to the country in question. Foreign currencies will appreciate in terms of the currency in question. This will reduce the money price–income–cost structure of the country concerned relatively to that of other countries. All over the world, within and outside the country concerned, people will be encouraged to shift their purchases from the goods and services of other countries on to the goods and services produced by the deficit country.

It is, of course, well known to the advocates of this system that such shifts of demand which are needed to restore equilibrium will take time. Purchases will be shifted only as the new opportunities are appreciated, existing contracts run out, new plans are matured, and so on. But in the meanwhile, so it is argued, the private foreign-exchange speculator will play a useful and social role in supporting the currency of the deficit country. In the absence of the speculator the country's currency might depreciate very heavily indeed during the period when there was an excess demand for foreign currencies and before the consequential alteration in relative price–income–cost structures had had time to have its effects on imports and exports. But the speculator would realise that this period of acute difficulty was temporary; he would expect the currency to recover its value as time passed and the necessary adjustments in imports and exports were made; the speculator would, therefore, have a straightforward profit incentive to buy up the currency concerned in exchange for foreign currencies while it was extra cheap in order to make a gain on its subsequent appreciation. In short it is argued that a system of freely floating exchange rates (i) brings about long-run structural adjustments in balances of payments through appropriate changes in relative price–income–cost structures and (ii) induces private speculators to give the necessary temporary support to currencies under pressure, a support which under other systems would have to be given by the use of official reserves of gold and foreign exchange.

There is only one possible snag to this system. Could one rely upon private speculation to fulfil adequately this vital role? True, speculators buy when they expect prices to go up. But on what do they base their expectations of future prices? Is it always on a correct anticipation of what is going to happen to the basic underlying elements of long-run supply and demand? But it is never easy to tell what the future holds in store for a country's imports, exports and international capital movements. Some speculators may base their expectations of future exchange rates mainly on what has happened recently to exchange rates; and when a currency falls in value because of some new strain on a balance of payments, they may expect a further fall simply because there has been a recent fall. Such speculation will intensify, not mitigate, the fall; the speculators' sales are added to the other pressures on the balance of payments. Then other speculators may sell the currency, although they realise that it has already fallen below its long-run value, simply because they expect this first group of less-well-informed speculators to go on selling. In other words, speculation could take a form which made completely free exchange rates subject to excessive fluctuations. And this could bring with it a further danger. An excessive depreciation of a currency could lead to a sharp rise in the price of imports. Such a price rise – particularly if, as in the United Kingdom, imports of food and other necessities make up a large element in the cost of living – could itself engender a rise in money wage claims and thus a rise in the domestic price–income–cost structure. And this rise in turn would justify increased pessimism about the future value of the currency.

(3) Now whether these fears be justified or not – and I would not myself be ready to assert that they are wholly imaginary – it is most unlikely that national governments would be prepared at one fell swoop to take the risk of letting the exchange rates go to fluctuate freely without any intervention. If the currency pegs were removed and exchange rates were allowed to fluctuate, the national authorities would undoubtedly insist on standing ready with their reserves of gold and foreign exchange to intervene in the exchange market from time to time. This we may call the system of *National Exchange Equalisation*. The system would work in the following way. As in the case just examined currency pegs would be removed; national currencies would fluctuate in terms of each other;

long-run adjustment would thus be achieved by changes in money price–income–cost structures due to alterations in the exchange rates between different domestic monies; and speculators would be free to speculate and – it would be hoped – to provide short-run support for the currency of a deficit country. But national monetary authorities would not rely wholly on private speculation. They would set up national exchange equalisation funds, endowed with resources in terms of their own currencies and of gold and foreign currencies. If private speculation appeared to them to be driving down excessively the value of the national currency, they would themselves support the currency by selling foreign currencies or gold and buying the domestic currency through their own exchange equalisation account, and *vice versa* if private transactions seemed to be raising the short-run value of the domestic currency excessively.

This system has in my view a great deal to recommend it. But it has its own peculiar difficulties which became obvious in the late 1930s when – so far as sterling and the dollar were concerned – something like it was in operation. At that time there was a fear that a national monetary authority would use its exchange equalisation fund to engage in competitive exchange depreciation. For example, the UK authorities by selling sterling and buying dollars could depreciate unnecessarily the value of sterling in terms of the dollar, thus enabling UK manufacturers to undercut US manufacturers even though there might be no underlying deficit on the UK balance of payments and no need, therefore, for such undercutting. The dangers of such action were undoubtedly much more real in the late 1930s than they would be in present conditions. Then there was mass unemployment; and national authorities were tempted to give employment to their own resources by beggar-my-neighbour international policies which stole markets from their neighbours even though their balance-of-payments position did not require such action. Nowadays there is not mass unemployment; and in any case national governments realise that they can give employment by measures which expand their own domestic markets, using measures which expand their exports and contract their imports only if they have a balance-of-payments deficit.

But even if competitive exchange depreciations are a much less real danger nowadays, it is pretty clear that the system of National Exchange Equalisation must be supplemented by an extensive system of international co-operation. To put it simply, if the UK Exchange Equalisation Account is intervening to control the sterling–dollar rate of exchange and the US Exchange Equalisation Account is intervening to control the dollar–sterling rate of exchange, it is clear that they would be well advised to co-ordinate their actions. But the obvious way to co-ordinate their actions is to agree on the rates at which they will peg their currencies and only to change the pegs from time to time in agreement; and this is, of course, in essence the present IMF system of the Adjustable Peg with which we started our discussion. In fact, it was the fear of competitive exchange depreciation engendered in the 1930s, combined with the obvious need to co-ordinate the actions of independent national exchange equalisation accounts, which led through the Tripartite Monetary Agreement of 1936 to the Articles of Agreement of the International Monetary Fund and the present excessively rigid exchange-rate structure.

(4) Thus National Exchange Equalisation cries out for international co-operation which appears to imply the system of the Adjustable Peg, which – as we have seen – is likely to imply a rigid exchange-rate structure. A possible escape from this dilemma is through *Supranational Exchange Equalisation*. Under this system national monetary authorities would renounce the use of national exchange equalisation accounts; exchange rates would be allowed to vary to give long-run balance-of-payments adjustments; private speculation would be supplemented not by the operations of a number of national exchange equalisation accounts but by a single Supranational Exchange Equalisation authority which – like the present International Monetary Fund – would be endowed with a large fund of the various national currencies, but – unlike the present International Monetary Fund – would be empowered on its own initiative to buy and sell these currencies in otherwise uncontrolled foreign exchange markets in order to control short-run fluctuations in exchange rates.

If I am frank, I must admit that I regard this as technically the best possible solution in present circumstances. For at heart I believe that in the free world we should develop real supranational authorities. It is in my view a quite mistaken form of monetary supranationalism to start by fixing rigidly the exchange rates between national currencies as a first step towards a supranational currency. We are at a very early confederal stage in our affairs. It is the national governments which have the great taxing powers and so the instruments for controlling budgetary inflations or deflations of demand; it is the national governments which have the great central banks which control the issue of money and so interest rates; and the nations have their own different modes of wage-rate determination. It is a wise and sensible division of powers in our present confederal stage that the national governments should exercise these budgetary, monetary and wage-fixing influences to control their own employment, growth and price stability. This implies, I am sure, some variations in the rates of exchange between their monies. It is in the necessary Exchange Equalisation between these monies that the first tentative supranational steps should be taken.

However, I am sufficiently realistic to admit that this supranational solution is politically not a starter in the year 1966. So reluctantly I pass on from Supranational Exchange Equalisation to other possible measures.

(5) If we abandon the heroic solution of Supranational Exchange Equalisation, can we do some useful but more mundane tinkering with the present excessively rigid Adjustable-Peg system? I believe that we can. First of all, we could introduce *Wider Bands* within which fluctuations could take place. I have so far treated the present system of Adjustable Pegs as if each currency were precisely and exactly pegged to

gold. But this is, of course, not the case. The present IMF obligation is for each member country to settle a par value for its currency in terms either of gold or of the dollar with its fixed gold content and then not allow the value of its currency to vary by more than 1 per cent above or below this par value. This means that if a country is in deficit it can allow the value of its currency to depreciate by 1 per cent before having to support it from its own reserves; if it is in surplus, it can allow the value of its currency to appreciate by 1 per cent. Such small variations[2] do not allow the exchange rate to be a significant instrument of long-run adjustment; but they can exercise an important and in general a beneficial effect on speculation in the exchange rates. Thus if a country is in deficit and the value of its currency has depreciated by the permitted 1 per cent, speculators (provided that there is no risk of a change in the currency's par value) will have some speculative incentive to purchase the depreciated currency; it cannot depreciate any further; it might, however, appreciate in the future by anything up to 2 per cent. This consideration will prompt speculators to support a currency when it is under pressure and thus helps the authorities to maintain the exchange rate with a smaller loss of reserves than would otherwise be necessary. This feature of a system which sets upper and lower limits to the band within which exchange rates may fluctuate gives it an advantage over the system of National Exchange Equalisation without any upper or lower limits. For a monetary authority to support its currency when it has fallen by x per cent will be much easier if speculators know that it will not fall any further than if they realise that at any time it may be still further reduced. As against this there must, of course, be set the reduction in the range of variations which can be used as an instrument of balance-of-payments adjustment.

But there is nothing sacred about 1 per cent. Suppose that the rules of the IMF were altered so that each member country were obliged only to prevent the value of its currency from deviating by more than 5 per cent from its par value. Changes in exchange rates could now begin to exert some, though still a moderate, influence on basic price–income–cost structures. Consider two currencies both of whose par rates were fixed in terms of gold. The most extreme permitted swing in the exchange rate

2 Consider two countries both of which have fixed the par values of their currencies in terms of gold. Suppose country A is in surplus and its exchange rate is 1 per cent above parity, while country B is in deficit and its exchange rate is 1 per cent below parity. Then B's money is 2 per cent devalued in terms of A's. If later B is in surplus and A is in deficit, B's money may be 2 per cent appreciated in terms of A's money. The maximum swing in the rate of exchange between the two currencies is, therefore, 4 per cent. The maximum conceivable swing could be somewhat greater if A had fixed its parity in terms of gold and B in terms of the dollar and if there were a margin between the United States' buying and selling prices of gold in terms of dollars. The swing in the rate of exchange between A's and B's currencies would be enlarged if (i) the dollar happened to be weak in terms of gold when A's currency was at its strongest (in terms of gold) and B's at its weakest (in terms of dollars) and (ii) the dollar happened to be strong in terms of gold when A's currency was at its weakest (in terms of gold) and B's at its strongest (in terms of dollars).

between the two currencies would now be 20 per cent,[3] though generally much smaller changes would be the rule. The possibility of these enlarged swings would also increase the incentive to speculators to aid the authorities in the support of a currency under pressure. For when the currency did reach its lower level there would, as before, be no possibility of a further fall in its gold value, but there would now be a possibility that its gold value might rise by anything up to 10 per cent instead of only 2 per cent.

The wider the band within which the exchange rate can vary, the greater its power as an instrument of basic adjustment of price–income–cost structures and the greater its power to induce the support of speculators when a currency is weak and at its lower level. Why then not advocate much Wider Bands? Why not 20 per cent above or below par? Unfortunately in this wicked world one cannot have one's cake and eat it. Fluctuations within the band raise all the problems already discussed of Freely Floating Exchange Rates or of Exchange Equalisation controls over fluctuations, of competitive exchange depreciation, and of the co-ordination of national exchange equalisation policies. If the band is kept reasonably narrow, one could without danger have a system in which exchanges were allowed to float freely without any official intervention within the permitted band. Or, as a second-best alternative, if national exchange equalisation were permitted within the band one could perhaps leave the necessary co-operation between national authorities in the exchange equalisation use of their national reserves of gold and foreign exchange to be worked out by suitable *ad hoc* arrangements. Simply because the band is limited, the dangers of anti-social speculation or of the misuse of national exchange equalisation funds will also be limited. Permission to fluctuate by 5 per cent either side of par value combined with freely floating exchange rates or with the uncontrolled national use of national monetary reserves within those limits might well provide a better mix than at present between international restraint and freedom of national action.

(6) There is one other way in which the present IMF rules might be modified in order to give a somewhat different mix between international restraint and national freedom in exchange-rate matters. At present the rule is that a member country can alter the par value of its currency only if it is in fundamental disequilibrium and only with the permission of the IMF, except that it can make an initial 10 per cent adjustment on its own initiative. These rules might be revised in the following way. Basic adjustments to meet a fundamental disequilibrium would be hedged around with even more safeguards and would be made even more exceptional than at present. The allowance of an initial 10 per cent adjustment would be abolished; but in its place member countries would be permitted to alter the par value of their currencies by not more than 1/6 per cent in any one month; moreover, they would undertake to

[3] At one extreme A's currency would be 5 per cent above par with B's 5 per cent below par; at the other extreme A's would be 5 per cent below par and B's 5 per cent above. The swing could be somewhat greater if A's parity were fixed in terms of gold and B's in terms of dollars. See the preceding footnote.

depreciate their currencies by 1/6 per cent in any one month if, but only if, they were faced with a continuing balance-of-payments deficit and to appreciate by this amount if, but only if, they were faced with a continuing surplus in their balance of payments. This system might perhaps be called that of the *Sliding Parity*. For if the right to change the parity were exercised every month, the exchange value of the currency would be changed continuously at 2 per cent per annum.[4]

Such a system is not, of course, a panacea. But it could be used as a partial but very useful supplement to other measures to achieve long-run equilibrium. If a country were in continuing balance-of-payments deficit it could by this means lower its price–income–cost structure by anything up to 2 per cent per annum – i.e. by 10 per cent over a five-year period. If at the same time some other country were in continuing surplus, it could have raised its price–income–cost structure through exchange-rate appreciation by anything up to 10 per cent over the same five-year period. A 20 per cent adjustment in five years is by no means to be despised. But this would be the very maximum, and clearly reliance could be placed on this method only if the countries concerned had very ample reserves of gold and foreign exchange to tide them over the fairly prolonged processes of adjustment.

The system raises also important problems of exchange-rate speculation. For this reason, to operate the system the monetary authorities would have to use their short-term interest rate policies for balance-of-payments reasons. Let us take the extreme possible case. Suppose that A's currency is confidently expected to appreciate at the maximum rate of 2 per cent per annum while B's currency is confidently expected to depreciate at the maximum rate of 2 per cent per annum. B's currency would then be expected to depreciate in terms of A's currency at the rate of 4 per cent per annum. To prevent the wholesale movement of short-term funds from B to A to take the prospective 4 per cent profit on the exchange rate the short-term rate of interest would have to be maintained in B four points above the level in A – for example, at 6 per cent per annum in B and 2 per cent in A. This means that to work a system of this kind the national monetary authorities would have to co-operate in setting their short-term interest rates in the interests of preserving balance-of-payments equilibrium. They would have to rely on budgetary policies and – in so far as they can be determined independently of short-term rates – upon long-term rates but not upon short-term rates, for the control of domestic economic expansion.

If a system of this kind were adopted, it might be sensible for the monetary authorities in each country to give a gold guarantee in respect of balances of its own currency which were held as monetary reserves by other monetary authorities. This is not an essential feature of the proposal, and the decision whether or not to give such a gold guarantee could be left to each individual country. If such guarantees were given, there would develop a structure of more or less uniform short-term

[4] The general idea of a *Sliding Parity* was first put forward by Mr Black of Merton College, Oxford, in an unsigned note in *The Economist* of 4 November 1961 ['Exchange rates on a moving average', p. 486].

interest rates in all the main financial centres for such currency balances as were backed by a gold guarantee, while divergent short-term rates would appear on balances of national currencies not subject to a gold guarantee – the short-term rate being higher in those centres where the exchange rate was expected to depreciate and *vice versa*.

Concluding Proposals

Let me sum up by putting forward proposals for the arrangements which in view of the above considerations I would myself advocate. There is no reason why a *Wider Band* should not be combined with a *Sliding Parity*. This could be achieved by two straightforward changes in the IMF rules.

(1) As at present member countries would fix a par value for their currencies. But their obligation would be to prevent deviations by more than 5 per cent (in place of the present 1 per cent) each side of this par value.

(2) As far as alterations in par rates were concerned the present allowance of a 10 per cent initial alteration at their own discretion would be removed and, in its place, each country would be permitted at its own discretion to change its parity by not more than 1/6 per cent per month.[5] Member countries would undertake to make such adjustments if, but only if, their balances of payments were in their view in continuing deficit or surplus.

Let us consider how such a system might operate. Suppose that we start in equilibrium with exchange rates at parity and that then some change in conditions occurs which puts country A into serious deficit and country B into serious surplus. As a result of the Wider Band A's currency would then depreciate by 5 per cent and B's would appreciate by 5 per cent. This would give at once a 10 per cent adjustment of relative price–income–cost structures which could begin to have a significant effect in bringing about the necessary basic adjustments. As long as the imbalance in international payments continued, as a result of the Sliding-Parity arrangements A's currency could further be depreciated at a rate of 2 per cent per annum while B's was appreciated at a rate of 2 per cent per annum, so that at the end of two and a half years there would have been another 10 per cent adjustment – or 20 per cent in all – in relative price–income–cost structures.

Thus these proposals could make a very serious contribution to the adjustment of balances of payments. At the same time they need not lead to insoluble speculative problems. As far as fluctuations of the exchange rates within the Wider Band were concerned, exchange rates could best be left to the free play of market forces. If speculators expected a fall in a currency, they could by their sale of it drive it down at once to its lower limit. Beyond this they would know for certain that it could not fall by

[5] At this rate it would take it five years to achieve an initial 10 per cent change.

more than 2 per cent per annum and might rise at any moment by 10 per cent. The expectation of a steady fall of 2 per cent per annum could induce speculative pressure and so loss of reserves on the deficit country, unless this was offset by a 2 per cent differential in short-term interest rates between the deficit country and other countries. For this reason the fully successful operation of the system would require real co-operation between the main central monetary authorities so that short-term rates were set at a lower level in surplus countries whose currencies were expected to appreciate and at a higher level in deficit countries. The financial authorities would have to rely rather on their fiscal policies and long-term interest-rate policies for the control of their domestic economies. Apart from this set of problems there is in my opinion very little to be said against the proposed system; and in my view this set of problems should not prove unmanageable. The degree of exchange-rate flexibility which the system would introduce would very greatly reduce the probability of there being (as at present) every now and then a huge once-for-all disturbing exchange-rate adjustment. It is the fear of such once-for-all government-determined devaluations of 10, 20, 30 or 40 per cent which cause the really big speculative runs on a currency; and with the new system such runs should quickly become a thing of the past.

I do not put these proposals forward as a cure-all. Although the amount of price–income–cost adjustment that they would make possible would, as we have seen, be really significant, there would, of course, be pressures on balances of payments while currencies were at their lower and upper limits on the edges of the Wider Band. Such pressures would have to be met by the use of national reserves of gold and foreign exchange or, if such reserves were not adequate, by the more drastic and more quickly operating measures of import restrictions or of otherwise undesirable deflations of domestic demand. The proposed system is not an alternative to other reforms of the international monetary mechanism designed to ensure that the amount and the nature of international liquid reserves are appropriate to modern conditions. It is a well-recognised fact that those methods of balance-of-payments adjustment which operate quickly (such as import restrictions or severe domestic deflations) are objectionable on other grounds, whereas acceptable methods of adjusting balances of payments through adjustments of relative price–income–cost structures (such as incomes policies or alterations in exchange rates) operate slowly and with considerable time-lags. One can, therefore, rely on these better policies only if there are adequate resources of international liquid reserves to tide over the periods of adjustment; and this is particularly true when, as with the present proposals, the changes in exchange rates are themselves expressly designed so as to be both moderate and gradual.

These proposals are, therefore, put forward only on the assumption that there are adequate supplies of international liquid reserves of an appropriate form. I have views on that set of subjects,[6] but I shall refrain

[6] I have expressed them in my paper, 'The International Monetary Mechanism' published in *The Three Banks Review*, no. 63 (September 1964), pp. 3–25. I have incorporated into

from expressing them in this paper. For it should be technically a relatively simple task to apply the principles of exchange-rate flexibility proposed in this paper to any form of international liquid reserves; and I do not want to prejudice consideration of these exchange-rate proposals by seeming to tie them to any particular form of international liquidity.

the present note two paragraphs from that paper dealing with the problem of speculation under a Sliding-Parity system.

313-23
[1978]
4113
4220
7130
1100

20

A Strategy for Commodity Policy

From the Scandinavian Journal of Economics, *vol. 80 (1978), pp. 349–359. The paper had been written for the Commodities Division of UNCTAD in October 1974.*

I Commodity Schemes

Let me first outline the general structure of commodity arrangements which I would advocate and then comment on the various items. There should be three elements in the structure.

(1) There should be an extensive system of buffer stocks for all commodities for which the costs of storage are reasonable.
(2) There should be price-compensation agreements for those commodities for which high costs of storage rule out the organisation of a buffer stock.
(3) There should be an extensive system of compensatory finance for developing countries which are hit by exceptionally low exports, or by the need for exceptionally high imports, of primary products.

These three elements together would form a comprehensive structure which would cover all commodities and would together fully meet the requirements of an integrated commodity policy programme. I will consider each element in turn.

(1) The buffer-stock system is one which can stabilise the price of the product concerned by buying for stock when price is exceptionally low and selling from stock when price is exceptionally high. It has the great advantage of being able to do this without in any way preventing the ordinary operation of the market in the commodity; and for this reason is much more likely to last than is a system which depends upon wide-ranging and strict control of market operations. While the stocks are being built up in the first place the prices of the products concerned will be maintained at levels higher than would otherwise be the case. The buffer-stock method has one other outstanding advantage, which recent events should have impressed upon our minds, namely that the existence of large stocks of vital foodstuffs and essential materials may serve to

avoid famine or other catastrophe when some unexpected misfortune (such as a series of widespread harvest failures) occurs. Stocks of grain and certain metals which were held privately or by national governments have now for the most part been used up. It is of vital importance that such emergency reserves should be rebuilt for the world as a whole; and this is just what an adequate international buffer stock can do – to the advantage of the producers of the primary product while the supplies for the stocks are being purchased.

(2) In the case of commodities which cannot be readily stored some of the same results can be achieved by means of price-compensation agreements. With an agreement of this kind the governments of the importing and exporting countries concerned agree on what may be regarded as a reasonable price for the commodity; when the actual market price falls appreciably below the target price, the governments of the importing countries transfer funds to the governments of the exporting countries to compensate for an agreed proportion of the shortfall in the price; and when the market price rises appreciably above the target price the governments of the exporting countries transfer funds to the governments of the importing countries to compensate for an agreed proportion of the excess of the market price over target prices.

This also is a system which can be operated without any governmental interventions in the actual operation of the market and for that reason is likely to be much easier to administer. Moreover, it has the great advantage that it can be operated on a large scale multilaterally between all importing and exporting countries or on a very small scale bilaterally between only one importing and one exporting country without in any way interfering with the operation of the market in the commodity concerned.[1] The government of exporting country A can simply agree with the government of importing country B to receive (or to make) compensation payments on a predetermined reference volume of trade between them according as the world price of the commodity falls below (or rises above) some pre-agreed target level. The higher the target price thus chosen, the more favourable is the outcome likely to be to the exporting country.[2]

The governments of the importing and exporting countries would be free to do what they liked with any price-compensation funds which they received or to raise in any way which they chose any price-compensation funds which they had to pay. Consider the case in which the market price is depressed below the target price and the importing country is, therefore, paying compensation to the exporting country. The government of the exporting country could use the compensation money to supplement the price received by the producers of the commodity or it could use the funds to promote the production of alternative and more repaying products. The importing country could similarly raise the compensation funds which it had to pay by means of a tax on the

[1] See my paper presented to the first UNCTAD conference: 'International Commodity Agreements' [Chapter 18 above].

[2] The mechanics of a price-compensation scheme are described in more detail in the Appendix to this paper [Chapter 20 pp. 320–3 below].

consumption of the product or it could allow the consumers to enjoy the low market price and could raise the funds by general taxation. But while each government would remain free to do what it chose in the use or the raising of the compensation funds, the scheme would not work if all the exporting countries chose to use the funds to supplement the selling price of the producers and all the importing countries to raise the funds by levying a charge on the buying price of the consumers. If this were to happen the producers would have no incentive to produce less and the consumers would have no incentive to consume more. In consequence the excess of supply over demand would continue and the market price would fall still further. This process of falling market price would go on indefinitely so long as (i) the price actually paid to the producers was not allowed to fall and thus lead to a reduced supply and (ii) the price actually charged to the consumer was not allowed to fall and thus to lead to an increased demand. Price-compensation schemes can be expected to work only if an appreciable part of the compensation funds are in fact used for purposes other than the direct supplementation of the price received by the producers concerned and/or are in fact raised by means other than the taxation of the price charged to the consumers of the product concerned. If it were desired to enable price-compensation agreements to be used to stabilise the net prices received by the producers concerned, it might be necessary in such agreements to prohibit the raising of compensation funds by the importing countries by means of the taxation of the consumption of the commodity and to prohibit the use of any compensation funds received by the importing countries for the subsidisation of the consumption of the commodity. With this requirement price-compensation agreements could be used to achieve for perishable commodities the same degree of producer price stabilisation as can be achieved for durable commodities by the buffer-stock mechanism. With the buffer-stock mechanism a gap between supply and demand at the stabilised price is closed by an excess of purchases or sales by the buffer stock; with the price-compensation agreement, if the stabilised price were maintained by the governments of the exporting countries for their producers, any gap between supply and demand would be closed by a rise or fall in the price charged to consumers on a scale sufficient to adjust demand to the supply.

(3) As we have seen, both the buffer-stock and the price-compensation techniques can be used to stabilise the price received by the producers of the commodity. But the stabilisation of the producer's selling price is not the same thing as the stabilisation of his income. Variations in the producer's output (for example, due to harvest variations) may still cause large variations in his income, even if the price is stabilised. A country which is much dependent upon the export of a single crop, the output of which is subject to large harvest variations, may be greatly hit by a fall in exports due to a bad crop. Nor is this problem confined to exporting countries. A developing country with a low income per head may nevertheless be dependent in an important way upon the imports of certain primary products in which it is not self-supporting. Such a country may, for example, need to import exceptionally large quantities of grain

if its domestic harvest is a failure and it is otherwise faced with famine. A developing importing country in this position can be as hardly hit by a harvest failure which leads to an exceptionally high need for imports as can a developing exporting country by a harvest failure which leads to an exceptionally low availability of supplies for export.

Buffer-stock and price-compensation schemes need, therefore, to be supplemented by a system under which developing countries can be compensated if their exports of primary products are exceptionally low or their need for imports of such products is exceptionally high. Such a scheme should be developed out of the existing IMF compensatory financing scheme. It is necessary to revise that scheme in a way which copes as well with the problem of exceptionally high import needs as with the problem of exceptionally low exports. For this purpose it is necessary to estimate for each country concerned the normal expected course of the net balance of its exports and imports of commodities and to provide compensatory finance if this balance is exceptionally unfavourable in any one year. There are a number of ways in which such a scheme can be made more or less favourable to the countries concerned: the normal target trend of its exports can be set at a generously high level and of its imports at a generously low level, so that more liberal compensation can be expected; any finance so provided can be granted or loaned on more or less favourable terms; and so on.

It is not my purpose in this short note to discuss the details of the various schemes. But a rounded integrated whole can be achieved in the commodity-policy field if the price stabilisation brought about by buffer stocks or by price-compensation schemes is accompanied by a really generous scheme of the kind just described for the support of export receipts and the curtailment of the burden of imports.

II The Case against Restriction Schemes

So much for the general nature of the positive commodity schemes which might be adopted. It is to be noted that there is no proposal for the maintenance of the prices of primary-product exports by means of quota or other schemes which restrict the volume of exports. Such schemes have been expressly omitted from the positive programme of Section I. This is not because they are thought necessarily to be ineffective. On the contrary it is clear that if all the exporters of a vital primary product agree, for example, by a system of quantitative export quotas, to restrict the sales of that product they may be able thereby substantially to increase their incomes. It is true that in the long run such restriction schemes often prove difficult to maintain, partly because with the help of modern ingenious technicians substitutes for the product are likely to be discovered or invented, and partly because there is a great temptation for each individual exporting country to increase its own exports, taking advantage of the high price maintained by the restriction of exports by the remaining exporting countries. And once one exporter breaks loose others are likely to follow.

But the basic reason for not including such schemes in the proposed positive programme is not simply that they are difficult to maintain, but rather that they should be given up in the context of a more profitable bargain with the developed countries. It is of the greatest importance for the developing countries that they should gain free access for their labour-intensive manufactures to the markets of the highly industrialised developed countries. The developing countries can hope to achieve good standards of living only if they develop their manufactures; and if they had free access to the vast markets for manufactured goods in the industrialised countries, their prospects of developing really large volumes of manufactures particularly of labour-intensive products would be improved out of all recognition.

The world is at the moment at one of its rare critical turning points. There is the opportunity for a bargain between the developing and the developed countries of enormous importance, which could be of the greatest benefit to both. The developing countries should say to the developed countries: 'We realise that by getting together we can restrict supplies of primary products which are vital to you in such a way as to gain a large income through the rise in their prices. There is, however, something which we want more than that, namely free access for our goods – and in particular for our manufactures – to your markets. If you will agree to that, we will agree to confine our commodity-policy programme to schemes of a kind which, while they will safeguard our export receipts, will in no way restrict the market in which you can obtain your supplies of primary products.'

An agreement on these lines could be of great benefit to all concerned; and the present is a moment when such an agreement might be reached. The opportunity presented by the current trade negotiations is not likely to recur and the developing countries should put a proposition of the above kind fairly and squarely into the GATT negotiations. It is not merely that positive agreement on these lines might bring great positive benefit to both sides. An equally forceful – perhaps more forceful – incentive for doing everything to achieve such an agreement is the prospect of what may well be the outcome if it is not achieved. Suppose that the developing countries do start to organise some effective restriction schemes. This may well make the developed countries less willing to liberalise their imports from the developing countries. Indeed, they might increase the severity of their existing restrictions. The developing countries in return might extend or intensify their restrictions on primary-product exports. The developed countries might in return cut down their aid. And so on, until the world finds itself not only unnecessarily impoverished but also – what is even more to be deprecated – divided into two distinct conflicting camps of developed and developing countries.

How much better a world in which the developing countries had free access to the domestic markets of the developed countries, while the developed countries could buy unrestricted supplies of primary products from the developing countries in free, but nevertheless stabilised and compensated, export markets.

III The Finance of the Commodity Schemes

So far nothing has been said about the finance of the schemes proposed in Section I.

The price-compensation schemes discussed under (2) of Section I would be self-financing in the simple sense that the countries which joined together in such schemes would themselves have undertaken to raise in any way which best suited them the finance necessary to make the agreed compensation payments. Whether or not, taking one year with another, the compensation payments by importers would exceed or fall short of the compensation payments by exporters would depend upon the setting of the 'target' prices. If these were set on the high side, then over the years payments by importing countries to exporting countries would tend to be higher than payments in the reverse direction; and this might be appropriate in the case in which the importers were on the whole developed countries and the exporters were developing countries. If the exporters were developed countries (such as the USA and Canada in the case of wheat) while the importers were developing countries (such as India in the case of wheat), it might be more appropriate to set target prices on the low side, so that compensation payments tended on the average to flow from exporting to importing countries.

The trade-balance compensation scheme discussed under (3) of Section I could be devised to as to be partly self-financing and partly dependent upon outside finance. A developing country which received financial compensation because its exports of primary products were unduly low or its imports unduly high could receive the finance in the first place as a loan, which it might be placed under an obligation to repay as and when the good years came when its exports were exceptionally high or its imports needs exceptionally low. If the scheme were devised in such a way that the good years on the average balanced the bad years, the scheme could be self-financing, though it would need an initial endowment with some capital fund in order to be ready to make the initial loans in the initial bad years. But there are various ways in which the scheme could be modified so as to rely to a greater or smaller degree on outside finance: (i) if the reference or target levels of a developing country's exports were set on the high side and of its imports on the low side, the years which were so defined as 'bad' would tend to outnumber those defined as 'good' and compensation payments would tend to exceed repayments; (ii) the terms of the outstanding loans as to interest and other charges might be set favourably for the borrowing countries; and (iii) any loans so made might be written off if they were not repaid out of the proceeds of 'good' years within a stated period.

There is one very important way in which the need for outside funds in any such trade-balance compensation scheme could be reduced, namely by introducing a mutual insurance element as between the developing countries which were members of the scheme. This could be done in the following way. Any developing country which was a member of the scheme and which enjoyed a 'good' year in which its exports were above target or its import needs below target would be required to make some contribution towards the finance of any compensation paid to any members whose exports had been below target or import needs above target. This would reduce the amount of support which would be needed over the years from sources other than the developing countries which were members of the scheme. Thus with this element of mutual insurance the target levels of exports and imports would be set at more generous levels without incurring any additional requirement of finance from outside sources other than the members of the scheme themselves.

The buffer-stock schemes suggested under (1) of Section I, if properly conducted, can aim at a commercial return on the capital invested in them. But they can hope to achieve this result only if they are conducted on proper principles. A buffer stock cannot be operated as an instrument for the purpose of maintaining the price of a product indefinitely above the normal level at which it would have stood in the absence of the buffer stock. A buffer stock is merely an instrument for (i) holding up the price as the stock is built up in the first place and (ii) then stabilising the price around the longer-run trend of the market. If this market trend is downwards, then the buffer-stock prices must themselves trend downwards. In such conditions the buffer stock could hold the market price up above the downward trend only through continuous and indefinitely expanding purchases of the commodity for storage. At some point it would have to desist; the buffer stock would disintegrate; and the market price would collapse.

The buffer stock must aim at purchasing only when the price in the market is well below the normal trend and at selling only when the price in the market is appreciably above the normal trend. If it is successful in doing so, it may make a good return on the capital funds invested in it.

But even the best conducted buffer stock may not be able to cover its costs. Consider a commodity whose costs of storage are high, whose market price has a downward trend, and whose market price does not in fact fluctuate very much. A buffer stock in such a commodity will have interest costs to pay on the funds borrowed to finance the purchase of its stock, will have important current storage costs to meet, will be holding in its stock a real asset whose market price has a downward trend, and will not be presented with any exceptional moments when it can purchase very cheaply or sell very dearly. And yet there may be good social reasons for operating such a stock, first because the stabilisation which it does achieve in the market price may be important to the producers in the developing countries concerned and second because an unforeseen world emergency may always occur in which a reserve stock of the commodity would be invaluable.

A really important network of buffer stocks would require very large capital funds to build up their stocks and would probably need some official guarantee for these loans to meet those cases where costs could not in fact be covered.

There is at present one and only one very large body of capital funds – namely, the oil funds – which need to find an appropriate investment outlet. Here is surely an opportunity for another mutually satisfactory arrangement. Capital funds are needed both to finance the trade-balance compensation scheme of (2) of Section I and the buffer-stock schemes of (1) of Section I; but in both cases there is more or less risk of greater or smaller losses. Might not an arrangement be made whereby the developed countries undertook in agreed proportions to meet losses incurred under these two schemes, so that oil funds might be safely invested in loans to finance these two schemes? As a result the owners of the oil funds might find a reliable form of investment which in the case of the buffer stocks would be backed not only by the guarantee of the developed countries, but also by the physical stocks themselves. The developing countries would receive payments for their exports to the buffer stocks and compensating support for their exports in general. With these additional funds the developing countries could buy additional manufactured goods from the developed countries. The developed countries could use these funds to cut down some of their oil debts, which would in turn finance the two schemes which had enabled the developing countries to expand and sustain their exports. The beneficial cycle would be complete.

Such then is the proper setting for an integrated commodity policy: buffer-stock, price-compensation, and trade-balance compensation schemes to stabilise and maintain the commodity trade of the developing countries; free access by the developing countries to the markets of the developed countries and unrestricted access by the developed countries to the primary-product supplies of the developing countries; oil funds invested profitably in the buffer-stock and trade-balance compensation schemes, backed by guarantees from the developed countries. An opportunity not to be missed.

Appendix

A Price-Compensation Model

Consider the following model:

$$x = Sp_s^{\sigma} = Dp_d^{-\delta} \tag{1}$$

$$xp_s - px + \alpha_s \beta(\bar{p} - p)\bar{x} \tag{2}$$

$$xp_d - px + \alpha_d \beta(\bar{p} - p)\bar{x} \tag{3}$$

x is total quantity bought and sold on the market.

p_s and p_d are the net prices obtained by the producers and paid by the consumers respectively, i.e. prices after adjustment for any governmental subsidies or taxes.

p is the market price before adjustment for taxes or subsidies.

$\bar{p}$ is the reference price.

$\bar{x}$ is the reference quantity.

β is the fraction of any divergence between $\bar{p}\bar{x}$ and $p\bar{x}$ which has to be compensated, so that the importing Government pays to the exporting government $\beta(\bar{p} - p)\bar{x}$.

α_s is the fraction of any compensation receipt which the exporting government uses to subsidise the price paid to its producers.

α_d is the fraction of any compensation payment which the importing government raises by taxation of its consumers.

Equations (1) express the market-clearing equality between supply and demand with a constant price elasticity of supply σ and a constant price elasticity of demand δ. S and D allow for shifts in the supply and demand curves, i.e. a 1 per cent rise in S or D represents a 1 per cent increase in the amount supplied or demanded at any given price.

Equations (2) and (3) express the factors determining the formation of the net prices received by producers (p_s) or paid by consumers (p_d). Thus from (2) we have the net price received by producers (p_s) equal to the ruling market price (p) plus that amount of the compensation receipts which is used to subsidise the producer ($\alpha_s\beta[\bar{p} - p]\bar{x}/x$).

Equations (1), (2), and (3) express the market equilibrium after compensation. Now let S and D change, i.e. autonomous shifts of supply and demand curves. We differentiate (1), (2), and (3) allowing x, S, D, p_s, p_d, and p to change. Write $\dot{x}$ for dx/x, i.e. for the proportionate change in x, and similarly for the other variables.

We then have:

$$\dot{x} = \dot{S} + \sigma\dot{p}_s = \dot{D} - \delta\dot{p}_d \tag{5}$$

$$xp_s(\dot{x} + \dot{p}_s) = xp(\dot{x} + \dot{p}) - \alpha_s\beta p\bar{x}\dot{p} \tag{6}$$

$$xp_d(\dot{x} + \dot{p}_d) = xp(\dot{x} + \dot{p}) - \alpha_d\beta p\bar{x}\dot{p} \tag{7}$$

Suppose that we start in 'full equilibrium', i.e. with actual price and quantity equal to reference price and quantity so that $\bar{p} = p$ and $\bar{x} = x$. From (2) and (3) we then have $p_s - p_d = p$. Substituting for these values in (6) and (7) and solving (5), (6), and (7) for $\dot{x}$, $\dot{p}_s$, $\dot{p}_d$, and $\dot{p}$ we obtain:

$$\dot{p}_s = \frac{1 - \alpha_s\beta}{\delta(1 - \alpha_d\beta) + \sigma(1 - \alpha_s\beta)}(\dot{D} - \dot{S}) \tag{8}$$

$$\dot{p}_d = \frac{1 - \alpha_d\beta}{\delta(1 - \alpha_d\beta) + \sigma(1 - \alpha_s\beta)}(\dot{D} - \dot{S}) \tag{9}$$

$$\dot{p} = \frac{1}{\delta(1 - \alpha_d\beta) + \sigma(1 - \alpha_s\beta)}(\dot{D} - \dot{S}) \tag{10}$$

$$\dot{x} = \frac{1}{\delta(1 - \alpha_d\beta) + \sigma(1 - \alpha_s\beta)}\{\sigma(1 - \alpha_s\beta)\dot{D} + \delta(1 - \alpha_d\beta)\dot{S}\} \tag{11}$$

Suppose that the compensation payments were complete in the sense that $\beta = 1$, and suppose that both the importing and the exporting countries decided to use any compensation receipts or to raise any compensation payments by subsidising or taxing their consumers or producers, $\alpha_s - \alpha_d = 1$. Then the system breaks down. From equation (10) it can be seen that with $\alpha_s \beta = \alpha_d \beta = 1$ any excess demand will lead to an infinite explosion of the market price. The reason is simple. With complete offset of the market price change due to any initial shift of D or S, there will be no incentive either for consumers or producers to change the quantities demanded or supplied; the excess demand or supply will persist indefinitely; and the market price will go up or down without limit.

Suppose that the rule was that the importing governments must not offset the market price change to consumers (i.e. $\alpha_d = 0$). Suppose that with a system of complete compensation the exporting countries offset the price change to their producers completely, but the importing countries did not offset the price change to their consumers at all. Then with $\alpha_d \beta = 0$ and $\alpha_s \beta = 1$ we have from (8), (9), (10), and (11):

$$\dot{p}_s = 0 \tag{12}$$

$$\dot{p}_d = \dot{p} = [\dot{D} - \dot{S}]/\delta \tag{13}$$

$$\dot{x} = \dot{S} \tag{14}$$

The net price to the suppliers will not change ($\dot{p}_s = 0$), since there is complete offset of the price change for the producers. The quantity on the market will, therefore, change by an amount equal to the shift in the supply curve ($\dot{x} = \dot{S}$). The price to consumers will change in the same way as the market price ($\dot{p}_d = \dot{p}$), since there is no offset to consumer price changes. This price change to consumers will have to be on a scale sufficient to cause a change in the amount demanded which offsets the whole of the initial gap between supply and demand ($\dot{D} - \dot{S}$), the change in price needed for this purpose being the greater, the smaller the price elasticity of demand ($[\dot{D} - \dot{S}]/\delta$).

Equations (8), (9), (10), and (11) can be used as a ready-reckoner to analyse the nature of various schemes according to the relative magnitudes of the various parameters δ, σ, β, α_s, and α_d and according to the probability of disturbances coming from the demand side ($\dot{D}$) or the supply side ($\dot{S}$) of the market. I will not indulge in the analysis of any more special cases. But these equations can be used for one other very obvious purpose. In what conditions are price-compensation schemes likely to lead to the stabilisation of the value of trade (px) and not merely to compensation for price changes? This question boils down to the question: In what conditions are variations in x likely to be small? For if x is constant, then compensation for variations in p obviously compensates also for variations in px.

From (11) we can see that one case in which $\dot{x}$ will be small is when $\dot{S}$ is small, σ is small, and $\alpha_s \beta$ is near unity. This is the case where (i) fluctuations are likely to originate on the demand side ($\dot{D}$ is large relatively to $\dot{S}$), (ii) the elasticity of supply is small, and (iii) price adjustment (through $\alpha_s \beta$) to exporters will in any case offset most of any price incentive to vary output. This is the ideal state of affairs for the use of a price-compensation scheme for the purpose of stabilising the producers' incomes.

There is apparently a symmetrical case where $\dot{S}$ is large relatively to $\dot{D}$, but δ is small and $\alpha_d \beta$ approaches unity. But this is not to be regarded in the same way for two reasons: first, because variability of S presumably involves supply factors like good or bad harvests which may hit some exporters and not others and equation (11) would in this case only indicate stability for total x and not for x for each individual exporting country; and, second, because for reasons outlined earlier in this note it would be wise for the scheme to require that $\alpha_d \beta$ approach zero rather than unity.

21

Structural Changes in the Rate of Interest and the Rate of Foreign Exchange to Preserve Equilibrium in the Balance of Payments and the Budget Balance

From Oxford Economic Papers, *vol. 36 (March 1984), pp. 52–66.*

The purpose of this note is to construct the simplest possible model to show how (1) the rate of interest and (2) the rate of exchange will affect the equilibrium growth paths of (1) the balance of international payments and of (2) the balance of governmental revenues and expenditures in a country which is successfully maintaining (a) a steady rate of growth of the total money demand for its products by means of fiscal policy and (b) a constant full-employment level of real economic activity by means of wage-rate adjustment.

We assume that we are dealing with a single small country in a large world economy so that what goes on in our single country does not appreciably affect what is going on in the rest of the world. We assume that in the rest of the world prices are rising at a constant rate, π^*; that the rate of interest ϱ^* is constant; and that the growth of real economic activity λ^* is constant.

I

The model of our small economy is as follows:

$$PQ = P_0 Q_0 e^{\alpha t} \tag{1}$$

where P is the price of domestic goods and Q is their output, the money expenditure on such goods being kept on a constant growth path, at a rate of growth α, by means of fiscal policy.

$$Q = A_1(Le^{\lambda t})^{(1-g)} K^g = A_1 L^{1-g} K^g e^{\lambda(1-g)t} \tag{2}$$

There is a Cobb–Douglas production function for Q with labour-expanding technical progress at a rate λ. L is kept constant at full employment by means of wage-rate flexibility. There is perfect competition so that L and K are paid the values of their marginal products.

If ϱ is the money rate of interest and π is the rate of price inflation, $\varrho-\pi$ is the real rate of interest. With capital receiving the value of its marginal product we would have $\varrho-\pi=\partial Q/\partial K$. Thus from (2) the capital–output ratio which we will call k could be expressed as

$$k \equiv \frac{K}{Q} = \frac{g}{\varrho-\pi} \tag{3}$$

From (2) and (3) we can obtain $(\varrho-\pi)^{1/1-g}/A_1 g = Le^{\lambda t}/K$. It follows that if $\varrho-\pi$ were constant, the growth rate of the capital stock which we will call γ would be the same as the rate of labour-expanding technical progress, λ, so that

$$\gamma \equiv \frac{1}{K}\frac{\mathrm{d}K}{\mathrm{d}t} = \lambda \tag{4}$$

From (2) it can be seen that with $\gamma=\lambda$, we have also $(1/Q)(\mathrm{d}Q/\mathrm{d}t)=\lambda$. From (1) we obtain $(1/P)(\mathrm{d}P/\mathrm{d}t)+(1/Q)(\mathrm{d}Q/\mathrm{d}t)=\alpha$ so that the rate of price inflation which we will call π can be expressed as

$$\pi \equiv \frac{1}{P}\frac{\mathrm{d}P}{\mathrm{d}t} = \alpha-\lambda \tag{5}$$

It follows from this analysis that if the real rate of interest $\varrho-\pi$ is kept constant at any given level, the rate of price inflation will be at the constant level $\alpha-\lambda$, no matter how high or low the level at which the real rate of interest is stabilised. It follows that, provided the real rate is kept constant, any change in that level will be the same for the money rate ϱ as for the real rate $\varrho-\pi$. It is the real rate of interest which is the true control variable whose effect we wish to examine. But since we are going to assume that it is kept constant at any given level, we can measure variations in the real rate $\Delta(\varrho-\pi)$ by variations in the level of the money rate $\Delta\varrho$.

$$PQ = P\frac{\mathrm{d}K}{\mathrm{d}t} + D + X - M$$

$$= PQk\lambda + D + X - M \tag{6}$$

The money demand for domestic products, PQ, is made up of the money demand for goods for new investment, $P(\mathrm{d}K/\mathrm{d}t)$, the money demand for goods for personal consumption, D, and the excess of the money value of receipts for the sale of exports, X, over money expenditure on imports,

M. The government is assumed to purchase no real goods and services; its fiscal function will be described in connection with equation (8).

$$D = (1 - s)\,Y \tag{7}$$

Individuals spend on consumption (D) a fixed proportion $(1 - s)$ of their spendable incomes (Y).

$$Y = PQ + G + (\varrho^* - \pi^*)\,EJ \tag{8}$$

In reaching the expression in (8) we assume that both persons and the government have adopted inflation-accounting methods of calculating their current incomes and expenditure. Thus we start with

$$Y = PQ + (\varrho - \pi)\,Z - \pi N + (\varrho^* + \epsilon - \pi)\,EJ_\varrho + \bar{G} \tag{8a}$$

where PQ measures the incomes received by persons from production either in the form of wages or return on capital, exclusive of inflationary capital gains on their capital (πPK). We assume that the government has financed any borrowing requirements by the issue either of notes (N) on which no interest is paid or of Treasury Bills (Z) on which the same nominal money rate of interest, ϱ, is paid as can be earned in private industry. But the recipients of debt interest ϱZ treat only the real interest $(\varrho - \pi)Z$ as current spendable income. They also deduct from their spendable incomes an amount πN to cover the loss of real value of their holding of notes. In addition persons receive income from their holding of foreign assets. We assume that foreign assets take the form of bills fixed in value in terms of foreign currency on which a nominal rate of interest (ϱ^*) is paid. Personal holdings of J are J_p, which are worth EJ_ϱ in terms of home currency where E is the rate of exchange (amount of home currency per unit of foreign currency). The money return on EJ_p (including capital gains) is therefore $(\varrho^* + \epsilon)\,EJ_p$, where

$$\epsilon \equiv \frac{1}{E}\frac{\mathrm{d}E}{\mathrm{d}t}$$

measures the capital gains in terms of home currency due to the depreciation, ϵ, of the home currency. The inflation-accounted return is thus $(\varrho^* + \epsilon - \pi)\,EJ_p$. Finally persons receive from the government lump-sum income subsidies (or, if negative, pay lump-sum taxes) equal to $\bar{G}$.

The government's fiscal function is simply to issue lump-sum income subsidies or to raise lump-sum incomes taxes in such amounts as to stabilise the total demand for the country's products, PQ, by the effect of these income subsidies or taxes on consumers' expenditure, D. The government's current budget deficit adjusted for inflation accounting can be expressed as

$$G = \bar{G} + (\varrho - \pi)Z - \pi N - (\varrho^* + \epsilon - \pi)EJ_g \tag{8b}$$

where $\bar{G}$ is its current payment of income subsidies, ϱZ is its national debt expenditure, and $(\varrho^* + \epsilon)EJ_g$ is its income (inclusive of capital gain) on governmental holding of a reserve of foreign assets worth J_g in terms of foreign currency. But inflation accounting implies that it should not include in its expenditures an amount equal to the reduction in the real value of its debts due to inflationary erosion, $\pi(Z+N)$, and that it should deduct from the gross yield on its foreign assets $(\varrho^* + \epsilon)EJ_g$ an amount (πEJ_g) to offset the inflationary erosion of the real value of its holding of foreign assets.

We are examining the equilibrium situation on the assumption that the competitiveness between home and domestic products is kept constant, which – as will be shown in (11) below – implies $\epsilon - \pi = -\pi^*$. Making use of this expression and eliminating $\bar{G}$ as between (8(a)) and (8(b)) we obtain the expression for Y given in (8). Personal disposable incomes are ultimately derived from their incomes from production, from the government's current budget deficit, and from the return on the country's foreign assets, EJ, where

$$J = J_p + J_g \tag{9}$$

We define the competitiveness of our country's products with foreign products as

$$C = \frac{EP^*}{P} \tag{10}$$

We will be examining structures in which C as well as ϱ are held constant in order to see what the implications are for the budget deficit and for the balance of payments. With C constant we would have from (10) and (5)

$$\epsilon = \pi - \pi^* = \alpha - \lambda - \pi^* \tag{11}$$

$$X = PA_2 Q_0^* e^{\lambda^* t} C^{\delta_x} \tag{12}$$

We assume that the amount of the country's goods bought for export, X/P, bears a certain ratio to the total real output in the rest of the world, $Q_0^* e^{\lambda^* t}$, this ratio depending upon the relative price of the goods, C, with a constant price elasticity of foreign demand of $-\delta_x < 0$.

$$m \equiv \frac{M}{D} = A_3 C^{1-\delta_m} \tag{13}$$

We assume that imports are purchased only for final consumption.[1] We assume that consumers allot a certain fraction of their total expenditure on consumption to the purchase of imports, and that this fraction,

1 We make this assumption solely to simplify the model. If foreign and domestic products are not perfect substitutes and if foreign goods were imported for investment, then in some form or another the production function in (2) would have to show output as dependent upon three inputs – labour, domestic products, and foreign products.

which we will call m, depends upon the relative price of imports with an elasticity of $1 - \delta_m$. This implies a price elasticity of demand for imports of $- \delta_m > 0$.[2]

$$\frac{\mathrm{d}(EJ)}{\mathrm{d}t} = X - M + (\varrho^* + \epsilon)EJ \tag{14}$$

The total increase in the value of foreign assets, whether held by the government as foreign-exchange reserves or by the private sector, must be equal to the amount earned by excess of exports over imports, $X - M$, plus the amount due to the rate of return (including capital gains) on existing foreign assets, $(\varrho^* + \epsilon)EJ$.

$$B = \frac{\mathrm{d}(EJ_\mathrm{g})}{\mathrm{d}t} - \pi EJ_\mathrm{g}$$

$$= E\frac{\mathrm{d}J_\mathrm{g}}{\mathrm{d}t} \pi^* EJ_\mathrm{g} \tag{15}$$

We measure the overall balance of payments (B) as that change in the value of its foreign-exchange reserves which the government must accept if it freely buys and sells foreign assets for domestic money at whatever level is needed to control the rate of exchange, E, in such a way as to keep the competitiveness index, C, constant.[3]

While we call $\mathrm{d}(EJ_\mathrm{g})/\mathrm{d}t - \pi EJ_\mathrm{g}$ the overall balance of payments, we will call $\mathrm{d}(EJ)/\mathrm{d}t - \pi EJ$ the level of foreign investment as contrasted with $P(\mathrm{d}K/\mathrm{d}t)$ which we call the level of domestic investment. It will be seen from (14) that the total holding of foreign assets, EJ, depends on what is accumulated from the balance of payments on current account before inflation-accounting adjustment – (i.e. balance of trade plus the return on existing foreign assets inclusive of any capital gains on such assets). $\mathrm{d}(EJ)/\mathrm{d}t - \pi EJ$ thus measures the rate at which current real resources are being saved and used to add to the stock of real capital abroad as contrasted with being saved and used to add to the stock of real capital at home. The finance of this level of real foreign investment is another matter. Private individuals, may, of course, 'invest' more funds abroad because, for example, the domestic rate of interest has fallen. But this in itself will not affect the level of foreign investment ($\mathrm{d}(EJ)/\mathrm{d}t - \pi EJ$) which depends simply on the balance of payments on current account (the excess of exports over imports plus the real return on foreign assets); it will affect the overall balance of payments by its effect on the flow of private funds. The private sector decides to hold more foreign assets (EJ_p up), and these are provided by the loss of

[2] If $\bar{M}$ is the quantity of imports and $\bar{P}$ $(= EP^*)$ is their price in home currency and if $(\bar{P}/M)(\mathrm{d}\bar{M}/\mathrm{d}\bar{P}) = - \delta_m$, then $(\bar{P}/\bar{P}\bar{M}) \cdot [\mathrm{d}(\bar{P}\bar{M})/\mathrm{d}\bar{P}] = 1 - \delta_m$.

[3] In (8(b)) we assumed that the government counted as current yield on its foreign assets only the excess of its gross receipts over the amount needed to preserve their real value intact. But from (15) it is clear that for this purpose with $\epsilon - \pi = - \pi^*$ the Government would have had to spend πEJ_g on the purchase of new foreign assets. $E(\mathrm{d}J_\mathrm{g}/\mathrm{d}t) - \pi^* EJ_\mathrm{g}$ thus measures the additional purchases which it has had to make in order to keep C constant.

government foreign-exchange reserves (EJ_g down) which are provided to finance the outflow of private capital without disturbing the rate of foreign exchange, E, needed to keep the competitiveness index, C, constant.

$$\frac{dW}{dt} = sY + \pi W \tag{16}$$

The increase in private wealth (W) is made up of two items. Wealth is increased by the amount saved (sY). But we have defined spendable incomes in such a way that savings exclude both capital gains on real capital (πPK) and the sums set aside to offset the inflationary erosion of other assets ($\pi(Z + N + EJ_p)$). This second element of increased wealth can thus be expressed as πW, where

$$W = PK + Z + N + EJ_p \tag{17}$$

since private wealth consists of privately held real capital (PK), bills (Z), notes (N), and foreign assets (EJ_p),

$$\frac{N}{W} = F_1(\varrho^* + \epsilon, \varrho) \tag{18}$$

$$\frac{EJ_p}{W} = F_2(\varrho^* + \epsilon, \varrho) \tag{19}$$

We assume that the proportions of personal wealth held in the form of money, N/W, and of foreign assets, EJ_p/W, depend upon the rates of return available at home and abroad. One can, of course, deduce from (17), (18) and (19) that the proportion of wealth held in bills and real capital $(PK + Z)/W = 1 - F_1 - F_2$. PK and Z are assumed to be treated as perfect substitutes by wealth holders in their portfolios since the rate of return (ϱ) is assumed to be the same for both.

With L, ϱ and C given and with constant parameters α, λ, ϱ^*, π^*, and λ^* we have the following 19 variables to be determined by these 19 equations, namely $Q, K, P, Y, D, G, Z, N, E, J, J_p, J_g, B, X, M, W, Y, \epsilon$ and π.

From (6), (7), (8), (16) and (17) we can derive

$$\frac{dN}{dt} + \frac{dZ}{dt} = G + \pi Z + \pi N - \pi^* EJ_g + E\frac{dJ_g}{dt} \tag{20}$$

(1) The government must issue cash or bills $((dN/dt) + (dZ/dt))$ to cover its purchase of foreign assets $(E(dJ_g/dt))$, its inflation-accounted budget deficit (G), and the net amount of cash payments which it has on inflation-accounting principles not included in its current outgoings $(\pi(Z + N) - \pi^* EJ_g)$.[4].

[4] It will have received in cash interest on its foreign assets $\varrho^* EJ_g$, but in its budget deficit in (8(b)) it has included $(\varrho^* + \epsilon - \pi) EJ_g$ in its current revenue. But from (11) $\epsilon - \pi = -\pi^*$ so that it has on inflation-accounting principles omitted $\pi^* EJ_g$ of its cash receipts from the calculation of its current revenue.

(2) It must keep its lump-sum cash subsidies or taxes and so its budget deficit G at the level necessary to maintain total demand, PQ, on its stable growth path.

(3) It must purchase or sell foreign assets ($E(\mathrm{d}J_g/\mathrm{d}t)$) at a rate necessary to control the foreign exchange rate so as to keep the competitiveness index, C, constant.

(4) It must be prepared to buy or sell bills for cash at a price for bills such as to yield a money return of ϱ on them.

Commercial bills issued by private persons are assumed to be perfect substitutes for Treasury Bills, both yielding a return of ϱ. Private producers will thus be able to sell bills of one kind or another to the government for cash to spend on real investment ($P(\mathrm{d}K/\mathrm{d}t)$) on the scale necessary to keep the yield on such investment (inclusive of any capital gains on it (πPK)) equal to ϱ and to leave themselves with their desired holding of cash.

The supply of cash necessary for this purpose can be derived from (18); but we shall not concern ourselves with this choice between liquid and less liquid domestic assets. The aspect of the capital market with which we are concerned is the choice between holding assets at home or abroad as shown in (19).[5]

II

We can now use (1) to (19) to determine the course of the budget deficit (G) and the overall balance of payments (B) as proportions of the national income (PQ), on the assumptions that ϱ and C are held constant.

From (4), (6), (7) and (8) we obtain

$$\frac{G}{PQ} = -1 + \frac{1 - k\lambda - x}{(1-m)(1-s)} - (\varrho^* - \pi^*)ej \tag{21}$$

and from (4), (6), (8), (14), (15), (16) and (19)

$$\frac{B}{PQ} = -(1-k\lambda)\frac{m + \dfrac{s}{1-s}f}{1-m} + \frac{x}{1-m}\left(1 + \frac{s}{1-s}f\right) + (\varrho^* - \pi^*)ej \tag{22}$$

where $$k \equiv \frac{K}{Q} = \frac{g}{\varrho - \pi}$$

$$m \equiv \frac{M}{D} = A_3 C^{1-\delta_m}$$

[5] The expression in (19) does not properly allow for a transactions demand for cash, that is to say, for an influence of PQ on the distribution of wealth holdings between cash, overseas assets, and other assets. This influence is neglected in the interests of simplification of the model.

$$x \equiv \frac{X}{PQ} = A_2 \frac{Q_0^*}{Q_0} C^{\delta_x} e^{(\lambda^* - \lambda)t}$$

$$f \equiv \frac{EJ_p}{W} = F_2(\varrho^* - \pi^* + \alpha - \lambda, \varrho)$$

and $$ej \equiv \frac{EJ}{PQ}$$

It may be observed that the real return on the country's foreign assets $(\varrho^* - \pi^*)EJ$, affects both G and B directly, being a direct addition to B and subtraction from G. The reason for this can be seen from (8) and (14). The receipt of interest on foreign assets by the private sector is part of the private sector's spendable income and thus reduces the amount of lump-sum income subsidies needed to maintain a given level of total demand; and the receipt of interest on its foreign-exchange reserves by the government reduces the level of the budget deficit needed to finance any given remaining level of lump-sum income subsidies. At the same time the receipt of interest on foreign assets by the private sector will enable the private sector to lend abroad to that extent without making a claim on the government's foreign-exchange reserves and the receipt of interest on the government's holding of foreign assets will directly add to such foreign-exchange reserves.

It is also to be observed that in equations (21) and (22) the terms k and f are functions of ϱ and the terms m and x are functions of C. If ϱ and C are held constant over time, all the terms in (21) and (22) will remain constant over time except x (which depends upon the value of $e^{(\lambda^* - \lambda)t}$) and ej, the determination of which remains to be examined. As far as x is concerned, the real income effect on X depends upon the rate of growth of the foreign real income and demand λ^*, while the real income element in PQ is λ. Thus with all relative prices constant (an effect achieved by keeping the competitiveness index C constant) X/PQ will rise or fall over time as $\lambda^* \gtreqless \lambda$. If, for example, $\lambda^* > \lambda$ then x will be rising; and from (21) G/PQ will be falling and from (22) B/PQ will be rising. Both these effects are easily understood. As X rises as a proportion of PQ, a lower level of consumption demand will be needed to keep PQ on its planned path, so that less lump-sum income subsidies will be needed. At the same time as X rises more quickly than PQ and than consumers' demand, X will rise more quickly than imports, M, so that – with any given level of private demand for foreign assets – the Government's foreign-exchange reserves will rise more quickly.[6]

[6] It is important to realise that if the foreign real growth rate exceeded the domestic real growth rate, it would in fact be impossible to continue *ad infinitum* with constant levels of C and ϱ. From (3), (4), (6) and (13) we can derive $D/PQ = (1 - k\lambda - x)/(1 - m)$. With k, λ, and m constant but $x \equiv X/PQ$ growing at a positive rate $(\lambda^* - \lambda)$, D would sooner or later be reduced to a negative figure. The demand for exports would come to exceed the total available supply of goods. As this situation developed the government would be having to reduce consumption by ever-increasing income taxes with a consequential ever-increasing budget surplus. On what may be called New Keynesian rules (see D. Vines, J. Maciejowski, and J. E. Meade, *Stagflation, Volume 2: Demand Management*

In order to obtain a complete account of what is happening to G/PQ and B/PQ, it is necessary to consider what determines $EJ/PQ \equiv ej$ in (21) and (22). This can be done in the following way.

From (1), (2), (3), (4), (6), (12) and (13)

$$X - M = X - \frac{m}{1-m}\{PQ(1-k\lambda) - X\}$$

$$= \frac{1}{1-m} X_0 e^{(\alpha-\lambda+\lambda^*)t} - \frac{m}{1-m} P_0 Q_0 (1-k\lambda) e^{(\alpha t)} \qquad (23)$$

so that from (14), (15) and (23)

$$\frac{d(EJ)}{dt} = (\varrho^* - \pi^* + \alpha - \lambda) EJ$$

$$+ \frac{1}{1-m} X_0 e^{(\alpha-\lambda+\lambda^*)t} - \frac{m}{1-m} P_0 Q_0 (1-k\lambda) e^{(\alpha t)} \qquad (24)$$

The solution of (24) gives:

$$\left.\begin{aligned} EJ = {} & (EJ)_0 e^{(\varrho^*-\pi^*+\alpha-\lambda)t} && \text{(i)} \\ & + \frac{X}{1-m} \cdot \frac{1 - e^{(\varrho^*-\pi^*-\lambda^*)t}}{\lambda^* - \varrho^* + \pi^*} && \text{(ii)} \\ & - \frac{mPQ(1-k\lambda)}{1-m} \frac{1 - e^{(\varrho^*-\pi^*-\lambda)t}}{\lambda^* - \varrho^* + \pi^*} && \text{(iii)} \end{aligned}\right\} \qquad (25)$$

where $X = X_0 e^{(\alpha-\lambda+\lambda^*)t}$ and $PQ = P_0 Q_0 e^{(\alpha t)}$

Element (i) in (25) represents the amount of foreign assets which would be accumulated from the reinvestment of the interest on an original stock of such assets. Element (ii) (which is >0 since the numerator and the denominator have the same sign) represents the addition to the stock due to the export element growing at a rate of $\alpha-\lambda+\lambda^*$, together with the continual reinvestment, at the compound interest rate of $\varrho^*-\pi^*+\alpha-\lambda$, of these export values. Element (iii) which is <0 represents the drain on the foreign assets resulting from the finance of imports due to the growth of consumers' demands.

From (25), dividing by PQ, one obtains

$$ej = (ej)_0 e^{(\varrho^*-\pi^*-\lambda)t}$$

$$+ \frac{x}{1-m} \frac{1 - e^{(\varrho^*-\pi^*-\lambda^*)t}}{\lambda^* - \varrho^* + \pi^*} \qquad (26)$$

(London: Allen & Unwin, 1983), Chapter V), the government should appreciate the real exchange rate (i.e. raise C) so as to restrict the foreign demand for exports and thus relieve the need for fiscal restriction of domestic consumption.

$$-\frac{m(1-k\lambda)}{1-m}\frac{1-e^{(\varrho^*-\pi^*-\lambda)t}}{\lambda-\varrho^*+\pi^*}$$

Thus the element $(\varrho^*-\pi^*)ej$ in (21) and (22) for G/PQ and B/PQ will not be constant over time. Its movement will depend upon the relations between λ^* and λ (which will determine the movement over time of $x=x_0e^{(\lambda^*-\lambda)t}$, between $\varrho^*-\pi^*$ and λ^*, and between $\varrho^*-\pi^*$ and λ. At any one point of time the terms x and m will be functions of C and the term k will be a function of ϱ. The other terms in (26) namely, $(ej)_0$, λ, λ^*, ϱ^* and π^* will be constant and independent of changes in C and ϱ.

III

We may now use (21) (22) and (26) to examine the effects upon the budget deficit (G/PQ) and the overall balance of payments (B/PQ) of a change, brought about by government policy, of the levels at which the rate of interest, ϱ, and the competitiveness index, C, are pegged. It is to be stressed that we are not concerned with the short-period turmoil caused by these changes of parameters, although these short-run dynamic changes are, of course, of the utmost importance. We are concerned in this paper only with the change in the structural equilibrium which will result when the short-run changes have converged (as we simply assume that they will do) on to a new structural equilibrium.

We start with the effect of changes in ϱ and C on ej. By partial differentiation of (26) we obtain

$$\frac{\partial(ej)}{\partial\varrho}=-\frac{g}{(\varrho-\pi)^2}\frac{m\lambda}{1-m}\frac{1-e^{(\varrho^*-\pi^*-\lambda^*)t}}{\lambda-\varrho^*+\pi^*} \tag{27}$$

and

$$\frac{\partial(ej)}{\partial C}=\frac{x\{(1-m)\delta_x+m(1-\delta_m)\}}{C(1-m)^2}\frac{1-e^{(\varrho^*-\pi^*-\lambda^*)t}}{\lambda^*-\varrho^*+\pi^*}$$
$$-\frac{m(1-k\lambda)(1-\delta_m)}{C(1-m)^2}\frac{1-e^{(\varrho^*-\pi^*-\lambda)t}}{\lambda-\varrho^*+\pi^*} \tag{28}$$

where

$$\delta_x=\frac{C}{x}\frac{\partial x}{\partial C}\quad\text{and}\quad 1-\delta_m=\frac{C}{m}\frac{\partial m}{\partial C}$$

From (27) it is clear that $\partial(ej)/\partial\varrho<0$. This is due solely to the fact that we are assuming the import content of domestic investment to be zero whereas m is the import content only of consumers' expenditure. When the rate of interest goes up, domestic investment falls. To maintain total demand, consumption must be stimulated and thus imports are stimulated and thus there is a *smaller* level of foreign investment as well as of domestic investment. Increased consumption takes the place of both. Foreign assets are less then they would otherwise have been. The increased domestic rate of interest may well (as we shall see below) improve the overall balance of payments in the sense of increasing the government's foreign-exchange reserves as the private sector 'invests' its money at home rather than abroad. This story illustrates clearly the difference between foreign investment (which depends upon the excess of exports over imports which, in our story, will have *fallen*) and the overall balance of payments (which increases the government's holding of foreign assets which in our story may well have *risen*).

In what follows we will assume that $\partial(ej)/\delta C$ in (28) is >0. The reason for this may be explained as follows. If we assumed $\lambda^* = \lambda$, then (28) could be rewritten as

$$\frac{\partial(ej)}{\partial C} = \frac{x\delta_x + \bar{m}(\delta_m - 1)}{C(1-m)} \frac{1 - e^{(\varrho^* - \pi^* - \lambda)t}}{\lambda - \varrho^* + \pi^*} \tag{29}$$

where $\bar{m} = M/PQ$. (Since $m/(1-m) = M/(D-M)$ and $D - M = PQ(1 - k\lambda - x)$, we have $[m/(1-m)](1 - k\lambda - x) = M/PQ \equiv \bar{m}$.) If $X = M$, then $\partial(ej)/\partial C$ in (29) is >0 if $\delta_x + \delta_m > 1$, which is the well-known Lerner–Marshall condition for an improvement in competitiveness to improve the balance of trade. We will simply assume that the elasticities δ_x and δ_m are sufficiently large for this to be true even though $X \neq M$ and $\lambda^* \neq \lambda$.

Partial differentiation of (21) and (22) gives

$$\left.\begin{aligned} \frac{\partial\left(\frac{G}{PQ}\right)}{\partial\varrho} &= \frac{g}{(\varrho - \pi)^2} \frac{\lambda}{(1-m)(1-s)} && \text{(i)} \\ &\quad - (\varrho^* - \pi^*) \frac{\partial(ej)}{\delta\varrho} && \text{(ii)} \end{aligned}\right\} \tag{30}$$

$$\left.\begin{aligned} \frac{\partial\left(\frac{G}{PQ}\right)}{\partial C} &= -\frac{x\delta_x + \bar{m}(\delta_m - 1)}{C(1-s)(1-m)} && \text{(i)} \\ &\quad - (\varrho^* - \pi^*) \frac{\partial(ej)}{\delta C} && \text{(ii)} \end{aligned}\right\} \tag{31}$$

$$\left.\begin{aligned} \frac{\partial\left(\frac{B}{PQ}\right)}{\partial\varrho} &= -\frac{s(1 - k\lambda - x)}{(1-s)(1-m)} \frac{\partial f}{\partial\varrho} && \text{(i)} \\ &\quad - \frac{g\lambda}{(\varrho - \pi)^2} \frac{(1-s)m + sf}{(1-s)(1-m)} && \text{(ii)} \\ &\quad + (\varrho^* - \pi^*) \frac{\partial(ej)}{\delta\varrho} && \text{(iii)} \end{aligned}\right\} \tag{32}$$

$$\left.\begin{aligned}\frac{\partial\left(\dfrac{B}{PQ}\right)}{\partial C} = \frac{1+\dfrac{s}{1-s}f}{C(1-m)}\{x\delta_x+\bar{m}(\delta_m-1)\} & \qquad \text{(i)}\\ +(\varrho^*-\pi^*)\frac{\partial(ej)}{\delta C} & \qquad \text{(ii)}\end{aligned}\right\} \quad (33)$$

From (30) it is clear that $\partial(G/PQ)/\partial\varrho>0$. Element (i) in (30) illustrates the fact that a rise in the rate of interest will reduce expenditure on domestic investment. In order to offset this, consumption expenditure must be stimulated, and this involves larger lump-sum income subsidies by the government. With $\partial(ej)/\partial\varrho<0$, element (ii) in (30) reinforces this need for a larger G. This influence is due solely to the fact that we are assuming the import content of the stimulated consumption expenditure to be greater than the import content of the reduced domestic investment. The increased demand for imports reduces foreign investment and this reduces the interest received on foreign assets, either by the private sector or by the government; but in both cases this calls for an increased budget deficit to stimulate domestic expenditure to the required level.

From (31) it is clear that $\partial(G/PQ)/\partial C<0$, provided that $x\delta_x+\bar{m}(\delta_m-1)>0$ and $\partial(ej)/\partial C>0$ both of which conditions rely upon the long-run foreign trade elasticities being sufficiently great. The reason is simple. If the increase in competitiveness improves the balance of trade, the national income can be held on target with a lower level of stimulation of domestic consumption by means of fiscal policy (element (i)) and the consequent reduction in the need for a budget deficit will be reinforced by the public and private receipt of interest on the increased foreign assets derived from the improved balance of trade (element (ii)).

In equation (32) there are two broad sets of factors pulling in opposite directions on the value of $\partial(B/PQ)/\partial\varrho$. Since $\partial f/\partial\varrho<0$ (i.e. a rise in home rate of interest will reduce the proportion of their wealth which people will decide to hold in the form of foreign assets), element (i) in (32) >0. This represents the fact that if people hold a smaller proportion of their wealth in foreign assets, then, as their total wealth grows through the accumulation of their new savings, a smaller proportion of these new annual savings will be used to purchase foreign assets; the annual overall balance of payments will be improved.[7] It is to be noted that the positive value of element (i) in (32) does not represent the large once-for-all improvement in the balance of payments during the turmoil of the process of adjustment to the new and higher domestic rate of interest. There will be a once-for-all inflow of capital funds into the government's foreign-exchange reserves as people shift their *existing* wealth from foreign to domestic assets. This large once-for-all improvement in EJ_g is not represented in (32) which, in element (i), reflects only the continuing annual improvement after the preliminary capital adjustment as the *new*

[7] This result strictly rests on the assumption that domestic wealth holders hold assets abroad but foreign wealth holders do not hold domestic assets.

savings are distributed in the new proportions between foreign and domestic assets.

Elements (ii) and (iii) of (32) pull in the opposite direction and are both <0. With a higher rate of interest domestic investment will be reduced. To keep the national income on target domestic consumption must be stimulated. But with a higher import content for expenditures on consumption than for those on domestic investment, this will stimulate imports and thus tend to worsen the overall balance of payments. This influence is reflected in the term $(1-s)m$ of the numerator in element (ii). But there is another factor also at work. The increased demand for imports will arise from that part of the consumers' increased spendable incomes which is spent and not saved. However, of the proportion which is saved a certain proportion will be used to purchase foreign as contrasted with domestic assets, and the resulting worsening of the overall balance of payments is represented in the term sf of the numerator in element (ii). If the government's fiscal policy simply took the form of the government purchasing the goods which because of the higher interest rate were no longer purchased for domestic investment, the whole of element (ii) in (32) would disappear. If the government fiscal policy took the form of stimulating domestic consumption by means of income subsidies in conditions in which there was no difference between the import contents of domestic investment and of consumption, the term $(1-s)m$ in element (ii) of (32) would no longer be operative. But the term sf would still have an effect. If people spend only 90 per cent of their spendable incomes, a fall of 90 in domestic investment would need a stimulation of spendable incomes by 100 to maintain total expenditures; but if the savings of 10 were partly used to purchase foreign assets, there would still be some strain on the overall balance of payments.

Element (iii) in (32) is also <0. This, as we have seen in discussion of (27), is due entirely to the greater import content of consumption expenditure, which by causing a reduced accumulation of foreign assets will reduce the credit item from interest on foreign assets in the overall balance of payments.

From (33) it can be seen that $\partial(B/PQ)/\partial C>0$ provided that $x\delta_x+\bar{m}(\delta_m-1)>0$. If the increased competitiveness improves the balance of trade, this will improve the overall balance of payments (element (i)). But this will be so not only because of the increase in $X-M$. The improved balance of trade will mean that domestic consumption need not be so greatly stimulated; this, as we have seen, means reducing spendable incomes by more than the desired reduction in domestic consumption; and this means that savings will be reduced, some part of which will cause a reduction in the demand for foreign assets. This is reflected in the term $[s/(1-s)]f$ in element (i) of (33). The improved balance of payments on current account will lead to a greater accumulation of foreign assets; and the consequential increase in interest on foreign assets will further improve the overall balance of payments (element (ii) of (33)).

If we assume that the basic element (i) is stronger than the elements (ii) and (iii) in (32) we can arrange the signs of the four factors in the following way:

	G	B
ϱ	$\dfrac{\partial\left(\dfrac{G}{PQ}\right)}{\partial\varrho} > 0$	$\dfrac{\partial\left(\dfrac{B}{PQ}\right)}{\partial\varrho} > 0$
C	$\dfrac{\partial\left(\dfrac{G}{PQ}\right)}{\partial C} < 0$	$\dfrac{\partial\left(\dfrac{B}{PQ}\right)}{\partial C} > 0$

With this pattern of effects, it would be possible to make any adjustment which was desired. Thus, to take one example, suppose that it was desired to keep G at its existing level but to increase B. An increase of ϱ accompanied by a suitable increase in C would keep G constant; since the reduced domestic investment would be matched by an improved balance of trade, there would be no need to change fiscal policy in order to stimulate or restrain consumption. But both the improved balance of trade (due to the increase in C) and the improved flow of new savings into domestic assets (due to the rise in ϱ) would serve to increase B.

It must, however, be remembered that, for the reasons discussed above, keeping ϱ and C constant will not suffice to keep G/PQ and B/PQ constant. The previous paragraph must be interpreted as showing only that a given combination of increases of ϱ and C, thereafter maintained unchanged at these higher rates, will after a period lead to a situation in which at every subsequent point of time B/PQ will be higher than it would otherwise have been without any change in G/PQ from what it would otherwise have been at that same point of time. If it were desired to control G/PQ and B/PQ at certain constant levels throughout their development (e.g. a balanced budget and a zero overall balance of payments with $G/PQ = B/PQ = 0$), it would be necessary for ϱ and C to be continually adjusted. But if one allowed for this, it would be necessary to take into account all the continuous dynamic turmoil due to the continuing adjustment of economic agents to changes in ϱ and C. That is a task which lies beyond the competence of the present author; and in any case it is perhaps best left to be dealt with in the construction of more complicated dynamic models which seriously attempt to simulate the actual behavioural adjustments which are to be observed in the real world.

22

A New Keynesian Bretton Woods

From The Three Banks Review, *no. 143 (June 1984), pp. 8–25. Meade presented an earlier version of this paper to an EEC seminar in Brussels in November 1983; he also put forward a similar set of rules, for the conduct of economic policy in the UK, in his evidence to the House of Commons Treasury and Civil Service Committee in April 1982 ('A proposed structure for international monetary arrangements', in House of Commons, Treasury and Civil Service Committee,* Memoranda on International Monetary Arrangements, *London: HMSO, July 1982, pp. 42–51).*

The purpose of this article[1] is to discuss the relationship between domestic macro-economic policies designed to maintain 'full employment' without a runaway inflation and international financial institutions and policies designed to facilitate these domestic objectives. The analysis itself is confined to the financial relationships between the developed, free-enterprise countries (basically the OECD countries). But it has important implications for the developing countries which are discussed at the close of the article.

The Onset of Stagflation

For some quarter of a century after World War II there was a general acceptance, at least in the United Kingdom, of what may be called the philosophy of Orthodox Keynesianism. It was regarded as a function of government to devise its financial policies – fiscal, monetary, and foreign-exchange-rate policies – so as to maintain total money expenditures on, and thus the demand for, the products of labour at whatever level was necessary to maintain 'full employment'. The effect of the public recognition of this governmental obligation to maintain full employment together with the building of a humane welfare state, designed to mitigate the hardships due to unemployment and other causes of poverty, was destined ultimately to lead to the threat of a

[1] I have to thank Dr Charles Goodhart, Mr John Odling-Smee, Professor John Williamson, and Mr Sam Brittan for comments on my original paper; but they are, of course, in no way responsible for the views expressed in this article.

runaway explosive inflation, so long as money wage-rates continued to be set by a process of *Free Collective* Bargaining or of what may perhaps more appropriately be called *Uncontrolled Monopoly* Bargaining. The welfare state made people less frightened of unemployment; the government obligation to expand money expenditures so as to maintain full employment made over-ambitious wage claims by monopolistic unions more insistent, since the fear of adverse effects on jobs was reduced; employers were more willing to grant wage increases since they expected in general that money expenditures would be expanded sufficiently to cover increased costs; this meant that they did not hesitate to raise selling prices to cover costs; and the consequent increase in the cost of living led to further increases in wage claims with the threat of a vicious spiral of runaway inflation so long as real demands were in excess of real productivity.

There were rumblings of this throughout the 1950s–60s with an increasing realisation that the logic of Orthodox Keynesianism required an incomes policy, that is to say, state intervention to control the money wage-rate. In fact the logic of Orthodox Keynesianism is that a centrally controlled money price of labour instead of, for example, a centrally controlled money price of gold is needed to form the monetary anchor for the economy.

The final explosion came with the OPEC rise in the price of imported oil in the early 1970s. Any failure to accept the fall in the real standard of living represented by this rise in the price of an important imported component in the cost of living was bound to cause an explosive inflation. Wages rose to offset the effect on the cost of living of the increased price of imported oil; this raised costs and prices still further so that wages rose still further which caused a further rise in costs and prices and thus a threat of explosive inflation so long as the inevitable fall in real income was not accepted.

The logic of Orthodox Keynesianism is to use the panoply of financial policies – fiscal, monetary, foreign exchange rate – to maintain *real* output and employment and to use the money wage-rate to control the inflation of *money* prices and incomes. It is, however, doubtful whether this can be made to work without excessive governmental intervention in the affairs of business at the micro level.

A New Keynesian Attack on Stagflation

This consideration suggests the advocacy of what may be called New Keynesianism, by which is meant the use of the whole panoply of Keynesian demand management financial policies for the control of money expenditures but with the objective, not of maintaining *real* output and employment, but of maintaining the total *money* expenditures on the products of labour (i.e. the money GDP or the money national income) on a moderate predetermined growth path, thus avoiding by Keynesian measures total monetary inflations or deflations. This would control inflation; but in order to be compatible with full employment it would need to be combined with a radical reform of wage-fixing arrangements so that money rates of pay were fixed so as to maintain *real* employment and output.

This is to use the wage-rate (price of labour) at the micro level in the natural market way to increase in any sector the demand for labour where there is an excess supply and *vice versa*. It is not suggested that this is an easy reform in modern conditions. It involves dealing somehow or other at the micro level with the monopolistic powers of companies, trade unions, and other bodies so as to ensure that, where unemployed resources exist, an increase in demand leads to an increase in output and employment rather than to an increase in prices and incomes for the sole benefit of the existing owners and workers.

To tackle this problem certainly requires a major change in institutions and attitudes whereby much less emphasis is put on wage settlements as the means of affecting the levels and the distribution of real incomes, while much more emphasis is put on other measures (fiscal, social security etc.) as the appropriate means for obtaining a socially acceptable distribution of real income. All this constitutes much the most difficult part of the problem politically and its solution depends very much in each country upon the particular institutions, customs, historical background, and political possibilities of that country. Its solution is essential for the future welfare of society in the countries of the free democratic way of life; but that is not the subject of the present article.

The present article concentrates on certain aspects of the other limb of New Keynesianism, namely the use of financial policies in each country for the demand management purpose of maintaining the total money national income or GDP (i.e. the total of money expenditures on the country's products) on a moderate predetermined growth path. This has, of course, an important feed-back upon the wage-fixing problem. If, for example, it is known that the total money national income is going to rise by 5 per cent and no more, then any individual claim for a rise of more than 5 per cent in pay must mean that someone else must get less – either a cut in profit margins, or a less than 5 per cent rise for some other group, or an increase in unemployment. Thus the public realisation of the true possibilities in the economy should be increased; and this should help with the reform of wage-setting procedures. In this respect to take the rate of increase in the money national income as the basic objective of counter-inflationary financial policy is much more sensible than to take a given rate of growth in some monetary aggregate. M_0, M_1, M_2, etc. to the man or woman in the street in the United Kingdom sounds like a reference to a series of motorways, whereas the total money income available for distribution is a much more meaningful idea. Moreover, any particular M may, as experience has shown, vary without a corresponding change in expenditures, as people change their preferences for one type of financial asset rather than another; and it is after all the total of money expenditures which one intends to control indirectly by controlling M. Why not then put resources into improving the statistics of the money GDP and watch that directly rather than movements in M?

The Budget Balance as a Policy Objective

The same sort of objection may be raised against trying to control the budget balance (i.e. the PSBR) as an indirect means of inflation control. It is the total expenditure on goods and services rather than the public sector borrowing or even total public expenditure which is the ultimate objective for control of monetary inflation and deflation.

This is not to argue that the budget balance should be disregarded. It is in itself of great importance quite apart from the control of monetary inflation or deflation. A large budget deficit, properly corrected for inflation accounting and after adjustment for true productive capital expenditures, means that the state is mopping up savings and using them to finance current public consumption. The size of the real current budget balance is thus a matter for legitimate concern in so far as it affects the long-run rate of growth in the economy through its effect upon the proportion of the national income which is saved and devoted to capital development rather than to current consumption. This is a long-run structural concern which is quite different from any short-run concern about the control of inflation. A structural maladjustment of the budget balance and investment ratio can well persist in macro-economic equilibrium conditions in which there is full employment and no threat of inflation or deflation.

The Domestic Aspects of Monetary and Budgetary Policies

In a closed economy there would then be two major forms of financial policy, namely monetary policy displaying itself in the form of variations in rates of interest, and budgetary policy displaying itself in the form of variations in government spending programmes or in rates of tax. To set against these two instruments there would be two objectives of macro-economic policy, namely the maintenance of the money GDP on its moderate predetermined growth path and the maintenance of the budget balance at a level which gives the desired structural balance between domestic investment and domestic consumption.

In a closed economy the general strategy for the use of these two weapons for the attainment of these two targets is clear and familiar. A constraint on the GDP can be achieved by a more restrictive budgetary policy and by tighter monetary policy; if, however, that results in too low a relation of investment to consumption, the balance can be put right by an increase in tax rates (which will largely restrict consumption) combined with a reduction in interest rates (which will largely stimulate investment).

Thus one can think of the problem in the way in which a control engineer would think of it. One needs a model of the dynamic, lagged, interrelationships between the main aggregate variables in the economy (consumption, investment, wage-rates, prices, earnings, profits, output, employment, tax rates, interest rates, etc., etc.) including equations which explain the formation of expectations about movements in these variables. One then asks a control engineer to apply his or her mysterious and magic powers to tell one what rules about the setting of rates of tax and rates of interest in the light of past and current events are most likely to keep the GDP on its planned path together with an acceptable budget balance.

Designed in this way one is not *a priori* linking one weapon to one target (e.g. tax rate to control GDP and interest rate to control the budget balance and investment ratio); one is designing the best possible package of tax rate and interest rate to obtain the most desirable package of GDP level and investment ratio. The best rules may turn out to put most stress on the GDP objective in determining the tax rate and on the investment ratio in determining the interest rate. Indeed, that will be the result if the tax rate has a rather more general effect on all forms of expenditure whether on consumption or investment, while the interest rate affects mainly investment.

But there is another very important reason why this allocation of weapons to targets may be desirable. It is very important to be able to nip in the bud deviations of the money national income from its steady growth path because monetary booms or slumps are apt to feed on themselves in a vicious circle due to multiplier effects, accelerator effects, and price-expectation effects.[2] On the other hand an imbalance between investment and consumption in an otherwise stable economy constitutes a structural growth problem which can be tackled in a more leisurely fashion. It is, therefore, important to use a quickly acting regulator to control the GDP and to relegate the less quickly acting instruments to the control of the investment ratio. The interest rate does probably work mainly on investment expenditures and does that slowly and with considerable lags since it involves revising investment plans. On the other hand it should be possible to devise some forms of tax regulator which could be varied fairly frequently and promptly and which would have a prompt effect upon expenditures. This consideration would strengthen the case for relying primarily on fiscal policy for the control of the GDP.[3]

The International Aspects of Monetary, Budgetary and Foreign-exchange Policies

This conclusion is greatly reinforced when one turns to the consideration of an open economy on the assumption that there is a basic freedom of trade and of capital movements between it and the rest of the world. We

[2] Once a boom in expenditures has started those whose incomes have risen will spend more (a multiplier effect), producers will spend more on capital equipment to meet the increased demand for their products (an accelerator effect), and rising prices may cause people to speed up their purchases to avoid paying still higher prices (a price-expectation effect). And conversely if a slump in expenditure occurs.

[3] This allocation of particular financial weapons to particular financial targets is not, of course, an absolute one. It is not suggested that the effects of tax policy on the investment ratio and of interest policy on the GDP can or should be ignored. But it is claimed that for the reasons given in the text most weight should be given to the tax rate effects on the

have now three instruments of financial policy – fiscal, monetary, and foreign-exchange-rate policies – to attain three objectives – control of GDP, of investment ratio, and of the balance of payments. A natural first reaction is to suggest that there should be a freely floating exchange-rate regime in which case the foreign exchange rate would automatically serve as the instrument to equate supply to demand in the foreign exchange market and thus keep the balance of payments in balance. In one sense that is more or less what will be proposed in what follows; but it is subject to some very important provisos.

The situation is fundamentally complicated by the fact that the international flow of capital funds constitutes a very important element in the balance of payments and that it is very sensitive to changes in interest rates. One cannot simply ignore this relationship in designing interest-rate policies; and this consideration strongly reinforces the argument for controlling the GDP primarily by tax policy which does not have the same sensitive effect upon the flow of capital funds in the balance of payments.

The international flow of capital funds is, of course, influenced by many factors besides the relative rates of yield on domestic and foreign assets. Political developments may influence expectations about the outlook for capital funds in different regions. Speculative bubbles may cause expectations of capital gains on given stock exchanges. Ill-informed 'chartism' or other fashionable simple predictors of future developments may affect the movements of funds. And so on. But relative rates of yields are also an important factor influencing the investment of funds.

Thus one must allow for the fact that international capital flows are sensitive to changes in national rates of yield and that at least for a time, while portfolio adjustments are being made, a reduction in interest rates in one country, other things being equal, will result in a substantial outflow of funds which will put a heavy pressure on that country's foreign exchange rate. Consider then a country – B for Britain – which lets its currency Sterling freely float so as to look after its balance of payments, which uses variations in its tax rate successfully to keep its GDP on target, and which keeps its interest rates low (and its tax rate therefore correspondingly high) so as to maintain a high desired investment ratio. Suppose the outside world to be made up of country A – A for America with a Dollar currency – which keeps its GDP on a reasonable path but with a very low tax rate and a very high rate of interest. Very low rates of interest in B combined with very high rates in A will cause a heavy flow of capital funds from B to A; with a floating exchange rate sterling will depreciate and the dollar appreciate until speculators think that sterling is so undervalued that it is bound to start appreciating at a rate which will offset the higher interest yield on dollar securities. If there were a 6 per cent difference in interest rates which was expected to last for 5 years, sterling would have to depreciate by some 30 per cent below its expected

GDP and to the interest rate effects on the investment ratio. Throughout this article any suggestion of the allocation of one particular financial instrument to the attainment of one particular objective should be subject to this qualification.

equilibrium level. The problem is complicated and intensified by the time-lags in the adjustment of imports and exports to changes in their prices – the perverse effects of the well-known J-curve.[4] A 30 per cent depreciation of sterling may at first worsen country B's balance of trade as the price of its imports rises, thus intensifying the immediate strain on the foreign exchange rate. Such overshooting of its exchange rates could play havoc with country B's domestic policies for full employment and price stability.

For this reason so long as there are free international capital movements it is not possible for country B to design its monetary policy and set its interest rates in such a way as to attain a desired domestic investment ratio regardless of monetary policies in the rest of the world, even though it allows free movements in its foreign exchange rate. But this does not mean that it has no control over its investment ratio provided that it is indifferent between investment at home and investment abroad.

Suppose country B by a successful New Keynesian combination of fiscal control and wage-setting institutions to be enjoying full employment without excessive inflation, but that because of high interest rates abroad it is doing so with undesirably high interest rates at home, matched by an undesirably low tax rate and an undesirably high budget deficit needed to offset the domestic deflationary effects of high interest rates. Country B wishes to maintain its GDP on its present growth path but with a higher tax rate and thus lower consumption expenditures, matched somehow or another by higher expenditures on capital development at home and abroad. It lowers its interest rate moderately; this gives some stimulus to domestic investment; it also causes some moderate depreciation of sterling; after the perverse J-curve has worked itself out and the sterling exchange rate has settled down to a new equilibrium level which balances supplies and demands in the foreign exchange market, there will result an increase in country B's balance of trade on a scale which matches the outflow of capital funds caused by the reduction in the interest rate, so that there is a corresponding increase in its investment of real resources abroad, i.e. in its foreign investment; the rise in expenditures on its home products due to the increase in its domestic investment and to the increase in its foreign investment (i.e. in the excess of its exports over imports of goods and services) means that it must now raise its tax rates and reduce its budget deficit in order to prevent an undesirable inflation of its money GDP. The ratio of total investment to consumption may well have been raised principally by a change in the exchange rate rather than by a change in the rate of interest and thus by an increase in foreign investment rather than in domestic investment. This will certainly be the case if domestic investment is not very sensitive to the rate of interest while international capital flows are very sensitive to the rate of interest and the balance of trade is ultimately sensitive to changes in the real rate of foreign exchange.

[4] The process whereby a depreciation, by raising the price of imports, *initially* worsens the balance of trade until a rising volume of exports and/or a falling volume of imports serves to improve it.

Principles of Financial Policy for a Single Country

To meet these basic interrelationships country B might well conduct its financial policies on the following principles.[5]

Rule (1) It relies primarily upon fiscal policy, in the form of an annual budgetary review backed by some tax regulators (such as a variation in the rate of VAT) which can be used in between the annual budget changes, to maintain its money GDP on a predetermined growth path.

Rule (2) Against the background of this controlled growth of the total money demand for the products of labour, it achieves a basic reform of its wage-fixing institutions in order to promote real output and employment.

Rule (3) It allows its foreign exchange rate freely to float subject to such official interventions in the foreign exchange market as are mentioned under Rule (9) below.

Rule (4) It chooses and announces a central target exchange rate between sterling and dollars at bW_b/aW_a where W_b is the value in sterling of an hour's work in country B and W_a is the value in dollars of an hour's work in country A and a and b are shift parameters which are discussed under Rule (8).

Rule (5) The central target exchange rate is announced at frequent regular intervals (e.g. monthly or once a quarter) after revision in the light of movements in W_a and W_b. Thus, in so far as differences in inflation rates are concerned, there is no element of cumulative disequilibrium ending inevitably with a cataclysmic change in a rigid adjustable peg such as delights the heart of the speculator, but rather a steady crawling peg offsetting the inflationary divergences of national policies.

Rule (6) The authorities in country B announce a zone or band around this central target exchange rate with upper and lower limits of $\pm x$ per cent from the central rate. At the one extreme, as proposed by Professor Williamson [in *The Exchange Rate System*, Washington DC: Institute for International Economics, September 1983], one might have a soft zone with variations of $\pm$ 10 per cent about the central rate, which would mean merely that the authorities hoped to keep the exchange rate within this wide zone. At the other extreme one might have a hard band with variations of $\pm$ 2 per cent which meant that the authorities in fact undertook to keep the rate within these narrow limits. The choice is of course, of basic importance; and it would probably be wise to adopt the less hard zone with its generous limits in order to allow erratic fluc-

[5] These principles are here stated in the form of precise, crisp rules in order to highlight the basic underlying relationships. In the real world their application would necessarily take a rather less strictly prescribed form. In particular they would be subject to the qualification already noted in footnote 3.

tuations in the international movements of capital funds to expend their impact effects in large measure on exchange-rate fluctuations.

Rule (7) The authorities would use monetary policy with its effect on interest rates and so on capital flows in the balance of payments as the normal instrument for trying to keep the foreign exchange rate within the stated zone or band.

Rule (8) In the periodic revisions of the central target exchange rate consideration would be given to making moderate small changes in the shift parameters a and b. A rise in W_b represents a rise in the price of labour; a rise in b may be thought of as a fall in the 'quality' of labour, so that bW_b measures the price of a unit of a given amount of 'labour efficiency'. A rise in b/a might, therefore, be appropriate if the productivity of labour were rising more rapidly in country A than in country B. This is not, however, certain. If productivity is rising more quickly in A than in B, selling prices will presumably be rising less rapidly in relation to wage-rates in A than in B. The substitution of A's products for B's products in world markets would then tend to put a pressure on B's balance of trade. But at the same time if successful full-employment policies are carried out in A and B, total real income and thus the total demand for imports will be rising more rapidly in A than in B which will put a pressure on A's balance of trade. It is not at all certain whether the substitution effect which is adverse to B's balance of trade or the income effect which will be adverse to A's balance of trade will be the stronger. It is for this reason that in this article the central target exchange rates have been described as being related to money wages rather than to money wage costs or to the money price per unit of tradeable output, though there are no doubt arguments in favour of the latter procedures.

In any case there is another and more basic criterion on which adjustments of the shift parameters a and b must be judged; and if this criterion is observed, any maladjustments due to the choice of money wage-rates as the index of monetary inflation will automatically be ultimately corrected. Suppose country A to be running an undesirably high budget deficit and low investment ratio. On the basis of the previous analysis it needs to depreciate its real exchange rate in order to promote a surplus on its balance of trade and thus its foreign investment. It needs a movement in its competitiveness in order to expand the sales of its products; and this requires its labour to be made 'cheaper' relative to country A's labour; and this can be achieved by a rise in the ratio b/a. Changes in these shift parameters ultimately affect the country's competitiveness and are thus the means for achieving a gradual structural adjustment of the budget balance and investment ratio.

Rule (9) The basic foreign-exchange regime would thus be freely floating exchange rates influenced by monetary policy designed to achieve appropriate adjustments in interest rates and so in capital flows. But such a regime should properly be modified by official intervention in the foreign exchange markets where such action was needed to prevent large, temporary, and unnecessary deviations of the exchange rate from a well-considered central target rate – fluctuations of a size and kind which could otherwise be contained, if at all, only by extreme and unacceptable changes in the rate of interest. Such occasions can well arise from movements of funds for speculative or political reasons or because of fashionable ill-informed analysis of the situation.

Intervention may also well be desirable on those occasions in which, on the principles discussed in Rule (8), a change is being made in the target real exchange rate in order to adjust the underlying competitiveness of the country's exports. Because of the perverse effects of the downward slope of the notorious J-curve the immediate, but temporary, effects of a rise in b/a might be to reduce instead of to increase the country's balance of trade. In order to prevent the perverse rise in interest rates which might then otherwise be needed to attract foreign funds so as to keep the exchange rate within its zone or band, there would be a clear case for temporary support of the foreign exchange rate by the use of official foreign-exchange reserves to tide over the period until the depreciation had its effect in increasing the balance of trade.

It is impossible to lay down precise rules to govern the occasions for official intervention. The general principle would be to prevent perverse movements in the foreign exchange rate which were likely to prove only temporary and whose control would otherwise need perverse and temporary adjustments of interest rates; but the application of this principle must inevitably remain a matter for informed judgement on the part of the authorities concerned.

Principles of Financial Policy for a Full Community of Nations

So much for the rules of action for one small country acting alone. At the other extreme the question arises what the rules would look like if all the free-enterprise countries of the world joined together in a community to attempt to apply these principles jointly.

One should not put much, if any, weight on harmonising the rates of inflation of money prices, money costs, and money incomes in the various countries. If the crawling peg principle of frequent and regular changes in the *W*'s and similar components of central target exchange rates is adopted, there is little or no cost in divergences in actual inflation rates. The extra degree of freedom for national governments may make it easier for them to maintain a high and stable level of employment; and it is the maintenance of a high level of *real* economic activity by methods which do not beggar my neighbour that really matters.[6]

[6] This is strikingly illustrated by one of the main exercises which the author of this article and two colleagues carried out in a recent book on demand management [D. Vines, J. Maciejowski and J. E. Meade, *Stagflation, Volume 2: Demand Management*, London: Allen & Unwin, 1983]. They asked what would have happened if during the years since 1972 the United Kingdom had by the use of fiscal policy and wage-setting reforms maintained full employment, on the lines discussed above for country B, in spite of the great world recession with its inevitable reduction in the *real* demand for United

In view of these *desiderata* the rules for the full community of nations might be as follows:

Rules (1) and (2) Each country would be free to design its own fiscal policy and wage-setting arrangements so as to achieve by these domestic measures a high and stable level of employment and real output. For the reasons given earlier in this article they might be well advised to do so by New Keynesian rather than Orthodox Keynesian means; and no doubt discussion and exchange of information on these methods would be helpful. But what really matters is the achievement of full employment by these innocuous domestic measures.

Rule (3) There would be a basic freely floating exchange regime.

Rule (4) The member countries would co-operate in setting a consistent structure of central target exchange rates. If the currency of country A (e.g. America's dollar) were taken for the numeraire these could be expressed as:

$$\frac{bW_b}{aW_a}, \quad \frac{cW_c}{aW_a}, \quad \frac{dW_d}{aW_a}, \quad \text{etc.}$$

The same result could be achieved by expressing the rates in terms of a Community Currency Unit (CCU).[7]

Rule (5) The Community would revise and announce at frequent and regular intervals the central target exchange rates in view of changes in the *W*'s.

Rule (6) The Community would announce given zones or bands for the target exchange rates with a given degree of variation between the upper and lower limits.

Kingdom products. The answer is that employment might have been maintained but only at the expense of a large strain on foreign-exchange reserves and of a corresponding increase in the national debt as relaxed fiscal policy was needed to maintain economic activity while the foreign demand for United Kingdom products was severely depressed. This increase in debt would have continued until the end of the perverse J-curve period when a reduction in the United Kingdom real exchange rate would have managed to restore her balance of trade in spite of the maintenance of her real demand for imports when the world's real demand for her exports had fallen.

7 Suppose one CCU to consist of A units of currency A, plus B units of currency B, plus C units of currency C etc. Then if a consistent structure of target exchange rates bW_b/aW_a, cW_c/aW_a, etc. were observed, the value in B's currency of one CCU would be

$$bW_b\left\{\frac{B}{bW_b}+\frac{A}{aW_a}+\frac{C}{cW_c}+\text{etc.}\right\}=bW_bQ$$

where Q measures the total amount of 'effective labour' which one CCU can command at any time throughout the community. The central target exchange rate for country B's sterling would be expressed as bW_bQ for one CCU; and B/bW_bQ would measure the proportional weight of sterling in the composition of a CCU.

Rule (7) The Community would co-operate continuously in national monetary policies so as to set a structure of national domestic interest rates which satisfied two conditions. First, the rates of interest relatively to each other would be adjusted so as to maintain foreign exchange rates within the agreed zones or bands. Secondly, the whole structure of rates of interest would be revised downwards if throughout the Community it was found that excessive budget deficits would otherwise be needed in order to offset the deflationary effects on the money GDP of high interest rates.

It is in this second requirement that the Community rules would differ from the single-country rules. In the case of a single country which found that it was having to run an undesirably high budget deficit and low investment ratio in order to prevent a deflation of its money GDP, the rule would be that it should depreciate its real exchange rate in order to improve its balance of trade and so its foreign investment. Clearly it would not make sense to say that every country should simultaneously depreciate its real exchange rate in terms of every other currency so that every country should improve its balance of trade with every other country. What is needed in these circumstances is a simultaneous reduction in interest rates in all countries in order to stimulate domestic investment in all the countries.

Rule (8) However, if only one country or a limited number of countries were experiencing undesirably high budget deficits as a result of the use of fiscal policy to prevent a deflation of their money GDPs, then a depreciation of the real exchange rates of this group of countries in terms of the currencies of the rest of the Community is the appropriate reaction; and this requires a rise in the shift parameters of the former group on the grounds which were discussed above at length for the single-country case.

Rule (9) There remains the problem of official intervention in foreign exchange markets. The ideal arrangement would be that the national monetary authorities should abstain from all intervention but that there should be some joint Community body which intervened when a temporary perverse movement or overshooting of exchange rates was otherwise likely to occur. Such intervention would have to be left to the joint judgement of the Community's monetary authorities on the principles discussed above for the single-country case. A particular example of such a case would be where a change in structural real exchange rates had been made on the principles just described in Rule (8), in order to expand the balance of trade of one set of countries with excess budget deficits at the expense of the balance of trade of another set of countries with excess budget surpluses; the temporary perverse effect of such a change in exchange rates on balances of trade could be offset by the use of official exchange interventions to the advantage of both parties concerned.

Principles of Financial Policy for a Regional Group

Finally one may consider what would be the sensible rules for a group of countries which wished to form a Community of this kind but which could not enlist the membership of all other free-enterprise countries. The relations between the members would be on the pattern just outlined for Community behaviour, but the relations between the members as a group and the outside world would have to be on the single-country pattern. The rules might be as follows:

Rules (1) and (2) The member countries would undertake to rely on fiscal policy and wage-setting as their domestic weapons for maintaining a high and stable level of real economic activity without a runaway inflation. It would be desirable though not essential that they should agree to do this on New Keynesian principles which would involve each member country in announcing a target path for the growth of its money national income or GDP.

Rule (3) The member countries would agree to rely basically on a regime of freely floating foreign exchange rates.

Rule (4) They would agree on a set of central target exchange rates for each country's currency in terms of a Community Currency Unit on the lines described under Rule (4) in the full Community case. Thus the sterling/CCU rate would be set at bW_bQ where

$$Q = \frac{B}{bW_b} + \frac{C}{cW_c} + \text{etc.}$$

and B, C, etc. were the amounts of the currencies of the member countries which were included in the CCU. They would also agree on a central target rate for the exchange between the CCU and outside currencies which would presumably be represented by the dollar. Such a rate could be expressed as one CCU $= aW_aQ$, since Q would measure the total amount of 'effective labour' which one CCU would command in the Community while $1/aW_a$ would measure the amount of 'effective labour' which one dollar would command in country A.

Rule (5) These rates of exchange would all be announced and revised at frequent regular intervals in view of changes in the W's.

Rule (6) The Community would decide on zones or bands with upper and lower limits for these rates of exchange.

Rule (7) The Community would continuously review the monetary and interest-rate policies of the members so as to achieve a structure of yields in the various member countries which satisfied two conditions; first, that the rates of interest relative to each other were such as to keep the rate of exchange of each member's currency in terms of the CCU within the agreed zone or band; and, second, that the absolute level of the whole structure of Community rates was raised or lowered so as to keep the CCU/dollar rate within the agreed zone or band.

Rule (8) If one member country had to incur an unduly large budget deficit as a result of fiscal policy designed to prevent a fall in its money GDP, then its shift parameter in the determination of its central target exchange rate on the CCU would be raised. If, on the other hand, all the members of the CCU were simultaneously experiencing unduly large budget deficits as a result of fiscal policies designed to maintain their money GDPs, then the shift parameter *a* in the CCU/dollar rate would be lowered.

Rule (9) All actual interventions in the foreign exchange markets would be carried out by a joint Community pool of currencies or other forms of official finance.

These would be the principles on which an institution such as the European Monetary System might well be developed – to summarise their implications, each member country would be free to devise its own fiscal and wage-setting policies and institutions so as to maintain economic activity without runaway inflation, but there would be a very extensive pooling of sovereignty in the case of monetary policy, foreign exchange rates, and official intervention. Central target exchange rates would be agreed and continuously adjusted in a crawl to offset differences in rates of domestic inflation. National monetary policies would be jointly managed with the object of keeping exchange rates within certain predetermined zones or bands. The real central target rates of exchange would be jointly adjusted so as to relieve members of any undesirably large budget deficits or surpluses which might result from their domestic use of fiscal policy for the maintenance of domestic equilibrium. Finally, all official interventions in foreign exchange markets would be undertaken by a Community authority for the purpose of avoiding temporary perverse strains on the members' balances of international payments.

The Interests of the Developing Countries

The preceding analysis has been concerned only with the reform of the financial relationships between the developed, free-enterprise countries which would enable these countries to maintain full employment without a runaway inflation. Success in such an enterprise is, however, of great importance for the developing countries.

First, the maintenance of a high level of economic activity in the developed countries would automatically lead to a high level of demand for many of the products of developing countries and thus to an improvement in their terms of trade.

Second, the reduction of trade barriers by the developed countries on imports from the developing countries is of the utmost importance; but it is politically very difficult, if not impossible, for the developed countries to go far in this direction so long as their own competing industries are depressed, their workers are unable to find jobs in expanding sectors, and there is in consequence pressure for increased protection from imports.

Third, the granting of financial aid or the provision of funds for capital development in the developing countries, as well as the removal of barriers on imports, may in some cases be difficult for developed countries which are themselves facing balance-of-payments problems. Such obstacles would be removed if there were a smoothly working mechanism for the adjustment of balances of payments by the developed countries.

In addition to such indirect benefits to the developing countries there is one aspect of the proposals made in this article which is of very direct concern to the developing countries.

One of the proposals is that the general structure of interest rates should be lowered (raised) if the developed countries agree that they are in general having to rely on excessive budget deficits (surpluses) to maintain their domestic national incomes on desirable levels. In other words, the international structure of interest rates should be lowered if the developed countries in general wished to change the 'mix' of their financial policies and to rely on a more restrictive budgetary policy combined with a less restrictive monetary policy as the means of controlling their total money expenditures at a given level; and *vice versa*.

The developing countries are vitally interested both in the maintenance of a high level of effective demand in the developed countries and also in the mix of policies by which demand is maintained. This dual interest is dramatically illustrated by the present policies in the United States, where a welcome growth of effective demand is at present making a substantial contribution to the market for the products of developing countries. But this favourable impact would be incomparably greater if this same expansion of demand were achieved by a more relaxed monetary policy offset to the necessary extent by a more restrictive fiscal policy.

Indeed, in order to prevent the present huge budget deficit from leading to an excessive inflation of money expenditures, interest rates are at present so high in the United States that capital funds are flowing into, rather than out of, the United States; this has caused the dollar to appreciate to such a high value, and United States products in consequence to become so expensive, that there is a large deficit on current account of the United States balance of payments; as a result the capital-rich United States instead of lending some real resources to the rest of the world is at present sucking in some of the real resources and savings of the rest of the world to supplement its own savings in the finance of its budget deficit.

This is of especial concern to the developing countries. High rates of interest in the developed countries mean that the balances of payments of developing countries will be burdened with large interest payments on past loans in so far as such loans have been made on terms which require their renewal; and high rates make it difficult for them to raise new loans for new developments since the productivity of the capital projects and the future ability to service them will have to be judged in the light of high rates of return. Both of these factors make it difficult for them to finance imports of real resources for development.

An international monetary institution such as the IMF in its present or revised form is not the appropriate body to concern itself with finance for development purposes; that is the function of the World Bank and other institutions and programmes. The financing function of the monetary body is concerned with foreign-exchange intervention in the widest sense of that term, i.e. to supply short-term funds to mitigate the foreign-exchange strains imposed by temporary balance-of-payment problems. The developing countries should not attempt to turn such a body into yet another source of development funds; but nevertheless they do have a very legitimate development concern with the functioning of such a monetary body, since, as has been argued in this article, such a body is properly concerned with the international structure of money rates of interest. And this, for the reasons outlined above, means that the appropriate mix of budgetary and monetary policies in the developed countries must inevitably become a matter of international concern to the developing as well as to the developed countries.

Conclusion

It is now Forty Years On since Bretton Woods. The present article is based on the belief that since then three basic, interrelated developments call for some revision of the system.

First, experience has made clear the disadvantage, on the one hand, of fixed exchange rates subject only to occasional cataclysmic adjustments when a fundamental disequilibrium has growth to an intolerable level and, on the other hand, of totally uncontrolled freely floating exchange rates. The present article seeks a regime between these two extremes.

Second, since Bretton Woods there has been a very marked increase in the international mobility of capital funds. The Bretton Woods system allowed for controls over capital movements; and, indeed, Keynes always insisted on the need for such controls. It would now probably be impossible, even if it were desirable, to rely on effective controls over capital movements as a major instrument of policy. It is suggested in the present article that this has made domestic monetary policies a matter for international concern.

Third, in the construction of the Bretton Woods system much thought was given to full employment and to equilibrium in balances of payments, but relatively little was given to the development of less developed countries. The atmosphere has changed dramatically in this respect, and, as is suggested in this article, that is another reason why domestic monetary policies must be regarded as a matter of international concern in a way which was not on the agenda forty years ago.

23

Monetary Policy and Fiscal Policy: Impact Effects with a New Keynesian 'Assignment' of Weapons to Targets[1]

By James Meade and David Vines. Meade presented an earlier version of this paper to the Centre for Economic Policy Research Conference on 'Exchange Rate Regimes, Money GDP Targets and Macro-economic Policy' in Cambridge on 6 July 1987. It is included here since it represents Meade's current views on the 'assignment problem' in an open economy. This revised version of his paper was issued as Centre for Economic Policy Research Discussion Paper No. 246, June 1988.

1 Introduction

In what may be called the Old or Orthodox Keynesian prescription, financial policy (covering monetary policy and fiscal policy) is to be designed to maintain a high and stable level of real economic activity (i.e. 'full' employment). Financial policies affect *money* expenditures on goods and services and any given increase in such *money* expenditures will stimulate *real* output and employment, only if the increased money expenditures are not absorbed by a rise in the money wage and the price of the existing level of employment and output. Thus the success of Orthodox Keynesian policy depends upon ensuring that wage- and price-setting institutions are such as to prevent any excessive or runaway inflation of money wage-rates and prices. In this system we may say that financial policies are assigned to the maintenance of full employment and that the design of wage-setting and price-fixing institutions ('incomes policies') are assigned to the control of inflation.

In what may be called the New Keynesian prescription, this assignment is reversed. It is proposed that financial policies should be designed to control the level of total money expenditures on the country's products (i.e. the level of the *money* national income) rather than the level of the country's total output and employment (i.e. the level of the

[1] We are greatly indebted to our colleagues Martin Weale and Andy Blake and to the discussants of an earlier draft of this paper at the CEPR Conference in Cambridge in July 1987.

real national income), and that the design of wage- and price-fixing institutions should then be directed towards the maintenance of full employment. The basic Keynesian analysis of the important causal relations in the economy is the same for both Old and New Keynesian prescriptions. The difference lies solely in the design of instruments of control, i.e. whether we should look mainly to the level of real output and employment in the formulation of monetary and fiscal policies and to the control of inflation in the formulation of incomes policy or whether we should look mainly to the control of total monetary expenditures (and so to the control of inflation) in the formulation of monetary and fiscal policies and to the reform of wage- and price-setting institutions to ensure that money wages and prices are held at levels which translate these money expenditures into high levels of output and employment rather than high levels of money prices.

Whether we are dealing with Old or with New Keynesianism, financial policy can be divided into two main parts, namely monetary policy and fiscal policy. In what follows we will assume that monetary policy is concerned with setting a short-term rate of interest (R) and that fiscal policy is concerned with setting a rate of income tax (S). We will for simplicity assume that the money price of domestic output is set by a given mark-up on money wage costs (W) so that control of price inflation goes hand in hand with control of wage inflation. In this model it is the setting of the variables S, R and W which determines the outcome both for inflation and employment.

But clearly there is a basic difference between W on the one hand and S and R on the other hand. The authorities can within limits simply decide to raise or lower the financial instruments S and R. They cannot in the same way put W up or down at will. All that can be done is to attempt to produce suitable structural changes in wage-setting institutions. The control problem, therefore, boils down to designing the best immediate adjustment of the financial controls S and R given whatever wage-setting institutions in fact exist, and attempting as a longer-run structural policy gradually to reform wage-setting institutions in a desirable direction.

Whether we are dealing with Old or New Keynesian systems, it is essential to add a third objective of policy (namely a control over the growth of national wealth) to the two objectives already specified (namely full employment and the control of inflation). Otherwise it would be all too easy, even with the most inflationary wage-setting institutions, to combine full employment with uninflated prices by means of a lax fiscal policy in which excessive government borrowing was used to raise funds to subsidise and thus keep down money costs and prices, while a tight monetary policy was adopted which seriously restricted all forms of expenditure on the maintenance of real capital resources, so that the excessive consumption due to the excessive subsidisation of expendable incomes was offset by deficient expenditures on real capital resources. Full employment combined with a control of price inflation would be achieved by living on capital (eating up the seed corn) with disastrous longer-term results.

The needed wealth target can take many forms. In this paper we will consider only three of these possible forms.[2]

(i) The government might take as its target the maintenance of a suitably chosen rate of investment in new capital resources by the country as a whole (I) (whether it was financed by official savings through a current account budget surplus or by private savings).

(ii) Or it might consider it more appropriate to take the ratio of total investment expenditures to total national income (I/Y) (i.e. the proportion of the national income devoted to national savings) as the target rather than the absolute level of total investment expenditures.

(iii) Or it might simply take a given level of budget surplus or budget deficit (B) as its wealth target. In this last case the government's contribution to, or calls upon, the country's savings would be the object of control (thus restricting the use of spendthrift fiscal policies for the control of wage and price inflation), while the contribution of private savings to the finance of the growth of the country's wealth would be uncontrolled.

The present paper is written on the assumption that a New Keynesian system of control is to be operated. Monetary policy and fiscal policy are to be devised for the control of the inflation of money national income[3] and for control over the division of national income between current consumption and capital investment. These controls are to be designed against the background of whatever wage-setting institutions in fact exist, the reform of such institutions being regarded as a long-run structural problem. The assignment problem then boils down to the question whether fiscal policy should be used to control inflation, leaving monetary policy to affect the accumulation of wealth, or whether these roles should be reversed.

What may be called a case of pure assignment would be a case in which, for example, the setting of the rate of tax (S) was decided solely with regard to its effect on the rate of inflation without any regard to its effect on the wealth target, while the rate of interest (R) was set solely with regard to its effect on the wealth target regardless of its effect on the rate of inflation, or *vice versa*.

But such an extreme disregard of the cross-effects of the different instruments on the different target objectives is, as will be argued later, normally an unwise strategy. Suppose the major effect of monetary

[2] These three forms concern themselves only with *flows* of savings and investment expenditures. Other possible forms would relate to *stocks* of assets (e.g. total real national wealth, the ratio of total wealth to national income, the size of the government's national debt, or the ratio of government national debt to national income). We confine ourselves in this chapter to flows rather than stocks in order to make possible the analysis of an *IS*/*LM* type of simplified model in the rest of this paper.

[3] We regard control of the country's total money income or money GDP as the most appropriate inflation target. However, in order to build as simple a model as possible to illustrate the main issues, in the following sections of this paper we use control of the money price of home product as the inflation target.

policy were on the rate of inflation but that it had some effect, though a relatively small effect, on the wealth target, whereas fiscal policy had a major effect on the wealth target and a relatively minor effect on the rate of inflation. In such a case in determining the setting of the rate of interest, it would be sensible to put the main emphasis on its effect on inflation but to pay some regard to the question whether a change in the rate of interest – which was desired on inflation grounds – would have a beneficial or adverse effect on the wealth objective. We may call such a case as one in which monetary policy should be 'assigned' to control of inflation, meaning by the use of the quotation marks around the terms 'assign' or 'assignment' that we are considering only a case in which the main emphasis in the determination of the use of the instrument should be in regard to its target to which it is 'assigned'. Thus the 'assignment' problem is merely part of the general problem how to combine the use of tax rate and interest rate to achieve a given combination of wealth target and inflation target.

This paper will not be concerned with the underlying dynamic problems which form an essential part of the analysis which is necessary before any final realistic policy prescriptions can be formed. It is confined to a form of the familiar *IS*/*LM* type of analysis in which certain basic dynamic relationships are neglected or assumed to be constant (such as the effect of investment upon the growth of the stock of capital and so upon the growth of output or the endogeneity of the formation of expectations) and in which the analysis is confined to a limited number of relationships which are assumed to operate without any time-lags. Such an analysis is obviously very incomplete; but the history of macroeconomic analysis since the work of Keynes suggests that it may provide certain insights which can be useful to those who are designing rules for realistic policy action which take account of the dynamics of the system.

2 *The Model of a Closed Economy*

We will start with a highly simplified model of a closed economy, the model being designed on lines which are suitable for a 'static' *IS*/*LM* type of analysis. For this purpose we will make use of the notion of what may be called a Marshallian–Keynesian short-period analysis with the following characteristics:

(i) The period is short enough for it to be reasonable to assume no significant change in any capital stocks.

(ii) Certain factors, however, such as labour can be varied and indeed are varied in amounts immediately at the beginning of each period.

(iii) There are no appreciable time-lags in the adjustment of consumption, investment, exports, imports, production etc. to the conditions ruling at the beginning of the period.

(vi) Expectations are given exogenously and are not influenced by the choice of policy variables at the beginning of each period.

(v) The money wage-rate is fixed at the beginning of each period, but the rate at which it will be set at the beginning of the next period depends upon what happened during this period, this difference measuring what we will call this period's rate of inflation ($\hat{w}_0 = (W_1 - W_0)/W_0$).

The questions which we then set to this model are of the following kind. What difference would be made to the rate of inflation ($\hat{p}$), the wealth target (I, I/Y, or B), the level of total output (Y), and the level of consumption (C) during this period if the control variables (the rate of tax (S) and/or the rate of interest (R)) were set at the beginning of the period at different levels? We are thus comparing two steady states which might rule during this short period according to the choice at the beginning of the period about the level of the control variables to operate during the period.

The *LM* side of the *IS*/*LM* is in this model represented by the fact that the monetary authorities are assumed to set the rate of interest which rules during the period under analysis by providing automatically whatever money or liquidity is necessary for that purpose. The *IS* side of the balance is represented by the fact that with the rate of interest together with the rate of tax being thus set by the authorities the multiplicand of the Kahnian multiplier (e.g. government expenditure and investment expenditure) and the consumption multiplier itself will be determined. The reader can then at his or her own pleasure interpret the following analysis in either of two ways:

(i) If the Keynesian 'short' period is imagined to be sufficiently 'long' for all the relevant relationships (e.g. the level of consumption dependent upon a given level of post-tax income) to have settled down to a reasonably long-term steady state, then the following model can be used to represent a full Keynesian type of analysis.

(ii) But alternatively – and this is the form in which the following model is precisely formulated – the 'short' period can be regarded as very 'short', indeed no longer than, say, the quarter which is often used as the relevant short period for a fully dynamic difference-equation type of analysis. The insights which are then gained from the model refer only to what may be called the 'impact' effects of changes in the policy variables, dealing with questions such as what would be the *immediate* effects of a given change in S or R on I, C, Y etc. regardless of their implications for any longer-period new steady state of the economy or of its subsequent path to, or away from, or around, such a steady state.

The actual level of money prices and costs ruling during the period under analysis is determined by assuming that a fixed money wage is set at the beginning of the period and that prices are determined by a fixed mark-up of prices on these money costs. But it is an essential feature of the model to consider the factors at work during the period under analysis which will influence, indeed will determine, the rate at which the money wage will be set at the beginning of the next period. In this respect the model does perhaps stray away from the strictly static nature of an *IS/LM* model.

Consider then the following nine equations of a greatly simplified short-period model of a closed economy:[4]

$$Y = L \tag{1}$$

Output (Y) per worker (L) is assumed constant.

$$P = (1 + m)W \tag{2}$$

The factor-cost price of output is equal to a marked-up $(1 + m)$ value of the money wage costs (W).

$$\begin{aligned} C &= c(1 - S)Y + (\bar{c} - c)(1 - S_{-1})Y_{-1} \\ &= c(1 - S)Y + \bar{C} \end{aligned} \tag{3}$$

The amount of product consumed in any given short-period (C) depends upon a proportion ($\bar{c}$) of the post-tax income from which it is financed. But there may be a distributed lag so that this period's consumption (C) is partly financed (c) out of this period's post-tax $(1 - S)$ income (Y) and partly $(\bar{c} - c)$ out of last period's post-tax $(1 - S_{-1})$ income (Y_{-1}). But for this period everything due to last period's events becomes a given constant effect ($\bar{C}$) on this period's consumption (C), so that the parameter (c) shows the impact effect of any change in this period's post-tax income on this period's consumption.

$$\begin{aligned} I &= \bar{I} - iR - (\bar{i} - i)R_{-1} + v(Y - Y_{-1}) + (\bar{v} - v)(Y_{-1} - Y_{-2}) \\ &= -iR + vY + \bar{I} \end{aligned} \tag{4}$$

The amount of product used by the private sector for capital development is equal to a constant ($\bar{I}$) minus a constant ($\bar{i}$) times the rate of interest (R) and an accelerator ($\bar{v}$) times the rate of increase in the total demand for the products of the economy $(Y - Y_{-1})$. But these two effects may be partially lagged. The parameters i and v show the impact effects on investment during the period of a reduction in R or a rise in Y during this period.

$$Y = \bar{J} + I + C \tag{5}$$

The amount of product produced this period is equal to the sum of consumption by the government sector which is assumed to be constant ($\bar{J}$) plus private investment (I) and consumption (C).

[4] In what follows the variables which are barred (such as $\bar{I}$) are assumed to remain constant throughout.

$$B = YS - \bar{J} \tag{6}$$

This period's budget balance (B) is defined as this period's income (Y) multiplied by this period's rate of tax (S) minus this period's government spending ($\bar{J}$). A major simplification of the model is to ignore the effects of the national debt and the payment of interest on the debt. Thus equation (3) neglects any effect on consumption of expenditures financed by the private sector's receipt of interest on the national debt and equation (6) neglects interest income both on the expenditure side of the budget and as an element of the tax base. A true dynamic analysis would necessitate the abandonment of these assumptions since the growth of national debt resulting from a growing interest charge upon the budget can be an important destabilising influence (Blinder and Solow (1973)).

$$k = \frac{I}{Y} \tag{7}$$

This simply defines (k) the ratio of investment (I) to income (Y).

$$V = \frac{W(1-S)}{P}$$

$$= \frac{1-S}{1+m}, \quad \text{using (2)} \tag{8a}$$

The real value of a worker's take-home pay (V) is his money wage (W) less tax (S) divided by the cost of living (P).[5]

$$\tilde{V} = \bar{V} + \frac{L}{\beta'} \tag{8b}$$

The term $\tilde{V}$ represents what may be called the workers' 'aspiration' level of real post-tax take-home pay, which is assumed to be an increasing function of the level of employment (L) and so a decreasing function of the level of unemployment.

$$L_s = \beta'(V - \bar{V}) \tag{8c}$$

This phenomenon of an aspiration rate of pay which may differ from the actual rate of pay can, if preferred, be translated into terms of a labour supply curve as given in (8c) by using (8a) write $V = \tilde{V}$ in (8b) and then solving for L. The term L_s then expresses what the level of employment would have to be to make the workers content with their actual pay.

[5] Equations (3), (6) and (8a) assume that all taxation takes the form of a direct proportionate tax on all incomes. It would be simple to represent taxation as a single rate of indirect tax on all purchases by replacing $(1-S)$ with $1/(1+S')$ where S' was the equivalent rate of indirect tax. In this case in (8a), while P would measure the factor-cost price of output, $P(1+S')$ would measure the market price of output, i.e. the cost of living.

Actual employment is demand-determined so that L represents the demand for labour. If $L>L_s$, the demand for labour exceeds the supply, which can in alternative language be stated as a situation in which workers aspire to, or demand, a wage which is higher than the actual wage.

$$\hat{w} \equiv \frac{W_{+1} - W}{W} = \alpha_1(\bar{V} - V) + \gamma(V_{-1} - V) \tag{9a}$$

Alternatively

$$\hat{w} = \alpha_2(L - L_s) + \gamma(V_{-1} - V) \tag{9b}$$

Equations (9a) and (9b) are alternative ways of expressing the pressures which build up during this period to cause the money wage-rate set at the beginning of the next period (W_{+1}) to exceed the money wage-rate which was set at the beginning of this period. In (9a) the rate of wage inflation is made to depend upon the excess of the aspired over the actual wage ruling during this period and in (9b) on the excess of labour demand over labour supply ruling during this period; and in both cases it is also made to depend upon a 'catching-up' term, i.e. upon any reduction of the rate of real post-tax pay ruling during this period below its level in the previous period. If one uses (1) to write $Y = L$ and also writes $\alpha_2\beta' = \alpha_1$ both formulations of $\hat{w}$ can be written as

$$\hat{w} = \alpha Y + \beta S + \hat{\hat{w}} \tag{9c}$$

where $\alpha = \alpha_1/\beta'$, $\beta = (\alpha_1 + \gamma)/(1 + m)$, and $\hat{\hat{w}} = \alpha_1\bar{V} + \gamma V_{-1} - (\alpha_1 + \gamma)/(1 + m)$. Thus if the parameter $\alpha_1 = \beta'$ times the parameter α_2 the two formulations are merely different ways of expressing the same real factors.

Thus the rate of wage inflation ($\hat{w}$) can be seen to depend upon two factors, Y and S.

The first is measured by αY and may be called the 'demand-pull' factor. The higher is the demand for output and so for labour, the greater will be the aspiration wage and thus the upward pressure on money wage-rates. This corresponds to the familiar Phillips-curve effect.

The second factor is measured by βS and may be called the 'cost-push' factor. It can be divided into two parts corresponding to the terms $\alpha_1/(1 + m)$ and $\gamma/(1 + m)$ which make up the term β. (i) The higher is S, the lower will be the actual post-tax real take-home pay and the greater, therefore, will be the gap between the aspired and the actual rate of pay. (ii) The higher is S, the lower will be this period's real post-tax pay relatively to that of the previous period and the greater, therefore, will be the catching-up pressure on wage claims.[6]

[6] In passing one may note a very important dynamic property implied by the distinction between these two 'cost-push' elements. The upward cost-push effects on money costs and prices due to a high rate of tax will be greater during the process of raising the tax than it will be subsequently when the rate of tax is stabilised at the higher level and the γ-effect will have fallen to zero.

If we eliminate L and W from equations (1) to (7) and use (9c) we obtain:

$$\begin{aligned} Y &= \mu\{\bar{J} + \bar{C} + \bar{I} - iR\} \\ C &= c(1-S)Y + \bar{C} \\ I &= -iR + vY + \bar{I} \\ B &= SY - \bar{J} \\ k &= I/Y \\ \hat{p} &= \alpha Y + \beta S + \hat{\bar{w}} \end{aligned} \tag{10}$$

where $\mu = 1/[1 - c(1-S) - v]$, the Kahnian multiplier, with $\bar{J} + \bar{C} + \bar{I} - iR$ as the multiplicand. By substitution of the value for Y from the first of these equations into the remaining five equations one can obtain expressions for the inflation target ($\hat{p}$) and the three possible wealth targets (I, B, and k) and also for total income (Y) and consumption (C) in terms of the two control variables (S and R). We assume that $c(1-S) + v < 1$; otherwise the amount of product consumed $[c(I-S) + \bar{C}]$ and the amount of product demanded to satisfy the investment needs $(\bar{I} - iR + vY)$ would exceed the total output even if $\bar{J} = 0$.

By differentiation of (10) in respect to S and R one obtains:

$$\begin{bmatrix} \delta\hat{p} \\ \delta B \\ \delta k \\ \delta I \\ \delta C \\ \delta Y \end{bmatrix} = \begin{bmatrix} p_s & p_r \\ b_s & b_r \\ k_s & k_r \\ i_s & i_r \\ c_s & c_r \\ y_s & y_r \end{bmatrix} \begin{bmatrix} \delta S \\ \delta R \end{bmatrix} \tag{11}$$

with the parameters in the matrix taking the following values:

$$p_s = -\alpha\mu cY + \beta \qquad p_r = -\alpha\mu i \qquad \sigma_p = -\frac{p_s}{p_r} = \frac{-\alpha\mu cY + \beta}{\alpha\mu i} = -\frac{\alpha\mu cY - \beta}{\alpha\mu cY} \cdot \frac{cY}{i}$$

$$b_s = (1 - c - v)\mu Y \qquad b_r = -S\mu i \qquad \sigma_b = -\frac{b_s}{b_r} = \frac{1 - c - v}{S_c} \cdot \frac{cY}{i}$$

$$k_s = (k - v)\mu c \qquad k_r = -\{1 - (k - v)\mu\}\, i/Y \qquad \sigma_k = -\frac{k_s}{k_r} = \frac{(k - v)\mu}{1 - (k - v)\mu} \cdot \frac{cY}{i} = \frac{k - v}{1 - c(1 - S) - k} \cdot \frac{\mathrm{cY}}{\mathrm{i}} \tag{12}$$

$$i_s = -\nu\mu cY \qquad i_r = -(1+\nu\mu)i \qquad \sigma_i = -\frac{i_s}{i_r} = -\frac{\nu\mu}{1+\nu\mu}\cdot\frac{cY}{i} = -\frac{\nu}{1-c(1-S)}\cdot\frac{cY}{i}$$

$$c_s = -(1-\nu)\mu cY \qquad c_r = -\{(1-\nu)\mu - 1\}i \qquad \sigma_c = -\frac{c_s}{c_r} = -\frac{(1-\nu)\mu}{\{(1-\nu)\mu-1\}}\cdot\frac{cY}{i} = -\frac{1-\nu}{c(1-S)}\cdot\frac{cY}{i}$$

$$y_s = i_s + c_s = -\mu cY \qquad y_r = i_r + c_r = -\mu i \qquad \sigma_y = -\frac{y_s}{y_r} = -\frac{cY}{i}$$

where σ in the last column measures the extent to which R must change, given a unit change in S, in order to keep the relevant variables ($\hat{p}$, B, k, I, C, or Y) at an unchanged level. We will call the value of σ_p 'the slope of the $\hat{p}$-contour' since it measures the change in R per unit change in S. It will be an upward or downward slope according as σ_p is positive or negative. We will call the absolute value of σ_p regardless of sign 'the steepness of the $\hat{p}$-contour slope'. Thus the steepness will be a *gentle upward* slope if a small increase in R is associated with a unit increase in S and a *steep downward* slope if a large decrease in R is associated with a unit increase in S; and *vice versa*. And similarly for σ_b, σ_k, σ_i, σ_c, and σ_y.

It should be emphasised that the small changes in the variables (δS, δR, $\delta\hat{p}$, δB etc.) in (11) and (12) do not represent the change in the variable over time. Changes in the variables listed in the left-hand vector in (11) may take place between one period and the next even if S and R remained unchanged; for example, in the consumption equation (3) C may be higher or lower in this period because Y was high or low in the last period, an influence which is captured by the element $\bar{C}$, even though S and R remained unchanged from one period to the next. All that the first equation in (11), namely $\hat{p} = p_s\,\delta S + p_r\,\delta R$, expresses is the extent to which $\hat{p}$ would be higher or lower than it would otherwise have been in the short period under examination if S and/or R were raised or lowered above or below what they would otherwise have been.

Thus the matrix (11) expresses the way in which a change in the levels of instrument variables S and R at the beginning of any one period would cause the values of the other variables in the system during the coming short period to differ from what they would otherwise have been. The six equations in (11) represent six independent relationships between the eight variables ($\hat{p}$, B, k, I, C, Y, S, and R). It is, of course, possible to rearrange these equations by selecting a pair of variables other than S and R to play the role of the 'knowns' in the right-hand vector in (11) while S and R join the unknowns in the left-hand vector.

Suppose one chooses to take $\delta\hat{p}$ and δB as two predetermined changes in the inflation targets and the budget targets which one wishes to achieve. One can then transform the six equations of (11) into the following six equations:

$$\begin{bmatrix} \delta S \\ \delta R \\ \delta k \\ \delta I \\ \delta C \\ \delta Y \end{bmatrix} = \frac{1}{\Delta_B} \begin{bmatrix} b_s & -p_s \\ -b_s & p_s \\ k_s b_r - k_r b_s & k_r p_s - k_s p_r \\ i_s b_r - i_r b_s & i_r p_s - i_s p_r \\ c_s b_r - c_r b_s & c_r b_r - c_r b_s \\ c_r p_s - c_s p_r & y_s b_r - y_r b_s y_r p_s - y_s p_r \end{bmatrix} \begin{bmatrix} \delta \hat{p} \\ \delta B \end{bmatrix} \tag{13}$$

$$\text{with } \Delta_B = p_s b_r - p_r b_s = \mu i\{\alpha Y - \beta S\}$$

In this case $\delta\hat{p}$ and δB represent the 'known' changes which are to be effected in the two target variables; δS and δR then measure the 'unknown' changes in the two control variables which are needed to effect the predetermined changes in the target variables; and δk, δI, δC, and δY indicate the changes which will result in these other variables.

If one took k instead of B as the target variable and sought an adjustment of k by δk instead of an adjustment of B by δB, one would obtain a series of the same form as (13) with the substitution throughout of δk for δB, k_r for b_r, and k_s for b_s, and Δ_k for Δ_B where

$$\Delta_k = p_s k_r - p_r k_s = \frac{1}{Y}\{\alpha\mu c Y - \beta(1 - [k - v]\mu)\} \tag{14}$$

And similarly if one took I instead of B as the wealth target, one would need in matrix (13) to substitute δI for δB, i_r for b_r, i_s for b_s, and Δ_I for Δ_B where

$$\Delta_I = p_s i_r - p_r i_s = \alpha Y \mu c - \beta(1 + v\mu) \tag{15}$$

In the following section of this paper we will illustrate the economic implications of the results of the formal analysis contained in equations (10) to (15) by examining in some detail the economic aspects of one particular short-period policy decision. But for this purpose it will be useful to note in advance certain features of these equations.

(1) The signs of all the parameters in the first two columns of (12) are unambiguous except in the cases of p_s and k_s.[7] In the case of p_s we have

[7] Note that $k_r<0$, since $1-(k-v)\mu = \{1-c(1-S)-k\}\mu$; and we must assume $c(1-S)+k<1$, since otherwise the products used for consumption and private investment would exceed the total national product. Similarly $c_r<0$, since $(1-v)\mu - 1 = \mu c(1-S)$. We simply assume b_s to be >0, though this depends upon $c+v<1$. In fact consumption plus the accelerator element in investment would take up less than the whole national product so long as $c+v<1+cS$. As we wish to apply the analysis to all values $0<S<1$ we simply assume $c+v<1$.

$$p_s \gtreqless 0 \quad \text{as} \quad \beta \gtreqless \alpha\mu cY \tag{16}$$

which expresses the fact that the effect of an increase in the rate of tax will lead to a net increase (or decrease) in the rate of inflation according as the cost-push element (β) exceeds (or is less than) the demand-pull element ($\alpha\mu cY$) in the wage equation. In the case of k_s we have

$$k_s \gtreqless 0 \quad \text{as} \quad k \gtreqless v \tag{17}$$

i.e. according as the existing average ratio of investment to income (k) is greater or less than the marginal accelerator ratio of investment-increment to income-increment (v). A rise in S will decrease consumption and thus lead to a decrease in income and this decrease in income will (if $v>0$) lead to a decrease in investment. If k is small and v large this will cause a proportionate fall in investment which is greater than the proportionate fall in income, and *vice versa* if k was large and v small.

(2) As already explained the expressions in the third column of (12) measure the slopes of the contour lines for the relevant variables. The signs of these contour slopes are all unambiguous except for σ_p and σ_k. The signs of these two slopes are ambiguous because of the ambiguity of the signs of p_s and k_s.

(3) In the economic analysis of the following section it will become clear that an important role is played by the comparative steepness of the various contour slopes, a comparison which is particularly important where any two slopes have the same sign (either upward or downward). In the third column of (12) we express all these slopes as multiples of cY/i, i.e. of the downward steepness of the Y-contour. (i) As can be seen from the first row of (12) the downward steepness of the $\hat{p}$-contour would be the same as that of the Y-contour if $\beta=0$, but if $\beta>0$ any downward slope of the $\hat{p}$-contour must be less steep than that of the Y-contour. (ii) In the case of the k-contour, suppose $v>k$ so that the slope is negative. We must, however, have $v-k<1-c(1-S)-k$, i.e. $c(1-S)+v<1$ since otherwise consumption plus the accelerator element of investment would account for more than the total national product. It follows that any negative slope for the k-contour must be less steep than for the Y-contour. (iii) Also in the case of the I-contour we must, for the same reason, have $v<1-c(1-S)$ so that the downward slope of the I-contour would be less steep than that of the Y-contour. (iv) In the case of the C-contour for the same reason we must have $1-v>c(1-S)$ so that the C-contour is more steeply sloped than the Y-contour.

(4) In the matrix (13) the expressions b_r/Δ_B and b_s/Δ_B in the first two rows represent the extent to which the control instruments S and R will need to be adjusted in order to lead to a change in the inflation target variables by $\delta\hat{p}$ without any change in the wealth target variable B; and similarly for the corresponding expressions in the other rows of the first column of the matrix for the resulting changes in the other variables. The signs of these expressions (such as b_r/Δ_B) thus depend not only upon the sign of the numerator (such as b_r) but also upon the sign of the

denominator (such as the determinant Δ_B). The signs of the determinants Δ_B, Δ_k, and Δ_I, will accordingly play an important role in the following economic analysis since they will determine in which direction, upward or downwards, the instruments of control must be adjusted in order to achieve a given adjustment of the levels of the target variables.

(5) In Section 1 of this paper it was shown that a proper 'assignment' of different instruments as means of control over particular target variables does not imply that each instrument should be exclusively tied to one particular target. Indeed the example given in the last paragraph illustrates the fact that if it is desired in (13) to change $\hat{p}$ by $\delta\hat{p}$ without changing B one should change S by b_r/Δ_B and R by $-b_s/\Delta_B$, which means that $|b_s/b_r|$ represents the relative emphasis which should be put on R as compared with S in the control of $\hat{p}$. Similarly if it is desired in (13) to change B by δB without changing $\hat{p}$, one would need to change S by $-p_r/\Delta_B$, and R by p_s/Δ_B, which means that $|p_s/p_r|$ represents the relative emphasis to be put on R as compared with S in the control of B. Thus if

$$\left|\frac{b_s}{b_r}\right| > \left|\frac{p_s}{p_r}\right| \tag{18}$$

emphasis should be put upon R relatively to S in the control of $\hat{p}$ and on S relatively to R in the control of B. R should be 'assigned' to the control of $\hat{p}$ and S to the control of B (cf. Mundell (1962)).

From (12) it can be seen that $\sigma_b = |b_s/b_r|$ measures the steepness of the slope of the B-contour and $\sigma_p = |p_s/p_r|$, the steepness of the slope of the $\hat{p}$-contour. Thus (18) states that R should be 'assigned' to the control of $\hat{p}$ if the $\hat{p}$-contour is less steeply sloped than the B-contour.

This rule can be generalised as follows: when two target variables are under consideration R should be 'assigned' to the control of that target whose contour line (regardless of sign) is the less steeply sloped. Thus R is to be 'assigned' to the control of the variable in whose control it is relatively effective, i.e. in whose control only a relatively small change in R is needed to offset the effects of a relatively large change in S.

3 The Control of Inflation in a Closed Economy

In this section we consider some of the economic policy implications of the formal analysis of Section 2 by applying the analysis to a particular policy objective. We suppose that it is desired so to change the setting of the control instruments (i.e. so to set δS and δR) as to cause a unit decrease in the rate of inflation below what it would otherwise have been (i.e. so as to cause $\delta\hat{p} = -1$) without having any effect upon the level of the wealth target variable (i.e. while keeping δB, δk, or $\delta I = 0$). In this section we will illustrate the problem for only two of these possible wealth targets, i.e. for $\delta B = 0$ and for $\delta I = 0$. We will neglect the possibility of choosing k as the wealth target variable.[8] In the analysis

[8] We do this because a major feature of the analysis will depend upon whether the wealth target variable has an upward or a downward contour slope as expressed in the third column of (12). As we have seen, the variable B has an upward and variable I a downward contour slope, while the contour slope of k may be upward or downward according as $k \gtreqless v$. To conduct the analysis for B and I will, therefore, suffice to cover the two possibilities which would need to be examined if k were adopted for the wealth target variable.

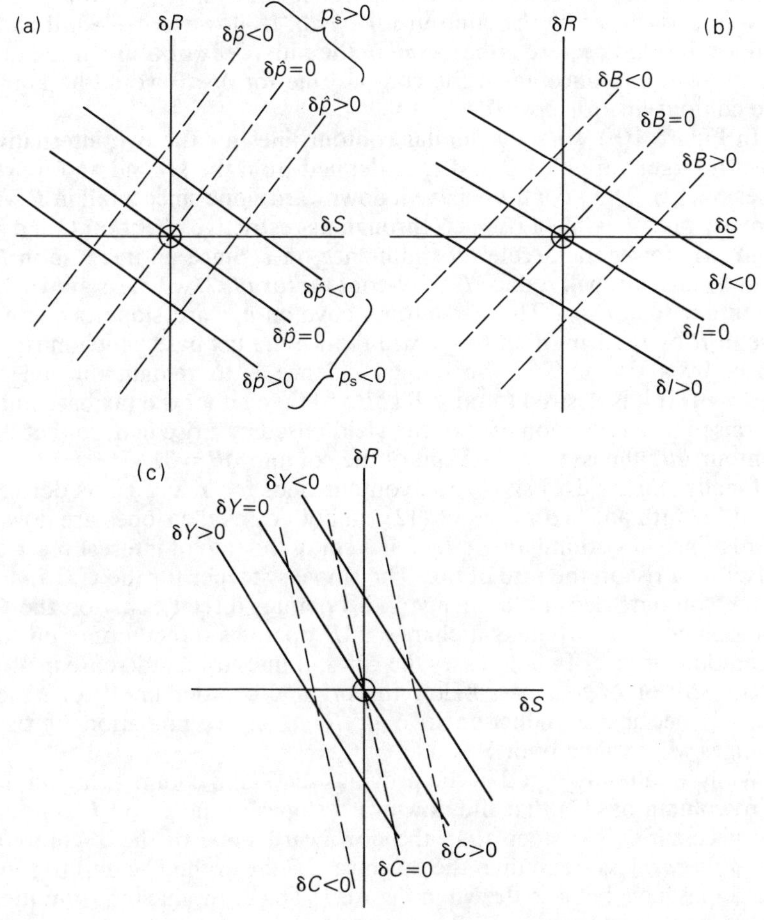

Figure 1

emphasis will be laid on the interaction between two features of the problem of control of inflation, namely (i) whether the demand-pull or the cost-push element is predominant in the wage equation (i.e. whether $p_s \gtrless 0$) and (ii) whether B (with an upward contour slope) or I (with a downward contour slope) is chosen as the wealth target variable.

In Figure 1 the relevant contour maps are illustrated, the slopes of the contour lines in this figure being as given in the third column of (12). We start in each case at an origin O where S and R are set at their existing levels. In Figure 1(a) we draw the line marked $\delta\hat{p} = 0$ which shows the combination of changes in S and R which would be needed to keep $\delta\hat{p} = 0$. The continuous line shows the combination if the demand-pull element exceeds the cost-push element ($p_s<0$), while the broken line shows the case in which the cost-push element is dominant ($p_s>0$). If it were desired to reduce $\hat{p}$ by a certain amount (e.g. $\delta\hat{p} = -1$) it would be necessary with $p_s<0$ to raise either the rate of tax or the rate of interest or some combination of both. The contour line for $\delta\hat{p} = -1$ would shift upwards as shown by the contour for $\delta\hat{p}<0$. If, however, $p_s>0$, then to reduce $\hat{p}$ would require either a *fall* in the rate of tax or a *rise* in the rate of interest; and once again the contour line for $\delta\hat{p}<0$ would lie above the contour line for $\delta\hat{p} = 0$.

In Figure 1(b) we show similar contour lines for the two alternative wealth target variables B and I, as defined from the second and fourth lines of (12). The I contours have a downward slope since a fall in R will directly raise I, while a *rise* in S through its restrictive effect on C and so on Y will *lower* the accelerator influence on I. Since an increase in R, with S constant, will reduce I, the I-contour for $\delta I<0$ will pass above the I-contour for $\delta I = 0$. The B-contours have an upward slope because a rise in R by reducing I and so Y will reduce the tax base which must be offset by a rise in S if the budget balance is to remain unchanged ($\delta B = 0$). If it is desired to raise B ($\delta B>0$) then either the tax base must be raised by a reduction of R or the yield raised by a rise in S, so that the contour $\delta B>0$ passes to the right of the contour $\delta B = 0$.

Finally, Figure 1(c) shows the contour lines for Y and C, as derived from the fifth and sixth rows of (12). In both cases the slopes are downwards since any stimulating effect of a cut in the rate of interest must be offset by a rise in the rate of tax. The slope is steeper for the C than for the Y contours because a change in S operates directly only on the C-component of Y, whereas a change in R operates directly only on the I-component of Y. In both cases the contour lines for an increase in Y or C (i.e. δY or $\delta C>0$) pass below the original contour line (i.e. δY or $\delta C = 0$) because a reduction in S or R or any combination of such changes will expand both Y and C.

We have already noted in the previous section in commenting on the third column of (12) that the downward slopes of the $\hat{p}$ and I-contours are necessarily less steep than the downward slope of the Y-contours and *a fortiori* less steep than the downward slope of the C-contours; and the slopes have been so drawn in Figure 1. The economic interpretation of these relationships is as follows.

As one moves to the left along any downward sloping $\hat{p}$-contour one will cross a higher and higher Y-contour. This means that as one controls any given level of inflation by reducing S and offsetting any inflationary effect by raising R, there will result a net increase in the level of Y. The reduction in S will reduce any upward cost-push pressure on inflation. The offsetting rise in R needs to exercise a downward demand-pull effect which is sufficient to offset only the *net* excess of the S-generated upward demand-pull effect over the S-generated downward cost-push effect.

Similarly as one moves to the left along any I-contour one will cross a higher and higher Y-contour. Consider any given reduction in S. For Y to be constant there must be a rise in R which causes a decrease in I equal to the impact effect on C of the reduction of S. For I to be constant there need not be so great a rise in R and thus there would be some increase in Y. There must be some rise in R because if there were no rise in R there would be an accelerator boost to I due to the rise in Y. The rise in R must exercise a sufficient restraint on I to offset the accelerator

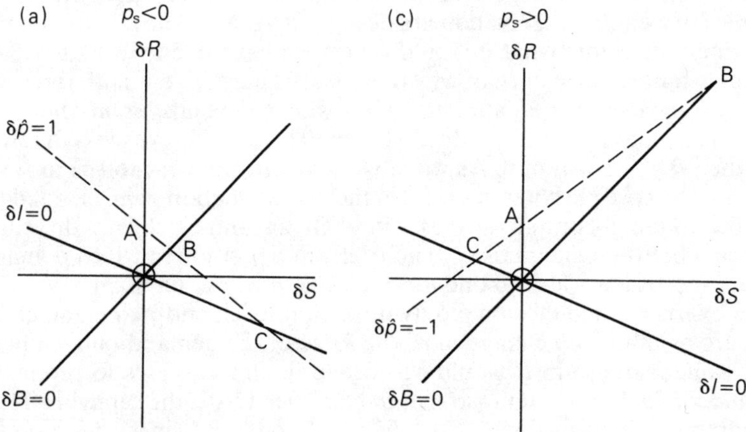

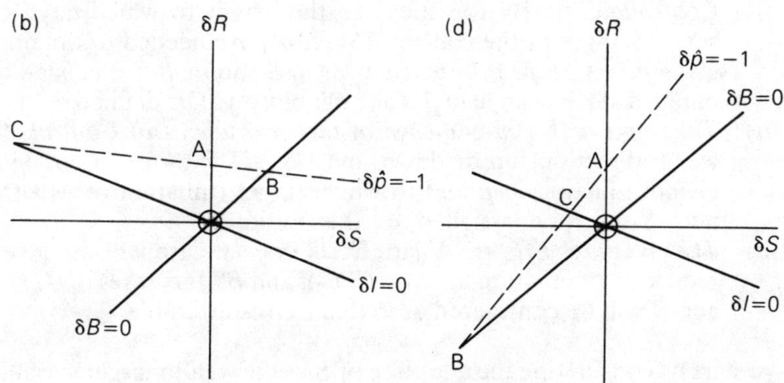

Figure 2

boost to I due to the rise in Y; but with I thus constant there will be some increase in Y as a result of the reduction in S combined with a moderate rise in R.

Since the B-contours slope upwards and the Y and C contours slope downwards, it follows that as one moves to the left along any B-contour, so one moves on to higher and higher Y and C contours.

Thus we may reach the following most important conclusion that *any* movement to the left along a wealth target contour will imply a rise in Y and C.[9]

[9] This conclusion is true also if k is taken as the wealth target variable. We have already shown in the previous section that any downward slope of a k-contour would be less steep than the downward slope of the Y-contour.

We now use the contours of Figure 1 to examine the effect of various combinations of the degree of cost-push in the wage equation and of the choice of wealth target on policies designed to reduce the rate of inflation by one unit below what it would otherwise have been. In Figure 2 we display four cases in each of which there are alternative wealth targets of $\delta B=0$ or $\delta I=0$, the attainment of which depends upon the same contour slopes in all four of the diagrams. The only difference is the slope of the $\delta\hat{p}=-1$ contour. As we move from diagram (a) to (b) to (c) to (d), so the cost-push parameter β in the wage equation increases and the slope of the $\hat{p}$-contour swings round in an anti-clockwise direction, passing between diagrams (b) and (c) from a position in which demand-pull exceeds cost-push to one in which cost-push is dominant.

R exerts its influence on $\hat{p}$ only through the demand-pull element. As we are assuming no change in α, the force of the demand-pull element, the same increase in R would be needed in all four cases to produce a reduction in $\hat{p}$ of one unit, so that the distance OA is the same in all four diagrams. Only the slope of the $\delta\hat{p}=-1$ contour swings round on the point A.

We will briefly comment on the outcomes in the four cases from the point of view of three features:

(i) *Controllability*. By this measure the extent to which large or small changes in the controls (S and R) are needed to obtain a given effect on $\hat{p}$. If large changes in S and/or R are needed to obtain a small change in $\hat{p}$, controllability will be defined as bad.
(ii) *The Signs and 'Assignments' of the Instruments of Control*. In which direction, up or down, must S and R move to obtain a given reduction in $\hat{p}$ and to which target (inflation or wealth) must S and R be 'assigned' for this purpose?
(iii) *The 'Welfare' Effects*. What effects in each case will the given reduction of inflation have on C, I, Y and B? Increases in C, I, Y and B will be considered as in themselves desirable.

We start by considering the adoption of B as the wealth target variable in conditions in which the demand-pull element is dominant (i.e. diagrams (a) and (b) in Figure 2). A reduction of inflation by one unit could be obtained by a rise in R of OA. But a $\delta B<0$ contour passes through A. To restore the budget balance S must be raised and R can be reduced somewhat below the point A to offset the deflationary effect of the rise in S. Equilibrium with $\delta B=0$ is reached at the point B. But $\delta Y<0$, $\delta C<0$, and $\delta I<0$ contours pass through the point B. In diagram (b) the point B is somewhat further to the right along the $\delta B=0$ contour and the reductions in Y, C and I are, therefore, somewhat greater in diagram (b) than in diagram (a). But in both cases one can say that controllability is good since only relatively small changes in S and R are needed and that welfare costs exist in reductions of Y, C and I but not on an excessive scale.

The signs for the control parameters are both positive in the sense that increases in both S and R are needed to attain the new equilibrium. The 'assignment' of S and R to the control of $\hat{p}$ and B depends on the relative steepness of the $\hat{p}$-contours and the B-contours regardless of sign in the way discussed above in connection with inequality (18). If the downward slope of the $\hat{p}$-contour were less steep than the upward slope of the B-contour, then R should be 'assigned' to the control of $\hat{p}$ and S to the control of B; and *vice versa*.

We know from (12) that the lower is the cost-push factor β, the steeper will be the downward slope of the $\hat{p}$-contour. However, we also know that the steepness of this slope will have a maximum value when $\beta = 0$ and that at this point the steepness of the downward slope of the $\hat{p}$-contour would be equal to cY/i (the same as the steepness of the downward slope of the Y-contour). Thus the maximum steepness of the downward slope of the $\hat{p}$-contour would be less than the steepness of the upward slope of the B-contour if

$$\frac{cY}{i} < \frac{1-c-v}{Sc} \cdot \frac{cY}{i}$$
$$\text{i.e. if} \quad S < \frac{1-c-v}{c} \qquad (19)$$

If this condition were fulfilled the $\hat{p}$-contour would be less steeply sloped than the B-contour for all values of β, since β cannot be <0. Since S cannot be >1 (otherwise consumption would be less than zero), condition (19) would necessarily be satisfied if c were small enough to make $(1-c-v)/c>1$; and even if this were not the case the condition would be satisfied for all low values of S. In such cases S would have to be 'assigned' to the control of B and R to the control of $\hat{p}$ for all values of β.

It is easy to understand why for high values of the cost-push element β, it is inappropriate to rely on the *net* excess of demand-pull over cost-push elements in the wage equation ($p_s<0$) to justify attempts to reduce $\hat{p}$ by raising S. But it may at first sight seem strange that for low values of S the cost-push element β cannot be low enough to justify the 'assignment' of S to the control of $\hat{p}$. This apparent paradox is to be explained as follows. Suppose S to be very small. Then from (12) it can be seen that b_r would be very small. In other words R would have a negligible effect on B because an expansion of the tax base would have a negligible effect on the budget balance if the rate of tax were very small. R could still have a substantial effect on $\hat{p}$ (the value of p_r being substantial). In this case, even if S would have a big net demand-pull effect on $\hat{p}$, it would be necessary to assign R to the control of $\hat{p}$ because R was insignificant as a controller of B. The effect of R on $\hat{p}$ relative to its effect on B would be greater than the effect of S on $\hat{p}$ relative to its effect on B.

If, however, condition (19) is not operational, there will be some initial range of values of β for which the downward slope of the $\hat{p}$-contour is steeper than the upward-slope of the B-contour, and over this range S should be 'assigned' to $\hat{p}$ to use its net demand-pull influence on the control of inflation.

As can be seen from diagram (c) the outcome can be very different if the cost-push element in the wage equation is dominant so that the $\delta\hat{p} = -1$ contour line is upward sloping. As in the previous cases a rise in the interest rate of OA with its unchanged pure demand-pull effect would cause a sufficient reduction in the rate of inflation and would cause the same reduction in the budget balance as a result of the restriction of the tax base. If the rate of tax is now raised in order to restore the budget balance, this will cause some revival of the rate of inflation due to the net cost-push effect of the rise in taxation. As a result the rate of interest will have to be raised beyond the point A in order to offset the net cost-push inflationary effect of the rise in S. Provided that this net cost-push effect is sufficiently moderate, there will be a point B in diagram (c) at which the budget balance is restored because the rise in interest rate has been sufficient to offset the net cost-push inflationary effect of the rise in the rate of tax.

But if the slope of the $\hat{p}$-contour is only a little steeper than that of the B-contour

(1) controllability will be bad because very large increases in R and S will be needed to obtain a unit decrease in $\hat{p}$,
(2) the welfare cost will be very great because at point B the levels of I, C, and Y will all be much reduced, while
(3) with the slope of the B-contour steeper than the slope of the $\hat{p}$-contour it will still be appropriate to 'assign' S to the control of B and R to the control of $\hat{p}$.

However, if the net cost-push element in the wage equation were very great, as depicted in diagram (d), the story would be very different. Starting once more with δR at the point A as a way of obtaining a unit reduction of the rate of inflation at the cost of a deterioration in the budget balance, it would no longer be sensible to try to restore the budget balance by raising the rate of tax. In this case if S is raised its very large net cost-push effect will cause a very large restoration of the inflation rate. To offset this a very large further rise in R will be needed to exert the necessary offsetting deflationary demand-pull effect on the rate of inflation. But this will cause such a reduction in the tax base that the budget balance will decrease in spite of the rise in the tax rate. Indeed, in order to improve the budget balance it will be necessary to *reduce* the rate of tax; this will cause a further net *reduction* in the rate of inflation below the target reduction of $\delta\hat{p} = -1$; this extra unneeded deflationary effect must be offset by a large fall in the rate of interest, which has so great an expansionary effect on the tax base that there is a restoration of the budget balance in spite of the reduction in the rate of tax. Equilibrium is restored at the point B in diagram (d).

In this case if the slope of the $\hat{p}$-contour is only slightly steeper than that of the B-contour,

(1) controllability is again very poor because huge reductions in S and R are needed to obtain a unit reduction in $\hat{p}$,

(2) at the new point of equilibrium B which is far down the *B*-contour from its origin at O there will be large increases in *I*, *Y*, and *C* so that a reduction in the rate of inflation will have been achieved without any strain on the budget balance but with the added bonus of large increases in output and employment both in the consumption section and in the investment sector, and
(3) with the slope of the $\hat{p}$-contour steeper than that of the *B*-contour the 'assignments' of controls to objectives and their signs are both reversed (*S* being lowered to reduce inflation instead of being raised to preserve the budget balance and *R* being lowered to preserve the tax base of the budget balance instead of being raised in order to reduce inflation).[10]

The controllability of the system is totally reversed if the level of investment (*I*) is taken as the wealth target instead of the budget balance (*B*). In diagrams (a) and (b) with $p_s<0$ the system now becomes difficult to control. In diagram (a) *S* is 'assigned' to the control of $\hat{p}$ and *R* to the control of *I*. Starting at point A the level of *I* is below target. *R* is lowered to stimulate *I*; this leads to some increase in $\hat{p}$; but with the slope of the $\hat{p}$-contour relatively steep this can be offset by a relatively small rise in *S* which causes only a small fall in *Y* and thus only a small acceleration fall in *I*; there is a net rise in *I* with the inflationary effect of the fall in *R* (below point A) being offset by the deflationary effect of the rise in *S*. A new equilibrium is achieved at point C with a large rise in *S* and a large fall in *Y* and *C* as a result of the movement towards the right along the wealth target contour.

If, however, the net balance of demand-pull over cost-push in the wage equation had been very small instead of very great, diagram (b) would be relevant with *S* assigned to the control of *I* and *R* to the control of $\hat{p}$. Starting once again at point A a reduction in *S* would be needed to restore the level of *I*; this reduction in *S* would lead to a small net inflationary effect the control of which would require a small offsetting rise in *R* with only a small negative repercussion on *I*. A final equilibrium would be found at point C with a very big reduction in *S* leading to a very big deterioration in the budget balance but with large increases in *Y* and *C* following the movement to the left along the wealth target contour.

If we compare diagrams (a) and (b) with *I* as the wealth target variable, both the signs and the assignments of the controls are reversed. In diagram (a) *S* is raised to reduce inflation and *R* is lowered to prevent a fall in *I*. In diagram (b) *R* is raised to reduce inflation and *S* is lowered to prevent a fall in investment. The determinant Δ_I in (15) has changed sign.

In the cases of diagrams (c) and (d) in which $p_s>0$, controllability is much improved by the choice of *I* instead of *B* as the wealth target.

[10] This corresponds to the case in which in (13) the determinant Δ_B changes sign with β greater than *Y*/*S*.

Whether S or R should be assigned to the control of $\hat{p}$ depends upon whether the upward slope of the $\hat{p}$-contour is greater or less than the downward slope of the I-contour. In either case a moderate reduction in R below its value at the point A (with its stimulating effect on the restoration of I towards its target level at the expense of some restimulation of inflationary pressure) combined with a moderate reduction in S (with its stimulating effect on the restoration of I combined with its cost-push net deflationary effect) will suffice to restore I to its original level while maintaining $\delta\hat{p} = -1$. There will in both cases at the point C be some moderate deterioration in the budget balance combined with some moderate increases in Y and C as the point of equilibrium moves moderately to the left along the wealth target contour.

4 The Availability of Free and Relatively Cheap Lunches

In the diagrams of Figure 2 there is one case (at the point B in diagram (d)) where a reduction of inflation is achieved with an increase in Y, C, and I and with no deterioration in the budget balance. Such a result makes one's mouth water and one may perhaps appropriately call it a case of a free lunch. There are other cases (at points C in diagrams (b), (c) and (d)) where a reduction of inflation is achieved with an increase in Y and C without any fall in I but at the expense of a deterioration in the budget balance. These we may perhaps call relatively cheap lunches. The possibility of an absolutely free or even of a relatively free lunch may seem startling at first sight. But two comments may be in order.

First, the result depends upon the assumption that the economy is below its full-employment level; it possesses unused resources which make an increase in output possible if the demand is forthcoming. No one who has heard of Keynes need be startled by the mention of the possibility of a free lunch if unemployed resources are available.

Second, as will be shown in the rest of this section even if unemployed resources remained available there is another strict limit to the extent to which free or cheap lunches can be obtained.

Figures 1 and 2 show that free or cheap lunches are available only if one moves to the left from the origin O along the constant-wealth-target contours ($\delta I = 0$ or $\delta B = 0$) onto higher Y and C contours ($\delta Y > 0$ and $\delta C > 0$). Thus there must be a fall in S (exerting less cost-push) to enable a decline in inflation to be combined with an increase in output and employment. Only in those cases in which equilibrium can be found at a point at which both $\delta S < 0$ and $\delta\hat{p} < 0$ can there be any free or cheap lunches. Free or cheap lunches are available only if $\delta\hat{p}/\delta S > 0$, i.e. only if a reduction in S can be combined with a reduction in $\hat{p}$.

The Figures 1 and 2 were, however, concerned with only small movements in S and R around the same origin (i.e. the same given original levels of S and R) in all the four diagrams of Figure 2. Thus where the fall in S showed a cheap or free lunch, this was true only for a small reduction in S, since the slopes of the $\hat{p}$, B, k, and I-contours (as can be seen from (12)) are not independent of the level of S. In particular, as S

falls, so the multiplier μ increases; and this raises the demand-pull element relatively to the cost-push element in the wage equation, because any initial increase in consumption or investment due to a reduction in S or R is by the multiplier swollen into a bigger increase in total output and thus into a greater ultimate demand-pull effect. Indeed it can be seen from the definition of μ in (10) that as S approaches the critical low value of $S = 1 - (1 - v)/c$ the multiplier and so the demand-pull in the wage equation will approach ∞.

It can be shown that as a result there is a strict limit to the process by which successive cumulative reductions in S can continue to provide free or cheap lunches. When S has been reduced to some critical level the slopes of the relevant contours will cease to be such as to allow still further increases in output to be combined with further falls in the rate of inflation. $\delta\hat{p}/\delta S$ will cease to >0. Suppose B^* to be taken as the wealth target. Then from the first row in (12) we have

$$\delta\hat{p} = (-\alpha\mu c Y + \beta)\,\delta S - \alpha\mu i\,\delta R \tag{20}$$

and from the third column of the second row in (12) we have the condition that B^* should remain unchanged, namely

$$\delta R = Y\frac{1 - c - v}{Si}\,\delta S \tag{21}$$

and from (10) the budget equation

$$SY = \bar{J} + B^* \tag{22}$$

If we eliminate δR and Y between (20), (21) and (22) we obtain the condition:

$$\frac{\delta\hat{p}}{\delta S} \gtreqless 0 \quad \text{as} \quad S \gtreqless \sqrt{\frac{\alpha}{\beta}(\bar{J} + B^*)} \tag{23}$$

A reduction in S can lead to a cheap or free lunch with $\delta Y>0$ and $\delta\hat{p}<0$ only so long as S remains above the critical level in (23). If the expression in (23) is >1, there can be no free or cheap lunches, since we must have $S<1$ to allow consumption to be positive. If, however, the expression in (23) was <1 there would be a range of values for S within which free or cheap lunches would be possible, namely

$$1>S> \sqrt{\frac{\alpha}{\beta}(J + B^*)} \tag{24}$$

A similar analysis can be applied to the case where the wealth target is I^*. We start once more with the equation (20) but we now add as the wealth condition from the fourth row in (12)

$$\delta R = -\frac{\nu\mu c Y}{i(1+\nu\mu)}\,\delta S \tag{25}$$

and the value of Y now becomes:

$$\begin{aligned} Y &= \bar{J} + I^* + \bar{C} + c(1-S)Y \\ &= \frac{\bar{J} + I^* + \bar{C}}{I - c(1-S)} \end{aligned} \tag{26}$$

Eliminating δR and Y between (20), (25) and (26) we obtain

$$\frac{\delta\hat{p}}{\delta S} \gtrless 0 \quad \text{as} \quad S \gtrless \sqrt{\frac{\alpha}{c\beta}(\bar{J} + \bar{C} + I^*) - \frac{1-c}{c}} \tag{27}$$

Once again if the critical value of S on the RHS of (27) is greater than 1 there is no possible value of $S<1$ which provides an opportunity for a cheap or free lunch. It is possible that the expression of the RHS of (27) is less than zero, in which case one would have to replace the tax S with a subsidy before free or cheap lunches became unavailable. But if the expression on the RHS of (27) were a positive fraction, there would be a range of positive values of S which would make a free or cheap lunch possible, namely

$$1 > S > \sqrt{\frac{\alpha}{c\beta}(\bar{J} + \bar{C} + I^*) - \frac{1-c}{c}} \tag{28}$$

Finally if k^* were taken as the wealth target one could combine equation (20) with

$$\delta R = \frac{(k^* - \nu)}{(1 - [k^* - \nu]\mu)i}\,\delta S \tag{29}$$

and

$$\begin{aligned} Y &= \bar{J} + k^* Y + \bar{C} + c(1-S)Y \\ &= \frac{\bar{J} + \bar{C}}{1 - c(1-S) - k^*} \end{aligned} \tag{30}$$

to obtain

$$\frac{\delta\hat{p}}{\delta S} \gtrless 0 \quad \text{as} \quad S \gtrless \sqrt{\frac{\alpha}{c\beta}(\bar{J} + \bar{C}) - \frac{1-c-k^*}{c}} \tag{31}$$

Once again if the expression on the RHS of (31) were >1, there would be no possible free or cheap lunches; if it were <0, the possibility of free or cheap lunches would exist for all possible positive values of S; and if it were equal to a positive fraction, there would be a limited range of free or cheap lunches as S was reduced from unity to this critical value.

We know from (10) that

$$\hat{p} = \alpha Y + \beta S + \hat{w} \tag{32}$$

In the cases in which there is a range of feasible values of S which offer the opportunity of a cheap or free lunch, we can find the minimum possible value of the rate of inflation by taking the relevant value for Y in (22), (26) or (30) and the critical value for S in (23), (27) or (31) and substituting these values for Y and S in (32).

The minimum possible value of $\hat{p}$ is then found to be

(i) $$\hat{p} = 2\sqrt{\alpha\beta(\bar{J} + B^*)} + \hat{w}$$

if B is to be kept constant at B^*

(ii) $$\hat{p} = 2\sqrt{\frac{\alpha\beta}{c}(\bar{J} + \bar{C} + I^*) - \beta\frac{1-c}{c}} + \hat{w} \tag{33}$$

if I is to be kept constant at I^*

or (iii) $$\hat{p} = 2\sqrt{\frac{\alpha\beta}{c}(\bar{J} + \bar{C}) - \beta\frac{1-c-k^*}{c}} + \hat{w}$$

if k is to be kept constant at k^*.

In all three cases $\hat{w}$ represents those forces which operate on $\hat{p}$ in the period in question and which remain unaffected by any adjustments to the current levels of S and R.

If these minimal values for the rate of inflation are unacceptable, *either* the wage-setting institutions must be reformed so as to reduce the inflationary parameters in the wage equation *or* the country must be prepared to make less provision for the future by relaxation of the wealth targets *or* the government must reduce its demand for goods and services. How easy it would be to devise endless employment subsidies to enable all money wage claims to be granted without any dire effects upon money labour costs or prices, so long as these subsidies could be happily financed by cutting expenditures on defence or the national health service or by living on the country's capital resources!

5 The Open Economy

We next consider a small open economy in which trading and financial transactions take place within a world economy, the single economy not being large enough to affect trading conditions in the rest of the world.

The equations of the previous model (1) to (9) are now modified in the following way:

$$Y = L \tag{34}$$

$$P = (1 + m)W \tag{35}$$

$$C = c(1 - S)Y + \bar{C} \tag{36}$$

$$I = -iR + vY + \bar{I} \tag{37}$$

The equations for Y, P, C and I remain unchanged.

$$Z = \bar{I} - iR + vY + X - M \tag{38}$$

We are now dealing with total investment (Z), i.e. with domestic plus foreign investment instead of only domestic investment.

$$Y = \bar{J} + Z + C \tag{39}$$

The national product now contains foreign investment as well as domestic investment.

$$M = \eta(Y - X + M) = \eta'(Y - X) \tag{40}$$

where

$$\eta' = \frac{\eta}{1 - \eta}$$

We assume that all imports take the form of finished goods and not of raw materials. This justifies the assumption in (35) above that the price of home products is set by a mark-up only on domestic labour costs. We assume that the expenditure and price elasticities of demand for imports are both unity so that the amount spent on imports in terms of home products (M) is a constant proportion (η) of total expenditures on finished goods bought for domestic use.

$$X = \bar{X}A^{-\epsilon} \tag{41}$$

where

$$A = \frac{EP}{\bar{P}_f} \tag{42}$$

A measures the real terms of trade where P is the price of home products, E is the rate of exchange (units of foreign money per unit of home money) and $\bar{P}_f$ is the price of foreign products in terms of foreign money.

ϵ then measures the price elasticity of the foreign demand for the country's exports (X).

$$F = \lambda\{\phi(\bar{R}_f - R) - \bar{H}\}$$
$$= -\theta R + \bar{F} \tag{43}$$

It is assumed that foreign capital movements (F = net outflows of capital funds measured in terms of domestic products) take the form solely of transactions initiated by residents of the home country. Such residents are assumed to wish to hold an amount of foreign assets which have a value in terms of domestic products ($\phi[\bar{R}_f - R]$) which depends upon the difference between the yield abroad ($\bar{R}_f$) and the yield at home (R) and to move funds abroad (F) at a rate (λ) which depends upon the extent to which this desired portfolio holding ($\phi[\bar{R}_f - R]$) falls below the portfolio holding actually held at the beginning of this period ($H_{-1} = \bar{H}$). With $\theta = \lambda\phi$ equation (43) then determines the value of this period's net outward flow of capital funds.

$$X = F + M \tag{44}$$

Equilibrium implies that the value of exports equals the value of imports plus the value of foreign lending, if one neglects interest earned on foreign assets. This neglect of interest payments in the balance of payments could represent a very serious distortion for dynamic analysis since accumulation of foreign interest can be a serious cause of instability (see Christodoulakis, Meade and Weale (1987)). But for a comparative-static analysis it is an acceptable simplification. Equation (44), using (41) and (43) could be written as $(1 + \eta')\bar{X}A^{-\epsilon} = \eta' Y + \theta(R_f - R$ and is in fact the equation which serves to determine the real terms of trade which will clear the market. If X were less than $F + M$, then the currency would depreciate, the terms of trade would deteriorate and the foreign demand for the country's exports would rise.

$$P_c = P^{1-\eta}(\bar{P}_f/E)^{\eta}$$
$$= PA^{-\eta}, \quad \text{using (42)} \tag{45}$$

The cost of living is a weighted average of the cost of domestic finished goods (P) and of imported finished goods ($\bar{P}_f/E$), the weights being dependent on the proportion of domestic expenditures spent on imports (η). If one uses (42) one can write (43) in the form of $P_c = PA^{-\eta}$.

$$k = \frac{Z}{Y} \tag{46}$$

This is merely an expression for the ratio of total investment to income which may be used as a wealth target.

$$B = SY - \bar{J} \tag{47}$$

This expression for the budget deficit is the same as for the closed economy in equation (6).

$$V = \frac{W(1-S)}{P_c} \tag{48a}$$

$$= \frac{(1-S)A^{\eta}}{1+m}, \quad \text{using (35) and (45)}$$

The real value of a worker's take-home pay (V) is his money wage (W) less tax (S) divided by the cost of living (P_c).

We have as in (8b) and (8c) for the closed economy:

$$\tilde{V} = \bar{V} + \frac{L}{\beta'} \tag{48b}$$

and

$$L_s = \beta'(V - \bar{V}) \tag{48c}$$

We can also express the two alternative ways of expressing the factors leading to wage inflation, as in (9a) and (9b) for the closed economy:

$$\hat{w} = \alpha_1(\tilde{V} - V) + \gamma(V_{-1} - V) \tag{49a}$$

and

$$\hat{w} = \alpha_2(L - L_s) + \gamma(V_{-1} - V) \tag{49b}$$

which can now both be expressed as:

$$\hat{w} = \alpha Y - \beta(1-S)A^{\eta} + \hat{\bar{w}} \tag{49c}$$

where, as before, $\alpha = \alpha_1/\beta'$ and $\beta = (\alpha_1 + \gamma)/(1+m)$ but $\hat{\bar{w}} = \alpha_1\bar{V} + \gamma V_{-1}$.

As before the terms in α and β express the demand-pull and the cost-push forces affecting the rate of wage inflation. But, while the price level of domestic products is determined by a mark-up on money wage cost in the same way as before, the cost of living now depends upon the price of imports as well as upon this marked-up price of home products; and this involves a modification of the formulation of the wage equations. The import-price modification of the cost of living (A^{η}) must now be applied to the post-tax $(1-S)$ value of the money wage to obtain the real value of take-home pay.

If we now eliminate L, W, I, M, X, E, F, P_c and V from equations (34) to (49) and rearrange terms we obtain:

$$Y = \bar{J} + C + c(1-S)Y + \bar{I} - iR + vY + \bar{F} - \theta R$$

$$= \mu\{-(i+\theta)R + \bar{Y}\} \tag{50}$$

where

$$\bar{Y} = \bar{J} + \bar{C} + \bar{I} + \bar{F}$$

and
$$\mu = \frac{1}{1 - c(1-S) - v}$$

$$C = c(1-S)Y + \bar{C} \tag{51}$$

$$Z = -(i+\theta)R + vY + \bar{I} + \bar{F} \tag{52}$$

$$B = SY - \bar{J} \tag{53}$$

$$k \equiv \frac{Z}{Y} = \frac{-(i+\theta)R + \bar{I} + \bar{F}}{Y} \tag{54}$$

$$\hat{p} = \alpha Y - \beta(1-S)A^{\eta} + \hat{\bar{w}} \tag{55}$$

$$A^{-\epsilon} = \frac{1}{(1+\eta')\bar{X}}\{\bar{F} - \theta R + \eta' Y\} \tag{56}$$

The assumptions that the international flow of capital funds measured in terms of the home product depends solely on the relative rates of interest and that the exchange rate and terms of trade adjust so as to maintain the balance of trade (i.e. the level of real foreign investment) equal to the flow of funds have two important effects upon these equations. First, total investment (Z) continues to depend solely on the rate of interest as it did in the closed economy, because foreign investment adjusts (through variations in the terms of trade) so as to be equal to the flow of funds which in turn depends solely on the rate of interest. Second, variations in S and so in Y have no effect upon foreign investment. It is true that a change in Y causes a change in M; but if F is constant, the terms of trade adjust so as to cause a change in X which exactly offsets the change in M. For this reason the multiplier (μ) in the open economy remains the same as it was in the closed economy. The multiplicand is changed by the addition of any positive foreign investment; but a change in Y does not affect this item, so the multiplier is unchanged.

By substituting the value of Y from (50) into equations (51) to (56) we can obtain expressions for Y, C, Z, B, $\hat{p}$, and A in terms of certain constant parameters and the two control variables S and R.

Differentiation of (56) and normalising by writing $A = 1$ (i.e. defining units of home and foreign products so that the real terms of trade are unity in the period under examination), we obtain

$$\delta A = \frac{\theta \delta R - \eta' \delta Y}{\epsilon(1+\eta')\bar{X}} \tag{57}$$

Differentiation of (50) to (55) using (57) to eliminate δA, gives matrix (58) which has for the open economy the same form as matrix (11) for the closed economy:

$$\begin{bmatrix} \delta\hat{p} \\ \delta B \\ \delta k \\ \delta Z \\ \delta C \\ \delta Y \end{bmatrix} = \begin{bmatrix} p_s & p_r \\ b_s & b_r \\ k_s & k_r \\ z_s & z_r \\ c_s & c_r \\ y_s & y_r \end{bmatrix} \begin{bmatrix} \delta S \\ \delta R \end{bmatrix} \tag{58}$$

where

$$p_s = \{-\alpha\mu cY + \beta(1-\psi\eta'\mu)\} \quad \text{with} \quad \psi = \frac{\eta(1-\eta)(1-S)cY}{\epsilon X}$$

$$p_r = -\left\{\alpha\mu(i+\theta) + \frac{\beta\psi}{cY}(\eta'\mu[i+\theta]+\theta)\right\}$$

$$\sigma_p = \frac{-\alpha\mu cY + \beta(1-\psi\eta'\mu)}{\alpha\mu cY + \beta\psi(\eta'\mu + \theta/(i+\theta))} \cdot \frac{cY}{i+\theta}$$

$$b_s = (1-c-v)\mu Y \qquad b_r = -S\mu(i+\theta) \qquad \sigma_b = \frac{1-c-v}{Sc} \cdot \frac{cY}{i+\theta}$$

$$k_s = (k-v)\mu c \qquad k_r = -\{1-(k-v)\mu\}(i+\theta)/Y \qquad \sigma_k = \frac{(k-v)\mu}{1-(k-v)\mu} \cdot \frac{cY}{i+\theta}$$

$$= \frac{k-v}{1-c(1-S)-k} \cdot \frac{cY}{i+\theta} \tag{59}$$

$$z_s = -v\mu cY \qquad z_r = -(1+v\mu)(i+\theta) \qquad \sigma_z = -\frac{v\mu}{1+v\mu} \cdot \frac{cY}{i+\theta}$$

$$c_s = -(1-v)\mu cY \qquad c_r = -\{(1-v)\mu - 1\}(i+\theta) \qquad \sigma_c = -\frac{(1-v)\mu}{(1-v)\mu - 1} \cdot \frac{cY}{i+\theta}$$

$$\begin{aligned} y_s &= z_s + c_s \\ &= -\mu cY \end{aligned} \qquad \begin{aligned} y_r &= z_r + c_r \\ &= -\mu(i+\theta) \end{aligned} \qquad \sigma_y = -\frac{cY}{i+\theta}$$

The forms of (58) and (59) are similar to the forms of (11) and (12) for the closed economy. There are, however, certain changes in the values of the various parameters.

(1) The expression for the parameters b_s, k_s, z_s (in place of i_s), c_s and y_s are all unchanged. These similarities all result from the fact noted above that changes in Y (resulting from a change in S) have no effect on $(X-M)$ and so no effect upon the multiplicand whether it includes or excludes $(X-M)$.

(2) On the other hand, the expressions for the parameters b_r, k_r, z_r (in place of i_r), c_r, and y_r are all multiplied by $(i+\theta)/i$. The reason for this is that the rise in R now causes total investment to fall by $\theta\delta R$ (the effect on foreign investment) as well as by $i\delta R$ (the effect on home investment).

The response to a change in R is thus multiplied up by the same factor in all these cases.

(3) The really notable changes are in the parameters p_s and p_r. As far as p_s is concerned there is a reduction in the cost-push element equal to $\beta\psi\eta'\mu$. This is due to the fact that a rise in S by reducing Y will cause a reduction in M which will lead to an appreciation of the exchange rate and so to a fall in the import-goods element in the cost of living. The aspiration wage will thereby be more fully met.

(4) But the changes in the parameter p_r will be even more striking. In this case the deflationary response to a rise in the rate of interest will be increased by three factors: (i) $\alpha\mu\theta$ (ii) $(\beta\psi/cY)\eta'\mu(i+\theta)$ and (iii) $(\beta\psi/cY)\theta$. Factor (i) occurs because the rise in the rate of interest will cause an inflow of funds which will cause an appreciation of the currency which will cause a fall in exports which after enlargement by the multiplier will result in a decreased inflationary demand-pull effect. Factor (ii) represents the fact that the decreased income due to the multiplier effect of the decreases in domestic and foreign investment caused by the higher rate of interest will cause a reduction in the demand for imports and so an appreciation of the currency which in turn will lower the cost of living and so reduce the cost-push element in the cost of living. Factor (iii) shows the favourable cost-push effect due to the appreciation of the currency which was noted in factor (i) to result from the reduction in the outflow of capital funds.

These changes in the parameters affect the changes in the contour slopes shown in the third columns of (12) and (59) respectively for the closed and the open economies.

It will be seen that all the contour slopes with the exception of the $\hat{p}$-contour slope are simply multiplied by the same factor $i/(i+\theta)$. This means that the steepnesses of all the slopes (except the σ_p slope) as shown in Figures 1 and 2 for the closed economy are reduced by a factor $i/(i+\theta)$, regardless of sign, simply because a smaller change in R is now needed to offset any change in S because R operates on foreign as well as domestic investment. We can, therefore, continue to use Figures 1 and 2 for all the contour slopes (except those for $\hat{p}$) since they all preserve an unchanged sign and an unchanged relationship to each other. For example, it is still true that as one moves to the left along any one wealth target contour, so one moves on to higher and higher Y and C contour lines.

In the third columns of (12) and (59) the slopes of the contour lines for B, k, Z and C are all expressed as multiples of the slope of the Y-contour line. In the first row of (12) and (59) we also express the slope of the $\hat{p}$-contour line as multiples of the cY/i or $cY/(i+\theta)$, i.e. of the absolute value of the slope of the Y-contour line. In the case of B, k, Z and C these multiples are the same in the open economy as in the closed economy. But this is not so in the case of the $\hat{p}$-contour lines where the multiple of the downward steepness of the Y-contour changes from Σ_c to Σ_0 as between the closed and open economies, where

$$\Sigma_c = \frac{-\alpha\mu cY + \beta}{\alpha\mu cY}$$

$$\Sigma_o = \frac{-\alpha\mu cY + \beta(1 - \psi\eta'\mu)}{\alpha\mu c\mathrm{Y} + \beta[\psi\eta'\mu + \psi\theta/(i+\theta)]} \tag{60}$$

Since all the other relationships remain unchanged it is the change in this relationship from Σ_c to Σ_o which expresses the basic change due to the opening of the economy. What changes must be made to the general behaviour of the $\hat{p}$-contour slopes in Figures 1 and 2 as a result of the changes in the relative slopes of the $\hat{p}$-contours shown in (60)?

(1) From (60) we have

$$\frac{\delta\Sigma_c}{\delta\beta} = \frac{\beta}{\alpha\mu cV} > 0 \quad \text{and} \quad \frac{\delta\Sigma_o}{\delta\beta} = \frac{\alpha\mu cY[1 + \psi\theta/(i+\sigma)]}{\{\ \cdot\ \}^2} > 0$$

so that it remains true that the relative slope of the open-economy $\hat{p}$-contour swings round anti-clockwise as one moves from diagram (a) to (b) to (c) to (d) in Figure 2.[11] If $\beta = 0$, then from (60) it can be seen that $\Sigma_c = \Sigma_0 = -1$. In other words it also remains true that the $\hat{p}$-contour can never have a negative slope which is steeper than the negative slope of the Y contour. However as $\beta \rightarrow \infty$ so $\Sigma_c \rightarrow \infty$, but $\Sigma_0 \rightarrow (1 - \psi\eta'\mu)/[\psi\eta'\mu + \psi\theta/(i+\theta)]$. Thus in the open economy there is a strict upper limit to Σ_o, a limit which will actually be <0 if $\psi\eta'\mu > 1$.[12] This is a most important effect of opening the economy. It may, with decreasing probabilities, rule out the existence of diagrams (d), (c) and (b) of Figure 2.

(2) The effect of changes in income on the demand for imports and so on the real terms of trade and the cost of living is shown by the introduction of the term $\beta'\psi\eta\mu$ in the slope Σ_0 in (60). Its appearance as a negative element in the numerator shifts the slope of the $\hat{p}$-contour in a clockwise direction and makes probable a movement of the actual situation in the direction from diagram (d) to (c) to (b). Its appearance as a positive element in the denominator leads to a decrease in the steepness of the slope of the $\hat{p}$-contour relative to the steepness of the slopes of all the other contours.

(3) The introduction of the term $\psi\theta/(i+\theta)$ into the denominator Σ_o has the unequivocal effect of decreasing the relative steepness of the slope of the $\hat{p}$-contour regardless of sign.

(4) The opening of the economy has one other effect on the contour

[11] From (59) we can obtain $p_s = -\alpha c(\bar{Y} - [i+\theta]R)\mu^2 + \beta(1 - \psi\eta'\mu)$ where $\bar{Y} - (i+\theta)R > 0$ is the multiplicand. It follows that $\delta p_s/\delta\mu < 0$. Since μ will $\rightarrow \infty$ as S is decreased without limit, there must in the open economy as in the closed economy be a limit to the possibility of reducing $\hat{p}$ by reducing S. The demand-pull effect will ultimately be dominant in the open economy as it was shown to be in the closed economy in the discussion of equations (20) to (33).

[12] This is not impossible if the volume of the country's exports and the elasticity of the foreign demand for them are sufficiently small.

for $\delta\hat{p} = -1$ in Figure 2. It can be seen from the expression δ for p_r in (12) and (59) that a rise in β has no effect on p_r in the closed economy whereas a rise in β will lower the value of p_r in the open economy; in the closed economy a rise in R has only its deflationary demand-pull effect, whereas in the open economy it has in addition a deflationary cost-push effect. This means that if one is to use Figure 2 for the analysis of the open economy, the distance OA (i.e. the rise in R needed to cause $\delta\hat{p} = -1$) falls as one moves from diagram (a) to (b) to (d).

With these interpretations of the sign, the relative slope, and the distance from origin on the vertical axis of the $\hat{p}$-contour, Figure 2 and its subsequent analysis can be used for the open economy as it was used for the closed economy. All combinations are still conceivable and it is difficult to reach any firm conclusions about the effect of opening the economy. There are, however, some important probabilities.

(1) A positive slope for σ_p becomes more unlikely, making diagrams (c) and (d) – and in particular diagram (d) with its completely free lunch – less probable as compared with the negative slopes for σ_p in diagrams (a) and (b).

(2) The steepness of the $\hat{p}$-contour relative to the steepness of the other contours is more likely to fall than to rise, which implies an increased probability that it would be appropriate to 'assign' R to the control of $\hat{p}$.

6 Conclusion

Certain insights may be gained from the greatly simplified comparative-static analysis of the preceding sections.

(1) Given (i) the initial position in the economy, (ii) the model of the economy, and (iii) the values of the target variables which are to be achieved, the use of the control variables (S and R) is determined. That is to say, the signs and the absolute values of the necessary δS and δR are in no sense arbitrary. This obvious conclusion is not without its importance. These matters are sometimes discussed as if it were an open matter of choice whether, for example, one should use fiscal policy or monetary policy as the primary instrument for the control of inflation. In a comparative-static model of the kind discussed in this chapter and with two instruments of control to achieve two objectives of policy, no open choice exists. 'Assignment' is not an arbitrary matter.

This conclusion cannot be carried over to a dynamic analysis of macro-economic policy without some modification. One would need to say that given (i) the initial position, (ii) the model of the economy, (iii) the values of the target variables to be achieved, and (iv) *the path to be taken by the economy to the new steady state*, the use of the control variables over time would be fully determined. A simple example may serve to show the need for the addition of condition (iv). Suppose the final wealth target to be a given level of expenditure. The path to the new steady state might be one on which the current investment expenditures were maintained at a high, or alternatively at a low, level. In the former case the new steady state will enjoy the advantage of a higher stock of real capital equipment than in the latter case. Thus the economy may in the new steady state enjoy the same final financial targets (rate of price inflation and level of investment expenditures) but may find itself in a different real situation because of the difference in the dynamic path with which it had chosen to attain the new target objectives.[13]

(2) The analysis in the preceding sections has indicated the basic importance which must be ascribed to the balance between demand-pull and cost-push factors in the determination of rates of pay. Different balances between these factors can cause basic changes in the signs and 'assignments' of financial instruments of control. For example, as we have seen, it may determine whether fiscal policy or monetary policy should be 'assigned' to the control of inflation; and it may even determine whether the rate of tax should be raised or lowered in order to reduce inflation.

(3) If the cost-push factor in wage-setting is extremely powerful and if tax rates are high, it is possible that a reduction of tax will provide an absolutely free lunch in the sense of leading to a simultaneous reduction of inflation, increase of investment, increase of consumption, increase of output, and increase of employment, without any deterioration of the budget balance. But in the model examined in this chapter it is clear that this possibility will reach a limit when the rate of tax has been reduced to a certain critical level; and at this point the rate of price inflation will have reached a minimum level which in turn may well still be unacceptably high.

(4) From the point of view of controllability (i.e. the possibility of attaining given changes in the target variables with relatively small changes in the instrument variables) it is important to choose a form of national wealth target which is compatible with the inflation target. This compatibility depends essentially upon the balance between demand-pull and cost-push in the wage equation. The need is to choose a national wealth target whose contour slope (as explained in Section 3) is orthogonal to the contour slope of the inflation target.

(5) The outstanding effect of opening a small economy to international influences shows itself through the sensitivity of capital movements to changes in the country's rate of interest relative to the rates of interest in the rest of the world. This has the result of making monetary policy a much more potent instrument of control in two quite different ways.

In the first place, the movement of capital funds affects the rate of foreign exchange and so the real terms of trade. This in turn affects the balance of trade and so the country's foreign investment, so that monetary policy now affects total demand through its effect on foreign investment as well as on domestic investment.

[13] It is, of course, possible in an international setting for the various countries to co-operate on choice of national financial targets which they will seek to attain and on the dynamic paths along which they will move to these final targets. Such agreements could very materially affect their 'assignments' of monetary and fiscal policies to the control of inflation and wealth.

In the second place, the change in the terms of trade affects the price of imports and thus the cost of living, so that monetary policy now exercises an important influence over the cost-push factor in wage determination. For this reason the probability of 'assignment' of monetary policy to the control of inflation is markedly enhanced.

References

A. Blinder and R. Solow (1973), 'Does Fiscal Policy Matter?', *Journal of Public Economics*, vol 2, pp. 319–337.

N. Christodoulakis, J. Meade and M. Weale (1987), 'Exchange Rate Regimes and Stock Instability'. Department of Applied Economics, University of Cambridge (mimeo).

R. A. Mundell (1962), 'The Appropriate Use of Monetary and Fiscal Policy for Internal and External Stability'. *IMF Staff Papers*, vol. 9, pp. 70–79.

Published Writings of James Meade

This bibliography is organised in the following sections: books (including books edited), articles in journals, pamphlets, chapters in books, reviews, articles in newspapers, letters to newspapers and unpublished papers included in this edition. We have tried to ensure completeness of the first three sections and are very grateful to Oxford University Press and Unwin Hyman for their efforts to locate all translations of Meade's books. With respect to chapters in books, however, we cannot pretend to have sought or located *all* the many collections in which Meade's articles have been reprinted. Furthermore, the main source of information on Meade's reviews of books and his articles and letters in newspapers has been the copies he has kept in his files.

Books

For translations the title is given where known; otherwise publication details only are provided. In some cases only the date of agreement is known and is given in square brackets.

(1933) *The Rate of Interest in a Progressive State* (London: Macmillan).

(1936) *An Introduction to Economic Analysis and Policy* (Oxford: Clarendon Press). (1937) 2nd edition (London: Oxford University Press). (1938) 3rd, American, edition, edited by C. J. Hitch, with introduction by A. H. Hansen (New York: Oxford University Press). Reprinted 1940, 1942.
Translations: French *Economie politique et politique économique* (Paris: Payot, 1939); Spanish *Economia, la ciencia y la politica* (Mexico: Fondo de cultura economica, 1943); Japanese *Keizaigaku Nyumon* (Tokyo: Tokyo Keizai Shimposha, 1952); Korean *Gyeongje Hag Weonri* (Seoul: Minjung-seongwan, 1964); Hindi (Delhi: Ranjit, 1970).

(with G. Ryle and K. C. Wheare) (1937) *Bibliography for the Honour School of Philosophy, Politics and Economics* (Oxford: Basil Blackwell).

(1937) *World Economic Survey, Seventh Year, 1937/38* (Geneva: League of Nations).

(1938) *Consumers' Credits and Unemployment* (London: Oxford University Press).

(1939) *World Economic Survey, Eighth Year, 1938/39* (Geneva: League of Nations).

(1940) *The Economic Basis of a Durable Peace* (London: Allen & Unwin; New York: Oxford University Press). Reprinted 1942, London: Allen & Unwin.

(with Richard Stone) (1944) *National Income and Expenditure* (London: Oxford

University Press). (1948) 2nd edition, Cambridge: Bowes & Bowes. (1952) 3rd edition, Cambridge: Bowes & Bowes. (1957) 4th edition, London: Bowes & Bowes. [Subsequent (5th–10th) editions (London: Bowes & Bowes, 1961–1977) were written by Richard and Giovanna Stone.] 1st edition reprinted in *Collected Papers*, Vol. I, Chapter 10.

Translations: Turkish *Ingiltere' de Milli Gelir v e Gider* (Ankara: Maliye Vekaleti Maliye Tetkik Kurulu, 1953).

(1948) *Planning and the Price Mechanism: The Liberal-Socialist Solution* (London: Allen & Unwin) (1949, New York: Macmillan). Reprinted 1953, 1957, 1962, London: Allen & Unwin.

Translations: Japanese *Keizaikeikaku to Kakaku kiko* (Tokyo: Shakaishiso Sha, 1950); German *Planung und Preismechanismus: Die Liberalsoziale Lösung* (Bern: Francke; Tübingen: Mohr, 1951); French *Plans et prix: entre socialisme et libéralisme* (Paris: Rivière, 1952); Korean *Gyeong'je'ge'hoeg Gwa Ga'gyeog'gi'gu* (Seoul: Il'sin'sa, 1959); Italian (La Nouva Italia Editrice, [1962]); Spanish (Editorial Tecnos, [1965]).

(1951a) *The Theory of International Economic Policy, Volume I: The Balance of Payments* (London and New York: Oxford University Press for Royal Institute of International Affairs). Reprinted 1952, 1954, 1956, 1960, 1962, 1963, 1966, 1970.

Translations: Spanish *El balance de pagos* (Buenos Aires: El Ateneo, 1976).

(1951b) *The Theory of International Economic Policy, Volume I: The Balance of Payments*: Mathematical Supplement (London and New York: Oxford University Press for Royal Institute of International Affairs). Reprinted 1960.

(1952) *A Geometry of International Trade* (London: Allen & Unwin; New York: Macmillan). Reprinted 1956, 1967, London: Allen & Unwin; 1966, 1969, New York: Kelly.

Translations: Spanish *Geometria del Comercio Internacional* (Madrid: Aguilar, 1957); Japanese (Bunga-do, [1964]).

(1953) *Problems of Economic Union*, Charles R. Walgreen Foundation Lectures (Chicago: Chicago University Press; London: Allen & Unwin).

Translations: German *Probleme der Wirtschaftsunion Souveräner Staaten* (Tübingen: Mohr; Zurich: Polygraph Verl., 1955); Spanish *Problemas de la Union Economica* (Madrid: Aguilar, 1957); French *Les Problèmes de L'Union Economique* (Paris: Institut pour le Développement Economique, 1963); Japanese: *Keizai Tago no Monda* (Tokyo: Bunga-do, 1960).

(1955a) *The Theory of International Economic Policy, Volume II: Trade and Welfare* (London and New York: Oxford University Press for Royal Institute of International Affairs). Reprinted 1960, 1961, 1962, 1964.

(1955b) *The Theory of International Economic Policy, Volume II: Trade and Welfare: Mathematical Supplement* (London and New York: Oxford University Press for Royal Institute of International Affairs).

(1955c) *The Theory of Customs Unions*, Professor Dr F. de Vries Lectures (Amsterdam: North-Holland). Reprinted 1966, 1968, Amsterdam: North-Holland; 1980, Westport, Conn.: Greenwood Press.

Translations: Spanish *Teoria de las Uniones Aduaneras* (Madrid: Moneda y Credito, 1969).

(1958) *The Control of Inflation* (Cambridge: Cambridge University Press). Reprinted in *Collected Papers*, Vol. I, Chapter 18.

Translations: Hebrew *Kezad Le-rassen Inflazya* (Tel Aviv: Histadderut Lapekidim, Hawa'ad ha-merkazi, 1964).

(with others) (1961) *The Economic and Social Structure of Mauritius, Report to the Governor of Mauritius* (London: Methuen; Port Louis: Mauritius Printing Co.). Reprinted 1968, London: Cass.

(1961) *A Neo-Classical Theory of Economic Growth* (London: Allen & Unwin; New York: Oxford University Press). (1962) Revised 2nd edition (London: Allen & Unwin). (1963) Revised 2nd edition (New York: Oxford University Press). Reprinted 1964, London: Allen & Unwin; 1984, Westport, Conn.: Greenwood Press.
Translations: Japanese (Diamond Inc. [1961]); Hungarian (Kozgazdasagi es Jogi Konyvkiado, [1964]; Spanish *Una Teoria neoclásica del crecimento economico* (Mexico: Fondo de Cultura Economica, 1976).

(with H. H. Liesner and S. J. Wells) (1962) *Case Studies in European Economic Union: The Mechanics of Integration* (London and New York: Oxford University Press).
Translations: Spanish *La union economica de Europe: estudios de diversos casas* (Buenos Aires: Instituto para la Integracion de America Latina, 1967).

(1964) *Efficiency, Equality and the Ownership of Property* (London: Allen & Unwin). (1965, Cambridge, MA: Harvard University Press). Reprinted 1969, London: Allen & Unwin.
Translations: Spanish *Eficiencia, justicia y propiedad* (Madrid: Editorial Tecnos, 1972); Hindi (Khosla & Co. [1974]); Japanese (Nihon Keizai Shinbusha, [1977]).

(1965) *The Stationary Economy (Principles of Political Economy, Vol. 1)* (London: Allen & Unwin; Chicago: Aldine Publishing Co.). Reprinted 1970, London: Allen & Unwin.
Translations: Japanese *Keizaigaku Genri (1)* (Tokyo: Diamond Inc., 1966); Spanish (Alianza Editorial, [1966]); Portuguese (Zahar Editores, [1966]); German *Die Stationäre Wirtschaft* (Cologne: Kiepenheuer und Witsch, 1971).

(with A. S. Parkes) (eds) (1965) *Biological Aspects of Social Problems: A Symposium held by the Eugenics Society in October 1964* (Edinburgh & London: Oliver & Boyd; New York: Plenum Press).

(with A. S. Parkes) (eds) (1966) *Genetic and Environmental Factors in Human Ability: A Symposium held by the Eugenics Society in September–October 1965* (Edinburgh & London: Oliver & Boyd; New York: Plenum Press).

(1968) *The Growing Economy (Principles of Political Economy, Vol. 2)* (London: Allen & Unwin; Chicago: Aldine Publishing Co.).
Translations: Japanese *Keizaigaku Genri (2)* (Tokyo: Diamond Inc., 1972); Portuguese (Zahar Editores, [1971]); Spanish (Alianza Editorial, [1972]).

(1970) *The Theory of Indicative Planning: Lectures given in the University of Manchester* (Manchester: Manchester University Press). Reprinted in *Collected Papers*, Vol. II, Chapter 9.

(1971) *The Controlled Economy (Principles of Political Economy, Vol. 3)* (London: Allen & Unwin). (1972, Albany: State University of New York Press).
Translations: Spanish (Alianza Editorial, [1972]).

(1973) *The Theory of Economic Externalities: The Control of Environmental Pollution and Similar Social Costs* (Leiden: A. W. Sijthoff for Institut Universitaire de Hautes Etudes Internationales).

(1975) *The Intelligent Radical's Guide to Economic Policy: The Mixed Economy* (London: Allen & Unwin).
Translations: Japanese *Riseiteki Kyushin Shugisha no Keizai seisaku* (Tokyo: Iwanami Shoten, 1977); Italian (Liguori Editore, [1976]).

(1976) *The Just Economy (Principles of Political Economy, Vol. 4)* (London: Allen & Unwin; Albany: State University of New York Press). Reprinted 1978, London: Allen & Unwin.
Translations: Spanish (Editorial Ariel, [1978]; Japanese *Kosei na Keizai* (Tokyo: Diamond Inc., 1980).

(1978) *The Structure and Reform of Direct Taxation: Report of a Committee chaired by Professor J. E. Meade* (London: Allen & Unwin for the Institute of Fiscal Studies).
Translations: Spanish (Instituto de Estudios Fiscales, [1979]).

(1982) *Stagflation Volume 1: Wage-Fixing* (London: Allen & Unwin). Reprinted 1983.
Translations: Spanish (Editorial Vicens-Vives, [1982]).

(with David Vines and J. M. Maciejowski) (1983) *Stagflation, Volume 2: Demand Management* (London: Allen & Unwin).

(1986) *Alternative Systems of Business Organization and of Workers' Remuneration* (London: Allen & Unwin).

Articles in Journals

For details of collections in which articles were reprinted, see *Chapters in Books*.

(1933a) 'Technical Improvement in Agriculture as a Cause of General Depression', *Journal of Proceedings of the Agricultural Economics Society*, vol. 2, no. 3 (June), pp. 168–76.

(1933b) 'International Economic Co-operation', *Journal of Proceedings of the Agricultural Economics Society*, vol. 2, no. 4 (November), pp. 275–82. *Collected Papers*, Vol. III, Chapter 1.

(1934a) 'The Elasticity of Substitution and the Incidence of an Imperial Inhabited House Duty', *Review of Economic Studies*, vol. 1, no. 2 (February), pp. 149–52. *Collected Papers*, Vol. II, Chapter 1.

(1934b) 'The Elasticity of Substitution and the Elasticity of Demand for One Factor of Production', *Review of Economic Studies*, vol. 1, no. 2 (February), pp. 152–3. *Collected Papers*, Vol. II, Chapter 1.

(1934c) 'The Amount of Money and the Banking System', *Economic Journal*, vol. 44, no. 173 (March), pp. 77–83. Reprinted in F. A. Lutz and L. W. Mints (eds) (1951); *Collected Papers*, Vol. I, Chapter 3.

(1937) 'A Simplified Model of Mr. Keynes' System', *Review of Economic Studies*, vol. 4 (February), pp. 98–107. Reprinted in Seymour E. Harris (ed.) (1947); *Collected Papers*, Vol. I, Chapter 5.

(with P. W. S. Andrews) (1938) 'Summary of Replies to Questions on Effects of Interest Rates', *Oxford Economic Papers*, vol. 1, no. 1 (October), pp. 14–31. Abbreviated version in T. Wilson and P. W. S. Andrews (eds) (1951). *Collected Papers*, Vol. I, Chapter 6.

(with Richard Stone) (1941) 'The Construction of Tables of National Income, Expenditure, Savings and Investment', *Economic Journal*, vol. 51, no. 202–3 (June–September), pp. 216–33. Reprinted in R. H. Parker and G. C. Harcourt (eds) (1969); *Collected Papers*, Vol. I, Chapter 8.

(with Richard Stone and D. G. Champernowne) (1942) 'The Precision of National Income Estimates', *Review of Economic Studies*, vol. 9, no. 2 (Summer), pp. 111–25; *Collected Papers*, Vol. I, Chapter 9.

(1944) 'Price and Output Policy of State Enterprise', and 'Rejoinder', *Economic Journal*, vol. 54, no. 215–216 (December), pp. 321–8, 337–9. Reprinted, with J. M. Fleming's 'Comment', in K. J. Arrow and T. Scitovsky (eds) (1969); *Collected Papers*, Vol. II, Chapter 3.

(1945) 'Mr. Lerner on "The Economics of Control"', *Economic Journal*, vol. 55, no. 217 (April), pp. 47–69. [Review article of Abba P. Lerner, *The Economics of Control: Principles of Welfare Economics*.] *Collected Papers*, Vol. II, Chapter 4.

(1948a) 'Bretton Woods, Havana and the United Kingdom Balance of Payments', *Lloyds Bank Review*, no. 7 (January), pp. 1–18. Appeared as appendix to *Planning and the Price Mechanism* (1948); *Collected Papers*, Vol. III, Chapter 6.

(with F. W. Paish) (1948b) 'Aggregate Supply and Demand at the End of 1948', *London & Cambridge Economic Service Bulletin*, vol. 26, no. 1 (February), pp. 9–16.

(1948c) 'Planning without Prices', *Economica*, new series, vol. 15, no. 57 (February), pp. 28–35. [Review article of Sir Oliver Franks, *Central Planning and Control in War and Peace* (1947).]

(1948d) 'Financial Policy and the Balance of Payments', *Economica*, new series, vol. 15, no. 58 (May), pp. 101–15. Revised version chapter V of *Planning and the Price Mechanism* (1948); *Collected Papers*, Vol. III, Chapter 5.

(1948–49) 'National Income, National Expenditure and the Balance of Payments', *Economic Journal*, vol. 58, no. 232 (December), pp. 483–505, and vol. 59, no. 233 (March), pp. 17–39; *Collected Papers*, Vol. III, Chapter 7.

(1949a) 'Next Steps in Domestic Economic Policy', *Political Quarterly*, vol. 20, no. 1 (January–March), pp. 12–24; *Collected Papers*, Vol. II, Chapter 16.

(1949b) 'Il controllo dell'inflazione e della deflazione', *Moneta e Credito*, no. 5 (1st quarter). Translation of Chapter 2 of *Planning and the Price Mechanism* (1948).

(1949c) 'A Geometrical Representation of Balance-of-Payments Policy', *Economica*, new series, vol. 16, no. 64 (November), pp. 305–20; *Collected Papers*, Vol. III, Chapter 8.

(1950a) 'Degrees of Competitive Speculation', *Review of Economic Studies*, vol. 17, no. 3, pp. 159–67; *Collected Papers*, Vol. II, Chapter 6.

(1950b) 'The Equalisation of Factor Prices: The Two-Country Two-Factor Three-Product Case', *Metroeconomica*, vol. 2, no. 3 (December), pp. 129–33.

(1951a) 'The Removal of Trade Barriers: The Regional versus the Universal Approach', *Economica*, new series, vol. 18, no. 70 (May), pp. 184–98. [Review article of W. A. Brown, jr, *The United States and the Restoration of World Trade*, J. Viner, *The Customs Union Issue*, and J. van der Mensbrugghe, *Les Unions Economiques*.]

(1951b) 'Some Economic Problems of Atlantic Union Rearmament', *Lloyds Bank Review*, no. 22 (October), pp. 35–51. Revised and shortened version appendix to *Problems of Economic Union* (1953).

(1952a) 'External Economies and Diseconomies in a Competitive Situation', *Economic Journal*, vol. 62, no. 245 (March), pp. 54–67. Reprinted in R. J. Staaf and F. X. Tannian (eds) (1973); *Collected Papers*, Vol. II, Chapter 7.

(1952b) 'Bretton Woods, GATT and the Balance of Payments: A Second Round?', *Three Banks Review*, no. 16 (December), pp. 3–22. Translated as 'Bretton Woods, GATT e bilancia dei pagamenti: una seconda tornata?', *Moneta e Credito*, vol. 5, no. 19–20, pp. 219–28; *Collected Papers*, Vol. III, Chapter 9.

(1953) 'The Convertibility of Sterling', *Three Banks Review*, no. 19 (September), pp. 3–26. Translated as 'Sterlingkonvertibilität', in G. von Haberler, P. Jacobssen, J. E. Meade et al. (1954).

(1955) 'The Case for Variable Exchange Rates', *Three Banks Review*, no. 27 (September), pp. 3–27. Reprinted in W. L. Smith and R. L. Teigen (eds) (1965); *Collected Papers*, Vol. III, Chapter 10.

(1956a) 'Benelux: The Formation of the Common Customs', *Economica*, new series, vol. 23, no. 91 (August), pp. 201–13; *Collected Papers*, Vol. III, Chapter 11.

(1956b) 'The Price Mechanism and the Australian Balance of Payments', *Economic Record*, vol. 32, no. 63 (November), pp. 239–56. Reprinted in H. W. Arndt and W. M. Corden (eds) (1963); *Collected Papers*, Vol. III, Chapter 12.

(1956c) 'The Building of Benelux', *The Banker*, vol. 106, no. 371 (December), pp. 757–64.

(with E. A. Russell) (1957a) 'Wage Rates, the Cost of Living, and the Balance of Payments', *Economic Record*, vol. 33, no. 64 (April), pp. 23–8; *Collected Papers*, Vol. III, Chapter 13.

(1957b) 'Japan and the General Agreement on Tariffs and Trade', *Three Banks Review*, no. 34 (June), pp. 3–32. Revised version of pamphlet *Japan and the General Agreement on Tariffs and Trade* (1956c).

(1957c) 'The United Kingdom and the European Common Market', *Economie*, no. 10 (July), pp. 453–9.

(1957d) 'The Balance-of-Payments Problems of a European Free-Trade Area', *Economic Journal*, vol. 67, no. 267 (September), pp. 379–96 and *The Advancement of Science*, vol. 14, no. 54 (September), pp. 68–79. Reprinted in P. Robson (ed.) (1971). Translated as 'Les problèmes de balance de paiements d'une zone Europèene de Libre-Echange', *Bulletin SEDEIS*, Etude no. 686 (November 1957), and 'Die Zahlungsbilanzprobleme einer Europäischen Freihandelszone', *Zeitschrift für die Gesamte Staatswissenschaft*, vol. 113, no. 4 (1957), pp. 581–601. *Collected Papers*, Vol. III, Chapter 14.

(1958) 'Is the National Debt a Burden?', *Oxford Economic Papers*, vol. 10, no. 2 (June), pp. 163–83. Reprinted in J. M. Ferguson (ed.) (1964); *Collected Papers*, Vol. II, Chapter 17.

(1959) 'Is the National Debt a Burden: A Correction', *Oxford Economic Papers*, vol. 11, no. 1 (February), pp. 109–10. Reprinted in J. M. Ferguson (ed.) (1964); *Collected Papers*, Vol. II, Chapter 17.

(1960) 'The Public Debt Reconsidered: A Reply', *Review of Economics and Statistics*, vol. 42, no. 3 (August), pp. 325–6.

(1961a) 'Solution Cannot Be Found by Britain and Europe Alone', *European Atlantic Review*, vol. 11, no. 1 (March–April), pp. 24–6, 30.

(1961b) 'The Future of International Trade and Payments', *Three Banks Review*, no. 50 (June), pp. 3–26. Also appeared as 'The Future of International Payments', in US Congress, Joint Economic Committee, *Factors Affecting the United States Balance of Payments* (1962), in H. G. Grubel (ed.) (1963) and in F. B. Jensen and I. Walter (eds) (1966). Translated as 'Die Zukunft des Internationalen Handels- und Zahlungsverken', *Konjunkturpolitik*, vol. 7, no. 6 (1961), pp. 355–73; *Collected Papers*, Vol. III, Chapter 15.

(1961c) 'Mauritius: A Case Study in Malthusian Economics', *Economic Journal*, vol. 71, no. 283 (September), pp. 521–34. Abbreviated version in P. H. Gray and S. S. Tangri (eds) (1970); *Collected Papers*, Vol. II, Chapter 20.

(1962a) 'Welfare Criteria: An Exchange of Notes, III. A Reply', *Economic Journal*, vol. 72, no. 285 (March), pp. 231–3.

(1962b) 'The Effect of Savings on Consumption in a State of Steady Growth', *Review of Economic Studies*, vol. 29, no. 3 (June) (Symposium on production functions and economic growth), pp. 227–34. Translated as 'Der Einfluss der Sparens auf den Konsum bei stetigen Wachstum', in H. König (ed.) (1970); *Collected Papers*, Vol. II, Chapter 21.

(1963a) 'The Adjustment of Savings to Investment in a Growing Economy', *Review of Economic Studies*, vol. 30, no. 3 (October), pp. 151–66. Reprinted in F. H. Hahn (ed.) (1971); *Collected Papers*, Vol. II, Chapter 22.

(1963c) 'The Rate of Profit in a Growing Economy', *Economic Journal*, vol. 73, no. 292 (December), pp. 665–74; *Collected Papers*, Vol. II, Chapter 23.

(1964a) 'International Commodity Agreements', *World Agriculture*, vol. 13, no. 2 (April), pp. 20–6. Earlier version of (1964b).

(1964b) 'International Commodity Agreements', *Lloyds Bank Review*, no. 73 (July), pp. 28–42; *Collected Papers*, Vol. III, Chapter 18.

(1964c) 'The International Monetary Mechanism', *Three Banks Review*, no. 63 (September), pp. 3–25. Reprinted in M. G. Mueller (ed.) (1966).

(with F. H. Hahn) (1965) 'The Rate of Profit in a Growing Economy', *Economic Journal*, vol. 75, no. 298 (June), pp. 445–8; *Collected Papers*, Vol. II, Chapter 24.

(1966a) 'Life-Cycle Savings, Inheritance and Economic Growth', *Review of Economic Studies*, vol. 33, no. 1 (January), pp. 61–78. Appeared as note to Chapter 13 of *The Growing Economy* (1968); *Collected Papers*, Vol. II, Chapter 25.

(1966b) 'The Outcome of the Pasinetti-Process: a Note', *Economic Journal*, vol. 76, no. 301 (March), pp. 161–5. Reprinted in G. C. Harcourt and N. F. Laing (eds) (1971).

(1966c) 'Exchange-Rate Flexibility', *Three Banks Review*, no. 70 (June), pp. 3–27. Also in American Enterprise Institute (1966); L. H. Officer and T. D. Willett (eds) (1969); W. L. Smith and R. L. Teigen (eds) (1970); B. Balassa (ed.) (1970); *Collected Papers*, Vol. III, Chapter 19.

(1966d) 'Economic Effects and Population Growth in the Developing Countries, Case Study I – Mauritius', *Royal Society Population Study Group, Abstracts of Proceedings, No. 1, 1965*, pp. 43–8.

(1967) 'Population Explosion, the Standard of Living and Social Conflict', *Economic Journal*, vol. 77, no. 306 (June), pp. 233–55. *Collected Papers*, Vol. II, chapter 26. Excerpt, 'Rates of Population Growth and Standards of Living', in US Department of Labor, *Monthly Labor Review*, September 1967, pp. 56–8.

(1968) 'Is "The New Industrial State" Inevitable?', *Economic Journal*, vol. 78, no. 310 (June), pp. 372–92. [Review article of J. K. Galbraith, *The New Industrial State*.] Translated as 'Ist die moderne Industriegesellschaft von J. K. Galbraith unvermeidlich?', *Hamburger Jahrbuch für Wirtschafts- und Gesellschaftspolitik*, vol. 14 (1969), pp. 226–47.

(with E. A. Wrigley, W. Brass, A. J. Boreham, D. V. Glass, and E. Grebenik) (1970a) 'Demography and Economics', *Population Studies*, vol. 24, Supplement (May), pp. 25–31.

(with J. M. Thoday, G. A. Harrison, W. Brass, J. A. Fraser Roberts, D. V. Glass, J. Maynard Smith, and E. A. Wrigley) (1970b) 'The Interrelation between Genetics and the Social Sciences', *Population Studies*, vol. 24, Supplement (May), pp. 49–54.

(1970c) 'The Use of a Social Welfare Function for Planning Purposes in a Free Enterprise Economy', *Economic Studies Quarterly*, vol. 21, no. 3 (December), pp. 19–41.

(1972a) 'The Theory of Labour-Managed Firms and of Profit Sharing', *Economic Journal*, vol. 82, no. 325 (March) Supplement (Special Issue in honour of E. A. G. Robinson), pp. 402–28. Reprinted in J. Vanek (ed.) (1975); *Collected Papers*, Vol. II, Chapter 10.

(1972b) 'Citizens' Demands for a Clean Environment', *L'Industria*, no. 3/4 (July–September/October–December), pp. 145–52.

(1972c) 'Poverty in the Welfare State', *Oxford Economic Papers*, vol. 24, no. 3 (November), pp. 289–326. *Collected Papers*, Vol. II, Chapter 18.

(1973) 'The Inheritance of Inequalities: Some Biological, Demographic, Social and Economic Factors', *Proceedings of the British Academy*, vol. 59, pp. 355–81. *Collected Papers*, Vol. II, Chapter 19.

(1974a) 'A Note on Border-Tax Adjustments', *Journal of Political Economy*, vol. 82, no. 5 (September–October), pp. 1013–15.

(1974b) 'The Optimal Balance between Economies of Scale and Variety of Products: An Illustrative Model', *Economica*, new series, vol. 41, no. 164 (November), pp. 359–67. *Collected Papers*, Vol. II, Chapter 11.

(1974c) 'Labour-Managed Firms in Conditions of Imperfect Competition', *Economic Journal*, vol. 84, no. 336 (December), pp. 817–24. *Collected Papers*, Vol. II, Chapter 12.

(1978a) 'The Meaning of "Internal Balance"', *Economic Journal*, vol. 88, no. 351 (September), pp. 423–35. *Collected Papers*, Vol. I, Chapter 21.

(1978b) 'A Strategy for Commodity Policy', *Scandinavian Journal of Economics*, vol. 80, no. 4, pp. 349–59. *Collected Papers*, Vol. III, Chapter 20.

(1978c) 'United Kingdom: The Structure and Reform of Direct Taxation', *Bulletin for International Fiscal Documentation*, vol. 32, no. 1, pp. 3–10.

(1979a) 'Della stagflazione', *Bancaria*, vol. 35, no. 7 (July), pp. 555–63. Translation of Snow Lecture 'On Stagflation' (printed in *The Listener*, 1978).

(1979b) 'The Adjustment Process of Labour Co-operatives with Constant Returns to Scale and Perfect Competition', *Economic Journal*, vol. 89, no. 356 (December), pp. 781–8. Reprinted in A. Clayre (ed.) (1980); *Collected Papers*, Vol. II, Chapter 13.

(1979c) 'Stagflation in the United Kingdom', *Atlantic Economic Journal*, vol. 7, no. 4 (December), pp. 1–10.

(1980) 'Companies, Inflation and Taxation – Comment', *Fiscal Studies*, vol. 1, no. 2 (March), pp. 13–16.

(1981a) 'Comment on the Papers by Professors Laidler and Tobin', *Economic Journal*, vol. 91, no. 361 (March), pp. 49–55. *Collected Papers*, Vol. I, Chapter 23.

(1981b) 'Note on the Inflationary Implications of the Wage-Fixing Assumption of the Cambridge Economic Policy Group', *Oxford Economic Papers*, vol. 33, no. 1 (March), pp. 28–41.

(1981c) 'Fiscal Devices for the Control of Inflation', *Atlantic Economic Journal*, vol. 9, no. 4 (December), pp. 1–11.

(1982) 'Domestic Stabilization and the Balance of Payments', *Lloyds Bank Review*, no. 143 (January), pp. 1–18. Reprint of pamphlet *Targets and Weapons for Domestic Stabilisation and the Balance of Payments* (1981). Translated as 'La estabilizacion interna y balanza de pagos', *Centro de Estudios Monetarios Latinoamericanos Boletin*, no. 29 (March–April 1983), pp. 65–74.

(1983a) 'A New Approach to the Balance of Payments', *Lloyds Bank Review*, no. 148 (April), pp. 42–7 [Letter to the editor].

(1983b) 'A New Keynesian Approach to Full Employment', *Nationaløkonomisk Tidsskrift*, vol. 121, no. 3, pp. 299–316, and *Lloyds Bank Review*, no. 150 (October), pp. 1–18. *Collected Papers*, Vol. I, Chapter 24.

(1984a) 'Structural Changes in the Rate of Interest and the Rate of Foreign Exchange to Preserve Equilibrium in the Balance of Payments and the Budget Balance', *Oxford Economic Papers*, vol. 36, no. 1 (March) pp. 52–66. *Collected Papers*, Vol. III, Chapter 21.

(1984b) 'Full Employment, New Technologies and the Distribution of Income', *Journal of Social Policy*, vol. 13, no. 2 (April), pp. 129–46. Revised version in D. Steel and R. Holme (eds) (1985).

(1984c) 'A New Keynesian Bretton Woods', *Three Banks Review*, no. 143 (June), pp. 8–25. *Collected Papers*, Vol. III, Chapter 22.

(1985) 'Lionel Robbins, 1898–1984', *Economica*, vol. 52, no. 205 (February), pp. 3–5. Also appeared in *The Economist*, 8 December 1984, p. 19.

Pamphlets

(1933) *Public Works in Their International Aspect*, NFRB pamphlet No. 4 (London: New Fabian Research Bureau). Reprinted 1972, Liechtenstein: Kraus; *Collected Papers*, Vol. I, Chapter 2.

(1940) *Economic Problems of International Government*, Federal Union Research Institute First Annual Report 1939–40 (London: Federal Union Research Institute).

(1953) *The Atlantic Community and the Dollar Gap* (London: Friends of Atlantic Union). Excerpt in W. R. Allen and C. L. Allen (eds) (1959).

(1956a) *The Belgium–Luxembourg Economic Union, 1921–1939: Lessons from an Early Experiment*, Princeton Essays in International Finance No. 25 (Princeton, NJ: International Finance Section, Princeton University). Reprinted as Chapter I of J. E. Meade, H. H. Liesner and S. J. Wells (1962).

(with D. C. Rowan and R. F. Holder) (1956b) *Developments in Monetary Policy*, Economic Papers No. 11 (Sydney: Economic Society of Australia and New Zealand).

(1956c) *Japan and the General Agreement on Tariffs and Trade*, Joseph Fisher Lecture, University of Adelaide (Adelaide: Griffin Press). Reprinted in *Three Banks Review* (1957b).

(1957) *Negotiations for Benelux: An Annotated Chronicle, 1943–1956*, Princeton Studies in International Finance No. 6 (Princeton, NJ: International Finance Section, Princeton University).

(1960) *An Analysis of Some Economic Aspects of Mauritius, A Lecture delivered by Professor James Meade at the Plaza Theatre on Thursday 13th April, 1960* (Port Louis: Mauritius Printing Co.). Also published as *Ile Maurice: quelques aspects économiques* (Port Louis: Mauritius Printing Co., 1960).

(1962a) *U.K., Commonwealth and Common Market*, Hobart paper no. 17 (London: Institute of Economic Affairs, April). Translated as 'Royaume-Uni, Commonwealth et Marché Commun', *Bulletin SEDEIS*, Etude no. 816 Supplement (April 1962), *Grossbritannien als Partner der EWG* (Frankfurt: Knapp, 1962), and 'Regno Unito, Commonwealth e Mercato Commune', *Quaderni di Orientamenti*, no. 37 (1962), pp. 7–64. *Collected Papers*, Vol. III, Chapter 16.

(1962b) *U.K., Commonwealth & Common Market: A Reappraisal* 2nd edition of *U.K., Commonwealth and Common Market* (London: Institute of Economic Affairs, November).

(1962c) *The Common Market: Is There an Alternative?* Prologue to 2nd edition of *U.K., Commonwealth & Common Market* (London: Institute of Economic Affairs, December). Translated as 'Royaume-Uni, Commonwealth et Marché Commun: Existe-t-il d'autres voies?', *Bulletin SEDEIS*, Etude no. 838 Supplement (December 1962). *Collected Papers*, Vol. III, Chapter 17.

(1970) *U.K., Commonwealth & Common Market: A Reappraisal* (3rd edition of *U.K., Commonwealth & Common Market*, with Introduction by Harry G. Johnson (London: Institute of Economic Affairs).

(1971a) *Common Market Debate No. 2: The Economic Arguments* (London: Open Seas Forum).

(1971b) *Wages and Prices in a Mixed Economy, Second Wincott Memorial Lecture*, IEA Occasional Paper no. 35 (London: Institute of Economic Affairs for the Wincott Foundation). *Collected Papers*, Vol. I, Chapter 19.

(1974) *The Inheritance of Inequalities: Some Biological, Demographic, Social and Economic Factors*, Keynes Lecture in Economics, 1973 (London: The British Academy). *Collected Papers*, Vol. II, Chapter 19.

(1981) *Targets and Weapons for Domestic Stabilisation and the Balance of Payments* (Hamburg: Verlag Weltarchiv GmbH for Institut für Wirtschaftsforschung). Reprinted as 'Domestic Stabilization and the Balance of Payments', *Lloyds Bank Review* (1982).

(1985) *Wage-Fixing Revisited*, IEA Occasional Paper no. 72 (London: Institute of Economic Affairs). *Collected Papers*, Vol. I, Chapter 25.

(1986) *Different Forms of Share Economy* (London: Public Policy Centre). *Collected Papers*, Vol. II, Chapter 14.

Chapters in Books

For bibliographical details of the articles and extracts from books and pamphlets reprinted see *Articles*, *Books* and *Pamphlets* above.)

(1947) 'A Simplified Model of Keynes' System', in Seymour E. Harris (ed.), *The New Economics: Keynes' Influence on Theory and Public Policy* (New York: Knopf), pp. 606–18. Reprint of article (1937).

(1951) 'The Amount of Money and the Banking System', in F. A. Lutz and L. W. Mints (eds), *Readings in Monetary Theory* (Philadelphia: R. Blakiston), pp. 54–62. Reprint of article (1934c).

(with P. W. S. Andrews) (1951) 'Summary of Replies to Questions on Effects of Interest Rates', in T. Wilson and P. W. S. Andrews (eds), *Oxford Studies in the Price Mechanism* (Oxford: Clarendon Press), pp. 27–30. Abbreviated version of Meade and Andrews (1938) article.

(1954) 'Sterlingkonvertibilität', in G. von Haberler, P. Jacobssen, J. E. Meade et al., *Die Konvertibilität der europäischen Währungen* (Zurich, Stuttgart: Rentsch), pp. 214–21. Translation of article (1953).

(1959) 'The Dollar Gap' in William R. Allen and Clark Lee Allen (eds), *Foreign Trade and Finance: Essays in International Economic Equilibrium and Adjustment* (New York: Macmillan), Chapter 10, pp. 206–19. Excerpt from pamphlet *The Atlantic Community and the Dollar Gap* (1953), pp. 13–25.

(1960) [Oral evidence to Radcliffe Committee, 1 July 1958] QQ. 9978–10042, in Committee on the Working of the Monetary System, *Minutes of Evidence* (London: HMSO), pp. 656–60.

(1962) 'The Future of International Payments', in US Congress, Joint Economic Committee, *Factors Affecting the United States Balance of Payments* (Washington, DC: US Government Printing Office), pp. 239–52. Slightly revised version of article (1961b).

(1962) 'The Belgium–Luxembourg Economic Union, 1921–1939', in J. E. Meade, H. H. Liesner and S. J. Wells, *Case Studies in European Economic Union: The Mechanics of Integration* (London and New York: Oxford University Press), pp. 13–57. Reprint of pamphlet *The Belgium–Luxembourg Economic Union 1921–1939: Lessons from an Early Experiment* (1956).

(with S. J. Wells) (1962) 'The Building of Benelux, 1943–1960', in J. E. Meade, H. H. Liesner and S. J. Wells, *Case Studies in European Economic Union: The Mechanics of Integration* (London and New York: Oxford University Press), pp. 59–194.

(1962) 'Background to the Problem', in William Clark and others, *War on Want, Report of a Conference on the United Nations Development Decade held at Christ's College, Cambridge, 13–15 April 1962* (Oxford and New York: Pergamon Press), pp. 6–19.

(1963) 'Comment by J. E. Meade on His Paper "The Future of International Trade and Payments"', in US Congress, Joint Economic Committee, *Outlook for United States Balance of Payments* (Washington, DC: US Government Printing Office), pp. 241–3.

(1963) 'The Future of International Payments', in H. G. Grubel (ed.) *World Monetary Reform: Plans and Issues* (Stanford, Calif.: Stanford University Press), pp. 301–19. Reprinted from US Congress, Joint Economic Committee (1962).

(1963) 'The Price Mechanism and the Australian Balance of Payments', in H. W. Arndt and W. M. Corden (eds), *The Australian Economy* (Melbourne: F. W. Cheshire), pp. 396–415. Reprint of article (1956b).

(1964) 'International Commodity Agreements', *Proceedings of the United Nations Conference on Trade and Development, Volume III: Commodity Trade* (New York: United Nations, 1964), pp. 451–7. Reprinted in *Lloyds Bank Review* (1964b).

(1964) 'Is the National Debt a Burden?' in J. M. Ferguson (ed.) *The Public Debt and Future Generations* (Chapel Hill, NC: University of North Carolina Press), pp. 19–44. Reprint of article (1958).

(1964) 'Is the National Debt a Burden?: A Correction' in J. M. Ferguson (ed.) *The Public Debt and Future Generations* (Chapel Hill, NC: University of North Carolina Press), pp. 44–6. Reprint of article (1959).

(1965) 'UK, Commonwealth & Common Market: A Reappraisal', in D. S. Lees, J. E. Meade et al., *Freedom or Free-For-All? Essays in Welfare, Trade and Choice* (London: Institute of Economic Affairs), pp. 95–156. Reprint of pamphlet *UK, Commonwealth & Common Market: A Reappraisal* (1962b).

(1965) 'The Case for Variable Exchange Rates', in W. L. Smith and R. L. Teigen (eds), *Readings in Money, National Income and Stabilization Policy* (Chicago: Richard D. Irwin), pp. 505–17. Reprint of article (1955).

(1966) 'Exchange-Rate Flexibility', in American Enterprise Institute, *International Payments Problems* (Washington DC: American Enterprise Institute for Public Policy Research), pp. 67–82. Also in *Three Banks Review* (1966c).

(1966) 'The Future of International Payments', in F. B. Jensen and I. Walter (eds) *Readings in International Economic Relations* (New York: Ronald Press Company), pp. 254–68. Reprinted from US Congress, Joint Economic Committee (1962).

(1966) 'The International Monetary Mechanism', in M. G. Mueller (ed.), *Readings in Macroeconomics* (New York: Holt, Rinehart and Winston), pp. 386–97. Reprint of article (1964c).

(1967) 'Gold and Reform: Other Views', in Randall Hinshaw, *Monetary Reform and the Price of Gold: Alternative Approaches* (Baltimore, Md.: John Hopkins Press), pp. 121–5.

(1967) 'Determinants of Inequality in a Property-Owning Democracy', and 'Towards a Property Owning Democracy', in Edward C. Budd (ed.), *Inequality and Poverty* (New York: Norton), pp. 105–13, 114–22. Extracts from *Efficiency, Equality and the Ownership of Property* (1964).

(with C. J. Hitch) (1967), 'How Should Income be Distributed?' in Edward C. Budd (ed.) *Inequality and Poverty* (New York: Norton), pp. 1–5. Extract from *An Introduction to Economic Analysis and Policy* (1938).

(1969) 'Price and Output Policy of State Enterprise' and 'Rejoinder', in K. J. Arrow and T. Scitovsky (eds), *Reading in Welfare Economics* (Homewood, Ill.: Richard D. Irwin) pp. 309–24. Reprint of article (1944).

(with Richard Stone) (1969) 'The Construction of Tables of National Income, Expenditure, Savings and Investment', in R. H. Parker and G. C. Harcourt (eds), *Readings in the Concept and Measurement of Income* (London: Cambridge University Press), pp. 329–46. Reprint of Meade and Stone (1941) article.

(1969) 'The Various Forms of Exchange-Rate Flexibility' in Lawrence H. Officer and Thomas D. Willett (eds), *The International Monetary System* (Englewood Cliffs, NJ: Prentice Hall), pp. 201–11. Reprint of article (1966c).

(1970) 'Der Einfluss des Sparens auf den Konsum bei stetigen Wachstum', in H. König (ed.) *Wachstum und Entwicklung der Wirtschaft* (Cologne & Berlin: Kiepenheuer & Witsch), pp. 366–75. Translation of article (1962b).

(1970) 'Exchange-Rate Flexibility', in W. L. Smith and R. L. Teigen (eds), *Readings in Money, National Income, and Stabilization Policy*, 2nd edition (Homewood, Ill.: R. D. Irwin), pp. 570–83. Reprint of article (1966c).

(1970) 'Exchange-Rate Flexibility', in B. Balassa (ed.), *Changing Patterns in Foreign Trade and Payments* (New York: Norton), pp. 203–22. Reprint of article (1966c).

(1970) 'Mauritius: A Case Study in Malthusian Economics', in P. H. Gray and S. S. Tangri (eds), *Economic Development and Population Growth: A Conflict?* (Lexington, Mass.: D. C. Heath and Co.), pp. 85–97. Abbreviated version of article (1961c).

(1971) 'The Adjustment of Savings to Investment in a Growing Economy', in F. H. Hahn (ed.), *Readings in the Theory of Growth* (London: Macmillan), pp. 202–17. Reprint of article (1963a).

(1971) 'The Theory of Customs Unions', in P. Robson (ed.), *International Economic Integration* (Harmondsworth, Middlesex: Penguin Books), pp. 48–58. Excerpt from *The Theory of Customs Unions* (1955), pp. 29–43.

(1971) 'The Balance of Payments Problems of a European Free Trade Area', in P. Robson (ed.), *International Economic Integration* (Harmondsworth, Middlesex: Penguin Books), pp. 219–41. Reprint of article (1957d).

(1971) 'The Outcome of the Pasinetti-Process', in G. C. Harcourt and N. F. Laing (eds) *Capital and Growth* (Harmondsworth, Middlesex: Penguin Books), pp. 287–94. Reprint of article (1966b).

(1972) 'Economic Efficiency and Distributional Justice', in Robert W. Crandall and Richard S. Eckhaus (eds), *Contemporary Issues in Economics: Selected Readings* (Boston: Little Brown), pp. 318–22. Extract from *Efficiency, Equality and the Ownership of Property* (1964).

(1973) 'European Monetary Union' and 'The Objectives of Economic Union', in Directorate-General for Economic and Financial Affairs of the European Communities Commission, *Report on European Economic Integration and Monetary Unification* (Brussels, 1973), Part II, Section F, pp. 141–53 and 155–9.

(1973) 'Factors Determining the Distribution of Property', in A. B. Atkinson (ed.), *Wealth, Income and Inequality* (Harmondsworth, Middlesex: Penguin Books), pp. 295–304. Extract from *Efficiency, Equality and the Ownership of Property* (1964), pp. 41–52.

(1973) 'External Economies and Diseconomies in a Competitive Situation', in R. J. Staaf and F. X. Tannian (eds), *Externalities: Theoretical Dimensions of Political Economy* (New York and London: Dunellen Publishing Company), pp. 61–75. Reprint of article (1952a).

(1973) 'The Galton Lecture 1972: Economic Policy and the Threat of Doom', in Bernard Benjamin, Peter R. Cox and John Peel (eds), *Resources and Population* (London and New York: Academic Press), pp. 119–46.

(1974) 'Preference Orderings and Economic Policy', in Ashok Mitra (ed.), *Economic Theory and Planning: Essays in Honour of A. K. Das Gupta* (Calcutta: Oxford University Press), pp. 17–25.

(1975) 'An Effective Social Contract', in Sir John Hicks et al., *Crisis '75 . . ?* IEA Occasional Paper no. 43 (London: Institute of Economic Affairs), pp. 28–33.

(1975) 'The Keynesian Revolution', in Milo Keynes (ed.), *Essays on John*

Maynard Keynes (London and New York: Cambridge University Press), pp. 82–8. *Collected Papers*, Vol. I, Chapter 20.

(1975) 'The Theory of Labour-Managed Firms and of Profit Sharing', in J. Vanek (ed.), *Self-Management: Economic Liberation of Man* (Harmondsworth, Middlesex, and Baltimore, Md.: Penguin Books), pp. 394–422. Reprint of article (1972a).

(1976) 'Conflicts between Internal and External Balance' in M. J. C. Surrey (ed.), *Macroeconomic Themes* (London: Oxford University Press), pp. 440–7. Extract from *The Theory of International Economic Policy, Vol. I: The Balance of Payments* (1951), Chapter X.

(1978) 'James Meade', in *Les Prix Nobel 1977* (Stockholm: Nobel Foundation), pp. 307–10. *Collected Papers*, Vol. I, Chapter 1.

(1978) 'The Meaning of "Internal Balance"', in *Les Prix Nobel 1977* (Stockholm: Nobel Foundation), pp. 311–23. Reprinted in *Economic Journal* (1978a); *Collected Papers*, Vol. I, Chapter 21.

(1980) 'Labour Co-operatives, Participation, and Value-added Sharing', in Alasdair Clayre (ed.), *The Political Economy of Cooperation and Participation: A Third Sector* (London and New York: Oxford University Press), Chapter 6, pp. 89–118.

(1980) 'Appended Mathematical Note: The Adjustment Processes of Labour Co-operatives with Constant Returns to Scale and Perfect Competition', in Alasdair Clayre (ed.), *The Political Economy of Cooperation and Participation: A Third Sector* (London and New York: Oxford University Press), Chapter 7. Reprint of article (1979b).

(1980) 'Movements of Capital and of Persons between a Country with an Income Tax and a Country with an Expenditure Tax Regime', in Peter Oppenheimer (ed.), *Issues in International Economics* (Stocksfield, Northumberland: Oriel Press Ltd), pp. 94–117.

(1981) 'The Fixing of Money Rates of Pay', in David Lipsey and Dick Leonard (eds), *The Socialist Agenda: Crosland's Legacy* (London: Jonathan Cape), pp. 75–106.

(1982) 'A Proposed Structure for International Monetary Arrangements', in House of Commons, Treasury and Civil Service Committee, *Memoranda on International Monetary Arrangements* (London: HMSO), pp. 42–51.

(1982) 'The Restoration of Full Employment', in Wayland Kennet (ed.), *The Rebirth of Britain* (London: Weidenfeld and Nicolson), pp. 171–85.

(1983) 'Impressions of Maynard Keynes', in David Worswick and James Trevithick (eds), *Keynes and the Modern World, Proceedings of the Keynes Centenary Conference, King's College, Cambridge* (Cambridge University Press), pp. 263–66.

(1985) 'Full Employment, Wage Restraint and the Distribution of Income', in David Steel and Richard Holme (eds), *Partners in One Nation: A New Vision of Britain 2000* (London: Bodley Head), pp. 13–33. Revised version of article (1984b).

Reviews

(1932) J. Akerman, *Economic Progress and Economic Crises*, *Economic Journal*, vol. 42, no. 167 (September) pp. 432–5.

(1933) Evans Clark (ed.), *Boycotts and Peace: A Report by the Committee on Economic Sanctions*, *The Spectator*, 3 March, p. 304.

(1935) Walter Lippman, *The Method of Freedom*, *The Spectator*, 11 January, pp. 54–5.

(1935) John Strachey, *The Nature of Capitalist Crisis*, *University Forward*, vol. 1, no. 3 (Summer), pp. 24–5.

(1936) L. E. Hubbard, *Soviet Money and Finance*, *The Spectator*, 14 August, pp. 279–80.

(1936) M. R. Bonavia, *The Economics of Transport*, *The Spectator*, 21 August, p. 316.

(1936) Wilhelm Röpke, *Crises and Cycles*, *Economic Journal*, vol. 46, no. 184 (December), pp. 694–5.

(1937) E. Ronald Walker, *Unemployment Policy with Special Reference to Australia*, *Economic Journal*, vol. 47, no. 185 (March), pp. 105–6.

(1937) R. G. Hawtrey, *Capital and Employment*, *The Listener*, 14 April, pp. 720, 723 [Anon].

(1937) H. L. McCracken, *Value Theory and Business Cycles*, *Economic Journal*, vol. 47, no. 186 (June), pp. 337–9.

(1937) Hans Neisser, *Some International Aspects of the Business Cycle*, *Economic Journal*, vol. 47, no. 187 (September), pp. 531–2.

(1939) H. V. Hodson, *Slump and Recovery 1929–1937: A Survey of World Economic Affairs*, *Economic Journal*, vol. 149, no. 193 (March), pp. 98–100.

(1939) M. Kalecki, *Essays in the Theory of Economic Fluctuations*, *Economic Journal*, vol. 49, no. 194 (June), pp. 300–5.

(1945) 'Mr Lerner on "The Economics of Control"', *Economic Journal*, vol. 55, no. 217 (April), pp. 47–69. [Review article of Abba P. Lerner, *The Economics of Control*.] *Collected Papers*, Vol. II, Chapter 4.

(1948) 'Planning without Prices', *Economica*, new series, vol. 15, no. 57 (February), pp. 28–35. [Review article of Sir Oliver Franks, *Central Planning and Control in War and Peace* (1947).]

(1948) John Jewkes, *Ordeal by Planning*, *The Listener*, 8 July, pp. 65–6.

(1950) Bertrand de Jouvenel, *Problems of Socialist England*, *Economic Journal*, vol. 60, no. 237 (March), pp. 114–17.

(1950) E. F. M. Durbin, *Problems of Economic Planning*, Ivor Thomas, *The Socialist Tragedy*, and W. Arthur Lewis, *The Principles of Economic Planning*, *Economic Journal*, vol. 60, no. 237 (March), pp. 117–22.

(1950) Clair Wilcox, *A Charter for World Trade*, *Economica*, new series, vol. 17, no. 66 (May), pp. 215–18.

(1950) *The Pattern and Finance of Foreign Trade, Lectures delivered at the Institute of Bankers' International Summer School, September 1949*, *Economica*, new series, vol. 17, no. 66 (May), pp. 218–19.

(1950) Bertil Ohlin, *The Problem of Employment Stabilisation*, *Economica*, new series, vol. 17, no. 67 (August), pp. 328–30.

(1951) 'The Removal of Trade Barriers: The Regional versus the Universal Approach', *Economica*, new series, vol. 18, no. 70 (May), pp. 184–98. [Review article of W. A. Brown, jr, *The United States and the Restoration of World Trade*, J. Viner, *The Customs Union Issue*, and J. van der Mensbrugghe, *Les Unions Economiques*.]

(1953) Jacob Viner, *International Trade and Economic Development*, *Economica*, new series, vol. 20, no. 79 (August), pp. 274–6.

(1953) William Diebold, jr, *Trade and Payments in Western Europe*, *Economica*, new series, vol. 20, no. 79 (August), pp. 276–7.

(1953) E. L. Hargreaves and M. M. Gowing, *Civil Industry and Trade*, *Oriel Record*, pp. 28–9.

(1954) Charles P. Kindleberger, *International Economics*, *Economica*, new series, vol. 21, no. 83 (August), pp. 261–2.

(1954) Ludwig Erhard, *Germany's Comeback in the World Market*, *The Listener*, 7 October, p. 585.

(1955) J. J. Polak, *An International Economic System*, *International Affairs*, vol. 31, no. 2 (April), p. 218.

(1955) A. H. Birch, *Federalism, Finance and Social Legislation in Canada, Australia and the United States*, *Economica*, new series, vol. 22, no. 88 (November), pp. 358–9.

(1956) Wolfgang Kohte, *Die Niederländische Volkwirtschaft Heute*, *International Affairs*, vol. 32, no. 1 (January), pp. 98–9.

(1956) Gove Hambidge, *The Story of FAO*, *Economica*, new series, vol. 23, no. 89 (February), pp. 81–2.

(1958) R. F. Harrod, *International Economics*, *Economic Journal*, vol. 68, no. 270 (June), pp. 365–6.

(1958) L. St Clare Grondona, *Utilizing World Abundance*, *Economic Journal*, vol. 68, no. 271 (September), pp. 550–4.

(1958) E. H. Chamberlin, *Towards a More General Theory of Value*, *Economic Journal*, vol. 68, no. 271 (September), pp. 541–3.

(1959) I. M. D. Little, *A Critique of Welfare Economics*, 2nd edition, *Economic Journal*, vol. 69, no. 273 (March), pp. 124–9. *Collected Papers*, Vol. II, Chapter 8.

(1962) Ragnar Nurske, *Patterns of Trade and Development*, *Economica*, new series, vol. 29, no. 113 (February), pp. 103–4.

(1963) J. M. Buchanan and G. Tullock, *The Calculus of Consent: Logical Foundations of Constitutional Democracy*, *Economic Journal*, vol. 73, no. 289 (March), pp. 101–4.

(1963) K. E. Boulding, *Conflict and Defense: A General Theory*, T. C. Schelling, *The Strategy of Conflict*, and A. Rapoport, *Fights, Games and Debates*, *Economic Journal*, vol. 73, no. 290 (June), pp. 284–95.

(1965) Sir Roy Harrod, *Reforming the World's Money*, *Economic Journal*, vol. 75, no. 300 (December), pp. 835–7.

(1968) 'Is "The New Industrial State" Inevitable?', *Economic Journal*, vol. 78, no. 310 (June), pp. 372–92. [Review article of J. K. Galbraith, *The New Industrial State*.]

(1971) P. R. Ehrlich and A. H. Ehrlich, *Population, Resources, Environment*, *Economic Journal*, vol. 81, no. 322 (June), pp. 428–30.

(1972) E. J. Mishan, *Cost–Benefit Analysis*, *Economic Journal*, vol. 82, no. 325 (March), pp. 244–6.

(1972) James M. Buchanan and Robert D. Tollison (eds), *Theory of Public Choice: Political Applications of Economics*, *Economic Journal*, vol. 82, no. 328 (December), pp. 1423–5.

(1973) James M. Buchanan and Robert D. Tollison (eds), *Theory of Public Choice: Political Applications of Economics*, *Revue Economique*, vol. 24, no. 5 (September), pp. 880–1.

(1973) E. J. Mishan, *Cost–Benefit Analysis*, *Revue Economique*, vol. 24, no. 5 (September), pp. 887–9.

(1974) Hugh Corbet and Robert Jackson (eds), *In Search of a New World Economic Order*, *Times Higher Education Supplement*, 18 October, p. 17.

(1978) David F. Heathfield, *The Economics of Co-Determination*, British Journal of Industrial Relations, vol. 16, no. 3 (March), pp. 392–3.

(1980) J. O. N. Perkins, *The Macro-economic Mix to Stop Stagflation*, Economic Record, vol. 56, no. 152, pp. 99–100.

Articles in Newspapers

(1936) 'Tariff Obstacles to World Peace. I. The Advantages of Free Trade', *Headway*, May, p. 92.

(1936) 'II. The Obstacles to World Trade Agreement', *Headway*, June, pp. 106–7.
(1936) 'III. How to Get Low Tariffs', *Headway*, September, p. 173.
(1950) 'A "Union of Free Peoples" – I. Defence', *The Listener*, 3 August, pp. 155–6.
(1950) 'A "Union of Free Peoples" – II. An Agenda for Economic Welfare', *The Listener*, 10 August, pp. 191–2.
(1950) 'A "Union of Free Peoples" – III. International Institutions', *The Listener*, 17 August, pp. 227–8.
(1950) 'A "Union of Free Peoples" – IV. Regional versus Universal Approach', *The Listener*, 24 August, pp. 263–4.
(1956) 'Outside Europe's Market. I – The British Dilemma', *Manchester Guardian*, 14 March.
(1956) 'Outside Europe's Market. II – A Free Trade Area', *Manchester Guardian*, 15 March.
(1956) 'Nato and Economic Development', *The Scotsman*, 31 May.
(1956) 'Free Trade with Europe?', *Sunday Times*, 14 October.
(1958) 'Defending the Pound', *The Listener*, 13 March, pp. 443–4.
(1958) 'Agenda for World Recession: What Britain Could Do', *Manchester Guardian*, 18 March.
(1958) 'Trade in a World Recession: A Floating Exchange Rate?', *Manchester Guardian*, 19 March.
(1961) 'A Plea for Flexible Exchange Rates', *Guardian*, 3 January, p. 6.
(1963) 'Alternatives to Common Market', *Guardian*, 16 January, p. 10. Extract from pamphlet *The Common Market: Is There an Alternative?* (1962c).
(1967) 'Professor James Meade looks at the Mauritian economy again' (Interview of Professor Meade by N. Akaloo, Enquiry TV programme, 21 September 1966), *L'Express*, 5 July.
(1968) 'A New Plan to Settle Pay Clashes', *The Times*, 5 September, p. 23.
(1970) 'On Becoming an Economist', *Christ's College Magazine*, May, pp. 123–5.
(1972) 'An Interview with James Meade', *Marginal Man*, no. 3 (October) pp. 3–7, 10–11.
(1974) 'How to Avoid Another Crisis', *Observer*, 3 February, p. 8.
(1978) 'On Stagflation' (Snow Lecture, November 1978), *The Listener*, 14 December, pp. 778–84. *Collected Papers*, Vol. I, Chapter 22. Revised version in *Atlantic Economic Journal*, (1979c). Translated as 'Della stagflazione' (1979a).
(1980) 'Full Employment without Inflation', *The Times*, 23 June, p. 7.
(with David Vines and Martin Weale) (1981), 'A New Financial Strategy', *Financial Times*, 8 December.
(1982) 'How to Achieve Full Employment without Stoking Up Inflation', *The Times*, 20 January, p. 13.
(1984) 'Tributes in Memory of Lord Robbins, C.H., C.B.', *The Times*, 11 October, pp. 5–7.
(1984) 'A Renaissance Man Remembered', *The Economist*, 8 December, p. 19.
(1985) 'We Can Conquer Unemployment', *New Democrat*, vol. 3, no. 3, pp. 13–14.
(1985) 'Reforms the Alliance Must Pursue to Beat Unemployment', *Guardian*, 11 September, p. 18.
(1987) 'Insiders and Outsiders', *Social Democrat*, vol. 5, no. 1.

Letters to Newspapers

(1936) To the editor, *Spectator*, 5 February, p. 385.

(1936) 'International Order', to the editor, *Spectator*, 17 July, p. 100.
(1937) 'Family Endowment', to the editor, *Spectator*, 5 February, p. 223.
(1949) 'Uneconomic Food Subsidies', to the editor, *The Times*, 27 June, p. 5.
(1949) 'The Dollar Gap', to the editor, *The Times*, 2 August, p. 5.
(1953) 'The Dollar Gap', Hartley Shawcross and Lord Tweedsmuir to the editor, *The Times*, 20 February, p. 7. [Drafted by Meade.]
(1953) 'The Dollar Gap', to the editor, *The Times*, 23 February, p. 7.
(1953) 'The Dollar Gap. Making British Goods More Competitive', to the editor, *The Times*, 3 March, p. 9.
(1954) 'Room for Japan', to the editor, *The Economist*, 18 September, p. 840.
(1955) 'Cures for No Confidence', to the editor, *The Economist*, 10 September, p. 846.
(1955) 'Case for Economic Streamlining', to the editor, *Daily Telegraph*, 21 December.
(1957) 'World Prices', to the editor, *The Times*, 30 October, p. 11.
(1957) 'World Prices, to the editor, *The Times*, 9 November, p. 7.
(1961) To the editor, *The Guardian*, 23 January.
(1961) 'Exclusion Need Not Be for Ever', to the editor, *The Times*, 13 March, p. 15.
(1961) 'The Lesson of Katanga. Strengthening UN Machinery', to the editor, *The Times*, 26 September, p. 11.
(1962) 'Britain, Free World, and the Six', to the editor, *The Times*, 9 January, p. 11.
(1962) 'Asia's Next Decade', to the editor, *New Statesman*, 15 June, p. 862.
(1962) 'Powers under US Trade Bill', to the editor, *The Times*, 13 July, p. 13.
(1962) 'In the Congo', to the editor, *The Times*, 23 August, p. 9.
(1963) 'A Time to be Radical. Britain's Dual Purpose', to the editor, *The Times*, 1 February, p. 13.
(1967) 'Arrests and Trials in Greece', to the editor, *The Times*, 3 May, p. 11.
(1967) 'Lack of Initiative', to the editor, *The Times*, 4 August, p. 9.
(1967) 'Devaluation', to the editor, *The Economist*, 5 August, p. 460.
(1967) To the editor, *The Times*, 27 October, p. 9.
(1968) 'The World's Economy', to the editor, *The Times*, 11 July, p. 9.
(1968) 'Wage-Bargaining and Cost Inflation', to the editor, *The Times*, 5 September.
(1968) 'Serious Threat', to the editor, *The Times*, 4 November, p. 9.
(1969) 'Troubles at LSE', to the editor, *The Times*, 5 February, p. 11.
(1973) To the editor, *The Guardian*, 26 September.
(1974) To the editor, *The Times*, 8 January, p. 13.
(1975) 'Domestic Inflation Threat to Economy', to the editor, *The Times*, 14 May, p. 17.
(1976) To the editor, *The Times*, 20 August, p. 13.
(1977) 'Control of Wage Bill', to the editor, *The Times*, 11 March, p. 19.
(1978) 'Tax Proposals', to the editor, *New Society*, 16 February, p. 386.
(1978) 'Revising the Tax Structure', to the editor, *The Times*, 4 April, p. 15.
(1980) To the editor, *The Times*, 26 March, p. 17.
(with Alec Cairncross and Henry Phelps Brown) (1980) 'An Alternative Route to Disinflation', to the editor, *The Times*, 20 November, p. 15.
(1981) 'Priorities for a Centre Party', to the editor, *The Times*, 3 February, p. 13.
(with Partha Dasgupta) (1981) To the editor, *The Times*, 29 April, p. 19.
(1981) To the editor, *Financial Times*, 30 December.
(1983) 'US Monetary Policy', to the editor, *The Times*, 6 July, p. 11.
(1984) To the editor, *The Times*, 6 April, p. 13.
(1985) 'A Welcome New Target', to the editor, *Financial Times*, 27 March.

(1987) 'In Economic Turmoil, a Keynesian Analysis May Be Useful', to the editor, *Financial Times*, 17 November.

Unpublished Papers Included in this Edition

The Meade Papers are in the British Library of Political and Economic Science; documents in the Public Record Office (PRO) appear by permission of the Controller of Her Majesty's Stationery Office.

(1934) 'The exchange policy of a socialist government' (Meade Papers 2/7). Vol. III, Chapter 2.

(1935) 'Outline of economic policy for a Labour government' (Meade Papers 2/9). Vol. I, Chapter 4.

(1940) 'Financial aspects of war economy' (Meade Papers 3/1; PRO T230/96). Vol. I, Chapter 7.

(1941) 'Internal measures for the prevention of general unemployment' (Meade Papers 3/2; PRO T230/66). Vol. I, Chapter 11.

(1942) 'Government intervention in the post-war economy' (Meade Papers 3/2; PRO T230/14). Vol. II, Chapter 2.

(1942) 'Variations in the rate of social security contributions as a means of stabilising the demand for labour' (Meade Papers 3/2; PRO T230/101). Vol. I, Chapter 12.

(1942) 'A proposal for an international commercial union' (Meade Papers 3/2; PRO T230/14). Vol. III, Chapter 3.

(1942) 'The effect on employment of a change in the employer's social security contribution' (Meade Papers 3/2; PRO T230/101). Vol. I, Chapter 13.

(1943) 'The maintenance of full employment' (Meade Papers 3/2; PRO T230/15). Vol. I, Chapter 14.

(1943) 'The post-war international settlement and the United Kingdom balance of payments' (Meade Papers 3/2; PRO T230/15). Vol. III, Chapter 4.

(1944) 'Sir William Beveridge's Full Employment in a Free Society and the White Paper on Employment Policy (Command 6527)' (Meade Papers 3/2; PRO T230/16). Vol. I, Chapter 15.

(1945) 'The Fiscal Problem set by the Debt' (Meade Papers 3/10; PRO T230/95). Vol. II, Chapter 15.

(1945) 'The Capital Levy' (Meade Papers 3/10; PRO T230/95). Vol. II, Chapter 15.

(1945) 'Debt Repayment and Employment Policy' (Meade Papers 3/10; PRO T230/95). Vol. II, Chapter 15.

(1945) 'The Socialisation of Industries. Memorandum by the Economic Section of the Cabinet Secretariat' (Meade Papers 3/2; PRO T230/19). Vol. II, Chapter 5.

(1945) 'Economic Planning' (Meade Papers 3/10; PRO T230/18). Vol. I, Chapter 16.

(1946) 'Control of Inflation' (Meade Papers 3/10; PRO T171/389). Vol. I, Chapter 17.

(1987) 'Monetary Policy and Fiscal Policy: Impact Effects with a New Keynesian "Assignment" of Weapons to Targets' (Centre for Economic Policy Research Discussion paper No. 246, June 1988). Vol. III, Chapter 23.

Index

absorption *see* domestic expenditure
accommodating finance 151–2, 159, 192–3, 215–17, 266, 271, 297 *see also* international liquidity
adjustable peg 55, 165–6, 172–3, 203, 239, 301–3, 305–8 *see also* exchange rates, fixed
Africa 229–32, 244, 259–60, 269, 272
aggregate demand 79–80, 90, 96–7, 106, 122, 162, 219, 225, 232, 239, 279, 325, 330, 339–41, 352, 354
  restricting of 29, 71, 75, 78, 92–3, 122, 202, 249, 268, 299 *see also* deflation
  see also domestic expenditure
Agricultural Economics Society 1
American Enterprise Institute for Public Policy Research 297
Amsterdam 204
Anglo-American Financial Agreement (1945) 71, 82, 86n, 87n, 148, 149, 160
Antwerp 186–7
Arndt, H. W. 190n
Article VII (of Mutual Aid Agreement, 1942), 28–30
Article VII of International Monetary Fund *see* scarce currency clause
Asia 229–32, 244, 259
assignment (of instruments to targets), New Keynesian 342, 345–51, 354–87
Australia 5, 7, 9, 150, 159, 174, 190–201, 215, 229n, 230, 248, 255–7, 259, 262–3, 269, 272, 277, 287
  balance-of-payments problems 169, 174–5, 190–211
  exports 5, 174, 194–8, 204, 206, 209, 211
  imports 169, 191–2, 194–201, 204, 206, 209, 211
  income distribution 198–200, 205–11
Australian National University 190
Austria 250, 276

balance of payments 101–3, 148–9, 156, 167, 168, 170–1, 232, 327–8, 330, 333–7, 343
  and national income 95–132
  Australian *see* Australia
  capital account *see* capital exports *and* international lending
  current account 3–4, 10, 18, 25, 63–6, 70, 97, 107, 122, 124, 163–5, 298, 328, 337 *see also* balance of trade
  UK *see* United Kingdom
  US *see* United States of America
balance-of-payments adjustment 29–30, 39–40, 43, 78, 83, 151–4, 158, 164, 194, 201, 237, 298–301, 305, 352 *see also* deflation, exchange-rate depreciation, import restrictions, inflation *and* tariffs
  in customs unions and free-trade areas 212–28, 266–72
balance-of-payments deficits 73–4, 134, 150–1, 162, 167, 174, 179, 191–3, 195, 201–2, 204, 209–10, 233–6, 239, 259, 266, 269, 270–2, 283, 297–303, 305, 307, 309–19, 353 *see also* balance-of-payments disequilibrium
balance-of-payments disequilibrium 4, 43, 66, 67, 79, 82, 88, 92, 93, 100, 127, 133–4, 151, 165, 236, 283 *see also* balance-of-payments problems
balance-of-payments equilibrium 6, 28, 38, 48–9, 54, 57, 60–1, 74, 79, 82, 100, 115, 120, 123n, 125, 127, 148, 156, 159, 161–2, 164, 167, 179, 188, 190, 209, 213–14, 233, 235, 238–9, 300, 310, 324, 336, 337, 343, 353, 379 *see also* external balance
balance-of-payments policy *see* balance-of-payments adjustment *and* exchange-rate policy
  geometrical representation of 133–47
balance-of-payments problems 9–10, 40, 48, 56–60, 62, 87, 90–1, 114, 131–2, 157–8, 159, 167, 170, 235–6, 267, 285–6, 290, 293, 313, 315–18, 352–3
  of Australia *see* Australia
  of customs unions and free-trade areas 212–28, 266–72
  UK *see* United Kingdom balance of payments

balance-of-payments surpluses 73–4, 134, 150–1, 162, 174, 233–7, 269, 270–1, 283, 297–301, 307, 309–10 *see also* balance-of-payments deficits
balance of trade 3–5, 10, 97, 101–3, 112–13, 117–20, 123–5, 130–1, 134, 136–41, 153–4, 164, 207–8, 301, 316, 328, 334–7, 344, 346–7, 349, 386
see also balance of payments, current account, exports *and* imports
Bank for International Settlements (BIS) 2, 18
Bank of England 5, 11, 14, 17–20, 24–6
Bank Rate 11, 18 *see also* interest rates
banking policy *see* monetary policy
banks 4–5, 8, 11–14, 19 *see also* monetary policy
Belgian Congo 185
Belgium 177–88, 212–14, 216, 255
Belgium-Luxembourg Economic Union 177–83, 186, 212–13, 223
Benelux 177–89, 212–14, 222, 224, 259, 263, 275
Benham, Frederic 67
bilateralism 28, 48–52, 74–6, 81, 215, 292, 314
Black, John 309n
Blake, Andy 354n
Blinder, A. S. 360, 387
Board of Trade 27
Brazil 154, 215, 232, 260
Bretton Woods *see* United Nations Monetary and Financial Conference
New Keynesian 338–53
British Association for the Advancement of Science 212
British Commonwealth 42, 47, 51–2, 92, 94, 160, 224, 231, 292
and UK entry to EEC 245–8, 250–2, 254–66, 272–8, 280–2
Brittan, Sam 338n
Brown, A. J. 120n
Brussels 189, 338
Budget 12–14, 19, 97–8, 104, 186–8, 192, 252, 254, 345
balance, as policy objective 324, 330, 337, 341–2, 356, 360, 363, 370–4, 386 *see also* wealth target
budget deficits 162, 219, 326–7, 329–33, 335, 341, 344, 346, 349, 351–2, 356, 380
budget surpluses 97, 104–5, 131, 162, 219, 331n, 351–2, 356
budgetary policy 4, 7, 12–14, 162–3, 190, 205, 209, 233–5, 299–301, 306, 309, 341, 352–3 *see also* fiscal policy
in customs unions and free-trade areas 188, 217–20, 224–5, 267–9
buffer stock schemes 30, 44–5, 62, 84–5, 288–9, 292, 313–16, 319–20
see also international commodity agreements
Cambridge University x
Canada 51, 94, 165, 230, 247–8, 256, 258–9, 262, 287, 318
Canberra 190
capital development *see* investment
capital exports, control of 21–6, 40–1, 47, 58, 62, 69–71, 75, 79, 86–7, 90, 100, 152, 298, 353 *see also* exchange control
capital movements 69–70, 90, 95, 100, 152, 191, 193, 218, 221, 233, 271, 299, 304, 343–6, 353, 379
and interest rates *see* interest rates
short-term 8, 18, 21, 23, 165, 167–8, 204, 236–7, 309
see also capital exports, international lending *and* speculation, exchange-rate
central banks 3, 18, 171, 219, 228, 243, 306 *see also* Bank of England, Federal Reserve System *and* monetary policy
Centre for Economic Policy Research (CEPR) 354
Ceylon 269
cheap money policy 9–10, 162, 232 *see also* interest rates *and* monetary policy
Christodoulakis, N. 378, 387
Churchill, Sir Winston 226
Clearing Union 27, 29–31 *see also* International Monetary Fund
Cole, G. D. H. 11
commercial policy 1–2, 20–1, 41–5, 48–52, 81, 134, 137, 149, 151, 153, 155–6, 159, 215, 220, 230, 255, 260, 263, 265, 274–5, 278, 281 *see also* commercial union, import restrictions, post-war international settlement *and* tariffs
Commercial Union, Meade's proposal for a (1942) 27–35 *see also* International Trade Organisation
commodity agreements *see* international commodity agreements *and* Wheat Agreements
commodity standard 19–20, 25
Common Market *see* European Economic Community
Commonwealth *see* British Commonwealth
compensatory finance 295–6, 314–16, 318–19, 320 *see also* international commodity agreements
competition ix, 230, 246–7, 248–9, 259, 267, 275–6, 290
perfect 211, 325
see also monopoly
competitiveness 327–8, 331, 333–7 *see also* terms of trade

consumption 96, 97, 99, 102–4, 105n, 130, 136–7, 187, 197, 256–7, 261, 285–6, 314–15, 325–7, 331–3, 335–7, 341–2, 355, 357–60, 362–3, 364n, 365, 370–1, 373, 375, 386
  restriction of 56, 68, 92, 100, 122, 231, 233, 253, 341, 344
controls 67–9
  on capital movements *see* capital exports, control of
  on imports *see* import restrictions
convertibility 51, 69, 75, 86–7, 151–3, 168, 214–15, 221 *see also* gold standard *and* US dollar
cost of living 170, 199, 203, 205, 252, 287, 360, 379–80, 383–4, 386–7
  and wage-rates 170, 199–201, 225, 238–9, 253–4, 304, 339, 360
customs unions ix, 177–89, 244–84
  Benelux 177–89, 212–14, 222, 224, 259, 263, 275
  Belgium-Luxembourg 178–83, 186, 212–13, 223
  European *see* European Economic Community
  see also free-trade areas

deflation 15, 114, 117, 119, 123n, 124–5, 127, 129–30, 133, 151, 153, 161–2, 165, 173, 175, 213, 225–7, 306, 339, 341, 344, 349
  for balance-of-payments adjustment 4–7, 22, 109, 112, 114, 132, 135, 150–1, 159, 164–5, 193, 217–19, 222, 233, 267–71, 285, 298–301, 312
  see also disinflation *and* gold standard
Denmark 250, 276
depression 5–6, 8, 41, 45–6, 63, 79, 81, 91, 131–2, 150–1, 160–2 *see also* unemployment
  of 1930s 40, 45–7, 91, 93, 161–2, 173, 220, 239, 278–9, 305
Detroit 221
development ix, 40, 45, 63, 83–4, 149, 151, 154, 193, 220, 229, 231, 258, 279, 282, 285, 290–1 *see also* less developed countries
  finance of 157–60, 230–5, 237, 241–3, 279, 293–4, 295n, 352–3 *see also* foreign aid *and* international lending to less developed countries
discrimination 28–33, 41, 47–50, 53, 73–4, 76, 78–9, 83n, 88, 92, 152, 255, 258–60, 262, 264, 266, 273, 276, 281 *see also* customs unions *and* Imperial Preference
disinflation 68–9, 75, 162–3, 170, 190–2, 202–4, 223 *see also* deflation
distribution
  of income *see* income distribution
  of wealth *see* wealth distribution
dollar *see* US dollar
domestic expenditure 97–103, 105–8, 112–15, 117–19, 122, 124–5, 127–31, 133–9, 190–2, 209
Downing, R. I. 190
Dublin 212

economic growth *see* growth
Economic Section (of Cabinet Offices) ix, x
economies of scale 230, 247–9, 275
effective demand *see* aggregate demand
Eisenhower, President 148
elasticity of demand 3n
  for exports 2–4, 23, 39, 63–6, 76–7, 153–4, 156, 163–4, 237, 288, 295–6, 327, 334, 379, 384n
  for imports 4, 23, 39, 63–6, 72, 76–7, 123n, 136–7, 139–41, 153–6, 163–4, 196–7, 223, 237, 328, 334–5, 378
elasticity of supply
  of exports 23, 64–5, 196–8, 285, 290, 295, 323
  of imports 23, 64–5, 197–8
employment, 4, 8, 95, 99, 114, 132–3, 161–2, 207, 210, 268, 278, 305, 354–5, 360–1, 374, 386
  maintenance of 11–17, 25, 44–5, 63, 150, 173, 209, 225, 301, 306, 339–40, 345, 347 *see also* full employment *and* internal balance
Employment Act (US, 1946), 150
England 5–7, 15–17, 22, 24, 218–19 *see also* United Kingdom
equilibrium
  domestic *see* internal balance
  growth *see* growth, steady-state
  in balances of payments *see* balance-of-payments equilibrium *and* external balance
European Economic Community (EEC) 223–4, 229–31, 233, 244–84, 338 *see also* customs unions
European Free-Trade Area (EFTA) 229–31, 245, 248–51, 275–7, 280–1
  see also free-trade areas
European Monetary System (EMS) 351
European Payments Union (EPU) 158, 172, 215–17
exchange controls 17–18, 24–6, 47, 58, 68, 82, 86–7, 100, 152, 154, 158–9, 164–8, 170, 221, 266 *see also* capital exports, control of *and* payments restrictions
Exchange Equalisation Account (EEA) 155, 173, 305
exchange equalisation funds *see* exchange-market intervention
exchange-market intervention 17–19, 152, 155, 166, 168, 171–3, 217, 227–8,

239–42, 268–9, 304–8, 345–7, 349–51, 353
exchange rate 2, 21, 95, 138–40, 154, 169
real *see* competitiveness
structural changes in 324–37
exchange-rate appreciation 15–16, 77, 79, 91, 136, 153, 168, 174, 204, 210, 222, 226, 236–7, 241, 283, 301, 304, 310, 331n, 352, 383
exchange-rate depreciation 3–7, 9, 15–17, 22–3, 37–44, 63–6, 74–80, 123n, 133–7, 139, 152–4, 156–8, 163–5, 167–8, 170–1, 193–5, 198–9, 201–4, 220, 222–3, 225–6, 236–7, 239, 241, 270, 285, 300–4, 310, 326, 346, 349, 379
and IMF rules 43, 47, 55, 61–2, 89–90 *see also* adjustable peg
competitive 37–8, 43, 64, 79, 89–90, 173, 228, 239, 242, 305, 308
expectations of 17, 21, 75, 167, 169, 171–2, 175, 193, 203, 225, 238–9, 302, 304, 309–11 *see also* speculation, exchange-rate
UK *see* pound sterling
exchange-rate policy 151, 194, 220, 338
of a socialist government 11–26
see also exchange rates, gold standard *and* international economic co-operation
exchange-rate speculation *see* speculation
exchange rates, fixed 15–17, 55, 153, 161–2, 164–5, 202, 206, 210, 219, 243, 267–70, 278–9, 301–3, 306, 353 *see also* adjustable peg *and* gold standard
exchange rates, flexible 17–18, 23, 60–1, 114n, 135n, 151–4, 159, 166, 179, 199, 235–43, 279, 283–4, 297–312
case for 15–17, 161–76, 297–301
in customs unions and free-trade areas 224–8, 267–71
see also exchange-rate depreciation
exchange rates, freely floating 166–70, 203–5, 227–8, 235–40, 303–4, 308, 343–51, 353 *see also* exchange-market intervention
exchange rates, target 345–51
export subsidies 32, 38, 40–2, 64, 82, 83n, 102n, 133, 137–41, 251, 253, 257, 267, 298
export taxes 139–41, 210
exports 2–6, 10, 15–16, 20–1, 22–3, 25, 33, 38, 56, 58–9, 77–8, 99–100, 102, 107, 115, 118, 122, 124, 127, 133, 135, 140–1, 152, 163–5, 167, 173, 187, 193, 200, 202, 207, 213, 215, 217, 224, 230–3, 235–7, 253, 259, 277, 291, 298, 304, 317, 325, 327, 331n, 332, 344, 357, 379, 383, 384n
Australian *see* Australia
of less developed countries *see* less developed countries
prices of 4, 9, 16, 22, 66, 77, 102n, 152–3, 158, 163–5, 174, 195, 197–8, 211, 239, 247, 280, 295, 300 *see also* terms of trade
UK *see* United Kingdom
external balance 101, 105–6, 114, 127, 151, 171, 207 *see also* balance-of-payments equilibrium
Externally Balanced Economy 100, 107, 109–12, 115–17, 119–20, 126–7, 129, 131–2

factor mobility 191, 197, 207–8, 218, 281–2, 286 *see also* labour mobility
Federal Farm Board 7
Federal Reserve System 5–7
fiscal policy 133, 149, 151, 199–200, 268, 279, 282–4, 300, 303, 311, 324, 335–8, 340, 342–3, 345, 347n, 348–51
New Keynesian assignment of 354–87
see also Budget, budgetary policy, government expenditure, investment, public, subsidies *and* taxation
foreign aid 230–2, 234–5, 237, 241–3, 298, 352 *see also* development, finance of
foreign-exchange reserves *see* international monetary reserves
foreign lending *see* capital movements *and* international lending
Forster, E. M. 226
forward exchange market 169, 227
franc, Belgian 179, 213
franc, French 75, 169, 221, 226, 235, 267, 269
France 7, 73, 75, 169, 180, 212, 214, 218–19, 221–3, 237, 248, 251–2, 255–9, 272, 276
free lunches 374–7, 385–6
free trade 1–2, 4, 6–8, 82, 134, 148, 152–3, 161–4, 212, 219, 226, 228, 230–1, 237, 247, 261, 274–5, 278–83, 342 *see also* trade barriers, reduction of
free-trade areas ix, 212–28, 262–4, 275–8, 280–1, 284 *see also* customs unions *and* European Free-Trade Area
Fremantle 194
Frisch, Ragnar 74
full employment 4, 20, 90–1, 99, 102n, 148, 150–1, 161–2, 170, 188, 202, 207, 210, 212, 217–18, 220, 225–6, 228, 232–5, 241–2, 268, 299–301, 303, 324–5, 338–9, 344, 346, 347n, 348, 351, 354–5, 374 *see also* internal balance
fundamental disequilibrium 43, 89, 165–6, 236, 239, 301–3, 308, 353 *see also* adjustable peg

Gardner, Richard N. 27
General Agreement on Tariffs and Trade (GATT) x, 27, 92, 148, 149, 155, 179–80, 184, 188–9, 222n, 230, 234, 249, 263, 280–1, 317
Geneva x, 27, 92, 188, 285
Germany 6–7, 28, 41–2, 50–1, 55–6, 85, 212, 214, 217–19, 221–4, 231, 233–4, 237, 246–8, 251–2, 255, 258, 259, 263–5, 269, 271–2, 276–7, 283
Ghana 234–5
Goodhart, Charles 338n
gold 3–7, 17–18, 51, 57, 69–70, 75, 86, 112, 135n, 165, 168, 170, 174–5, 217–18, 228, 239–42, 267, 269, 271, 301, 307n *see also* international monetary reserves
  price of 17–18, 25, 155, 242, 302, 339
gold standard 1–2, 5, 17–18, 25, 82, 112, 135, 151, 159, 161–2, 164, 217–20, 233, 268, 278–9
government borrowing 9, 12–14, 326, 355 *see also* national debt
government expenditure 69, 92, 96, 103–4, 105n, 114, 122, 130, 138n, 232, 252, 326–7, 336, 341, 358–60, 377 *see also* investment, public, national debt, interest on *and* subsidies
Great Britain *see* United Kingdom
growth 30, 229, 230, 232–5, 241–3, 246–9, 268, 279, 281–2, 299–300, 303, 306, 341 *see also* development
  steady-state 324–37
guilder, Dutch 179, 267, 269

Hague Club 215
Harvard University 148
Hawtrey, R. G. (Sir Ralph Hawtrey) 162
Hill, M. 194
Hong Kong 257–60, 264

Imperial Preference 30, 42, 92, 255, 258, 260, 265, 281
import duties *see* tariffs
import licensing 71–3, 80n, 152, 191–2, 194–7, 200, 202, 209–10, 270
import quotas *see* quantitative restrictions on imports
import restrictions 3, 15–16, 28, 37, 42, 53–4, 59, 72–6, 78–9, 83n, 91–2, 106, 112, 133, 139, 153–4, 158–9, 163–6, 169–70, 220, 233–4, 255, 274–6, 278–83, 285, 298
  for balance-of-payments adjustment 37–8, 40–4, 47, 54, 57–9, 62, 86–7, 90, 194, 220–4, 226, 266–8, 270–1, 311
  in Australia 191, 195, 198–203, 205, 209–10
  see also quantitative restrictions *and* tariffs
import subsidies 139
imports 3, 5–6, 15–16, 20–2, 33, 56, 78, 97–103, 106–9, 112–13, 115, 117, 119n, 120, 122, 124–5, 127, 130–1, 133–6, 138–9, 141, 150, 152–3, 155, 163–6, 167, 173, 185–6, 193, 200, 202, 209, 213, 215, 217, 223–4, 232–3, 235, 237, 262, 289–91, 298, 304, 325, 327–8, 333, 335–6, 344, 346, 357, 378, 383–4
  Australian *see* Australia
  of less developed countries *see* less developed countries
  prices of 3–4, 8, 20, 22–3, 38, 66, 71–2, 77, 137–8, 139–40, 152–3, 158, 163–5, 170, 190, 195, 197–8, 200, 208, 225, 238, 252–3, 280, 285–6, 300, 339, 386 *see also* terms of trade
  UK *see* United Kingdom
income, money 3–4, 6, 9, 15–16, 18–19, 69, 153, 161–2, 164, 170, 201, 217–18, 227, 233, 270, 298–301, 303, 305, 308–10, 339, 347, 354, 356 *see also* national income
  real 207, 209, 285–7, 290, 315–16, 331, 339, 346, 355
income distribution ix, 131, 170, 198, 211, 253–4, 283–4, 287, 290, 340
  in Australia *see* Australia
incomes policy 300–1, 311, 339, 355
India 231–2, 255, 257–61, 263, 269, 271–2, 277, 281n, 298n, 318
infant industries 83, 161, 231, 259, 275
inflation 109, 112, 114, 117–19, 123n, 124–5, 127, 219–30, 132–3, 135, 159, 170–3, 175, 178, 188, 191–3, 199–200, 205, 213, 219, 225, 238–9, 246, 301, 304, 306, 325, 338–9, 345–6, 354–5, 363, 365, 377, 386–7 *see also* stagflation
  control of ix, 9, 12–13, 68–9, 75, 92–3, 122, 162, 165, 170–1, 188, 191, 193, 200, 206, 217, 224–7, 232–3, 242, 268, 300, 338–41, 344, 351–2, 355–7, 366–74 *see also* deflation *and* wage-fixing
  demand pull vs. costpush *see* wage equation
  for balance-of-payments adjustment 5, 15–16, 150–1, 162, 164, 217, 222, 233, 267, 269–71, 298–9
Institut National de la Statistique et des Etudes Economiques (INSEE) 177n
Institute of Economic Affairs 244
integration 218–20, 222, 228, 276–7 *see also* customs unions *and* free-trade areas
interest rates 4–6, 8, 11, 13, 19, 95, 131, 218, 309–11, 325, 341–2, 347, 349–50, 352–3

and capital movements 21, 95, 218, 328, 343–4, 346, 352–3, 379, 381, 383, 386
and investment 8, 11–12, 19, 96–7, 105, 122, 333, 335–6, 342, 359, 381–2
in New Keynesian assignment 355–87
structural changes in 324–337
see also monetary policy
internal balance 101, 106, 114, 133, 170, 175–6, 219 *see also* full employment, internal stability *and* price stability
Internally Balanced Economy 99–101, 109–12, 115–20, 122–4, 129, 131–2
internal stability 11, 14–16, 23, 26 *see also* internal balance
International Bank for Reconstruction and Development (IBRD) x, 81, 90, 94, 148, 353
international cartels 44–6, 86n, 156
International Commerce Commission 31–4 *see also* International Trade Organisation
international commodity agreements 30, 32, 40–1, 43–4, 81, 84–5, 285–96, 313–23
buffer stock schemes 30, 44–5, 62, 84–5, 287–8, 292, 313–16, 319–20
compensatory finance 294–6, 314–16, 318–19, 320
price compensation agreements 290–4, 314–15, 318, 320–3
restriction schemes 40–1, 43–4, 46, 84–5, 91, 287–90, 292–3, 316–17
international economic co-operation 1–10, 17–18, 24, 28–30, 44–5, 48, 63, 92–4, 148–60, 217, 222–3, 226–8, 240–3, 267–70, 305–6, 309, 311, 347–51
see also commercial policy, commercial union *and* post-war international settlement
international economic policy *see* commercial policy, exchange rates *and* international economic co-operation
international lending 2–6, 9, 21–4, 30, 41–2, 44–5, 59–61, 63, 90–1, 96–102, 106, 112–17, 119–20, 122n, 123–7, 131, 154, 157, 169–70, 193, 213–14, 217, 242, 301, 328–9, 333–4, 344, 346, 349, 378, 381–2, 386 *see also* capital movements
control of *see* capital exports, control of *and* exchange control
to less developed countries 40–1, 45, 90, 154, 157–8, 159–60, 352–3 *see also* foreign aid
international liquidity 154–5, 159, 215, 219–20, 227–8, 236, 240–2, 267, 311–12 *see also* international monetary reserves
International Monetary Fund x, 43, 47, 54–5, 57–8, 60, 62, 80, 82, 94, 148, 155, 173, 193, 216, 239–43, 272, 295, 297, 301–3, 305, 307–12, 316, 353
Articles of Agreement 41, 47, 55, 82, 86–9, 90, 149, 152, 166, 306
see also Bretton Woods *and* Clearing Union
international monetary reserves 40–2, 44, 47, 51, 57, 86, 90, 97, 100, 154, 165–8, 174–5, 191–3, 214–17, 219, 226–8, 233, 240–2, 268–9, 271–2, 282–3, 297, 304, 307–12, 328–9, 331, 334, 335, 347
see also gold, US dollar, international liquidity
UK *see* United Kingdom
US *see* United States of America
international monetary standard 2–4, 6–8, 17, 165, 240–2 *see also* adjustable peg, commodity standard, gold standard
international payments, reform of 229–43, 267 *see also* International Monetary Fund, multilateralism *and* post-war international settlement
International Trade Organisation (ITO) 27, 53–4, 62, 74, 76, 78–82, 83n, 84–94, 184 *see also* Commercial Union
investment 12–14, 69, 92, 98, 102, 105n, 113n, 130, 220–1, 231–3, 235, 249, 325, 328, 337, 342, 344, 356–9, 364–5, 373–5, 378, 386
and interest rates *see* interest rates
international *see* capital movements *and* international lending
private 8–9, 11–12, 96–7, 103–5, 114, 192, 285, 301
public 8–9, 11–12, 96–7, 124 *see also* public works
investment ratio 341–4, 346, 349, 356, 360, 364–5, 379 *see also* wealth target
Ireland 49
Italy 220, 223, 255, 258–9, 263, 271–2, 276–7

J-curve 344, 347
Japan 55–6, 85, 229n, 232, 248, 258, 262

Kennedy, President 249, 263–4, 273–7, 280
Keynes, John Maynard (Lord Keynes) 27, 81, 150, 156, 290, 353, 357, 374
see also Clearing Union
Keynesian model 357–66, 378–85
Keynesian policies (Old) 161–2, 239, 338, 348, 354–6
New *see* New Keynesian approach

labour
demand for 5, 133, 190, 205, 281–3, 299, 340, 361

marginal product of 207, 209
migration 250, 272–3
mobility 191, 197, 220, 281–2
supply of 231, 360–1
see also employment *and* unemployment
Labour governments 2, 15, 17, 20
economic policy for 11–26
Labour Party, Meade's work for ix–x *see also* New Fabian Research Bureau
Latin America 47–8, 50, 273 *see also* South America
Law Mission (1943) 27, 36, 41, 43–6, 48, 52–3, 57–9, 61, 66
League of Nations x, 2, 178
lend-lease 58–61
Lerner, Abba P. 138n
Lerner-Marshall condition 334
less developed countries 76, 83–4, 149, 151, 157–8, 161, 229–32, 234–5, 241, 257–8, 260, 263, 266, 271, 275–6, 279–83, 286–7, 293–4, 298, 313, 315–17, 319, 338, 351–2 *see also* development
exports of 286–7, 289, 295, 313, 315–19
imports of 84, 258–9, 285, 287, 313, 315–16, 318–19, 353
Liesner, H. H. 177
London 27, 148, 168–9, 175, 204, 220
London School of Economics ix, 67, 177n
Lundberg, Erik 194
Luxembourg 177–81, 188, 255 *see also* Belgium-Luxembourg Economic Union

MacDougall, G. D. A. (Sir Donald MacDougall) 74, 93–4
Machlup, Fritz 130–1
Maciejowski, J. 331n, 347n
Malaya 50, 269
marginal propensity to import 97, 105–6, 108–9, 119, 130–1, 135–6, 141
mark, German 221, 226, 235, 237–8, 241, 267, 269, 283
Marshall Aid 71, 149
'Marshall Aid' 134, 135n, 137, 139
Mauritius 281n, 286–8, 296
Meade, James
An Introduction to Economic Analysis and Policy (1936) ix
Case Studies in European Economic Union (1962) 177
Negotiations for Benelux: An Annotated Chronicle (1957) 177
Nobel Memorial Prize ix
Planning and the Price Mechanism (1948) 67
Problems of Economic Union (1953) 148, 177
The Balance of Payments (1951) ix, 95, 133
The Belgium-Luxembourg Economic Union 1921–1939 (1956) 177
The Common Market: Is there an Alternative? (1962) 274–84
The Theory of Customs Unions (1955) ix, 177
Trade and Welfare (1955) ix
UK, Commonwealth and Common Market (1962) 244–73, 274
other publications 388–405
Meade Papers x, 11, 27, 81
Melbourne 204
monetary policy 11–14, 20, 96–7, 105, 133, 149, 162–3, 190, 192, 193, 205, 209, 219, 233–5, 279, 282, 299–301, 303, 338, 341–4, 346, 349, 351–2
in customs unions and free-trade areas 188, 217–20, 224–5, 267–9
New Keynesian assignment of 354–87
money, demand for 8, 105, 137, 330
money supply 8, 11, 19, 105, 217–19, 306, 330, 340, 358
monopoly ix, 72, 76, 82, 168, 194, 230, 339 *see also* international cartels
most-favoured-nation 52, 183–4, 230, 262, 277
multilateralism 28, 49, 74, 76, 82, 90, 158, 184, 280, 292–3, 314 *see also* rules of the game
multiplier 95–6, 99, 105, 112–19, 132–3, 342
Kahnian 358, 362, 375, 381, 383
Mundell, R. A. 366, 387
Mutual Aid Agreement (1942) 28–30, *see also* lend-lease
Myrdal, Gunnar 93n

national debt 9, 12–13, 347n, 356n, 360
interest on 7, 12, 326–7, 360
national expenditure, and balance of payments 95–132 *see also* domestic expenditure
national income 7, 45–6, 57, 66, 134, 136, 139–41, 162, 211, 247, 286, 293, 330, 335–6, 339–43, 352, 354–6
and balance of payments 95–132
National Investment Board 12–14, 24
Netherlands 177–88, 212–14, 216, 223, 255, 257, 271
Neutral Economy 99–101, 108–10, 112, 115–22, 123n, 124–5, 127, 131–2
New Fabian Research Bureau x, 11
New Keynesian approach 331n, 339–53, 354–87
New York 168, 169, 204
New Zealand 211, 229n, 230, 255–9, 261, 269, 271–2, 287
North America 73, 229n, 244, 258, 274

North Atlantic Treaty Organisation (NATO) 149, 156–7, 159
Norway 250, 276

Odling-Smee, John 338n
Ohlin, Bertil ix
Organisation for Economic Co-operation and Development (OECD) 230, 263, 338
Organisation for European Economic Co-operation (OEEC) 158, 215, 227
Organisation of Petroleum Exporting Countries (OPEC) 339
Organization of American States 294n
Ouchy Convention (1931) 183
Oxford University ix, 11

Pakistan 269, 281n
Paris 204
payments restrictions 29, 152, 161, 163, 165, 213, 266, 270
  on current transactions 32, 34, 54–5, 60, 62, 85–7, 154, 167, 221, 266
  on capital transactions 47, 54–5, 58, 62, 69, 86–7, 152, 167, 221, 266
  see also exchange control
Philippines 47
Phillips curve 361
population growth 272, 287
Portugal 276
post-war international settlement 36–62, 81–94, 149, 159–60 *see also* General Agreement on Tariffs and Trade, International Bank for Reconstruction and Development *and* International Monetary Fund
  second round 148–60
post-war transition 28, 34–6, 52–63, 86, 148, 182
pound, Australian 169, 174, 193–5, 199, 203–4, 214
pound sterling 16–17, 19–21, 24, 38, 47, 61, 69, 152, 159, 167–9, 172–5, 195, 214–15, 227, 235, 237–8, 240–1, 245, 250, 265–9, 282–3, 302, 305, 343, 345, 348n, 350
  depreciation of 38, 40, 47, 63–6, 75, 153, 156–7, 220, 238–9, 241, 268, 270, 279–80, 283, 343–4
  devaluation of (1949) 148, 179
  see also sterling area
preferences *see* discrimination *and* Imperial Preference
price compensation agreements 290–4, 314–15, 318 *see also* international commodity agreements
price-compensation model 320–3
price control 68, 200, 283, 300
price mechanism 67–8, 71–2, 79–80, 164, 194, 290–1, 298
  and Australian balance of payments 190–205
price stability 2, 15–16, 19–20, 22, 26, 46, 63, 160, 175, 225, 232–5, 241, 300–1, 344 *see also* inflation, control of *and* internal balance
prices, general level of 2, 4–10, 15–16, 18, 69, 95, 99, 161–2, 164, 170–1, 175, 213, 217–18, 225–7, 233, 265, 270, 283, 298–301, 303, 305, 308–10, 324, 339, 347, 355, 358–9
  in Australia 190–1, 195, 198–9, 202, 209–10
  see also inflation *and* wage-rates
prices, of primary products 9–10, 40, 84–5, 91, 158, 197–8, 203, 206–7, 285–8, 290–4, 313–15, 320–3 *see also* international commodity agreements
production function 325
productivity 16, 162, 170, 192, 202, 212, 225, 232, 265, 283, 346
profits 4–5, 8, 12, 15–16, 98, 103–4, 161, 167, 169, 193, 299, 301, 304, 340–1
protection 31–2, 48, 83, 156, 159, 179, 182, 194, 278–9, 352
  agricultural 250–4, 256–7, 259, 262, 264–5, 273, 281–3
  see also import restrictions *and* tariffs
protectionism 29, 48, 50, 82, 84, 89, 91 *see also* protection
public investment *see* investment, public
public works, 6, 9, 10, 14, 99–100, 118 *see also* investment, public

quantitative restrictions
  on exports 32–3, 40, 43–4 *see also* restriction schemes
  on imports 21, 26, 32–5, 37–8, 40–1, 48–9, 53, 62, 64, 68, 71–2, 82, 85–9, 152, 164, 188, 192–4, 199, 264 *see also* import restrictions

rationing 68, 200
rents 207–10
reparations payments 6, 22, 56, 96–8, 114, 128–30
reserves *see* international monetary reserves
restriction schemes for primary products 40–1, 43–4, 46, 84–5, 91, 288–90, 292–3, 316–17 *see also* international commodity agreements
restrictions
  on consumption *see* consumption
  on imports *see* import restrictions
  on payments *see* payment restrictions *and* exchange control
risk 168–70, 175, 227, 320
Robinson, Joan 120n
Rome Treaty (1957) 259, 266–9, 272

Rotterdam 186–7
Royal Institute of International Affairs 95, 177n
rules of the game 52, 76, 79–81, 83, 88, 90
see also International Monetary Fund, Articles of Agreement *and* International Trade Organisation
Russell, Eric 206

saving 96, 98, 103–4, 106, 113n, 128, 130–1, 192, 300, 328–9, 335–7, 341, 352, 356
scarce currency clause 41, 47, 55, 87–8
Schuman plan 158
small open economy assumption 206–7, 324, 377
socialisation 15, 21, 26 *see also* state trading
Solow, Robert 360, 387
South America 229–32, 248 *see also* Latin America
speculation 285, 343
exchange-rate 8–9, 17–18, 21–2, 25, 165, 167–8, 170–2, 175, 203–4, 225, 227–8, 236–40, 302–11, 345, 347
stagflation 338–9
state trading 21, 26, 28–30, 33–4, 49, 53, 82, 83n, 188
sterling *see* pound sterling
sterling area 51–2, 154, 158–9, 174–5, 214–15, 217, 224, 266–7, 269–73
see also sterling balances
sterling balances 51–2, 57–8, 62, 69–71, 86–7, 154, 158–9, 175, 240, 271
subsidies 69, 102n, 104, 138, 188, 201, 251–4, 264, 282, 315, 321–2, 326–7, 330–1, 335–6, 355, 376–7
on exports *see* export subsidies
Swan, Trevor 190n
Sweden 93n, 247–8, 250, 276
Switzerland 250, 276
Sydney 194, 204

target exchange rates *see* exchange rates, target
targets (of economic policy) 11, 14–16, 90, 99–100, 209, 218, 226, 230, 232, 301, 338–42 *see also* external balance, full employment, growth, internal balance, price stability *and* wealth target
and instruments *see* assignment
tariff revenues 71–2, 97, 138, 209–10
in customs unions 186–8, 252–3, 257, 261
tariffs 15, 38, 48, 64, 92, 177–89, 207, 209–10, 246–8
common *see* customs unions
imposition of 3–4, 6, 9, 16, 47, 64, 97, 134, 137–8, 161–2, 194, 197–8, 234
reduction of 1, 6, 10, 16, 21, 26, 28, 38, 40–2, 82, 91, 123n, 249, 262, 264, 277–8
US *see* United States of America
see also free trade, General Agreement on Tariffs and Trade *and* trade barriers
taxation 7, 12–13, 32, 69, 92, 96, 98–100, 102n, 193–4, 114, 122, 128, 130–1, 139–41, 188, 192, 199, 201–2, 224, 232, 252–4, 257, 269, 283, 314, 321–2, 326, 330, 331n, 341–4, 360n
in New Keynesian assignment 354–87
terms of trade 22, 45–6, 66, 77–9, 134, 135n, 158, 160–1, 198, 207–11, 231, 247–8, 280, 327–31, 333, 351, 378–9, 381, 384, 386 *see also* competitiveness
The Hague 189
Trade Agreements Act (US) 149, 155
trade balance *see* balance of trade
trade-balance compensation schemes *see* compensatory finance
trade barriers 21, 79, 86, 164, 198, 278 *see also* customs unions, tariffs and import restrictions
reduction of 28–30, 48, 79–80, 81, 155–6, 161, 164, 218, 224, 230, 234–5, 241–2, 246, 249, 262–3, 265–8, 273, 279–80, 351–2 *see also* free trade, free-trade areas *and* General Agreement on Tariffs and Trade
Trade Charter *see* International Trade Organisation
trade unions 5, 162, 170, 225, 246, 339–40
tradeable goods 191, 195–6, 198–201, 346
transfer payments 98, 100, 103, 125, 292
see also reparations payments
transitional period *see* post-war transition
Tripartite Monetary Agreement (1936) 306

underdeveloped countries *see* less developed countries
unemployment ix, x, 4–5, 11–12, 25, 44, 91, 93, 99, 104, 150–1, 161–3, 165, 173, 190–2, 205, 209, 210, 225, 231, 235, 239, 278–9, 299–300, 305, 338–40, 360, 374 *see also* depression *and* employment
unemployment benefit 5, 7, 104–5, 131, 190, 261
Unemployment Insurance Fund 104
United Kingdom 15–17, 27–9, 36, 38, 42–3, 45, 49, 52, 57, 66, 81–2, 88n, 107n, 149–53, 157–8, 160–1, 164, 168, 173, 175–6, 183, 194, 201, 214–15, 217–20, 223–4, 227, 237–9, 247, 274–5, 287, 295n, 296, 338, 347n
and EEC 231, 244–84
balance of payments 27–9, 36–66,

67–80, 81–94, 148–9, 169, 174, 194, 249, 253–4, 265–73, 278–9, 282–3, 303
exports 27–8, 36–9, 40, 42, 46, 48–50, 56–9, 63–6, 68–70, 74–7, 83–5, 91–3, 149, 152–3, 158, 161–2, 169, 197, 246–8, 264–5, 275, 278, 280
imports 27–8, 36–40, 42, 44, 46, 48–50, 57–8, 63–6, 68, 70, 72–7, 83–4, 92, 152, 158, 161, 168–9, 224, 248, 253–9, 265–6, 275, 278–9, 280
reserves 59, 70–1, 154–5, 158–60, 168, 170, 173–4, 216–17, 227, 240, 266–7, 269, 271–2
see also pound sterling
United Nations 294n
United Nations Conference on Trade and Development (UNCTAD) 285, 295n, 314
United Nations Conference on Trade and Employment (Havana, 1948) 27, 82
United Nations Monetary and Financial Conference (Bretton Woods, 1944) 81–2, 148, 173, 353
United Nations Relief and Rehabilitation Administration (UNRRA) 56
United States of America 5–7, 15–17, 27–9, 36, 40, 43, 45–52, 55, 58–9, 75, 81–2, 90, 92–4, 148–9, 150–1, 154–7, 160–2, 169, 183–4, 186, 220, 223, 229–30, 232–5, 237, 245, 247–8, 255, 259–60, 262–4, 270, 273, 276–80, 287, 318, 352–3
balance of payments 42, 46, 47, 73, 75, 77–8, 162, 234–5, 237–8, 259, 263–5, 300, 303, 352
reserves 162, 215, 234, 240
tariff 15–16, 28, 42, 92, 155, 234, 249, 273, 277–8
University of Adelaide 190
University of Chicago 148
University of Indiana 148
US dollar 41, 47, 51, 86, 90, 154, 174–5, 179, 195, 214–16, 228, 235, 239–41, 267, 269, 271, 301, 305, 307, 343, 345, 348, 350, 352
depreciation of 237–8
shortage 70, 74, 77, 88, 90–1, 154, 229
US Loan *see* Anglo-American Financial Agreement
USSR 28, 244

Vines, David 331n, 347n, 354

wage equation 360–1, 365, 367, 372–3, 377, 380
wage-fixing 191, 201, 225, 265, 300, 303, 306, 339–40, 343, 345, 347n, 348, 350–1, 354–5, 377
wages
money 4–6, 12, 15–17, 68, 75, 95, 99, 133, 135, 153, 160, 170, 211, 225, 233, 238, 246, 253–4, 265, 283, 299–300, 325–6, 339, 346, 354, 357–61, 380
in Australia 190–1, 193–5, 198–203, 205–11
real 199–201, 207–11
Wales 218–19
Washington 27, 36, 81, 148, 297
Anglo-American conversations at (1943) *see* Law Mission
Weale, Martin 354n, 379, 387
wealth 329, 335–6
wealth distribution 68, 283–4, 287
wealth target 355–8, 362, 366–70, 373, 375–6, 379, 385–6
Weisglas Max 177n
Wells S. J. 177
West Indies 260, 272, 281n
Western Europe 73, 94, 212–28, 229n, 244, 246, 251, 258, 274–5, 277
see also European Economic Community *and* European Free-Trade Area
Wheat Agreements 81, 85n, 294 *see also* price compensation agreements
Williamson, John 338n, 345
World Bank *see* International Bank for Reconstruction and Development
World Economic and Financial Conference (1933) 1
World Economic Conference (1927)

Zurich 168–9, 204